ENFORCEMENT OF CORPORATE AND SECURITIES LAW

This book is the first of its kind in focusing on the enforcement of corporate and securities laws, both public and private. This relatively understudied issue is critically important for the development and health of global capital markets. In addition to a special focus on the young system coming into being in the People's Republic of China (PRC), this book also examines the enforcement of corporate and securities laws across the globe and across different legal and political systems from an in-depth comparative perspective. This single volume assembles a veritable 'dream team' of the very best scholars and legal specialists in the many national jurisdictions covered in the book. Hence, it is of significant value to corporate and securities regulators, judicial officials, prosecutors, litigation specialists, corporate counsel, legal and economic policy makers, scholars, think tanks, students and investors alike.

ROBIN HUI HUANG is Professor of Law in the Faculty of Law, The Chinese University of Hong Kong, and is currently serving as Assistant Dean (External Affairs, Asia) and Executive Director of the Centre for Financial Regulation and Economic Development. He is also Adjunct Professor in Faculty of Law at the University of New South Wales, Sydney, and Guest Professor at the China University of Political Science and Law, Beijing. He is the author of *International Securities Markets: Insider Trading Law in China* (2006) and *Securities and Capital Markets Law in China* (2014).

NICHOLAS CALCINA HOWSON is Professor of Law at the University of Michigan Law School, and is a former partner of the international law firm Paul, Weiss, Rifkind, Wharton and Garrison LLP. In addition to Michigan, he has taught law at the University of California, Berkeley; Columbia University, Cornell University, and Harvard University. He publishes widely on Chinese (PRC) corporate and securities law as well as Chinese law and legal institutions, and he acts regularly as a Chinese law expert in US and international litigation and arbitration proceedings.

ENFORCEMENT OF CORPORATE AND SECURITIES LAW

China and the World

Edited by

ROBIN HUI HUANG

The Chinese University of Hong Kong

NICHOLAS CALCINA HOWSON

University of Michigan Law School

CAMBRIDGE
UNIVERSITY PRESS

CAMBRIDGE
UNIVERSITY PRESS

University Printing House, Cambridge CB2 8BS, United Kingdom

One Liberty Plaza, 20th Floor, New York, NY 10006, USA

477 Williamstown Road, Port Melbourne, VIC 3207, Australia

4843/24, 2nd Floor, Ansari Road, Daryaganj, Delhi – 110002, India

79 Anson Road, #06–04/06, Singapore 079906

Cambridge University Press is part of the University of Cambridge.

It furthers the University's mission by disseminating knowledge in the pursuit of education, learning, and research at the highest international levels of excellence.

www.cambridge.org
Information on this title: www.cambridge.org/9781107164994
DOI: 10.1017/9781316691397

First published 2017

A catalogue record for this publication is available from the British Library.

Library of Congress Cataloging-in-Publication Data
Names: Huang, Robin Hui, 1976– editor. | Howson, Nicholas Calcina, editor.
Title: Enforcement of corporate and securities law : China and the world / edited by Robin Hui Huang, Nicholas Calcina Howson.
Description: New York : Cambridge University Press, 2017.
Identifiers: LCCN 2016057936 | ISBN 9781107164994 (hardback)
Subjects: LCSH: Corporation law – China. | Tort liability of corporations – China. | Business ethics – China. | Securities – China. | Fines (Penalties) – China. | Sanctions, Administrative – China. | Corporation law. | Tort liability of corporations. | Securities. | Fines (Penalties) | Sanctions, Administrative.
Classification: LCC KNQ1060 .E54 2017 | DDC 346.51/066–dc23
LC record available at https://lccn.loc.gov/2016057936

ISBN 978-1-107-16499-4 Hardback

CONTENTS

FIGURES

TABLES

NOTES ON CONTRIBUTORS

JOHN ARMOUR is Hogan Lovells Professor of Law and Finance at Oxford University and an ECGI Fellow. He has held visiting posts at various institutions including Columbia Law School and the Universities of Chicago, Frankfurt and Pennsylvania. He is an executive editor of the *Journal for Corporate Law Studies* and the *Journal of Law, Finance and Accounting*, and he has been involved in policy-related work for the UK's Department of Trade and Industry (now BIS), Financial Services Authority (now FCA), the Commonwealth Secretariat and the World Bank. He currently serves as a member of the European Commission's Informal Company Law Expert Group.

MICHAEL S. BARR is the Roy F. and Jean Humphrey Proffitt Professor of Law at the University of Michigan Law School, Professor of Public Policy at the Gerald R. Ford School of Public Policy, Faculty Director of the Center on Finance, Law, and Policy at the University of Michigan, and a nonresident senior fellow at the Center for American Progress and at the Brookings Institution. He served under President Obama as the US Department of the Treasury's Assistant Secretary for Financial Institutions and was a key architect of the Dodd-Frank Wall Street Reform and Consumer Protection Act of 2010.

BERNARD S. BLACK is Nicholas D. Chabraja Professor at Northwestern University, with appointments in the School of Law and the Kellogg School of Management (Finance Department), and he is Faculty Associate at Northwestern's Institute for Policy Research. He is also Managing Director of the Social Science Research Network, and Founding Chairman of the annual Conference on Empirical Legal Studies. Professor Black received a BA from Princeton University, an MA in physics from the University of California at Berkeley and a JD from Stanford Law School. His principal research areas include health policy and medical malpractice, law and finance, international corporate governance, and corporate and securities law.

BRIAN R. CHEFFINS, since 1998, has been the S. J. Berwin Professor of Corporate Law at Cambridge University, having begun his academic career at the University of British Columbia's Faculty of Law. Professor Cheffins has held visiting appointments at Columbia, Duke, Harvard, Oxford, Stanford, the University of British Columbia and the University of Western Ontario. Professor Cheffins has written widely on corporate law and corporate governance, including *Company Law: Theory, Structure and Operation* (1997), *The Trajectory of (Corporate Law) Scholarship* (2004), *Corporate Ownership and Control: British Business Transformed* (2008) and *The Modern History of U.S. Corporate Governance* (2011) (as editor).

DONALD CLARKE is a professor at the George Washington University Law School in Washington, DC, where he specialises in modern Chinese law, focusing particularly on corporate governance, Chinese legal institutions and China's economic reforms. In addition to his academic work, he founded and maintains Chinalaw, the leading Internet listserv on Chinese law, and writes the Chinese Law Prof Blog. He was educated at Princeton University (AB), the University of London (MSc) and Harvard Law School (JD), where he was a member of the *Harvard Law Review*. He is a member of the New York bar and the Council on Foreign Relations.

JAMES D. COX is Brainerd Currie Professor of Law at Duke University School of Law. In addition to his texts *Financial Information, Accounting and the Law*, *Corporations* (with Hazen & O'Neal), *Business Organizations Cases and Materials* (with Eisenberg), and *Securities Regulations: Cases and Materials* (with Hillman & Langevoort), Professor Cox has published extensively in the areas of market regulation and corporate governance, as well as having testified before the US House and Senate on insider trading, class actions and market reform issues. He served as a member of the PCAOB Standing Advisory Committee (2008–2015), the corporate law drafting committees in California (1977–1980) and North Carolina (1984–1993) and the ABA Committee on Corporate Laws.

GUIDO FERRARINI is Professor of Business Law at the University of Genoa, Department of Law and is Director of the Centre for Law and

Finance and Chair in Governance of Financial Institutions at Radboud University Nijmegen. He holds a JD (University of Genoa, 1972), an LLM (Yale Law School, 1978) and a Dr. jur. (h.c., Ghent University, 2009). He is founder and fellow of the European Corporate Governance Institute (ECGI), Brussels. He is the author of many articles in the fields of financial law, corporate law and business law. He is also the editor of several books, including *Boards and Shareholders in European Listed Companies* (with M. Belcredi, 2013).

CARSTEN GERNER-BEUERLE is Associate Professor of Law at the London School of Economics and Political Science. His research focuses on corporate governance, securities regulation and economic analysis of law. He studied law and economics at Humboldt University Berlin, the University of Minnesota and the University of London. He has worked or held visiting positions at various universities in Europe and the United States including Humboldt University Berlin, King's College London, the University of California at Berkeley and Duke University. Carsten is also admitted to the bar in Germany and the United Kingdom, regularly advises a German law firm on matters of corporate law and corporate insolvency and has prepared studies for the European Commission and the European Parliament on the reform of corporate governance, financial regulation and private international law.

PAOLO GIUDICI is Professor of Business Law at the University of Bozen-Bolzano, Italy. He is a graduate of Genoa Law School (1987, magna cum laude). He is on the board of editors of *Le Società*, the most-read company and securities law journal in Italy, where he is in charge of capital markets law. He has published three books and a long list of articles and book chapters on Italian and European law in top journals and books.

Before starting his academic career, he was a practicing business lawyer for fifteen years, with extensive international experience. In the continental Europe tradition, he continues to serve as legal counsel and advocate in matters concerning his areas of academic expertise. He serves as an expert witness as well.

GEN GOTO is Associate Professor of Law at the University of Tokyo, Graduate Schools for Law and Politics, in Japan (since 2010). After graduating from the Faculty of Law at the University of Tokyo in 2003 (LLB), Professor Goto has been Assistant Professor at the University of

Tokyo (2003–2006), and Lecturer (2006–2008) and Associate Professor (2008–2010) at Gakushuin University in Tokyo. Also, he assisted Japanese Government on law reforms as Researcher of Japanese Ministry of Justice (2010–2013) (for reform of Companies Act), and as Professional Member of Financial System Council of Japanese Financial Services Agency (2011–2013) (for reform of Insurance Business Act).

NICHOLAS CALCINA HOWSON is Professor of Law at the University of Michigan Law School, and is a former partner of the international law firm Paul, Weiss, Rifkind, Wharton and Garrison LLP. In addition to Michigan, he has taught law at the University of California, Berkeley; Columbia University, Cornell University, and Harvard University. He publishes widely on Chinese (PRC) corporate and securities law as well as Chinese law and legal institutions, and he acts regularly as a Chinese law expert in US and international litigation and arbitration proceedings.

ROBIN HUI HUANG is Professor of Law in the Faculty of Law, The Chinese University of Hong Kong, and is currently serving as Assistant Dean (External Affairs, Asia) and Executive Director of the Centre for Financial Regulation and Economic Development. He is also Adjunct Professor in Faculty of Law at the University of New South Wales, Sydney, and Guest Professor at the China University of Political Science and Law, Beijing. He is the author of *International Securities Markets: Insider Trading Law in China* (2006) and *Securities and Capital Markets Law in China* (2014).

VIKRAMADITYA KHANNA is William W. Cook Professor of Law at the University of Michigan Law School and graduated from Harvard Law School with an SJD. His interest areas include corporate and securities laws, law in India, corporate crime, the globalising legal profession, comparative corporate governance, and law and economics. His publications include papers in the *Harvard Law Review, Journal of Finance, Journal of Econometrics, Michigan Law Review, Supreme Court Economic Review* and *Georgetown Law Journal*, and he is the current and founding editor of *White Collar Crime eJournal* and *India Law eJournal* at SSRN. He has testified before the US Congress and has presented papers at many venues in the US and internationally.

HWA-JIN KIM is Professor of Law at Seoul National University and William W. Cook Global Law Professor at University of Michigan Law

School. He has also taught at Tel Aviv University and Stanford Law School. He is the founding chair of the Seoul Corporate Governance Forum. He received his BS from Seoul National University; Dr jur *magna cum laude* from University of Munich; and his LLM from Harvard Law School. He won the Book Prize from the Korean National Academy of Sciences in 2005, 2010 and 2015. He has advised the Office of the President of Korea, the Korea Financial Supervisory Service and the Ministry of Justice of Korea.

RAINER KULMS is Senior Research Fellow, head of the US Law Department at the Max Planck Institute for Comparative and International Private Law, and Editor-in-Chief of the European Business Organization Law Review. He graduated from Hamburg University (Dr iuris, and Postgraduate Degree of Habilitation), obtained an LLM from the University of Michigan and was Visiting Fellow at the University of Cambridge (Wolfson College). After several years in industry, he has taught at Chinese, German and other European universities. He has published on German, European and US corporate and commercial laws, mediation law, class actions and private law in Eastern Europe.

ALEXA LAM is Professor of Legal Practice at the Law Faculty of the University of Hong Kong (HKU). She teaches Securities Law and Regulation, a new course designed to take students from the policy behind market regulation to the enforcement of securities law and regulation. Before joining HKU, Professor Lam was Deputy Chief Executive Officer and Executive Director of the Securities and Futures Commission in Hong Kong (SFC). While at the SFC, Professor Lam co-chaired the Working Group on Margin Requirements, an international group tasked with formulating principles for the regulation of uncleared OTC derivatives, a financial reform item mandated by the G-20 leaders.

MICHAEL LEGG is Associate Professor of Law at University of New South Wales Australia (UNSW). He researches in the areas of civil procedure and corporate and securities law, including on the interaction between public and private enforcement, class actions and litigation funding. He is admitted to practice in Australia and in the State and Federal courts of New York. He holds accounting and law degrees from UNSW and an LLM from the University of California, Berkeley. Michael is a member of the Law Council of Australia's Class Actions Committee.

JUNHAI LIU is Professor of Law, Renmin University of China (since 2006). He is Vice President and Secretary General of China Consumers Protection Law Society. He is also an adviser for the State Authority of Industry & Commerce, Ministry of Commerce and All China Federation of Trade Unions (ACFTU). His representative publications are *Protection of Shareholders' Rights* (1995, 1997, 2004), *Corporate Social Responsibility* (1999), *Modern Corporate Law* (2008, 2011, 2015) and *Modern Securities Law* (2011). In addition to advising NPC (National People's Congress) on the reform of Corporate and Securities Law, he has advised the Supreme Court on numerous judicial interpretations and controversial cases on business law. He was Adjunct Senior Research Fellow at China Securities Regulatory Commission (2013–2015, Vice Chairman of China Consumers' Association (2008–2015) and Professor at Institute of Law, Chinese Academy of Social Sciences (CASS) from 1995 to 2006.

XIAOCHUN LIU is the President of Shenzhen Court of International Arbitration (also called South China International Economic and Trade Arbitration Commission). He received his LLB, Master of Economics and PhD in Law from Peking University, and his MBA from Roosevelt University (Chicago).

He is Panel Arbitrator of SCIA, SHIAC and HKIAC. He is also Co-founder and Vice Chairman of Shenzhen Securities and Futures Dispute Resolution, and Co-founder and Vice Chairman of Guangdong-Hong Kong-Macau Mediation Alliance.

JEFFREY MACINTOSH holds the Toronto Stock Exchange Chair in Capital Markets at the Faculty of Law and is a past director of the Capital Markets Institute at the University of Toronto. He holds law degrees from Harvard and the University of Toronto, and a Bachelor of Science degree from MIT. He was appointed John M. Olin Fellow at Yale Law School in 1988–1989. Professor MacIntosh has published widely on various topics related to corporate law, securities law, venture capital and innovation policy, and he is the co-author of a popular student-oriented text on Canadian securities law.

RICHARD NOLAN has been Professor of Law at the York Law School since September 2012. Previously he was Reader in Corporate & Trust Law at the University of Cambridge and a Fellow of St John's College, where he taught for 19 years. He has given courses and papers as a visiting academic both at home in England and abroad in Australia, Hong Kong, New Zealand, Poland, Singapore and the US. He has advised on law reform in several projects by the Department of Trade and Industry and the Law Commission for England and Wales.

He is a barrister and door tenant (a part-time practitioner) at Erskine Chambers, Lincoln's Inn, widely regarded as the leading corporate law set of chambers in the United Kingdom. Before he became an academic, he qualified and practised as a solicitor with Macfarlanes, a leading firm in the City of London.

JED S. RAKOFF has served since March, 1996 as a United States District Judge for the Southern District of New York. He also frequently sits by designation on the 2nd, 3rd and 9th Circuit Courts of Appeals. In addition, Judge Rakoff holds the position of Adjunct Professor at Columbia Law School, where he teaches courses in white collar crime, science and the law, class actions and the interplay of civil and criminal law. He has co-authored five books, written over 135 published articles, delivered over 550 speeches and authored over 1500 judicial opinions. He is also a regular contributor to the *New York Review of Books*.

MATHIAS REIMANN is Hessel E. Yntema Professor of Law at the University of Michigan Law School. He received his basic legal education in Germany (1st and 2d state examination; Dr iuris, University of Freiburg, 1982), before completing graduate studies in the United States (LLM, University of Michigan, 1983). He held a chair for private law, legal history and comparative at the University of Trier 1995–1999 and has taught as a visiting professor in more than half a dozen countries around the world. He served as Editor-in-Chief of the American Journal of Comparative Law 2003–2012 and is a titular member of the International Academy of Comparative Law.

CAROLINE SCHMIDT is a qualified lawyer and member of the Brazilian Bar Association. She held a research fellowship in Law and Finance at University of Oxford, working with Professor John Armour on an ESRC-funded project on law, development and finance in the 'rising powers' (Brazil, India, Russia and China). She holds a DPhil at University of Oxford/UK, an LLM in International Commercial and Business Law from the University of East Anglia/UK, an LLM in Business Law and Fundamental Rights from the Pontifical Catholic University of Paraná/BR and an MBA with an emphasis in finance from the Federal University of Paraná/BR. She earned her Bachelor in Law from the Pontifical Catholic University of Paraná/BR.

RANDALL THOMAS is John S. Beasley II Professor of Law and Business Director, Law and Business Program at Vanderbilt University, and he is Professor of Management at the Owen Graduate School of Management. He has earned the reputation of being one of the most productive and thoughtful corporate and securities law scholars in the nation. His recent work addresses issues such as hedge fund shareholder activism, executive compensation, corporate voting, corporate litigation, shareholder voting, and mergers and acquisitions. He joined the Vanderbilt Law faculty in 2000 to develop and direct the Law and Business Program.

JIANGYU WANG is Associate Professor at the National University of Singapore Faculty of Law. His teaching and research interests include international economic law, corporate and securities law, and law and development. He is also an executive member on the Governing Council of the WTO Institute of the China Law Society, an executive editor of the *Asian Journal of Comparative Law* and deputy editor-in-chief of the *Chinese Journal of Comparative Law*.

LIMING WANG is Professor of Law and Vice President of Renmin University, and he was one of the drafters of Chinese Contract Law, Property Law and Tort Law. Professor Wang has specialised in a wide range of fields of legal studies, such as methodology of jurisprudence, general principles of civil law, commercial law, property law, contract law, and tort law. He has published more than twenty books and 200 articles in various influential academic journals.

WEN-YEU WANG is Law Professor at National Taiwan University and has authored over 100 academic books and papers in Chinese or in English. Notable among them are 'Corporate versus Contractual Mutual Funds', *Washington Law Review* (1994) and 'The Best of Both Worlds? On Taiwan's Quasi-Public Enforcer of Corporate and Securities Law', *The Chinese Journal of Comparative Law* (2015). In addition, he has edited two books: *Codification in International Perspective* (2014) and *Codification in East Asia* (2014). He is the Chair of the Taiwan Committee, International Academy of Comparative Law. During the past two decades, he has offered formal courses at some leading law schools, including Stanford, Columbia, Tsinghua and Peking Law Schools.

XIANCHU ZHANG is a Professor of the University of Hong Kong. He is a Council Member of Chinese Judicial Studies Association of the Supreme People's Court, and a member of the Expert Committee of Foreign Related Trials Studies of China Law Society. He serves as a member of the editorial board of the *British Journal of Interdisciplinary Studies* and the Edward Elgar Asian Commercial, Financial and Economic Law and Policy Book Series. He is also an arbitrator of CIETAC and International Arbitration Commissions in Shanghai, Shenzhen and Tianjin. His main teaching and research interests have been on Chinese commercial law, regional conflict of laws and comparative law.

PREFACE

This volume collects the fruits of an unprecedented international academic conference, 'Public and Private Enforcement of Company Law and Securities Regulation – China and the World', which was held at the Chinese University of Hong Kong (CUHK) in December 2014 and convened by the Centre for Financial Regulation and Economic Development (CFRED) of the Faculty of Law of CUHK, the University of Michigan Law School and the Lieberthal Rogel Center for Chinese Studies at the University of Michigan.[1] The aim of the conference was to gather, in one place and at one time, some of the world's top academic specialists, legal practitioners and judicial personnel concerned with public and private enforcement of these two critical aspects of the legal system that govern the global economy and its capital markets, and to engage in an explicitly comparative discourse centred on a rapidly developing China, on one hand, and other developed and developing jurisdictions, on the other.

With ever-globalising capital markets, and particularly in the aftermath of the Global Financial Crisis of 2008, the enforcement of corporate law and securities regulation – both inside one country and across national borders – has garnered significant attention worldwide. While a great deal has been written about comparative corporate governance and the role of law – and specifically different legal and political systems – in the development of capital markets and overall economic development, the focus of that scholarship has been mainly on substantive law and institutional development, with much less attention paid to actual enforcement mechanisms and effects. This collection represents an effort to start filling this critical gap.

In our view, this book has at least four important features. First, and as noted above, it is devoted to relatively understudied but critically

[1] See conference website and list of participants and papers delivered at https://webapp1.law.cuhk.edu.hk/2014conference/1213/cfred/index.php.

important issues for corporate law and securities regulation. To be sure, the well-known 'law and finance' school of academic writing does take into consideration enforcement-related variables in explaining different levels of development amongst global financial markets. However, this particular approach to enforcement issues must be questioned because it focuses largely on formal, rather than applied, enforcement mechanisms. Accordingly, this book seeks to examine how these enforcement mechanisms are actually applied in practice across a wide number of legal and political systems that have firms which issue securities and capital markets, and what factors have determined the institutional environment for the making and application of these enforcement mechanisms.

Second, the book has a special focus on the case of the People's Republic of China (PRC). Compared with other jurisdictions, the PRC has received much less attention in both the analytical and empirical scholarship on comparative corporate and securities law, despite the fact that it is now the world's second largest economy and its issuer firms and increasingly institutional investors have a very significant role in the global capital markets. As an emerging as well as a transitional economy, China presents a particularly interesting case study, thanks to its distinctive political economy, its reconstructed and under-construction legal and regulatory system, and apparently its successful development model. In the PRC, the enforcement of corporate governance and capital markets norms impact directly on areas of critical import and some sensitivity, such as economic reform and the efficient allocation of capital; the development of Chinese capital markets under the much-discussed 'state capitalism' model; the power of China's strongest political economic actors and their impact on China's legal and regulatory system; and the form and function of China's law and legal institutions, from courts to the private bar. Hence, it is our hope that this book will be a first step in giving PRC corporate law and securities regulation enforcement the relatively detailed and comprehensive treatment it deserves in order to embrace a broader global comparative context.

Third, the book tries to broaden its scope from a necessary concern with the PRC to the examination of the enforcement of corporate and securities laws across the globe from a comparative perspective. To this end, the book covers a total of 13 jurisdictions: the US, the UK, Australia, Canada, Germany, Italy, Japan, Korea, India, Brazil, Taiwan and Hong Kong, as well as the PRC. These jurisdictions were carefully selected to cover the various divides – such as the purported fundamental differences between the common law and civil law systems, 'the West' and 'the rest', and 'developed' and 'developing' economies – that are traditionally drawn in the comparative law literature on these questions, notwithstanding the broadly accepted convergence driven by increasingly transnational capital markets. While it was, in concept, a daunting task to attempt to meaningfully discuss and compare so many jurisdictions, it was made a reality by a fourth and final feature of this book and its contributing authors: the assemblage of a veritable 'dream team' of conference participants and then contributors who are among the very best scholars and legal specialists in their respective jurisdictions.[2]

This book is divided into four parts. The first part, comprised of five chapters, lays the foundations of a theoretical framework and provides the context for the remaining three parts of the book. The second part consists of six chapters focusing on enforcement issues in the PRC. The third and fourth parts have six chapters each and are devoted to common law jurisdictions (the US, the UK, Australia, Canada, India and Hong Kong) and civil law jurisdictions (Germany, Italy, Japan, Korea, Brazil and Taiwan), respectively.

In the first chapter of Part I, we have included a *cri de coeur* by the Honourable Judge Jed S. Rakoff of the US District Court for the Southern District of New York, originally published in the 9 January 2014 issue of the *New York Review of Books*, which bemoans the lack of criminal enforcement after the Global Financial Crisis. Judge Rakoff is one of the most forceful and articulate judges ruling on the enforcement of corporate and securities law today. He is also a former US federal prosecutor with extensive experience in this area. We were honoured to have Judge Rakoff keynote our conference in Hong Kong, at which time he delivered an equally impassioned critique of the use (and abuse) of so-called 'deferred prosecutions', which was afterwards published as a review of Professor Brandon Garret's book *Too Big to Jail: How Prosecutors Compromise with Corporations* (Belknap Press/Harvard University Press, 2014) in the 9 February 2015 issue of the *New York Review of Books.*[3] In Chapter 2, Professor Mathias Reimann of the University of Michigan Law School provides a provocative and informative comparative view of private enforcement in the United States and Europe, adding what he understands to be the lessons for what are said to be 'civil law' Asian legal and economic systems. For Chapter 3, Professor

[2] For brief biographies of the contributors, see Notes on Contributors. For the names of the participants in the December 2014 conference, and their biographies, see https://webapp1.law.cuhk.edu.hk/2014conference/1213/cfred/speaker.php.

[3] Available at www.nybooks.com/articles/2015/02/19/justice-deferred-justice-denied/

Carsten Gerner-Beuerle of the London School of Economics and Political Science effects a unique historical consideration of the role of disclosure regulation and enforcement in the development of efficient capital markets in Germany and Britain of the late nineteenth and early twentieth centuries. Chapter 4 is a contribution by Professor Michael S. Barr, also of the University of Michigan Law School and a former Obama administration Assistant Secretary of the US Treasury for Financial Institutions (and key participant in the drafting of Dodd-Frank Wall Street Reform and Consumer Protection Act of 2010), on the pervasive use of mandatory arbitration clauses in consumer and financial contracts, and their impact on enforcement questions. In Chapter 5, Professor Donald Clarke of George Washington University then interrogates the reality of a much-theorised 'bonding' effect for PRC issuers listing overseas and asks whether or not such apparent 'bonding' should conjure a price premium apparently attributable to better enforcement.

Part II of the volume turns specifically to the PRC. Chapter 6 presents a paper given at the December 2014 Hong Kong conference by Renmin University of China's Vice President Liming Wang on his ideas for amelioration of the regulatory and statutory system for private enforcement against false and misleading disclosure in the PRC securities markets. The chapter was translated and annotated by Professor Nicholas Calcina Howson of the University of Michigan Law School. Given before the collapse of the Shanghai and Shenzhen Exchanges in the summer of 2015 and again at the start of 2016, Vice President Wang's views on private enforcement in this area are nonetheless of critical importance given his stature in China as a technical legislative drafter and master of China's developing hybrid civil-common law legal system and the still-ongoing wholesale amendment of the PRC Securities Law 2006. Professor Xianchu Zhang of the University of Hong Kong similarly addresses the in-process amendment of China's Securities Law in Chapter 7, with a special emphasis on the proposed introduction of a class action mechanism – or something close to it – in the PRC. In Chapter 8, Professor Robin Hui Huang of the Chinese University of Hong Kong gives readers perhaps the most comprehensive survey in existence of the progress of private securities law enforcement in the PRC. Junhai Liu, Professor of Law at Renmin University of China, in Chapter 9, records his own broad-ranging views on desired amendment of the PRC Securities Law. Professor Liu's contribution is important, as he has taken an active and very public role inside the PRC in suggesting the way forward for China's securities regulation program, and he participates in an Asian Development Bank expert group (with Professor Howson), advising the PRC legislature on this amendment of the PRC Securities Law. In Chapter 10, the National University of Singapore's Jiangyu Wang records his revealing conception of how the PRC courts actually enforce orthodox fiduciary duties in connection with China's company law, asserting that PRC judges are using something like tort law doctrine (and defences) in applying this most critical aspect of corporate law. Finally, Dr Xiaochun Liu, President of the newly autonomous Shenzhen Court of International Arbitration writes authoritatively in Chapter 11 on the possible use of arbitration – and not judicial enforcement – in sorting financial disputes arising in China's recently augmented 'Free Trade Zones'.

Part III of this book turns to common law jurisdictions and begins with Chapter 12 by Duke University's James D. Cox and Vanderbilt University's Randall S. Thomas. These two most authoritative observers of the US system argue that, perhaps surprisingly, more efficient corporate governance and market mechanisms have increasingly been used to address management agency costs over a progressively weakened representative shareholder litigation mechanism. Chapter 13 is a previously published paper by conference participant John Armour of Oxford University, writing with Bernard S. Black of Northwestern University, Brian R. Cheffins of Cambridge University and Richard Nolan of University of York. The authors attempt an empirical comparison of the 'law in action' (specifically, private enforcement of corporate law via fiduciary claims) in the US and the UK in the mid-2000s. Professor Jeffrey G. MacIntosh of the University of Toronto follows in Chapter 14 with an inventive and wide-ranging consideration of securities law enforcement, public and private, and how it contradicts or supports basic notions of 'rule of law'. Chapter 15 has Michael Legg of Sydney's University of New South Wales discussing the class action in Australia as presently implemented, and Chapter 16 is University of Michigan Law School Professor Vikramaditya Khanna's consideration of the class action in a jurisdiction that is both common law and 'Asian' – India. Finally in the common law jurisdictions part of the book, Chapter 17 provides a writing by the University of Hong Kong's Alexa Lam, a former Deputy Chief Executive of the Hong Kong Securities and Futures Commission, with a high-level and broadly philosophical analysis of how the Hong Kong SAR's securities laws are enforced, invoking some fascinating examples taken from her time as a leader of the Hong Kong enforcement apparatus.

The final section of this book, Part IV, addresses the enforcement of corporate law and securities regulation in civil law jurisdictions, or jurisdictions that are understood to be closer to the civil law system than the traditional common law nations. In Chapter 18, Professor Rainer Kulms of the Max Planck Institute for Comparative and International Private Law provides an expert appraisal of the enforcement problem with respect to a whole range of corporate or legal person entities in the German context and in the civil and criminal spheres. Professor Guido Ferrarini of the University of Genoa and Professor Paolo Giudici of the Free University of Bozen-Bolzano turn to Italy – 'ten years after Parmalat' – in Chapter 19, bemoaning the continuing lack of effectiveness in the particular Italian circumstance. Chapter 20 has University of Tokyo Professor Gen Goto's presentation on the progress of private securities litigation against securities issuers in Japan. Chapter 21 offers the same consideration but with respect to South Korea by Hwa-Jin Kim, a professor at Seoul National University and William W. Cook Global Law Professor at University of Michigan Law School. In Chapter 22, National Taiwan University's Professor Wen-Yeu Wang studies, in a comparative manner, what he and others have called Taiwan's 'semi-public' enforcement model – the Investor Protection Center starting in 2003 (and successor to a similar body from 1998) – a mechanism which continues to attract significant attention in the PRC across the Taiwan Straits. The last chapter in this book, Chapter 23, sees Professors John Armour and Caroline Schmidt, both of Oxford University, describe the developing institutional basis for enforcement of corporate and securities law in Brazil, a jurisdiction which has, over the decade, attracted a great deal of study.

This book was made possible only with the generous financial and moral support of many individuals and institutions, not least the Chinese University of Hong Kong Law Faculty, the University of Michigan Law School and the Lieberthal Rogel Center for Chinese Studies at the University of Michigan. As conference convenors and editors of this volume, we have benefitted immensely from the vision and commitment of the respective leaders of those three institutions in enabling the December 2014 international conference which provided the vehicle for creation of this book: Dean Christopher Gane of the Chinese University of Hong Kong Law Faculty; Dean Mark West of the University of Michigan Law School; and Professor Mary Gallagher, Director of the Lieberthal Rogel Center for Chinese Studies at the University of Michigan. We are also immensely grateful for the financial support provided by the Hong Kong Research Grants Council Theme-Based Research Scheme, 'Enhancing Hong Kong's Future as a Leading International Financial Centre'. Moreover, we wish to express our thanks to the participants in the conference and, thus, the contributors to this volume, who travelled to Hong Kong from seemingly every corner of the globe to participate in an intensive and uniquely productive meeting.

Special thanks must also go to CFRED Research Assistant Ms. Susanna Leone who worked tirelessly, creatively and efficiently in organising every aspect of the December 2014 conference and in editing this book. Lastly, our gratitude goes to the staff of Cambridge University Press for their invaluable assistance with this book project.

PART I

Theoretical Framework

1

The Financial Crisis

Why Have No High-Level Executives Been Prosecuted?

JED S. RAKOFF

Five years have passed since the onset of what is sometimes called the Great Recession. While the economy has slowly improved, there are still millions of Americans leading lives of quiet desperation: without jobs, without resources, without hope.

Who was to blame? Was it simply a result of negligence, of the kind of inordinate risk-taking commonly called a 'bubble', of an imprudent but innocent failure to maintain adequate reserves for a rainy day? Or was it the result, at least in part, of fraudulent practices, of dubious mortgages portrayed as sound risks and packaged into ever more esoteric financial instruments, the fundamental weaknesses of which were intentionally obscured?

If it was the former – if the recession was due, at worst, to a lack of caution – then the criminal law has no role to play in the aftermath. For in all but a few circumstances (not here relevant), the fierce and fiery weapon called criminal prosecution is directed at intentional misconduct and nothing less. If the Great Recession was in no part the handiwork of intentionally fraudulent practices by high-level executives, then to prosecute such executives criminally would be 'scapegoating' of the most shallow and despicable kind.

But if, by contrast, the Great Recession was in material part the product of intentional fraud, the failure to prosecute those responsible must be judged one of the more egregious failures of the criminal justice system in many years. Indeed, it would stand in striking contrast to the increased success that federal prosecutors have had over the past fifty

Jed S. Rakoff, 'The Financial Crisis: Why Have No High-Level Executives Been Prosecuted?' *New York Review of Books* (9 Jan 2014). First appeared in *New York Review of Books*. Reproduced by permission.

years or so in bringing to justice even the highest-level figures who orchestrated mammoth frauds. Thus, in the 1970s, in the aftermath of the 'junk bond' bubble that, in many ways, was a precursor of the more recent bubble in mortgage-backed securities, the progenitors of the fraud were all successfully prosecuted, right up to Michael Milken.

Again, in the 1980s, the so-called savings-and-loan crisis, which again had some eerie parallels to more recent events, resulted in the successful criminal prosecution of more than 800 individuals, right up to Charles Keating. And again, the widespread accounting frauds of the 1990s, most vividly represented by Enron and WorldCom, led directly to the successful prosecution of such previously respected CEOs as Jeffrey Skilling and Bernie Ebbers.

In striking contrast with these past prosecutions, not a single high-level executive has been successfully prosecuted in connection with the recent financial crisis, and given the fact that most of the relevant criminal provisions are governed by a five-year statute of limitations, it appears likely that none will be. It may not be too soon, therefore, to ask why.

One possibility, already mentioned, is that no fraud was committed. This possibility should not be discounted. Every case is different, and I, for one, have no opinion about whether criminal fraud was committed in any given instance.

But the stated opinion of those government entities asked to examine the financial crisis overall is not that no fraud was committed – quite the contrary. For example, the Financial Crisis Inquiry Commission, in its final report, uses variants of the word 'fraud' no fewer than 157 times in describing what led to the crisis, concluding that there was a 'systemic breakdown,' not just in accountability, but also in ethical behaviour.

As the commission found, the signs of fraud were everywhere to be seen, with the number of reports of suspected mortgage fraud rising twentyfold between 1996 and 2005 and then doubling again in the next four years. As early as 2004, FBI Assistant Director Chris Swecker was publicly warning of the 'pervasive problem' of mortgage fraud that was driven by the voracious demand for mortgage-backed securities. Similar warnings, many from within the financial community, were disregarded, not because they were viewed as inaccurate, but because, as one high-level banker put it, 'a decision was made that "We're going to have to hold our nose and start buying the stated product if we want to stay in business".'

Without giving further examples, the point is that, in the aftermath of the financial crisis, the prevailing view of many government officials (as well as others) was that the crisis was, in material respects, the product of intentional fraud. In a nutshell, the fraud, they argued, was a simple one. Subprime mortgages, i.e. mortgages of dubious creditworthiness, increasingly provided the chief collateral for highly leveraged securities that were marketed as AAA, i.e. securities of very low risk. How could this transformation of a sow's ear into a silk purse be accomplished unless someone dissembled along the way?

While officials of the Department of Justice have been more circumspect in describing the roots of the financial crisis than have the various commissions of inquiry and other government agencies, I have seen nothing to indicate their disagreement with the widespread conclusion that fraud at every level permeated the bubble in mortgage-backed securities. Rather, their position has been to excuse their failure to prosecute high-level individuals for fraud in connection with the financial crisis on one or more of three grounds:

First, they have argued that proving fraudulent intent on the part of the high-level management of the banks and companies involved has been difficult. It is undoubtedly true that the ranks of top management were several levels removed from those who were putting together the collateralised debt obligations and other securities offerings that were based on dubious mortgages, and the people generating the mortgages themselves were often at other companies and thus even further removed. And I want to stress again that I have no opinion whether any given top executive had knowledge of the dubious nature of the underlying mortgages, let alone fraudulent intent. But what I do find surprising is that the Department of Justice should view the proving of intent as so difficult in this case. Who, for example, was generating the so-called 'suspicious activity reports' of mortgage fraud that, as mentioned, increased so hugely in the years leading up to the crisis? Why, the banks themselves. A top-level banker, one might argue, confronted with growing evidence from his own and other banks that mortgage fraud was increasing, might have inquired why his bank's mortgage-based securities continued to receive AAA ratings. And if, despite these and other reports of suspicious activity, the executive failed to make such inquiries, might it be because he did not want to know what such inquiries would reveal?

This, of course, is what is known in the law as 'wilful blindness' or 'conscious disregard'. It is a well-established basis on which federal prosecutors have asked juries to infer intent, including in cases involving complexities, such as accounting rules, at least as esoteric as those involved in the events leading up to the financial crisis. And while some federal courts have occasionally expressed qualifications about the use of the wilful blindness approach to prove intent, the Supreme Court has consistently approved it. As that Court stated most recently in *Global-Tech Appliances, Inc.* v. *SEB S.A.* (2011):

> The doctrine of willful blindness is well established in criminal law. Many criminal statutes require proof that a defendant acted knowingly or willfully, and courts applying the doctrine of willful blindness hold that defendants cannot escape the reach of these statutes by deliberately shielding themselves from clear evidence of critical facts that are strongly suggested by the circumstances.

Thus, the department's claim that proving intent in the financial crisis is particularly difficult may strike some as doubtful.

Second, and even more weakly, the Department of Justice has sometimes argued that, because the institutions to whom mortgage-backed securities were sold were themselves sophisticated investors, it might be difficult to prove reliance. Thus, in defending the failure to prosecute high-level executives for frauds arising from the sale of mortgage-backed securities, Lanny Breuer, the then head of the Department of Justice's Criminal Division, told PBS:

> In a criminal case ... I have to prove not only that you made a false statement but that you intended to commit a crime, and also that the other side of the transaction relied on what you were saying. And frankly, in many of the securitizations and the kinds of transactions we're talking about, in reality you had very sophisticated counterparties on both sides. And so even though one side may have said something was dark blue when really we can say it was sky blue, the other side of the transaction, the other sophisticated party, wasn't relying at all on the description of the color.

Actually, given the fact that these securities were bought and sold at lightning speed, it is by no means obvious that even a sophisticated counterparty would have detected the problems with the arcane, convoluted mortgage-backed derivatives they were being asked to purchase. But there is a more fundamental problem with the above-quoted statement from the former head of the Criminal Division, which is that it totally misstates the law. In actuality, in a criminal fraud case, the government is never required to prove – ever – that one party to a transaction relied on the word of another. The reason, of course, is that that would give a crooked seller a licence to lie whenever he was dealing with a sophisticated buyer. The law, however, says that society is harmed when a seller purposely lies about a material fact, even if the immediate purchaser does not rely on that particular fact, because such misrepresentations create problems for the market as a whole. And surely there never was a situation in which the sale of dubious mortgage-backed securities created more of a problem for the marketplace, and society as a whole, than in the recent financial crisis.

The third reason the department has sometimes given for not bringing these prosecutions is that to do so would itself harm the economy. Thus, Attorney General Eric Holder himself told Congress:

> It does become difficult for us to prosecute them when we are hit with indications that if you do prosecute – if you do bring a criminal charge – it will have a negative impact on the national economy, perhaps even the world economy.

To a federal judge, who takes an oath to apply the law equally to rich and to poor, this excuse – sometimes labelled the 'too big to jail' excuse – is disturbing, frankly, in what it says about the department's apparent disregard for equality under the law.

In fairness, however, Holder (who later claimed his comment was misconstrued) was referring to the prosecution of financial institutions, rather than their CEOs. Moreover, he might have also been influenced, as his department unquestionably was, by the adverse reaction to the Arthur Anderson case, where that accounting firm was forced out of business by a prosecution that was ultimately reversed on appeal. But if we are talking about prosecuting individuals, the excuse becomes entirely irrelevant; for no one that I know of has ever contended that a big financial institution would collapse if one or more of its high-level executives were prosecuted as opposed to the institution itself.

Without multiplying examples further, my point is that the Department of Justice has never taken the position that all the top executives involved in the events leading up to the financial crisis were innocent; rather it has offered one or another excuse for not criminally prosecuting them – excuses that, on inspection, appear unconvincing. So, you might ask, what's really going on here? I don't claim to have any inside information about the real reasons why no such prosecutions have been brought, but I take the liberty of offering some speculations.

At the outset, however, let me say that I completely discount the argument sometimes made that no such prosecutions have been brought because the top prosecutors were often people who previously represented the financial institutions in question and/or were people who expected to be representing such institutions in the future: the so-called 'revolving door'. In my experience, most federal prosecutors, at every level, are seeking to make a name for themselves, and the best way to do that is by prosecuting some high-level person. While companies that are indicted almost always settle, individual defendants whose careers are at stake will often go to trial. And if the government wins such a trial, as it usually does, the prosecutor's reputation is made. My point is that whatever small influence the 'revolving door' may have in discouraging certain white-collar prosecutions is more than offset, at least in the case of prosecuting high-level individuals, by the career-making benefits such prosecutions confer on the successful prosecutor.

So, one asks again, why haven't we seen such prosecutions growing out of the financial crisis? I offer, by way of speculation, three influences that I think, along with others, have had the effect of limiting such prosecutions.

First, the prosecutors had other priorities. Some of these were completely understandable. For example, before 2001, the FBI had more than 1,000 agents assigned to investigating financial frauds, but after September 11, many of these agents were shifted to antiterrorism work. Who can argue with that? Yet the result was that, by 2007 or so, there were only 120 agents reviewing the more than 50,000 reports of mortgage fraud filed by the banks. It is true that after the collapse of Lehman Brothers in 2008, new agents were hired for some of the vacated spots in offices concerned with fraud detection, but this is not a form of detection easily learned, and recent budget limitations have only exacerbated the problem.

Of course, while the FBI has substantial responsibility for investigating mortgage fraud, the FBI is not the primary investigator of fraud in the sale of mortgage-backed securities; that responsibility lies mostly with the SEC. But at the very time the financial crisis was breaking, the SEC was trying to deflect criticism from its failure to detect the Madoff fraud, and this led it to concentrate on other Ponzi-like schemes that emerged in the wake of the financial crisis, along with cases involving misallocation of assets (such as stealing funds from a customer), which are among the easiest cases to prove. Indeed, as Professor John Coffee of Columbia Law School has repeatedly documented, Ponzi schemes and misallocation-of-asset cases have been the primary focus of the SEC since 2009, while cases involving fraud in the sale of mortgage-backed securities have been much less frequent. More recently, moreover, the SEC has been hard hit by budget limitations, and this has not only made it more difficult to assign the kind of manpower the kinds of frauds we are talking about require, but also has led the SEC enforcement staff to focus on the smaller, more easily resolved cases that will beef up their statistics when they go to Congress begging for money.

As for the Department of Justice proper, a decision was made in 2009 to spread the investigation of financial fraud cases among numerous US Attorney's Offices, many of which had little or no previous experience in investigating and prosecuting sophisticated financial frauds. This was in connection with the president's creation of a special task force to investigate the crisis, from which remarkably little has been heard in the intervening four-plus years. At the same time, the US Attorney's Office with the greatest expertise in these kinds of cases, the Southern District of New York, was just embarking on its prosecution of insider-trading cases arising from the Raj Rajaratnam tapes, which soon proved a goldmine of prosecutable cases that absorbed a huge amount of the attention of the securities fraud unit of that office.

While I want to stress again that I have no inside information, as a former chief of that unit, I would venture to guess that the cases involving the financial crisis were parcelled out to assistant US attorneys who were also responsible for insider-trading cases. Which do you think an assistant would devote most of her attention to: an insider-trading case that was already nearly ready to go to indictment and that might lead to a high-visibility trial, or a financial crisis case that was just getting started, would take years to complete and had no guarantee of even leading to an indictment? Of course, she would put her energy into the insider-trading case, and if she was lucky, it would go to trial, she would win and, in some cases, she would then take a job with a large law firm. And in the process, the financial fraud case would get lost in the shuffle.

In short, a focus on quite different priorities is, I submit, one of the reasons the financial fraud cases have not been brought, especially cases against high-level individuals that would take many years, many investigators and a great deal of expertise to investigate. But a second, and less salutary, reason for not bringing such cases is the government's own involvement in the underlying circumstances that led to the financial crisis.

On the one hand, the government, writ large, had a part in creating the conditions that encouraged the approval of dubious mortgages. Even before the start of the housing boom, it was the government, in the form of Congress, that repealed the Glass-Steagall Act, thus allowing certain banks that had previously viewed mortgages as a source of interest income to become instead deeply involved in securitising pools of mortgages in order to obtain the much-greater profits available from trading. It was the government, in the form of both the executive and the legislature, that encouraged deregulation, thus weakening the power and oversight not only of the SEC but also of such diverse banking overseers as the Office of Thrift Supervision and the Office of the Comptroller of the Currency, both in the Treasury Department. It was the government, in the form of the Federal Reserve, that kept interest rates low, in part to encourage mortgages. It was the government, in the form of the executive, that strongly encouraged banks to make loans to individuals with low incomes who might have previously been regarded as too risky to warrant a mortgage.

Thus, in the year 2000, HUD Secretary Andrew Cuomo increased to 50 per cent the percentage of low-income mortgages that the government-sponsored entities known as Fannie Mae and Freddie Mac were required to purchase, helping to create the conditions that resulted in over half of all mortgages being subprime at the time the housing market began to collapse in 2007.

It was the government, pretty much across the board, that acquiesced in the ever-greater tendency not to require meaningful documentation as a condition of obtaining a mortgage, often preempting in this regard state regulations designed to assure greater mortgage quality and a borrower's ability to repay. Indeed, in the year 2000, the Office of Thrift Supervision, having just finished a successful campaign to preempt state regulation of thrift underwriting, terminated its own underwriting regulations entirely.

The result of all this was the mortgages that later became known as 'liars' loans'. They were increasingly risky; but what did the banks care, since they were making their money from the securitisations? And what did the government care, since it was helping to create a boom in the economy and helping voters to realise their dream of owning a home?

Moreover, the government was also deeply enmeshed in the aftermath of the financial crisis. It was the government that proposed the shotgun marriages of, among others, Bank of America with Merrill Lynch and JP Morgan with Bear Stearns. If, in the process, mistakes were made and liabilities not disclosed, was it not partly the government's fault? One does not necessarily have to adopt the view of Neil Barofsky, former special inspector general in charge of oversight of TARP, that regulators made almost no effort to hold accountable the financial institutions they were bailing out, to wonder whether the government, having helped create the conditions that led to the seeming widespread fraud in the mortgage-backed securities market, was all too ready to forgive its alleged perpetrators.

Please do not misunderstand me. I am not suggesting that the government knowingly participated in any of the fraudulent practices alleged by the Financial Inquiry Crisis Commission and others. But what I am suggesting is that the government was deeply involved, from beginning to end, in helping create the conditions that could lead to such fraud and that this would give a prudent prosecutor pause in deciding whether to indict a CEO who might, with some justice, claim that he was only doing what he fairly believed the government wanted him to do.

The final factor I would mention is both the most subtle and the most systemic of the three, and arguably the most important. It is the shift that has occurred, over the past thirty years or more, from focusing on prosecuting high-level individuals to focusing on prosecuting companies and other institutions. It is true that prosecutors have brought criminal charges against companies for well over a hundred years, but until relatively recently, such prosecutions were the exception, and prosecutions of companies without simultaneous prosecutions of their managerial agents were even rarer.

The reasons were obvious. Companies do not commit crimes; only their agents do. And while a company might get the benefit of some such crimes, prosecuting the company would inevitably punish, directly or indirectly, the many employees and shareholders who were totally innocent. Moreover, under the law of most US jurisdictions, a company cannot be criminally liable unless at least one managerial agent has committed the crime in question; so why not prosecute the agent who actually committed the crime?

In recent decades, however, prosecutors have been increasingly attracted to prosecuting companies, often even without indicting a single person. This shift has often been rationalised as part of an attempt to transform 'corporate cultures', so as to prevent future such crimes; and as a result, government policy has taken the form of 'deferred prosecution agreements' or even 'nonprosecution agreements', in which the company, under threat of criminal prosecution, agrees to take various prophylactic measures to prevent future wrongdoing. Such agreements have become, in the words of Lanny Breuer, the former head of the Department of Justice's Criminal Division, 'a mainstay of white-collar criminal law enforcement', with the department entering into 233 such agreements over the last decade. But in practice, I suggest, this approach has led to some lax and dubious behaviour on the part of prosecutors, with deleterious results.

If you are a prosecutor attempting to discover the individuals responsible for an apparent financial fraud, you go about your business in much the same way you go after mobsters or drug kingpins: you start at the bottom and, over many months or years, slowly work your way up. Specifically, you start by 'flipping' some lower- or mid-level participant in the fraud who you can show was directly responsible for making one or more false material misrepresentations but who is willing to cooperate and maybe even 'wear a wire' – i.e. secretly record his colleagues – in order to reduce his sentence. With his help, and aided by the substantial prison penalties now available in white-collar cases, you go up the ladder.

But if your priority is prosecuting the company, a different scenario takes place. Early in the investigation, you invite in counsel to the company and explain to him or her why you suspect fraud. He or she responds by assuring you that the company wants to cooperate and do the right thing, and to that end, the company has hired a former assistant US attorney, now a partner at a respected law firm, to do an internal investigation. The company's counsel asks you to defer your investigation until the company's own internal investigation is completed, on the condition that the company will share its results with you. In order to save time and resources, you agree.

Six months later, the company's counsel returns with a detailed report showing that mistakes were made but that the company is now intent on correcting them. You and the company then agree that the company will enter into a deferred prosecution agreement that couples some immediate fines with the imposition of expensive but internal prophylactic measures. For all practical purposes, the case is now over. You are happy because you believe that you have helped prevent future crimes; the company is happy because it has avoided a devastating indictment; and perhaps the happiest of all are the executives, or former executives, who actually committed the underlying misconduct, for they are left untouched.

I suggest that this is not the best way to proceed. Although it is supposedly justified because it prevents future crimes, I suggest that the future deterrent value of successfully prosecuting individuals far outweighs the prophylactic benefits of imposing internal compliance measures that are often little more than window dressing. Just going after the company is also both technically and morally suspect. It is technically suspect because, under the law, you should not indict or threaten to indict a company unless you can prove beyond a reasonable doubt that some managerial agent of the company committed the alleged crime; and if you can prove that, why not indict the manager? And from a moral standpoint, punishing a company and its many innocent employees and shareholders for the crimes committed by some unprosecuted individuals seems contrary to elementary notions of moral responsibility.

These criticisms take on special relevance, however, in the instance of investigations growing out of the financial crisis, because, as noted, the Department of Justice's position, until at least recently, is that going after the suspect institutions poses too great a risk to the nation's economic recovery. So you don't go after the companies, at least not criminally, because they are too big to jail, and you don't go after the individuals, because that would involve the kind of years-long investigations that you no longer have the experience or the resources to pursue.

In conclusion, I want to stress again that I do not claim that the financial crisis that is still causing so many of us so much pain and despondency was the product, in whole or in part, of fraudulent misconduct. But if it was – as various governmental authorities have asserted it was – then the failure of the government to bring to justice those responsible for such colossal fraud bespeaks weaknesses in our prosecutorial system that need to be addressed.

2

Private Enforcement in the United States and in Europe

A Comparative Perspective and Potential Lessons for Asia

MATHIAS REIMANN

Introduction: Three Levels of Comparison (and Three Caveats)

The private enforcement of regulatory agendas is a major issue of increasingly global dimensions. This is especially true in the areas of antitrust, securities regulation, and company law. It also plays a role in consumer protection (such as product liability), anti-discrimination law, and the environmental field.

In the United States, such private enforcement has a long history.[1] In Europe, it has become an important agenda since the 1990s. Today, the developed economies of Asia face it as well. Can the third major economic area of the world learn something by looking at the approaches of the other two?

In pursuit of that question, I will present some comparative perspectives on the self-confident US-American regime and its more hesitant European counterpart, proffering potential lessons for an Asian audience. I will compare the two sides of the Atlantic on three levels. First, I will, very briefly, consider the *practical importance* of private enforcement in the United States and Europe. Second, I will, also quite briefly, look at the respective *legal environments*, especially the procedural, institutional, and professional frameworks. Third, and most extensively, I will ruminate about the different *cultural contexts* in order to show how they entail different deeper meanings of private enforcement. In addition, I will ask how all this relates to the traditional dichotomy between the civil and the common law. Finally, I will consider the role of the European Union in this context.

[1] For an overview, see Maria Glover, 'The Structural Role of Private Enforcement Mechanisms in Public Law', 53 Wm.& Mary L.R. 1137 (2012), 1146–1153.

At the outset, three caveats are in order. Most importantly, I am no specialist in any of the substantive areas involved – I'm not an antitrust, securities, or corporate law scholar; instead, I am a European–American comparativist. Also, I will generalise almost to the point of recklessness. Speaking of 'the United States' as a whole is quite brave to begin with because there is much diversity within that country even with regard to private enforcement. Discussing 'Europe' as a unitary culture is even more questionable because there the diversity is even greater than in the US. And lumping the legal systems on the Pacific Rim together under the label of 'Asia' is excusable at best because I involve them merely as an audience. Yet, such generalisations are the price for trying to bring some fundamental assumptions and structures into sharp relief. Finally, it is an orthodoxy in comparative law that drawing 'lessons' from one system for others is risky business in light of the law's notorious contingency on almost everything. My 'lessons for Asia' can thus be no more than food for further thought.

1 Practical Importance: How Much Does Private Enforcement Matter?

Assessing the practical importance of private enforcement in the United States and Europe is both very simple and somewhat dubious.

1.1 The Simple Case

Let us begin with the simple case. Private enforcement of regulatory agendas plays a central role in the United States while it is of merely marginal importance in Europe. This is both largely uncontested and fairly obvious.[2] To be sure, this practical importance varies – and quite considerably – across areas of substantive law. In the United States, it is predominant in antitrust law, corporate law, and even more so in products liability;[3] it is very significant in securities law and employment discrimination;[4] and it is still quite substantial in environmental and civil rights protection.[5] In European countries, it plays some role with regard

[2] For an impressive graph depicting the situation in the United States, see David Freeman Engstrom, 'Agencies as Litigation Gatekeepers', 123 YALE L.J. 616 (2013), 626.

[3] See, e.g. Kip Viscusi, *Regulation through Litigation*, AEI-Brookings Joint Center for Regulatory Studies, Washington, DC (2002).

[4] Stephanie Bornstein, 'Rights in Recession: Toward Administrative Antidiscrimination Law', 33 *Yale Law and Policy Review* 119 (2014).

[5] See, e.g. David Engstrom, 'Agencies as Litigation Gatekeepers', 123 YALE L.J. 616 (2013), 627–629.

to securities fraud, remains low in antitrust, company, and consumer protection law, and is almost unknown in the environmental and civil rights context.[6]

1.2 The Dubious Foundation

In what sense is such an assessment 'somewhat dubious'? It is true that almost all observers would at least roughly agree with almost all of my description, but comparisons between the United States and the European side are largely based on general impressions, not on sound empirical evidence.[7] To be sure, in the United States, there are many empirical studies,[8] but on the European side, there are very few, and on the comparative level, there are almost none.[9]

Still, it is fairly safe to say that, on the whole, the transatlantic differences are very large. A thought experiment shows that very nicely: assume that all private enforcement of regulatory policies is abolished tomorrow. In the United States, that would dramatically change the nature of the game; in European countries, it would merely require some, fairly limited, adjustment.

1.3 A Lesson for Asia?

If there is a lesson for Asia here, it is quite simple – but nonetheless very significant: modern economies can succeed with or without a lot of private enforcement. Of course, this does not mean that it is irrelevant.

[6] For antitrust law (usually termed competition law in Europe), see Thomas Möllers and Andreas Heinemann, eds., *The Enforcement of Competition Law in Europe*, Cambridge University Press, Cambridge and New York (2008) 389–390; David Gerber, 'Private Enforcement of Competition Law: A Comparative Perspective' in Möllers and Heinemann (eds.), *The Enforcement of Competition Law in Europe*, 431; for corporate law especially in the United Kingdom, John Armour, Bernard Black, Brian Cheffins, and Richard Nolan, 'Private Enforcement of Corporate Law: An Empirical Comparison of the United Kingdom and the United States', 6 *Journal of Empirical Studies* 687 (2009).

[7] For a fuller discussion of this problem, see Mathias Reimann, 'Präventiv-administrative Regulierung oder *Private Law Enforcement*, Bitburger Gespräche, Jahrbuch 2009/I, 105, 107–109.

[8] See, e.g. Joshua Davis and Robert Lande, 'Toward an Empirical and Theoretical Assessment of Private Antitrust Enforcement', 36 SEATTLE U.L.REV. 1269 (2013) (finding that private antitrust actions lead to substantial damage recoveries and have a strong deterrent effect).

[9] An exception is the study by Armour, Black, Cheffins, and Nolan, 'Private Enforcement of Corporate Law'.

Reliance on private enforcement may very well increase efficiency, enhance competition, and strengthen investor protection, though these effects are very hard to measure. Still, the very different levels of practical importance in the United States and Europe show that a strong regime of private enforcement is not indispensable for economic success. In other words, reliance on private enforcement is an option, not a must.

2 The Legal Frameworks: Procedural, Institutional, and Professional Conditions

It is widely assumed that the differences in the practical importance of private enforcement are largely due to differences in the broader *legal frameworks* on both sides of the Atlantic. This explanation is quite plausible although it is, again, based on very little empirical evidence. It is also, as I will show later (Section 3), remarkably incomplete. While there is thus no need for an elaborate discussion here, the impact of the respective legal frameworks needs to be put on the table at least in summary fashion, in part because it calls for an important note of caution.

2.1 The Traditional Account: Favourable versus Unfavourable Conditions

The traditional account has been that in the United States, the broader legal framework creates highly favourable conditions for private enforcement, while in Europe, it does not. On both sides of the Atlantic, this is assumed to be due to a combination of legal, institutional, and professional factors.

In the United States, private enforcement is fostered by potent private remedies that create strong incentives to sue, both for plaintiffs and their lawyers – most obviously in the form of treble damages in antitrust actions, but also through punitive damages and a generally high level of awards. In addition, US-American plaintiffs operate in a favourable procedural environment: they bear little risk of high litigation costs because their lawyers usually work on a contingency fee basis and because costs are normally not shifted to the losing party.[10] Class actions allow them to band together, be it to aggregate small claims or simply to increase the pressure

[10] In some areas, such as antitrust or civil rights actions, statutes even provide for one-way fee shifting: the victorious plaintiff can recover court and lawyer fees from the vanquished defendant, but not the other way around; see 15 U.S.C. § 15(a) (Clayton Act); 42 U.S.C. § 1988(b) (Civil Rights Attorney's Fees Award Act of 1976).

on defendants. And notoriously sharp discovery tools permit an extensive search for damning evidence, even if it is in the possession of the other side. In addition, there are important institutional factors, such as (especially federal) courts endowed with ample power and resources to handle high-impact litigation, and, of course, civil jury trials. Last, but not least, there is a plaintiffs' bar which is highly specialised, well-funded, and aggressive – willing and capable to take on even the most formidable business entities. In short, in the United States, the overall legal framework has traditionally provided a powerful tailwind for private actions.

In Europe, as observers have easily noted, almost none of these favourable conditions have existed. To be sure, private causes of action are not lacking; this is well known, especially in European antitrust law,[11] but it is also true in securities and company law.[12] Yet, they are risky to pursue, hard to win, and, at best, modestly rewarding. Suing for damages often holds little promise without class actions, effective discovery, and (at least the threat of) jury trials.[13] The risk of having to bear enormous litigation costs is high without contingency fee arrangements and especially because the loser often has to make the winner whole. There are virtually no multiple damages, punitive damages are rarely allowed and even more rarely imposed,[14] and awards are often modest. In addition, there are few lawyers specialised, powerful, and hungry enough to take on big corporations, banks, and other deep pockets. In sum, in Europe, the wind blows hard into the face of private enforcement at almost every turn.

2.2 A Note of Caution: Recent Convergence

While this traditional view suffers from overgeneralisation and thus presents somewhat of a caricature, there is much truth in it: the legal

[11] See Council Regulation (EC) No. 1/2003 of 16 December 2002 on the implementation of the rules on competition laid down in Articles 81 and 82 of the Treaty, O.J. L1 (4 January 2003) 1–25.

[12] In Germany, for example, private causes of action are provided in §§ 37 (b) and (c) Wertpapierhandelsgesetz (Securities Trade Law) (liability for insider trading); §§ 93 and 148 Aktiengesetz (Securities Law) (liability of corporate directors, admissibility of derivative actions); and § 826 BGB (Civil Code) (general tort liability for intentional misconduct harming others in a manner contrary to standards of decency).

[13] For antitrust law, see Möller and Heinemann, The Enforcement of Competition Law in Europe, at 266–267; for company law, see Ulrich Schmolke, Die Aktionärsklage nach § 148 AktG – Anreizwirkungen de lege lata und Reformanregungen de lege ferenda, *Zeitschrift für Unternehmens- und Gesellschaftsrecht* 40 (2011) 398–442.

[14] But see below note 70.

frameworks in the United States and Europe differ substantially, and they have a significant impact on the frequency and effectiveness of private enforcement. Still, one must sound a major note of caution, which is that the traditional picture has become dated in important respects.

In the United States, conditions for private enforcement have recently become considerably less favourable in several, though not in all, regards. Today, punitive damages are often capped and have become subject to constitutional control for excessiveness.[15] Legislative reforms as well as the Supreme Court have made class actions much more difficult to maintain than a decade or two ago,[16] discovery has often been curtailed, and standards of pleading and proof have been raised.[17] Jury trials have diminished almost to the vanishing point.[18] Private securities litigation has been curtailed, largely through Congressional legislation[19] but in part also by the US Supreme Court.[20] And in antitrust law, the US Supreme Court has recently pursued a conservative course, cutting back on remedies[21] and also on the extraterritorial reach federal legislation.[22]

In Europe, the trend has been in the opposite direction. More private remedies have been recognised, in part by the courts (*inter alia* the

[15] *BMW of North America* v. *Gore*, 517 U.S. 559 (1996); *State Farm Mutual Automobile Insurance Co.* v. *Campbell*, 538 U.S. 408 (2003); *Philip Morris* v. *Williams*, 548 U.S. 346 (2007).

[16] See, e.g. through the Class Action Fairness Act of 2005 (28 U.S.C. 1332(d), 1453, and 1711–1715). Notably, the Supreme Court has secured the right of providers of services and products to exclude class arbitration, *AT&T Mobility* v. *Concepcion*, 563 U.S. 321 (2011).

[17] At least in the federal courts, pleading requirements were rendered more stringent by the US Supreme Court in *Bell Atlantic Corp.* v. *Twombly*, 550 U.S. 544 (2007), an antitrust case; see also *Ashcroft* v. *Iqbal*, 556 U.S. 662 (2009); Alex Reinert, 'Measuring the Impact of Plausibility Pleading', 101 *Virginia Law Review* 2117 (2015). Proof was made more demanding in *Daubert* v. *Merrel Dow Pharmaceuticals*, 509 U.S. 579 (1993), a products liability case. For an overview, see Glover, 'The Structural Role of Private Enforcement Mechanisms in Public Law', at 1160–1175.

[18] Robert Burns, *The Death of the American Trial*, Chicago University Press, Chicago (2009). The threat of a jury trial remains, of course, but even that has become fairly remote in practice.

[19] Especially the Private Securities Litigation Reform Act of 1995 (codified as amended in various sections of 15 U.S.C.) and the Securities Litigation Uniform Standards Act of 1998 (ibid.).

[20] Adam Pritchard, 'Securities Law in the Roberts Court: Agenda or Indifference?', 37 *Journal of Corporation Law* 105 (2011).

[21] See, e.g. *Leegin Creative Leather Products, Inc., v. PSKS*, 551 U.S. 877 (2007); *Texaco, Inc., v. Fouad N. Dagher et al.*, 547 U.S. 1 (2006); *Independent Ink, Inc., v. Illinois Tool Works, Inc.*, 547 U.S. 1002 (2006); *Bell Atlantic Corp. v. William Twombly*, 548 U.S. 903 (2006).

[22] *Hoffmann-La Roche* v. *Empagran*, 542 U.S. 155 (2004); *Morrison* v. *National Australia Bank Ltd.*, 561 U.S. 247 (2010).

European Court Justice[23]), in part by legislatures.[24] Many countries have begun to allow various forms of success-oriented fees, litigation insurance, and outside litigation funding, all of which relieve plaintiffs of some of the cost risk.[25] Group or representative actions have become possible in many European legal systems,[26] and the creation of collective redress mechanisms has been a major agenda on the EU level.[27] There is also a general trend, especially at the EU level, to encourage, rather than discourage private enforcement. In October of 2014, the EU Council and Parliament issued a directive requiring the member states to facilitate private antitrust actions by allowing more extended discovery, rendering a public authority's finding of a violation binding in subsequent civil actions, and allowing damage claims by final victims, etc.[28]

As a result, there has been considerable convergence between the legal frameworks in the United States and in Europe: in the former, private enforcement has become harder, in the latter, easier.

2.3 *Lessons for Asia?*

What, if any, lessons does this provide for Asia? Let me suggest two.

The first is so time-worn that it borders on the trivial, and I hesitate even to mention it: if policy makers want to exercise the option of promoting greater private enforcement, they must recognise that providing private causes of action alone is not sufficient. Instead, successful implementation requires a favourable procedural, institutional, and professional environment. That, in turn, may require changing some fundamental features of the legal system as a whole, ranging from cost and fee allocation in civil procedure to the management of evidence-taking to the structure of the bar and attitudes towards collective action.

[23] Especially in antitrust law, *Courage Lts.* v. *Bernhard Crehan*, C-453/99, E.C.R. [2001] I-6267; *Manfredi* v. *Lloyd Adriatico*, C-295/04, E.C.R. [2006] I-6619.

[24] See, e.g. the provisions cited above note 12.

[25] Mathias Reimann, *Cost and Fee Allocation in Civil Procedure*, Springer, Dordrecht, Heidelberg, New York, London (2012), 39–42, 44–50.

[26] Ibid., at 42–44; see also Tiana Russell, 'Exporting Class Actions to the European Union', 28 *B.U.Int'l L.J.* 141 (2010), 168–170. More recently, France enacted a law providing for group actions in consumer cases, Loi no. 2014–344 (17 March 2014).

[27] Arnaud Nuyts and Nikitas Hatzimihail (eds.), *Cross-Border Class Actions: The European Way*, Sellier, Munich (2013).

[28] Directive of the European Parliament and of the Council on certain rules governing actions for damages under national law for infringement of the competition law provisions of the Member States and of the European Union, 2014/104, 26 November 2014.

The second lesson is that today, Asian observers of the situation in the United States and in Europe must take the traditional comparative view with a large grain of salt. In particular, they must recognise that the frameworks for private enforcement are not cast in stone on either side of the Atlantic. Legislatures and courts can change them, and they have done so quite seriously in recent years. This has caused some convergence. To be sure, important differences remain, but the United States is no longer the heaven of private enforcement, nor is Europe still the hell.

3 The Cultural Context: Conceptions of State, Law, and Litigation

Interestingly, however, the partial convergence of the legal frameworks on both sides of the Atlantic has not entailed an equal convergence of the practical impact. In particular, in Europe, the impact of private enforcement has remained very low, the long list of facilitating reforms notwithstanding. Why?

Three answers come to mind. They are all compatible as well as plausible. The first is that the reforms in Europe have not gone far enough. It is true that for potential plaintiffs, the procedural hurdles are still very high, winning is still fairly unrewarding, and losing can still be crushingly costly. The second answer is that it may be too early to tell. The reforms may require more time to take effect because victims, lawyers, and courts often react to new options with a considerable time lag. The third answer is that the legal framework is not the only, and perhaps not even the most important, factor determining whether private enforcement takes root. This may also depend – and rather heavily – on the respective legal tradition and culture into which private enforcement of public policies may, or may not, fit.[29]

[29] To be sure, the concepts of legal tradition and legal culture are highly amorphous as well as contested. This is not the time or place to enter such swampy terrain. Suffice it to say that by tradition, I mean how the concept and role of law have been shaped through historical development. By legal culture, I mean both the (objective) practices and behaviours of actors in a legal system, see Erhard Blankenburg, 'Civil Litigation Rates as Indicators for Legal Culture', in David Nelken (ed.), *Comparative Legal Cultures*, Oxford University Press and Aldershot, Hants, England (1997), 41, and the legal consciousness consisting of (subjective) elements, especially as attitudes towards, opinions about, and expectations from law, see Lawrence Friedman, 'Is There a Modern Legal Culture?', 7 *Ratio Juris* 118 (1994), 119.

This last aspect has not been explored as much as the other two.[30] Yet, from an Asian observer's perspective, it may ultimately be the most interesting dimension of an American–European comparison. This is because looking at the broader cultural context shows that private enforcement of public policies means different things on the two sides of the Atlantic. As we shall see, in the United States, it easily fits fundamental features of the legal culture, while in Europe, it runs by and large counter to them.[31]

In exploring the cultural context, we will consider two main aspects: first, the conception and role of the state, and then the conception and role of private law and litigation. In doing so, we will focus mainly on the transatlantic *differences*. Obviously, the US-American and European legal cultures show many similarities, ranging from broadly shared Western conceptions of public power and private markets to assumptions about political legitimacy and economic efficiency. But our purpose here is to bring the *differences* into sharp relief, in part because of their greater explanatory power and in part because they are more easily overlooked from an Asian perspective.[32]

3.1 The Conception of the State: Task, Administration, and Power

To begin with, there are significant differences between the conceptions of the state in Europe and in the United States. They pertain, *inter alia*, to

[30] A notable exception for the area of antitrust law is the thoughtful essay by David Gerber, 'Private Enforcement of Competition Law: A Comparative Perspective', at 431–452.

[31] The following analysis draws in part on Robert Kagan, *Adversarial Legalism: The American Way of Law*, Harvard University Press, Cambridge, MA (2001). Kagan defines 'adversarial legalism' as 'policymaking, policy implementation, and dispute resolution by means of lawyer dominated litigation,' ibid., 3. He claims that it is much more prevalent in the United States than anywhere else in the world, and that this prevalence is one of the distinctive hallmarks of US-American political and legal culture. Since he considers this to be true with regard to both private rights and public regulation, his analysis does not focus on private enforcement of public policies in particular. Yet, along the way, he proffers numerous observations that are relevant in our context as well – about the underlying conceptions of the state and its power, about law and litigation, and about courts and lawyers.

[32] In addition to the two aspects emphasised here, one could also look at the differences in the structure of the respective economies; see, e.g. Kagan, *Adversarial Legalism*, at 51–54. In the United States, the economy is highly decentralised and clearly separated from the state; in such an environment, private enforcement promises fairly effective self-policing of market actors. In most of Europe, asset ownership is more concentrated, and economic activity is often more closely tied to the state, especially in countries with a corporatist tradition; in such an environment, reliance on enforcement of market rules by private actors is much more dubious.

the state's essential task, administrative apparatus, and the distribution of power. In looking at these elements, we will, again, need to generalise in order to perceive some fundamental differences.

3.1.1 Task: The Proactive v. the Reactive State[33]

The modern European state has traditionally been comprehensively tasked with the regulation of the public welfare, at least in principle. Throughout the period of its creation and consolidation (mainly through the early modern period and into the nineteenth century), it took over the regulatory domains of feudal lords, merchant guilds, the church, and a diversity of other actors. It eventually assumed the primary responsibility for the well being of society at large and of its members. The result has been an essentially 'activist' state. Its 'activism' has two major dimensions. First, in such a state, the regulation of market activity and the protection against abuse of market power is first and foremost a public responsibility.[34] Second, the state's typical instrument is *ex ante* regulation, e.g. through (administrative) control of market entry.[35]

The US-American state has been tasked with the regulation of the public welfare only insofar as it is demonstrably necessary. Its origins lie in a reaction against the – overweening – power of a European nation. As a result, it has become an essentially 'reactive' state. Again, this has two major consequences. First, such a state does not assume sole responsibility to protect market actors against the abuse of economic power; instead, it counts on, and encourages, society to help itself.[36] Second, the state prefers to respond to particular problems *ex post*, as expressed in the

[33] These terms are borrowed from Mirjan Damaska, *The Faces of Justice and State Authority*, Yale University Press, New Haven and London (1986).

[34] Note that '[i]n Europe, competition law was originally conceived as an administrative tool, a means for the state to intervene in market processes in order to achieve public goals'. Gerber, 'Private Enforcement of Competition Law: A Comparative Perspective', at 442. Thus, administrative enforcement (e.g. by the European Commission) became the rule, and private enforcement 'has been non-existent or marginal', ibid., 445.

[35] Such a state must, of course, collect enough revenue to pay for extensive public enforcement which inevitably drives up taxes; at the same time, however, it does not burden private parties with the costs of litigation for purposes of public enforcement.

[36] This fits the broader picture of a state and society in which self-help is much more widely allowed, required, and often prized than in Europe. This is true not only in the context of protection against the abuse of economic power but also in the pursuit of compensation for injury (through tort claims rather than public insurance schemes), against unemployment or disability (again, mainly through private lawsuits), and even against crime where the right to armed self-defence is broadly protected.

popular phrase 'we cross that bridge when we get to it', e.g. through (public or private) sanctions for the breach of market rules.[37]

To be sure, there has, again, been considerable convergence. In twentieth-century America, the state has assumed more and more wide-ranging responsibilities for the public welfare, especially since the New Deal, and *ex ante* regulation is dominant in several contexts. By contrast, in late twentieth-century Europe, the state began to retreat from the full-scale social welfare model and to privatise many formerly public services and functions, and reliance on *ex post* sanctions now is increasingly common. As a result, the transatlantic differences today are not nearly as marked as they were a century ago. Still, they remain significant, not only in particular areas (such as health insurance or employment protection) but also more generally in form of opposite presumptions – in favour of a more involved state and of public regulation in Europe, and in favour of more limited state and of reliance on private action in the United States.

Private enforcement occupies different positions under these respective conceptions of the state. The European (activist) state operates on the assumption that public enforcement is the norm – and also that it is preferable because it is considered more effective and efficient.[38] It resorts to private enforcement (through the civil courts) only if, and to the extent that, public measures (by the administration) fail, i.e. as a second-best. In other words, private enforcement is a deviation from the default rule of state action.[39] *In dubio pro re publica*. The US-American (reactive) state inherently prefers private action, i.e. market self-regulation.[40] It supports public regulation mainly in the event of 'market failure'[41] or to the extent

[37] See Samuel Issacharoff, 'Regulating After the Fact', 56 DePaul L.R. 375 (2007).

[38] Rolf Stürner, *Markt und Wettbewerb über Alles*, Beck, Munich (2007), 98–100, 283–287. Thus, when European countries, first of all Germany, developed a distinct antitrust law, it seemed entirely natural that its rules would be enforced by public authorities, Gerber, 'Private Enforcement of Competition Law: A Comparative Perspective', at 442, 444.

[39] Stürner, Markt und Wettbewerb über Alles, at 283 ("allerletzte und glanzlose Notlösung"). In fact, private enforcement of competition law is *meant* merely to supplement administrative action, see Möllers and Heinemann, The Enforcement of Competition Law in Europe, at 430.

[40] Thus, US-American antitrust law involved private enforcement from the very beginning – not as a result of a conscious choice but rather because it seemed like the normal way of enforcement, Gerber, 'Private Enforcement of Competition Law: A Comparative Perspective', at 434.

[41] See Francis Bator, 'The Anatomy of Market Failure', 72 *Quarterly Journal of Economics* 351 (1958).

private remedies are ineffective.[42] Private enforcement thus complies with the default rule of state abstention. *In dubio pro libertate.*[43]

These different conceptions of the state entail different attitudes of the respective private actors. In Europe, private parties do not consider themselves responsible for the enforcement of public policies; thus, they accept invitations to do so reluctantly at best. In the United States, members of society are much more willing to take charge of public policy enforcement, if need be through litigation; thus they often respond to incentives quite readily, if not eagerly.

3.1.2 Administration: Belief v. Skepticism

There are also subtle but important differences in the attitudes towards the administrative apparatus.

European states have long presented themselves to their citizens in form of a hierarchically organised administrative structure. They have maintained a career bureaucracy since the early modern period. Citizens expect officials to be specialised, competent, and impartial, and they tend to trust their bureaucrats' professional training. Thus, the legitimacy of administrative action is heavily based on the decision makers' expertise. The result is an ideology of belief in the ability of professional, qualified officials to make and enforce regulations about all public concerns, including market behaviour.

The US-American state defines itself more through the democratic process than through official hierarchies. It began to build modern bureaucratic structures only towards the end of the nineteenth century, and on a large scale only in the twentieth. Administrative expertise is less rigorously required and not necessarily the most important qualification for public office.[44] The competence of bureaucrats is not easily taken for

[42] See, e.g. Michael Waterstone, 'A New Vision of Public Enforcement', 92 MINN.L.REV. 434 (2007).

[43] This does not mean that private enforcement is universally supported; even in the United States, it is often contested and subject to critique. For a summary, see Engstrom, 'Agencies as Litigation Gatekeepers', at 630–641. See also Glover, 'The Structural Role of Private Enforcement Mechanisms in Public Law', at 1140 ('Americans have a love-hate relationship with private enforcement of their laws').

[44] In the United States, mid- and high-level government officials are often recruited from the private sector on the basis of their political affiliation or economic status and are expected to acquire the requisite special knowledge on the job. They tend to serve short terms of office, usually ending with the tenure of the appointing head of the executive. Many state governors are not professional politicians but come from private business or other walks of life, including, as in the cases of Ronald Reagan and Arnold Schwarzenegger in California, the entertainment industry.

granted, and their impartiality is quickly doubted for reasons of 'agency capture'.[45] Thus, the legitimacy of public decisions rests less on professional competence than on democratic input. The result is an ideology of scepticism towards the ability and neutrality of public officials effectively to regulate society, including the market.[46]

From this perspective as well, private enforcement looks quite different on both sides of the Atlantic. In Europe, the basic trust in administrative competence implies a presumption in favour of public, and against private, action. In the United States, the scepticism towards administrative capability and impartiality results in the opposite presumption. None of this means that bureaucrats in Europe are de facto more competent or neutral than in the United States; it only means that Europeans have, largely for historical reasons, greater trust in them – and thus hesitate to entrust regulatory policies to private actors.

3.1.3 Power: The Centralised v. the Fragmented State

Finally, there are differences regarding the locus and distribution of state power.

In Europe, state power has traditionally been concentrated. The modern European nation state was born when a central authority (mostly a prince, sometimes a representative assembly) absorbed the power of regional or local actors. To be sure, eventually such power became distributed both among different institutions (legislature, executive, judiciary) and, in some systems, within a federal structure. But in most European states, such distribution has been carefully circumscribed: the constitutional separation of powers is not strict (especially in parliamentary systems), and federalism has mostly been created top-down and remained limited. In Europe, decentralising power remains counterintuitive and requires effort.[47]

In the United States, state power has, from the beginning, been fragmented.[48] The nation was born in a revolt against centralised

45 See George Stickler, 'The Theory of Economic Regulation', *Bell Journal of Economics and Management Science* 2 (1971), 3–21. For a more recent discussion, see Davniel Carpenter and David Moss (eds.), *Preventing Regulatory Capture*, Cambridge University Press, New York (2011).

46 In certain areas, such as consumer product safety or employment and housing discrimination, public enforcement in the United States is notoriously deficient, see Glover, 'The Structural Role of Private Enforcement Mechanisms in Public Law', at 1203–1207.

47 This characterisation is similar and related to, but not identical with, Mirjan Damaska's 'hierarchical ideal' of state power. Damaska, *The Faces of Justice and State Authority*.

48 Kagan aptly speaks of the 'structurally fragmented state', *Adversarial Legalism*, at 15.

authority. It is true that pretty soon, the individual colonies delegated power to a centre under a federal constitution, but that delegation was undertaken reluctantly, it was carefully limited, and its extent has remained constantly contested. It is also true that there has been much centralisation throughout the twentieth century, and yet, government power has remained much more fragmented than in Western Europe and in countries modelled after it, like Japan.[49] Note that the constitutional separation of powers is much stricter than in Europe and that federalism is much more pronounced. In addition, much governmental power has always been exercised on the municipal level or even below, resulting in the notorious US-American localism.[50] In the United States, decentralised power is not counterintuitive but easily accepted.[51]

These traditions react differently to private enforcement of public policies because it requires a relinquishment of state power. The European state, with its tradition of centralised authority, does not share power lightly, and relinquishing even part of it is a big step. The US-American state, with its tradition of wide distribution of authority, is used to sharing power, and leaving part of it to actors beyond central control is more easily accepted.

All this is particularly true if the power to enforce public policies is to be shared not with other, e.g. local, government actors but rather with private parties. In Europe, that conflicts with the traditional notion of sovereignty. Since Bodin and Hobbes, (internal) sovereignty has been vested in the *state*. Leaving public-policy enforcement to private parties thus requires the European state to entrust part of its sovereign function to non-state actors – which, again, does not come naturally at all. In the United States, private enforcement does not raise the same sovereignty concerns. Sovereignty has from the beginning rested with 'the people'.[52] Thus leaving public policy enforcement to private parties in a sense

[49] Kagan, *Adversarial Legalism*, at 43–45. Samuel Huntington, *Political Order in Changing Societies*, Yale University Press, New Haven and London (1968), sees the fragmentation of political power in the United States as a continuation of the medieval, pluralistic legal order. In contrast to Continental Europe, the United States has, in his view, failed to modernise the political system, i.e. to build a centralised, hierarchically organised, and professionally administered state, ibid., at 93–139.

[50] It was already described by Alexis de Tocqueville, *Democracy in America I*, Random House, New York (Vintage Classics 1990, French orig. 1835), 60–83, 271–272.

[51] This is related to, but again is not identical with, Damaska's 'coordinate ideal' of state power, *The Faces of Justice and State Authority*.

[52] US Constitution, Preamble.

means leaving (some) sovereign power where it lies to begin with, which is more easily acceptable.

3.2 Private Law and Litigation: Conceptions, Functions, and Actors

3.2.1 Private Law: Corrective Justice v. Social Agenda

It is well known that private law plays somewhat different roles on both sides of the Atlantic.

In Europe, the traditional function of private law is to ensure corrective justice: *suum cuique tribuere* – to give each his due. It regards rights-holders strictly in their private capacity. At least in principle, it is not concerned with public affairs. In particular, it is not supposed to be used as a political instrument. This is reflected in the basic distinction between private and public law, which dates all the way back to classical Roman jurisprudence.[53]

In the United States, private law has a dual function. On the one hand, it should, like in Europe, ensure justice among private parties. On the other hand, however, it has also long been regarded as a viable instrument for the promotion of regulatory goals.[54] This instrumentalisation and politicisation has its origins in the early nineteenth century,[55] was boosted by legal realism in the mid-twentieth,[56] and received its ultimate imprimatur from the law and economics movement in the last forty years.[57] Since private law often serves the promotion of social and economic goals, a clear distinction between private and public law is not common in the United States.[58]

[53] Ulp. D.1.1.1.2.

[54] For example, when public regulation of certain contested product categories, such as tobacco, firearms, or breast implants, was widely considered lacking or at least ineffective, plaintiff groups brought product liability class actions to provide 'regulation through litigation,' though with varying success, see Viscusi, Regulation through Litigation.

[55] At least if one believes Morton J. Horwitz, *The Transformation of American Law 1780–1860*, Harvard University Press, Cambridge, MA, and London, England (1977).

[56] Legal realism entailed a jurisprudential turn towards functionalism, pragmatism, and – most importantly for our purposes – an emphasis on social policy; see the classic article by Felix Cohen, 'Transcendental Nonsense and the Functional Approach', 35 COL.L.REV. 809 (1935).

[57] See, e.g. Guido Calabresi, *The Cost of Accidents*, Yale University Press, New Haven and London (1970), 24–31.

[58] Beyond these different conceptions of private law in particular lie different views of law in general. The traditional European view, especially in the civil law tradition prevailing on the Continent, has been that law is a set of positive and systematically organised (and ideally, codified) rules. These rules belong to the state which creates and develops them.

To be sure, we must not overstate this difference. In Europe, private law is not entirely free from instrumentalism nor from politics. It has always been infused with a dose of public purpose, and in recent decades, that dose has become much stronger, especially in certain areas, such as consumer contracts or product liability. The private/public law distinction has also been blurred with the rise of fields like labour law and environmental protection. Yet, the essential functions of private law continue to differ on both sides of the Atlantic. In Europe, the public function of private law is merely incidental to its principal purpose, which remains doing justice between private parties, while in the United States, the instrumental use of private law is part of its core mission. This is why employing damage remedies to punish wrongdoers is essentially alien to European private law[59] and either not permitted or very rarely used, while it is generally accepted and fairly common in the United States. And this is why openly political arguments are disparaged in European private-law discourse but clearly tolerated, if not prized, in the United States.

In summary, in Europe, enlisting private rights for public purposes raises systemic concerns because it is at odds with the basic conception of private law and it cuts across a dividing line that continues to be regarded as essential. In the United States, there are no systemic issues because linking private rights to public policies has a long tradition and does not conflict with any basic jurisprudential categories.

3.2.2 Litigation: Dispute Resolution v. Policy Making

In the same vein, in Europe, the traditional purpose of private litigation is simply to decide an individual dispute; in the United States, it is also used to serve broader, especially social and economic, goals.[60] Again, we should not exaggerate. At least on the appellate level, European court decisions are often informed by considerations of broader policies; and at least in routine cases, US-American judges have scant occasion to think

Private litigants can use, and benefit from, these rules, but enforcing them is quintessentially a state function. The modern (twentieth century) American view has been that law is a social process to which many institutions and actors constantly contribute. As a result, law does not belong to the state alone, it also belongs to society; witness the constitutionally guaranteed role of lay jurors in adjudication. As a result, the pursuit of regulatory policies is not a state monopoly and can be left in private hands as well.

59 For a clear statement and explication of this view, see the Decision by the Supreme Court (Bundesgerichtshof) of 4 June 1992, Enscheidungen des Bundesgerichtshofs in Zivilsachen (BGHZ) 118, 312 (English summary in 32 I.L.M. 1320, 1993).

60 Richard Marcus, 'American Exceptionalism in Goals for Civil Litigation', 34 *IUS Gentium* 123 (2014).

beyond the parties and facts before them. Still, the difference remains significant: European parties have traditionally not sought social or economic change through private lawsuits,[61] while American litigants have done so routinely, openly, and often successfully.[62] On this general level, all this is familiar terrain. This difference, however, also entails more specific conceptions of the bench and bar.

3.2.3 Judges: Disinterested Arbiters v. Political Actors

In private litigation, judges on both sides of the Atlantic occupy different positions and play different roles.

European judges deciding private lawsuits are apolitical specialists, essentially for two reasons. First, at least on the Continent, they operate in a system of strict separation of dockets. Those deciding private lawsuits sit on private law courts which are separate from administrative courts hearing public law disputes. As a result, private law judges are tasked with private law concerns only. The impact of their decision on public affairs is, in principle, none of their business. Second, they have been selected for their doctrinal prowess and professional reliability, and they get promoted in a career system based on performance and seniority. As a result, private law judges are not used to thinking in broader political terms. They are, or at least see themselves as, distinctly apolitical figures who leave public concerns to the legislature.

US-American judges handling private lawsuits are politically conscious generalists – again for two principal reasons. First, they operate in a system with weak docket specialisation. There is no fundamental distinction between private and public law courts. As a result, most judges face a wide array of cases and cannot avoid issues with obvious political implications. Second, US-American judges come to office through a politicised process – be it through popular election or through executive appointment. For them, the political function of courts, and the need to be responsive to political and social concerns, is as clear as it is inevitable, and thinking in broad policy terms is quasi second nature.[63]

61 See Klaus Hopt, 'Comparative Company Law', in Mathias Reimann and Reinhard Zimmermann, *The Oxford Handbook of Comparative Law*, Oxford University Press and Aldershot, Hants, England (2006), 1161, 1191 ('Continental European lawmakers and academics tend to underestimate the role of courts and litigation').

62 See below. *d*.

63 Huntington, *Political Order in Changing Societies*, at 113. Kagan, *Adversarial Legalism*, at 16. The uniquely political function of US-American courts was already noted by de Tocqueville, Democracy in America I, at 98–103.

Obviously, asking judges to enforce public policies through private litigation is a different matter in these respective contexts. The European private law judge suddenly having to decide cases with massive regulatory implications is forced to do a job he or she is neither trained nor appointed for, and to think in terms which are neither comfortable nor familiar. His US-American colleague, by contrast, is quite at ease with such implications and has, if not the ability, at least the self-confidence and political mandate to handle them.

3.2.4 Lawyers: Private Attorneys v. Political Activists

These different roles and functions of private law judges are mirrored by the roles and functions of the lawyers appearing before them.

In Europe, lawyers involved in private litigation are merely representatives of individual interests. They bring private lawsuits in order to protect their clients, not to promote political views, economic agendas, or social justice. The private bar is not considered a venue for organised political activism. Thus, lawyering in private litigation is largely technical and narrowly focused. Broadly political, economic, or social arguments are eschewed – in part simply because courts would not consider them appropriate. In short, private litigation is one thing, and political activism is quite another.

In the United States, lawyers engaged in private law litigation often pursue agendas way beyond their clients' interests. Even when they sue primarily on behalf of a private plaintiff, they can simultaneously act as 'private attorneys general' enforcing public interests;[64] this is not only tolerated by the state but also actively encouraged by the promise of financial rewards.[65] Moreover, they often bring cases openly to pursue a political or social cause;[66] in these instances, the concrete client is just a placeholder, e.g. as the named party in a class action or the carefully selected plaintiff in a test case. Such litigation is often conducted by public interest groups committed to a certain

[64] It is true that more commonly, this term is applied to the plaintiffs themselves, but in practice it is often the lawyer representing the client who really plays that role.

[65] Most notably through the award of treble damages and the award of attorney fees in antitrust suits under section 4 of the Clayton Act (15 U.S.C. § 15), but also through a multitude of one-way fee-shifting statutes under which the victorious plaintiff (really his or her lawyer) can recover attorney fees from the defendant – but not the other way around; see above supra note 10.

[66] See Kagan, *Adversarial Legalism*, at 7–8.

cause.[67] Crusades for broader agendas are a widely accepted function of the private bar, which thus assumes an overtly political role. Here, private litigation becomes part of the political process.

Asking lawyers to bring private actions for the enforcement of public policies thus has different implications. In Europe, it means asking them to tread on unfamiliar ground. Like private law judges, they are rarely used to thinking in instrumental terms. It is not something they are trained to do; it is not something their professional self-image includes; and it is not something they expect judges to want to hear. His or her US-American colleagues are likely to be much more familiar with such considerations and arguments. They are trained to think beyond the individual case; they are members of a profession comfortable with pursuing political agendas; and they expect the court to listen.

3.3 *Lessons for Asia?*

What can an outside observer, e.g. from an Asian country, learn from looking at these divergent cultural features? Let me, again, suggest two possible lessons – or, rather, issues to think about. The first is pretty straightforward: it arises from the impact of legal culture on private enforcement. The second is more thought provoking: it concerns the impact of private enforcement on legal culture.

3.3.1 The Impact of Legal Culture on Private Enforcement

As we have seen, the meaning and role of private enforcement depend on the broader cultural context. In the United States, entrusting the enforcement of public regulation, e.g. of market behaviour, to private actors is an easy fit with defining features of the legal tradition and culture: a still largely 'reactive' state marked by a basic penchant for private self-regulation; an ideology of skepticism vis-à-vis the competence and neutrality of the administrative apparatus; and a system of widely dispersed regulatory power. In addition, there is a tradition in which private law is easily instrumentalised for social purposes and in which even private litigation often serves broader political agendas. In Europe, enlisting private action for regulatory purposes is at odds with the cultural context: an essentially 'activist' state *prima facie* responsible for all public

[67] It is often supported through so-called legal defense funds created by NGOs and supported by donations. The name is somewhat misleading because these funds finance not only defensive action but also the bringing of claims to begin with.

concerns, thus a preference for public regulation; an ideology of belief in the competence and neutrality of its administrative apparatus; and a system of concentrated sovereign power which is shared with other, and especially private actors, at best reluctantly. There is also a tradition in which the purpose of private law has been limited to corrective justice and in which private litigation has been carefully separated – institutionally and professionally – from political functions.

Asian observers should consider how entrusting the enforcement of regulatory agendas to private action fits their own legal culture. The more that culture resembles that of Europe, the more tension it will create; the more it is like that of the United States, the easier the fit will be. To be sure, even in a legal culture like Europe's, private enforcement is not impossible, but it is harder to implement, destined to play a more limited role, and less likely to fulfil the hopes of its proponents.

3.3.2 The Impact of Private Enforcement on Legal Culture

The second issue is more thought provoking. Just as legal culture has an impact on the role and effect of private enforcement, so too does the reliance on private enforcement have an impact on legal culture. Some of this impact is fairly predictable, some is not, and much is a matter of more or less plausible speculation. It suffices here to point out some of the more likely consequences.[68]

To begin with, entrusting private parties with the enforcement of public policies means not only that the state shares power over the enforcement of the law but also that it loses some control over its growth. Where the state relies on private action, it leaves it up to private parties which cases are brought, litigated, settled, appealed, etc., and thus which issues are decided or avoided. Private decisions thus influence the development of the law. Note that since these decisions are based on private motives rather than public agendas, they can easily push the law's development in directions that differ from the preferences of government authorities.

At the same time, enlisting private action means distributing enforcement power among a much larger crowd of actors. Next to public officials, private businesses, their lawyers, and judges play important roles. Since their actions are not necessarily coordinated, the law no longer follows a unitary course. Instead, it becomes more complex and

[68] See (for the antitrust context) Gerber, 'Private Enforcement of Competition Law: A Comparative Perspective', 448–451.

uncertain – and thus less predictable. This, in turn, will make compliance more burdensome because firms will face more rules (especially in the form of court decisions) and thus risk more violations.

Furthermore, reliance on private enforcement will affect the relative importance, status, and perhaps even the numbers of the actors involved. Since it shifts (more or less) enforcement power from regulation to litigation, lawyers gain power because they decide which cases to bring and how to pursue them. Judges become more important since they decide which actions prevail and thus have a private enforcement effect. Public officials, by contrast, lose part of their power and thus possibly some of their status. Such a shift will also affect the respective actors' numbers: a system relying – more or less heavily – on private enforcement needs more lawyers and judges but fewer bureaucrats.

The greater involvement of lawyers and judges will also change the style of enforcement decisions. In addition to the top-down style of administrative orders, there will be the adversarial style of litigation and the deliberative style of judicial opinions. This can, though it does not have to, broaden the spectrum of arguments and increase the aggressiveness of contests.

The US-American experience suggests that outcomes of private litigation will often be determined less by the underlying merits and more by the parties' relative resources, ability to create or tolerate delays, and overall tenaciousness. And ultimate dispute resolution will often, if not predominantly, take the form of settlement rather judgment. All this will, again, lower the predictability of results.

In addition, enforcement through private action is likely to cause greater publicity. Administrative decisions do not lend themselves to media attention: high-stakes litigation does. This entails greater public awareness of market regulation policies and issues. A positive effect can be greater consciousness in the business world and more self-policing; a more ambivalent consequence could be a further increase in lawsuits.

Finally, a shift from public to private enforcement has noteworthy financial consequences. It is often claimed that the overall cost of litigation is greater than that of administrative action,[69] although this claim is very difficult to substantiate and even harder to prove, and its veracity is ultimately unclear.[70] It is clear, however, that such a shift has an impact

69 See, e.g, Kagan, *Adversarial Legalism*, at 9.

70 The costs of administrative action may simply be more hidden because they are absorbed by large state bureaucracies and thus are not separately billed like court costs and lawyer fees.

on cost distribution: public enforcement is largely funded by taxpayers while private litigation is largely paid for by the litigants. This is why the reliance on and the push for private enforcement is often motivated by the promise to save tax expenditures. The social importance and political pay-off of such a promise, however, vary. They are greater in the United States with its culture of (at least allegedly) low taxes and of skimping on public expenditures than in Europe with its tradition of higher revenue rates and a more generously funded state apparatus.[71]

As these examples demonstrate, policy makers favouring private enforcement should carefully think about what they unleash. Once the genie is out of the bottle, it will be difficult to constrain even with regard to the predictable effects. Beyond that lies the law of unintended consequences.

4 Common Law and Civil Law? The Channel and the Atlantic

So far, we have not looked at the traditional civil v. common law distinction at all. That was not an oversight. Tempting as it may be to analyse private enforcement under this time-honoured dichotomy, it is really of marginal relevance in our context.

4.1 The Case of England: Mainly on the Side of Europe

Most of the features we have considered have rather little to do with the respective legal systems' membership in the civil or common law families, at least as classically defined. The perfect test case is, of course, England. In the context of private enforcement, England belongs more on the side of Europe than on that of the United States. This is, by and large, true on all three levels we have considered.

The practical impact of private enforcement in England is still, as in Continental Europe, fairly marginal and is not, as in the United States, of central importance.

The legal framework in England does not favour private enforcement nearly as much as in the United States either. There are no multiple

[71] How much money the state can really save by shifting from public to private enforcement is less clear than one might think. It depends, *inter alia*, on the extent to which public enforcement continues parallel to private action; on how much money the state wins in enforcement actions (especially in fines); on how the courts handling (potentially massive and protracted) private litigation are funded (i.e. through taxes or by user fees); and on the extent to which firms can deduct litigation expenses from their tax liability.

damages nor American-size damage awards; punitive damages are allowed only under very limited circumstances[72] and rarely imposed in practice. Discovery is less powerful than in the United States. There is no American-style class action and virtually no civil jury trial. And under the (in)famous 'English rule', litigation is financially risky because the loser pays (at least a large part of) the winner's costs. It is true that in England as well, the situation has recently become somewhat more favourable to private enforcement, for example when 'exemplary damages' have been imposed in some antitrust litigation.[73] In addition, success fees are now common, litigation insurance and financing are on the rise, and some forms of collective action are allowed. Yet, none of this has given rise to private enforcement on the US-American level.

Even the English legal culture is, in most of the respects discussed here, closer to Continental Europe than to the United States. The English state has traditionally been quite 'activist'; it has trusted in the regulatory prowess of its civil service rather than extensively relying on private parties to enforce public policies, and it has long kept sovereign power concentrated rather than fragmented and dispersed, recent devolution notwithstanding. Finally, English private law and litigation have, as on the Continent, traditionally served the limited function of pursuing corrective justice in the case before the court. Private law has not been broadly instrumentalised for social purposes, and English courtrooms are not easily considered venues for the promotion of political agendas.[74]

4.2 Some Qualifications: The Bench and Bar

To say that the civil v. common law dichotomy is of marginal importance in our context is not to say that it is entirely meaningless. Some relevant features of the English legal culture differ from the Continent and resemble those of the United States. But they do not necessarily favour private enforcement as a result.

The nature of the English bench, for example, does not. It is true, of course, that English judges are similar to their American peers in that

[72] *Rookes* v. *Barnard*, 64 1 All ER 376.

[73] See 2 *Travel Group Plc* v. *Cardiff City Transport Services Ltd.*, [2012] CAT 19 (Competition Appeal Tribunal).

[74] The English–American differences are in large part due to the fact that notions of popular sovereignty, federalism, legal realism, and the economic analysis of law have crucially shaped the United States legal culture while they have had a minor impact in England.

they are typically generalists recruited from the senior echelons of the legal profession; they are not, like their typical continental colleagues, highly specialised career officials. Yet, in marked contrast to the United States, English judges are not political figures or champions of an instrumentalised use of private law. They do not see it as their job to promote particular social or economic agendas.

By contrast, the English bar *is* a factor in favouring private enforcement, at least to some degree. In the last few decades, it has rapidly become more entrepreneurial than most of its continental counterparts. Today, the English bar is at least partially geared towards the representation of private actions in pursuit of public agendas. This makes the English cultural environment somewhat more hospitable to private enforcement than most legal systems on the Continent.

Thus, in some regards, the Channel separating England from continental Europe matters, but it matters less than the Atlantic separating Europe from the United States. In other words, as on a world map, England is, at least in the context of private enforcement, closer to the European continent than to the United States.

4.3 A(nother) Lesson for Asia: The Scant Relevance of the Traditional Dichotomy

In this respect, the lesson for Asia is quite simple: thinking about the conditions for and implications of private enforcement from the traditional civil v. common law perspective promises very limited pay-off. In fact, attributing the differences between the United States and the (Continental) European systems primarily to their respective memberships in these traditions is by and large misleading.

5 The European Union: The Uneasy Hybrid

A look at Europe today cannot be limited to its national legal systems. Instead, it must also consider the enormous role played by its supranational structure, the European Union. This is particularly true in our context: note that the initiative for private enforcement has come largely from the European Union rather than from the member states. From the perspective of legal culture, this makes eminent sense because in several respects, the EU is actually closer to the US than to its own member states. Let us again look at the concept of the state and the function of private rights and litigation.

5.1 The European Union: Activist Tradition and Market Competition

As an organisation exercising (legislative, executive, and adjudicatory) governmental power, the European Union shares features both with European nation states and the United States.

On the one hand, the European Union is, like most of its members, an 'activist' governmental power: it is officially committed to and actively pursues various substantive social goals.[75] Later, other policies were added, such as the protection of fundamental rights and of the environment.[76] Also like its members, the EU stands in the tradition of the 'regulatory state'.[77] It thus entrusts promoting these goals largely to an extensive administrative apparatus consisting of professional career bureaucrats whose legitimacy rests much more on (at least presumed) expertise than on democratic input. And it has increasingly concentrated power in a centre at the expense of its subunits (and successfully claimed supremacy of its law over theirs).[78]

On the other hand, the European Union, like the United States, is also the constitutional framework for a common market. The creation of such a market was its original purpose, and the promotion of the free movement of people, goods, capital, and services remains a core function. The freedoms it originally sought to guarantee were market freedoms, although a much longer list has now been added.[79] As the constitutional structure for a common market, the EU is committed to the freedom of economic activity and in particular to the promotion of competition.[80]

[75] From the very beginning, among these goals were the 'constant improvement of the living and working conditions of [the member states'] peoples', Treaty Establishing the European Economic Community (Treaty of Rome, 1957), Preamble; more particular goals were the promotion of 'employment opportunities for workers' (ibid., Article 3 (i); see also Articles 48–51), as well certain elements of broader 'social policy' (ibid., Articles 117–128). However, these objectives were often considered instrumental to its basic mission of creating an integrated market.

[76] Treaty on European Union (Maastricht Treaty, 1992), Preamble, Article F 2.

[77] Lukacz Gorywoda, Nitikas Hatzimihail and Arnaud Nuyts, 'Introduction: Market Regulation, Judicial Cooperation and Collective Redress', in Nuyts and Hatzimihail, *Cross-Border Class Actions*, at 1, 5–17.

[78] *Flaminio Costa* v. *E.N.E.L.*, European Court of Justice Case 6/64, 1964 E.C.R. 585.

[79] Charter of Fundamental Rights and Freedoms of the European Union (2000, in force 2009).

[80] The Treaty Establishing the European Economic Community already contained substantive competition (antitrust) provisions in Arts. 85 and 86. Pursuant to the insane European practice of constantly renumbering articles in subsequent treaties, these

The EU's ambivalent character entails an ambivalent attitude towards private enforcement. This is most obvious in the antitrust context. As an activist, bureaucratic, and power-concentrating governmental body, the EEC (and later the EC) originally took full control over the enforcement of its antitrust rules; as long as it had the resources to enforce these rules through its central bureaucracy, it did so in an increasingly eager fashion. Yet, as the constitution of a market committed to economic freedom and competition, it also wanted market actors to police each other. As soon as its resources became insufficient to guarantee effective public enforcement (mainly because of the doubling of its member states), it began to favour enforcement through private action.[81] Ever since, the EU has remained ambivalent. It now wants private enforcement[82] – but only in a supplemental manner and not on the US-American level. It orders its member states to create a more favourable legal framework – but not a US-style litigation environment.[83] And it wants to enlist private litigation to support public enforcement largely because its public authorities can no longer provide sufficient control and deterrence.

5.2 *Law and Litigation: The Instrumentalisation of Rights*

The EU occupies a similar middle ground between its members and the United States also with regard to the function of private law and litigation.

On the one hand, it operates against the background of the European tradition in which private law and litigation have served the narrow functions of corrective justice and individual case decision. On the other hand, however, the EU (formerly the EEC, then the EC), like the United States legal culture, has instrumentalised citizen suits for public purposes.[84] As early as in 1963, the original driver of this instrumentalisation was the European Court of Justice (ECJ). In its seminal *Van Gend and Loos* decision, the court construed Article 12 of the Treaty of Rome

provisions later became Arts. 81 and 82 and, eventually Articles 101 and 102 in the Treaty on the Functioning of the European Union (Lisbon Treaty, in force 2009).

81 See Gerber, 'Private Enforcement of Competition Law: A Comparative Perspective', at 446.

82 See Council Regulation (EC) No. 1/2003 of 16 December 2002; *Courage* v. *Crehan; Manfredi* v. *Lloyd Adriatico.*

83 Directive of the Council and the European Parliament.

84 See Martin Hesselink, 'The New European Legal Culture' (2001), 37–40; Gorywoda, Hatzimihail and Nuyts, 'Introduction: Market Regulation, Judicial Cooperation and Collective Redress', at 17–24.

(against its wording) to create a private cause of action for aggrieved citizens and businesses. The primary motivation was not, mind you, to protect private interests, but rather that the '[t]he vigilance of individuals' provide 'an effective supervision' of state action[85] (necessary because public supervision could not be fully trusted[86]). In short, individual rights were created in order to allow private enforcement of the treaty. And indeed, in the subsequent decades, suits by individuals and businesses became the primary vehicle through which questions of community law came before the ECJ, enabling the court to pursue a vigorous course of legal and economic integration. In 2001, the ECJ boldly pushed for private enforcement of EU antitrust law when it held that the competition law provisions of the treaty created directly enforceable private rights.[87] The European legislator has often followed suit. The Council, Commission, and Parliament have routinely justified rule harmonisation in areas such as product liability or consumer contracts in instrumental terms, not only (or even primarily) as a means of consumer protection but rather as a tool to create a level playing field for market actors in the member states.[88]

Such an instrumentalised understanding of private law encourages a litigation culture of regulation through litigation similar to the United States,[89] in particular the use of private enforcement. Yet, it also has its costs. Again as in the United States, EU private law has become more politicised, which in turn has rendered it increasingly fragmented and incoherent.[90] And its employment for regulatory purposes has blurred,

[85] *NV Algemene Transport-En Expeditie Onderneming Van Gend & Loos* v. *Netherlands Inland Revenue Administration*, European Court for Justice Case 2–26/62, 1963 E.C.R. 585, par. 18.

[86] Ibid., par. 17.

[87] *Courage* v. *Crehan*, E.C.R. [2001] I-6297; see also *Manfredi* v. *Lloyd Adriatico*, E.C.R. [2006] I-6619.

[88] See, e.g. Directive 85/374 EEC on the Approximation of the Laws, Regulations and Administrative Provisions of the Member States Concerning Liability for Defective Products, OJ L210 (7 August 1985) 29–33, Preamble (1); Directive 1999/44/EC of the European Parliament and of the Council of 25 May 1999 on Certain Aspects of Consumer Goods and Associated Guarantees, OJ L 171 (7 July 1999) 12–16, Preamble (3).

[89] See Daniel Kelemen, *Eurolegalism: The Transformation of Law and Regulation in the European Union*, Harvard University Press, Cambridge, MA (2011).

[90] Hesselink, 'The New European Legal Culture', at 40–44; Anthony Sebok and Lars Trägårdh, Adversarial Legalism and the Emergence of a New European Legality: A Comparative Perspective, in Austin Sarat et al. (eds.), *Imagining New Legalities*, Stanford Law Books, Stanford, CA (2012) at 154, 168.

and at times obliterated, the traditional distinction between private and public law, for better or worse.

5.3 *A Lesson for Asia: The Two Sides of Europe*

All this entails a final lesson for Asia. A transatlantic comparison of private enforcement must distinguish two sides of Europe: the legal culture of European nation states and that of the European Union. Private enforcement goes much more against the grain of the former than the latter.

Conclusion: Insights from a Comparison of Legal Cultures

Policy makers in Asia (and elsewhere) contemplating private enforcement face myriad conflicting arguments, ranging from the technical to the economic. At some point, they should take a very broad perspective and consider how enlisting private action for public purposes relates to their legal tradition and culture. In this regard, looking at other highly developed economies can be helpful because it shows that private enforcement fits into some legal cultures much more easily than others.[91]

In particular, a cultural perspective generates two important insights.

First, the question of whether or not to enlist private enforcement is not merely a technical matter; it touches on broad and fundamental questions. Does the state assume the sole responsibility for enforcing public policies – or is it willing to enlist private actors and thus to relinquish (at least some) control? Does the state want to train, maintain, and pay for an expert, neutral, and efficient administrative apparatus, and does it trust its bureaucrats to enforce the law effectively and efficiently? Or does it want to leave some of the job to market participants acting in their self-interest, and does it trust them to police each other? Does the state want to keep concentrated control over the enforcement of law – or is it willing to decentralise such control, even to the point of delegating it to private parties? Should private law and litigation merely serve private purposes – or should they be instrumentalised (and thus politicised) so that they serve public agendas as well?

[91] Of course, legal cultures are not immutable – they can be changed. But they are usually pretty tenacious, and change is mostly slow and incremental. It can be initiated and fostered by governments, but it can scarcely be imposed. At least for starters, policy makers are therefore well advised to take their legal culture as they find it.

Second, a cultural perspective shows that reliance on public enforcement also inevitably affects the surrounding legal culture: the degree of state control over the development of the law; the law's unity, coherence, and predictability; the status of bureaucrats, judges, and lawyers; the range of arguments in and the style of decision making; and possibly a host of other features as well.

None of this means that relying on private enforcement is a bad idea – it may very well be worth its price and risks. But it does mean that the implications are more complex, and the stakes higher, than it seems at first glance.

3

Disclosure Regulation and the Rise of Capital Markets

Nineteenth-Century Britain and Germany Compared

CARSTEN GERNER-BEUERLE

1 Introduction

A perennial concern of policy makers around the world is the construction of a framework of financial regulation that is effective, efficient, and – most importantly – conducive to the emergence of a deep and liquid financial market. While the channels through which financial development influences economic growth are not yet fully understood, there is broad agreement that developed financial markets are instrumental in fostering economic growth.[1] Thus, the importance of regulatory design for the prosperity of nations can hardly be overestimated.

The essential ingredients of any regulatory regime governing the capital markets are rules mandating the disclosure of financial information, both transaction-specific and ongoing, and liability rules that allow investors to recover losses from those who are responsible for misstatements to the market. Legal institutions requiring, for example, the disclosure of the company's annual accounts and the publication of a prospectus containing particulars of the company and the securities to be offered to the public were formulated for the first time in the nineteenth century. This period saw the transformation of largely agrarian economies into industrial ones, first in Western Europe and then in

[1] The first in-depth consideration of the nexus of finance and economic growth is commonly attributed to Joseph Schumpeter, *The Theory of Economic Development: An Inquiry into Profits, Capital, Credit, Interest, and the Business Cycle* (Harvard University Press, 1911). For two more recent contributions providing empirical evidence see Robert G. King and Ross Levine, 'Finance and Growth: Schumpeter Might Be Right', 108 Q. J. ECON 717 (1993); Raghuram G. Rajan and Luigi Zingales, Financial Dependence and Growth', 88 AM. ECON. REV. 559 (1998).

the United States. With it came the mobilisation of capital, expansion of the banking system, and increased use of the capital markets as a means of financing industrial enterprises.[2]

One country was ahead of all other industrialising nations in terms of financial development over the course of the nineteenth century: Great Britain. The number of joint stock companies incorporated in Britain was seven to eight times higher, and their paid-up capital three to four times larger than in the next largest economies on the Continent,[3] and the London Stock Exchange was the leading exchange in the world, with a deeper and more liquid market than anywhere else.[4] The different financial trajectory is particularly astonishing when compared with another European economy that was rapidly growing in the latter half of the nineteenth century and overtook Britain as the leading industrial powerhouse of Europe by the early twentieth century: Germany. In spite of the fact that Germany was home to a considerable number of expanding industrial corporations, available comparative data show consistently that, until the eve of World War I, Germany's financial markets lagged behind those in Britain in respect of almost every measure of financial development: number of incorporated firms, volume of securities issues, stock market capitalisation as a percentage of gross domestic product, and financial assets as a proportion of national assets.[5]

[2] Caroline Fohlin, *Mobilising Money* (Cambridge University Press, 2012), 15–47.

[3] In 1906, 40,995 joint-stock companies with a combined paid-up capital of £2,000 million were incorporated in Britain, compared with 5,061 companies with a paid-up capital of £685 million in Germany (also 1906) and 6,325 companies with a paid-up capital of £540 million in France (1898), see Ranald Michie, 'Different in Name Only? The London Stock Exchange and Foreign Bourses, c. 1850–1914', 30 *Business History* 46 (1988), 52.

[4] Ranald Michie, *The London Stock Exchange: A History* (Oxford University Press, 2001), 70–73. For comparative data on stock market capitalisation and the number of listed companies per million people, see also Raghuram G. Rajan and Luigi Zingales, 'The Great Reversals: The Politics of Financial Development in the Twentieth Century', 69 J. FIN. ECON. 5 (2003), 15.

[5] Deutsche Bundesbank, *Deutsches Geld- und Bankwesen in Zahlen, 1876–1975* (Knapp, 1975). Detailed annual information on listings on the London Stock Exchange are contained in Burdett's Official Intelligence of Securities (Couchman, from 1882), later renamed Stock Exchange Official Intelligence. Secondary sources summarising the data include George W. Edwards, *The Evolution of Finance Capitalism* (Longman, 1938), 392–393, 404–405; Raymond W. Goldsmith, *Comparative National Balance Sheets: A Study of Twenty Countries 1688–1978* (University of Chicago Press, 1985), 221–226; Alfred Neymarck, 'La statistique internationale des valeurs mobilières', 56 *Journal de la Société Française de Statistique* 353 (1915), 360–366.

One explanation for these striking differences in financial development, often advanced in the finance and legal literature, is epitomised by the following quote:

> Disclosure legislation by the end of the nineteenth century armed British investors . . . with the best information possessed by investors anywhere. We consider this to be a reason, possibly a major reason . . . why the British capital markets were the world leaders in the same era.[6]

Thus, a central role in the development of financial markets is attributed to financial regulation and more generally the legal environment. Legal rules that impose comprehensive disclosure requirements on issuers and allow investors to recover losses incurred as a consequence of incorrect market disclosures give the necessary assurances to the public to part with their savings and invest in the capital markets. Since such legal mechanisms were in place in the UK by the end of the nineteenth century, it is not surprising, so the argument goes, that Britain's financial system was more diversified and market-oriented than those on the Continent.

However, a detailed legal historical analysis of the regulatory framework in key countries, such as Britain and Germany, which could corroborate or refute the hypothesis that disclosure regulation plays an essential role in financial development, is largely absent from the debate. This article seeks to fill this gap. It maps the evolving disclosure framework, as well as the evolution of legal institutions imposing liability for incorrect disclosures to the market, during the formative stages of the capital markets in Europe – the nineteenth century and the beginning of the twentieth century. Even though the regulatory framework was incomplete by modern standards, legal concepts such as prospectus disclosure or liability for incorrect statements to the market that continue to constitute essential building blocks of securities regulation to this day were promulgated in a fairly well-defined form as early as the second half of the nineteenth century. Importantly, this legal development could be observed not only in the UK, but also in Germany. By comparing the existing regulatory strategies in the two countries, we can therefore

[6] Richard Sylla and George David Smith, 'Information and Capital Market Regulation in Anglo-American Finance' in Michael D. Bordo and Richard Sylla (eds.), *Anglo-American Financial Systems: Institutions and Markets in the Twentieth Century* (Irwin, 1995), 179. The studies of Rafael La Porta, Florencio Lopez-de-Silanes, Andrei Shleifer, and Robert Vishny (LLSV), who express similar views, are well known, see for example, 'Legal Determinants of External Finance', 52 J. Fin., 1131 (1997).

provide additional contextual information that may contribute to a better understanding of the relationship between regulation and stock market development.

The remainder of this chapter is organised as follows. Section 2 analyses the evolution of disclosure regulation in the UK and Germany, focussing on the two most important items of disclosure in nineteenth century regulation, the company's financial accounts and the offering prospectus. Section 3 examines private enforcement mechanisms, notably liability for incorrect prospectus disclosure. Section 4 concludes.

2 Elements of Disclosure Regulation

In order to facilitate comparison of disclosure regulation between Germany and the UK, this section analyses the regulatory regime along four dimensions: first, the requirement to disclose financial accounts on an annual basis; second, the mandatory audit of the accounts; third, the requirement to publish a prospectus before shares can be offered to the public and/or listed on a stock exchange; and fourth, rules providing for a relatively comprehensive list of relevant information to be contained in the prospectus.

In Germany, disclosure requirements were imposed for the first time when the concession system was replaced with a system of incorporation by registration in 1870.[7] The reasons justifying the policy shift were similar to those that we find in other jurisdictions transitioning to incorporation by registration.[8] The German legislator acknowledged

[7] The new system was introduced for the states of the North German Confederation, which included Prussia, in Art. 211 Allgemeines Deutsches Handelsgesetzbuch (ADHGB) [General German Commercial Code], as amended by Gesetz, betreffend die Kommanditgesellschaften auf Aktien und die Aktiengesellschaften [Act Concerning Limited Partnerships by Shares and Joint Stock Corporations], BGBl. Norddt. Bund [Federal Law Gazette of the North German Confederation] 1870, 375. Some German states, in particular the Hanseatic cities of Bremen, Hamburg, and Lübeck, but also Württemberg and Saxony, abolished the concession system earlier than 1870, making use of the authority under Art. 249 General German Commercial Code of 1861.

[8] For example in the UK, see the House of Commons debates on the Joint Stock Companies Act 1856, Hansard, 3rd Series, vol. 140 (1856), 116–138. The German policy makers were well aware of the legal developments in the UK (and also in France and Italy) and did indeed refer to them to justify the German reforms, see for example Stenographische Berichte über die Verhandlungen des Reichstages des Norddeutschen Bundes, I. Legislatur-Periode, Session 1870 [Stenographic Protocols of the Proceedings of the Reichstag of the North German Confederation, 1st Parliamentary Term, Session 1870], vol. 4, document no. 158, 651–652.

that a concession system was not only incapable of protecting the public effectively, but was prone to increasing the risks for investors by giving them a false sense of confidence in the prospects of the business and thus encouraging imprudent investment behaviour. The only viable solution, it was argued, was reliance on the investors' own vigilance and care in making investments.[9]

As opposed to the British Act of 1844, the Companies Act of 1870, however, only embraced one aspect of disclosure, the periodic publication of the company's books and accounts, and not the transaction-specific disclosure triggered by the intention to access public capital markets. Even the former type of disclosure was not fashioned in a particularly stringent manner. The management board was required to draw up a balance sheet which had to be presented to the shareholders and published in the official gazette.[10] The act also contained some relatively basic provisions on the form of the accounts[11] and criminal sanctions,[12] but prospectus disclosure was not mentioned. This approach was maintained in later company law amendments.

To some extent, the regulatory lacuna was filled by the rules and regulations of the stock exchanges adopted since the 1880s, which required the publication of a prospectus before securities could be admitted to trading and specified in detail the content of the prospectus, distinguishing between type of issuer and security.[13] For example, for shares of domestic industrial corporations, the prospectus had to contain information on the articles of association; objects; domicile and duration of the company; legal capital and amount of shares to be issued; rights attached to the shares, including pre-emptive rights and dividend rights; contributions in kind and payments made or other benefits granted in relation to the formation of the company; applicable accounting principles and principles on dividend distribution; and the names of the members of the management and supervisory boards. In addition, the company's articles and the last annual report had to be appended to the application.[14]

[9] Stenographische Berichte über die Verhandlungen des Reichstages des Norddeutschen Bundes, at 650.

[10] Act Concerning Limited Partnerships by Shares and Joint Stock Corporations of 1870, n 7 above, Art. 239.

[11] Ibid., Art. 239a. [12] Ibid. Art. 249.

[13] See, for example, the regulations of the Berlin Stock Exchange of 1884, reproduced in Bericht der Börsen-Enquete-Kommission [Report of the Stock Exchange Commission of Inquiry] (1893), 47–51.

[14] Report of the Stock Exchange Commission of Inquiry, ibid., at 51.

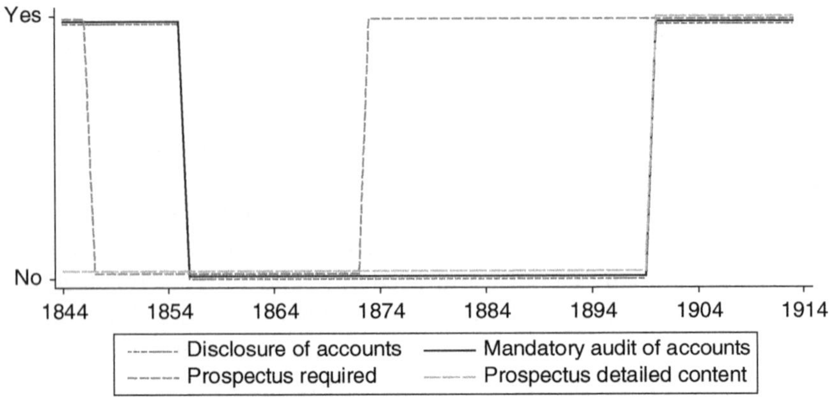

Figure 3.1 Evolution of disclosure regulation in Germany, 1870–1914

This regulatory framework remained largely unaltered until after World War I. Figure 3.1 visualises the legal changes in the four dimensions of disclosure mentioned above in a binary way.

In Great Britain, similar to Germany, disclosure became a central element of company law when the Joint Stock Companies Act of 1844[15] replaced the concession system with a liberal system of incorporation by registration. The 1844 Act, informed by the conviction of its primary author, William Gladstone, that publicity was 'the most effectual remedy' in that it brought 'the power of public opinion to bear on the proceedings of joint-stock companies',[16] required for incorporation only the filing of a list of particulars with the registrar of companies that included information on the name, purpose, and principal place of business of the company; disclosed its promoters, officers, and subscribers; and provided a copy of every prospectus or other statement addressed to the public with a view to issuing and allotting the company's shares.[17] The latter requirement is noteworthy for its wide scope which applied to any 'prospectus or circular, handbill or advertisement, or other such document at any time addressed to the public, or to the subscribers or others, relative to the formation or modification of [the] company'.[18] Thus, the legislator intended to establish control over any form of communication with the public that could potentially influence the investors' decision to subscribe for securities. These obligations upon the formation of companies were supplemented by detailed, mandatory rules on the

[15] 7 & 8 Vict., c. 110. [16] *The Economist*, 6 April 1844, 655.
[17] Joint Stock Companies Act 1844, s. 4. [18] Ibid., s. 4, no. 8.

drawing-up, auditing, and disclosure of the company's financial accounts.[19] The directors were responsible for producing periodical accounts and balance sheets which had to be audited by external auditors appointed by the annual general meeting. Printed copies of the balance sheet and auditors' reports were sent to all shareholders before the ordinary general meeting, read at the meeting, and filed with the registrar of companies.

Only a few years later, the ambitious disclosure regime of the 1844 Act, however, started to be hollowed out. The first step towards a liberal regime characterised by light-touch regulation and limited intervention in the workings of companies came with the Joint Stock Companies Act 1847, which repealed the registration requirement for prospectuses because it was 'found to be very burdensome to the Promoters'.[20] The only remaining restriction on the use of prospectuses was the prohibition against publishing any prospectus or other document addressed to the public containing information that had to be filed with the registrar of companies before the required particulars were so filed, or statements that were at variance with the particulars previously filed.[21] Then, in 1856, an act consolidating the various amendments to the Companies Act 1844 moved the rules on audited accounts into an appendix to the act which laid down model articles that could be disapplied by the incorporators.[22] The 1856 act introduced a number of other changes facilitating the formation of companies, allowed registration with the most basic information to be filed,[23] and did not undertake to regulate primary market disclosure in any way.

The amendments of 1847 and the Joint Stock Companies Act 1856 were said to have been adopted 'in the heyday of *laissez-faire*'.[24] Both the requirement to register prospectuses and mandatory auditing would not be reinstated until the Companies Act 1900.[25] However, with the Act of 1856, the pinnacle of the deregulatory movement was probably reached, and subsequent amendments began to make careful alterations to the free

[19] Ibid., ss. 34–43. [20] Joint Stock Companies Act 1847, 10 & 11 Vict., c. 78, s. 4.

[21] Ibid., s. 7. [22] Joint Stock Companies Act 1856, 19 & 20 Vict., c. 47, s. 9 and Table B.

[23] Ibid., ss. 5, 12.

[24] Laurence C.B. Gower, *The Principles of Modern Company Law* (3rd ed., Stevens 1969), 49. However, Gower observes that most companies continued to adopt the relevant provisions, and the change, therefore, seems to have had a smaller impact in practice than could have been expected, see Ibid., fn. 59.

[25] Companies Act 1900, 63 & 64 Vict., c. 48, ss. 9–10, 21–23. The requirement to publish audited accounts was reinstated earlier for banking corporations, Companies Act 1879, 42 & 43 Vict., c. 76, s. 7.

market system. As far as disclosure regulation is concerned, the Companies Act 1867 is notable. It reintroduced the term 'prospectus' and prescribed that prospectuses should set out the dates and names of all contracts entered into by the company, promoters, and directors before the issue of the prospectus.[26] The rules and regulations of the London Stock Exchange also served to strengthen the disclosure regime somewhat.[27] Quotation of companies in the official list required, *inter alia*, that a prospectus in agreement with the articles of association be published and that both the prospectus and the articles were filed with the stock exchange.[28] However, it would be an exaggeration to claim that the stock exchange rules effectively filled the void in disclosure regulation that was left by the legislator. Rather, they operated within the ambit of the existing legislative framework, amplified some disclosure obligations, for example regarding payments made to the promoters, and sought to ensure that a meaningful portion of the capital issued and subscribed was paid up and at the free disposal of the directors[29] and the

[26] Companies Act 1867, 30 & 31 Vict., c. 131, s. 38. However, the requirement to disclose contracts was often waived in practice; for references, see Brian R. Cheffins, *Corporate Ownership and Control: British Business Transformed* (Oxford University Press, 2008), 194.

[27] Contemporary discussions of the rules and regulations of the London Stock Exchange include Bertram O. Bircham and Frederick G.C. Morris, *Public Companies: A Treatise on the Law and Practice Relating to the Formation and Flotation of Such Joint Companies Limited by Shares as Invite the Public to Subscribe for Their Capital* (E. Wilson 1911); B.E. Spencer Brodhurst, *The Law and Practice of the Stock Exchange* (W. Clowes 1897); Rudolph E. Melsheimer and Walter Laurence, *The Law and Customs of the London Stock Exchange* (H. Sweet 1879; further editions 1884, 1891, and 1905); Frederick J. Varley, *Rules & Regulations of the Stock Exchange. With notes and references to decided cases* (E. Wilson 1925).

[28] Mihill Slaughter, *Rules and Regulations for the Conduct of Business on the Stock Exchange* (London Stock Exchange, 1873), Rules 128–129.

[29] See, for example, Brodhurst, The Law and Practice of the Stock Exchange, 283–284, reproducing the stock exchange regulations of 1897. The central provision was Rule 136, which stipulated that an application for quotation of a company in the official list had to be accompanied by 'the prospectus, . . . the original application for shares, the allotment book, signed by the chairman and secretary to the company, and a certificate verified by the statutory declaration of the chairman and the secretary, stating the number of shares applied for and unconditionally allotted to the public, the amount of deposits paid thereon, and that such deposits are absolutely free from any lien, the bankers' pass-book and a certificate from the bankers stating the amount of deposits received'. Further, Rule 136 required 'that the prospectus shall have been publicly advertised, and that it agrees substantially with . . . the articles of association . . . that it provides for the issue of not less than one-half of the nominal capital, and for the payment of ten per cent, upon the amount subscribed, and sets forth the arrangements for raising the capital, whether by

articles of association contained certain mechanisms designed to protect investors.[30]

Major changes finally came with the Companies Act 1900, which adopted four amendments significantly affecting disclosure regulation. First, it re-established the registration requirement for prospectuses that had been abolished in 1847.[31] Second, it defined prospectuses widely – but arguably not as widely as the 1844 Act – to capture any statement offering securities to the public.[32] Third, it required more comprehensive disclosures in the prospectus, including the number and amount of shares issued for a consideration other than in cash and the consideration for which they were issued, incorporation expenses, underwriting commissions, material contracts, and related party transactions, defined as any interest of a director in property to be acquired by the company and compensation for services rendered in connection with the formation of the company.[33] Fourth, the provisions on external audits of the balance sheet were again made binding for all companies.[34]

If we visualise the legal situation as before by coding changes from the Joint Stock Companies Act of 1844 to the Companies Act 1900 in a binary way, we obtain the picture reproduced in Figure 3.2.

Comparing both legal systems, it is difficult to conclude that one disclosure regime is clearly superior to the other. The German rules were less stringent than their British counterparts in that they did not require the mandatory auditing of annual accounts. In addition, the prospectus requirement was linked to the application for admission to trading on a stock exchange, since it was imposed not by general company legislation, but by the regulations of the stock exchanges. The British legislation, on the other hand, used a wide definition of prospectuses to ensure that the regulation applied to any communication to the public was intended to attract subscriptions for securities. However, these differences emerged relatively late, in 1900, when the

shares fully or partly paid-up, with the amounts of each respectively, and also states the amount paid, or to be paid, in money or otherwise to concessionaires, owners of property, or others on the formation of the company, or to contractors for works to be executed, and the number of shares, if any, proposed to be conditionally allotted; that two-thirds of the whole nominal capital proposed to be issued has been applied for and unconditionally allotted to the public (shares reserved or granted in lieu of money payments to concessionaires, owners of property, or others, not being counted to form part of such public allotment)'.

30 See, e.g. Rule 136, Ibid., at 284, requiring 'that the articles of association restrain the directors from employing the funds of the company in the purchase of its own shares'.

31 Companies Act 1900, s. 9(3). 32 Ibid., s. 30. 33 Ibid., s. 10. 34 Ibid., ss. 21–23.

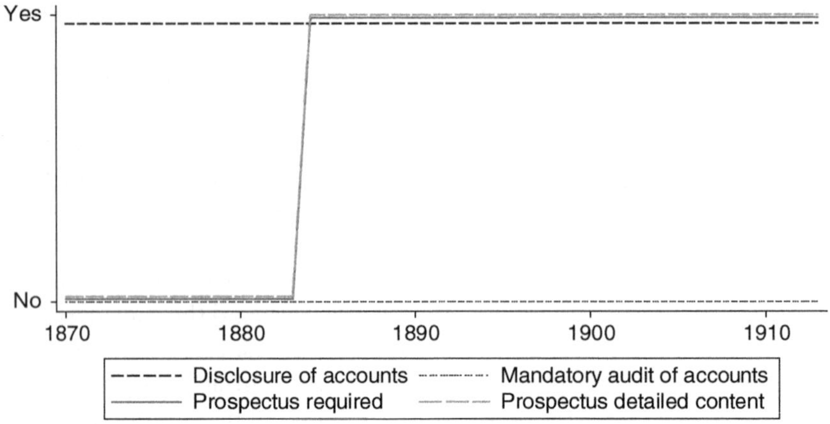

Figure 3.2 Evolution of disclosure regulation in Great Britain, 1844–1914

British capital markets were already well developed and leading in the world.

3 Enforcement of Disclosure Regulation

A strong public regulator of the financial markets was not part of the nineteenth-century regulatory landscape in any country. Public enforcement mechanisms consisted primarily of the supervision of the operations of stock exchanges by means of the appointment of a state commissioner,[35] unless the stock exchange was set up as a self-regulatory organisation.[36] Disclosure obligations were mainly enforced at the time of admission to trading when the stock exchange had to approve the offering prospectus[37] or by requiring the company to file a prospectus with the registrar of companies before any shares could be allotted to investors.[38] Thus, private enforcement played an essential role as a tool to protect investors in a regulatory environment that had only recently emerged from a heavy-handed system of concession requirements and had not yet produced effective substitute mechanisms of public enforcement. This section, therefore, focuses on private enforcement mechanisms.

[35] See, for example, the German Börsengesetz [German Stock Exchange Act] of 22 June 1896, RGBl (1896), 157, s. 2.

[36] Michie, The London Stock Exchange, 35. [37] German Stock Exchange Act, s. 36.

[38] Companies (Consolidation) Act 1908, 8 Edw. 7, c. 69, ss. 80, 85.

3.1 Germany

For most of the nineteenth century, the courts in both countries grappled with the problem of interpreting common law concepts developed in different contexts in ways that made them operational in impersonal capital markets. They did so with limited success. In Germany, the liability of issuers and underwriters for incorrect market disclosures had been a controversial policy issue since the first joint stock corporations, mainly railways, started to offer securities to the public in greater numbers in the 1840s and 1850s. Before the adoption of a codified prospectus liability provision in the Stock Exchange Act of 1896, the courts generally took recourse to a concept of Roman law, the *actio doli*, which was somewhat comparable to the common law tort of deceit[39] and required a showing of intent to defraud.[40] This meant that possible avenues of purchasers to claim damages were limited. The investor had to provide evidence that the issuer of the prospectus intended to deceive, and did deceive, the purchaser and that the investor relied on the prospectus. These requirements made it, in most cases, impossible for purchasers on the secondary market to bring a claim. In addition, they did not provide any incentive for those who drafted and published a prospectus to verify the information they had obtained about the issuer. The gatekeeper function of reputational intermediaries that is reinforced by the private enforcement machinery of modern securities regulation, therefore, was not utilised by these early attempts to formulate principles of prospectus liability.

The law remained largely unchanged until the end of the century, when the legislator proposed the adoption of a statutory prospectus liability provision as part of a comprehensive overhaul of the regulatory architecture governing stock exchanges. The structure of the liability provision was the subject of considerable debate. The report of the government commission of enquiry on the reform of stock exchange law stressed the importance of balancing the interests of the investing public, who placed trust in the fact that the issuing house had agreed to underwrite and offer securities to the public, and the interests of underwriters and other issuers of prospectuses not to be subject to excessive liability, which, it was feared, would impede the

[39] For a comparison of the Roman *actio doli* and the tort of deceit, see W. W. Buckland and Arnold D. McNair, *Roman Law and Common Law: A Comparison in Outline*, 2nd ed., (Cambridge University Press, 1952), 383–390.

[40] Friedrich Carl von Savigny, *System des heutigen Römischen Rechts, vol. 3* (Veit 1840), 118.

market for public offerings and harm the position of German stock exchanges.[41] The commission's final suggestion, however, sided more with the industry than with investors, proposing to limit responsibility to knowing misstatements or bad faith failure to verify information.[42] The prospectus liability provision eventually codified represented a better compromise between the views expressed during the commission hearings, which ranged from qualifying prospectuses as recommendations or imposing liability for the failure to employ the care of a conscientious manager to restricting responsibility to *dolus*. The Stock Exchange Act distinguished between misstatements and omissions, stipulating that gross negligence was sufficient for the former, whereas bad faith was required for the latter. As adopted in 1896, Section 43 of the act, laying down prospectus liability, provided:

> Where securities have been admitted to stock exchange trading on the basis of a prospectus containing incorrect statements that are material for an assessment of the value of the securities, those who issued the prospectus or initiated the issue of the prospectus shall be jointly and severally liable to pay compensation for any loss suffered as a consequence of the incorrect statement to any person acquiring such security, provided that they knew of the untruth, or should have known of it without gross negligence. The same applies where the prospectus omits to state a material fact and those who issued the prospectus or initiated the issue of the prospectus, acting in bad faith, concealed the fact or failed to conduct an adequate investigation.
>
> The obligation to pay compensation shall not be excluded by virtue of the fact that the statement is identified as stemming from a third party.

The Stock Exchange Act was revised in 1908,[43] however without amending the rules on prospectus liability.[44] It may be useful to analyse the provision along five dimensions: (1) standing; (2) defendants; (3) incorrect prospectus or other publication; (4) fault-based elements or defences; and (5) causation.

First, the drafters of the act were of the opinion that it was the function of an offering prospectus to inform the investing public at large, not only

[41] Report of the Stock Exchange Commission of Inquiry, 66–67. For similar considerations see the Explanatory Notes to the Stock Exchange Act, Reichstags-Drucksache 1895–1897, Erster Anlageband [Journal of the Parliament, First Supplementary Volume], 23.

[42] Report of the Stock Exchange Commission of Inquiry, 68.

[43] RGBl (1908), 193.

[44] Only the numbering was changed, and the provision became s. 45. Now it can be found in s. 21 of the Securities Prospectus Act [Wertpapierprospektgesetz], BGBl. I 2005, p. 1698, as last amended by Article 11 of the Law of 20 September 2013, BGBl. I 2013, p. 3642.

the subscribers for securities in the primary market. 'With the prospectus', the explanatory notes to the Stock Exchange Act explained, 'the issuing house turns to the public to furnish investors with the necessary information to assess the intrinsic value of the offered security. The trust placed in the correctness and completeness of the information is crucial for the acquisition of the securities.'[45] Importantly, in the view of the drafters, the published information not only influenced the decision of the initial subscribers whether or not to invest, but it continued to affect subsequent transactions in the securities, even if purchasers in the after-market had not read the prospectus. Accordingly, it was provided that all buyers of securities admitted to stock exchange trading on the basis of the defective prospectus, both in the primary and secondary market, had standing to bring a claim.[46] However, the effectiveness of the cause of action was compromised by the additional requirement that the claimant was still the owner of the securities at the time when compensation was claimed.[47]

Second, two classes of defendant were responsible for the content of the prospectus: those who issued the prospectus and those who 'initiated' the issue. The former was anyone who signed the prospectus and thus accepted responsibility for it, which included the issuer of the securities.[48] The latter referred to those who had initiated the drafting of the prospectus, because they pursued their own financial interests with the offering, for example, under appropriate circumstances, the directors or owners of the issuer. However, it is clear from the explanatory notes to the Stock Exchange Act and the report of the government commission of enquiry on the reform of stock exchange law that the main addressees of the liability provisions were not the issuer or its directors, but the issuing houses.[49] The policy makers were well aware of the fact that investors relied on the reputation of the underwriters and the underwriters implicitly vouched for the quality of the issue by making use of the information

45 Explanatory Notes to the Stock Exchange Act, 23. 46 Stock Exchange Act, s. 44(1).

47 This requirement was criticised in the contemporary literature, see for example Arthur Nußbaum, *Kommentar zum Börsengesetz* (C.H. Beck 1910), 198. It was a consequence of the regulation of damages in s. 44(2) Stock Exchange Act. Section 44(2) provided that the defendant, instead of paying damages, could elect to compensate the plaintiff for the purchase price paid or the initial stock market price and return the securities.

48 The Stock Exchange Act 1896 did not specify who had to sign the prospectus. In practice the issuer of the securities usually signed, see Nußbaum, ibid., at 170.

49 Explanatory Notes to the Stock Exchange Act, 23–24; Report of the Stock Exchange Commission of Inquiry, 66–70.

in the prospectus to place the securities. It was also pointed out that underwriters had an incentive to verify the information provided by issuers to protect their reputational capital. However, the policy makers were concerned that the sanctioning mechanism of the market was not sufficiently effective without being supplemented by a liability provision going beyond common law fraud, in particular because of the market's 'short memory'.[50] These arguments attest to the sophistication of the debate that informed the legislative reforms and show that the prospectus liability provisions already incorporated some of the considerations that were later conceptualised as gatekeeper liability.[51] In addition, it was argued that the issuer in a liability case will often be insolvent or in financial distress. In order to ensure effective investor protection, it was therefore necessary to extend liability to intermediaries that were in a position to assess the quality of the offering.[52]

Third, liability depended on an incorrect statement in the admission prospectus. Other publications, for example promotional material or newspaper announcements of the intended offering, did not fall within the scope of the provision. Misstatements in such publications were, therefore, governed by the general law with the consequence that liability was, for most purposes, restricted to fraudulent actions.[53] Furthermore, given that the Stock Exchange Act required the publication of a prospectus only for securities to be admitted to stock exchange listing and not for public offers without admission,[54] the codification left some regulatory gaps.[55]

Fourth, as mentioned above, after a controversial debate, the legislator adopted a gross negligence standard for misstatements and a bad faith standard for omissions. While this standard is fairly lenient,[56] it allowed

50 Max Weber, *Gesamtausgabe, vol. 5: Börsenwesen*, Knut Borchardt and Cornelia Meyer-Stoll (eds.), (J.C.B. Mohr 1999), 471–472.

51 Highly influential were two articles by Rainier H. Kraakman, 'Corporate Liability Strategies and the Costs of Legal Controls', 93 *Yale L.J.* 857 (1984); and 'Gatekeepers: The Anatomy of a Third-Party Enforcement Strategy', 2 *J.L. Econ. & Org.* 53 (1986).

52 Nußbaum, Kommentar zum Börsengesetz, 192.

53 Ibid., at 193–194.

54 Stock Exchange Act, s. 38(2).

55 See, for example, Imperial Court, Decision of 19 October 1910, *Leipziger Zeitschrift für Handels-, Konkurs- und Versicherungsrecht* 1911, 155, where liability was rejected because the investors had relied on a report given by the management board to the general meeting, and the prospectus was only published later.

56 Gross negligence has been defined as the failure to exercise a degree of care that would have prevented the harm or injury 'without effort', Imperial Court, Decision of 22 June 1896, RGZ 46, 83, 85. Bad faith [bösliches Verhalten] is comparable to recklessness; it does not require the intention to cause harm or to defraud (it is, accordingly, less

investors to recover damages both from the issuer who had made the misstatement[57] and from intermediaries who had not verified the information provided by the issuer.[58] As far as the latter point is concerned, it was disputed during the reform discussions whether underwriters should have a duty to investigate and, for example, review the books and records of the issuer.[59] The courts clarified that such a duty did not exist per se, but that it was also not sufficient to assume simply that information provided by third parties was correct.[60] Especially if the underwriter had reason to suspect that the information was not accurate, i.e. 'red flags' existed, for example because dividend payments were unusually high in comparison with other companies in the same industry, it would be necessary to obtain the opinion of an outside expert or perform on-site inspections.[61]

Fifth, section 43 seems to require proof of a causal connection between the loss suffered by the investor and the incorrect statement in the prospectus. This element of the cause of action is not easy to interpret, given that the law does not clearly distinguish between reliance and loss causation. As far as the latter point is concerned, the Imperial Court held that damages were not restricted to the difference between the purchase price and the true value of the securities. Rather, investors were able to claim that they would not have acquired the securities had they been aware of the true facts. The acquisition as such, therefore, could be qualified as the damaging event, with the consequence that the investor could recover the purchase price against return of the securities to the defendant.[62] This holding is in line with general principles of German tort law and, by itself, is not remarkable.[63] However, in combination with another doctrine, which the policy makers and courts developed in a rather ingenious way without taking recourse to established legal principles, it transforms, for most purposes, the causation requirement into a presumption of reliance and loss causation, provided that the claimant bought the securities after the prospectus was published and

than *dolus*), but the conscious disregard of the risk to others posed by the defendant's conduct, Higher Commercial Court of the Reich [Reichsoberhandelsgericht], Decision of 20 May 1875, ROHGE 10, 218.

57 For example, Imperial Court, Decision of 22 June 1896, RGZ 46, 83.

58 For example, Imperial Court, Decision of 11 October 1912, RGZ 80, 196.

59 Weber, Gesamtausgabe, vol. 5: Börsenwesen, 475.

60 Imperial Court, Decision of 19 October 1910, 157; Decision of 11 October 1912, RGZ 80, 196.

61 RGZ 80, 196, 200.

62 Imperial Court, Decision of 2 May 1900, RGZ 46, 83, 86–87.

63 See ibid., 87. The relevant principles are now laid down in s. 249 of the Civil Code [BGB].

the misstatement was material. During the reform discussions that led to the adoption of the Stock Exchange Act the government commission of enquiry expressed the view that 'it could be expected that . . . the offering prospectus, given its function, can and will generate a certain investment mood on the part of the public invited to subscribe to the offering'.[64] Investors were entitled to rely on this 'investment mood', even if they had not read the prospectus and were not familiar with its detailed content, unless they must have been aware of the true circumstances.[65] The courts adopted this approach and held that the necessary causal connection was given if the investor was influenced by the investment mood created by the prospectus to acquire the securities.[66]

This approach bears some resemblance to the US fraud-on-the-market theory, which can be used to establish reliance in Rule 10b-5 actions.[67] Both notions create rebuttable presumptions; both are informed by the consideration that the price of the securities is influenced by the incorrect information and that the investor would not have acquired the securities, at least not at the respective price, if the true facts had been disclosed. The German approach is somewhat crude compared with the fraud-on-the-market theory because the courts seemed to be prepared to invoke an 'investment mood' fairly quickly, without considering whether conditions were conducive to a wide dissemination of the incorrect statement or the market was sufficiently efficient to allow the assumption that misstatements would be priced in quickly. On the other hand, considering that the policy makers and courts could not benefit from two decades (at the time of *Basic, Inc.*) of research into market efficiency,[68] it is probably not surprising that the theory was not yet well developed.

64 Report of the Stock Exchange Commission of Inquiry, 70. 65 Ibid.

66 Imperial Court, Decision of 11 October 1912, RGZ 80, 196, 204; Decision of 19 October 1910, 156–157; Decision of 2 May 1903, *Holdheims Monatsschrift für Handelsrecht und Bankwesen, Steuer- und Stempelfragen*, vol. 13 (1904), 253–254 (rejecting liability because the plaintiff had bought before publication of the defective prospectus). The Court used the same line of reasoning under the law that applied before the Stock Exchange Act entered into force, arguing that the notion of 'investment mood' was not a legal presumption introduced by s. 43 of the Stock Exchange Act, but that it was based on general experience and rebuttable under appropriate circumstances, see Imperial Court, Decision of 25 February 1905, *Zeitschrift für Rechtspflege in Bayern*, vol. 1 (1905), 304.

67 *Basic Inc.* v. *Levinson*, 485 U.S. 224 (1988).

68 The first theorems and empirical evidence concerning market efficiency appeared in the 1960s; see Andrei Shleifer, *Inefficient Markets: An Introduction to Behavioural Finance* (Oxford University Press, 2000), 1–10, for a historical sketch.

In spite of its shortcomings, the approach that they chose is remarkable for considering the function of information in capital markets at a time when such markets were a relatively new phenomenon in Germany.

We now turn to English law and compare the German legal strategies with their English counterparts at successive points in time until 1913. Since the relevant English principles are well known,[69] the rules will be approached with a view to assessing the comparative effectiveness of both legal systems' investor protection mechanisms.

3.2 Great Britain

In Great Britain, similar to Germany, the leading cases on common law prospectus liability made it clear that the claimant in an action of deceit must prove actual fraud. In *Derry* v. *Peek*, fraud was held to require a showing 'that a false representation has been made (1) knowingly, or (2) without belief in its truth, or (3) recklessly, careless whether it be true or false.'[70] Thus, a statement, even if made without reasonable ground for believing it, will not necessarily give rise to liability, provided that it was 'made honestly, and in the full belief that it was true'.[71] In addition, it was pointed out that the proper purpose of an offering prospectus was 'to invite persons to become original partners in a company, that is to say, allottees of shares'.[72] The prospectus was therefore not addressed to investors other than the original allottees, and the issuer of the prospectus did not intend others to act on it. These cases made it, for most purposes, impossible for the purchaser in the aftermarket and very difficult for the original subscribers for shares to claim compensation for misstatements in the offering prospectus or in other documents published on the occasion of a public offering.

The law was reformed shortly after *Derry* v. *Peek* in reaction to the restrictive holding in that case[73] by the Directors Liability Act 1890,[74] which added a prospectus liability provision to the existing company legislation, providing in relevant part:

69 For a comprehensive treatment and critical discussion, see Michael Lobban, 'Nineteenth Century Frauds in Company Formation: *Derry* v. *Peek* in Context' (1996) 112 *LQR* 287; Geoffrey Morse (ed.), *Palmer's Company Law* (Sweet & Maxwell, 2014), ch. 5.7.

70 *Derry* v. *Peek* (1889) LR 14 App Cas 337, 374. The defendant did not, however, need to have intended the claimant to suffer a loss.

71 Ibid., 368. 72 *Peek* v. *Gurney* (1873) L.R. 6 H.L. 377, 401.

73 See *Clark* v. *Urquhart* (1930) A.C. 28, 55; *McConnel* v. *Wright* (1903) 1 Ch. 546, 558.

74 53 & 54 Vict., c. 64.

(1) Where . . . a prospectus or notice invites persons to subscribe for shares in or debentures or debenture stock of a company, every person who is a director of the company at the time of the issue of the prospectus or notice, and every person who having authorised such naming of him is named in the prospectus or notice as a director of the company or as having agreed to become a director of the company either immediately or after an interval of time, and every promoter of the company, and every person who has authorised the issue of the prospectus or notice, shall be liable to pay compensation to all persons who shall subscribe for any shares, debentures, or debenture stock on the faith of such prospectus or notice for the loss or damage they may have sustained by reason of any untrue statement in the prospectus or notice, or in any report or memorandum appearing on the face thereof, or by reference incorporated therein or issued therewith, unless it is proved –

(a) With respect to every such untrue statement not purporting to be made on the authority of an expert, or of a public official document or statement, that he had reasonable ground to believe, and did up to the time of the allotment of the shares, debentures, or debenture stock, as the case may be, believe, that the statement was true; and

(b) With respect to every such untrue statement purporting to be a statement by or contained in what purports to be a copy of or extract from a report or valuation of an engineer, valuer, accountant, or other expert, that it fairly represented the statement made by such engineer, valuer, accountant, or other expert, or was a correct and fair copy of or extract from the report or valuation. Provided always, that notwithstanding that such untrue statement fairly represented the statement made by such engineer, valuer, accountant, or other expert, or was a correct and fair copy of an extract from the report or valuation, such director, person named, promoter, or other person, who authorised the issue of the prospectus or notice as aforesaid, shall be liable to pay compensation as aforesaid if it be proved that he had no reasonable ground to believe that the person making the statement, report, or valuation was competent to make it; and

(c) With respect to every such untrue statement purporting to be a statement made by an official person or contained in what purports to be a copy of or extract from a public official document, that it was a correct and fair representation of such statement or copy of or extract from such document . . .

This provision was later incorporated without major changes into the Companies (Consolidation) Act 1908[75] and carried over into the Companies Act 1929, again only with slight amendments that did not change the substance of the provision or the level of investor protection.[76] Parts of the Companies Act 1929 served as a template for the US Securities Act of 1933,[77] and the structure of the 1890 prospectus liability provision can still be discerned in its US counterpart, Section 11 of the 1933 Act, notably in the reversed burden of proof in the form of the due diligence defence and the distinction between statements from experts, non-experts, and official persons.[78]

Relying on the same five dimensions that were used above to analyse the codified prospectus liability provisions of the German Stock Exchange Act,[79] we can note the following differences and similarities. First, the class of claimants is defined more narrowly than under the German act. Claimants are 'persons who shall subscribe for any shares, debentures, or debenture stock'. Thus, only purchasers in the primary market have standing to bring a claim,[80] whereas the German provision protects 'any person' acquiring securities.

Second, compensation can be claimed from any director of the issuer, any promoter, and anyone who has authorised the issue of the prospectus. Intermediaries that offer shares to the public will often be caught as promoters,[81] but the concept is notoriously fact-specific,[82] and the role of

[75] 8 Edw. 7, c. 69, s. 84. [76] 19 & 20 Geo. 5, c. 23, s. 37.

[77] See the account of James M. Landis, member and second chairman of the SEC and one of the drafters of the Securities Act of 1933, 'Legislative History of the Securities Act of 1933', 28 GEO. WASH. L. REV. 29 (1959–1960), 34.

[78] Securities Act 1933, s. 11(b)(3). An important difference is the requirement under US law to show that the defendant had no reasonable ground to believe and did not believe that statements purporting to be made on the authority of an expert were untrue, whereas it was (and still is) sufficient under UK law to prove that the director had no reasonable ground to believe that the expert 'was competent' to make the statement. Thus, the relevant point of reference is not the correctness of the statement, but only the position of the person making the statement; see Alistair Alcock, *The Financial Services and Markets Act 2000: A Guide to the New Law* (Jordan, 2000), para. 12.4.2. The prospectus liability provision is now contained in s. 90 Financial Services and Markets Act (FSMA) 2000, c. 8, and Schedule 10 to the FSMA.

[79] The five dimensions are (1) standing; (2) defendants; (3) incorrect prospectus or other publication; (4); fault-based elements or defences; and (5) causation.

[80] Morse, Palmer's Company Law, para. 5.708.

[81] See, for example, *McConnel* v. *Wright* (1903) 1 Ch. 546.

[82] For an overview of the case law see Paul L. Davies and Sarah Worthington, *Gower & Davies' Principles of Modern Company Law*, 9th ed., (Sweet & Maxwell, 2012), paras 5–1 to 5–4.

promoter has been said to end once formation of the company is completed.[83] Similarly, who authorises the issue of the prospectus will depend on the facts of the case, notably on who signs the prospectus.[84] Therefore, the Directors Liability Act 1890 gives rise to some degree of legal uncertainty, and the intention to employ reputational intermediaries to enforce disclosure obligations is not as pronounced as under the German Stock Exchange Act. On the other hand, as has been seen, the German prospectus liability provision also uses somewhat ambivalent terms to define the class of defendants, which has produced inconsistent case law.[85]

Third, the term 'prospectus' is understood broadly as 'any prospectus, notice, circular, advertisement, or other invitation, offering to the public for subscription or purchase any shares or debentures of a company'.[86] This goes beyond the German regime, which attaches liability only to incorrect statements in prospectuses used to obtain admission to stock exchange trading and thus leaves an important regulatory gap where offers are made to the public without seeking a listing or misleading statements are disseminated in other types of publications. It is clear that investors are as much in need of protection where unlisted securities are offered to the public, as they are where the securities are traded on a stock exchange. For this reason, the German provision was criticised in the literature,[87] and modern regimes usually provide for a uniform set of rules that apply to both public offers and admissions to stock exchange listing.[88]

Fourth, the main innovation of the Directors Liability Act 1890 is a shift of the burden of proof to those responsible for the prospectus, who can exculpate themselves by showing that they had reasonable ground to believe, and did believe, that the information in the prospectus was correct. This constitutes a significant improvement compared with

[83] *Twycross* v. *Grant* (1877) 2 C.P.D. 469, 540.

[84] For a discussion of this point see Carsten Gerner-Beuerle, 'Underwriters, Auditors, and Other Usual Suspects: Elements of Third Party Enforcement in US and European Securities Law', 6 *ECFR* 476 (2009), 494.

[85] See Landgericht I Berlin [Regional Court I Berlin], *Plutus, Kritische Wochenschrift für Volkswirtschaft und Finanzwesen* 1905, 467 (expressing the view that only the issuer, and not the underwriter, was to be qualified as issuer of the prospectus).

[86] Companies Act 1900, s. 30. [87] Nußbaum, *Kommentar zum Börsengesetz*, 193.

[88] For example, the EU Prospectus Directive, Directive 2003/71/EC of the European Parliament and of the Council of 4 November 2003 on the prospectus to be published when securities are offered to the public or admitted to trading, OJ L 345/64, art 3.

the gross negligence and bad faith standards under German law; although it seems that in most cases in which the claimant prevailed, the common law action of deceit would also have been well founded.[89]

Fifth, the Directors Liability Act 1890 did not change the common law on reliance and loss causation. Claimants bear the burden of proving that they relied on the misstatement (they acted 'on the faith of [the] prospectus')[90] and suffered a loss as a consequence of the action taken upon misrepresentation.[91] The English courts did not introduce a presumption comparable to the investment-mood concept that can be found in German law. They accordingly required that the investor must have received and read the prospectus, but they accepted a showing that the claimant 'was misled by the prospectus as a whole [rather than by a specific misrepresentation] . . . that he was induced to put his money into this concern by representations in the prospectus'.[92]

If the interpretation offered here is correct, it is again difficult to identify a clearly superior regulatory approach, both in the pre-codification decades and after adoption of a statutory prospectus liability regime. The two enforcement mechanisms under German and English common law most likely to be applied in the relevant circumstances, the *actio doli* in Germany and the tort of deceit in the UK, both posed significant obstacles to recovery. Most importantly, they generally required a showing of intent to defraud or reckless indifference to the truth and proof that the claimant relied on the incorrect statement and suffered a loss as a result. The two earliest comprehensive prospectus liability provisions, codified in the German Stock Exchange Act of 1896 and the UK Directors Liability Act 1890, constituted a marked improvement on the common law, but they also exhibited weak elements that impeded private enforcement. In the case of the Stock Exchange Act of 1896, the most problematic element was the requirement to show that the defendant acted with gross negligence or in bad faith, and in the case of the Directors Liability Act 1890, it was the failure to introduce any presumption of reliance and loss causation. On the other hand, both legal systems developed innovative reforms over the course of the nineteenth century to improve investor protection, such as shifting the burden of proof and establishing a due diligence defence (Britain) or using the notion of 'investment mood' (Germany).

[89] See, for example, *Broome* v. *Speak* [1903] 1 Ch. 586; *McConnel* v. *Wright* [1903] 1 Ch. 546, 558.

[90] *McConnel* v. *Wright*, ibid., at 550–551. [91] Ibid., at 555–556. [92] Ibid., at 551.

4 Conclusion

The essential role in the development of deep and liquid capital markets that some commentators ascribe to disclosure regulation rests on an intuitive observation: A broad range of indicators of financial development show that one country was far ahead of the rest of the world in the nineteenth century: Great Britain. At the same time, it is uncontroversial that Great Britain had progressive legislation in place governing companies, administered by a competent government and adjudicated in sophisticated courts, which could draw on a rich body of case law. However, a more granular analysis of the legal system and a comparison with another leading industrial nation of the time, Germany, calls this narrative into question. There is no evidence that Britain's capital markets were more developed because British investors were 'armed . . . with the best information possessed by investors anywhere'[93] and because they had more effective instruments at their disposal to recover damages if they had purchased securities in reliance on misstatements.

In the two countries, the required level of disclosure and the ease with which investors could claim compensation for incorrect statements to the market were broadly comparable during the period under investigation. Both countries relied on publicity in the form of the requirement to publish annual accounts to protect investors when the concession system was replaced with a system of incorporation by registration. However, for most of the nineteenth century, the company laws in neither country required the mandatory auditing of accounts, and accounting rules were generally rudimentary. Similarly, prospectus disclosure, while mentioned in UK legislation as early as 1844, did not ensure that investors were informed in any comprehensive manner until the end of the century.

Furthermore, recovery of damages for incorrect disclosures was difficult in both countries. Before the adoption of codified prospectus liability provisions in the last decade of the nineteenth century, investors had to take recourse to common law mechanisms, which had been developed under different economic conditions. They were not designed to operate in impersonal capital markets, but to regulate personal interactions giving rise to contractual or tortious relationships. It is therefore not surprising that the courts struggled to render them operational in the anonymous capital markets that emerged during the nineteenth century.

[93] Sylla and Smith, 'Information and Capital Market Regulation in Anglo-American Finance', 179.

The situation improved somewhat with the adoption of the British Directors Liability Act 1890 and the German Stock Exchange Act of 1896. Both prospectus liability provisions had drawbacks, but the legislators in the two countries also showed considerable sophistication in fashioning the liability regime in a way that took account of the particularities of capital markets. The German provision extended liability to the underwriters, based on considerations reminiscent of the modern-day gatekeeper theory. The British provision pioneered what is now called, in American parlance, 'due diligence defence': a reversal of the burden of proof concerning the fault-based elements of the cause of action. In addition, the German policy makers and the Imperial Court displayed remarkable regulatory creativity in using the notion of 'investment mood' to establish a presumption of reliance, provided that the claimant had bought the securities at a time when the misleading prospectus could be assumed to have influenced 'the public's appraisal of the securities'.[94]

Thus, the level of investor protection was strengthened in both countries over the course of the nineteenth century. However, this development was incremental and was a reaction to changing economic conditions or harmful practices that had already taken hold in the markets, rather than the deliberate attempt to fashion a disclosure regime that would create vibrant capital markets by providing optimal conditions for investment. Causality is a vexed issue, and it may well be the case that stringent disclosure regulation is an important factor in sustaining well-functioning capital markets, but in the case of the two countries analysed in this study, there is no clear evidence that it was a causal factor in the initial emergence of capital markets. Rather, the trajectory of regulatory reform in Britain and Germany points in the opposite direction. In Britain, markets arose before the regulator took a more interventionist stance, and in Germany, their development slowed down just as policy makers and courts began to formulate modern concepts of disclosure regulation.

94 Explanatory Notes to the Stock Exchange Act, 23.

4

Mandatory Arbitration in Consumer Finance and Investor Contracts

MICHAEL S. BARR*

1 Introduction

Arbitration is widely used as an effective alternative to litigation in a variety of contexts in the United States and in many other jurisdictions. The Supreme Court has touted the benefits of arbitration over litigation, noting that 'parties forgo the procedural rigor and appellate review of the courts in order to realise the benefits of private dispute resolution: lower costs, greater efficiency and speed, and the ability to choose expert adjudicators to resolve specialised disputes'.[1] These benefits explain why arbitration is widely used, for example, in commercial contracts and labour-management agreements. For commercial actors, arbitration often has greater flexibility than court proceedings and has long been considered essential for cross-border transactions. For labour unions and management, resolving disputes through arbitration 'minimize[s] industrial conflict over worker grievances' and permits the business to continue to run during dispute resolution.[2]

In addition to agreements between sophisticated parties, arbitration clauses are now also nearly ubiquitous in American consumer contracts. Consumers are typically presented with contracts on a 'take it or leave it' basis, with no meaningful ability to negotiate over terms. Arbitration provisions are often not clearly disclosed and, even when disclosed, are not salient for consumers, who generally do not focus on the importance of the provisions in the event that a dispute over the contract later arises

* I would like to thank Jessica Kraft and Angela Xu for research assistance. This chapter first appeared, under the same title and in similar form, in NYU J. of Law & Business, vol. 11, no. 4, pages 793–817 (2015), and appears here with permission.

1 *Stolt-Nielsen S.A.* v. *AnimalFeeds Int'l Corp.*, 559 U.S. 662, 685 (2010).

2 Linda J. Demaine and Deborah R. Hensler, '"Volunteering" to Arbitrate Through Pre-Dispute Arbitration Clauses: The Average Consumer's Experience', 67 *Law & Contemp. Probs.* 55 (2004), 55.

and who may mis-forecast the likelihood of being in such a dispute. As has been pointed out in a variety of contexts, non-salient contract terms that reduce consumer welfare can be offered without offsetting effects on price.[3] The lack of salience at time of sale also means that there is no meaningful competition to provide contracts without arbitration provisions or with more consumer-friendly arbitration provisions. Some arbitration proceedings lack the procedural protections and unbiased arbitrator selection processes essential for fair outcomes. In addition, many arbitration provisions prohibit written opinions and bar consumers from disclosing any information about the arbitration proceedings or evidence backing claims from such proceedings. Moreover, arbitration clauses today typically preclude consumers from banding together in aggregated actions. The lack of ability to aggregate claims may diminish consumer access to effective redress, particularly for small-value claims, and may diminish the deterrent value of private litigation in enforcing legal norms.

This chapter focuses on the use of mandatory pre-dispute arbitration clauses in a subset of consumer contracts – those involving consumer finance and investor products and services. Arbitration clauses are pervasive in financial contracts – for credit cards, bank accounts, auto loans, broker-dealer services, and many others. In the wake of the recent financial crisis, Congress enacted the Dodd-Frank Wall Street Reform and Consumer Protection Act of 2010 (Dodd-Frank).[4] Dodd-Frank authorises the new Consumer Financial Protection Bureau (CFPB)[5] and the Securities and Exchange Commission (SEC)[6] to prohibit or condition the use of arbitration clauses in consumer finance and investment contracts, respectively.

This chapter outlines the need for increased regulation over mandatory pre-dispute arbitration clauses and suggests the need for key reforms. This paper begins by exploring arbitration clauses in consumer finance and investor contracts and then highlights the problems caused

[3] See, e.g. Michael S. Barr, Sendhil Mullainathan and Eldar Shafir, 'The Case for Behaviorally Informed Regulation' in David Moss and John Cisternino (eds.), *New Perspectives on Regulation* (The Tobin Project, 2009), 25, 41.

[4] Wall Street Reform and Consumer Protection Act (Dodd-Frank) § 1–1601, 12 U.S.C. §§ 5301–5641 (2013).

[5] Dodd-Frank Act § 1028. The author served as Assistant Secretary of the Treasury for Financial Institutions, 2009–2010, and was responsible for developing and working with Congress to enact Dodd-Frank, including the relevant provisions discussed in this article.

[6] Dodd-Frank Act § 921.

by mandatory pre-dispute arbitration clauses. A full treatment of potential solutions to these problems is beyond the scope of this chapter.

2 Background

2.1 History

Congress enacted the Federal Arbitration Act (FAA) in 1925.[7] The Supreme Court has ascribed this statute a broad purpose, perceiving it as a 'congressional declaration of a liberal federal policy favouring arbitration agreements, notwithstanding any state substantive or procedural policies to the contrary'.[8] The Supreme Court has not only all but foreclosed state regulation of arbitration agreements, but it has also severely limited access to the courts generally for consumers seeking to challenge arbitration agreements.

The FAA provides that agreements to arbitrate 'shall be valid, irrevocable, and enforceable, save upon such grounds as exist in law or in equity for the revocation of any contract'.[9] Under this exception to enforceability, states tried to regulate the use of arbitration clauses in consumer contracts, but the Supreme Court has interpreted this statutory carve-out very narrowly, noting that the FAA was enacted '[t]o overcome judicial resistance to arbitration'.[10] State courts tried to use the doctrine of unconscionability to set aside arbitration provisions that violated the state's procedural and substantive norms. The Supreme Court, however, has repeatedly upheld the validity of arbitration clauses in consumer contracts. The court has held that the Federal Arbitration Act of 1925 pre-empts a wide swath of state legislative and judicial efforts at regulation that, in the Supreme Court's view, interfered with the ability of commercial firms to use mandatory pre-dispute arbitration clauses in consumer contracts.[11]

The Supreme Court has interpreted the FAA broadly to uphold the enforceability of arbitration clauses. Even fraud in the formation of the contract is not grounds for evading arbitration; fraud must be found specifically in the formation of the arbitration clause itself.[12]

[7] 9 U.S.C. § 1 (1947).
[8] *Moses H. Cone Mem'l Hosp.* v. *Mercury Constr. Corp.*, 460 U.S. 1, 24 (1983).
[9] 9 U.S.C. § 2 (1947).
[10] *Buckeye Check Cashing, Inc.* v. *Cardegna*, 546 U.S. 440, 443 (2006).
[11] E.g. *Perry* v. *Thomas*, 482 U.S. 483 (1987).
[12] *Prima Paint Corp.* v. *Flood & Conklin Mfg. Co.*, 388 U.S. 395, 402–406 (1967) ('[T]he federal court is instructed to order arbitration to proceed once it is satisfied that the

Additionally, the arbitrators, not the courts, determine the arbitrability of the underlying dispute.[13] Even where state courts have been inclined to explore whether arbitration clauses are unconscionable, delegation clauses allow parties to delegate the decision about an arbitration clause's unconscionability to an arbitrator.[14] Most controversially, perhaps, the Supreme Court has ruled that arbitration clauses can exclude class-action arbitration or litigation.[15]

The Supreme Court has also narrowly interpreted the grounds for *vacatur*. Congress laid out in the FAA four circumstances under which a court can vacate an arbitral award: (1) 'where the award was procured by corruption, fraud, or undue means', (2) 'where there was evident partiality or corruption in the arbitrators', (3) 'where the arbitrators were guilty of misconduct', and (4) 'where the arbitrators exceeded their powers'.[16] Even the arbitrator's misinterpretation or disregard of the law is not grounds for *vacatur*.[17] Instead, the courts have developed the doctrine of manifest disregard of law, which requires plaintiffs to overcome a high hurdle in the form of a three-part test.[18] To make matters even more difficult for plaintiffs, the parties are not allowed to

making of the agreement for arbitration ... is not in issue. Accordingly, if the claim is fraud in the inducement of the arbitration clause itself – an issue which goes to the making of the agreement to arbitrate – the federal court may proceed to adjudicate it. But the statutory language does not permit the federal court to consider claims of fraud in the inducement of the contract generally' (internal quotation marks omitted).); see also *Buckeye Check Cashing, Inc.* v. *Cardegna*, 546 U.S. 440, 445–448 (2006).

[13] E.g. *Buckeye Check Cashing, Inc.* v. *Cardegna*, 546 U.S. 440, 445–446 (2006) (noting that 'as a matter of substantive federal arbitration law, an arbitration provision is severable from the remainder of the contract' and that 'unless the challenge is to the arbitration clause itself, the issue of the contract's validity is considered by the arbitrator in the first instance'); see also *First Options of Chicago, Inc.* v. *Kaplan*, 514 U.S. 938, 943 (1995) (deciding that the primary power to decide arbitrability belongs to either the arbitrators or the courts as the parties agreed).

[14] *Rent-A-Center, W., Inc.* v. *Jackson*, 561 U.S. 63, 71–72 (2010).

[15] *AT&T Mobile LLC* v. *Concepcion*, 131 S. Ct. 1740 (2011). I discuss limitations on collective relief in arbitration more extensively in Section 3.4.

[16] 9 U.S.C. § 10 (2002).

[17] E.g. In *re Goldman Sachs Execution & Clearing L.P.* v. *Official Unsecured Creditors' Comm. of Bayou Group, LLC*, No. 10-5049-CV, 2012 WL 2548927 (2d Cir. July 3, 2012); *United Paperworkers Int'l Union* v. *Misco, Inc.*, 484 U.S. 29, 38 (1987) ('But as long as the arbitrator is even arguably construing or applying the contract and acting within the scope of his authority, that a court is convinced he committed serious error does not suffice to overturn his decision'.).

[18] E.g., In *re Goldman Sachs Execution & Clearing L.P.* v. *Official Unsecured Creditors' Comm. of Bayou Group, LLC*, No. 10-5049-CV, 2012 WL 2548927 (2d Cir. July 3, 2012) (applying the three-part test: (1) the court must determine whether the law that was allegedly ignored was clear, and explicitly applicable to the matter before the

supplement grounds for *vacatur* in the contract,[19] so the arbitration clause itself cannot stipulate that mere legal error is sufficient to trigger judicial review.

2.2 *The Dodd-Frank Act's New Authority to Regulate Arbitration*

After the recent financial crisis, Congress enacted the Dodd-Frank Wall Street Reform and Consumer Protection Act of 2010 (hereafter Dodd-Frank).[20] Bucking the trend towards greater enforcement of arbitration clauses, Congress gave the new CFPB and the SEC the respective authority to regulate and even prohibit the use of arbitration clauses in consumer finance[21] and investment contracts.[22] Thus, Congress has provided clear and unambiguous legislative authority to these financial regulatory agencies to regulate arbitration agreements in these contracts. To date, however, neither the CFPB nor the SEC has taken regulatory action under these broad authorities, but the CFPB has already flatly banned arbitration clauses in mortgage contracts and for whistleblowers, as required under the act.[23]

2.3 *Arbitration Clauses in Consumer Finance and Investor Contracts Today*

2.3.1 Consumer Finance Contracts

Dodd-Frank instructed the CFPB to 'conduct a study of . . . the use of agreements providing for arbitration of any future dispute between covered persons and consumers in connection with the offering or providing of consumer financial products or services'.[24] In December

arbitrators; (2) the court must find that the law was improperly applied; and (3) the court must find that the arbitrator possessed the subjective intent to disregard the law).

19 *Hall Street Associates, LLC* v. *Mattel, Inc.*, 552 U.S. 576, 578 (2008). However, parties may be able to alter the scope of judicial review in state courts. *Cable Connection, Inc.* v. *DirecTV*, 44 Cal. 4th 1334 (Cal. 2008).

20 Dodd-Frank Act §§ 1–1601. 21 Ibid., § 1028. 22 Ibid., § 921.

23 The CFPB has issued rules flatly barring mandatory pre-dispute arbitration clauses in residential mortgage loan contracts and home equity lines of credit, as required by Dodd-Frank. Dodd-Frank Act § 1414(e). Whistleblowers are also protected under Dodd-Frank against any reduction in their rights to legal redress pursuant to mandatory arbitration provisions. Ibid., § 748 (providing protections to whistleblowers reporting to the Commodity Futures Trading Commission); Ibid., § 922 (providing protection to whistleblowers reporting to the SEC).

24 Ibid., § 1028(a).

2013, the CFPB issued a preliminary report on pre-dispute arbitration clauses,[25] and followed up with a second study in March 2015.[26]

Arbitration clauses appear in contracts representing 50.2 per cent of outstanding credit card loans, 58.8 per cent of checking accounts, and 83 per cent of general purpose reloadable (GPR) prepaid cards.[27] Currently, nearly all consumer financial contracts include no-class arbitration provisions.[28] Larger financial institutions are more likely to use arbitration clauses than smaller ones.[29] This holds true across all products and services the CFPB studied. To illustrate, only 7.7 per cent of banks include arbitration clauses in checking account contracts, yet 44 per cent of checking accounts are subject to arbitration clauses.[30] Currently, 53 per cent of credit card loans contain arbitration clauses in the agreement.[31] However, this figure is artificially deflated because several large issuers settled an antitrust class action by agreeing to remove arbitration clauses for a defined period. If these issuers reinstate arbitration clauses once the period expires, then approximately 94 per cent of outstanding credit cards will be subject to arbitration clauses.[32] As another example, 81 per cent of prepaid cards, which are often used by lower-income consumers, are subject to arbitration clauses.[33]

2.3.2 Broker-Dealer Agreements

As with its recommendations on consumer finance contracts, the Treasury Department recommended in its 2009 financial reform

[25] Consumer Finance Protection Bureau, *Arbitration Study Preliminary Results: Section 1028(a) Study Results to Date* (2013), http://files.consumerfinance.gov/f/201312_cfpb_arbitration-study-preliminary-results.pdf. Industry pushback has been understandably fierce, given the stakes. Many financial institutions and law firms have vociferously criticised the CFPB's report. See, e.g. Christine A. Scheuneman, Joseph T. Lynyak III, and Amy L. Pierce, *CFPB's Arbitration Study – A Warning to Consumer Financial Service Companies*, Pillsbury (8 January 2014), www.pillsburylaw.com/publications/cfpbs-arbitration-study-a-warning-to-consumer-financial-service-companies ('In point of fact, however, while the tone of the Study appears to be somewhat hostile to the use of arbitration clauses, an objective reading of the research indicates that the conflict resolution system that has developed is working well'.); Michael Mallow and Christine Reilly, *The CFPB's Unfair and Misleading Report on Arbitration*, Law 360 (24 January 2014), www.law360.com/articles/502651/the-cfpb-s-unfair-and-misleading-report-on-arbitration.

[26] Consumer Financial Protection Bureau, *Arbitration Study: Report to Congress, pursuant to Dodd-Frank Wall Street Reform and Consumer Protection Act § 1028(a)* (2015), http://files.consumerfinance.gov/f/201503_cfpb_arbitration-study-report-to-congress-2015.pdf [hereinafter *CFPB Arbitration Study*].

[27] Ibid., at 19–28. [28] Ibid., at 10. [29] Ibid., at 19. [30] Ibid., at 25–26.

[31] Ibid., at 9–10. [32] Ibid., at 11. [33] Ibid., at 27.

proposal that the SEC prohibit or condition mandatory arbitration clauses in broker-dealer and investment adviser agreements.[34] As mentioned above, Dodd-Frank contains the authorization for such a prohibition or condition.[35]

The Financial Industry Regulatory Authority (FINRA), a self-regulatory body governing broker-dealers, is responsible for administering arbitration between broker-dealers and their clients.[36] The vast bulk of disputes between broker-dealers and their clients involves arbitration, and as with consumer arbitration clauses, the Supreme Court has repeatedly upheld mandatory pre-dispute arbitration clauses in investor-broker contracts.[37] Filed claims can end with an arbitrator award or with a settlement achieved through direct negotiation or mediation. Between 21 and 23 per cent of cases were decided by arbitrators from 2011 to 2015.[38] During that same time period, 51–55 per cent of cases were settled via negotiation, and 7–10 per cent via mediation.[39] Also during that period, the percentage of cases where the customer was awarded damages decreased from 47 per cent to 41 per cent.[40]

There has long been some concern about the process by which FINRA selects its arbitrators. For claims of $50,000 or less, FINRA appoints one arbitrator.[41] For claims for more than $50,000 but less than $100,000, the parties will select an arbitrator and FINRA will appoint that person, unless the parties agree in writing to three arbitrators.[42] For claims of more than $100,000, the parties will select and FINRA will appoint three arbitrators. In the latter two situations, FINRA generates a random list of arbitrators from its rosters and sends that list to the parties.[43] Each party

[34] Department of Treasury, *Financial Regulatory Reform, A New Foundation: Rebuilding Financial Supervision and Regulation*, 72 (2009), www.treasury.gov/initiatives/Documents/FinalReport_web.pdf.

[35] Dodd-Frank Act §§ 921, 1028.

[36] FINRA, *Arbitration Process*, www.finra.org/ArbitrationAndMediation/Arbitration/Process/.

[37] See *Shearson/American Express* v. *McMahon*, 482 U.S. 220, 238, 242 (1987) (holding that the claims under § 10(b) of the Securities Exchange Act of 1934 and under RICO were arbitrable per the Federal Arbitration Act); *Rodriguez de Quijas* v. *Shearson/American Express*, 490 U.S. 477, 480 (1989) (holding that the claims under § 14 of the Securities Act of 1933 were arbitrable).

[38] FINRA, *Dispute Resolution Statistics*, www.finra.org/ArbitrationAndMediation/FINRADisputeResolution/AdditionalResources/Statistics/.

[39] Ibid. [40] Ibid.

[41] FINRA, *Arbitrator Selection*, www.finra.org/ArbitrationAndMediation/Arbitration/Process/ArbitratorSelection/index.htm.

[42] Ibid. [43] Ibid.

strikes from the list arbitrators they do not want, and ranks the remaining choices. FINRA then combines the parties' rankings and appoints the highest-ranked available arbitrator from each list to serve on the panel. Critics charge that the arbitrators on FINRA's rosters are biased or otherwise unqualified. Generally speaking, the pool of arbitrators has close ties to the financial industry,[44] lacks diversity,[45] and is infrequently updated.[46]

In response to critics and industry concern about the potential for SEC regulation, in June 2014, FINRA filed a proposed rule change with the SEC to redefine 'public arbitrators'.[47] Parties can choose whether they want public arbitrators on their panel or not. Currently, FINRA allows people who have been out of the securities industry for at least two years to be classified as public arbitrators as long as they have spent fewer than twenty years total in the industry.[48] The proposed rule would require public arbitrators to be at least five years out of industry and would permanently disqualify professionals who worked longer than fifteen years total on behalf of industry clients.[49] It also classifies attorneys, accountants, and other professionals who devote more than 20 per cent

[44] See Matthias Rieker, 'FINRA to Limit Use of Arbitrators with Industry Ties', *The Wall Street Journal* (11 February 2014), www.wsj.com/articles/SB10001424052702304104504579377300739589882; Mason Braswell, 'FINRA Approves Rule to Redefine Public Arbitrators', *Investment News* (13 February 2014), www.investmentnews.com/article/20140213/FREE/140219936/finra-approves-rule-to-redefine-public-arbitrators; see also Peter Robison, 'FINRA's Arbitrators: Dubious, Asleep – Sometimes Dead', *Bloomberg Businessweek* (24 April 2014), www.businessweek.com/articles/2014–04-24/finra-seeks-reform-for-broker-investor-arbitration-system ('Lawyers complain about . . . arbitrators who are reluctant to make big rulings against the industry because they won't be asked back').

[45] Mark Schoeff Jr., 'PIABA Claims Arbitrator Bias – FINRA Lashes Back', *Investment News* (7 October 2014), www.investmentnews.com/article/20141007/FREE/141009934/piaba-claims-arbitrator-bias-finra-lashes-back (noting that most FINRA arbitrators are white males over sixty who hold advanced degrees, which 'puts them out of touch with the average investor').

[46] See Robison, 'FINRA's Arbitrators' (observing that FINRA has provided the names of dead people as potential arbitrators).

[47] Mason Braswell, 'FINRA Approves Rule to Redefine Public Arbitrators', *Investment News* (13 February 2014), www.investmentnews.com/article/20140213/FREE/140219936/finra-approves-rule-to-redefine-public-arbitrators; George H. Friedman, 'The Camel and the Last Straw or the Frog and the Boiling Water: Pick Your Parable', *Securities Arbitration Commentator* (4 August 2014), www.sacarbitration.com/blog/camel-last-straw-frog-boiling-water-pick-parable/.

[48] Mark Schoeff Jr., 'FINRA Seeks to Tighten Investor Dispute Rules', *Investment News* (18 June 2014), www.investmentnews.com/article/20140618/FREE/140619905/finra-seeks-to-tighten-investor-dispute-rules.

[49] Ibid.

of their professional time to representing investors in securities claims as non-public. In February 2015, the SEC approved the new rule.[50] FINRA and the SEC have garnered praise for this move,[51] but its actual impact is not yet clear.

Recently, FINRA rejected a Schwab broker-dealer contract on the grounds that it contained a bar on class-action litigation.[52] FINRA reasoned that its rules have long barred such clauses, and that FINRA Rule 2268(d), promulgated under the Securities Exchange Act, is not prohibited by the Federal Arbitration Act.[53] Some have speculated that FINRA rejected the contract in order to avoid provoking the SEC into using its Dodd-Frank authority to bar mandatory arbitration provisions altogether.[54]

2.3.3 Investment Advisers Agreements: No Mandatory Pre-Dispute Arbitration

Investment advisers owe a fiduciary duty to their clients.[55] Accordingly, the SEC has long taken the position, even prior to Dodd-Frank, that mandatory pre-dispute arbitration clauses do not constitute a waiver of rights provided under the Investment Advisers Act of 1940 (including the right to choose the forum, whether arbitration or adjudication, of dispute resolution), and that investment contracts should disclose this

[50] SEC, 'Order Approving Proposed Rule Change Relating to Revisions to the Definitions of Non-Public Arbitrator and Public Arbitrator', 80 Fed. Reg. 11695 (4 March 2015).

[51] Mark Schoeff Jr., 'FINRA Proposal on Public Arbitration Wins Praise', *Investment News* (3 October 2010), www.investmentnews.com/article/20101003/REG/310039991/finra-proposal-on-public-arbitration-wins-praise.

[52] Decision, *Dep't of Enforcement* v. *Charles Schwab & Co.* (Complaint 2011029760201) (FINRA Board of Governors 24 April 2014). FINRA does not permit class action arbitration, but requires broker-dealer contracts to permit class action lawsuits.

[53] Ibid.

[54] Ibid. See Letter from Sen. Franken to the SEC, Office of Senator Franken (30 April 2013), available at www.franken.senate.gov/?p=press_release&id=2381; Mark Schoeff Jr, 'States Urge SEC to Chuck FINRA's Schwab Decision', *Investment News* (4 May 2013), available at www.investmentnews.com/article/20130504/FREE/130509954/states-urge-sec-to-chuck-finras-schwab-decision; Mark Schoeff Jr. and Mason Braswell, 'Seeing Writing on Wall from FINRA, Schwab Throws in Towel on Class Action Lawsuit', *Investment News* (25 April 2014), www.investmentnews.com/article/20140425/FREE/140429929/seeing-writing-on-wall-from-finra-schwab-throws-in-towel-on-class; Susan Antilla, 'Schwab Case Casts Spotlight on Securities Arbitration and Its Flaws', *The New York Times* (4 September 2013), http://dealbook.nytimes.com/2013/09/04/schwab-case-casts-spotlight-on-securities-arbitration-and-its-flaws/?_r=0.

[55] *SEC* v. *Capital Gains Research Bureau, Inc.*, 375 U.S. 180, 191–92 (1963) (holding that § 206 of the Investment Advisors Act of 1940 imposed a fiduciary duty on investment advisers).

fact.[56] However, the SEC took these positions before several Supreme Court decisions upheld arbitration clauses under the federal securities laws, and a subsequent federal district court citing those opinions upheld pre-dispute arbitration clauses in an advisory client agreement.[57]

The SEC now has the clear power under Dodd-Frank to prohibit or restrict mandatory pre-dispute arbitration clauses in these agreements going forward.[58] At present, investment advisers who deploy mandatory arbitration clauses may operate in what some see as 'gray area', where they use arbitration clauses at their own risk.[59] Recently, however, the SEC is reported to have pressured the Carlyle Group to remove a mandatory arbitration clause from its initial public offer filing,[60] suggesting that the SEC's prior views that the fiduciary duty standard already bars use of these agreements have not changed. Moreover, the SEC is authorised under Dodd-Frank to harmonise the differing standards of care for investment advisers and for broker-dealers offering individualised investment advice by requiring that the advice be in the best interest of the investor.[61] Under that approach, both broker-dealers (when providing individualised advice) and investment advisers would be prohibited from using mandatory pre-dispute arbitration clauses.

3 Problems with Arbitration Clauses in Investor and Consumer Finance Contracts

Proponents of arbitration often note the benefits to arbitration over litigating, stressing the faster process, reduced costs, and ability to choose expert adjudicators.[62] For consumers and investors, however,

[56] SEC, *Staff Study on Investment Advisers and Broker-Dealers* 44 (2011), www.sec.gov/news/studies/2011/913studyfinal.pdf.

[57] Ibid. [58] Dodd-Frank Act § 921.

[59] Suzanne Barlyn, 'Do Arbitration Pacts Go Against Clients' Best Interests?', *Chicago Tribune* (13 February 2013), http://articles.chicagotribune.com/2013–02-13/news/sns-rt-us-arbitration-advisersbre91c1fj-20130213_1_mandatory-arbitration-arbitration-agreements-federal-arbitration-law.

[60] Carter Dougherty, 'Consumers May See New Limits on Mandatory Arbitration', *Bloomberg Businessweek* (21 May 2012), www.bloomberg.com/news/articles/2012–05-21/consumers-may-see-new-limits-on-mandatory-arbitration.

[61] SEC, 'Order Approving Proposed Rule Change Relating to Revisions to the Definitions of Non-Public Arbitrator and Public Arbitrator', § vi.

[62] E.g. *Stolt-Nielsen S.A.* v. *AnimalFeeds Int'l Corp.*, 130 S. Ct. 1758, 1775 (2010) (citing *Gilmer* v. *Interstate Johnson Lane Corp.*, 500 U.S. 20 (1991); *Mitusbishi Motors Corp.* v. *Soler Chrysler-Plymouth, Inc.*, 473 U.S. 614 (1985); *Penn Plaza LLC* v. *Pyett*, 556 U. S. 247 (2009); *Alexander* v. *Gardner-Denver Co.*, 415 U.S. 36 (1974)).

the many problems with mandatory pre-dispute arbitration clauses often significantly outweigh these benefits. Consumers and investors are not making any meaningful choice in agreeing to arbitration clauses. They face a significant imbalance of power in bargaining, if any such bargaining actually occurs. If a dispute does arise, consumers and investors often proceed without the advice of counsel and are faced with a process that is often inadequate and unfair.[63] Furthermore, arbitration clauses often limit consumers' and investors' access to collective redress, which meaningfully impedes both recovery and deterrence.

3.1 Lack of Meaningful Consumer Consent

Even in the best of circumstances, it is hard to believe that consumers give anything like meaningful consent to arbitration clauses.[64] At the moment of signing a financial contract, consumers are not focused on dispute resolution; they are focused on the financial product or service, or more likely on the underlying thing they are trying to get done by obtaining the financial product (for example, buying a car). Even if they were focused on dispute resolution, they are unlikely to be able to forecast the circumstances under which they would find themselves in a dispute or to understand the ways in which the choice of dispute resolution might influence the outcome. These problems are compounded by the complexity of arbitration clauses, the lack of clear disclosure of the provisions (or the clear disclosure alongside many other 'clear' disclosures that seem more pertinent), and the limited ability of consumers to opt out of arbitration clauses. Given that consumers pay little or no attention to arbitration clauses at the time of contracting, competition does not drive firms to offer contracts without arbitration clauses or with more consumer-friendly arbitration clauses, and importantly, it is unlikely that these provisions have a significant effect on the price of consumer financial goods and services.[65]

[63] See Section 3.3.

[64] See, e.g. Margaret Jane Radin, *Boilerplate* 12 (Princeton University Press, 2013) (noting that consumers often do not even read boilerplate contracts and hypothesizing seven reasons for that, including a belief that they would not even understand the terms even if they read them; a lack of awareness of being subject to those terms; and a belief that it would be unenforceable if it were harmful).

[65] See Russell Korobkin, 'Bounded Rationality, Standard Form Contracts, and Unconscionability', 70 U. Chi. L. Rev. 1203 (2003), 1253 n. 189.

3.1.1 Complexity of Arbitration Clauses

The CFPB analysed the complexity of arbitration clauses in credit card contracts by measuring clause length, readability, and grade level.[66] It found that the average arbitration clause comprised 14.1 per cent of the words in the contract and consisted of 1,108.8 words.[67] The average grade level (which translates total words, total sentences, and total syllables into the level of education required to understand the text) for the arbitration clauses averaged 15.6.[68] This score indicates that the text is best understood by those with some college education. In contrast, the average grade level for the remainder of the contract was 11.6, which roughly corresponds to a high school–level education.[69] The meaning of delegation or anti-severability clauses, for example, likely escapes most readers. The length and complexity of arbitration clauses makes consumers less likely to understand (or even to read) them.

3.1.2 Limited Consumer Ability to Opt Out

Some arbitration clauses give consumers the ability to opt out of or reject the arbitration clause within a defined time period, but they appear only in a small share of agreements,[70] and their exercise is typically subject to restriction. To exercise an opt-out, a consumer generally must submit a signed writing by mail within thirty or sixty days.[71] If there are multiple authorised users on the account, they may each need to submit written consent for the opt-out to be effective.[72] Most consumers are unlikely to exercise the opt-out options because of hassle factors and an incomplete understanding of the consequences of their decisions.

3.1.3 Behavioural Factors

Even if consumer contracts better disclosed mandatory pre-dispute arbitration provisions and permitted consumers to opt out, the problem of meaningful consumer consent would remain. The use of arbitration clauses should be not measured against some abstract notion regarding

66 Consumer Finance Protection Bureau, *Arbitration Study Preliminary Results*, app. A at 27–29.

67 Ibid., at 28 (To put that in perspective, that is two pages of single-spaced text in 12-point Times New Roman font.)

68 Ibid. 69 Ibid.

70 Ibid., at 31. (Opt-out features appear in 27.3 per cent of credit card agreements, 26.2 per cent of checking account agreements, and 17.6 per cent of prepaid card agreements.)

71 Ibid. 72 Ibid.

rational agents who fully understand the implications of disclosed arbitration provisions, but rather considered alongside empirical evidence regarding how real human beings actually process information and make decisions.[73] The empirical evidence is clear that consumers do not read or understand standard contract terms.[74] It is highly unlikely that consumers find the relevant arbitration terms salient at the time of entering into the contract. Consumers routinely underestimate the likelihood of financial firms violating the law in a way that would affect them.[75] Moreover, they are highly unlikely to understand the consequences of different choices of forum or law.

3.2 Imbalance of Power

A significant proportion of consumers go through the arbitration process without legal representation, whereas companies never do. From 2010 to 2012, 53 per cent of consumers had counsel in AAA arbitrations reviewed by the CFPB.[76] This percentage drops to 42 per cent in debt collection proceedings.[77] In contrast, companies 'almost always' retained outside or in-house counsel in both debt collection and non-collection arbitrations.[78] With lawyers representing companies, the purported benefits of an informal, low-cost proceeding are largely dissipated.

[73] Michael S. Barr, Sendhil Mullainathan, and Eldar Shafir, 'Behaviorally Informed Financial Services Regulation', *Asset Building Program Policy Paper* (New America Foundation 2008); Michael S. Barr, Sendhil Mullainathan, and Eldar Shafir, 'Behaviorally Informed Home Mortgage Credit Regulation', in Nicholas P. Retsinas and Eric S. Belsky (eds.), *Borrowing to Live: Consumer and Mortgage Credit Revisited*, (Brookings Institution Press & Harvard University Joint Center for Housing Studies, 2008), 170; Michael S. Barr, Sendhil Mullainathan, and Eldar Shafir, 'The Case for Behaviorally Informed Regulation', in Moss and Cisternino (eds.), *New Perspectives on Regulation*, (2009), 25; Michael S. Barr, Sendhil Mullainathan, and Eldar Shafir, 'Behaviorally Informed Regulation', in Edlar Shafir (ed.), *Behavioral Foundations of Public Policy* (2012), 440.

[74] Yannis Bakos et al., 'Does Anybody Read the Fine Print? Consumer Attention to Standard Form Contracts', 43 J. Legal Stud. 1 (2014), 2–3; Florencia Marotta-Wurgler, 'Does Contract Disclosure Matter?', 168 J. Institutional & Theoretical Econ. 94 (2012), 100–106.

[75] See Michael S. Barr, Sendhil Mullainathan, and Eldar Shafir, 'Behaviorally Informed Regulation', *No Slack: The Financial Lives of Low-Income Americans* (2012), 246, 257–261, 267–271, 274–276; Daylian M. Cain, George Lowenstein, and Don A. Moore, 'The Dirt on Coming Clean: Perverse Effects of Disclosing Conflicts of Interest'. 34 *Journal of Legal Studies* 1–25 (2005).

[76] Consumer Finance Protection Bureau, *Arbitration Study Preliminary Results*, § 5, at 28

[77] Ibid., app. A, at 74. [78] Ibid., app. A, at 14.

Additionally, most arbitration clauses contain carve-outs for small claims court.[79] Small claims carve-outs exclude from arbitration claims that could be or had been brought in small claims court. These carve-outs are neutral in theory and have the potential to benefit consumers significantly. However, small claims court carve-outs are 'significantly more likely' to be used by credit card issuers to sue consumers rather than the other way around.[80]

3.3 *Procedural Barriers to Full and Fair Adjudication*

In addition to the problem of whether or not consumers can be considered to have actually consented to arbitration, there are procedural barriers within arbitration itself, as it is often currently conducted, that may lead to substantively unfair outcomes.

3.3.1 Lack of Transparency

Arbitrators are not required to issue written opinions explaining their decisions.[81] This lack of transparency creates several problems for consumers. First, it prevents parties from understanding how the arbitrator arrived at his decision.[82] The absence of a written record also makes it harder for the consumer to prove whether the arbitrator has displayed a manifest disregard of law when seeking judicial review. Furthermore, this opacity precludes the application of *stare decisis*, which in any event does not generally apply to arbitration. Since arbitrators have no body of precedent to consult, arbitration awards may suffer from unpredictability and lack of uniformity.

While arbitrators are of course free to issue written decisions, institutional factors often weigh against them doing so. Financial institutions retain control over drafting arbitration clauses, and contracts for consumer financial products and services will rarely require arbitrators to issue reasoned opinions. Moreover, the American Arbitration Association

79 Ibid., app. A, at 32 (finding that the incidence of small claims court carve-outs was 59 per cent, 62.7 per cent, and 66.7 per cent in contracts for checking accounts, prepaid cards, and credit cards, respectively).

80 Ibid., app. A, at 15.

81 *O.R. Sec., Inc.* v. *Prof'l Planning Assocs.*, 857 F.2d 742, 747 (11th Cir. 1988) (citing *Wilko* v. *Swan*, 346 U.S. 427 (1953), overruled on other grounds by *Rodriguez de Quijas* v. *Shearson/Am. Express, Inc.*, 490 U.S. 477 (1989)).

82 See Lynn Katzler, Comment, 'Should Mandatory Written Opinions Be Required in All Securities Arbitrations? The Practical and Legal Implications to the Securities Industry', 45 AM. U. L. REV. 151 (1995), 193–194.

(AAA) Commercial Rules and the Uniform Arbitration Act contain a presumption that a reasoned opinion shall not be issued unless the parties so require.[83]

Moreover, arbitration clauses often contain various forms of confidentiality or 'gag' rules that prevent consumers from disclosing arbitration outcomes, or from revealing evidence used in the arbitration process, or from otherwise disparaging companies with whom they are in dispute. As a result, arbitration may result in hiding information from the public even when widespread and serious legal violations that gave rise to the arbitration proceeding may have occurred.

3.3.2 Selection of Arbitrators

The ability of the parties to choose their own arbitrator is touted as an advantage because parties can theoretically choose a mutually acceptable, impartial person or panel possessing relevant expertise. Commonly, the arbitration clause stipulates an arbitration organization such as the AAA, which is currently the predominant administrator for consumer arbitration about credit cards, checking accounts, and GPR prepaid cards.[84] The arbitration organization then determines the pool of prospective arbitrators, if not the actual arbitrator(s).[85] Professional arbitrators can be preferable to judges due to their subject-area expertise, and they are generally bound by codes of conduct, as are AAA arbitrators, to ensure neutrality. However, arbitrators may be biased if they are affiliated with the industry that is the subject of the dispute. Even when arbitrators are truly neutral, the perception of unfairness may lead consumers to lose faith in the process.

There have been notorious examples of highly biased arbitration organizations, such as the National Arbitration Forum, that were essentially working on behalf of debt collection agencies and offering 'neutral' arbitration services that were in the interests of the debt collection firms.[86] NAF has since been forced to terminate its consumer arbitration services. The current market leader in consumer arbitrations, AAA, has

[83] Abraham J. Gafni, 'Written Opinions in Arbitration Aren't a Given', *Legal Intelligencer*, (22 September 2008), www.adroptions.com/pdfs/08SEPT-WrittenOpinions_in_Arbitration Arent_a_Given.pdf.

[84] Consumer Finance Protection Bureau, *Arbitration Study Preliminary Results*, § 2, at 34–35.

[85] Ibid. § 2, at 40.

[86] See, e.g. *State* v. *Nat'l Arbitration Forum, Inc.*, No. 27-CV-09–18550, 2009 Minn. Dist. LEXIS 340 (Minn. Dist. Ct., 17 July 2009).

voluntarily agreed not to hear firm-initiated debt collection cases on the grounds that its own inquiry into such arbitrations gave it serious doubt about the fairness of the process.[87]

A recent study of securities arbitration found that the arbitrator's background had a significant impact on arbitration outcomes.[88] For example, industry experience tends to decrease arbitral awards for claimants. The influence of arbitrator background on outcomes is tempered, however, when claimants are represented by counsel in the arbitral proceedings.[89]

3.3.3 Limits on Damages

Arbitration clauses can limit consumers' ability to recover damages in a number of ways. Oftentimes, arbitration clauses preclude the award of punitive damages or consequential damages, or both.[90] Alternatively, they may specify strict guidelines for the arbitrator to follow in calculating the award.[91] Some type of limitation on damages appears in 15 per cent of credit card contracts with arbitration clauses and over 60 per cent of both checking account and prepaid card contracts with arbitration clauses.[92]

3.4 Collective Redress and the Interplay between Public and Private Enforcement

3.4.1 The Role of Mandatory Pre-Dispute Arbitration Clauses in Thwarting Efforts for Collective Redress

Arbitration clauses increasingly bar access to collective redress.[93] Class proceedings are essential for effective redress of many small value legal

[87] Consumer Finance Protection Bureau, *Arbitration Study Preliminary Results*, app. A, at 65–66. See also *Arbitration or Arbitrary: The Misuse of Mandatory Arbitration to Collect Consumer Debts: Hearing Before the Subcomm. on Domestic Policy of the H. Comm. on Oversight & Gov't Reform*, 111th Cong. (2009) (statement of Richard W. Naimark, Senior Vice President, American Arbitration Association).

[88] See Stephen J. Choi, Jill. E. Fisch and Adam C. Pritchard, 'The Influence of Arbitrator Background and Representation on Arbitration Outcomes', 9 VA. L. & BUS. REV. 43 (2014).

[89] Ibid.

[90] Consumer Finance Protection Bureau, *Arbitration Study Preliminary Results*, § 2, at 47.

[91] Ibid. [92] Ibid., § 2, at 47–49.

[93] Ibid., § 1, at 10 ('Nearly all the arbitration clauses studied include provisions stating that arbitration may not proceed on a class basis . . . Although these terms effectively preclude all class proceedings, in court or in arbitration, some arbitration clauses also expressly waive the consumer's ability to participate in class actions in court').

claims.[94] Class action arbitration, like class action litigation, solves the problem that occurs when a company's practice defrauds many people, but individual lawsuits would be impracticable because each consumer could only hope to recover a relatively minor amount. Though the amount is negligible for each individual, the error adds up to a significant windfall for the company, and the lack of collective redress diminishes the deterrent value of private litigation in shaping corporate behaviour.

For those reasons, the California Supreme Court struck down waivers of class arbitration in adhesive contracts as unconscionable, in the *Discover Bank* rule.[95] The US Supreme Court, however, held in *AT&T Mobility v. Concepcion* that the FAA pre-empted the *Discover Bank* rule, with the result that class arbitration waivers are not permitted to be ruled unconscionable under state law, at least not under similar facts and circumstances.[96] The Court reasoned that class-wide arbitration sacrifices 'the principal advantage of arbitration – its informality – and makes the process slower, more costly, and more likely to generate procedural morass than final judgment'.[97] *Concepcion* has been widely decried for its negative impact on public access to justice.[98]

3.4.2 Reduced Private Enforcement

Class proceedings are critical components of the mix of public and private enforcement of many legal norms. Many consumer financial protection statutes contemplate that class proceedings will be conducted to enforce those norms.[99] '[W]e have come to assume, quite correctly, that private actors will be the frontline enforcers in actions redressing broadscale securities fraud, consumer fraud and deceptive trade

[94] See, e.g. *Mace* v. *Van Ru Credit Corp.*, 109 F.3d 388, 344 (7th Cir. 1997) (noting the importance of aggregating claims in transforming 'relatively paltry recoveries into something worth someone's (usually an attorney's) labour' to bring).

[95] See *Discover Bank* v. *Superior Court*, 36 Cal. 4th 148, 156–158, 160 (2005).

[96] *AT&T Mobile LLC* v. *Concepcion*, 131 S. Ct. 1740, 1753 (2011).

[97] Ibid., at 1751.

[98] See, e.g. Frank Blechschmidt, Comment, 'All Alone in Arbitration: *AT&T Mobility* v. *Concepcion* and the Substantive Impact of Class Action Waivers', 160 U. Pa. L. Rev. 541 (2012), 567–570; Jean R. Sternlight, 'Tsunami: *AT&T Mobility LLC* v. *Concepcion* Impedes Access to Justice', 90 Or. L. Rev. 703 (2012), 720–725; Ann Marie Tracey and Shelley McGill, 'Seeking a Rational Lawyer for Consumer Claims after the Supreme Court Disconnects Consumers in *AT&T Mobility LLC* v. *Concepcion*', 45 Loy. L.A. L. Rev. 435 (2012), 466–469.

[99] See, e.g. Truth in Lending Act § 130, 15 U.S.C. § 1640 (2012); Equal Credit Opportunity Act § 706, 15 U.S.C. § 1691e (2012); Fair Debt Collection Practices Act § 813, 15 U.S.C. § 1692k (2012); Electronic Funds Transfer Act § 916, 15 U.S.C. § 1693m (2012); Credit Repair Organizations Act § 409, 15 USC § 1679g (2012).

practices, ... and many other areas'.[100] Penalty levels set by statute necessarily contemplate a given mix of public and private enforcement. Thus, if consumer class relief were not available, penalty levels (and the extent of public enforcement) would need to be increased to achieve the same overall level of enforcement.[101]

The traditional use of private litigation to enforce individual rights in the United States has become increasingly supplemented with public enforcement. Recently, the United States 'increasingly relies on states attorneys general, federal prosecutors, agencies, and legislative compensation to compensate victims on a massive scale' as reformers have moved for a focus on victims' rights.[102] Although it is true that there has been an emerging trend in America towards increased public enforcement, private litigation is still an essential enforcement mechanism.[103] It is, moreover, an important check on lax public enforcement.[104] Notably, even many European countries, long considered to be focused on civil enforcement over private litigation, have adopted increasingly expansive collective redress procedures. In fact, there has been a 'convergence' in how the United States and the European countries have attended to collective redress.[105] This demonstrates that the ideal mix of public and private enforcement is fluid and can change over time. However, Congress has legislated against a backdrop of enforcement policies and has established many privately actionable statutory schemes that depend on individuals bringing suit, individually and collectively, for enforcement.[106]

[100] Myriam Gilles and Gary Friedman, 'After Class: Aggregate Litigation in the Wake of *AT&T Mobility* v. *Concepcion*', 79 U. Chi. L. Rev. 623 (2012), 625–626.

[101] David Noll, Assistant Professor of Law, Rutgers Univ. Sch. of Law – 'Newark, Contract Procedure, Regulatory Breakdown', Remarks at *New York University School of Law Conference: The Future of Class Action Litigation* (7 November 2014) (noting that Congress controls the amount of enforcement by adjusting the incentives to litigate).

[102] Adam S. Zimmerman, 'The Convergence of Global Settlements', *PrawfsBlawg* (1 February 2012), http://prawfsblawg.blogs.com/prawfsblawg/2012/02/the-convergence-of-global-settlements.html.

[103] See Gilles and Friedman, 'After Class', 624–626.

[104] Luigi Zingales, *A Capitalism for the People: Recapturing the Lost Genius of American Prosperity*, (Basic Books, 2012).

[105] Zimmerman, 'The Convergence of Global Settlements' (noting that '[t]he 'bottom up' approach of the United States to aggregate litigation appears to be converging with other countries' 'top-down approach').

[106] See, e.g. Blechschmidt, 'All Alone in Arbitration', 567–570; Gilles and Friedman, 'After Class', 624–625; Sternlight, 'Tsunami', 720–725; Tracey and McGill, 'Seeking a Rational Lawyer for Consumer Claims', 466–469.

4 Arbitration Agreements in Other Contexts

The use of arbitration agreements in other contexts informs the use of mandatory pre-dispute arbitration clauses in consumer contracts. Arbitration agreements in the labour context are individually negotiated between sophisticated parties and are highly touted as beneficial for both sides. Arbitration agreements are also used by commercial actors, but, surprisingly, much less used for commercial disputes by the very same firms that impose mandatory pre-dispute arbitration agreements on consumers.

4.1 Labour Agreements

Collective bargaining agreements often feature mandatory arbitration provisions. Both labour unions and management are sophisticated parties who individually negotiate for these provisions. Both parties believe that dispute resolution through arbitration causes less friction than litigation.[107] Additionally, both parties have more trust in arbitrators that the parties have selected themselves and tend to have more expertise in labour relations than judges with only general knowledge.[108] Labour unions and management also have similar goals in maintaining a strong and competitive business, and so both stress 'a conflict resolution process that would keep businesses running and avoid losses in productivity and employment'.[109]

Unlike consumer and investor contracts, collective bargaining agreements are individually negotiated between sophisticated parties with equal bargaining power.[110] As such, the specific details that are commonly found in these labour agreements can inform what should be enforced in the consumer context. One of the reasons that labour unions

[107] Linda J. Demaine and Deborah R. Hensler, '"Volunteering" to Arbitrate through Pre-Dispute Arbitration Clauses: The Average Consumer's Experience', 67 Law & Contemp. Probs. 55 (2004), 55.

[108] See, e.g. Julius H. Cohen, 'The Law of Commercial Arbitration and the New York Statute', 31 Yale L.J. 147 (1921), 150 ('Presumably men of commercial experience today need no guardianship for determining, at the time of making a contract, whether they prefer the opinion of their own trade upon technical questions, or the hazardous judgment of a jury of their vicinage').

[109] Ibid. See also Allison Anderson, 'Labor and Commercial Arbitration: The Court's Misguided Merger', 54 B.C. L. Rev. 1237 (2013), 1246 (comparing the purpose of labor arbitration which is to 'stabilize the workplace by preventing work stoppages' and the purpose of other arbitration which is as a replacement for litigation).

[110] See, e.g., Demaine and Hensler, '"Volunteering" to Arbitrate', 55–56.

and management negotiate for arbitration in collective bargaining agreements in the first place is the ability to choose the arbitrator.[111] One key safeguard for unionised workers is that 'unions and management repeatedly arbitrate and jointly select the arbitrator'.[112] Joint selection helps to ensure a neutral arbitrator,[113] and repeated arbitration incentivises the arbitrator 'to perform consistently without favouring one party over the other'.[114] Instead, labour unions and management use the outcomes to renegotiate the terms of their agreements if they want future outcomes to differ from the arbitrator's decision.[115] Additional safeguards include: a duty on both parties to share information[116] and a duty on the union to fairly represent its workers.[117] The National Labor Relations Act requires employers to share information throughout the entire arbitration process. In labour arbitrations, arbitrators often write opinions, which allows for future arbitrators and future parties to explore patterns in prior adjudications.[118]

4.2 *Commercial Actors*

Notably, the same commercial actors that inflict mandatory pre-dispute arbitration agreements on their consumers do not choose to bargain for these agreements in other contracts. One study found that with large public corporations, over 75 per cent of the studied consumer agreements imposed mandatory arbitration of disputes, yet *less than 10 per cent* of their 'negotiated nonconsumer, non-employment contracts' included arbitration clauses.[119] The authors concluded that '[t]he absence of arbitration provisions in the great majority of negotiated business contracts suggests that companies value, even prefer, litigation as the means for resolving disputes with peers'.[120] They further noted that

[111] Ibid., at 55. [112] Anderson, 'Labor and Commercial Arbitration', 1255–1256.
[113] Julius G. Getman, 'Labor Arbitration and Dispute Resolution', Paper 4403, *Faculty Scholarship Series*, 916 (1979), 929–930. Compare this with the consumer and investor context, in which the firm may be a repeat player in arbitration whereas the consumer may only arbitrate the one time.
[114] Anderson, 'Labor and Commercial Arbitration,' 1256. This author also notes that the joint bargain for the particular arbitrator may justify limited judicial review of the final award.
[115] Ibid. [116] Ibid. [117] Ibid. [118] Getman, 'Labor Arbitration', 920–921.
[119] Theodore Eisenberg, Geoffrey P. Miller, and Emily Sherwin, 'Arbitration's Summer Soldiers: An Empirical Study of Arbitration Clauses in Consumer and Nonconsumer Contracts', 41 U. Mich. J.L. Reform 871 (2008), 876.
[120] Ibid.

'[t]he systematic eschewing of arbitration clauses in business-to-business contracts also casts doubts on the corporations' asserted beliefs in the superior fairness and efficiency of arbitration clauses'.[121] It appears, therefore, that at least some commercial actors may be using arbitration clauses against consumers for the strategic advantages it provides. Those strategic advantages are diminished, however, when dealing with other sophisticated parties. This is shown in the revealed preferences of large companies, which choose arbitration with consumers but prefer litigation for business-to-business disputes.

5 Conclusion

Although arbitration can provide some benefits over litigation in a variety of commercial contexts, consumers are often subject to mandatory pre-dispute arbitration clauses that diminish their legal protections, reduce recoveries, and attenuate deterrence. It can hardly be said that consumers meaningfully consent to such arrangements, and so it has often been left to courts to police these provisions through doctrines such as unconscionability. Over the years, the Supreme Court has significantly cabined the ability of courts to exercise this critical oversight role. In 2010, however, Congress stepped in through the passage of Dodd-Frank to provide the authority for the CFPB and SEC to prohibit or condition the use of arbitration agreements in consumer finance and investor contracts, respectively.

The CFPB and SEC should use this authority to prohibit or condition contractual requirements on consumers and investors to arbitrate. At a minimum, significant conditions on arbitration agreements are needed. These include both up-front protections, including prominent disclosures and easy methods to opt out of arbitration at any time, as well as protections embedded in arbitration processes that are used in consumer finance and investor contract disputes, to ensure that they provide a fair and efficient method for resolving claims. In addition, the agencies should bar provisions in consumer finance and investor contracts that limit the ability to seek collective relief or otherwise inhibit full redress of consumer and investor claims. In fact, the CFPB has signalled its intent to propose rules that would move in just that direction.[122] While this

[121] Ibid.

[122] Consumer Financial Protection Bureau, Small Business Advisory Review Panel for Potential Rulemaking on Arbitration Agreements, Outline of Proposals Under

chapter does not provide the space necessary to work out these proposals in detail, continued progress on regulating arbitration clauses is essential for protecting consumers and investors from abuse and for supporting financial markets with integrity.

Consideration and Alternatives Considered, (7 October 2015), www.consumerfinance.gov/newsroom/cfpb-considers-proposal-to-ban-arbitration-clauses-that-allow-companies-to-avoid-accountability-to-their-customers/.

5

The Bonding Effect in Cross-Listed Chinese Companies

Is It Real?

DONALD CLARKE

1 Introduction

Why do Chinese companies[1] list abroad, and more specifically, in the United States? One explanation is that they wish to reduce their cost of capital by increasing investor confidence, and cross-listing in the United States accomplishes that by credibly committing the company to a regime of enhanced disclosure and greater exposure to a shareholder-protective legal regime (the bonding hypothesis).

The cause-and-effect proposition of the bonding hypothesis has been challenged from time to time, notably in a recent paper by Licht et al.[2] This paper takes a different tack. It accepts for the sake of argument that investors believe that cross-listing produces the promised benefits and are accordingly willing to pay more for cross-listed companies.[3] It asks instead whether, in the case of Chinese cross-listings in the United States, that belief is well founded. If not, then it follows that the stock of Chinese

[1] The term 'Chinese [or PRC] company' is used in this study to mean a company headquartered in the People's Republic of China and managed predominantly by Chinese nationals, even though it may be incorporated in another jurisdiction.

[2] Amir N. Licht, Christopher Poliquin, Jordan I. Siegel, and Xi Li, 'What Makes the Bonding Stick? A Natural Experiment Involving the Supreme Court and Cross-Listed Firms', *Harvard Business School Working Paper* 11-072, 27 August 2013, http://ssrn.com/abstract=1744905.

[3] This is not necessarily true. Li Xian Liu, Fuming Jiang, and Milinde Sathye, 'Does Bonding Really Bond? Cross-Listing Location, Corporate Governance and Value of Chinese Firms', 28 January 2015, http://ssrn.com/abstract=2556689, find that firms listed only on Chinese domestic stock exchanges command a higher value than those that are cross-listed on overseas exchanges. On the other hand, Hongbo Shen, Li Liao, and Guanmin Liao, 'Cross-Listing and Bonding Premium: Evidence from Chinese Listed Companies', FRONT. BUS. RES. CHINA 4(2) (2010), 171–184 found that there *was* a cross-listing premium. Resolving the issue is beyond the scope of this chapter.

companies in United States markets is generally overpriced both in the United States and in China (if the company has also listed stock there), and that the semi-strong form of the efficient capital markets hypothesis, which holds that all publicly available information is rapidly incorporated into stock prices, does not hold in this particular case.

2 Analysis

2.1 Cross-Listing Generally

A number of explanations have been offered for cross-listing generally, including a desire to overcome inefficiencies in pricing caused by market segmentation, a desire for increased liquidity, a belief that cross-listing will enhance stock prices through the increased availability of information that results from increased analyst and media coverage, a belief that the cost of capital will be reduced through the increased disclosure that comes from cross-listing in a market that requires such disclosure, and the belief that the cost of capital will be reduced because cross-listing can bind the company to a regime that protects minority shareholder interests better than the home jurisdiction.[4] It is this last theory – the 'bonding hypothesis'[5] – that will be examined in this paper with reference to China.

2.2 The Bonding Hypothesis

2.2.1 Bonding in General[6]

As applied to cross-listings in the United States, the bonding hypothesis has two parts. First, it states that companies commit to a higher level of

[4] See generally Olga Dodd, 'Why Do Firms Cross-List Their Shares on Foreign Exchanges? A Review of Cross-Listing Theories and Empirical Evidence', July 2013, http://ssrn.com/abstract=2271371.

[5] The bonding hypothesis is generally credited to John C. Coffee, Jr., 'The Future as History: The Prospects for Global Convergence in Corporate Governance and Its Implications', 93 *Northwestern University Law Review* (1999), 641–708 and René M. Stulz, 'Globalization, Corporate Finance, and the Cost of Capital', 12 *Journal of Applied Corporate Finance* (1999), 8–25, although Coffee ('The Future as History', 674 n.114) notes that Edward B. Rock, 'Mandatory Disclosure as Credible Commitment: Going Public, Opting In, Opting Out and Globalization', 9 September 1998, abstract available at http://ssrn.com/abstract=145528 (full text no longer available), comes up with the 'same bonding thesis'. Rock's 1998 paper was subsequently published as Edward B. Rock, 'Securities Regulation as Lobster Trap: A Credible Commitment Theory of Mandatory Disclosure', 23 *Cardozo Law Review* (2002), 675–704.

[6] For a particularly helpful review of the literature, see Liu et al., 'Does Bonding Really Bond?' and its bibliography.

disclosure. Second, it states that companies expose themselves to the more investor-protective laws of the United States. Both actions give investors greater confidence and thus lower the cost of capital for cross-listing companies. A typical statement is that of Coffee:

> [C]ross-listing may also be a bonding mechanism by which firms incorporated in jurisdictions with weak protection of minority rights or poor enforcement mechanisms can voluntarily subject themselves to higher disclosure standards and stricter enforcement in order to attract investors who would otherwise be reluctant to invest (or who would discount such stocks to reflect the risk of minority expropriation).[7]

More specifically,

> Listing on a US exchange [commits the listing firm to respect minority investor rights and to provide fuller disclosure] because (1) the listing firm becomes subject to the enforcement powers of the Securities and Exchange Commission (SEC); (2) investors acquire the ability to exercise effective and low-cost legal remedies, such as class actions and derivative actions, that are simply not available in the firm's home jurisdiction; and (3) entry into the US markets commits the firm (at least when it lists on an exchange or Nasdaq) to provide fuller financial information in response to SEC requirements and to reconcile its financial statements with US generally accepted accounting principles (GAAP).[8]

2.2.2 Bonding as Applied to Chinese Firms

A number of scholars have attributed the cross-listing of Chinese firms on United States exchanges to precisely this motivation. Moreover, the consensus in the literature seems to be that bonding is more than simply perceived; it is real:

> Issuers migrate from 'low disclosure' domestic exchanges to 'high disclosure' overseas exchanges and voluntarily subject themselves to higher disclosure and corporate governance standards and greater threat of enforcement. Laws and regulations of a foreign jurisdiction, such as the US, may effectively deter malfeasance by a foreign issuer's insiders. As a result, cross-listing signals to their investors the issuer's strong commitment not to expropriate the minority shareholders' interests. In accordance with this strategy, many Chinese companies choose to list themselves on overseas stock exchanges, including exchanges in Hong Kong, the US, Singapore,

[7] John C. Coffee, Jr., 'Racing Towards the Top? The Impact of Cross-Listings and Stock Market Competition on International Corporate Governance', 102 *Columbia Law Review* (2002), 1757–1831, 1767.

[8] Ibid., at 1780–1781 (internal footnote omitted).

> and the UK. Among those foreign exchanges, exchanges in the US and the UK are considered to have the highest disclosure standards.[9]
>
> [When Chinese firms cross-list], [t]hey become subject to stricter insider trading prohibitions, limitations on tender offers, stricter corporate governance requirements, and private shareholder actions under Rule 10b-5 for fraudulent statements or omissions by the issuers.[10]
>
> When a firm from a less strict institutional environment decides to cross-list on a US-based exchange, the firm subjects itself to much stricter reporting requirements and must play by US rules.[11]

There is some support for the proposition that there is a cross-listing premium for Chinese firms listing in Hong Kong,[12] a premium that might well exist for Chinese firms listing in the United States as well. But we do not know the reason for this premium. It may not be attributable to bonding, and even if it is, it does not answer the question posed by this chapter, which is whether the bonding is real or simply perceived.

2.3 *Is Bonding by Chinese Companies Real?*

There are a number of reasons for doubting that bonding by Chinese companies when they list in the United States is real. By this I mean two things. First, one of the most frequently cited benefits of bonding – more and better disclosure of corporate information – can be undertaken entirely voluntarily by the company and does not require a listing in the United States. Second, the protection offered to minority shareholders by state and federal law in the United States is illusory. The actors that need to be deterred from expropriatory actions are not realistically subject to suit. I explore each of these themes below.

2.3.1 Bonding through Disclosure

The bonding hypothesis states that investors value disclosure and will pay a higher price for companies listed in jurisdictions with high disclosure standards. Yet there is nothing preventing Chinese companies from disclosing all the information required by the SEC in companies listed

[9] Hua Cai, 'Bonding, Law Enforcement, and Corporate Governance in China', 13 *Stanford Journal of Law, Business & Finance* (2007), 82–119, 102.

[10] Ibid.

[11] Mike W. Peng and Dane P. Blevins, 'Why Do Chinese Firms Cross-List in the United States?', in Abdul A. Rasheed and Toru Yoshikawa (eds.), *The Convergence of Corporate Governance: Promise and Prospects* (Palgrave McMillan, 2012), 249–265, 250.

[12] Qian Sun, Wilson H.S. Tong, and Yujun Wu, 'Bonding Premium as a General Phenomenon', March 2006, http://ssrn.com/abstract=890962.

on American exchanges or from adopting GAAP for presenting their financial results. Leuz and Verrechia found that when German firms switched from German accounting principles to IAS or GAAP, the market reacted positively even though the firms were not required to do so.[13]

It could be argued that investors will not trust the appearance of disclosure unless it is backed up by the threat of sanctions for misleading disclosures that cross-listing supposedly entails. As I will argue below, however, this threat is largely illusory in the first place, at least for Chinese firms, and so there is no actual distinction in this respect between Chinese firms that list in the United States and subject themselves to US disclosure standards and Chinese firms that remain at home and voluntarily disclose the same information.

2.3.2 Bonding through Self-Subjection to State and Federal Law

As noted above, a key element of the bonding hypothesis as applied to China is that listing in the United States imposes real discipline on Chinese companies and those who manage them[14] because it exposes them to lawsuits if they fail to act according to the higher US standards. But does it? The question can be examined both generally and with respect to China.

2.3.2.1 Generally There is scepticism in the literature as to the degree to which cross-listing companies and their senior management really subject themselves to the risk of litigation for violating US standards.[15] MacNeil argues that the commitments made by foreign firms listing in London are not as strong as they might first appear.[16] Coffee notes that both public and private enforcement against foreign firms listed in the United States appeared (as of the time of his writing) to be rare, although he goes on to argue that for various reasons he finds the evidence 'far from dispositive'.[17] Siegel examined Mexican companies cross-listed in the United States in the period during and after the crisis of 1994–1995.

[13] Christian Leuz and Robert Verrecchia, 'The Economic Consequences of Increased Disclosure', 38 *Journal of Accounting Research* (Supplement, 2000), 91–124.

[14] The latter group is rarely specifically mentioned, but since companies can only act through people, it is a necessary element of the claim.

[15] See generally Anywhere Sikochi, 'The Effect of Shareholder Litigation Risk on the Information Environment: The Case of Cross-Listed Firms', 4 November 2014, http://ssrn.com/abstract=2515091.

[16] Iain MacNeil, 'Competition and Convergence in Corporate Regulation: The Case of Overseas Listed Companies', 1 August 2001, http://ssrn.com/abstract=278508.

[17] Coffee, 'Racing Towards the Top?', 1794.

He concluded that the SEC and minority shareholders had not effectively enforced the law against those firms and that their insiders were not deterred from expropriating corporate resources.[18] Cheng et al. found that 'US listed foreign companies experience securities class action lawsuits at about half the rate as do US firms with similar levels of ex ante litigation risk.'[19]

There is also the general problem that litigation and sanctions targeting the *company* do not by themselves punish, and therefore do not deter, the individuals responsible for corporate wrongdoing. As Arlen writes,

> Private actions against corporations cannot be justified as a mechanism for ensuring that wrongdoers compensate victims because the burden of this litigation does not fall on wrongdoers. Instead, it falls on the firm's shareholders, many of whom were victims of the fraud.[20]

Thus, even if cross-listing means that sanctions can in fact be imposed on the cross-listed firm, there is no particular reason why investors should be comforted by that fact.[21]

2.3.2.2 China When it comes to Chinese cross-listed companies, there are a number of reasons for doubting that they and their senior management are in fact subject to public or private enforcement.

2.3.2.2.1 Prospectus Disclosure Certainly investors who read the companies' prospectuses can blame only themselves for thinking that companies and their management can be made accountable. I examined a random sample of eleven F-1 statements from Chinese companies listed on US exchanges.[22] Every single one contained a statement along the lines of the following, in virtually identical language:

[18] J. Siegel, 'Can Foreign Firms Bond Themselves Effectively by Renting US Securities Laws?', 75 *Journal of Financial Economics* (2005), 319–359.

[19] Beiting Cheng, Suraj Srinivasan, and Gwen Yu, 'Securities Litigation Risk for Foreign Companies Listed in the US', June 2014, http://ssrn.com/abstract=2163864.

[20] Jennifer Arlen, 'Public versus Private Enforcement of Securities Fraud', 2007, weblaw.usc.edu/assets/docs/Arlen.pdf, 3.

[21] John C. Coffee Jr., 'Reforming the Securities Class Action: An Essay on Deterrence and Its Implementation', 106 *Columbia Law Review* (2006), 1534–1586, 1556–1561, provides a detailed analysis of which shareholder groups win or lose by the wealth transfer involved when a company pays damages in a shareholder class action.

[22] The set of companies from which I made a random selection is a list purporting to include all Chinese ADR issuers as of September 2014, with 'Chinese' apparently applying to companies with the headquarters and principal place of business in China; many were

> Substantially all of our operations are conducted in China, and substantially all of our assets are located in China. A majority of our directors and executive officers are nationals or residents of jurisdictions other than the United States and a substantial portion of their assets are located outside the United States. As a result, it may be difficult for a shareholder to effect service of process within the United States upon these persons, or to enforce against us or them judgments obtained in United States courts, including judgments predicated upon the civil liability provisions of the securities laws of the United States or any state in the United States.[23]

In other words, Chinese cross-listed companies and their management regularly declare that they do not believe they are realistically subject to discipline imposed by American legal institutions. That should count for something.

2.3.2.2.2 Enforcement of US Judgments The confidence of management in their untouchability is well founded. Should investors manage to bring a successful action against a Chinese company or its senior management, they would have to get that judgment enforced where the defendant has assets, i.e. in China. Unlike the home countries of a large number of other cross-listed companies – Canada, Israel, and the United Kingdom, for example, to name some important ones – China does not enforce US court judgments.[24]

2.3.2.2.3 Experience to Date As of November 2015, there were approximately 100 Chinese companies listed on the New York Stock Exchange or the Nasdaq, and approximately another 200 traded on the over-the-counter market in the United States.[25] In order to assess the

incorporated in non-Chinese jurisdictions such as the Cayman Islands. The list appears at topforeignstocks.com/foreign-adrs-list/the-full-list-of-chinese-adrs/. The procedure used here is not good for more than a quick and dirty estimate of what the prospectuses of Chinese ADR issuers say, but given the strength of the results, I doubt a more rigorous inquiry would show anything different.

The companies whose prospectuses I examined are 21Vianet, Autohome, China Sunergy, Ctrip, Hurray! Holding, iDreamSky Technology, New Oriental, Renesola, Trina Solar, and Yingli Green Energy.

23 Autohome, Inc. 'Form F-1 Registration Statement', 5 November 2014, www.sec.gov/edgar/searchedgar/companysearch.html, 57.

24 Donald C. Clarke, 'The Enforcement of United States Court Judgments in China: A Research Note', 27 May 2004, http://ssrn.com/abstract=943922; Marc Davis, 'Chinese Companies Doing Business in the US Build Barriers to Legal Remedies', *ABA Journal*, 1 November 2015, available at perma.cc/TPA3-UDGB.

25 This datum is from a list of American Depository Receipts of China-based companies available at topforeignstocks.com/foreign-adrs-list/the-full-list-of-chinese-adrs/.

actual effect of bonding, I hand-collected a set of recent public and private enforcement actions under US securities law against Chinese companies and their senior management. I included not only companies incorporated in China, but also companies controlled by Chinese citizens whose main place of business was China, even though they may have incorporated outside of China. I have attempted to find every case, but as the cases are nowhere systematically collected it is possible I have missed some.

2.3.2.2.3.1 Private Enforcement To assess private enforcement, I examined class actions involving Chinese companies from January 2011 through October 2015 inclusive that were listed on the Securities Class Action Clearinghouse (SCAC) website.[26] There has been considerable action in the realm of private enforcement, although it has not necessarily been successful. In 2011, a record number of class actions – sixty-two – were filed against foreign issuers.[27] This is the only recent year in which more than half of the cases against foreign issuers – thirty-seven – were against Chinese companies (see Figure 5.1). That year also marked the beginning of a reversal of a long-term pattern in which foreign issuers were underrepresented as targets.[28] Foreign issuers were overrepresented in 2011, but underrepresented in 2012 and 2013[29] (see Figure 5.2). In 2014 and 2015, however, they were over-represented again.[30]

[26] The website is at securities.stanford.edu. Cases listed at this website do not constitute a complete set of all the cases one would wish to examine in a study of private enforcement of corporate law standards; the site does not list, for example, derivative suits brought by shareholders against management for inflicting damage on the company through connected transactions. On the other hand, listing abroad does not necessarily entail subjecting the company to the corporate law of the foreign jurisdiction where listing occurs; the issuer could be incorporated anywhere (for example, the Cayman Islands or even China itself) and thus governed by that jurisdiction's corporate law, not the corporate law of any state in the United States.

[27] This surge in lawsuits is attributable to a number of Chinese reverse mergers, Kevin LaCroix, 'Year-to-Date Securities Suit Filings Disproportionately Involve Non-US Companies', *The D&O Diary*, 15 June 2015, available at perma.cc/6AYF-JFHD. Thirty-one of the thirty-seven filings in 2011 against Chinese companies were related to Chinese reverse mergers, Cornerstone Research, *Securities Class Action Filings: 2014 Year in Review* (2015), available at perma.cc/428M-GXK2.

[28] LaCroix, 'Year-to-Date Securities Suit Filings'.

[29] Renzo Comolli and Starykh Svetlana, 'Recent Trends in Securities Class Action Litigation: 2013 Full-Year Review', *NERA Economic Consulting*, 21 January 2014, available at perma .cc/E6C5-2W4F, 9.

[30] Kevin LaCroix, 'Year-to-Date Securities Suit Filings'.

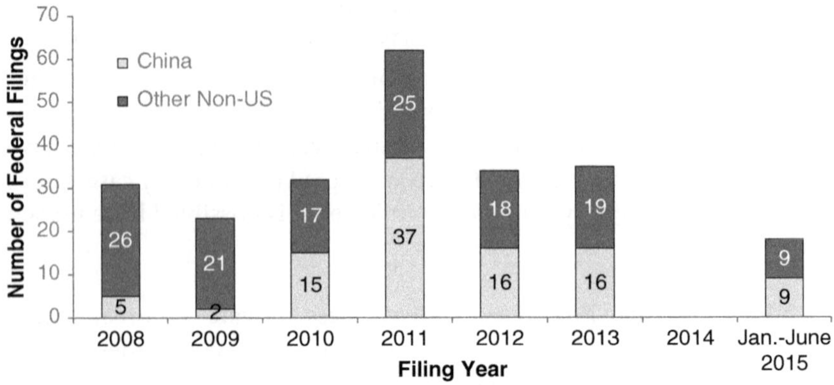

Figure 5.1 Class action filings by foreign company domicile and year, January 2008–June 2015
Sources: Renzo Comolli and Starykh Svetlana, 'Recent Trends in Securities Class Action Litigation: 2013 Full-Year Review', *NERA Economic Consulting*, 21 January 2014 (for years 2008–2013); Kevin LaCroix, 'Year-to-Date Securities Suit Filings Disproportionately Involve Non-US Companies', *The D&O Diary*, 15 June 2015 (for 2015).

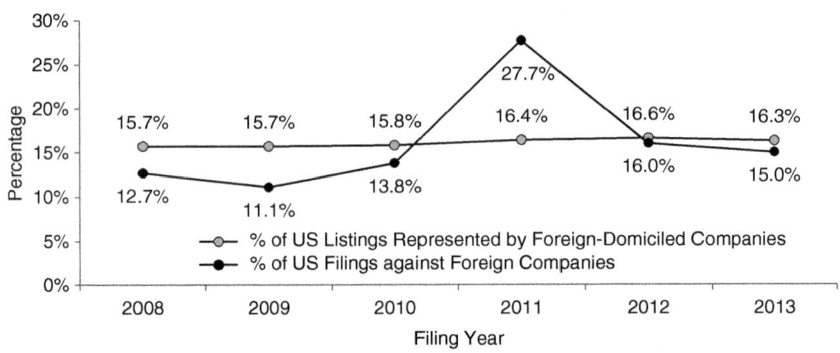

Figure 5.2 Foreign-domiciled companies: Share of filings and share of companies listed in the United States, January 2008–December 2013
Source: Renzo Comolli and Starykh Svetlana, 'Recent Trends in Securities Class Action Litigation: 2013 Full-Year Review', *NERA Economic Consulting*, 21 January 2014.

The SCAC website lists a total of eighty-eight cases involving Chinese companies filed between January 2011 and October 2015 inclusive. The result is pending or unknown in thirty-five cases. Twenty-five cases were dismissed and twenty-eight were settled. In three cases, plaintiffs won a default judgment (see Figure 5.3).

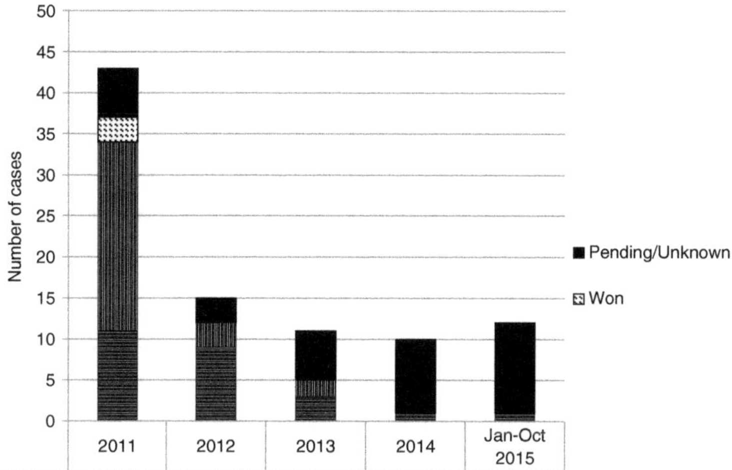

	2011	2012	2013	2014	Jan-Oct 2015
Pending/Unknown	6	3	6	9	11
Won	3	0	0	0	0
Settled	23	3	2	0	0
Dismissed	11	9	3	1	1

Year

Figure 5.3 Securities class actions involving Chinese companies

It is unlikely that the plaintiffs will ever collect from the default judgment. Such cases can therefore be excluded from cases where bonding had bite. Similarly, the dismissed cases imposed no penalty on corporate management beyond the cost of defending the suits, which would have been borne by the company and not by individuals. We are left, therefore, with the settled cases.

If all the settled cases resulted in monetary damages being paid by individuals, one could find a modest bonding effect: fully twenty-three out of forty-three cases in 2011, when lawsuits surged because of reverse mergers, although only two of fifteen and three of eleven cases in 2012 and 2013, respectively, and none so far in 2014 and 2015 (to the extent the outcome is known). The problem, however, is that this is almost certainly not happening; the consensus of those who have researched the question is that insiders – directors, executive officers, and controlling shareholders, or in other words, those who need to be deterred – personally pay a vanishingly small proportion of any settlement amount (less than one per cent).[31]

[31] John C. Coffee, Jr., 'Reforming the Securities Class Action: An Essay on Deterrence and Its Implementation', 106 *Columbia Law Review* (2006), 1534–1586, 1534–1535. A more recent study concludes: Out-of-pocket payments by officers or directors are rare. Among

Might settlements with Chinese companies not follow this pattern? Given that it is difficult as a practical matter to force individual Chinese defendants to pay, there is no reason for thinking that plaintiffs will be *more* likely in Chinese cases than otherwise to insist on individual liability as part of a settlement. On the other hand, a substantial proportion of payments in US class action settlements comes from directors' and officers' insurance (D&O insurance). Here Chinese corporate insider defendants appear to be very different from their US counterparts; apparently only five per cent of Chinese A-share listed companies have purchased D&O insurance for their officers and directors.[32] Nevertheless, given that cases that are not dismissed appear almost always to be settled, it is plausible to suppose that the individual defendants are willing to settle because they do not feel harmed by the terms.

2.3.2.2.3.2 Public Enforcement Experience to date in the realm of public enforcement has not been encouraging. In his study of Chinese firms listed in Hong Kong, Cai finds that the Hong Kong Stock Exchange and Hong Kong authorities in general have been weak in enforcement actions against Chinese companies.[33]

To assess public enforcement in the United States, I examined all civil suits brought in federal courts by the Securities and Exchange Commission involving companies headquartered in China for which there was a result on or after 1 January 2011.[34] I found no such cases for 2011 and 2012. From 2013 to October 2015 inclusive, there were twelve actions involving Chinese companies. These actions, however, involved only nine cases of fraud perpetrated upon investors.[35] In six of

cases filed from 2006 through 2010, 2 per cent of settlements have included an out-of-pocket payment by an officer and none has involved a payment by an outside director. From 2000 through 2005, 5.45 per cent of settlements included payments by officers and 2 per cent included payments by outside directors. Michael Klausner, Jason Hegland, and Matthew Goforth, 'How Protective Is D&O Insurance in Securities Class Actions? – An Update', 23 April 2013, http://ssrn.com/abstract=2260815, 8.

32 Hui Jia, 'D&O Liability Insurance: Legal Issues under the PRC Laws', *Lexology*, 8 May 2015, available at perma.cc/XAR9-YCWQ (citing an unnamed report).

33 Cai, 'Bonding, Law Enforcement, and Corporate Governance in China'.

34 These cases are listed on the SEC's website at www.sec.gov/litigation.shtml.

35 According to the bonding hypothesis, the importance of bonding lies in its assurance it provides to potential investors that the company and its management will follow relevant disclosure rules and not expropriate shareholders. As a result, investors are more willing to trust management with their money and this lowers the company's cost of capital. For this reason and for the purposes of this project, I have excluded cases of insider trading

those nine cases, individual perpetrators who were Chinese citizens resident in China ended up paying a penalty.[36]

3 Implications and Conclusion

The results of this survey of private and public enforcement of securities laws against Chinese cross-listed companies do not, unfortunately, speak for themselves. The results for private enforcement actions suggest that scepticism about the actual bonding effect of cross-listing is justified. In no case is it clear that individual wrongdoers actually suffered adverse consequences.

The number of public enforcement actions appears, as an absolute number, to be small; whether this is good or bad depends on one's assessment of the number of actions there *should* have been. Among the public enforcement actions brought for fraud perpetrated upon investors, two-thirds resulted in Chinese citizens resident in China paying a penalty, a result that suggests a stronger than expected bonding effect. At the same time, Chinese executives have not suffered anything worse than liability for monetary amounts and temporary bans from serving as officer or director. Since US authorities could not have forced the defendants to pay the penalty, the result suggests that some other factor – perhaps the desire to travel to or otherwise continue to do business in the United States – makes paying the penalty preferable to not paying it.

On the whole, it appears that the actual bonding effect of cross-listing by Chinese companies is greater than zero, but not by much. Investors should take seriously the disclosures in the risk factors section of the prospectuses of Chinese companies to the effect that it will be difficult to hold companies and their executives accountable under US law. To the extent that the stock prices of those companies incorporate a bonding premium of any significance, they are therefore probably overpriced.

and market manipulation, since those offences do not amount to improper diversions of corporate funds that expropriate shareholders.

36 I have assumed that where a case was disposed of by a settlement or other form of consent, the penalty was in fact paid, and that where a defendant failed to appear and the case was disposed of by a default judgment, the penalty was not in fact paid. I am looking only at penalties paid by individuals, not by companies, on the theory that only the former penalties act as the realistic deterrent required by the bonding hypothesis. As noted in Section 2.3.2.1 above, sanctions on companies hit the wrong target; they merely add insult to injury by hurting the very investors intended to be protected. Arlen, 'Public Versus Private Enforcement of Securities Fraud', 3.

This in turn suggests that stock markets do not efficiently reflect all publicly available information;[37] instead, it is more likely that markets treat cross-listed shares similarly – that is, as making companies and management equally accountable under US law – regardless of the country in which the company is based.

[37] This is not inherently implausible, despite the obvious objection that anyone in possession of publicly available information that has not been reflected in stock prices should be able to make a killing. The key is to know which publicly available information is already reflected in stock prices and which is not. A recent study finds, for example, that over the last fifteen years, US Supreme Court decisions have been responsible for changes in wealth of over $140 billion. Yet the study also finds that the informational content of those decisions has been incorporated only very slowly in the price of affected securities, implying 'a market ripe for arbitrage where an event-based trading strategy could be successful'. See Daniel Martin Katz, Michael J. Bommarito II, Tyler Soellinger, and James Ming Chen, 'Law on the Market? Evaluating the Securities Market Impact of Supreme Court Decisions', 24 August 2015 (Version 1.01), http://ssrn.com/abstract=2649726.

PART II

China (Mainland)

6

Improving the Civil Liability System for False and Misleading Disclosure in the Chinese Securities Markets

LIMING WANG[1]

1 Introduction

Investor protection is the most important aspect of securities markets. A critical legal mechanism for implementing this aim is the guaranty of a right to civil compensation for investors who have been harmed by securities fraud. Since the Supreme People's Court (SPC) of the People's Republic of China (PRC) issued the 'Several Regulations on the Adjudication of Civil Compensation Securities Suits Involving False or Misleading Disclosure in the Securities Markets' (hereafter, the 'Securities Misrepresentation Regulations' or 'Regulations')[2] on 1 January 2003, China has already accumulated more than 10 years of experience with

1 Vice President of China People's University, Professor of Law and Dean *Emeritus* of China People's University Law School. Professor Wang Liming is one of the most highly regarded legal academics and legislators in China, and has had an important role in shaping important aspects of China's substantive civil law, such as the PRC Contract Law, China's Tort Law, the Civil Procedure Law of the PRC, and even a draft Civil Code. Accordingly, his views on possible revisions of any aspect of China's substantive law in the civil and economic spheres should be afforded significant weight, especially at a time when China is in the process of completely amending its Securities Law. Note also that Vice President Wang's presentation was given at the end of 2014, and thus before the several 'crashes' in the Chinese stock markets in the summer of 2015 and the beginning of 2016, and the direct central government financial and regulatory interventions they elicited. This paper was translated into English and annotated by Nicholas Calcina Howson, Professor of Law, University of Michigan Law School. Footnotes and references in the original presentation by Vice President Wang Liming are indicated as such.

2 'Zuigao Renmin Fayuan Guanyu Shenli Zhengquan Shichang Yin Xujia Chenshu Yinfa De Minshi Peichang Anjian De Ruogan Guiding' (effective 1 February 2003). These are SPC 'regulations' (*guiding*), not, as they are often referred to in Chinese and English, a 'judicial interpretation' (*sifa jieshi*). The difference in these norms issued by the SPC (and in addition the 'approving response', or *pifu*) is detailed at Xi Xiaoming and Jia Wei,

a civil compensation system for false and misleading securities disclosure.[3] So-called false or misleading disclosure occurs when a party obligated to make disclosure into the securities markets makes a false or misleading disclosure in violation of law and regulation that in turn causes securities investor losses. The Securities Misrepresentation Regulations issued by the SPC in January 2003 provide stipulations regarding the definition and scope of fraudulent disclosure, case jurisdiction, the defendants in false or misleading disclosure cases, principles for the determination of false or misleading disclosure, liability exemptions, and the determination of damages, etc.[4] Looking back on the past to reflect on the present, as we legal specialists analyse the more than ten years of data on the effectiveness of the legal regulation of false and misleading disclosure civil compensation, we can broadly confirm that it has had an overall positive effect in preserving the basic ordering of fair and even capital markets and in protecting the lawful rights and interests of investors. The system represents a beneficial and timely element of our 'rule of law' markets which have been continuously under reform over the past decade. At the same time, however, we must clearly acknowledge that the Regulations were of course conceived during the initial stage of the tentative construction of our socialist market economy. Because of the accelerated development of China's capital economy [market] over these more than ten years, the legal

'Zhengquan Shichang Xujia Chenshu Minshi Peichang Zhidu' [The Civil Compensation System for False and Misleading Disclosure in the Securities Markets], 3 *Zhengquan Falu Pinglun* [Securities Law Review] 33 (October 2003), 41. The subsequent amendment of the 1999 PRC Securities Law in 2006 added a statutory basis for the false and misleading disclosure civil claims addressed in the 2003 Regulations at Articles 69 and 173. For some of the English-language writing on the Regulations and associated claims, see: Walter Hutchens, 'Private Securities Litigation in China: Material Disclosure About China's Legal System?', 24 U. PA. J. INT'L. ECON. L. 599 (2003); Guiping Lu, 'Private Enforcement of Securities Fraud in China: A Critique of the Supreme People's Court 2003 Provisions Concerning Private Securities Litigation', 12 PAC. RIM. L. & POL'Y J. 795 (2003); Sanzhu Zhu, 'Civil Litigation Arising from False Statements on China's Securities Market', 31 N.C.J. INT'L L. & COM. REG. 377 (2005); and Robin Hui Huang, 'Private Enforcement of Securities Law in China: A Ten-Year Retrospective and Empirical Assessment', 61 AM. J. COMP. L. 757 (2013).

3 The following two sentences are taken from the introduction Vice President Wang offered in connection with his conference paper. The rest of the first paragraph of this translation is taken from the revised paper he submitted for publication in this book.

4 See Securities Misrepresentation Regulations, Arts. 17 (different types of misrepresentation), 2 and 3 (eligible plaintiffs), 7 (potential defendants), 21–25 (defences available), 18 and19 (presumptions of causation and reliance), 29–35 (calculation of damages), and 9 (jurisdiction awarded to the Intermediate People's Court of the *situs* of the securities issuer).

regulation of false and misleading disclosure, and the regulatory system for civil compensation in particular, as applied has not completely kept up with changes in our economic life. Often, the system has not served as a reliable weapon for investors to clean up the capital markets, but instead it has become a 'blunted sword' for investors who seek to protect their rights, and it has even – because of illogical aspects of the system's design – blocked a channel through which investors might have protected their rights. As our new Securities Law attempts to 'scatter the clouds and show us the bright moon' [while also] reflecting institutionally the command in the Report of the Eighteenth National Congress [of the Chinese Communist Party] to deepen financial reform, perfecting financial regulation reform policy so as to implement in regulation the post [Global Financial Crisis] assurance of financial stability, and protecting the real demands of financial investors, I believe that we must undertake supplementary regulation of the false and misleading disclosure civil compensation litigation [system] in the context of revising the PRC Securities Law. As a legal academic, I propose we can take the next step in perfecting the false and misleading disclosure civil litigation system starting with the following aspects.

2 Eliminate or Restrict Use of the Pre-Action Procedural Requirement for Civil Misrepresentation Suits

Article 6 of the Securities Misrepresentation Regulations states,

> The People's Courts shall accept civil compensation lawsuits complying with Article 108 of the PRC Law on Civil Procedure brought by investors because such investors have been harmed by false or misleading disclosure, against persons who have engaged in false or misleading disclosure, based upon the relevant organ's administrative punishment decision or a criminal judgment rendered by the People's Courts.

This rule creates a procedural precondition (hereinafter, the 'Procedural Requirement') for false or misleading disclosure lawsuits so that when injured persons make a claim against those who have engaged in false or misleading disclosure to take responsibility for rights infringement, there is a precondition which requires the existence of an administrative penalty decision by the relevant organ or a criminal judgment by a court of law.[5] It should be clear that the stipulated rule to the effect that

[5] There is a long-running dispute in China and abroad as to whether or not the Procedural Requirement inhibits private enforcement. See, for example, Sanzhu Zhu, 'Civil Litigation

the court should accept the claim only if at the time of the lawsuit by the injured party there already exists an administrative penalty decision or if a criminal judgment by a court of law is in some ways reasonable. If before the lawsuit there is an administrative penalty decision or a criminal judgment by a court of law in existence, then the court in the subsequent civil lawsuit can use that decision directly as evidence in the determination of civil liability, or as a substantial factor for reference, and will not be required to undertake a separate adjudication on [the question of] whether the defendant in the proceeding has engaged in behaviour which constitutes false or misleading disclosure. This is beneficial for the conservation of judicial resources and the resolution of disputes. And it can at a certain level solve the difficulties faced by plaintiffs with respect to the gathering of evidence at the inception of a claim.[6] In practice, this requirement has already had good effect. For example, in the Dongfang Electronics false and misleading disclosure civil compensation case[7], because the court's criminal judgment decision had already confirmed the fact of Dongfang Electronics' false and misleading disclosure, there was no need in the civil claim process for the [civil] court to determine that fact.[8]

However, making the existence of an administrative penalty decision or criminal judgment by a court of law a precondition to any civil claim

Arising from False Statements on China's Securities Market', 427 and Luo Peixin, 'Qianzhi Chengxu Quliu Kunjing' [Difficulties Over Whether to Eliminate or Keep the Procedural Precondition], 19 *Caijing* [Finance] 28 (2007) (it does inhibit); and Robin Huang Hui, 'Private Enforcement of Securities Law in China', 764–766 (it does not necessarily inhibit).

6 [Footnote in original] See Xi Xiaoming and Jia Wei, '"Guanyu Shenli Zhengquan Shichang Yin Xujia Chenshu Yinfa De Minshi Peichang Anjian De Ruogan Guiding" De Lijie He Shiyong' ['Understanding and Use of the "Several Regulations on the Adjudication of Civil Compensation Securities Suits Involving Misrepresentation in the Securities Markets"'], *Renmin Sifa* [People's Judiciary] 2000, No. 2. [Annotators footnote:] Vice President Wang elaborated in his remarks to the conference: 'The advantages of the [Procedural Requirement] are to ease the burden of proof on the part of plaintiff investors, and to minimise disputes regarding the fact of misrepresentation. The reason is that misrepresentation is very complicated in reality, as it is disputed whether a certain statement amounts to misrepresentation or not. Furthermore, it is not certain whether investor loss causation can be tied to a specific misrepresentation'.

7 There is a huge literature on the Dongfang Electronic case, which is considered China's first securities false or misleading disclosure case under the SPC's Securities Misrepresentation Regulations. See, for example, Song Yixin, 'Dongfang Dianzi An De Weiquan Gushi' ['The Story of [Property] Rights Defense in the Case of Dongfang Electronics'], *Zhongguo Zhengquan* Bao [China Securities News], 27 November 2006, available at http://vnetcj.jrj.com.cn/2012/02/22091212309457.shtml.

8 [Footnote in original] See Shandong Qingdao Municipal Intermediate People's Court Civil Mediation Document, 2007 *qingminchuzi* No. 70.

by investors may also work against the protection of investors. The major reasons for eliminating or restricting the Procedural Requirement are as follows:

First, the Procedural Requirement unreasonably heightens requirements for the bringing of lawsuits by injured parties, and does not help investor protection. According to Article 119 of the Law of the PRC on Civil Procedure, parties need only meet the following conditions in order to bring a lawsuit: first, that the plaintiff has an interest at stake in the case; second, that there is a clearly-identified defendant; third, that there are specific claims and facts in the litigation; and fourth, that the claim falls within the scope of a civil action and comes within the jurisdiction of the People's Courts. According to these stipulations, where there is false or misleading disclosure in the securities markets, an investor should only need to demonstrate it has a stake in the case and that there is a specific individual or entity [which] has [allegedly engaged in] false or misleading disclosure in order to fulfil the conditions precedent for the bringing of a lawsuit. It is clear that the precondition in Article 6 of the Securities Misrepresentation Regulations for the bringing of an investor lawsuit – that there be in existence an administrative penalty decision or criminal judgment by a court of law – unreasonably raises the bar for the bringing of lawsuits by injured parties, and [therefore] does not benefit investor protection.

Second, some false or misleading disclosure cases do not meet the conditions for an administrative fine, and others do not involve what constitutes a criminal breach, and yet they may still have resulted in financial losses for investors. If the existence of an administrative penalty decision or criminal judgment by a court of law is a condition precedent for any lawsuit by investors, that condition may result in a large number of investors having no way to procure an effective remedy, and in addition does not help the effective regulation of false and misleading disclosure behaviour in the securities markets.[9]

Third, the Procedural Requirement may result in investors having no way to receive effective compensation for their injury.[10] Pursuant to

[9] [Footnote in original] See Liu Min, 'Lun Minshi Susong Qianzhi Chengxu'['On the Procedural Pre-Condition for Civil Litigation'], *Zhongguo Faxue* [China Jurisprudence] 2011, No. 6.

[10] [Footnote in original] See Chen Yijun, 'Zhengquan Shichang Xujia Chenshu Minshi Peichang Chengxu Ruogan Wenti Tantuo' ['Discussion of Several Problems in the Civil Compensation Procedure for False and Misleading Disclosure in the Securities Markets'], *Zhengzhi Yu Falu* [Politics and Law] 2003, No. 2.

Article 6 of the Securities Misrepresentation Regulations, only once the administrative penalty decision or criminal judgment by a court of law is made can the investor bring a civil lawsuit against the relevant people responsible. In practice, however, many cases demonstrate that after implementation of the administrative penalty decision or criminal judgment by a court of law, the defendant may already be bankrupt or have no residual assets to offer in enabling the enforcement of compensation for investor damages by the defendant adjudicated as liable, and that the relevant defendant may already have lost the ability to shoulder its [compensation] liability. This is clearly detrimental to the full protection of investors.[11]

3 Civil Infringement Liability for False or Misleading Disclosure Should Be 'Modified Joint and Several Liability'[12]

Article 21 of the Securities Misrepresentation Regulations stipulates the following:

> promoters, issuers and listed companies bear civil liability for the losses suffered by investors arising from their false or misleading disclosure. Promoters, and the directors, supervisory board members and CEO and other high level managers of listed companies, responsible [for false and misleading disclosure] bear joint and several liability for the losses described in the preceding clause. However if there is evidence demonstrating that [such persons] are without fault, then they shall be exempted from liability.

From the face of this article, joint and several liability among promoters, issuers and listed companies, and listed company directors, supervisory board members, CEOs and other high level managers who are responsible [for the false and misleading disclosure] is stipulated. Said another way, when an investor suffers financial losses because of false or misleading disclosure by [any of] the promoters, issuer or listed company, then the investor can claim that any of these parties bear joint and several liability for its losses. Although beneficial for the full protection of

[11] Vice President Wang elaborated another reason in his conference remarks, '. . . it can be very time consuming for the plaintiff investors to wait for the defendants to be punished by regulators or criminally sentenced by a court'.

[12] Vice President Wang uses the Chinese language term, 'bu zhenzheng de liandai zeren', which could be translated literally as 'not true' or 'not complete' or 'not traditional' joint and several liability. I use 'modified joint and several liability' as an English term of art to encapsulate the concept he describes in the body of Section 3.

investors, this stipulation of joint and several liability by the identified parties for the financial losses suffered by investors may violate the principle holding that civil parties should only bear responsibility for their own faults (*zeren zefu*). This is because, although the [named] responsible party may have some level of fault in causing the false or misleading disclosure and thus should bear some responsibility for compensating investor losses, in accordance with the principle of each bearing responsibility for its own fault, the [civil] actor should bear liability only for the injury caused by its own mistakes. Moreover, each [defendant] party has a different causal relationship with the losses suffered. And further, there should be a certain difference between their internal allocations of liability [among the defendants for investor losses].

Specifically based upon the foregoing reasons, we believe that the above-described liability scheme should be changed into [a scheme for what I will call] modified joint and several liability. So-called modified joint and several liability means that where a number of different persons for different reasons are determined to be legally responsible for the totality of compensation to persons who have had their rights infringed upon, and where, after one of the responsible defendants has borne that liability, that defendant has the right to seek full contribution from the [other] defendant or defendants having ultimate responsibility. The major rationales for stipulating modified joint and several liability with respect to civil liability for rights infringement related to false and misleading disclosure include the following:

First, this scheme conforms to the principle of each bearing responsibility for its own faults. Under this principle, a party should only bear liability for injury brought about by itself, and should not bear responsibility for injury brought about for other reasons [or by other persons].[13] According to the stipulations of Article 21 of the Securities Misrepresentation Regulations, promoters and the directors, supervisory board members, CEOs and other high level managers of listed companies should bear joint and several liability to investors for the losses suffered by such investors arising from false or misleading disclosure; only if able to demonstrate that they themselves were not at fault are they exempted from liability. However, if the above-named parties have only committed a relatively minor mistake and thus the

[13] [Footnote in original] See Jiang Zhanjun, 'Qinquan Goucheng De Feixiandingxing Yu Xiandingxing JI Qi Jiazhi' ['Infringement Structured as Limited and Unlimited and Its Value'], *Faxue Yanjiu* [Jurisprudence Research] 2006, No. 5.

injury to investors [they are liable for] is also relatively small, they (along with all of the other defendants) nonetheless have joint and several liability for [all of the] investor losses. This clearly contravenes the principle of each bearing responsibility according to its own faults. Now if we change this liability scheme to one of modified joint and several liability, where the relevant party's fault is relatively minor and after that party bears liability [for compensation to investors], it can seek compensation [contribution] from the main defendants responsible [for the injury]. This [scheme] conforms better to the principle of each bearing responsibility for its own faults. Moreover, changing the nature of civil liability for false or misleading disclosure to modified joint and several liability would help ascertain where ultimate responsibility [for the injury to investors] lies, clarify the party ultimately responsible [for investor losses], help discipline the behaviour of directors, supervisory board members, CEOs and other senior management, protect against their abuse of power, and promote the internal balance of applicable corporate governance structures.

Second, this scheme would benefit the accurate determination of party responsibility. From the standpoint of loss causation, [the application of] joint and several liability is usually grounded in [the existence of the same cause], such as when there is harm visited upon a common group and there exists a common subjective fault among the individual tortfeasors. But the application of modified joint and several liability [in these cases of false and misleading disclosure] is not based in the cause of the losses experienced [by investors]. [Instead, in these cases] several obligors have liability [for the same injury but] for different reasons. [So,] modified joint and several liability [can be appropriately] applied where liability [of several defendants] is determined to exist independently and arise from different causes [and levels of fault]. With respect to false or misleading disclosure cases, defendants such as promoters, issuers, listed companies and listed company senior management, etc., rarely share the same subjective intent, and thus the causes of investors' financial losses are not of the same kind.[14] Therefore, each of the defendants [in false and misleading disclosure cases] should not bear joint and several liability for

[14] Vice President Wang explained this point slightly differently in his conference remarks, focusing on the legal duties owed by different actors in the corporate law and securities law schemes: '. . . the content of the fiduciary duties owed by the directors, supervisory board members and senior managers of issuers and listed companies are quite different. If the real wrongdoers are not held ultimately liable, that would be unfair to the directors, supervisory board members and senior managers [who have not breached any legal duty]'.

investor losses, but instead should have modified joint and several liability.

Third, a scheme of modified joint and several liability will not affect investor remedies. Regardless of whether joint and several liability or modified joint and several liability is applied, injured parties all have the right to make a claim for joint and several compensation against some or all of the defendants. The major issue differentiating the modified joint and several liability scheme [from traditional joint and several liability] concerns the internal relationship among the responsible parties, such that after one of the defendants has borne liability for compensation liability, does that party have the right to seek compensation [contribution] from the party or parties that have ultimate responsibility? With respect to the external relationship [between defendants and plaintiffs], the injured parties [will regardless of the scheme employed] always have the right to make a claim for joint and several liability against some or all of the defendants. Accordingly, even though the nature of civil liability for false and misleading disclosure would be characterised as modified joint and several liability, this would not affect the remedies available to investors.[15]

4 Perfect the Method for Calculating Compensation for Financial Losses Resulting from False or Misleading Disclosure

The scope of compensation for financial losses arising from false or misleading disclosure is limited under Article 30 of the Securities Misrepresentation Regulations to the actual losses (*shiji sunshi*) suffered by investors. According to this article, the exact scope of 'actual losses' suffered by investors includes: first, the investment differential loss [the difference between the purchase and sales prices of the affected securities], and second, those portions of the commission paid [to securities firms] and stamp tax charged [by the state] attributable to that investment differential. Although this article of the Regulation sets forth the scope of investor financial losses, it does not clearly stipulate the details of how such financial losses should be calculated. Because the trading price

[15] Vice President Wang does not address why such claims for what other legal systems call 'contribution' among joint and severally liable defendants are not somehow permitted at present in China, or why the right to contribution needs to be provided affirmatively in statute or regulation. Perhaps he knows of civil judgments in false or misleading disclosure cases where defendants who have paid compensation to investors have not been permitted subsequently to seek contribution from co-defendants.

for securities in securities markets is constantly in flux, it is difficult for investors to demonstrate the exact *quantum* of their financial loss, and even more difficult for them to demonstrate the causal relationship between false or misleading disclosure and their [asserted] financial losses.[16] In practice, China employs a multiplicity of methods for the calculation of compensation [of investors' losses] in false or misleading disclosure lawsuits, with those seen most frequently including: the price differential method, the systemic risk method, the event study method, the discount method, the median price method, etc.[17] Faced with the same fact of a loss, the methods for calculation of the amount of the losses suffered is different, and [thus] the amount of [adjudicated] compensation can be different. We believe the method for calculating compensation for financial losses arising from false and misleading disclosure should be perfected with the following two ideas in mind.

The first is to distinguish different situations involving false or misleading disclosure, and specify different methods of calculating financial losses [according to those situations]. In the course of securities issuance and trading, false or misleading disclosure can take different forms such as misstatement, misleading disclosure, inappropriate disclosure, etc. There are also multiple parties responsible for false or misleading disclosure. And different kinds of false or misleading disclosure cause different kinds of losses for investors. We should therefore classify [different varieties of] false and misleading disclosure and apply different methods for calculating financial losses with respect to each variety.

The second thing to do when specifying a method of calculating financial losses is to adopt a loss calculation method that takes account of the reasonable inclinations of investors. In the securities markets different actors grasp market information in different degrees. Compared to securities issuers and the senior management of listed companies, the ability of investors to grasp [understand] relevant information [in the market] is weaker. When a party obligated to make information disclosure [into the market] makes false or misleading disclosure, it can result in huge losses for such investors. In order to provide investors with a complete remedy and avoid or reduce false or misleading disclosure, when specifying the

16 [Footnote in original] See Lai Wu, 'Zhengquan Xujia Chenshu Minshi Zeren De Rending' ['Ascertaining Civil Liability for Securities [Market] False and Misleading Disclosure'], *Fazhi Yu Shehui Fazhan* [Law and Society Development] 2003, No. 2.

17 [Footnote in original] See Wang Dan, 'Zhengquan Xujia Chenshu Sunhai Peichang Jisuan Fangfa Lun' ['On the Method of Calculating Losses for Securities [Market] False and Misleading Disclosure'], *Faxue* [Jurisprudence] 2003, No. 6.

method of calculating losses we should adopt a loss calculation method that takes account of the reasonable inclinations of investors.[18]

5 The Question of the Scope of Investors' Losses

In principle, Article 18 of the Securities Misrepresentation Regulations only provides a [compensation] remedy for investor losses caused by false or misleading disclosure arising from the *purchase* of [the related] securities, and does not provide a [compensation] remedy for investors who have suffered financial losses by *selling* securities as a result of false or misleading disclosure. For financial losses suffered by investors because of false or misleading disclosure, this Article of the Regulations only provides a remedy for financial losses suffered by investors who have sold the affected securities after the date of [truthful] disclosure or correcting disclosure. It is [of course] true in practice that most of the parties engaging in false or misleading disclosure seek to exaggerate profits or hide losses, etc., and thus investor losses generally arise from such investors' purchase of the securities in mistaken reliance upon this [false or misleading] information. However, if the parties obligated to make information disclosure breach their information disclosure obligations by making disclosure of the related information that is false or misleading because it purposely understates company revenues or exaggerates losses, thereby causing investors to sell the related securities [at a lower price than is warranted], then investors can also suffer certain financial losses.[19] These financial losses are also a result of false or misleading disclosure, and thus investors should also have a right to make a claim for compensation from those obliged to make information disclosure [concerning such securities]. The Securities Misrepresentation Regulations do not have any stipulation allowing compensation for this kind of financial loss, and thus as we go forward with amending the PRC

[18] Vice President Wang alluded to a related issue in his conference remarks, what amounts to a loss causation element or the relevance of evaluating systemic risk in the losses actually suffered by investors: '. . .. it remains controversial as to whether systematic risk should be considered as an element in discounting the financial losses actually suffered by investors. Some Chinese courts do take account of systemic risk in evaluating loss causation. However, many investors push back against excessive discounts reflecting systematic risks of the stock market, as investors assert they would never have purchased the securities if they had not been misled or lied to'.

[19] [Footnote in original] See Duan Jie, 'Zhengquan Xujia Chenshu Minshi Zeren Zhidu' ['On the Securities [Market] False and Misleading Disclosure Civil Liability System'], Faxue [Jurisprudence] 2003, No. 6.

Securities Law the scope of the remedy for investors' financial losses should be appropriately broadened to cover this kind of situation.[20]

6 Perfect Dispute Resolution Mechanisms for False and Misleading Disclosure in the Securities Markets

Article 4 of the Securities Misrepresentation Regulations states, 'When adjudicating securities [market] false and misleading disclosure compensation cases, the People's Courts should emphasise mediation and encourage the parties to reconcile'. In accordance with this article, in resolving securities market false and misleading disclosure cases, the People's Courts are to emphasise mediation. The preference for mediation has been lauded as [arising from] the 'East Asian experience', and comes to us directly from China's traditional legal system. The mediation system is seen as an important method for resolving social contradictions in China. Mediation has some advantages over the litigation process in respect of dispute resolution – it reduces dispute resolution costs and very importantly provides for final resolution of disputes; at the same time, mediation procedures are comparatively flexible and also easier to implement. Therefore, we should acknowledge the importance of mediation with respect to dispute resolution. Because mediation can conserve costs associated with litigation, [we should] in principle allow the mediation system to play the fullest role possible, such that mediation is an important component of a multifaceted dispute resolution mechanism. In false and misleading disclosure cases, the courts should also use mediation where appropriate, and not contravene any [expressed] desire of the parties to use mediation in resolving such disputes.

Notwithstanding, first, in false and misleading disclosure cases it is not advisable to overemphasise the use of mediation procedures and ignore the intention of investors in choosing a dispute resolution mechanism, which can also be detrimental to investor protection. We should correctly ascertain the positive contribution of the mediation system, but cannot make mediation a procedural condition precedent for all cases, or even the primary method for dispute resolution. Use of the mediation system should respect the desires of the disputing parties, so that when the

20 This transaction is captured in the private enforcement of US securities regulation, which goes to the purchase or sale of the affected securities. See, for example, *Basic* v. *Levinson*, 485 U.S. 224 (1988) (plaintiffs *sold* shares in reliance upon false denial of merger negotiations).

parties choose a litigation process for dispute resolution, courts should not force mediation onto the parties. Second, when mediation is employed in dispute resolution, the principle of voluntarism should be upheld. For many courts faced with case disputes, regardless of whether or not a case dispute is suitable for mediation or the parties want to use mediation for dispute resolution, courts will generally prefer a mediation procedure. Thus, for many courts a mediation procedure has gradually become a kind of pre-condition for litigation. In false and misleading disclosure cases, overuse of mediation for dispute resolution can contravene mediation's [own] principle of voluntarism. Regardless of whether it is mediation before litigation or mediation in the course of litigation, we believe that for securities market false and misleading disclosure cases the guiding principle should be the parties' desires [for choice of a dispute resolution procedure].

7 Establish a Multifaceted System for the Compensation of Investor Losses

In false and misleading disclosure cases, investors can suffer huge financial losses caused by a given party's false or misleading disclosure. Although litigation can provide a remedy for investors, the litigation process can be rather tedious and continue for a comparatively long period of time, which is not beneficial for provision of a convenient investor remedy. Even if investors are successful in obtaining a remedy through litigation, they still face a risk that the party liable will forfeit or be unable to pay. For example, listed companies can go bankrupt, or the senior management of listed companies can be judgment proof, all of which will result in investors losing any [compensation] remedy for their financial losses. To address this [problem], we should establish a multifaceted system for the compensation of investor losses.[21] For example, we could establish an investor compensation fund mechanism. It is precisely

[21] Vice President Wang detailed a different, extra-judicial example of an investor compensation mechanism in his conference remarks: 'The actions undertaken by the Ping An securities firm offer a very good example for a non-judicial compensation mechanism. By the time it was revealed that Chinese listed firm Wanfu Shengke had made misrepresentations in its IPO prospectus, the public investors also learned that the company was unable to pay out any substantial compensation. In this unique case, Ping An Securities, as the lead underwriter and sponsor for the Wanfu Shengke IPO, voluntarily and without any judicial process contributed almost RMB 300 million yuan to the China Securities Investor Protection Corporation to establish a special compensation fund available only to the Wanfu Shengke investors'.

the investor compensation fund mechanism's ability to address the above-described problem that makes the use of it such a good idea. As a fund that helps investors protect their rights and compensate for the losses they suffer, it functions as a material guaranty for the protection of investor rights. The [investor compensation fund] can be financed from [sources such as] a special fee extracted from securities issuance or trading, the receipts from securities trading stamp tax levies, trading commissions, annual fees paid by securities firms or securities investment funds, or even from the penalties paid or illegal gains disgorged by trading violators. The assets of the fund could be entrusted to the securities regulatory agency or a financial institution designated by the judiciary, and used only to compensate investor losses. When [injured] investors make a common or group claim for their rights, the party entrusted [with managing the fund] would determine disbursement of compensation to [investor] victims in accordance with law. This would provide investors with a more complete remedy [for false or misleading disclosure].

8 The Statute of Limitations Issue

Pursuant to Articles 135 and 137 of the General Principles of the Civil Law of the PRC (GPCL), the statute of limitations for civil claims is two years unless otherwise stipulated in law, calculated as starting from the time the [plaintiff] rights holder knows or should have known its rights were infringed upon. In false or misleading disclosure cases and in accordance with general statute of limitation principles for civil litigation, the start of the statute of limitations period should be [the time when] the investor knows that its rights have been harmed. However, Article 5 of the Securities Misrepresentation Regulations makes the issuance date of the relevant administrative penalty decision or the effective date of the criminal judgment the starting date for calculating the statute of limitations. This may not be beneficial for rights holders trying to procure remedies, because it is relatively easy for such rights holders to gain knowledge of false or misleading disclosure, but more difficult [for them] to gain knowledge of the issuance of either the relevant administrative penalty decision or criminal judgment. By the time investors have gained knowledge that their rights were infringed upon, the issuance [date] of the relevant administrative penalty decision or criminal judgment may be more than two years before. This may force some investors to have to forfeit their right to bring a legal claim, and it is clearly not beneficial for investors seeking a remedy [for false and misleading disclosure breaches].[22]

9 Lawyers' Contingency Arrangements

Consideration of a [lawyer's] contingency mechanism is driven primarily by the ever-pronounced imbalance between defendants and plaintiffs with respect to the ability to litigate in false or misleading disclosure cases. Therefore, it is [deemed] necessary to introduce a specific mechanism in order to bring about a reasonable incentive for the plaintiffs to litigate, and reverse the litigation capability imbalance between the parties. The contingency fee arrangement is one kind of very effective mechanism in this line. It ties the result of the lawsuit to the lawyers' fees, and thereby assigns the risk of financing the litigation to litigators who want to accept such a risk. It encourages lawyers to use fully their professional knowledge in making the litigation balance among the parties more equal. In the US, it is usually special class action attorneys who organise and lead investor class action suits, controlling almost the entire course of cases, from strategy at the start to the final conclusion of the litigation, even representing the investor class in collecting any damages award. For investors, from the time they make an agreement to entrust the lawyers at the start and all the way to the end of the litigation, there is no need to be involved in any specific matters connected to the lawsuit. If the case is successful, the investors will pay a stipulated portion of the compensation award to the lawyers as their fees. If the case is unsuccessful, then in accordance with the retention agreement they will pay no fees or reduced fees. We can say that the contribution of the investor class action lawsuit mechanism [in the US] – which in the final analysis constitutes a very robust force for enforcement against illegal activity in the US securities markets – is only made possible because of the contingency fee system. Pursuant to China's current regulations, the PRC Ministry of Justice allows lawyers and the parties they represent to agree to fee arrangements, which can be seen as the initial basis for contingency arrangements.[23] However, China at present has

[22] [Footnote in original] See Chen Yijun, 'Zhengquan Shichang Xujia Chenshu Minshi Peichang Chengxu Ruogan Wenti Tantao' ['Consideration of Several Issues Concerning the Civil Compensation Procedure for Securities Market False and Misleading Disclosure'], *Faxue* [Jurisprudence] 2003, No. 2.

[23] See Robin Huang Hui, 'Private Enforcement of Securities Law in China', 767 (explaining the current limited space for contingency fee-type arrangements in China, but noting that

only introduced the embryo of a contingency fee model. I therefore suggest that we should think about how to ascertain the legal effectiveness of any contingency fee system (with specific arrangements determined by the market) that may appear via new legislation for use in the false or misleading disclosure litigation area, and formulate appropriate standards to regularise [these arrangements].

10 The Chinese Judiciary

The present system of incentives for civil lawsuits on false or misleading disclosure will have to rely on positive reinforcement from the judiciary. Because of competence constraints, lack of independence and other reasons, the PRC courts act extremely sluggishly at present, forcing investors to overcome a parade of obstacles which include case establishment (*li'an*), hearing, judgment and enforcement hurdles, all of which seriously affect the lawsuit activism of investors. First, many courts erect very serious obstacles at the case establishment phase, as they do not want to accept the cases; in some cases they reluctantly accept a case but then add all kinds of constraints on its progress. For example, in the Yinguangxia case, the court was only open to receive claims for a three-month period; in many cases, the courts restrict the numbers [of plaintiffs] included in group lawsuits, thereby increasing the costs of establishing claims. Moreover, according to interviews with lawyers, courts often delay case establishment for civil compensation cases, justifying that delay with the complexity of the cases and the need for more time to determine whether or not case establishment is warranted. At times, courts refuse outright to give case establishment without offering any reason for such refusal. And sometimes, the decision on case establishment is entirely determined by the personal connections of the lawyers. Furthermore, even after case establishment the court often holds endless hearings on the case. In reality, the practice of 'separate case establishments, collective hearings' is fairly common, whereby courts will wait through to the end of the two-year statute of limitations period before beginning any hearings on the case, with final conclusion of the case coming even later. For example, in the Dongfang Electronics case, the court waited until the end of the statute of limitations period before undertaking merged hearings on all of the claims, so that for some of the

such arrangements can only be used in property disputes, and are not allowed with respect to so-called 'mass litigation' (*qunti susong*)).

cases the period between case establishment and final judgment was almost five years.[24] Pursuant to the Civil Procedure Law of the PRC, hearings on civil cases should normally be concluded within six months of case establishment, but where there are special circumstances and the President of the court system approves, that period can be extended another six months; when such an extension is given, it must be reported to the next higher level of the People's Court for approval. And yet, according to data from academic studies, both the median and average time periods for hearings [in false and misleading disclosure cases] are very long. Furthermore, it appears that in adjudicating these cases some courts invoke substantive law in a way that is seemingly biased against the interest of the plaintiffs. The SPC's 2003 Securities Misrepresentation Regulations provide substantive law on a large number of issues, and thus there are fairly clear stipulations on the determination of causation, the calculation of compensatory damages, etc. Notwithstanding, the way in which some courts determine the 'disclosure date' [of the false or misleading disclosure] or handle consideration of loss causation [tied to] systemic risk, etc. is clearly inappropriate. This gives observers a feeling of unfairness or that [the courts] are acting purposely to disadvantage the plaintiffs. For example, in the December 2011 judgment on the Huawen Media case, the court unexpectedly determined that the disclosure by the listed company of false financial information did not constitute the [actionable legal] fact of false or misleading disclosure. This very clearly contravened jurisprudential understanding, and was completely different from the way other courts handled the same kind of case.

Finally, even when investors eventually get a court judgment or mediation result, the [subsequent] enforcement stage may also present difficulties. In the Daqing Lianyi case, China's first securities civil compensation lawsuit that went to final judgment, many scholars celebrated when the court issued a judgment for the plaintiffs. In reality, however, after the effectiveness of that judgment, very serious obstacles to enforcement arose for many different reasons, resulting in a failure to deliver compensation [to investors] in a timely way. In practice, there are many reasons for the enforcement problem. Sometimes there are objective reasons, such as the

[24] See ibid., 769–780. 'After Dong Fang Electronics was found guilty in a criminal judgment for falsifying earnings and accounting statements in December 2002, a total of 6,983 shareholders submitted civil claims, which were divided into a total of 2,716 suits, either as individual or joint actions. In 2007, the court hearing the case, the Intermediate [People's] Court of Qingdao [Municipality], completed all the suits, primarily through mediation'.

bankruptcy of the defendant company. Yet, more often we should look to the judiciary in finding the root causes [for these obstacles]. In sum, it is my hope that we can reassert the principle of appropriately inclining toward the protection of investors in the regulation of false and misleading disclosure through the above-described substantive designs and procedural ameliorations.

11 A Public Interest Litigation Mechanism

We should promote the practice of a public interest litigation system for false and misleading disclosure civil cases. Two aspects are 'new' with respect to the situation facing regulation of false and misleading disclosure. First, the [Chinese] capital markets have seen accelerated development from the time of initial regulation of false and misleading disclosure under the 1993 'Provisional Regulations on the Prohibition of Fraudulent Securities Behaviour' through to [and beyond] the [SPC's] 2003 Securities Misrepresentation Regulations. The degree of difficulty in regulating [this behaviour] is very high, as the different kinds of false and misleading disclosure we need to combat proliferate, and the methods used become ever more sophisticated. Second, China's capital markets presently face a profound opportunity for reformation, and many issues such as the powers and responsibilities of the [securities] regulatory agency and the repositioning of investors, etc. await a new disposition. In this environment, we ask that investors be given more systemic incentives so they can influence democratic rule of law reform of the capital markets at the same time as they seek their lawful remedies, and that with respect to this aspect of system change the regulatory departments are transitioned to a 'service' role. Specifically, the promotion of a public interest litigation system for false and misleading disclosure is the most evocative system design [responsive to] this new kind of change.

Presently, civil litigation on false or misleading disclosure is based in relevant judicial regulations, and limited to individual and common (*gongtong*)[25] lawsuits. For individual lawsuits, because the number of [aggrieved] investors is so large, when individual claims are pursued efficiency is low, and they create a waste of social resources. Moreover,

[25] I translate Vice President Wang's term as 'common' because the plaintiffs share the same basic underlying legal claim against the same defendant or defendants. Other English language terms conventionally used to translate this character set – such as 'group', 'collective', 'joint' or 'class action' – can have misleading implications.

because listed companies are so complex organisationally, the costs of suing a listed company for rights infringement are very high. In many cases, the amount of damages awarded to any individual investor will be small, so that the benefit obtainable from the lawsuit is not enough to compensate for the costs of the litigation or the litigation risk. Accordingly, individual investors who have suffered harm never want to bring an individual lawsuit against a listed company or the related responsible parties. And common lawsuits are never able to satisfy the legal claims of all the investors whose rights have been harmed. This is because in that type of lawsuit claimants must first register with the People's Court before they can be part of the common litigation. As retail investors in securities issuance transactions are very many and widely dispersed, the costs associated with assembling the common group in large scale lawsuits are exorbitant. Forcing injured parties to register with the court and select a [litigation] representative only increases the complexity and costs associated with this kind of litigation. Moreover, such common group lawsuits do not have wide effect because the litigation representative's claim in litigation is only effective with respect to the parties it represents who have registered to participate [in the common claim]. Thus, it is difficult to guaranty the rights and interests of those investors who have been harmed by the same false or misleading disclosure but who are not registered as participants in the common group lawsuit. In the new situation, reliance solely on individual and common lawsuits will not fulfil the twin aims of investor protection and the inhibiting of false and misleading disclosure, and will make difficult compensation of losses for injured parties and a re-imposition of normal securities market operation. Therefore it is imperative that we focus intently on the establishment of an economical public interest litigation system for false and misleading disclosure based upon the public interest litigation system provided for under the new Civil Procedure Law of the PRC. I believe that any future economical public interest litigation system for false and misleading disclosure should have the following characteristics: First, the scope of plaintiffs should be expanded beyond just those who have been injured, so that individuals and organisations without a direct interest in the legal claim can also enjoy the right to sue. This will evoke the idea that public interest litigation is a lawsuit for the public, and enhance the special character of 'public enforcement'. Second, the nature of these cases is multifaceted: there are private enforcement claims, where the injured party brings a lawsuit before a court; and there is public enforcement, where the competent regulatory agency sues in a court; and there are mixed claims cases, where one or more public enforcement bodies and private claimants together bring the lawsuit. Even though the China Securities Regulatory Commission (CSRC) does not have the right or power to sue on behalf of injured parties, when as the securities regulator it participates in the lawsuit, it can make the provision of evidence by the private claimants much easier. Therefore, the CSRC must have a role in the public interest litigation system in the securities sector, and where necessary be allowed to act as the plaintiff in lawsuits seeking compensation for damages. To bring about this transition in the role of the securities regulator, other than the CSRC, we can also establish an Investor Protection Association with the mission of protecting the rights and interests of investors to specifically handle matters related to the protection of retail investors. Finally the mediation principle should be employed, but in the normal case only with respect to individual claims and not those common claims on false or misleading disclosure that impact the national or public interest.

12 Conclusion

In the foregoing, I have offered some specific thoughts on how we might conform [the system for] false and misleading disclosure [cases]. I hope that these issues will be fully addressed in the process of amending the PRC Securities Law so as to fully protect the rights and interests of financial investors.

7

A Question of Class Action in China

XIANCHU ZHANG

1 Introduction

Public investor protection has been a serious concern in China's securities market. The recently initiated overhaul of the Securities Law[1] has triggered a new round of debate on introducing class action as a legal mechanism into China to improve the condition of investor protection. Although the idea was raised a long time ago and a promise was made in as early as 2005 by Shang Fulin, the then Chairman of the China Securities Regulatory Commission (CSRC) to establish such a system by 2010,[2] the latest draft amendment submitted to the national legislature seems to retreat from the commitment. Some experts have warned that failure to adopt class action rules this time would be self-defeating to the very purpose of the amendment.[3] This chapter will briefly examine the practice, policy and debate in this regard in the past two decades and reflect the difficulties and institutional challenges concerning the introduction.

1 Report, 'Draft Amendments to the Securities Law Goes to the Standing Committee of the National People's Congress in April with an Expectation to Be Adopted by the End of the Year', *Xinhua Net*, 10 March 2015. The amendments to the Securities Law, however, have been apparently delayed with change of the leadership of the CSRC due to the unstable market condition and the controversies on the reform measures. Xie Yu and Daniel Ren, 'Key Chinese Reform Delay: Securities Market Overhual Will Take Time, Says Watchdog Chief', South China Morning Post, 12 March 2016, www.scmp.com/news/china/policies-politics/article/1922396/key-chinese-reform-delay-securities-market-overhaul.

2 Shang Fulin, 'A Class Action System Expected to Be Established by 2010', Official Website of the Central Government of China, 3 November 2005, http://big5.gov.cn/gate/big5/www.gov.cn/ztzl/2005-11/03/content_90241.htm.

3 Cao Zhongming, 'Lack of Class Action Will Be Self-Defeating of the Securities Law Amendments', *Tengsun Caijing* (Tencent Finance), 16 March 2015, http://finance.qq.com/a/20150316/044271.htm.

2 The Market Conditions and the Legal Framework

The securities market in China has celebrated the twenty-fifth anniversary of its establishment in 1990. In this short period the market has experienced rapid developments and at the same time suffered from limited institutional capacity and political paradox in the economic transition. Today some distinctive Chinese characteristics are still well attached to the market, such as socialist ideology, government control, domination of state shares and lack of effective regulation and enforcement.[4]

For a long time the market has been labelled with different bad names, such as 'worse than a casino', to describe its rampant violations.[5] However, the goal of the party state to use the market as a political means to promote the socialist market economy, the close relations between the government and most listed companies, corruption and poor bureaucratic efficiency have led to failure of effective regulation and supervision in the market. Xiao Gang, the current CSRC Chairman, openly admitted that thus far two-thirds of more than 200 liability provisions embodied in the current market legal framework have never been used; in recent years, the CSRC took about 110 investigations each year, but only about half of them could be carried out smoothly with some criminal charges, and more than half of investigations ended with nothing settled.[6] According to a recent survey, the actual number of violation cases dealt with went down in the years 2007–2011, with some years seeing no investigations on market manipulation or inside trading at all, although violations have never gone down.[7] Hong sharply pointed out that 'the history of the securities market development is in fact a history of violations'.[8] This environment has rendered public investors very vulnerable victims with huge losses. According to a study, investors' total losses in 1991–2011 piled up to RMB 2 trillion.[9]

[4] Chao Deng, 'China's Stock Markets: Nearly 25 Years of Wild Swings', *The Wall Street Journal*, 31 July 2015, www.wsj.com/articles/chinas-stock-markets-nearly-25-years-of-wild-swings-1438328914.

[5] Stephen Green, *China's Stock Market* (The Economist Newspaper Ltd., London, 2003); and Comment, 'China's Securities Market: A Crazy Casino', *The Economist*, 26 May 2015.

[6] Xiao Gang, 'Supervision and Enforcement: The Corner Stone for Healthy Development of the Capital Market', *Qiushi* [Seeking Truth], 28 August 2013, 29–31.

[7] Miao Yinzhi, 'Critics of Government Led Regulation on the Securities Market in Comparison with Private Litigations', *Jiaoda Faxue* [SJTU Law Review], No. 1 (2015), 147–148.

[8] Wu Hong, *Zhongguo Zhengquan Shichang Fazhan de Falu Tiaokong* [Legal Regulation of Securities Market Development in China] (Law Press, Beijing, 2001), 255.

[9] Report, 'Average Loss of ￥40000 Each Investor in 2011', *Xinwen Chengbao* [Morning News], 26 April 2012.

Indeed, the government has repeatedly promised to enhance public investor protection. However, when come down to the legal remedies, the party state has insisted a bureaucrat led approach with hostile attitude to private enforcement actions.[10] Such bias has been well reflected in a series of policy and provisions of the Supreme People's Court (SPC) on dealing with mass litigations against securities market wrongdoings. In 2001, when several hundred investors filed their first bunch of lawsuits, the SPC rushed out its first circular in this regard to ask all the lower courts 'temporarily not to accept' any civil cases of insider trading, fraud and manipulation on securities market 'due to the constraints of the legislative and judicial conditions.'[11] This circular was harshly criticised as a political decision without legal ground at the cost of judicial justice.[12]

In fact, the Civil Procedure Law of 1991 set out two types of multiparty ligations: lawsuits with more than two persons on one side with the same subject matter, or same type of claim subject ('common litigation on the same subject') under Art. 54, where representatives may be selected with their litigation conducts binding all the parties on their side and a combined hearing may be ordered with the parties' consent; and lawsuits with representatives for mass litigations with an undetermined number of participants when the case is filed under Art. 55 ('mass litigations with representatives'). The people's court may ask potential participants to register their interest to join the litigation by public notice. In this type of mass litigation, the conduct of the representative will bind all the participants he represents, and the court decision will be effective on all the participants. Due to lack of detailed provision, practical application of these rules has met with confusion and controversy.

The SPC, however, has taken the position that mass litigations for compensation for securities market wrongdoings should be governed by Art. 54, instead of Art. 55, and treated as representative cases on the same subject. For example, the SPC stipulated in its 'Notice on Receiving Civil Tortious Cases Caused by False Statements in Securities Markets dated 15 January 2002' (hereafter '2002 Notice') that in dealing with claims for market misrepresentations, the people's courts should hear them in forms of either individual cases or representative cases on the same

10 Yinzhi, 'Critics of Government Led Regulation', 142–158.

11 The circular is dated 21 September 2001, http://baike.baidu.com/view/438807.htm.

12 Guo Feng, 'What Type of Value the Judiciary Should Pursue?', *Zhengquan Falu Pinglun* [Securities Law Review], Vol. 3 (2003), 319–322.

subject, but 'it was inappropriate to accept civil cases for false statements on the securities market in form of class action'.[13]

In its 'Certain Provisions on Trials of Cases for Civil Compensation Caused by False Statements in Securities Markets of 1 February 2003' (hereafter, 2003 Provisions) the SPC reaffirmed that plaintiffs could choose to file their claims as either individual cases or representative cases on the same subject.[14] However, the 2003 Provisions as the most applied judicial interpretation dealing with securities market misrepresentations have proved highly defective on several aspects. First, they very narrowly cover false statements in the securities market, leaving other wrongdoings punishable under the Securities Law, such as insider dealing and market manipulation, untouched.[15] Such a narrow approach has rendered many claims, even if the defendant had been found guilty of market crimes, dismissed by the people's courts due to lack of legal ground for civil compensation.[16] Secondly, for the political security, only intermediate people's courts at the capital cities of each province, cities specifically designated in the state plan and special economic zones are permitted to exercise their jurisdiction over compensation claims for false statements on the securities market.[17]

Thirdly, the 2003 Provisions only allow the plaintiffs to carry out their claims in form of single individual lawsuits or mass litigation with undetermined participants when the case is filed subject to judicial discretion for any combined trial.[18] As such, the American-style class action was not permitted. Finally, the SPC intended to hide the judiciary behind the administrative authorities before any case could be accepted. Art. 6 of the 2003 Provisions mandated a decision of either administrative or criminal penalty imposed by a government authority or criminal proceedings as a pre-condition for parties to initiate their civil compensation claims. This rule not only completely gives up the judicial independence to make its own determination on the evidence presented, but it also deprives public investors of the right to sue and the entitlement to

[13] The SPC Notice on Acceptance of Civil Tortious Cases Caused by False Statements on the Securities Market dated 15 January 2002.

[14] 2003 Provisions, Art. 12.

[15] For a recent discussion, see Li Weiqun and Wu Danqing, 'Confidence Construction of Small Investors on the Securities Market from the Perspective of Civil Compensation Litigations', *Zhengfa Xuekan* [Journal of Political Science and Law], No. 3 of 2013, 77–82.

[16] See 'Failure of the Civil Claims against Wang Jianzhong Due to Lack of Legal Basis', *Renmin Wang* [People's Net], 20 December 2011, http://finance.sina.com.cn/stock/yjdt/20111220/074011022470.shtml.

[17] 2003 Provisions, Art. 8. [18] Ibid., Arts. 11 and 12.

convince the court through introducing their own evidence in such civil actions. As a result, the provision may be used as a means of political control over cases at the costs of public investor protection and market integrity.[19]

3 Judicial Handling in Practice

The judicial preference is closely related to the political environment in China. In his working report of 1999, the then president of the SPC, Xiao Yang, called for properly handling various mass class litigations to safeguard social stability.[20] In 2005 he further pointed out that 'one important feature of civil trials presently was the upward trend of class actions and mass litigations to reach 538,941 among more than 4.3 million civil cases, or a 9.5 per cent increase from the number of the previous year'.[21] As a response to the party state's call to actively prevent and properly deal with mass incidents to maintain social and political stability,[22] the SPC warned all the local courts to deal with mass incidents very carefully. In addition to setting up early warning and emergency action procedures, the people's courts were required to make sure to settle the concerned mass disputes at the local level with a personal responsibility system.[23] Later an even more rigid policy to prioritise mediation over adjudication was adopted and enforced at the cost of the strict compliance with the law and due punishment to market violators.[24] Thus, the political sensitivity in dealing with the mass demands for right protection has overtaken the judicial justice in legal proceedings. As some scholars observed, despite the explicit provision of Art. 55 of the Civil Procedure Law on mass representative litigations, in practice it has been 'almost useless',[25] thus leading to a strange phenomenon in China that a large number of securities

19 Chen Zhiwu, 'Judicial Independence, Case Law and Shareholders' Right Protection', *Nanfang Zhoumo* [Southern Weekend], 28 February 2003, quoted from www.people.com.cn/GB/guandian/29/173/20030228/932865.html.

20 The Working Report of the SPC of 1999.

21 The Working Report of the SPC of 2005.

22 Report, 'The SPC: Actively Preventing and Properly Dealing with Massive Incidents', *Xinhua Wang* [Xinhua News Agency Net], 17 December 2004, available at http://news.sina.com.cn/c/2004-12-17/16304553950s.shtml.

23 Ibid.

24 Xianchu Zhang, 'Rethinking the Mediation Campaign', *Journal of Comparative Law*, Vol. X (2015), Issue 2, 44–64.

25 Yang Yanyan, 'Common Lawsuits or Mass Actions?', *Xiandai Faxue* [Modern Law Science], No. 2 of 2007, 101.

compensation claims cannot be settled through legal proceedings while the applicable rules are being disregarded in practice.[26]

According to a comprehensive study by Professor Howson of Michigan Law School on company law practice, even in Shanghai, which is one of the most developed cities, the heavy influence of political ideology had allowed the people's courts there limited judicial independence, sometimes even 'actually work[ing] against the law in the service of the state policy aims' while dealing with large state-owned or -controlled companies, including refusal to accept investors' cases on the ground of social stability priority.[27]

Various measures have been further developed at the local level to reduce the size of mass securities litigations. For instance, it is reported that in Shanghai, joint actions were limited to no more than nine persons, whereas in the Daqing Lianyi Case heard by Haerbin Intermediate People's Court against false statements in the securities market, 381 plaintiffs were forced to be divided into smaller groups of ten to twenty individuals,[28] which drove the litigation fee up to RMB 600,000.[29] In the Oriental Electronic case, the mass action of 6,989 plaintiffs against the same listed company was broken up into 2,716 small cases.[30] Moreover, such practice was later endorsed by the SPC. In its 'Guiding Opinions on Provision of Judicial Safeguards by the People's Courts for Preventing Financial Risks and Promotion of Financial Reform dated 10 February 2012', it was stated that civil cases concerning securities market violations should be properly handled to eliminate any hidden dangers of both market and social stability. In doing so, the people's courts at all levels shall consciously obey and serve the overall situation of the national development and enhance their coordination in centralised handling under the guidance of the upper level courts. In line with such policy, the All China Lawyers

[26] Yuan Dasong and Liao Yawen, 'On Construction of Public Interest Securities Litigations', *Jinrong Fuwu Fa Pinglun* [Financial Service Law Review], No. 6 of 2014, 266.

[27] Nicholas C. Howson, 'Judicial Independence and the Company Law in Shanghai Courts', in R. Peerenboom (ed.), *Judicial Independence in China: Lessons for Global Rule of Law Promotion* (Cambridge University Press, 2010), 134–153.

[28] Donald C. Clarke and Nicholas C. Howson, 'Pathway to Minority Shareholder Protection: Derivative Action in the People's Republic of China' in Dan W. Puchiak, Harald Baum, and Michael Ewing-Chow (eds.), *The Derivative Action in Asia: A Comparative and Functional Approach* (Cambridge University Press, 2012), 243–295.

[29] Liu Yunliang, 'Feasibility of Securities Civil Litigation with Representatives', *Fazhi Yanjiu* [Rule of Law Study], No. 7 (2013), 75.

[30] Song Yixin, 'Right Protection in Oriental Electronic Case', *Zhongguo Zhengquan Bao* [China Securities Daily], 27 November 2006.

Association as a quasi-government organisation has also mandated lawyers to accept the government supervision and guidance in all mass actions with more than ten plaintiffs.[31]

In practice the institutional barriers have in many occasions rendered refusal to accept private claims, long delay of the trials and judgments, and difficulties in execution of court judgments, which to a large extent explains why public investors have been reluctant to participate in mass litigations.[32] Moreover, under the current regime, quite a few other biased provisions need to be reformed, such as the short statute limitation of two years, placement of the onus of the burden proof on the plaintiffs, limitation on group size, and the grand total court fee charge on each individual claim rather than a fee based on the entire class claim.[33]

With respect to effectiveness of private enforcement, there seem to be different assessment results. According to Professor Robin Huang of the Chinese University of Hong Kong, although the number of private securities lawsuits is much smaller, the percentage of recovery in China is significantly higher than that in the United States. His conclusion was based on the sixty-five cases that had been decided in a ten-year period (2002–2011) in China. Plaintiffs received their recovery in fifty-nine cases out of the total sixty-five cases in his study with the mean and median of the compensation ratio to provable losses being as high as between 78.6–83.1 per cent. Compare that to the mean and median ratio of the settlement amount to provable losses being 13.5 per cent and 9.6 per cent before the Private Securities Litigation Reform Act was adopted and the even lower numbers to 12.3 per cent and 5.1 per cent, respectively, afterwards in the US.[34] This assessment, however, seems to provide an incomplete and inaccurate picture of private securities

[31] All China Lawyers Association, 'Guiding Opinion Regarding Lawyers Handling Cases of a Mass Nature dated 20 March 2006'; an English translation is available at www.cecc.gov/resources/legal-provisions/guiding-opinion-of-the-all-china-lawyers-association-regarding-lawyers.

[32] Tang Xin, 'Private Litigation and Securities Law Enforcement', *Qinghua faxue* [Tsinghua Law Review], No. 3 (2007), 92–117; and Yunliang, 'Feasibility of Securities Civil Litigation, 73–78.

[33] For a recent discussion in this regard, see Jin Sheng, 'Private Securities Litigation in China: Passive People's Courts and Weak Investor Protection', 26 *Bond Law Review* (2014), 94–147.

[34] Robin Hui Huang, 'Private Enforcement of Securities Law in China: A Ten-Year Retrospective and Empirical Assessment', 61 *The American Journal of Comparative Law* 757 (2013), 770–772.

litigation in China and thus may not be fairly comparable to the assessment results of the United States.

Despite controversies and criticism, class action has been one of the most powerful legal tools in the United States. According to a study, since enactment of the Private Securities Litigation Reform Act in 1995 (PSLRA) 4,226 federal securities class actions had been filed by 2014, with over 40 per cent of listed companies on major American exchanges being targeted[35] and the average value of private litigation settlements over 400 cases in 2009–2013 was about US $41 million.[36] The database of Securities Class Action Alert Service (SCAA) shows that 2,169 class actions were filed between January 1998 and June 2004. Of these actions, at least 851, or 39.2 per cent, reached final settlements, and 472, or 21.8 per cent, were dismissed on various grounds. It was argued on the basis of these litigation results that 'class actions are more effective in obtaining investor restitution recovering on average almost four times more than corresponding enforcement actions'.[37]

As reflected above, since China's adoption of the 2003 Provisions, most mass securities litigations failed due to various institutional obstacles. In the past decade, the average number of mass securities litigations for false market statements that were eventually accepted by the people's court is less than ten, with a mere total of 60 listed companies being targeted. The average conclusion time of these proceedings is more than five years.[38] A recent survey found that since 2001, indeed 16,000 investors, or 90 per cent of the plaintiffs of private securities actions, received compensations of total RMB 170 million in China. However, the number represented a 10 per cent participation rate of all the qualified victims, and all the claims filed only amounted to 5 per cent of the investors' total

[35] US Chamber of Commerce Institute for Legal Reform, *Economic Consequences: The Real Costs of U.S Securities Class Action Litigation* (US Chamber of Commerce Institute for Legal Reform, Washington, DC, 2014), 5.

[36] PricewaterhouseCoopers LLP, 'Are Changes on the Horizon? 2013 Securities Litigation Study', April 2014, 29, www.pwc.com/us/en/forensic-services/publications/2013-securities-litigation-study.html.

[37] Nishal R. Ramphal, 'The Role of Public and Private Litigation in the Enforcement of Securities Laws in the United States', (Rand, 2007), 4 and 24.

[38] Guo Silu and Li Xingli, 'Re-opening of Mass Litigation for Right Protection? A Review of Litigations on False Statements in the Past 10 Years', *Nanfang Zhoumo* [Southern Weekend], 24 January 2014, at www.infzm.com/content/97734; and Song Yixin, 'A Summary of Investor Rights Protection on Chinese Securities Market (2002–2011)', *Zhongguo Jiazhi* [China Value], 20 January 2012, www.chinavalue.net/Finance/Blog/2012-1-20/874623.aspx.

wealthy losses.[39] Such conditions are even well acknowledged by the state authority. In a working paper that appeared on the CSRC official website, the Hunan Branch of the CSRC reported that in 2002–2012, three of twelve listed companies that had been penalised by the CSRC for their misrepresentations on the market became the targets of lawsuits for compensation in eighty-seven cases with merely ninety-six plaintiffs. Four cases were eventually withdrawn. The remaining eighty-three, or more than 95 per cent of the litigations, ended in settlements with an average conclusion time of about 500 days and total compensations of RMB 1.748 million, or 52 per cent of the total claims. In other words, the final compensations received by plaintiffs in each case were just about RMB 20,000. As such, lack of interest to participate, high costs of litigation and less meaningful compensation are considered the major reasons of weak private enforcement actions.[40] As such, a limited number of 'successful' compensation cases may not truly reflect the huge losses suffered by public investors, the very low costs of market violation, or the much larger number of failed claims due to the institutional and political filtration.

In this environment, although Professor Huang believed that, like the US, 'China's securities civil cases are also lawyers-driven, and there is no shortage of entrepreneurial lawyers in China',[41] the harsh reality – which is completely different from the US – of political sensitivity, unfavourable rules, high initial and overhead costs, and the long course with great uncertainties have driven many lawyers away from the business. It is reported that, after a decade of struggling, there are less than ten specialised lawyers who were active in early year mass claims that still make their living on securities right litigations in China.[42]

4 Continued Debates and the Latest Draft

There has been an appeal for a long time to introduce a class action mechanism into China. Although the social, cultural and legal differences may inevitably require necessary adaptive adjustments, private enforcement,

39 Liu Wenliang, 'Lawyers Fighting for Rights through Thorns', *Zhengquan Shibao* [Securities Times], 19 October 2013.

40 Hunan Branch of the CSRC, 'Considerations and Suggestions on Securities Litigations for Civil Compensation', 3 August 2012, www.csrc.gov.cn/pub/hunan/xxfw/hngzjx/201208/t20120803_213469.htm.

41 Huang, 'Private Enforcement of Securities Law in China', 798.

42 Silu and Xingli, 'Re-opening of Mass Litigation'.

particularly class action, is considered by many scholars and experts to be an urgently needed institution in China to support healthy development of the entire market, not just the securities market.[43] The mechanism will not only provide public investors with much better protection and thus improve the overall market integrity and deterrence to violations, but also streamline civil procedural practice. Regardless of the final decision on the introduction, the people's courts need to improve the current regime and find their sensible solutions to some key concerns, including filing requirements, defining duties of the representatives of the mass/class, notice procedures, parties' right to opt out, permitted ways to finance mass litigation, binding effect of the judicial decision on the people concerned, and effective judicial supervision over the settlement and proceeding conducts.[44] In all these areas, valuable experience and reference can be drawn from the American style class action.

Moreover, the introduction of class action into China may also play a role in correcting the political imbalance by reducing the party state intervention. As Dr. Huang Tao of Shanghai Jiaotong University pointed out, for a long time in the securities market in China, investor protection was actually dealt with more by political means than judicial institutions.[45] As a result, legal protection to public investors may still be just a pleasant but empty promise unless the judiciary is empowered with the necessary legal tools and liberalised from political control.

In addition to the political concerns, scholars are also divided on the value and utility of class action as a legal institution in China. The views in favour of introduction have met some strong disagreement and resistance. For instance, Professor Xue Yonghui of China University of Political Science and Law argued that introduction of the American-style class action into China was neither feasible, nor necessary, even in

[43] Jiang Wei and Jia Changcun, 'On Class Action', (Part II), *Zhongguo Faxue China Legal Science*, No. 1 (1989), 103–113; Tang Weijian and Chen Wei, 'Gap Strategy: A Study on the Path to Transplant Class Action into China', *Falu yu Zhengzhi* [Law and Politics], No. 1 of 2008, 111–116; Zhang Wusheng, 'On Solving Mass Disputes – An Analysis with Reference to Class Action in the US', *Zhongguo Faxue* [China Legal Science], No. 3 of 2007, 24–26; and Yinzhi, 'Critics of Government Led Regulation', 142–145.

[44] For a brief discussion, see Janet C. Alexander, 'An Introduction to Class Action Procedure in the United States', Paper presented to the Conference on Debate over Group Litigation in Comparative Perspective on 22 July 2000, https://law.duke.edu/grouplit/papers/classactionalexander.pdf.

[45] Huang Tao, 'Why Are the Courts Not That Important? An Analysis on Government Regulations on the Securities Market in China', Conference paper presented to the Legal and Economic Form of China 2011, www.financiallaw.sjtu.edu.cn/Pages/Detail.aspx?id=251.

a long future, because the soil in the US for growing its class action system is quite different from that in China in all political, judicial and cultural aspects, and the current conditions of the judicial system in China cannot allow such risk taking.[46] Thus, given the conditions in China as a transitional economy, a more viable strategy for better investor protection should be to further strengthen public enforcement rather than private litigation.[47] Professor Huang believed it was the court's dysfunction, not the policy restrictions, that should be blamed, and he cast doubts on the approach to adopt the US-style class action.[48] One senior judge was quoted as saying the American class action was developed after the people's survival problems had been solved; in China, judicial priority should be given to the remedies to people's basic rights. Application of class action in China may only increase the difficulties and pressure on the judiciary.[49]

At this time the political complexity and the academic debates seem to lead to a compromise by seeking an alternative way to channel securities mass litigations in the course of overhauling the Securities Law. In 2012 the amendments to the Civil Procedure Law officially introduced public interest litigation as a new means to deal with conducts infringing public interests, such as environment pollution and consumer protection cases. Such claims can be initiated by the institutions or organisations stipulated by the law.[50]

On this basis, a new chapter entitled 'Protection of Investors' has been added to the new Draft Securities Law that has been submitted to the Standing Committee of the National People's Congress for the first reading in April 2015 where two provisions on investors' mass litigation are stipulated. Art. 175 allows investors protection institutions designated by the CSRC to file derivative litigation to protect the interest of the company concerned, and Art. 176 permits mass actions with representatives elected where investor protection institutions designated by the CSRC may participate in as a representative in both litigation and

[46] Xue Yonghui, 'Representative Action or Class Action – China's Choice on Mass Litigation Institutions', *Journal of China University of Political Science & Law*, No. 5 (2009), 103–115; also see Tang Xin, 'On Alternative Mechanism to Class Action', *Zhengquan Fayuan* [Securities Law Forum], Vol. 4 (2011), 174–200.

[47] Marlon A. Layton, 'Is Private Securities Litigation Essential for the Development of China's Stock Market?' 83 *New York University Law Review* 1948 (2008).

[48] Huang, 'Private Enforcement of Securities Law in China', 34.

[49] Quoted from Fan Yu, *Jituan Susong Wenti Yanjiu* [A Study of Mass Litigation Problems) (Beijing University Press, 2005), 429.

[50] Civil Procedure Law of 2012, Art. 55.

liquidation proceedings. The court's decisions on this type of litigations will bind all the investors concerned, except those who have made it clear they are not to be bound by such decisions in an express way.

After the first reading of the draft, some experts have openly expressed their disappointment in the draft's failure to include class action in the new law. They believe the current Arts. 175 and 176 will not be enough to provide public investors with sufficient legal protection and address to the institutional deficiency.[51] Professor Wu Xiaoqiu of People's University further emphasises the point that, without class action, investor protection in China will still be just a lip service.[52]

The current draft, on the one hand, may have some positive implications since the CSRC or CSRC-designated institutions may bring in more political strength and influence and have stronger financial capacity in the legal proceedings so as to correct the current market imbalance and enable public investors to better fight for their lawful interests.[53] On the other hand the current draft raises questions. Thus far, the provision of Art. 176 is still very vague without sufficient procedural and substantive details. Moreover, to include public interest to securities litigation by blurring the public and private boundary may cause new problems because the logic and purposes of the two types of litigation may not be the same. For example, in private enforcement, reasonable investors may dispose their rights in a sensible way, including rejection or acceptance of compromises according to their conditions and strategies, whereas public interest institutions may have their own prioritised goals. For example, the first public interest litigation after the amendment to the Environment Law in 2014 initiated by the Volunteers Association of Environment Protection of Dalian City against China National Petroleum Corporation for a disastrous accident in the city ended with a settlement of RMB 200 million without any appeal. Although the proceedings were delayed for four years and the compensation is far below the total claims of RMB 645 million, the associate held that its goal in calling public attention had been realised.[54] In this regard, it should be further noted that the draft

[51] Zhongming, 'Lack of Class Action Will Be Self-Defeating'.

[52] Report, 'Without Class Action Investor Protection Is Just a Lip Service', *Xin Jing Bao* [Beijing News], 16 March 2015, at B04.

[53] Liu Shuilin and Gao Feng, 'Theoretical Basis to Construct a System of Public Interest Securities Litigations', *Shanghai Caijing Daxue Xuebao* [Journal of Shanghai University of Finance and Economics], No. 6 of 2014, 81–96.

[54] Lucy Hormby, 'CNPC Settles China Oil Spill Lawsuit', *Financial Times*, 26 June 2015, www.ft.com/content/035cdc42-1bca-11e5-8201-cbdb03d71480.

seems again to fail to stipulate any specific provision for establishing investors' own private rights protection organisation, although this has been demanded almost from the very beginning of enactment of the first Securities Law in China since 1998[55] and was promised by the Central Government in 2013 as a direction to explore.[56]

Besides the technical details, the current draft has clearly reflected some institutional challenges facing the party state to modernise the securities law of the country. First, Art. 176 seems intended to add official flavours to the current mass litigation regime since freedom of association in China is still highly politically sensitive;[57] as a result the administrative designation would inevitably, to a certain extent, subject the institutions concerned to the CSRC's control or influence. In 2011 an Investor Protection Bureau in charge of coordination, organisation and supervision of investor protection activities and pushing forward legal remedies for victims of market violations was established in the CSRC.[58] Thus, with the expectation for the bureau to play a more active role in private securities litigations, the government-led approach, directly or indirectly, may continue in securities market enforcement despite its poor record thus far.

Secondly, the judicial independence and activism still seemed tested in the rounds of comprehensive reforms since 2012 with the goals to let the market play a decisive role and improvement of property right protection.[59] In this regard the judiciary is facing challenges from at least two aspects: to delink the adjudication from the political ideology and to modernise the judicial mechanisms and philosophy according to the needs and conditions of China with open-minded reference to experiences of other market economies. For instance, as early as 1946 a judge in the US made it clear that 'there was a private right of action under Rule 10b-5 ... in view of the general purpose of the Act the mere

[55] Song Yixin, 'Draft Amendments to the Securities Law Provides Investors with Insufficient Protection and Should Be Enhanced from Six Aspects', *Xinhua Wang* (Xinhua News Net), 26 May 2005, http://news.xinhuanet.com/stock/2005-05/26/content_3004029.htm.

[56] Sec. 9 of 'Opinions on Further Enhancement of Small Investors' Interest Protection issued by the General Office of the State Council on 25 December 2013'.

[57] Chris King-Chi Chan, 'Promotion of Freedom of Association in China? Putting Transnational Corporate Social Responsibility into a National Context', *Journal of Comparative Asian Development*, Issue 1 of 2013, 6–34.

[58] See the mission statement on the CSRC Website, www.csrc.gov.cn/pub/newsite/tzzbhj/.

[59] The Decision of the Central Committee of the Communist Party of China on Certain Major Issues Concerning Comprehensively Deepening Reform dated 12 November 2013.

omission of an express provision for civil liabilities is not sufficient to negate what the general law implies'.[60] This view was later supported in a decision of the Supreme Court where Justice Clark stated that while the language of the 1934 act made no specific reference to a private right of action, 'It is the duty of the court to be alert to provide such remedies as are necessary to make effective the congressional purpose'.[61] Later the US Supreme Court further developed its judicial doctrine, such as the theory of 'fraud on the market', to enable investors to seek civil compensations by way of class actions.[62] Although the common law approach may not be squarely copied to China, the professional philosophy could be shared to certain extent in promoting social and market justice.

Last but not least, the real institutional question facing the party state and the legislature in the present securities law amendment is to what extent in China, as a socialist market economy, can private ownership and rights be respected, protected and tolerated. In a sense, the socialist market economy itself is a concept with inherent contradiction.[63] After the paradoxical implementation for two decades, the tension between the socialist ideology and governance, on the one hand, and the market demands, on the other, has reached a critical stage. The securities market in China alone has thus far attracted more than 100 million investors[64] who have become not only stock owners with legitimate concerns with their property rights and investment returns, but also an increasingly political force to demand social justice and legal protection. This development may have some profound implications similar to the path leading to the victory of capitalism over the feudal monarchy and the downfall of the former Soviet Union, where property rights and related institutions were the most crucial factors.[65] As such,

[60] *Kardon* v. *National Gypsum Co.*, 69 F. Supp. 512 (1946), per Judge Kirkpatrick.

[61] *J. I. Case Co.* v. *Borak*, 377 U.S. 425 (1946).

[62] *Basic Inc.* v. *Levinson*, 485 U.S. 224 (1988); and *Halliburton Co.* v. *Eric P. John Fund. Inc. (Halliburton II)*, 134 S. Ct. 2398 (2014).

[63] Robert Well, 'Red Cat, White Cat: China and the Contradictions of "Socialist Market Economy"', *Monthly Review Press* (1996); and Edward Cody, 'China Confronts Contradiction between Marxism and Market', *Washington Post*, 5 December 2005, www.washingtonpost.com/wp-dyn/content/article/2005/12/04/AR2005120400982.html.

[64] By the end of 2014, the effective stock investment accounts opened in China exceeded 140 million. Wu Xiaoqiu, 'Deepening Reform and Further Opening to Promoting Healthy Development of Securities Market in China', *Zhongguo Renda Wang* [The Website of the National People's Congress], 4 January 2015, www.npc.gov.cn/npc/xinwen/2015-01/04/content_1892418.htm.

[65] James Fulcher, *Capitalism: A Very Short Introduction* (Oxford University Press, 2004); and Hans-Hermann Hoppe, *A Theory of Socialism and Capitalism* (The Ludwig von Mises Institute, 2010).

control of political threat and using the tools borrowed from capitalist countries to maintain economic growth, which has been the most important legitimacy justification for the party state, have to be carefully balanced. As Professor Wu recently pointed out, at this moment the major obstacle to the introduction of class action is still more focussed on worries about political stability than market integrity.[66]

5 Concluding Remarks

After rapid developments and expansion of the securities market for twenty-five years, the party state is under increasingly built-up pressures to fulfil its promise to improve investor protection. In the course of the new round of reforms and overhauling the Securities Law of China, private enforcement in the form of class action is gaining momentum as an effective and powerful means of investor protection. However, thus far the introduction still faces a great deal of uncertainties. In addition to the technical details, the potential political and social implications have apparently cautioned the party state with its profound institutional challenges. From this perspective, the answer to the question of introducing class action into China may be considered as a significant test of the seriousness of the party state commitment to a real market economy.

[66] Report, 'Without Class Action'.

8

Private Enforcement of Securities Law in China

Past, Present and Future

ROBIN HUI HUANG

1 Introduction

China is currently considering a fundamental reform of its regulatory regime for securities offerings, commonly referred to as the Registration Reform (*Zhucezhi Gaige*), under which the existing merits-review regulation will switch to the disclosure-based regulation as adopted in many developed markets overseas. The central tenet of the disclosure-based regulation is that regulation is affected not by direct governmental intervention in the form of merits tests but by requiring adequate information disclosure from the issuer and imposing sanctions for misrepresentations. As I have argued before, therefore, the success of the reform will depend on the development of relevant market and institutional preconditions, one of which is the liability regime for securities misrepresentations.[1]

China has set up a liability regime for securities misconduct since the early stage of the development of its securities market. There are generally three types of legal liability, namely criminal liability, administrative liability and civil liability. Under the current 2005 Securities Law, if the contravention of the Securities Law is serious enough to constitute a crime, criminal liability shall be pursued.[2] The administrative liability is imposed by the regulator, namely the China Securities Regulatory Commission (CSRC). These two types of legal liability are obtained through proceedings initiated by bodies with public power, which is collectively called public enforcement.

[1] Robin Hui Huang, 'The Regulation of Securities Offerings in China: Reconsidering the Merit Review Element in Light of the Global Financial Crisis', 41(10) *Hong Kong Law Journal* 261 (2011).

[2] Zhonghua Renming Gongheguo Zhenquan Fa [Securities Law of the People's Republic of China] (promulgated on 29 December 1998 and effective from 1 July 1999, amended in 2004, 2005 and 2013) (2005 Securities Law), Article 193. Unless indicated otherwise, reference to Securities Law is to the 2005 Securities Law.

Finally, the person committing misrepresentation will also be subject to civil liability in private civil suits, which are brought by aggrieved investors seeking compensation. Private securities litigation is commonly known as private enforcement, as opposed to public enforcement as noted above. There has been an ongoing debate as to the relative importance of private enforcement versus public enforcement of investor protection laws.[3] What is clear though is that the two forms of law enforcement have their own strengths and weaknesses. For instance, public enforcement has advantages vis-à-vis private enforcement in terms of the power to investigate and impose severe penalties. Private enforcement, however, has its own strengths. To begin with, while the function of deterring misconduct is common to both public and private enforcement, private enforcement also has the important function of compensating investors, which public enforcement usually cannot perform. Further, the regulator is subject to resource constraints and incentive issues in dealing with securities fraud, whereas investors – often driven by lawyers who are dubbed 'private attorneys general' – are relatively well resourced and well incentivised in pursuing relevant cases. In sum, public enforcement and private enforcement are both important, and they complement each other in setting up a comprehensive and effective system of legal liability for securities fraud.

As with other civil law countries, China has traditionally relied on public enforcement of securities law. Only in recent years has China started utilising private enforcement of securities law in the form of civil suits brought by investors. This chapter will focus on private securities litigation in China, examining its past and present situation as well as the future direction in which it is likely to develop.

2 The Legal Framework for Civil Liability

2.1 Historical Development

Under China's first securities law, namely the 1998 Securities Law, while civil liability for market misconduct like misrepresentation was provided for in principle, there were no detailed provisions to implement the

[3] See e.g. LLSV, 'What Works in Securities Laws?', 61 *Journal of Finance* 20 (2006) (arguing that compared with private enforcement, the importance of public enforcement is at best modest); cf Howell E. Jackson and Mark J. Roe, 'Public and Private Enforcement of Securities Laws: Resources-Based Evidence', 93 *Journal of Financial Economics* 207 (2009) (finding that public enforcement is more important than private liability rules in explaining financial market outcomes around the world).

remedy. Indeed, the law was silent on relevant issues concerning civil liability, such as who is the eligible plaintiff, how to calculate the damages and how to bring the suit, thus rendering the private civil liability provision virtually a dead letter. To be sure, the statutory remedies in the Securities Law are not exhaustive, and those committing misrepresentation could be theoretically based on the general contract law or on the tort regime. However, due to the special nature of on-market securities transactions, for example, being impersonal and anonymous, it is extremely difficult, if not impossible, particularly in terms of the causation and reliance requirement, to bring private civil suits on those conventional grounds.

The above problem was well illustrated in the 1998 case of *Liu Zhongmin* v. *Bohai Group*, which is widely regarded as the first ever securities civil case in China. There, the court rejected the plaintiff's claim to compensation on the grounds that the plaintiff failed to prove the causal link between his trading loss and the defendant's misrepresentation. Although the case was not successful, its significance should not be underestimated. For the very first time, Chinese investors tried to vindicate their rights in the courtroom, showing the potential utility of this legal mechanism as well as the problems with the then prevailing Chinese law in this area. The case marked the beginning of the history of private securities litigation in China, serving as a wake-up call for China to consider the value of private enforcement of securities law.

The simmering development of China's legal regime for private securities litigation finally reached its boiling point in 2001. As was the case in many overseas markets such as the US at that time, there was a sudden outburst of corporate scandals on the Chinese securities market. As a result, many Chinese investors suffered large losses, and a spate of civil cases were filed for compensation across the nation. It was against this backdrop that the Supreme People's Court (SPC) issued three important circulars on private securities litigation in 2001, 2002 and 2003 respectively.

On 21 September 2001, the SPC issued the first circular (hereinafter the SPC First Circular), instructing China's courts not to accept civil compensation claims over securities market misconduct, on the grounds that the courts were not ready to hear such cases due to 'legislative and judicial limitations at the moment'.[4] This circular was vehemently

[4] Zuigao Renmin Fayuan Guanyu she Zhengquan Minshi Peichang Anjian Zan Buyu Shouli de Tongzhi [The Notice of the Supreme People's Court on Temporary Refusal of Filings of Securities-Related Civil Compensation Cases] (21 September 2001).

criticised by many, and the public pressure forced the SPC to change its position less than four months later. On 15 January 2002, the SPC issued its second circular (hereinafter the SPC Second Circular), to lift the restriction on civil cases arising from misrepresentation, but not those arising from other forms of market misconduct such as insider trading and market manipulation.[5] The SPC Second Circular has only five brief provisions and leaves unaddressed many issues concerning the bringing and hearing of civil compensation suits. Hence, although some cases were accepted according to this second circular, they were all stayed pending further guidance from the SPC. On 9 January 2003, the SPC circulated the eagerly awaited third instrument (hereinafter the SPC Third Circular), which, while not without problems, contains thirty-seven detailed provisions to set up a relatively complete legal framework for private securities litigation arising from misrepresentation in China.[6]

In the 2005 overhaul of the Securities Law, the legal basis for civil suits on securities misrepresentation was written into the statute, with all detailed aspects left in the SPC Third Circular. This is a significant development, because in the hierarchy of the Chinese legislative system, the Securities Law as a national law enjoys a much higher level of legal force than the rules issued by the CSRC, thereby providing a more solid foundation for private securities litigation over misrepresentation in China. Since detailed rules are still to be found in the SPC Third Circular, it remains the centrepiece of China's legal regime for private securities litigation and, therefore, the focus of analysis in this chapter.

2.2 *Key Elements of the Current Law*

The SPC Third Circular has attracted intense attention both inside and outside China. As detailed accounts of the content of the SPC Third Circular have been provided elsewhere,[7] only a brief discussion of its key

[5] Zuigao Renmin Fayuan Guanyu Shouli Zhengquan Shichang Yin Xujiachengshu Yinfa de Minshi Qinquan Jiufen Anjian Youguan Wenti de Tongzhi [The Notice of the Supreme People's Court on Relevant Issues of Filing of Civil Tort Dispute Cases Arising from Misrepresentation on the Securities Market] (15 January 2012).

[6] Zuigao Renmin Fayuan Guanyu Shenli Zhengquan Shichang Yin Xujia Chenshu Yinfa De Minshi Peichang Anjian De Ruogan Guiding [Provisions of the Supreme People's Court Concerning the Acceptance and Trial of Civil Compensation Securities Suits Involving Misrepresentation] (effective from 1 February 2003).

[7] Robin Hui Huang, *Securities and Capital Markets Law in China* (Oxford University Press, 2014), Chapter 6.

elements is offered below to set the stage for further analysis in the parts that follow.

First, although the SPC bowed to public pressure to open the door to private securities litigation, it is at best a half-opened door in the sense that private securities litigation is limited to misrepresentation only. Investors harmed by other forms of market misconduct, such as insider trading and market manipulation, cannot bring civil cases under the SPC Third Circular.[8] Hence, this chapter will be focused on securities civil cases arising from misrepresentation under the SPC Third Circular.

Second, the purpose of private securities litigation in China is explicitly stated to be compensatory. The official Chinese term used in the SPC Third Circular to refer to 'private securities litigation' literally means 'securities civil *compensation* cases' (*Zhengquan Minshi Peichang Anjian*), and the rules contained in the SPC Third Circular all serve to clarify how investors can be awarded compensation. Hence, one of the main inquiries of this paper is to examine the extent to which the SPC Third Circular has achieved its stated mission of generating meaningful compensation to aggrieved investors.

Third, the SPC Third Circular contains a rather complete set of rules to cover both substantive and procedural issues. For instance, it stipulates the different types of misrepresentation,[9] the scope of eligible plaintiffs,[10] a list of potential defendants,[11] the availability of defences,[12] the rebuttable presumption of causation and reliance,[13] the calculation of damages,[14] and the territorial jurisdiction rule under which jurisdiction goes to the place where the issuer is established.[15] This set of rules provides very useful guidelines for bringing and hearing private securities cases in China.

Fourth, a unique feature of the SPC Third Circular is the procedural prerequisite that in order to bring a securities civil suit, there must be

[8] On 30 May 2007, a vice president of the SPC stated at a national conference that courts should also accept securities civil cases arising from insider trading and market manipulation. A very small number of such cases have since been brought, but most of them, if not all, are rejected or withdrawn for lack of detailed rules from the SPC as to how to hear them. On 30 September 2015, several civil cases arising from the insider trading of Everbright Securities were adjudicated as a batch at the Second Intermediate Court of Shanghai, and six plaintiffs won their cases. This is the first time that civil cases against insider trading have achieved success in China. In hearing the cases, the court applied by way of analogy the 2003 SPC Circular.

[9] SPC Third Circular, Article 17.

[10] SPC Third Circular, Articles 2, 3.

[11] SPC Third Circular, Article 7.

[12] SPC Third Circular, Articles 21–25.

[13] SPC Third Circular, Articles 18, 19.

[14] SPC Third Circular, Articles 29–35.

[15] SPC Third Circular, Article 9.

a prior criminal judgment or administrative sanction by the relevant bodies, notably the CSRC.[16] This prerequisite has been a subject of controversy ever since the SPC Third Circular was issued. The SPC's rationale behind the prerequisite is that the courts lack the resources and expertise needed to decide the complicated question of whether there is indeed misrepresentation; rather, the relevant specialised regulatory bodies, notably the CSRC, would be better equipped to handle that issue. Critics argue, however, that the prerequisite unduly limits the scope of private securities litigation – investors might not be able to bring suits in the event that regulatory bodies fail to take appropriate action due to factors like limited resources and even corruption problems. Which side of the debate has more merit? Should the procedural requisite be abolished? These questions will be answered in light of my empirical findings.

Last but not least, China does not allow investors to bring private securities suits in the form of a class action (*jituan susong*); rather, investors can sue either in the form of individual action (*dandu susong*) or joint action (*gongtong susong*). The court can, depending on the circumstances, decide whether the civil suit should be filed as an individual or a joint action: if one or both parties to individual actions consist of two or more persons and the object of the action is the same or in the same category – as is often the case in securities civil suits – the court can, with the consent of the parties, combine the individual actions into a joint action. Are the individual action and joint action effective forms of litigation for securities civil cases? Should China adopt the US-style class action? This chapter attempts to answer these questions from a comparative perspective.

3 Empirical Findings

As discussed above, the SPC Third Circular contains a quite complete set of rules to cover both substantive and procedural issues in relation to private securities litigation. For instance, it stipulates the types of misrepresentation activities, the scope of eligible plaintiffs, a list of potential defendants, the availability of defences, the rebuttable presumption of causation and reliance, the calculation of damages, and the territorial jurisdiction rule under which jurisdiction goes to the place where the issuer is established. This set of rules provides very useful guidance on the bringing and hearing of private securities action in China.

[16] SPC Third Circular, Article 6.

Table 8.1 *Civil cases arising from securities misrepresentation, 2002–2011*

	2002	2003	2004	2005	2006	2007	2008	2009	2010	2011
Cases	0	7	7	5	9	5	6	9	7	10

It is worth noting that the main purpose of private securities litigation in China is explicitly stated to be compensatory. The official Chinese term used in the SPC Third Circular to refer to private securities litigation literally means 'civil *compensation* cases' (*Minshi Peichang Anjian*), and the rules contained in the SPC Third Circular all serve to clarify how investors get compensation. Hence, when evaluating the efficacy of the law governing private securities litigation in China, it is important to examine the extent to which the SPC Third Circular has achieved its stated mission of generating meaningful compensation to aggrieved investors. To this end, this author has recently conducted an empirical study by looking at the relevant cases brought during the first decade since private securities litigation was formally permitted in 2002.[17]

3.1 How Popular Is Private Securities Litigation in China?

The research located a total of sixty-five securities civil cases during the period under study. Table 8.1 shows the temporal distribution of cases. There have been some fluctuations in the number of cases along the ten-year research period, but the number has stayed within a range of five to ten. The numbers are generally too low for statistical analysis, and no trend is discernible over time.

As shown above, a total of sixty-five securities civil cases arising from misrepresentation have been found during the period from 2002 to 2011. This is a rather modest number given the high incidence of misrepresentation in China's securities market. Why has the number of cases been so small?

3.1.1 Is the Procedural Prerequisite to Blame?

The prime suspect is the procedural prerequisite; that is, bringing a civil compensation action requires a prior criminal judgment or administrative

[17] Robin Hui Huang, 'Private Enforcement of Securities Law in China: A Ten-year Retrospective and Empirical Assessment', 61(4) *American Journal of Comparative Law* 757 (2013).

sanction. Many commentators have argued that the procedural prerequisite may unduly limit the number of securities civil suits. Intuitively, this argument sounds appealing, as the prerequisite naturally has some screening effect, but the deeper question is whether the prerequisite is in fact the primary reason for the small number of cases. I therefore tested the above hypothesis by comparing the number of eligible civil cases that could have been filed to the number of civil cases that have actually been filed.

After careful calculation, the total number of eligible suits was found to be 253. This means that the sixty-five securities civil suits brought represent only about 25.7 per cent of all the eligible criminal/administrative sanctions which may lead to securities civil suits. To be sure, one cannot expect all eligible cases to be actually brought, but the above suing rate is truly extraordinary. It is fair to say that even within the boundaries set by the procedural prerequisite, many more securities civil suits could have been brought. Hence, the procedural prerequisite does not seem to be the primary factor contributing to the small number of securities civil suits.

3.1.2 Is There a Lack of Entrepreneurial Lawyers?

If a securities civil case is eligible to be filed but is not, one possible explanation could be the lack of incentive to litigate on the part of the plaintiff. From a law and economics perspective, a case will not be brought if, viewed *ex ante*, the cost of litigation exceeds the result of the amount of compensation discounted by the possibility of success. A distinctive feature of securities civil suits is 'large scale, small claim', that is, overall a large number of investors are injured by the misrepresentation, but individually the injury to each of the investors is small. Hence, most investor plaintiffs would not initiate any action as the costs may well exceed the benefits derived from the litigation. It is in this situation that entrepreneurial lawyers could play a significant role.

The US experience illustrates rather well the role of entrepreneurial lawyers. In the United States, there are many securities civil cases in form of class action, and entrepreneurial lawyers are believed to be one of the main reasons.[18] Indeed, due to the free-rider and other collective action problems that make individual suits not cost-effective, the

[18] See, e.g. John C. Coffee, Jr., 'Rescuing the Private Attorney General: Why the Model of the Lawyer as Bounty Hunter Is Not Working', 42 MD. L. REV. 215 (1983); Jonathan R. Macey and Geoffrey P. Miller, 'The Plaintiffs' Attorney's Role in Class Action and Derivative Litigation: Economic Analysis and Recommendations for Reform', 58 (1) U. CHI. L. REV. 1 (1991).

entrepreneurial lawyers are actually the driving force behind securities class actions. A key element in this process is the contingency fee system under which the legal fees are contingent on the case being successfully litigated or settled. That is, the entrepreneurial lawyer usually bears the costs of litigation, and in case of success withholds a percentage of the amount recovered as his fee. This provides an incentive for the investor plaintiffs, because they will not incur any financial risk, no matter how the case ends up, yet could gain something, however small it might be, in the event of a successful outcome.

The contingency fee system is more commonly known as 'risk agency fee' (*fengxian daili Shoufei*) in China, and despite some ambiguity over the law in the books, it has long been used in the context of securities civil actions. The availability of the risk agency fee has greatly facilitated the bringing of securities civil suits, and has led to the emergence of many entrepreneurial lawyers in China, who are also called securities rights lawyers (*zhengquan weiquan lvshi*). Hence, there is no shortage of entrepreneurial lawyers in China. This then makes it even more interesting to ask why the suing rate is so low. Why have those entrepreneurial lawyers let almost seventy-five percent of eligible cases slip through their fingers?

3.1.3 It Is about the Court, Stupid

In order to solve the puzzle over the exceedingly low suing rate, one needs to look at the possible problems in the litigation process itself. If the judicial process were fair and efficient, most, if not all, securities civil cases would present very good litigation opportunities: the civil case could simply piggyback on the criminal judgment or administrative penalty decision which has already established the factual finding of wrongdoing, and the company's misrepresentation would therefore be an easy target.

The court, however, has behaved very unsatisfactorily at almost every stage of the judicial process in handling securities civil cases. To start with, the court appears to have been very inhospitable in accepting securities civil cases. Second, even if a securities civil case is accepted, the time the court takes to hear the case is often so long as to make the suit unattractive. Finally, according to interviews with plaintiffs' lawyers and judges, even if the plaintiffs receive the long-awaited judgment in their favour, they may still face uncertain enforcement prospects. A combination of these problems may be responsible for the low number of securities civil cases.

Table 8.2 *The ratio of compensation amounts to provable losses*

	Mean	Median
Ratio	78.6%	83.1%

3.2 *How Compensatory Is Private Securities Litigation in China?*

As discussed earlier, the main purpose of securities civil action in China is to provide compensation to the aggrieved investors; to what extent has this purpose been fulfilled? There are three important findings. While a majority of cases are concluded through court-facilitated mediation (*tiao jie*) or out-of-court settlement (*he jie*), there are a good number of cases that have gone through adjudication (*pan jue*). Then, in fifty-nine cases, or about 90.7 per cent of the total sixty-five cases under study, the plaintiff has successfully received recovery, and last but not least, the ratio of compensation amounts to provable losses is very high, as shown in the table below.

This rate of recovery is impressive by any standard and certainly compares very favourably with overseas data. In the United States for instance, research shows that the sums recovered in securities private suits represent a small fraction of provable losses. In a 2006 paper, Professors Cox and Thomas found that the mean and median of the ratio of settlement amount to provable losses are 13.5 per cent and 9.6 per cent in the pre-PSLRA (Private Securities Litigation Reform Act) period, and the situation in the post-PSLRA is even worse, with the mean and median dropping to 12.3 per cent and 5.1 per cent respectively.[19] Why is the recovery rate so high? Why can't the defendant pay less?

3.2.1 The Piggyback Effect

In contrast with the United States, where the fact-finding of misrepresentation is often a difficult task, it is not an issue at all for the civil court in China, thanks to the piggyback effect – that is, securities civil cases can be brought only after there has been a criminal or administrative sanction regarding misrepresentation, so the civil court can simply refer to the fact-finding in the prerequisite procedure.

[19] James D. Cox and Randall S. Thomas, 'Does the Plaintiff Matter? An Empirical Analysis of Lead Plaintiffs in Securities Class Actions', 106 COLUM. L. REV. 1537 (2006), 1627.

3.2.2 Clear Rules Governing Civil Claims

Apart from the general fact-finding of misrepresentation, there are other difficult issues specific to the filing of securities civil suits, including the establishment of reliance or causation and the measure of damages. As discussed earlier, the SPC Third Circular sets out detailed rules on these issues. Although these rules have been criticised by some commentators for their rigidity, they are clear and certain so that parties to the dispute are able to predict the outcome of the suit, including the amount of compensation, with a fair degree of precision. In the United States, for instance, a variety of methods to assess damages has been used, and it is hard to predict which method will be adopted in a given case. This uncertainty adds to the difficulty in predicting the litigation outcome, thereby making it more likely for the plaintiff to accept lower compensation.

3.2.3 Weak Incentives to Defend

In general, compared to corporate/entity liability, personal/individual liability generates more deterrence.[20] Individual liability has a direct impact on the person to be punished and usually meets more strenuous opposition. Hence, if individuals such as directors get sued and also need to pay out of their own funds in a securities civil action (in China, it is very rare for public companies to carry directors' and officers' liability insurance), they have a stronger incentive to fight against the civil claims. Plainly, this would affect the outcome of the suit.

It is found that corporate insiders, namely, individuals such as directors and senior management personnel, were listed as co-defendants alongside the listed company in a small minority of cases. This stands in stark contrast with the US usage, where corporate insiders almost always are named as co-defendants. As they are not listed as defendants in most cases, Chinese corporate insiders have less incentive to care about the final results of the cases. Even in those cases where corporate insiders are originally sued as co-defendants, the plaintiffs almost invariably drop the cases against them in the process of a settlement. It may well be that Chinese corporate insiders prefer to offer a favourable settlement in exchange for having the cases against them dropped.

The incentive of corporate insiders to defend against the civil suits may be further reduced by the fact that for various reasons, the costs of

[20] See John C. Coffee, Jr., 'Reforming the Securities Class Action: An Essay on Deterrence and its Implementation', 106 Colum. L. Rev. 1534 (2006).

securities civil actions are frequently not borne by the listed company, but by its controlling shareholder. As securities civil suits do not have direct financial impact on the listed company itself, corporate insiders are under less pressure to worry about the amount of payment.

4 The Way Forward

4.1 *Should the Procedural Prerequisite Be Abolished?*

The procedural prerequisite rule has been a subject of heated debate ever since the SPC Third Circular was issued. It has been severely criticised as unduly limiting the scope of securities civil litigation in China. First, the prerequisite, it is argued, can leave investors without remedy if the criminal court or relevant administrative bodies, for whatever reason, fail to address the underlying misrepresentation.[21] Indeed, both the courts and regulators in China may be prevented from effectively responding to securities frauds due to a variety of reasons, such as lack of independence, bureaucratic inefficiency, inadequate enforcement resources, regulatory capture or outright corruption. A second line of attack upon the prerequisite is directed to the difference in standards of proof between civil proceedings and criminal/administrative proceedings. For instance, the criminal standard of proof, being 'beyond reasonable doubt', is significantly higher than that for civil proceedings, which is the balance of probabilities; that is, the evidence of the party to win is 'more forceful'. Yet, the prerequisite essentially requires the criminal standard of proof for civil cases and thus may deprive investors of civil claims arising from securities frauds which fall short of constituting a crime.[22]

On the other hand, proponents of the prerequisite argue that it is necessary for the time being for the following reasons. First, without the prerequisite, there could be a flood of private securities litigation which would disturb the stable development of the securities markets and overstretch the limited resources of China's judicial system. Second,

[21] Guiping Lu, 'Private Enforcement of Securities Fraud Law in China: A Critique of the Supreme People's Court 2003 Provisions Concerning Private Securities Litigation', 12 *Pacific Rim Law and Policy Journal* 795 (2003), 800; Sanzhu Zhu, *Securities Dispute Resolution in China* (Ashgate Publishing, 2007), 167.

[22] The standard of proof for administrative proceedings in China seems to be flexible, and it can range from the civil standard to criminal standard, depending on the nature of the administrative case. See Xiangjun Kong, *Administrative Litigation Evidence Rules and Legal Applications* (Law Press, 2005), 226–227.

compared to the Chinese judiciary, the specialist regulatory bodies, notably the CSRC, are more competent to handle complicated securities cases, particularly on determining whether there is misrepresentation and who should be held liable. Finally, as discussed above, the prerequisite rule has beneficial evidentiary effects for investors, allowing them to piggyback on the efforts of the regulator or prosecutor in the prerequisite proceedings.

Which side of the debate has more merits? Does the prerequisite unduly limit the number of private securities litigation? Is it needed in China's current institutional environment? These questions should be assessed in light of empirical evidence. As found earlier, only sixty-five of eligible securities civil suits have actually been brought to date. This suggests that even within the bounds set by the procedural prerequisite, many more securities civil suits could have been brought. Further, the usage of the piggyback benefits of regulatory actions is also seen elsewhere. In the US, for example, up to 55 per cent of enforcement actions by the SEC have had parallel securities class actions.[23] Hence, at present, the prerequisite does not seem to be a 'devastating weakness' as asserted by some commentators,[24] and there is no pressing need to abolish the prerequisite, at least for now as there is still much scope for more securities civil cases to be brought even within the confines of the prerequisite.

To be sure, the above view is not to deny the problems with the prerequisite. The main weakness of the prerequisite as a screening mechanism is that it makes civil litigation simply a copycat effort, thereby reducing the utility of 'private attorneys-general' as a supplement to the regulators to enforce securities law. In order to harness the power of 'private attorneys-general' while maintaining some level of control over private litigation, it is necessary to gradually relax the prerequisite so as to expand the scope of securities civil action.

It is proposed that the procedural prerequisite be extended beyond the administrative penalty decision by the governmental regulators to include the enforcement activities by other relevant entities such as the stock exchanges. As a self-regulatory body, the stock exchange is charged with the task of supervising the information disclosure by listed companies and other relevant disclosing entities. To this end, the stock

[23] Verity Winship, 'Fair Funds and the SEC's Compensation of Injured Investors', 60 *Florida Law Review* 1103 (2008), 1134.

[24] Walter Hutches, 'Private Securities Litigation in China: Material Disclosure about China's Legal System?', 24 U. PA. J. INT'L. ECON. L. 599 (2003), 634.

exchanges in Shanghai and Shenzhen have issued their listing rules. If a listed company breaches the listing rules, these rules empower the exchange to take appropriate enforcement actions, including correction orders (*Zeling Gaizheng*), internally-circulated criticism (*Neibu tongbao piping*), public censure (*Gongkai qianze*), punitive damages against management of the listed company and referral of the matter to the CSRC for consideration. In addition, the stock exchange has the option to suspend or, in the extreme case, to delist the company. Like the administrative penalty decisions issued by the CSRC, the above enforcement actions taken by the stock exchange could arguably also serve as evidence of misrepresentation and consequently prompt securities civil suits.

This proposal would address some structural concerns about the current role of private securities litigation in China. If securities civil suits are strictly limited to the CSRC's enforcement actions, then why not simply empower the CSRC to recover private damages and distribute them to injured investors? In the United States, the SEC has such power under the so-called Fair Funds provisions of the federal securities laws, although they have not done much with it. As noted earlier, the CSRC may not be a good enforcer due to resources constraints, lack of independence and even outright corruption. The above reform proposal could provide a solution to this problem in the sense that it would allow private enforcement independent of CSRC action in certain circumstances. In sum, to enhance the utility of private securities litigation as an enforcement tool, the prerequisite should be relaxed to make private enforcement a more meaningful supplement to public enforcement.

4.2 Should China Adopt the US-Style Class Action?

As noted earlier, securities civil suits in China may take the form of either individual or joint action, but not class action. Many commentators have criticised this and suggested that China adopt the US-style class action. A closer examination of this issue in light of empirical findings, however, may suggest otherwise.

First and foremost, it is argued that because the court does not consolidate multiple suits into one class suit, the current litigation form for securities civil action causes inefficient use of the limited judicial resources. On the face of it, this argument seems to make sense, but in reality, the force of the argument has proved widely exaggerated. In some cases, the misrepresentation gives rise to a quite small number of suits, in which case the litigation form would have little impact on judicial resources. Further, even when there are a large number of suits arising from the same misrepresentation, the consumption of judicial resources may not be significantly more than if there was just one class action.

In practice, the Chinese court has tried to achieve judicial economy through a procedural innovation called 'test suits', under which the court will choose a representative suit, from the multiple suits arising from the same misrepresentation, to be fully adjudicated, and then apply the judgment to other suits.[25] This works because all the cases arising from the same misrepresentation involve similar legal issues, such as the presumption of causation and measure of damages, and they only differ in relation to the number of shares each of the plaintiffs can get compensation for. In fact, even if the multiple cases were consolidated into one class action, the court would still need to separately calculate the damages for each plaintiff. Interviews with judges having heard such cases suggest that there is no significant difference in terms of the substantive issues the court needs to address.

The only difference thus lies in the number of judgments or settlements as the case is more likely to be (for brevity, collectively referred to as judgments in this part) – in the current system, the court will need to issue a judgment for each case, but if it was a class action, there would be only one super-judgment covering all plaintiffs. Compared with the one super-judgment, however, the making of multiple judgments involves minimum extra work, because, once the first judgment for the model case is written, it can serve as a template for other judgments with just a couple of items changed, such as the case number, the plaintiff's name and the compensation amount.

The above point is well exemplified in the case of Dongfang Electronics, which has been the largest securities civil action so far in terms of the number of plaintiffs (6,989) and cases (2,716). The cases were filed either as individual action or joint action. Faced with the large number of cases arising from the same statement, the court chose first to hear one exemplary case on 24 August 2004, dealing with relevant issues such as the presumption of causation, the determination of the relevant dates (e.g. the misrepresentation day, the exposure day and the benchmark day), the measure of damages and other relevant issues which apply to all other cases. Thereafter, the court could simply use the exemplary case as a model

[25] This practice is broadly similar to the German 'model case proceedings' introduced under *Act on Model Case Proceedings in Disputes under Capital Markets Law* ('Capital Markets Model Case Act').

to hear other cases, and the issues already addressed in the exemplary case would not be examined again. Hence, this practice also dispels the concern over the inconsistency of judgments for a series of cases arising from the same misrepresentation.

Another criticism of the current regime is that it does not promote investor protection as it is financially burdensome for plaintiffs to bring action. It is asserted that 'litigation costs would prevent most investors from making separate claims'. The litigation cost in China is comprised mainly of the attorney and court fees. As to the attorney fee, it is not an issue for the plaintiffs due to the availability of the contingency fee/risk agency fee system. The court fee requires some more discussion – indeed, when a case is filed before the court, the plaintiff needs to prepay a filing fee, which is calculated as a percentage of the claim's value.[26] The requirement to advance the filing fee, some commentators argue, may 'make it impossible for small plaintiffs to assert large claims.'

Again, while there is some merit to this argument, the problem is not as serious as suggested by the critics. The US securities civil actions are driven by lawyers who are incentivised by the prize at the end, and so they are in China. Interviews with plaintiffs' lawyers and judges suggest that the filing fee has rarely been an insurmountable hurdle for bringing securities civil actions. In the first place, the filing fee does not usually represent a big financial problem for most investors. The filing fees are calculated on a sliding scale and are reasonable. Second, even in those cases where the potential plaintiffs are unable or unwilling to pay the filing fee, the entrepreneurial lawyers may choose to pay the fee for their clients – with a higher risk agency fee in return. Further, in China, the filing fee is subject to the so-called loser pays rule under which the losing party has to bear the fee. Since the success rate of securities civil actions is very high, it means that in the end the prepaid filing fee will be returned to the payer.

Apart from the fact that the current litigation form has functioned reasonably well, some other factors work against the idea of an immediate and wholesale transplantation of the US-style class action to China. For one thing, while securities class action has played an important role in the United States, it has its own problems such as strike suits. Further, when

[26] Susong Feiyong Jiaona Banfa [Measures of Charging Litigation Fees] (Promulgated by the State Council on 29 December 2006, effective from 1 April 2007), Article 13. The court fee consists of the filing fee (*Anjian Shouli fei*) and other litigation fees (*Qita Susong feiyong*) such as the costs of travel, accommodation, living allowances, and expenses paid to expert witnesses, accountants, translators, etc. As other litigation fees are contingent on actual needs, the focus of discussion is on the filing fee.

looking to foreign experience for solutions to local problems, one needs to consider the compatibility of the foreign experience with local conditions. For instance, it is doubtful that institutional investors in China can perform the role of lead plaintiff to address the classic issue of agency costs in the lawyer-client relationship in the US-style class action.

4.3 Suggestions for Improvements

4.3.1 More Freedom to Choose the Court

Based on the previous discussions, it seems clear that the real problem with China's securities civil action does not lie in the substantive rules, but rather in the way the court handles such action. As discussed earlier, in practice, the courts have been unsympathetic towards securities civil suits, as evidenced by the difficulty and delays in getting the case accepted and heard and the judgment enforcement problems. To be sure, there are many factors contributing to this. For instance, most listed companies are former state-owned enterprises (SOE), and thus the courts are naturally cautious about hearing securities civil cases. Those cases usually involve a large number of litigants, and if not handled properly, they may pose a threat to social stability. The court would rather stay away from this minefield as far as possible, given that social stability is currently the top priority of the Chinese government. For well-known reasons, however, the above factors will not disappear any time soon.

It is proposed that the plaintiff should have the option to bring securities civil cases in the courts in the locality where the issuer company is listed, including Shanghai, Shenzhen, Beijing, Tianjin and Wuhan (the 'Five Cities').[27] This proposal would address two main factors responsible for the problematic performance of the court in hearing securities civil actions.

To start with, the court lacks resources and expertise in hearing securities civil suits. Compared with ordinary civil cases, securities civil cases are more technical and complicated. As noted above, the SPC was actually honest about this, citing the lack of judicial resources and expertise as one of the main reasons why it initially refused securities civil litigation and later put in place the prerequisite to control securities civil cases. The reform proposal can help alleviate this problem as the

[27] Apart from the two national stock exchanges in Shanghai and Shenzhen, China has recently established OTC markets, known as Third-Board markets in China, first in Beijing, and later on 3 August 2012, expanded to Shanghai, Tianjin and Wuhan.

courts in the Five Cities have more adequate resources and better trained staff amongst Chinese courts to hear securities civil cases. In general, the judges there are well-educated, and in particular, due to their proximity to the securities markets, are very experienced in handling financial disputes. For instance, this study finds that the two intermediate courts in Shanghai have heard nine cases, the most cases one single city has handled so far in China. Altogether, the courts in the Five Cities have heard nineteen cases, accounting for close to one-third of all cases in my dataset.

Furthermore and more importantly, the above proposal can address the problem of local judicial protectionism in handling securities civil cases. Local protectionism means that in dealing with litigation, courts are often biased in favour of parties from their own region. This problem is well-known and deep-rooted in China due to the lack of the courts' independence – the local courts are dependent on the local government in terms of funding, and personnel decisions relating to the local judiciary are also in the hands of the local government. The problem is particularly severe in the area of securities civil cases, because listed companies are usually the mainstay of the local economy and thus the main source of revenue for the local government. Under the proposal, the problem of local protectionism would be avoided by allowing the plaintiff to choose not to bring the case before the local courts.

The above proposal may beg the question of whether it is proper, both legally and practically, for the courts in the Five Cities to hear non-local securities civil cases. In fact, under Article 28 of the Civil Procedure Law as amended in 2012, for tortious claims such as securities civil cases, courts at the place where a defendant is located or where the tortious conduct occurred have territorial jurisdiction. Misrepresentation as a form of tortious conduct can be said to occur at the stock exchange where the company is listed, because the information as prescribed by law has to be disclosed by the listed company to the stock exchange for public review. This would also make it easier to gather and cross-examine evidence if the case were to be heard where the company is listed, because the required evidence will normally come from the stock exchange. Hence, the courts in the Five Cities should have jurisdiction over securities civil cases.

4.3.2 Public Interest Group Litigation

Apart from giving aggrieved investors more freedom in choosing the court under the current system, another possible way to improve private enforcement of securities law is to bring securities civil cases in the form of public interest group litigation (*gongyi tuanti susong*).

In 2012, China significantly revised its Civil Procedure Law, introducing the regime of public interest group litigation. The provision governing this regime is couched in very broad terms, stating that an authority or relevant organisation as prescribed by law may instigate a suit against conduct damaging the public interest such as those that pollute the environment, or infringe upon the lawful rights and interests of vast consumers.[28] Although securities fraud is not explicitly mentioned in the provision, there is little doubt that as is often the case in practice, securities fraud may harm a large number of investors and thus give rise to public interest concerns. The draft amendment to the Securities Law as tabled in April 2015 builds on the above framework of civil procedural law, adding one provision to give effect to the public interest litigation in the context of China's securities market. Under Article 176, investor protection organisations recognised by the CSRC may participate in securities civil cases as the representative of investors who are harmed by securities misconduct such as misrepresentation, insider trading and market manipulation.

It appears that Article 176 borrows from the experience of Taiwan. On 17 July 2002, Taiwan promulgated the Securities Investors and Futures Traders Protection Act (Taiwan SIFTP Act) to 'safeguard the rights and interests of securities investors and futures traders and promote the sound development of the securities and futures markets'.[29] To this end, the Taiwan SIFTP Act authorises the establishment of a protection institution, namely the Securities and Futures Investors Protection Center (SFIPC), which perform a range of functions including, amongst others, the provision of litigation services on behalf of investors.[30]

Under the Taiwan SIFTP Act, there are some special arrangements made to facilitate the SFIPC bringing cases for the benefit of aggrieved investors. First, the SFIPC may institute an action in its own name with

[28] Zhonghua Renmin Gongheguo Minshi Susongfa [Civil Procedure Law of the People's Republic of China] (passed on 9 April 1991, amended on 28 October 2007, and on 31 August 2012) (Civil Procedure Law), Article 55.

[29] Zhengquan Touziren ji Qihuo Jiaoyiren Baohu Fa [Securities Investors and Futures Traders Protection Act] (passed on 17 July 2002, effective from 1 January 2003, amended on 20 May 2009 and 04 February 2015), Article 1.

[30] For a detailed discussion of the SFIPC, see Wallace Wen-Yeu Wang, Chapter 22 of this book.

respect to a securities or futures matter arising from a single cause that is injurious to multiple securities investors or futures traders, if no less than twenty securities investors or futures traders have empowered it to do so.[31] Second, after the SFIPC has initiated the action, other securities investors or futures traders suffering damages due to a securities or futures matter arising from the same cause can join the litigation prior to the conclusion of oral arguments or examination of witnesses in the court of first instance.[32] In a similar vein, the securities investors or futures traders may withdraw from the litigation prior to the conclusion of oral arguments or examination of witnesses. Third, the SFIPC has the power to perform all procedural acts in relation to an action it is empowered to institute by securities investors or futures traders, but securities investors or futures traders may restrict its power to make waivers, accept liability, withdraw, or enter into a settlement.[33]

Fourth, to overcome the difficulty to obtain relevant information for the purposes of bringing suits, the SFIPC has the power to request issuers, securities firms, securities service industries, futures enterprises, or relevant bodies in securities and futures markets to provide relevant documents or materials. If those bodies fail to provide the documents or materials requested, the SFIPC can request the financial regulator in Taiwan, namely the Financial Supervisory Commission, to handle the matter.[34] Fifth, the SFIPC enjoys some preferential treatments of litigation costs. For instance, the application of the SFIPC for a provisional injunction or a provisional attachment can be exempted by the court from the usual requirement for provision of security.[35] Similarly, in the event that the SFIPC applies for execution of a court judgment even before it becomes final and unappealable on the grounds that failure to do so may result in damages that would be excessive or not easily calculated, the court shall declare provisional execution exempt from provision of security in accordance with the protection institution's application.[36] Moreover, the SFIPC is entitled to be exempted from court costs on that portion of the value of the object of litigation or the compensation sought that is in excess of NT$30 million.[37]

Finally, the SFIPC shall disburse compensation it receives in an action to the securities investors or futures traders who empowered it to

[31] Taiwan SIFTP Act, Article 28(1). [32] Ibid., Article 28(2).

[33] Ibid., Article 31(1). The effect of a restriction set by one member of the group of securities investors or futures traders does not extend to other securities investors or futures traders (Article 31(2)).

[34] Ibid., Article 17. [35] Ibid., Article 34. [36] Ibid., Article 36. [37] Ibid., Article 35.

institute the action after deducting the relevant costs of litigation. The protection institution is not entitled to seek remuneration for itself, let alone make a profit out of the services; therefore the SFIPC is called a non-profit organisation (NPO).[38] The operation of the SFIPC is funded by the securities and futures industry in the form of donations and levies.[39]

The above special arrangements make it easier for the SFIPC to bring cases, and by effectively shifting the litigation risks and costs from investors to the SFIPC, encourage investors to take advantage of the litigation services offered by the SFIPC. Moreover, the SFIPC model has the ability to avoid the issue of strike suits as seen in the US, because as a NPO, the SFIPC can review the cases and only bring those that it believes meritorious and socially beneficial. To date, the SFIPC appears to have achieved some noticeable success, judging from the number of cases brought and the amount of compensation obtained. According to official statistics, by the end of 2014, there were eighty-four class action cases pending in the court and more than 93,000 investors empowered the SFIPC to file class action suits in civil claims for a total amount of more than NT$37.31 billion. A total of 103 cases had been either settled or rendered final judgment, favourable or unfavourable, and these cases altogether represented more than 18,000 investors and concerned more than NT$6.6 billion.[40]

However, the SFIPC model is not without its problems, particularly the independence and accountability of the SFIPC.[41] Although it is nominally a private NPO, the SFIPC has strong official colour due to the way in which it is funded and staffed. As discussed earlier, the SFIPC is funded by donations and contributions from the industry under the coordination of the financial regulator. In terms of its governance structure, the highest authority of the SFIPC is its board of directors, but the directors of the SFIPC are either selected by the financial regulator from among representatives recommended by a contributor, or appointed by the financial regulator from among academics, experts, and impartial

[38] Curtis J. Milhaupt, 'Nonprofit Organisations as Investor Protection: Economic Theory and Evidence From East Asia', 29 *Yale Journal of International Law* 169 (2004), 171–174.

[39] Taiwan SIFTP Act, Articles 7, 18.

[40] The Securities and Futures Investors Protection Center, Annual Report 2014, 20, www.sfipc.org.tw/MainWeb/Index.aspx?L=2 (last accessed 28 December 2016).

[41] See e.g. Yu-Hsin Lin, 'Modeling Securities Class Actions Outside the United States: The Role of Nonprofits in the Case of Taiwan', 4 *New York University Journal of Law and Business* 143 (2007).

members of the public.[42] Further, the selection of a chairman of the board of directors needs approval by the financial regulator.[43] This may lead to the erosion of independence of the SFIPC with the possibility that the SFIPC is unduly influenced by the government. On the other hand, accountability may be an issue for the SFIPC which, as the only NPO officially authorised to bring securities class actions in Taiwan, effectively enjoys a monopoly over the provision of litigation services to investors. Hence, it would be hard to evaluate the performance of the SFIPC. As the SFIPC has no direct financial interest in the bringing of cases, there is a legitimate concern over whether the SFIPC has the right incentive to work diligently and efficiently.

In sum, like any other legal mechanisms, the SFIPC model has its advantages as well as disadvantages, and overall, it presents an option worthy of serious consideration for Mainland China.[44] It has the potential to provide an important and valuable way for aggrieved investors to seek remedies by way of litigation, while at the same time address the issue of strike suits which has long plagued the US securities market. Further, it seems quite feasible to transplant the SFIPC model in that it fits well with the existing framework of China's civil procedural law.

Hence, Article 176 of the draft amendment to the Securities Law represents an interesting reform idea which is certainly worth trying. Of course, the extent to which it may succeed in practice will depend on the details of implementation. To start with, Article 176 simply allows the investor protection organisations recognised by the CSRC to act as representatives in bringing securities civil cases, without setting out detailed rules to govern the bringing of such cases. As discussed above, the SFIPC is given many preferential treatments which are very important in enabling it to perform its functions smoothly at low costs. It is submitted that China put in place similar rules to address those technical issues. Further, it is not clear who will be the 'investor protection organisations recognised by the CSRC'. As Professor Xianchu Zhang rightly pointed out in Chapter 7 of this book, 'the administrative designation would inevitably, to a certain extent,

[42] Taiwan SIFTP Act, Article 11. [43] Ibid., Article 12.

[44] See e.g. Wen-Yeu Wang and Chen Jian-Lin, 'Reforming China's Securities Civil Actions: Lessons from PSLRA Reform in the US and Government-Sanctioned Non-Profit Enforcement in Taiwan', 21(2) *Columbia Journal of Asian Law* 115 (2008); Xin Tang, 'Private Litigation and Securities Law Enforcement', 3 *Qinghua Faxue* [*Tsinghua Law Review*] 92 (2007).

subject the [recognised organisations] to the CSRC's control or influence'.[45] Indeed, the lack of independence has been a concern for the SFIPC in Taiwan, and it can only be more serious in a jurisdiction like Mainland China where the rule of law is yet to be fully established. This issue may be alleviated by recognising more than one organisation, including private NPOs. Presumably, if aggrieved investors have several organisations to choose from, the pressure of competition may help incentivise those organisations to work hard for the interest of aggrieved investors.

5 Conclusion

Although China's first securities law, namely the 1998 Securities Law, provided for private civil liability for securities market misconduct, it could not be meaningfully enforced due to the lack of detailed guidance on the bringing and hearing of such cases. This situation changed in 2002 when private securities litigation was formally permitted by China's highest court. Overall, private securities litigation has since played a visible role in the enforcement of securities law and protection of small investors in China, judging both from the quantity and quality of relevant cases brought during the period of 2002 to 2012.

A total of sixty-five cases were located for the ten-year study period, which is an encouraging number from a comparative law perspective – apart from the United States known for litigiousness, private securities litigation is rarely seen in many other jurisdictions covered in this book. However, the number is still much lower than expected, representing only a quarter of all cases which could have been brought. In search of reasons behind this, this chapter first refutes the conventional wisdom that the procedural prerequisite built into the Chinese private securities litigation regime is the main factor to blame. Then, it finds that like its counterparts in the United States, China's securities civil cases are also lawyer driven, and there is no shortage of entrepreneurial lawyers in China. Finally, it seems that the main obstacle to bringing securities civil actions in China actually rests with the courts, which has caused significant difficulties and delays in the pursuit of securities civil claims.

Another significant empirical finding is that the rate of recovery generated by private securities litigation in China is significantly higher than that in the United States. To explain this, the paper identifies and

[45] Xianchu Zhang, Chapter 7 of this book, 123.

examines several possible contributing factors, including the piggyback effect of the procedural prerequisite, the clarity of the relevant rules governing securities civil action, and the defendants' weak incentive to defend against such actions.

In choosing a regime for private enforcement of securities law, the guiding principle is to maintain an appropriate balance of providing investor protection by way of litigation while at the same time preventing the problem of strike suits as seen in the US. In light of relevant empirical findings, doubt is cast on the popular belief that China should adopt the US-style class action. As the local courts are found to be ineffective in handling private securities litigation, it is suggested that the plaintiffs be given the option to bring securities civil actions before the courts in the locality where the issuer company is listed. Under the current round of securities law reform, there is a possibility of introducing the regime of public interest group litigation to bring private civil suits against securities fraud. This is an interesting reform effort, but it remains to be seen what exactly the regime may look like and whether it can function effectively as expected.

9

Improving Investor-Friendly Legal Environments in the Chinese Capital Market

JUNHAI LIU

1 Introduction

Public investors, especially minority shareholders, are the backbone of modern corporations and the capital market. At the macro-level of capital market, capital would not be able to be formed without the strong confidence of investors. At the micro-level of a specific corporation, the governance powers of the corporation shall be from the shareholders, for the shareholders, by the shareholders. Shareholders are supposed to enjoy sovereignty in the corporation and the capital market.

Therefore, a good capital market based on the rule of law is supposed to be an investor-friendly environment and should respect shareholder sovereignty. The most serious concern for every stock market is not insufficient funds, but weak investor confidence. The paramount mission of corporate law and securities law is to protect investors, especially minority shareholders. Without investor justice, there would be no sustainable globalization of capital markets.

However, investor-friendly environments and shareholder sovereignty is still an unachieved dream in China and many jurisdictions. This chapter will start by analysing reasons why public investors and minority shareholders may become vulnerable in the capital market, and will then proceed to outline the modern governance of capital markets, and will finally focus on the way to ensure investors justice in direct and indirect actions, but especially derivative actions.

2 Why Are the Public Investors a Vulnerable Group?

Public investors are both significant and vulnerable. As many parties claim to be vulnerable in the litigations before the court, it is vital to decode the root causes for the classification of public investors as vulnerable groups. This is a very critical issue for the legislature, regulator and judiciary in terms of formulating legislative rules, regulatory policy and judicial rulings in favour of public investors. The exploration of the root causes is also valid for the similar positions of consumers, creditors and employees, among others.

2.1 Information Asymmetry

Information is the most effective leverage. Reliable information or intelligence is always at the core of competitiveness in the battlefield and the market. Different from the controlling shareholder or insiders, the minority shareholder always has a shortage of sufficient and credible top-quality information. Despite the overwhelming amount of 'trash' information released by the issuers, the public investors' need for credible information is always difficult to satisfy.

The separation between ownership and management in the listed corporations deprives the public investors of the power of daily management. Futhermore, the public investors are unable to afford the cost for investigating management activities. It is extremely difficult for the public investors, especially the retail investors, to gather and analyse the meaningful information necessary for informed decisions. On the other hand, the issuers, the insiders and the affiliated gatekeepers always disclose information in favour of the issuers and the insiders. Most frequently, only the issuers and the insiders are capable of committing frauds, including misrepresentation, insider trading or manipulation of the market.

To strike the reasonable balance between the insiders and the public investors, many jurisdictions anticipate the gatekeepers, including but not confined to the lawyers, public certified accountants, rating agencies and sponsors, that will counteract the negative effects of information asymmetry. Unfortunately, good philosophy and good rules are not necessarily implemented in the reality. In fact, the pro-investor institutional arrangements of gatekeepers have been turned against the public investors. Professional information is always supplied in favour of the strong insiders and issuers due to the issuer's dominant influence in selecting and paying the professionals. Therefore, a new question is raised. To whom should the professionals owe their fiduciary duty? Issuers, end investors or financial consumers?

A good example is the institutional arrangement of mandatory sponsorship in Chinese Securities Law.[1] The mandatory sponsorship of the securities firms has put public investors in even more danger although a rule aiming to improve the public investors' vulnerable positions was introduced in 2005. The real reason for the sponsoring securities firm to turn into tortfeasors against public investors is that many sponsors consider themselves as the trustee and agent of the issuers, instead of the public investors. In other words, the sponsors tend to be responsible to their clients, the listed corporations or the issuers.

Such misunderstanding is deeply rooted in the mere fact that the sponsors are chosen and paid by the issuers instead of by public investors, although the public investors ultimately pay the bill of mandatory sponsorship. Therefore, it is a hidden rule for the sponsors to consider themselves as the gatekeepers in favour of issuers, rather than the gatekeepers in favour of public investors who are vulnerable to information asymmetry. The legislative mistake has not alleviated the suffering of the public investors, but it has furthermore exacerbated the suffering of the public investors by imposing ultimate financial burdens on the investors and deploying sophisticated enemies against the public investors. That is why I urge the legislature to change the Securities Law, abolish the mandatory sponsorship, and permit the proposed issuers to select the sponsors on voluntary basis. However, the sponsoring securities firms and the representatives should be oriented as the joint and several liability guarantors of the issuer in case of fraud or misrepresentation.

Less information on the part of public investors implies their lack of capacity to shoulder the burden of proof. Unfortunately, the information asymmetry and capital markets are twin brothers. The issue of information asymmetry exists and will exist in the capital market permanently.

2.2 Comparatively Weak Financial Power

Only the strongest survive in the market. The winners take all. The rich always take all. The financial power could also lead to political, emotional, behavioural and social advantage and influence.

[1] Paragraph of Article 11 of Securities Law of 2005 says: 'When an application is made for public issuance of shares or corporate bonds convertible into shares and such issuance shall take place by way of underwriting pursuant to law, or when an application is made for public issuance of other securities which is subject to the sponsorship system as prescribed by laws or administrative regulations, the issuer shall engage the institution with sponsorship qualifications to act as a sponsor'.

Public individual investors are always vulnerable in terms of their insufficient financial resources that make it difficult to efficiently control investment risks compared with the issuers, the insiders, the controlling shareholders, the professional agencies allied with the issuers and the major institutional investors. The truth is that rich people and organisations are able to mobilise more resources to exploit public investors. Classic investment advice for public investors is that a smart investor should not put a hundred eggs into a hundred baskets. But this advice does not work when the investor has only one egg.

There is a widespread misleading argument that individual investors should be replaced by institutional investors gradually in the future. Following this reasoning, the individual investor is held accountable for the over-speculation feature of the Chinese stock market.

When I was involved in the process of the legislation on Securities Investment Funds Law from 1999 to 2003, all the working group including myself anticipated that this piece of legislation would help to minimise the risks of individual investors. In fact, speculation is not unique to individual investors. Institutional investors, under the pressure of the mutual fund holders, are even more speculative than individual investors in China. There is no evidence indicating that institutional investors are less speculative than individual investors and are therefore a better alternative to individual investors.

Cultural tradition does matter. The traditional Chinese culture tends to encourage individualism instead of collectivism. In Hong Kong, the individual investors still predominate in the current capital market. The right policy should address the root cause of the overly excessive speculation by improving the governance of listed corporations and encouraging listed corporations to declare reasonable dividends in cash to the public investors. Of course, it is left to the market to decide the competitiveness of individual investors or the institutional counterparts. In the US, the growth of institutional investors is the outcome of the market choice, rather than governmental regulations.

2.3 The Magical Negative Effects upon the Transfer of the Wealth

When the agents acquire control of other people's money, there are always subsequent moral hazards, regardless if the agent uses the money to advance his own interest or the interest of the principal. In the former situation, the agents are likely to breach their duty of loyalty. In the latter situation, the duty of diligence is likely to be breached. The reason is that the controlling power over the property puts the principal on the side of the vulnerable and puts the agent on the side of the stronger.

In addition to the doctrine of agency or trust, the real operation of commercial transaction also reveals the different negotiation positions of different parties. Buyers, consumers and investors usually lose control of their wealth from the very moment of the transfer of the funds or wealth to the seller and the issuers of securities. The tricky issue is that the loss of wealth control on the part of the buyer is certain, while the consideration, including the investment return, from the seller or the issuers is unfinished or even uncertain yet.

Regardless of the antifraud regulatory policy, it is very frequent that the tricky sellers tend to be very friendly to the buyers before, and only before, the buyers make the payment. Once the payment is over, the seller becomes stronger in contrast to the buyer.

2.4 Unique Ability to Externalise the Costs on the Part of Business Firms

In China and many jurisdictions, the business firms including the issuers and professional firms have the unique ability to externalise costs, including but not confined to litigation costs, to outside taxpayers including the victim vulnerable groups.

It is legal and natural for corporate taxpayers to book the litigation expenses into the deductible cost for the purpose of tax law. In this way, the corporate wrongdoers will pay less tax than the normal situation without litigation with the victim investors. It means that the whole society and all the taxpayers are financing the dishonest, stronger firms' litigation against the public investors and minority shareholders.

In contrast, the victim investors, especially the individual investors, find no efficient and effective channels to externalise the litigation cost in the same format used by the business firms. That partly explains why most victim investors choose to tolerate the wrongdoing of the issuers and the insiders in cases where there is no meaningful mechanism of class action or public interest litigation.

2.5 Imperfect Market Structure with Unfair Bargaining or Insufficient Competition

There are many presumptions and expectations about the characteristics of a perfect market. First, there is a substantially equal and informed bargaining process between the buyer and the seller, which usually leads to fair dealing and free transaction. Second, there are many honest sellers, including ever-increasing sellers of top-quality products or services, and the sellers are competing for the same group of potential target buyers at a level playing field. However, the perfect market does not exist in any given economy. The reason is very simple. The honest buyer is unable to bargain with the fraudulent seller on equal footing. The honest firm is unable to compete on level playing field with competitors that abuse monopoly positions or unfair competition strategies. Therefore, there is not a perfect or ideal market nor are there rational or reasonable market actors in absolute terms on the earth. Of course, many jurisdictions do have good, although not necessarily perfect, markets characterised by freedom and justice.

In Chinese capital markets, there are also unfair competitions between securities issuers, investment bankers, law firms and accounting firms in the primary market based on the two decades of the IPO approval system. The ongoing investigation into the former vice chairman of CSRC, Yao Gang, and other corrupted former IPO officers in November 2015 is a good footnote to shine the light on unfair competition in the primary market.[2] As the issuer is not directly selected by public investors, but by CSRC on behalf of public investors, it is difficult, if not impossible, to ensure equal and free bargaining between the investors and the issuers, or to ensure fair and transparent competition between issuers in a meaningful way.

Theoretically speaking, because CSRC as a government agency, unlike Warren Buffet and other sophisticated investors, is not professionally qualified to evaluate the merit of the investment value of thousands of issuers, the race to the bottom between issuers is made possible. Some issuers are competing to be the least loyal to public investors. As public investors have no voice in selecting and setting the service fees of gatekeepers, unfair competition between professionals exists in the primary market.

In the secondary market, unfair competition between brokerage firms could also occur. For instance, commission fights between securities firms in the secondary market have been triggered as more securities firms compete for the limited resources of public investors.

[2] Liyan Chen, 'China's 'King Of IPOs' Is Arrested On Corruption Probe', (2015) www.forbes.com/sites/liyanchen/2015/11/13/chinas-king-of-ipos-is-arrested-on-corruption-probe/#5d6a5faf4e47.

2.6 *Concentrated Shareholding Structure: Good or Bad?*

The shareholding structure in the American capital market is much more highly dispersed compared with the Chinese capital market. There is always a paramount controlling shareholder, either a state-controlled shareholder, or a private individual or a family in most of the listed corporations.

Powerful and paramount controlling shareholders of both the private and public sectors in Chinese listed corporations are reluctant to give up controlling power. Of course, one possible trend is that the shareholding structure of the state-shareholder controlled listed corporations will become more flexible in the commercial, competitive industries. It is also possible for the state shareholder to convert their shares from the common shares with voting and controlling powers into preferred non-voting shares, as indicated by the Guidance Opinions of SOE Reform of September 2015.

In my opinion, either the paramount shareholder or the related party transaction based on the corporate group or controlling shareholders is neither the angel nor the devil per se. Smart controlling shareholders are supposed to be responsible, trustworthy, transparent and inclusive. There are opportunities and possibilities for the related party transaction to achieve the win-win outcome. Truly smart controlling shareholders are supposed to advance the interests of the corporation and all the shareholders as a whole for their own sake.

However, the tricky issue is that not every controlling shareholder behaves in this way. Consequently, many related party transactions between the members of corporate groups are not based on the arm's-length principle, and are detrimental to the interests of the minority shareholders and the creditors of the subsidiaries.

2.7 *Free Ride Preference and Cost of Collective Action*

In the event of a massive violation of investor rights, victims have the right to seek judicial remedy. It is true that Chinese investors have become active in taking private litigations to protect their rights.[3] However, the litigation and ADR are not always cheap in terms of time,

[3] For part of the court rulings of securities fraud litigations, please see: Junhai Liu and Yixin Song, *The Court's Judgements Collection of Civil Compensation Cases in Securities in China (*中国证券民事赔偿案件司法裁判文书汇编, Zhongguo zheng quan min shi pei chang an jian si fa cai pan wen shu hui bian, Press of Beijing University, 2013.

emotional pressure and financial resources. Therefore, some victim investors wish for a free white knight to help them out. The most qualified white knight seems to be the regulator. However, China has begun to differentiate the different roles of private litigation and public enforcement based on the rule of law. Therefore, the regulator has the power to punish the violators in the capital market, but it has no power to enforce the private litigation. Even when the wrongdoers pay the bill ticketed by the regulator, the payment will go to the treasury, instead of the victim investors. It is natural for the government to consider the private enforcement of securities law as a market choice of investors to address the injustice. That is why the government is reluctant to step in as a white knight in the context of private litigation. Even if attorneys and NGOs or NPOs are better candidates to organise the victims' investors and advocate before the courts in the form of class action, the cost of collective action should not be ignored. That is why many law firms need to work together and make financial contributions to support the class action in one single case.

In the Chinese capital market, it is also difficult for public investors to be well organised. Many investors choose to suffer as victims not because of tolerance (REN), one of the virtues of Chinese traditional culture, but because of the substantial cost of being organised. Public interest litigation, or the Chinese version of class action, was not recognised by the Civil Procedure Law before 31 August 2012. Although I have called for the establishment of the Chinese Investor Association, a twin sister of the Chinese Consumer Association for over twenty years, such an idea has not come true yet. Although Chinese lawyers have become active in representing the investors in securities fraud cases, the clients they represented only account for an ignorable percentage.

2.8 *Agency Cost and Moral Hazards*

There is no free lunch or free agency service. Agents are not only costly, but they also trigger serious concern about moral hazards, a core agency cost. The agent is the last resort for the principal to conduct transactions. It is unlikely or even impossible for the agents to demonstrate the same diligence, skill, experience, expertise, care or prudence when he serves the principal or the beneficiary as he would demonstrate in dealing with his own business.

The agents serving the public investors include but are not confined to the issuers, directors, senior executives, controlling shareholders, de facto controllers and a great number of gatekeepers. First, irresponsible controlling shareholders consider the capital market as a free pocket to raise capital, rather than as a goose to lay eggs for the investors. Ignorable or no dividends is one of the reasons for public investors to be addicted to highly speculative trades in the market in China. Average individual investors have no choice but to risk irrational speculations in the market.

Second, theoretically speaking, the directors and senior executives are the best custodian of public investors, as they are capable of preventing or counteracting or at least buffering the threat from the controlling holders or the de facto controllers against the public investors. However, the directors and senior executives are confused with the issue of divided and competing loyalties toward the controlling shareholder and the public shareholders. If the directors and senior executives say no to unfair instructions from the controlling shareholder, they will be fired. If the directors and senior executives say no to the reasonable claims of the public shareholders, they will be condemned by the public. Although rational directors and senior executives are good at striking a good balance between and among the controlling shareholder and public shareholder, it is very challenging to implement the doctrine of golden mean.

Third, as indicated above, the gatekeepers of the public investors are in fact the gatekeepers of the issuers, controlling shareholders, de facto controllers and insiders of the listed corporation.

Fourth, although paid by the public investors, agents are not selected by their principal, the public investors in many listed corporations, due to the concentrated shareholding structure. Without fundamental changes with the nomination and selection process of agents, it is impossible for the agents to be loyal to the public investors. That is also part of the reason for me to advise the Chinese legislature to impose mandatory obligation of guarantor on the controlling shareholder for the fraudulent issue of securities by the issuers, to reserve majority seats on the board for independent directors selected only by public investors, to hold the negligent gatekeepers jointly and severally liable for the victim public investors.

In summary, public investors are always the vulnerable groups in the Chinese capital market for the reasons outlined above.

3 How Can Investor-Friendly Governance in Chinese Capital Markets Be Promoted?

As the economic reform is deepening, a new framework of governance is being incepted in Chinese capital markets, including good corporate governance, self-regulation of industries, rational governmental regulation, efficient judicial remedy and ADR, reasonable media oversight, advocates for public investors activism and impartial academic criticism.

3.1 Investor-Friendly Corporate Governance

The first pillar is the autonomy or self-governance of market participants, including issuers, listed corporations, directors, senior executives, gatekeepers and professional intermediaries. Autonomy implies both freedom and self-discipline. The market participants should not only comply with the external rules made by the legislature and the regulator, but also endorse their internal rules and investor policies.

Corporate governance is extremely important in the aftermath of the Global Financial Crisis. Financial crises reflect both the failures of regulation and the failures of corporate governance. Good governance is a better alternative than government regulation. Good governance does little harm to the market and entrepreneurship, while it efficiently enhances freedom of contracts, financial and commercial innovations, and free and fair competition. Good governance is not only a philosophy, but also a set of institutional arrangements and commercial practice. Good institutional arrangements, good people and good culture are three equally important factors. However, good corporate law and corporate governance in any given jurisdiction is unable to be achieved without the higher level of mutual learning and transplanting of successful international and foreign experiences.

Investor-friendly corporate governance demands our attention on the business ethics, justice, fairness and transparency. If they behave themselves in a good manner, the legal rules will be voluntarily complied with without further intervention of the regulators or judiciary. If disputes arise, the investors and the firms should do their best to settle disputes and restore mutual confidence.

Although many listed corporations claim to be concerned about the public investors, such attention is only paid at the lower level of public relations, not at the higher level of governance strategy.

3.2 Self-Regulation of Stock Exchanges and Chambers of Commerce

The second pillar is self-regulation of stock exchanges and chambers of commerce including the association of listed corporations, the association of securities industry, and the association of securities investment fund industry. In case of failure of the compliance by the market participants, self-regulatory bodies should step in. If the self-regulatory bodies actively play their roles, the government agency should stay away from the market.

The legislation on the chamber of commerce is in the drafting process led by State Development and Reform Commission. Generally speaking, many self-regulatory bodies are closely affiliated with government agencies. It is necessary to disconnect the tie between the self-regulatory bodies and the government agencies including CSRC, and empower the self-regulatory bodies to effectively function for the benefit of public investors. These efforts are not only in the best interests of the investors, but also in the long-term interest of the members of self-regulatory bodies.

My policy suggestion is to transform the stock exchanges into listed business corporations. The shares of Shanghai Stock Exchange could be listed on Shenzhen Stock Exchange, while the shares of Shenzhen Stock Exchange could be listed on Shanghai Stock Exchange. Moreover, the stock exchange would have the authority to monitor the performance of good governance of the listed corporations and security firms, and take necessary self-regulatory measures to protect the public investors according to the listing rules, listing agreement with the listed corporations and the articles of incorporations passed by the securities firms. In my opinion, the self-regulatory penalties imposed on the listed corporations and securities firms should be subject to judicial review.

3.3 Public Enforcement by Governmental Regulation

The third pillar is the governmental regulation, which is supposed to start to work only in case of market failure, which implies failures of both market participants and self-regulatory bodies. As the trustee of the public interest and the guardian of the taxpayers, the government should fulfil their constitutional duties to protect the investors and restore the investors' confidence. If a few patients, namely the disobedient actors, refuse or fail to comply with the rule of law, they should be subject to medical treatment by the public doctor, the governmental regulator.

The mission of the government is not to kill the market, but to reactivate the immunization of the market. Once the market recovers, the market participants get rational, and law and order is respected by the market, the public enforcement should be terminated. Even when the stock market collapses, the regulator needs to follow the due process of law and satisfy the criteria of market failure. The toolbox of market rescue programs needs to be further enriched and prioritised. The less costly and more efficient tools should be given the top priority. One such ideal tool is to investigate the frauds and relevant crimes, and to prosecute the real wrongdoers.

The government has a duty to guarantee the transparency and fairness of the stock market, but it is not obligated to guarantee the booming price of the stocks. The regulator should be also aware that market failure does not necessarily mean no government failure. Government failure could make even more trouble than the market failure. When governmental regulation steps in to address market failure, it is possible to produce double failures: market failure and governmental failure, which compound together and could lead to derivative disasters in the short term and long term.

The investor-friendly regulatory system needs to be further strengthened. CSRC, as the regulator of the securities market and the futures market, has become active in investigating market frauds. In 2011, CSRC investigated 209 cases of insider trading, manipulation and rat trading, and made sixty-eight administrative decisions on punishments and market entrance forbiddance.[4]

Although the watchdogs including the central bank, People's Bank of China, CSRC, CBRC and CIRC take care of their own financial industries, the booming of Internet industries has enabled many financial innovations to extend beyond the traditional boundaries of current financial regulatory bodies, whose regulatory duties were originally designed before the advent of the Internet financing boom.

The stock disaster of late June 2015 offered a great opportunity for the decision makers to adapt the current regulatory framework and regime to the changing business environment. This point was also confirmed by the Suggestion of the Thirteenth Five-Year Plan passed by the Central Committee of Chinese Communist Party in November 2015. Although loose information-sharing between CSRC and other government bodies has been established, it does not function very well. To eliminate the regulatory loopholes, this author advises the legislature to create a uniform comprehensive regulatory body based on the CSRC, CBRC and CIRC.

[4] http://roll.sohu.com/20120518/n343557248.shtml.

Since 2011, People's Bank of China, CSRC, CBRC and CIRC have built their consumer protection agencies based on the American experience under Dodd-Frank Act. In early November, 2015, the State Council published the Guidance Opinions on the Protection of Financial Consumers. More efficient collaboration between administrative regulator and criminal investigator is urgent.

I have three suggestions to restructure the regulatory powers. First, the approval powers should be further minimised. Second, the regulatory authorities need to be strengthened to prevent and cure market failures. Third, the regulator should be reorienting it as the guardian of the public investors, instead of the guardian of the issuers and professional gatekeepers. Namely, the regulator has the mission and duty to guard the vulnerable market actors' rights, especially shareholder's rights. Traditionally, regulators tend to favour the interest of the business industry instead of consumers.

3.4 *Judicial Remedy and ADR*

The fourth pillar is judicial remedy and alternative dispute resolutions (ADR). If the investor or their advocates takes litigations, the court should hear the cases based on investor-friendly philosophy and make the fair rulings capable of withstanding the test not only by the law, but also by the market and the history. In addition to the civil cases, administrative cases and criminal cases relevant to the protection of the investors are also heard by the courts in China.

In addition to the judicial remedy, ADR have been also innovated and upgraded in China. In the ADR pyramid, negotiation between the dispute parties sits on the bottom. It should be encouraged as the first resort to solve the majority of disputes. In case of negotiation failure, an independent third-party mediator, such as consumer organizations, China Securities Investor Protection Fund Company, China Securities Middle and Small Investor Service Center, and Asset Management Association of China (AMAC),[5] should step in for mediation. If the private mediation fails, the third resort will be administrative mediation organised by governmental agencies, including People's Bank of China, CSRC, CBRC and CIRC. If the administrative mediation fails, the parties should be encouraged to submit their disputes to the arbitration bodies,

[5] For the functions of this corporation, please see: www.amac.org.cn/cms/site/preview?ID=23.

as arbitration is faster, cheaper, more confidential and more professional. In the absence of an arbitration clause, the investor disputes could only be heard by the court, which sits on the top of the pyramid.

Restrictively speaking, the judicial system is the hybrid of private enforcement and public enforcement, because the litigation between the investors and the defendants is the private litigation, while the judiciary branch is part of public powers. Therefore, the private enforcement refers to the civil procedure for enforcing civil liabilities, while the public enforcement refers to the administrative and criminal process for enforcing administrative punishment and criminal penalties.

3.5 *Media Oversight*

Mass media is an important part of the governance framework of the capital market. In many cases, the investor fraud cases are covered by the media. Newspapers and journals have become more and more active in covering the investor fraud cases. For instance Guangxia (Yinchuan) Industry Co. Ltd. was first reported by the cover article on the journal *Caijing* on 5 August 2001.[6] Of course, the mass media need to separate their business of advertising from their mission as watchdogs of public interests.

In addition to rational media, new media or social media such as Weibo and Wechat are widely used for voicing different criticism and suggestions, and they disseminate the information flowing in the capital market. Of course, tort liability of defamation might arise from the abuse of websites.

3.6 *Advocates for Public Investor Activism*

It is necessary to support the growth of the diversified NGOs or NPOs for building an investor-friendly society. Based on the experience of China Consumers' Association and other local consumer organisations, it is necessary to set up China Investors' Association and other local investor organisations. Their core mission is to provide investor education, to take public interest litigations on behalf of public investors, to support the individual investor litigation and to mediate the investor disputes.

To ensure the independence and impartiality, it is necessary to finance the investor association by public funds from taxpayers. It is not fair for

[6] http://finance.ifeng.com/zq/20030107/182549.shtml.

the investors to make the payment of the membership fee, as the investors are usually individuals. It is not appropriate for the investor association to collect membership from the listed corporations and the professional gatekeeper, as the public will be concerned about the independence of the investor association. Of course, if the investors win the case, the mediation fee or the court fee needs to be borne by the business firms.

There is an investor protection company called 'China Securities Investor Protection Funds' (SIPF), a wholly state-owned company, which was set up under the 'Measures for the Administration of Securities Investor Protection Funds' on 30 August 2005. SIPF is under the regulation of the CSRC and its register capital is RMB 6.3 billion injected by the State Council via the Ministry of Finance. The principal functions of SIPF are: 1) to raise, manage and operate a securities investor protection fund; 2) to monitor risks of securities companies and participate in the risk disposition and the liquidation of the dissolved, closed or bankrupt securities companies; 3) to indemnify eligible creditors in case a securities company is subject to compulsory regulatory measures by the CSRC and trustee operation; 4) to manage and dispose of foreclosed assets and safeguard the fund's rights and interests; 5) to put forward regulatory and disposal suggestions to the CSRC in case a securities company's operation and management have material risks that may damage investors' interests and the safety of the securities market; 6) to join relevant authorities in establishing a rectification mechanism for the potential risks arising from operation of securities companies; 7) to strengthen the monitoring of securities market risks by setting up and improving the monitoring system on a transaction settlement fund at the securities market and the XBRL information system; 8) to conduct investor protection assessment of both securities companies and listed companies; 9) to build a routine investor protection mechanism mixing 'monitoring, appraisal and service'; and 10) to increase the independence of IPFC from the government, and enable it to take litigations on behalf of the investors.[7]

Although SIPF has made substantial progress in disposing the bankrupt securities firms, it still has many differences with China Consumer Association, which is more influential in representing Chinese consumers in daily life. I believe it is also an alternative to restructure the SIPF into Chinese Investor Association based on the successful model of China Consumer Association.

[7] www.sipf.com.cn/NewEN/aboutsipf/corporateprofile/03/40081.shtml.

3.7 *Impartial Academic Criticism*

Impartial academic criticism is an indispensable pillar to support the modern governance platform of Chinese capital market. Impartial academic criticism could help the business industry, the regulators, the judiciary, the arbitration bodies, the media and investor advocates to coordinate their efforts in the process of investor protection. Of course, academia should contribute both criticism and solutions to the complicated issues of capital market.

4 Ensuring Every Investor Has Access to Justice In Private Litigations

4.1 *Direct Actions in Corporate Law*

The shareholders are entitled to take direct actions to enforce their individual rights. Direct actions could be classified as individual actions and class actions. Compared with the indirect litigations, direct actions are most relevant to the plaintiff shareholder. That is why most of the shareholders litigations are direct actions, rather than the indirect litigations.

The Corporation Law offers several types of direct actions for minority shareholders. First, the minority shareholder may take action based on the right to information under Article 33 of Corporate Law of 2013. The shareholder may inspect and copy the books and records of the corporation. In certain circumstances, the former shareholder, who depended on the inspection of books and records to support another litigation claiming insufficiency of the price agreed in the equity transfer contract, should be also granted the right of inspection.

Second, the existing shareholder, based on existing shareholders' preemptive right to buy under Article 71 of Corporate Law of 2013, may challenge the transfer of equity interest from other fellow shareholders to outsiders.

Third, the dissenting shareholders may take actions of appraisal right based on Article 74 of Corporate Law of 2013.

Fourth, if the interest of an individual shareholder, instead of the corporation, is damaged by the directors or senior executives, the victim shareholders may take direct action against the wrongdoers under Article 152.

Fifth, the qualified shareholder may take action to wind up the corporation in case of corporate governance deadlock under Article 182 of Corporate Law of 2013.

Sixth, although not recognised by the legislation and judicial interpretation, the minority shareholders may request the court to declare mandatory dividend in extremely exceptional cases. For instance, while the corporation has been profitable for more than five years, the minority shareholder has received neither dividends nor the opportunities of substantial income from the corporation; controlling shareholder or insiders have received substantial benefits via generous compensation and related-party transaction but not in the form of dividends. It seems that this embarrassing situation is designed to bully the minority shareholder.

Of course, it is very rare for Chinese courts to declare mandatory dividends in reality. Although mandatory declaration of dividends is controversial, in the opinion of this author, such judicial remedy should be open to certain minority shareholders who have been trapped into dead ends but do not want to leave the corporation.

4.2 Direct Actions in Securities Law

Securities Law of 2005 recognised several direct actions as individual actions. First, the investors may take direct action against misrepresentation wrongdoers under Article 69 of Securities Law in the primary market. Second, the investors may take direct action against insider trading under Article 76 of Securities Law. Third, the investors may take direct action against manipulation under Article 77 of Securities Law. Fourth, the investors may take direct action against fraudulent securities firms and their employees under Article 79 of Securities Law.

Although the direct litigations in the area of insider trading and manipulation of the market began to be active especially after the Everbright Securities Firm was sued by some investors based on the doctrine of manipulation of the market, most direct actions focus on the misrepresentations in the prospectus and other disclosure documents.

4.3 Public Interest Litigation Is Expected to Function in the Securities Market

Neither Corporate Law of 2005 nor Securities Law of 1998 has recognised the class action. In early 2002, the Supreme People's Court issued a notice entitled 'Acceptance of Cases of Disputes over Civil Tort Arising from False Statements in the Securities Market' ('2002

Securities Notice').[8] Although it permitted courts to accept securities fraud suits, the 2002 Securities Notice prohibited plaintiffs from bringing 'group actions.' This author agrees with the commentators who believe that it has been applied in Chinese securities litigation to mean that those cases must, in effect, be brought as either individual actions or joint actions.

However, depending on one's definition, two cases vie for designation as the 'first' Chinese class action securities fraud lawsuit.[9] In 2001, 363 investors filed a class action suit against Yorkpoint Science & Technology Co. However, the following day, the Supreme People's Court promulgated a notice temporarily prohibiting lower courts from accepting securities lawsuits from private parties. The main reason was that courts were not yet well prepared for hearing securities lawsuits in terms of social responsibility and professional expertise.

After the Supreme Court issued the Judicial Interpretation on the Civil Liabilities Arising from the Misrepresentation on the Securities Market on 9 January 2003, investors brought a suit against Daqing Lianyi Co. and Shenyin Wanguao Securities Corporation, the entity that was the listing recommender and main underwriter of the securities during the public offering. The court required the 381 original plaintiffs to divide into groups of ten to twenty. As a result, the plaintiff investors were successfully awarded some of the damages they claimed. This chain of litigations was the first set of comparatively large-scale litigations in the securities market, although they were substantially different from the typical class actions in the US.

Article 55 of the Civil Procedure Law of 2012 introduced the new mechanism of public interest litigation as 'relevant authorities and social organisations may take litigations against the infringements of the public interest especially those involving environmental pollution or damaging mass consumers' legal rights and interests.' As the relevant authorities and social organisations play the leading role of the plaintiff in the public interest litigation, such public interest litigation is different from

[8] 《关于受理证券市场因虚假陈述引发的民事侵权纠纷案件有关问题的通知》(guan yu shou li zheng quan shi chang yin xu jia chen shu yin fa de min shi qin quan jiu fen an jian you guan wen ti de tong zhi), issued by Chinese Supreme Court (最高人民法院，zui gao ren min da yuan) on 15 January 2002. For the details of the process of making this notice, see then Justice Li Guoguang's introduction under www.chinacourt.org/article/detail/2008/12/id/333945.shtml.

[9] Dana M. Muir, Junhai Liu, and Haiyan Xu, 'The Future of Securities Class Actions Against Foreign Companies: China and Comity Concerns', 46 *University of Michigan Journal of Law Reform*, (2013), 1315–1360.

American class action in which the lawyers are always the active organisers of the class action for the purpose of contingency fee.

Article 47 of Consumer Protection Law further extends the public interest litigation to the consumer disputes, and authorises Chinese Consumer Association and the consumer organisations at the provincial level to act as the plaintiff. Influenced by the consumer-friendly philosophy, Chinese Supreme Court is busy drafting two separate judicial interpretations on the public interest litigation in the field of consumer disputes and in the field of environmental protection.

In my opinion, the public interest litigation should also be extended to the societies market. The idea of China Investors' Association is an ideal qualified plaintiff to represent the public investors in the direct litigations. If the Investors' Association holds the shares in many listed corporations, it is also qualified take derivative actions against the controlling shareholders, the insiders and other third parties infringing the interest of the corporation in the event the internal remedy is exhausted.

This author argues that as Article 28 of Consumer Law of 2013 considers the consumers in the industries of securities, banking and insurance as the target of the Consumer Law, China Consumers' Protection Corporation should be empowered to take class actions on behalf of the public investors, before investor association is established.

4.4 Indirect Derivative Actions Including Derivative Actions Remain to Be Reactivated

The shareholders are entitled to take indirect derivative actions to enforce the corporate rights as a whole. The most significant indirect action is the shareholder's derivative action.

Traditional civil procedure rules are designed based on the hypothesis that every party, including a plaintiff and defendant, is rational and reasonable. Namely, every party except the mentally incompetent know very well whether to bring litigation to the court or not. As mentioned above, Article 119 of the Civil Procedure Law requires the plaintiff to have direct interest in the litigation. Although the victim corporation is supposed to sue the wrongdoer's directors, it chooses not to sue in many cases when the defendant controls the victim corporation. In this way, the victim corporation has been 'kidnapped' by the defendant. Once kidnapped, the victim corporation will be unable to sue the defendants in its own name. In such cases, the traditional civil procedure rules leave corporate victims no justice.

Therefore, it is critically important to encourage and enable the shareholder's derivative actions in the interest of the victim corporation pursuant to Article 151 of Corporate Law of 2013. Therefore, any eligible minority shareholder may, in their own name, but on behalf of the interest of the corporation, take legal actions against the wrongdoing directors, supervisors and the controlling shareholders for the damage suffered by the corporation.

The functions of the shareholder's derivative action are not limited to corporate governance, but also cover the secondary capital market. For instance, under Article 47 of Securities Law, shareholder's derivative action could also be used for disgorgement of short-term trading or short swing profits acquired by the directors, senior executives and shareholder with more than 5 per cent of the outstanding shares of the listed corporation.

Shareholder's derivative action is not only tailor-made for the minority shareholders. In fact, any vulnerable non-controlling shareholder might be qualified to use this tool. For instance, this author was once consulted in a derivative action taken by a non-controlling majority shareholder holding 65 per cent of shares in a real estate company taking derivative actions against controlling minority shareholder holding 35 per cent of shares for embezzlement of corporate funds.

To make sure that the plaintiff shareholders fairly and adequately represent the victim corporation, and to deter the strike suits abused by the evil-hearted shareholders, Article 151 of Corporate Law only permits certain minority shareholders to act as the plaintiff, who in fact is a self-appointed representative of the victim corporation, to take derivative actions. The qualification requirements vary in different types of corporations.

Any shareholder of a limited liability company, regardless of the size or duration of her shareholding size, is entitled to take derivative actions. The rationale behind this is that the number of shareholders in typical LLCs is very limited, and the fellow shareholders are usually family members, relatives, colleagues or close friends. Therefore, rational minority shareholders would not take derivative actions if their fellow majority shareholders or the management behave themselves very well. However, if a minority shareholder is determined to take derivative actions, she must have compelling good reasons to enforce the rights of the corporations in good faith, and she is very unlikely to abuse the derivative actions. The relatively lower threshold for the derivative actions is very helpful to deter the moral hazards of directors, to hold the directors accountable and diligent, and therefore to strengthen the solidarity and mutual confidence of between and among the fellow shareholders and the directors in closely held corporations.

Quite contrary to the case of closely held corporations, not every single shareholder in publicly held corporations has the standing to take derivative actions. In order to prevent the abuse of derivative actions, Article 151 of Corporate Law has rigid requirements in terms of both size and duration of the shareholding by the plaintiff. First, the plaintiff has to possess at least 1 per cent of the total outstanding shares issued by the company. For listed corporations with giant capital, 1 per cent of the total shares are not easy to satisfy. Therefore, the legislature permits two or more minority shareholders to work together as joint plaintiffs, and to accumulate their shares together to satisfy the shareholding size requirements. Second, the plaintiff must have been a shareholder in the particular corporation for at least 180 days or six months. The philosophy is to make sure that the plaintiff is a genuine investor instead of speculator, as it is not easy for a speculator to stay in a corporation more than six months. Although it is doubtful whether the 180-day test is convincing or not, the basic idea is that speculators or too speculative investors are not justified morally to represent the corporation. The Chinese Supreme Court interprets the 180 days as the duration before the plaintiff files her complaint to the court of justice.[10] Therefore, the plaintiff need not be the shareholder when the wrongdoings were committed, nor does the plaintiff need to maintain her shareholding through the end of the whole hearing process of the court.

In reality, many investors use the doctrine of trust to invite their close friends to act as the nominal shareholder, and hide themselves behind the nominal shareholder. In this way, the anonymous shareholder could keep her privacy, while she receives the investment fruits and bears the investment risks or losses. The legislature is silent on the eligibility of anonymous shareholder for taking derivative actions. This author argues that an anonymous shareholder remains eligible in case her nominal shareholder fails to take derivative actions, because the anonymous shareholder acts as the beneficiary shareholder and the nominal

[10] Provisions of the Supreme People's Court on Several Issues Concerning the Application of the Company Law of 2005 (promulgated by the People's Supreme Court, 28 April 2006), Judicial interpretation No. 3 (2006), Art. 4, published by the News of People's Court (China), www.chinacourt.org/law/detail/2014/02/id/147551.shtml. The Chinese title of this document is: 《最高人民法院关于适用〈中华人民共和国公司法〉若干问题的规定（一）》(法释〔2006〕3号.

shareholder acts as a trustee in their trust relationship. The court has no reason to deny the eligibility of the beneficiary shareholder when moral hazards against the beneficiary occur on the part of the trustee.

The non-voting shareholders are also not clearly excluded from the scope of the plaintiff shareholders. Although the voting right is different for the right to take derivate suits, and the non-voting shareholders have more good reasons to start derivate suits, as the nonvoting shareholders are more vulnerable than the voting shareholders.

The rule of exhaustion of internal remedies could be abused by the insiders, and the directors and supervisors would scratch each other's backs. For instance, if the wrongdoing directors and supervisors are close friends, the supervisors would promise the proposed plaintiff shareholder that the supervisors will file suit against the wrongdoing directors. In this way, requesting shareholders may not take derivative actions, as the victim corporation would enforce its own rights. But the problem is that the dishonest supervisors would easily lose the corporate claim, therefore benefitting the wrongdoing directors. Thus, I propose that if the directors or supervisors claim themselves to exhaust corporate internal remedies, the proposed plaintiff shareholder has the right to oversee the performance of the corporate litigation. If the proposed plaintiff shareholder has evidence that the directors or supervisors have not demonstrated their due loyalty and diligence in the course of the trial, the proposed plaintiff shareholder should be entitled to step in to file derivative suit.

In China, the derivative actions have not been very active yet since the reform of Corporate Law in 2005, partly because of the requirement of prepaid court fees calculated based on the amount of the claim under the Regulations on the Litigation Fees.[11] Since any recovery in derivative actions generally runs to the victim corporation, instead of the shareholder plaintiff, the derivative actions could be loosely regarded as the 'public interest litigations' in the kingdom of the corporations. Therefore, this author argues that the shareholder plaintiff only needs to prepay a small amount of fees ranging from 50 to 100 Chinese Yuan as the court fee, pursuant to Item 3 of Article 13(2) of the Regulations on the Litigation Fees on the non-pecuniary cases. Another alternative is to allow the shareholder plaintiff to petition the court to postpone, reduce,

[11] 《诉讼费用交纳办法》(su song fei yong jiao na ban fa), issued by the State Council on 19 December 2006, effective on 1 April 2007, www.gov.cn/ziliao/flfg/2006-12/29/content_483682.htm.

or waive the prepayment of the court fee, as Article 118 (2) of Civil Procedure Law offers such a remedy to the parties who truly have difficulties to pay litigation expenses.[12]

Regardless of the amount of the prepaid court fee, the successful shareholder plaintiff will be reimbursed from the unsuccessful defendant directors, under the traditional rule that loser bears the court fee in China. Article 29 (1) of the Regulations on the Litigation Fees also makes it very clear, 'the litigation expenses should be borne by the losing party, unless the winning party is willing to bear'.[13]

5 Conclusion

Public investors, especially the minority shareholders, are the most important but also most vulnerable stakeholders of the corporations for the reasons outlined above. To build an investor-friendly market, it is necessary to promote the modernisation of the governance of capital market through good corporate governance, self-regulation of industries, rational governmental regulation, efficient judicial remedy and ADR, reasonable media oversight, advocates for public investors activism and impartial academic criticism.

To restore the confidence of the investors, it is necessary to ensure that every investor has access to justice in private litigations, including but not confined to direct and indirect actions, especially derivative actions. The bottom line is that wrongdoers should be ordered to pay a price that is more than their unjust benefits on the one hand, while the victim shareholder should gain more profits than the litigation cost on the other hand. For this purpose, the court and arbitration bodies should take shareholder-friendly hearing policy, such as allocating less of the burden of proof on the minority shareholder than the controlling shareholders or the insiders.

[12] 《民事诉讼法》(min shi su song fa), enacted by the Standing Committee of National People's Congress on 9 April 1991, as amended on 31 August 2012.

[13] 《诉讼费用交纳办法》(su song fei yong jiao na ban fa).

10

Enforcing Fiduciary Duties as Tort Liability in Chinese Courts

JIANGYU WANG

1 Introduction: Attempted Transplant of Fiduciary Duties in Civil Law Countries

The directors and officers of a company or corporation in common law jurisdictions are subject to a set of legal obligations which can generally be referred to as fiduciary duties. Specifically, under American corporate law, the duties of these corporate insiders include, among others, the duty of care and duty of loyalty. For the duty of care, 'a director or officer has a duty to the corporation to perform the director's or officer's functions in good faith, in a manner that he or she reasonably believes to be in the best interest of the corporation, and with the care that an ordinarily prudent person would reasonably be expected to exercise in a like position and under similar circumstances'.[1] On the other hand, the fiduciary duty of loyalty prohibits the directors and officers 'from taking advantage of their beneficiaries by means of fraudulent or unfair transactions'.[2] In English law, fiduciary duties of the directors require the directors to act within powers which have been conferred upon them, to act in good faith to promote the success of the company, and to exercise independent judgment. In addition, they should avoid conflicts of interest involving self-dealing transactions with the company, personal exploitation of the company's property, information or opportunities, or conflicts 'out of the receipt from a third party of a benefit for exercising their directorial functions in a particular way'.[3]

[1] American Law Institute (1992), §4.01(a) (hereinafter the *ALI Principles*). See also Robert C. Clark. *Corporate Law* (New York: Aspen Law & Business, 1986), 123.

[2] Clarke, *Corporate Law*, 141.

[3] See Paul L. Davies, *Gower and Davies' Principles of Modern Company Law*, 8th ed., (London: Sweet & Maxwell, 2008), 496–497. Under the English Companies Act, the term 'fiduciary

Once a core concept in Anglo-American corporate law, fiduciary duties have now been borrowed by many civil law countries, China being one of them.[4] Needless to say, when the rules and standards of fiduciary duties are transferred to these jurisdictions, they have to appear in the form of legislations, most likely as provisions in the company law act or statute.[5] It is however fundamentally important to stress that the laws of fiduciary duties in common law countries have been mainly developed by judges through case law rather than by the lawmakers through written laws. As noted by the American Law Institute, '[h]istorically, courts rather than legislatures have played the central role in shaping the law regarding the duty of care of corporate directors and officers'.[6]

Thus the very nature of fiduciary duties may have determined that they could not be transplanted merely through written legislations. As Robert C. Clark pointed out, '[m]ost importantly, this general fiduciary duty of loyalty is a residual concept that can include factual situations that no one has foreseen and categorised'.[7] As such, Lynn Stout has observed that,

> [T]here seems reason to question how easily one can export the formal legal rules of one nation to another. Commentators have raised concerns about 'transplant shock' – the possibility that legal rules that work well in one nation may not work well, and ultimately may be rejected, in a nation with a different historical, political, or cultural background.[8]

China offers a third possibility on how the transplanting of fiduciary duties may work in a civil law jurisdiction. It appears to be a rather simple model: the concept – or name – of fiduciary duties has been used by the courts to apply the doctrine of torts in civil law to the wrongdoings of corporate insiders such as the directors, officers and supervisors. In other

duties' traditionally refer to conflict of interest situations. See Nicholas Bourne, *Bourne on Company Law*, 6th ed., (London and New York: Routledge, 2013), 182.

4 See Katharina Pistor and Chenggang Xu, 'Fiduciary Duty in Transitional Civil Law Jurisdictions: Lessons from the Incomplete Law Theory', in Curtis J. Milhaupt, *Global Markets, Domestic Institutions: Corporate Law and Governance in a New Era of Cross-Border Deals*, (Columbia University Press, 2003), 77–106 (surveying case law concerning fiduciary duties from Poland, Russia and Germany).

5 Pistor and Xu, 'Fiduciary Duty in Transitional Civil Law Jurisdictions', 87–96.

6 *ALI Principles*, Part IV, 'Introductory Note '.

7 Clarke, *Corporate Law*, 141.

8 Lynn A. Stout, 'On the Export of U.S.-Style Corporate Fiduciary Duties to Other Cultures: Can a Transplant Take?', in Curtis J. Milhaupt, *Global Markets, Domestic Institutions: Corporate Law and Governance in a New Era of Cross-Border Deals* (Columbia University Press, 2003), 46–76.

words, the codification of fiduciary duties by China's Company Law offers room for the courts to use this concept as an authorisation by the law to impose tort liability on corporate wrongdoers, which they were not able to do before the codification. In this sense, the adoption of fiduciary duties in China's corporate law plays an instrumental role in improving investor protection in China, although the judicial understanding and interpretation of fiduciary duties are probably far different from what the duties are understood to be in the origin countries.

2 The Introduction of Standards and Rules of Fiduciary Duties into China's Corporate Law

In 2005, the National People's Congress of the People's Republic of China adopted a set of amendments which were seen as the most important revision to China's Company Law in history. The PRC Company Law, originally adopted in 1993, was regarded as a law merely serving the interest of state-owned enterprises (SOEs). The 2005 revision, which rewrote about two-thirds of the provisions, is so significant that the current corporate law statute is often referred to as the '2005 Company Law'.[9]

One of the major changes in the 2005 Company Law is the adoption of a framework of fiduciary duties 'resembling common law fiduciary duties'.[10] Like the major origin jurisdictions, China has now adopted in its corporate law a mixture of rules and standards, under the umbrella of 'fiduciary duties', to minimise the 'agency costs' arising out of the separation of ownership and control.[11] Not surprisingly, this has been regarded

[9] The Company Law was most recently revised in December 2013 to abolish the rules on compulsory minimum registered capital.

[10] Braig Anderson and Bingna Guo, 'Corporate Governance under the New Company Law (Part 1): Fiduciary Duties and Minority Shareholder Protection', *China Law & Practice*, April 2006, and 'Corporate Governance under the New Company Law (Part 2): Shareholder Lawsuits and Enforcement', *China Law & Practice*, May 2006. (noting that 'the Chinese framework [of management duties] appears to patterned on common law concepts').

[11] For analytical purposes, it is useful here to distinguish between 'rules' and 'standards'. As Reinier Kraakman et al., *The Anatomy of Corporate Law: A Comparative and Functional Approach*, 2nd ed. (Oxford University Press, 2009), 39 point out, 'The most familiar pair of regulatory strategies [in addressing agency problems] constraints agents by commanding them not to make decisions, or undertake transactions, that would harm the interests of their principles. Lawmakers can frame such constraints as *rules*, which require or prohibit specific behaviors, or as general *standards*, which leave the precise determination of compliance to adjudicators after the fact'.

as a successful move to transplant an Anglo-American doctrine into Chinese law, as remarked by Nicholas Howson:[12]

> [I]n October 2005 China introduced Anglo-American-style corporate fiduciary duties into the nation's corporate law. In addition, and as in the 1994 Company Law (but in a different article), the 2005 Company Law sets forth in accompanying Article 149 a number of bright-line prohibitions, violation of which would constitute breach of loyalty-type obligations.

With Articles 147, 148, 149, 151, and 152 in the PRC Company Law, China appeared to be one of the first major jurisdictions to have systematically – not yet entirely – codified the contents and enforcement of fiduciary duties.[13] Article 147 of the Company Law requires the senior personnel in a company to act in accordance of due care and loyalty:

> Directors, supervisors and senior management executives shall abide by laws, administrative regulations and the corporate charter, and have a duty of loyalty (zhongshi yiwu) and duty of care (qinmian yifu) to the company.[14]

This provision sets forth a general, statutory standard of corporate fiduciary duties in China. Other than this, there are no general principles or guidelines to elaborate upon the contents the standards of fiduciary duties. As Nicholas Howson observes, with respect to the duty of care, 'the 2005 statutory formulation passes upon the opportunity to ... articulate a specific *standard* for the duty of care prong, or any instruction to regulators or judges who might be employed as a 'business judgment rule' for newly authorised duty of care inquiries'.[15]

An interesting comparison is the articulation of the general standard for directors' 'duty to promote the success of the company' in the UK Companies Act 2006, which, as mentioned above, requires the directors of a company 'act in the way he considers, in good faith, would be most

12 Nicholas C. Howson, 'The Doctrine That Dared Not Speak Its Name: Anglo-American Fiduciary Duties in China's 2005 Company Law and Case Intimations of Prior Convergence', in Hideki Kanda, Kon-Sik Kim and Curtis J. Milhaupt (eds.), *Transforming Corporate Governance in East Asia*, (Routledge, 2008), 193–254, 198.

13 After the 2005 PRC Company Law, the United Kingdom codified its body of directors' duties in Part 10 of the Companies Act 2006.

14 Company Law, Article 148, para. 1 (Chinese pinxin added). There is a similar general standard of fiduciary duty in Article 33 of the Code of Corporate Governance, which states, 'Directors should act in the best interest of the company and all the shareholders, performing their duties loyally, in good faith and diligently'.

15 Howson, 'The Doctrine That Dared Not Speak Its Name', 198.

likely to promote the success of the company for the benefits of its members as a whole'.[16]

Noticeably, words such as 'good faith', 'benefit', 'success', etc., which feature a high degree of flexibility and uncertainties, all require clarification and interpretation whenever they are applied to specific facts. Likewise, the duty of loyalty in the US requires a director to act 'in the good faith belief that her actions are in the corporation's best interest'.[17] Flexible terminology like 'good faith', 'best interest', 'fair', 'reasonable', 'adequate', etc. also compels judicial interpretation. That is to say, in applying a standard of fiduciary duties, courts everywhere will always have to interpret the doctrine and terminology to determine, on the facts and context of each case, whether the standard was met.[18] China in theory is not an exception, but it is very questionable that the Chinese judiciary is able to undertake such a task to understand the original meaning of corporate fiduciary duties as they are in the American or English common law context.[19]

Although it is overwhelmingly agreed upon that the doctrine of fiduciary duties in Chinese corporate law has its Anglo-American origins, it can also find part of its roots in Chinese civil law, which was styled after the Continental legal family. The majority view is that the relationship between the company and its directors, supervisors and executives is built upon an agency-based 'contract of mandate' (*weiren hetong*, officially called *weituo hetong* in the PRC Contract Law), in which the principal and the agent agree that the agent will handle the principal's affairs.[20] Leading civil law textbooks in China have suggested 'the mandatory [agent] shall perform the duty of care of a good manager [*shanliang guanli ren*] in contracts of mandate with remunerations'.[21]

[16] UK Companies Act 2006, Article 172(1).

[17] *Stone, ex rel. AmSouth Bancorporation* v. *Ritter*, 911 A 2d 362, 370 (2006), cited in Andreas Cahn and David C. Donald, *Comparative Company Law: Text and Cases on the Laws Governing Corporations in German, the UK and the USA* (Cambridge University Press, 2010), 344.

[18] Cahn and Donald, *Comparative Company Law*, 343.

[19] See Howson, 'The Doctrine That Dared Not Speak Its Name', at 202 (noting 'the application of fiduciary duties requires extraordinary flexibility and complex fact analysis, and thus a demanding level of technical competence among the judicial corps (or state regulator) wielding the doctrine').

[20] PRC Contract Law, Article 396. Leading textbooks on civil law in China suggest that *weiren* and *weituo* mean the same and can be used interchangeably. See Liming Wang (ed.), *Minfa*, (Di Wu Ban)[*Civil Law*, (5th ed.)], (Renmin University Press, 2010), 483; Mingrui Guo (ed.), *Minfa* [*Civil Law*], (Higher Education Press, 2007), 507.

[21] See e.g. Wang, *Civil Law*, 485; Guo, *Civil Law*, 508.

Since the modern civil law system on the Chinese mainland is, to a large extent, built upon the civil law of Republic of China (ROC) which is still applicable in Taiwan now, Chinese academic writing is accustomed to using laws, judicial decisions and scholarly opinions in Taiwan to interpret concepts in contemporary PRC civil law. The above treatment of the mandatory/agent as a 'good manager' with duty of care in Chinese textbooks on civil law is such an example. Article 535 of the ROC Civil Code states, 'The mandatory who deals with the affair commissioned, shall be [acting] in accordance with the instructions of the principal and with the same care as he would deal with his own affairs. If he has received the remuneration, he shall do so with the care of a good administrator'.[22] Article 192 of the ROC Company Law, governing the legal relationship between the company and its directors, was largely derived from Article 535 of the Civil Code. It provides, 'The relationship between a company and its directors, unless otherwise stipulated in this law, shall be [understood] in accordance with the civil code stipulations for mandate (*weiren*)'.[23]

Since the doctrine of fiduciary duties has been formally introduced but the traditional doctrine of 'mandate' is here to stay, how Chinese courts will reconcile the two in disputes on director/management duties appears to be an interesting question. Some pragmatic academics and judges in China have optimistically – but probably mistakenly – understood the two as having the same result. After the much hailed but rarely used PRC Trust Law was adopted in April 2001, they now have further reasons to believe that the two doctrines can coexist in China's corporate law regime. Article 25 of the Trust Law requires the trustee to 'be attentive to duties and perform his obligations honestly, trustworthily, prudently and effectively'. Liu Junhai, one of the leading corporate law scholars in China, thus concludes,[24]

> The generally agreed view in our country is that the relationship between the company and its directors, supervisors is one of contractual relations based on *weituo* (*weiren*). The directors, supervisors and senior management executives should perform both the obligations conferred upon him by the Contract Law and the contract of mandate, and the obligations arising from the provisions in the Company Law and its special laws.

[22] The bilingual versions of the ROC Civil Code were provided at the website of the ROC Ministry of Justice, http://mojlaw.moj.gov.tw.

[23] Translation provided in Howson, 'The Doctrine That Dared Not Speak Its Name', at 203.

[24] Junhai Liu, *Xiandai Gongsi Fa* (Di Er Ban) [*Modern Corporation Law* (2nd ed.)] (Law Press China 2011), 506–507.

> Although the respective duties of the directors, supervisors and senior management executives are a bit different, they share the common duty of being honest, trustworthy, and diligent.
>
> The Anglo-American legal family usually relies on the concept of fiduciary duties to interpret the legal relationship between the company and its directors and senior executives. As our country adopted the Trust Law in April 2001 and the trust obligations stipulated in the Trust Law are higher than the obligations in the contract of mandate under the Contract Law, we could also use trust obligations to describe the relationship between the company and its directors, supervisors and senior executives in our country. Of course, no matter one uses the contract of mandate or the trust obligations to explain the relationship between the company and its directors, supervisors and senior executives, it will lead to the same result though from different paths. [In this sense], the two paths do not fundamental differences.

The zeal to embrace fiduciary duties in Chinese corporate law however ignores a basic fact in the development of the duties in their origin countries: they are not just some plain and simple rules that could be easily copied from the statute book of one jurisdiction to another. In fact, these rules and standards of great longevity were developed by courts over several centuries in Anglo-American jurisdictions and embedded in a vast body of cases which is impossible to entirely copy into a civil law jurisdiction. As Paul L. Davies has remarked, 'These rules for directors were developed by the courts at an early stage, often on the basis of analogy with the rules applying to trustees. The substantial corpus of learning on the nature and scope of these general fiduciary duties and duties of skill and care has remained until now largely within the common law'.[25]

It is still an open question whether Chinese courts could apply these duties in a way that is roughly in line with both the fundamental principles and legal reasoning for applying such duties in their origin countries. As will be seen later, Chinese courts, because of a lack of understanding of the common law in which the fiduciary duties are embodied, have to resort to the traditional doctrines and legal reasoning in their own civil law system to interpret and apply the newly established 'fiduciary duties' in the PRC Company Law. Of course there is probably nothing wrong with this per se, but eventually we will have a Chinese doctrine of fiduciary duties with distinctive Chinese characteristics. We look at how the fiduciary duties provided in the 2005 Company Law are understood and applied in Chinese courts in the following sections.

[25] Davies, Gower and Davies' Principles, 477.

3 Fiduciary Duties as Provided and Understood in China

3.1 *Duty of Loyalty: The Rules and Standard*

First, paragraph 2 of Article 147 sets forth a general prohibition for all directors, supervisors and senior management executives, which reads: 'Directors, supervisors and senior executives shall not take advantage of their positions and powers to collect or accept bribes or other illegal income, and shall not encroach upon the property of the company'. This is explicitly a statutory provision of a duty of loyalty that applies to the 'key players' inside a company, namely all the directors, supervisors and senior management executives. It covers the typical conflicts of interest situations in a company. The key players, holding company offices, possess certain decision-making powers and also have unique access to company resources, information, and secrets. These key players will be subject to civil and/or criminal liability if they use their position to gain personally or to gain advantage for someone else with a view to seeking or accepting bribes or other illegal income. They are also prohibited from expropriating the company's property in any form.

Article 148 of the Company Law provides a number of additional bright-line prohibitive rules, violation of which would constitute breach of the duty of loyalty by only the directors or senior management executive (and not the supervisors). In essence, a director or senior management executive must not do the following:

1. He shall not misappropriate the company funds, or deposit company funds in a bank account opened in his personal name or in the name of another individual.[26] Obviously this is flagrant stealing of corporate money and a plain breach of the director's or executive's duty of loyalty, which very likely will also lead to punishment of the wrongdoers under the PRC Criminal Law.
2. He shall not lend company funds to others or use company property as collateral to provide security for others, without the consent of the shareholders' general meeting or of the board of directors.[27] This especially refers to a director or executive who has the authority to dispose of corporate assets and uses this position to gain advantage for someone else, regardless of whether he has received anything in return. In the Chinese context, because the directors do not have managerial rights unless he also serves as a senior management

[26] Company Law, Articles 148 (1) and (2). [27] Ibid., Article 148 (3).

executive, such wrongdoing is most often committed by the executives. Such a transaction could however be approved or ratified by either the general meeting or the board of directors.

3. He shall not enter into a contract or transaction with the company in violation of the corporate charter or without the consent of the shareholders' general meeting.[28] This provision covers the typical self-dealing transactions where the director/executive and the company are on opposite sides. Often such transactions are concluded on terms unfair to the company. In essence, the effect of an unfair transaction is the same as if the director or executive has appropriated the financial difference between the transaction's fair value and the transaction's concluded price. But even if he can prove the 'fairness' of the transaction, it will still be voided by the court if the deal violated the corporate charter or was not approved by the general meeting. Such deals are often related-party transactions, whereby the controlling shareholder (or actual controller) of the company ordered the company's board or management to sign and perform contracts preferential to the controlling shareholder but at the expense of the minority shareholders. In such a case, the controlling shareholder or actually controller, together with the directors or executives concerned, violates also Article 21 of the Company Law.
4. He shall not use his position to seek or seize, for himself or for other persons, commercial opportunities that belong to the company without consent from the general meeting.[29] This is apparently the Chinese version of the 'usurping corporate opportunity' doctrine, which prohibits the director or executive to seize for himself or someone else desirable business opportunities that the company likely would have taken and profited from. The court will invoke the corporate opportunity doctrine only when the director's or executive's taking of the opportunity was not approved by the general meeting. It is not clear in the law what would be the consequence if the director/executive takes the opportunity for himself after he presented the opportunity to the company but the company declined to take it. It is of course likely that a wise court interprets this as an 'approval' of the company.
5. He shall not operate for himself or any other person the same type of business as that of the company without the consent of the general meeting.[30] This is a statutory recognition of the non-compete clause

[28] Ibid., Article 148 (4). [29] Ibid., Article 148 (5). [30] Ibid., Article 148 (5).

in many private contracts. The directors and senior management executives are thus prohibited from pursuing a similar profession or business in competition against the company. Of course, as with other types of conflicts of interest, disloyal competition may be approved or ratified by the general meeting of shareholders. It also refers to the situation where the director/executive is competing with the company while still on the payroll. Competition after the director or executive has ended his employment with the company is not governed by the Company Law. In fact, it might largely depend on whether the company has a non-competition agreement with said directors or executives. It is also important to note that this non-compete provision could be related to the above-mentioned corporate opportunity doctrine, as the competitive business the director/executive runs might also be a desired opportunity for the company.

6. He shall not accept commissions for transactions between the company and other parties and turn them into personal gains.[31] This is to be distinguished from taking bribes referred to in paragraph 2 of Article 148 of the Company Law. Here the other party in the transaction is understood to have no intention to bribe the director or senior management executive. He simply mistakenly believed that the director/executive was a broker for the transaction who deserved the commission. It is not relevant whether the director/executive who pocketed the commission also held the same belief.
7. He shall not disclose company secrets without authorisation. The unique decision-making and leadership position of the directors and supervisors provide them with access to all the key information and business secrets of the company.
8. He shall not harm the interest of the company in related-party transactions.

The above prohibitions could be generally classified into two groups whether they are absolutely prohibited or could be approved/ratified. The director/executive is 'absolutely prohibited' from engaging in taking bribes, commissions and other illegal incomes, expropriating company property, misappropriating company funds or depositing the funds in the personal name of his or other individuals, harming company interest in related-party transactions or arbitrarily disclosing confidential information. Other acts can be put into the 'approvable group' as they are conditional

[31] Ibid., Article 148 (6).

upon the in-advance approval or after-the-fact-ratification of the board or the general meeting. That is to say, an act of the director or supervisor which otherwise violates the duty of loyalty may be validated if it is approved in advance or ratified afterward ('consent'). In line with the shareholder-centred nature of China's corporate law, all transactions with such conflict of interest must be approved by the general meeting with one exception: lending company funds to or providing security for others may be consented by the board of directors. Implicitly, to obtain the consent, a full disclosure of the nature of the conflict and material facts of the transaction to the general meeting or board would be necessary.

Conflicted interest transactions shall only be approved by disinterested holders of the voting rights. In the case the board's consent could suffice, it is important to note that, especially in listed companies, the board approval or ratification could only be passed by the majority of disinterested directors under Article 125 of the Company Law. It has been suggested however that the court should adopt an 'expanded interpretation' of Article 125 and apply it to non-listed companies.[32] As noted above, most of such transactions must be approved by the general meeting. Similarly, interested shareholders shall recuse themselves under certain circumstances. Based on Article 16 of the Company Law, company's investment in another enterprise or provision of security for others may be approved by either the board of directors or the general meeting. But if the company provides security for a shareholder or the *de facto* controlling person of the company, it must be approved by the general meeting in the form of a resolution.[33]

[32] Liu, *Modern Corporation Law*, 490–491.

[33] Any other forms of company approval other than a formal resolution would be regarded as invalid by the courts. In *Weiyan Ltd.* v. *Xu Naihong and Others* (2006), the defendant, Mr. Xu, was a deputy general manager of the plaintiff, a Japanese-invested LLC. During his term of office at Weiyan Ltd., the defendant formed another company and served as the legal representative of the company, which had a similar scope of business as that of the plaintiff. The defendant argued that he was approved by the defendant's legal representative, in an approval letter which carried even the official stamp of the plaintiff, to serve as another company's executive director and general manager. The court, which was a basic court in Wuxi City, Jiangsu Province, ruled that Mr. Xu violated the duty of loyalty rule that a senior management executive of a company 'shall not operate for himself or any other person the same type of business as that of the company without the consent of the general meeting'. The approval letter signed by the company's legal representative together with corporate seal was not the same as a resolution of the general meeting. The facts and decision of the case were summarised and discussed in Xiaofeng Huai, *Zhongguo Zuixin Gongsifa: Dianxing Anli Pingxi* [*Latest PRC Company Law: Cases and Commentaries*], (Beijing: Law Press China, 2007), 322–329.

A violation of any of the prohibitive rules above might lead to the following legal consequences. First, all the income as a result of the violation shall belong to the company – that means the wrongdoer will have to disgorge the income.[34] Second, the wrongdoer might be sued by the company or shareholders for damage under Article 150 of the Company Law. If the court invalidates the transactions, restitution will follow and the wrongdoer might also be ordered to return the corporate property he illegally possessed. In addition, the wrongdoer might be subject to administrative and criminal liabilities. In particular, a criminal offence for breaching the duty of loyalty was introduced by the National People's Congress by way of the Amendment (VI) to the PRC Criminal Law in June 2006.

3.2 The Lack of the 'Fairness' Factor

The disclosure and approval requirements above appear to be procedural in nature. A legalistic interpretation of the requirements will lead to the following understandings:

(1) The courts will void any transactions in the 'absolutely prohibited group'.
(2) The courts will dismiss a claim that challenge a transaction of the 'approvable group' if the statutorily required consent is obtained from the general meeting or the board, regardless of whether the transaction is fair to the company or not.
(3) On the other hand, the courts will invalidate a transaction that is not approved or ratified by the board or the general meeting, regardless of whether the transaction is actually fair or not to the company.

This legalistic but rigid interpretation, which might very likely be adopted by courts in China, demonstrates a major loophole in the legal test under the duty of loyalty rules examined above. By contrast, under the US law, the director or executive concerned will avoid self-dealing problems if the conflict-of-interest transaction (1) was ratified by an impartial director approval or impartial shareholder approval after he disclosed the material facts to the board or general meeting; or (2) was proven to be basically 'fair' to the company.[35] That is, if the self-dealing

[34] Company Law, Article 149, para. 2.
[35] James D. Cox and Thomas Lee Hazen (2003), *Corporations*, 2nd ed., (New York: Aspen Publishers, 2003), 210.

transaction is found to be fair to the company, it will be allowed to stand by the courts. This is true whether or not the transaction was approved or ratified by the board or general meeting. However, it will not be a surprise if some Chinese courts opt for ignoring a rigid textual reading of those disclosure and approval requirements as seen above with the view to determining the case based on the 'fairness' of the transaction.

3.3 *The Duty of Care*

Apart from mentioning the duty of care in Article 148, the Company Law has neither a clear definition nor guiding principles as to how to understand this duty. One textbook in China defines it as follows:[36]

> The duty of care, also known as the duty of good management or duty of attention, means that the directors, supervisors and senior management executives shall exercise the rights granted by the company prudently, seriously and diligently, and act with the kind of prudence, care and diligence and skills that a reasonably prudent person would behave like under similar circumstances.

Other leading corporate law textbooks or treaties have adopted rather similar definitions.[37] There is little doubt this kind of definition was borrowed from American corporate law.[38] Indeed, § 4.01(a) of the ALI Principles of Corporate Governance has an almost identical provision about the duty of care:

> director or officer has a duty to the corporation to perform the director's or officer's functions in good faith, in a manner that he or she reasonably believes to be in the best interests of the corporation, and with the care that an ordinarily prudent person would reasonably be expected to exercise in a like position and under similar circumstances.

The Company Law does not define the basic standard of care and diligence. As noted above, civil law jurisdictions (including China) treat the legal relationship between the company and its directors as one based

[36] Yousu Zhou, *Xin Gongsi Fa Lun* [*New Survey on Corporation Law*], (Law Press China, 2006), 391.

[37] See Liu, *Modern Corporation Law*, 513; Tiantao Shi, *Gongsifa Lun (Di'er Ban)* [*Corporation Law*, 2nd ed.], (Law Press China, 2006), 401; Peizhong Gan, *Qiye yu Gongsi Faxue* [*Enterprise and Company Law*], (Peking University Press, 2007), 405.

[38] The leading textbooks noted above rely heavily on the relevant rules, concepts, principles and explanations in American corporate law to interpret the duty of care in Chinese Company Law. See Gan, *Enterprise and Company Law*, 405–407; Shi, *Corporation Law*, 400–403; Junhai, *Modern Corporation Law*, 513–514.

on the contract of mandate, in which the mandatory must act with the duty of care of a 'good manager', although the specific requirements for a good manager have not been spelled out. Two judges of the PRC Supreme People's Court (SPC), in their academic writing, have boldly – but not surprisingly – suggested Chinese courts to adopt the 'three criteria of the duty of care decided in the case law of Anglo-American countries', which are interpreted by them as the following:[39]

1. *Good faith.* The directors and executives must act in good faith, which is understood as a subjective standard. That is to say, whether the good faith standard is met depends on the mental state of the director or executive when he was committing the alleged wrongdoing. Whether he understood the consequences of his action and had bothered take due care to ensure negative consequences would not happen would be an essential factor here.[40]
2. *Care.* The director or executive should act as an ordinarily prudent person would reasonably do in a like position under similar circumstances. He would however need to exercise the necessary care of an expert if he does have such professional capabilities.[41]
3. *Reasonable belief that his action is in the best interest of the company.*[42]

One has no difficulty in discerning the similarities between the above standard and the one provided in § 8.30(a) of the Revised Model Business Corporation Act (RMBCA), which provides, 'A director shall discharge his duties as a director . . . (1) in good faith; (2) with the care an ordinarily prudent person in a like position would exercise under similar circumstances; and (3) in a manner he reasonably believes to be in the best interests of the corporation'.[43]

3.4 *Return to the Civil Law Doctrine of Tort Liability*

It is however not difficult to discover a doctrinal misunderstanding in the two SPC judges' interpretation of the American duty of care. That is, the standard of care enumerated in the RMBCA is basically an

[39] Xiaoming Xi and Jianfeng Jin, *Gongsi Susong: Lilun yu Shiwu Wenti Yanjiu* [*Corporate Litigation: Theory and Practices*], (People's Court Press, 2008), 468–469.

[40] Ibid., at 469. [41] Ibid. [42] Ibid.

[43] Note this provision has been replaced by §8.30(a) of the new Model Business Corporation Act (MBCA) which simply requires a member of the board of directors to act '(1) in good faith, and (2) in a manner the director reasonably believes to be in the best interests of the corporation'.

'objective one', rather than the 'subjective standard' understood above:[44]

> [T]he director will be held to the standard of care that would be exercised by a 'reasonable person' in the director's position. Consequently, a director who is simply less smart, less able or less innately diligent than an 'ordinary' reasonable director will nonetheless have to meet this higher ordinary standard.

The difference here may be only linguistic in nature. After all, the two judges' interpretation above also require the director/executive to behave with the care an ordinarily prudent person in a like position would exercise, which was a literal reproduction of the relevant American corporate law rules in Chinese. 'Subjective standard', a rather peculiar expression, is used here to emphasise a key element in the Chinese doctrine of the duty of care as understood by the courts, which is the mental fault of the wrongdoers. In doing so, the application of fiduciary duties was casually translated into the application of the traditional doctrine of general tort liability that has long existed in Chinese civil law. In essence, a cause of action for general tort liability require the following four key elements:[45]

- An infringing action (*jiahai xingwei*), which is essentially illegal and harmed the civil rights and interests of injured. The action is characterised as 'illegal' to presume the presence of a duty. Harming others by breaching any laws, which is defined here in its broadest sense, would constitute an illegal action.[46]
- Injury (*sunhai shishi*) in the form of economic losses, or physical, mental or emotional damages.[47]
- Causation (*yinguo guanxi*), which means it can be proven that there is a causal link between the injury and the infringing action.[48]
- Fault (*guocuo*), which means the infringer is at fault. Fault was the subjective mental state of the infringer when committing the infringing action, which could either be based on the infringer's intention or negligence.[49]

Not coincidentally, Judge Xi and Judge Jin explicitly stated in their academic writing that the duty of care liability would require the showing of the following four factors:[50]

[44] Steven L. Emanuel, *Corporations*, (Emanuel Publishing Corp., 1997), 175.
[45] Liming Wang, *Minfa Xue* [*The Science of Civil Law*] (Fudan University Press, 2004), 834–853.
[46] Ibid., at 836. [47] Ibid., at 838–843. [48] Ibid., at 843–847. [49] Ibid., at 847–853.
[50] Xi and Jin, *Corporate Litigation*, 470.

- *Jiahai xingwei*: The director or senior executive violated laws, administrative regulations or the corporate charter in their conduct of corporate affairs.
- *Guocuo*: The director or senior executive must be mentally at fault when he failed to meet the duty of care, which was a result of either intentions or negligence.
- *Sunshi*: The company must have suffered financial losses, which include both direct and indirect losses.
- *Yinguo guanxi*: The losses suffered by the company must be caused by the breach of the duty of care.

It is fairly reasonable to say that the above view applies to the judicial practice in China. In *Xiangjia Ltd. vs. Tai Jianying* (2007),[51] the defendant, Mr. Tai Jianying ('Tai'), was hired by the plaintiff in August 2004 as its manager. On 31 August 2005, Tai signed, on behalf of the plaintiff, a sale contract with Baiqiang Ltd. in which the plaintiff was committed to provide goods worthy of RMB 16,310 to Baiqiang. The contract was signed by the representatives of Baiqiang without however affixing Baiqiang's corporate stamp. Tai left the plaintiff on 30 September 2005. The goods were delivered to Baiqiang, but Baiqiang never made any payment to the plaintiff. The plaintiff, however, also never attempted to go after Baiqiang through litigation, arbitration or any other effective means. In a beautifully written judgment which linguistically interpreted the common-law's fiduciary duty of care according to the doctrine of tort liability in Chinese civil law, the court ruled that[52]

> Tai Jianying ('Tai'), as the company's hired manager to be in the charge of business operations, should meet his obligations and conduct the company's affairs with diligence and care, otherwise he should be liable for the losses suffered by the company. This liability would be established if the following four constituent elements were shown: (1) he violated laws, administrative regulations or the corporate charter in managing the company's business; (2) he was subjectively at fault; (3) the company suffered losses; and (4) there is a causal link between the violations and the losses suffered by the company. In the case in question, Tai's signing the contract and performing the contractual obligations on behalf of the company were actions that he had taken to execute his managerial duties in good faith, which did not violate any national laws, administrative

51 The facts and decision of the case were summarised and discussed in Liu Lanfang, *Xin Gongsifa Yinan Anli Panjie* [*Understanding the Difficult Cases under the New Company Law*] (Law Press China, 2009), 432–435.

52 Ibid., at 433–434.

regulations or provisions in the corporate charter. Baiqiang Ltd. was a legal person enterprise lawfully registered with the company registration authority, which had secured in its own name a contract for building a construction project. Xiangjia Ltd. could certainly benefit from the sale contract for supplying concrete to the project, and the payment of the price was also guaranteed to a certain degree. For these reasons, Tai had already exercised the due care required for an ordinarily prudent person in signing and performing the sale contract. As such, Tai should not be expected to be liable for any loss as a result of his actions above. Further, the economic loss which Xiangjia Ltd. had asked Tai to compensate was actually because Baiqiang Ltd. did not perform its obligation of making payment under the sale contract. [Under normal circumstances], Xiangjia should raise claims to Baiqiang in time after the payment was delayed. An economic loss would be incurred only when Xiangjia still could not get paid after it tried to pursue its claims through litigation, arbitration or other effective means. Since Xiangjia Ltd. had never raised any claim to Baiqiang, the economic loss claimed by Xiangjia had actually never been incurred. Furthermore, there is no direct causal link between Tai's above actions and Xiangjia Ltd.'s alleged loss. It is thus ruled that this court will not support the plaintiff Xiangjia Ltd.'s claims for compensation by Tai.

3.5 The Business Judgment Rule Applied in Chinese Courts

There is no mention of the business judgment rule (BJR) whatsoever in any of the corporate law legislations in China, but Chinese judges and scholars seem to truly like the rule and prefer to see it being applied in corporate litigation in China, although they publicly admitted that the BJR was a creation of American corporate law.[53] In essence, the BJR is a presumption that the directors or executives acted on an informed basis, in good faith and in the honest belief that the action taken was in the best interest of the company. The courts will thus not easily second-guess business decisions of the company and 'will abstain from reviewing board decisions unless those decisions are tainted by fraud, illegality, or self-dealing'.[54]

Chinese jurists' understanding of the BJR is largely in line with the above spirit. Immediately after the new Company Law was promulgated in 2005, two SPC judges, one of them being a vice president of the SPC, published an article in the *People's Court Daily* to encourage Chinese

[53] See e.g. Xi and Jin, *Corporate Litigation*, at 476 (stating 'the business judgment rule is a legal institution created by American courts to exempt directors from bearing liability for reasonable mistakes in business operation'. See also Junhai, *Modern Corporation Law*, 517–518; Gan, *Enterprise and Company Law*, 411–413; Shi, *Corporation Law*, 403–408.

[54] Stephen M. Bainbridge, *Corporate Law* (2nd ed.) (Thomson Reuters/Foundation Press, 2009), 109.

courts to 'respect the principle of party autonomy in private law' and apply the business judgment in judicial resolution of disputes.[55] This article states, among other things, that[56]

> The key to the trial of corporate disputes by the people's courts is to stick to the principle of safeguarding the autonomy in private law, respect the self-governance and self-control of decision-making of the corporate bodies, and properly handle the relationship between lawful judicial interference and the company's self-governance .... A major problem of the [1993] Company Law is that it has left very little room for corporate self-governance, having the law to decide on both the big and trivial matters of the company. The practice has shown that making the law to decide on everything is not only impractical but also impossible. The numerous differences in corporate activities necessarily mean that corporate governance could not follow the same patter at all. For these reasons, the people's court, when stepping in to look at the internal legal relations inside a company, must be cautious enough to leave enough room for corporate self-governance. The people's courts should not substitute judicial power for the company's ordinary business judgment, but should instead respect the ordinary business judgment. Judges are not always able to make wise and fair decisions under all circumstances, even though they have the good will to do so. Generally speaking, a company's internal affairs should be carried out by the company in accordance with its charter. As long as self-governance does not pose barriers to transactional security and social stability, we should respect the companies to make decisions based on commercial considerations, respect their freedom in declaring intention and carrying out civil acts, and recognise the legal effect and corporate self-governance. The people' courts should intervene to replace the business judgment with judicial judgment only when issues relating to the health of the corporate structure or transactional security are concerned, such as that the controlling shareholders, directors or senior executives abuse the autonomy of private law and the freedom of carrying out civil acts and therefore harm the rights and lawful interests of the parties in corporate legal relations.

In Xi and Jin (2008), the judges advocated that the Supreme People's Court should enact a judicial interpretation to incorporate the BJR into Chinese law for three reasons:

> (1) The BJR is suitable for dealing with the complexities of business operation of the companies. As the company's scale expands its operation

[55] Guoguang Li and Chuang Wang, 'Shenqi Gongsi Susong Ruogan Wenti (I)' ['Several Questions on the Courts' Adjudication of Corporate Disputes (Part I)'], *People's Court Daily*, 29 November 2005, http://old.chinacourt.org/public/detail.php?id=187288.

[56] Ibid.

> becomes increasingly complicated, and therefore it is impossible to expect the directors to make all decisions correct. (2) The BJR is consistent with the nature of commercial decision-making. Market risks and uncertainties predetermines that business decisions cannot always only bring benefits to the company, and one simply could not predict in advance the negative consequences of a decision before it was made. If the requirement is that a business judgment should always be correct, the results would be that commercial opportunities will be missed, corporate operational efficiency will be reduced and the protection for the company and the shareholders will be undermined. (3) The BJR is consistent with nature of the operation of the corporate organs. It positively encourages the directors to be more risk-taking in business operation to bring value for the company and its shareholders.[57]

Despite the enthusiastic embracing of the BJR by influential SPC judges, neither judicial interpretations nor typical cases related to the BJR have emerged in China. It is hence still an open question, from a doctrinal perspective, how Chinese courts will consider the constituent elements of the BJR in judicial practice.

4 Transplant of Fiduciary Duties into China: Implications in Comparative Law

The transplant of foreign legal institutions into any country's domestic legal order is doomed to be difficult. Any such transplant might result in the transplant shock, which describes the phenomenon that the foreign institutions may not work well or even be rejected by actors of the domestic legal order. The transfer of Anglo-American fiduciary duties into civil law jurisdictions or transition economies is especially difficult as the concept of fiduciary duties itself is open-ended, thus any codification – which is normally how foreign laws are transplanted – could only capture a small portion of the whole meaning of the duties as understood in their origin jurisdictions.

The adoption of 'fiduciary duties' by China's legislature and enforced by Chinese courts suggests that legal transplant may offer two lessons in comparative law. First, a transplant may generate an unexpected result which hasn't been adequately studied in comparative law. Namely, the legal transplant may give the courts a legal authorisation to do something that they could not do before the transplanting. Although judges of the host jurisdiction may not fully understand the 'authentic' meaning of the

[57] Xi and Jin, *Corporate Litigation*, 476.

transplanted rules, they may seek help from local legal resources – legal doctrines which have long-existed in their domestic legal system. That they could not employ these local resources for disputes in an area in the past was probably because the civil law doctrines of their country prohibit them from protecting rights which are not provided in the legislations.

Before the codification of the fiduciary duties in 2005, the then prevailing 1993 Company Law offered little legal protection for minority shareholders. Very few of the legal rights of shareholders and almost none of the legal liabilities and remedies against corporate insiders which can be seen in the Company Law today were available to shareholders in the 1993 Company Law.[58] In essence, the corporate law culture underlining the 1993 Company Law displayed the suppression of private enforcement of minority shareholders' rights.[59] The legal provisions concerning private enforcement contained in the 1993 Company Law were vague, rudimentary and largely unenforceable. Article 111 of the 1993 Company Law provided the only legal basis for private enforcement, allowing shareholders to bring a legal action to 'enjoin such violation or infringement if a resolution adopted by the shareholders' meeting or board of directors violates national laws, administrative regulations, or infringe upon the rights and interests of the shareholders'. It is pretty clear from this provision that shareholders in China were only empowered to petition the court to stop the implementation of a corporate resolution, be it adopted by the shareholders' meeting or board of directors, but were not allowed to bring a legal action against individual directors who are personally responsible for the resolutions or have committed wrongdoings. As remarked by this author in a previous paper,

> Due to its inherent defects, Article 111 was rarely replied upon by the court to solve shareholder civil disputes. Instead, courts would simply reject almost all private enforcement initiatives, being unwilling to adjudicate on such cases in the absence of clear guidance from the statue and judicial interpretations.[60]

As can be seen from the analysis on the understanding and application of fiduciary duties in China, Chinese courts and judges have demonstrated

[58] See generally, Jiangyu Wang, 'Rule of Law and Rule of Officials: Shareholder Litigation and Anti-Dumping Investigation in China', Paper No. 4 in the *Rule of Law in China: Chinese Law and Business Series*, Oxford: The Foundation for Law, Justice and Society (2007).

[59] Ibid., at 2. [60] Ibid., at 3.

a pro-active attitude to protect the rights of minority shareholders in the name of enforcing fiduciary duties provided in the Company Law after the fiduciary duties were codified in the 2005 Company Law. To compensate for their lack of understanding of the original meaning of Anglo-American fiduciary duties, the courts have resorted to the conventional wisdom of tort liability to interpret such duties in the Chinese context. They can do it now because the 2005 Company Law has, through codifying fiduciary duties, outlawed a number of looting behaviours and conflict of interest situations which were not prohibited by the previous Company Law. Whatever doctrine the Chinese courts use to approach fiduciary duties, the wrongdoings were punished in many cases. Frankly, as we have already seen, the legal reasoning in the tort law based approach used by Chinese courts as enunciated in the judgments and scholarly writing of Chinese judges has a system of its own. In essence, it has begun to form a distinctive but workable Chinese doctrine of fiduciary duties which does not necessarily need to be identical to the understanding of fiduciary duties in Anglo-American countries, although the concept of fiduciary duties in Chinese law was unquestionably borrowed from common law.

A second implication of China's adoption of fiduciary duties is rather ironic. That is, it again proves that the transplant of Anglo-American fiduciary duties into a civil law jurisdiction – and a transition economy – is particularly difficult, if not entirely impossible. Although the result is not necessarily bad; after all, the unexpected result of turning fiduciary duties into tort liability by Chinese courts enhances the legal protection for minority shareholders to probably the equal extent. However, exactly for this reason, the fiduciary duties now in China are so much different from those in their origin jurisdictions that we would be looking hypercritical if we still call this a transplant of fiduciary duties.

5 Conclusion

The codification of fiduciary duties in the PRC Company Law has raised again the question of whether and to what extent Anglo-American fiduciary duties can be exported to other countries through legal transplant. An empirical examination of the judgments and scholarly writing by Chinese judges suggests that the courts have been proactively using enforcement of fiduciary duties to protect minority shareholders' rights in China. This, however, is not necessarily a successful example of legal transplantation. In fact, Chinese courts and judges have almost totally disregarded the relevant overseas jurisprudence. Instead, they relied on the traditional civil law doctrine of tort liability to interpret fiduciary duties. In other words, fiduciary duties have been given substance, content and effect by Chinese courts and judges not through careful learning of the relevant case law in Anglo-American countries, but through the application of domestic legal resources which the Chinese judges are familiar with. The results are almost equally good, as investor protection in China is also improved.

The Chinese case of transplanting fiduciary duties probably proves again the non-transplantability of open-ended foreign institutions such as fiduciary duties. On the other hand, the codification of the name and a few principles of fiduciary duties have achieved an unexpected result which equally enhanced the quality of Chinese corporate law. This is a phenomenon that is worthy of further study in comparative law.

11

China's Free Trade Zone and Latest Development of the Resolution Mechanism for Financial Disputes

A Perspective from the Innovation of Qianhai International Arbitration

XIAOCHUN LIU[1]

1 Experiment of China's Free Trade Zone Reform and Financial Reform

At the beginning of 2015, China expanded the free trade zones and the State Council laid down particular emphases in the approval of each specific free trade zone; for example, in respect of Guangdong Free Trade Zone, the State Council proposed specific requirements for Qianhai-Shekou Area in the field of financial innovation and clearly required it to build 'the window for trial and demonstration of the opening of China's financial industry'.[2]

In fact, before the release of the above approval, Qianhai had already promoted the financial industry by listing it among the key industries of Shenzhen-Hong Kong Cooperation Area. After the free trade zone policy is approved, the financial enterprises are more willing to take Qianhai as their place of establishment. Up to 27 November 2015, a total of 56,550 enterprises have been established in Qianhai, including 28,972 financial enterprises (accounting for 51 per cent). Why do so many financial enterprises choose to establish in Qianhai? Financial innovation is a key factor. Qianhai not only has the policy advantage regarding the offshore RMB loans, but also the innovations in respect of overseas bonds and foreign-invested venture capital funds, etc. The perfect support of

[1] This chapter was prepared with the support from Xin An, Feng Zhao, Tao Yang and Yi Zhou.

[2] Article 2, *Reply of the State Council on Relevant Policies to Support the Development and Opening up of Shenzhen-Hong Kong Modern Service Cooperation Zone in Qianhai* (Guo Han [2012] No.58).

surrounding industries is also another key factor, but the most important factor is the expectations of financial enterprises for the financial innovation of Qianhai. As a special area of Shenzhen Special Economic Zone, Qianhai has inevitably acquired Shenzhen's gene of innovation; therefore, the whole society is eager to expect and has full confidence in the leading role of Qianhai in financial innovation in the new era.

An innovation must be protected by other innovations. As the financial industry innovates constantly and quickly, the corresponding dispute resolution mechanism must satisfy the demand of such innovation. As the first arbitration institution established in the region of Guangdong, Hong Kong and Macau, which has over thirty years' experience in commercial arbitration, the South China International Economic and Trade Arbitration Commission (also known as Shenzhen Court of International Arbitration, hereinafter the SCIA), in order to support the construction of international and law-based environment and the development of finance and other leading industries in Qianhai, has been actively engaged in the innovation of international arbitration of Qianhai and has established the corporate governance structure surrounding the international and society-based council. The SCIA is the first and the only arbitration institution that adopts the mode of administration by a statutory body in Mainland China and thus strengthened the independence of arbitration in the Free Trade Zone. On the basis of the characteristics of financial industry, the SCIA created the 'quaternity' dispute resolution mechanism for capital markets together with the CSRC's Shenzhen Bureau and Shenzhen Stock Exchange in 2013, and established the Free Trade Zone Financial Arbitration Centre together with Guangdong Provincial Financial Office and the Authority of Qianhai in 2015, which further enhances the professionalism in financial disputes resolution.[3]

2 The Innovation of the 'Quaternity' Dispute Resolution Mechanism of Shenzhen Securities and Futures Dispute Resolution Centre

Mediation, arbitration and litigation are the most common methods to resolve commercial disputes; yet, among these methods, which one is

[3] South China International Economic and Trade Arbitration Commission (also called Shenzhen Court of International Arbitration) was established in 1983. It was originally called China International Economic and Trade Arbitration Commission Shenzhen Sub-Commission and China International Economic and Trade Arbitration Commission South China Sub-Commission.

the favourite method for disputes resolution in capital markets? The parties of these disputes usually have a strict demand in regards to cost, efficiency, confidentiality and professionalism in dispute resolution, and litigation may not be the favourite method. On the contrary, in the current framework of law, there are still some deficiencies to resolve disputes in capital markets through mediation only or through arbitration only. As regards mediation, the mediation agency may lack professionalism (e.g. the mediation agency established by local governments usually do not engage any specialists to act as mediators) or impartiality (e.g. the mediation department established by a professional association can hardly obtain the trust of an external party). Even if the parties finally reach a settlement, the settlement agreement does not have any legal force for it to be implemented; therefore, when a party does not respect the settlement agreement, it will increase the cost and trouble of dispute resolution. As regards arbitration, although an arbitral award is legally binding and enforceable, it requires a valid arbitration agreement between the parties for the dispute to be accepted by the arbitration institution. As a result, many requests for arbitration are refused due to the 'distance' between the arbitration institution and the capital market, i.e. the parties fail to reach a valid arbitration agreement.

To effectively prevent and harmoniously resolve the disputes in capital markets, to improve the environment of finance and to promote the robust development of capital market, the SCIA, together with the CSRC's Shenzhen Bureau, Shenzhen Stock Exchange, Shenzhen Securities Association, Shenzhen Futures Association, and Shenzhen Asset Management Association, etc., fully borrowed the experience from the US mediation and arbitration of securities-related disputes in the current framework of law and established the Shenzhen Securities and Futures Dispute Resolution Centre (hereinafter the 'Dispute Resolution Centre') in Qianhai. They created the quaternity mode for resolving disputes in capital markets: professional mediation + commercial arbitration + industry discipline + administrative regulation. The 'quaternity' mode enables the Dispute Resolution Centre and the professional arbitration institution, the securities regulatory agency and the industrial discipline organisations to cooperate with each other so that the mediation by the Dispute Resolution Centre may play a more effective role with the support of arbitration, self-discipline and regulation.

The 'quaternity' mechanism has the following advantages:

(1) It sticks to the principles of independence and impartiality. The Dispute Resolution Centre is an independent agency with its council and secretariat operate independently pursuant to its articles of association. Therefore, as an independent third party, it can easily obtain trust from the parties, especially the investors;
(2) It emphasises professionalism and industrial practice. All mediators are selected professionals of the capital market who are not only equipped with sound credibility, mediation ability and professional ethics, but are also familiar with the rules and mode of operation of the industry so that they can mediate the disputes and resolve the conflicts on the basis of the characteristics and professional issues of the industry;
(3) It focuses on the protection of small and medium investors. The Dispute Resolution Centre does not charge any mediation fee for disputes between small and medium investors and members of the securities associations, futures associations, asset management associations, or for the disputes between small and medium investors and companies listed in the Shenzhen Stock Exchange;
(4) The mediation result can be enforced. Thanks to the integration between the mediation by the Dispute Resolution Centre and the arbitration by the SCIA, the parties may, after reaching a settlement agreement, apply to an arbitral tribunal of the SCIA to issue an arbitration award instantly according to the terms of the settlement agreement, which can be recognised and be enforceable throughout China and in the other 155 contracting states of the New York Convention (up to November 2015); and
(5) Fully reflects the regulation and self-discipline of the industry. If one party refuses to execute the settlement agreement or arbitration award, the other party or the Dispute Resolution Centre may report the relevant situation to the self-discipline organisations or the administrative regulatory agency of the capital market for it to be recorded in the record of good standing. For a member who refuses to execute or fails to actively execute the settlement agreement, the self-discipline organisations or the administrative regulatory agency may take disciplining measures pursuant to the rules of self-discipline.

The practice has proved that the 'quaternity' mechanism adopted by the Dispute Resolution Centre can harmoniously resolve disputes and conflicts in the capital market. Since its official establishment

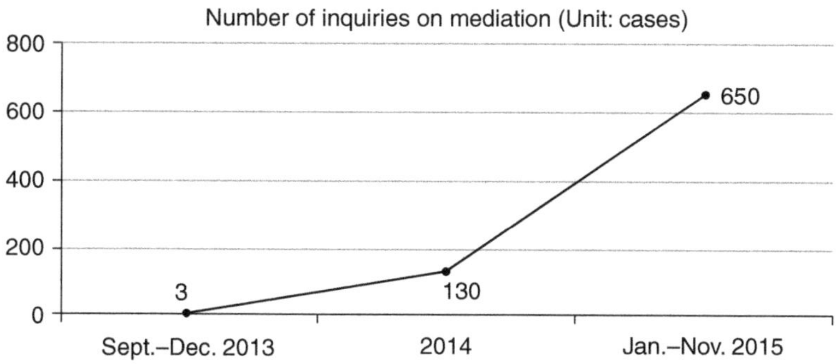

Figure 11.1 Number of inquiries on mediation received by the Dispute Resolution Centre since September 2013

in September 2013, the Dispute Resolution Centre has properly handled a lot of enquiries concerning disputes in capital market, including disputes between listed companies and their investors due to false representation and other disputes related to securities, futures and fund transactions. The total amount involved in these disputes was nearly RMB 200 million.

As a result of the violent fluctuation of China's securities market since July 2015, the disputes and complaints received by the Dispute Resolution Centre due to compulsory close of positions in margin transactions of securities has increased abruptly. To properly resolve the disputes arising from margin transactions, the Dispute Resolution Centre timely released announcements through the professional media to direct the investors and securities companies to solve dispute rationally through mediation conducted by the Dispute Resolution Centre and called the mediators and professional experts up to discuss the solutions and techniques for resolving these disputes. The Dispute Resolution Centre and its mediators properly resolved many disputes arising from compulsory close of margin transaction positions in line with the principle of objectivity and impartiality, thus effectively protecting the legitimate rights and interests of investors and securities companies, and made a positive contribution to the stability and long-term development of China's capital market.

After the implementation of the Shanghai-Hong Kong Stock Connect program and the mutual recognition of funds between mainland China and Hong Kong, the Shenzhen-Hong Kong stock connect program will be put forward soon; therefore, the Dispute Resolution Centre pays more

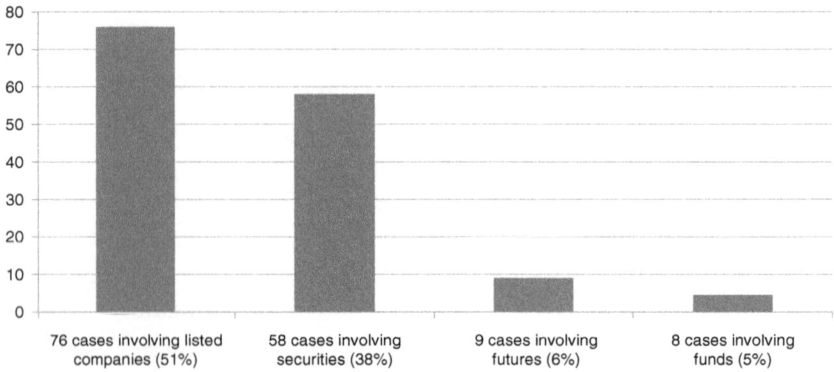

Figure 11.2 Specific types of dispute of the 151 mediation cases officially received by the Dispute Resolution Centre pursuant to its mediation rules and their respective number and ratio

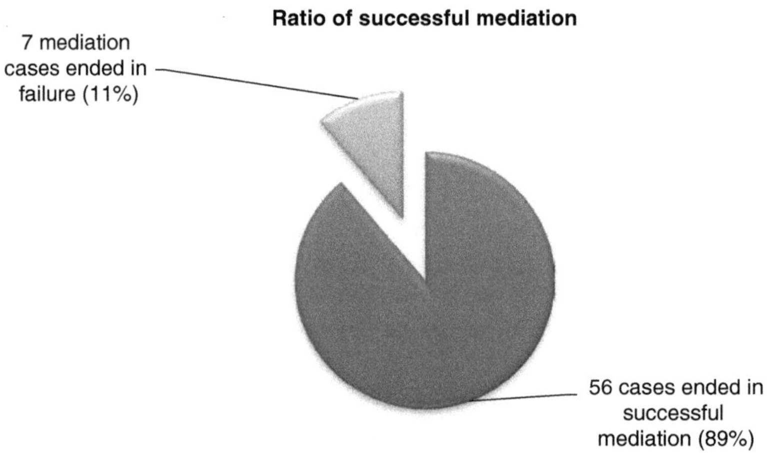

Figure 11.3 Except for the seventy-one cases involving listed companies transferred to the relevant court in 2014, the Dispute Resolution Centre has completed sixty-three cases with a ratio of successful mediation up to 89 per cent, and the other seventeen cases are in the process of mediation

attention to dispute resolution related to cross-border capital market businesses. At present, the Dispute Resolution Centre is strengthening the exchange and cooperation with relevant associations of capital market and commercial mediation institutions in Hong Kong, and plans to absorb a number of Hong Kong professionals of capital market in the panel of mediators to accommodate the demand for dispute resolution

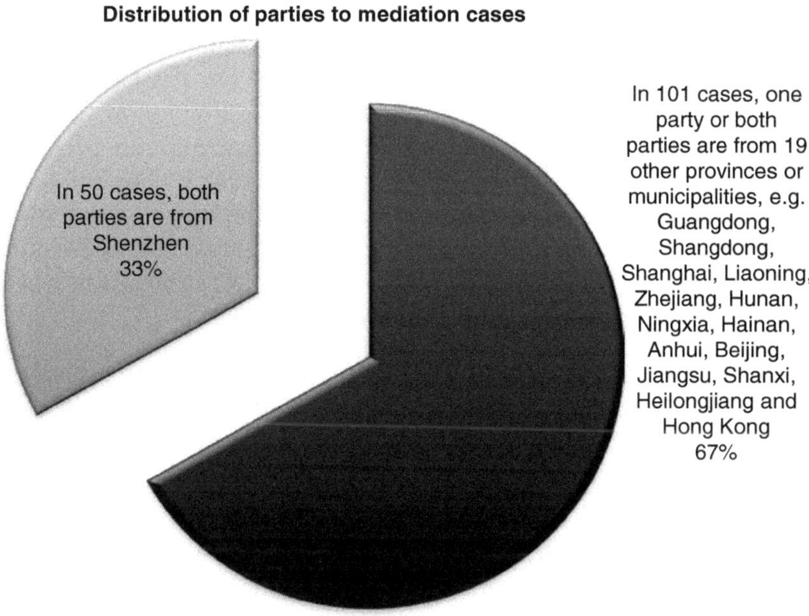

Figure 11.4 Most of the mediation cases accepted by the Dispute Resolution Centre involve cross-regional disputes, i.e. one party or both the parties are from areas outside Shenzhen, and the remote mediation is adopted

related to cross-border capital market businesses and provide better dispute resolution services to the financial enterprises of Qianhai.

2.1 Case of Securities Dispute Between Listed Companies and Investors Resolved by the Dispute Resolution Centre

In April 2014, a listed company, H, encountered a dispute with investors due to false representation, which involved over 9,800 investors from all over China and the total amount of claims is nearly RMB 100 million. In July 2014, the majority of H company's shareholders established the special compensation fund and invited the Dispute Resolution Centre to participate in the design and implementation of the compensation fund program. The compensation fund program provided the listed company and investors with various dispute resolution methods, including reconciliation, mediation and arbitration: if the investors accepted the compensation program, they were deemed as having reached a reconciliation with the fund provider; in case the investors refused to accept the compensation program, they could apply to the Dispute Resolution Centre for mediation or execute an arbitration agreement with the fund provider and apply to the SCIA for arbitration. On the basis of the compensation program offered by H, the Dispute Resolution Centre's staff persuaded most investors to accept the compensation program by phone or e-mail. However, there were still investors who refused to accept the compensation program and applied to the Dispute Resolution Centre for mediation. In this case, the mediator appointed by the Dispute Resolution Centre helped the fund provider and these investors to reach a settlement and sign a mediation agreement.

2.2 Case of Dispute Arising from Compulsory Close of Positions in Margin Transactions of Securities

Investor, B, was a client engaging in margin transactions of the securities company, A. On 9 July 2015, the 600,000 shares of stock issued by Oceanwide Holdings held in B's credit account was closed forcefully at 9:42 a.m. (hereinafter the 'compulsory close'), and the ratio of guarantee of B's credit account was 136 per cent after the transaction ended on the previous transaction day, i.e. 8 July. Investor B claimed that the securities company A should not have forcefully closed his credit account and thus applied to the Dispute Resolution Centre for mediation, requesting the securities company A to restore the stock sold forcefully from his credit account and compensate the traffic cost and mediation cost arising from the claim, with the total amount of claims exceeding RMB 2 million.

The mediator appointed by the Dispute Resolution Centre fully investigated the applicant's claims and the issues in dispute between the parties and organised a mediation conference for them.

The mediator raised the following opinions and suggestions to investor B: First, the investor had a false understanding of the benchmark for compulsory close prescribed by the regulatory agency, i.e. he falsely believed that the securities company may not close the positions as long as the ratio of guarantee was over 130 per cent. In fact, the ratio of 130 per cent was just the minimum benchmark for compulsory close prescribed by the regulatory agency, and the actual benchmark, 140 per cent, established by the securities company A was consistent with the regulation and the agreement between the parties. Second, investor B's claim that the securities company A failed to perform the duty of notification before the compulsory close was not consistent with the truth. The recording of telephone communication indicates that, after the ratio of guarantee of investor B's account fell below the benchmark, the investment adviser and margin transaction specialist of the securities company A had notified B several times to make up the guarantee or sell the stock within two business days. In addition, investor B should not attribute his failure in understanding the rules of margin transactions to the staff's failure in explaining A's special rules of margin transactions and failure to deliver the business contract in time. On the contrary, as a qualified investor of the securities market, B had both the right and the duty to actively learn the transaction rules and request for the business contracts.

The mediator raised the following opinions and suggestions to the securities company A: First, on 7 July, the securities company A failed to close the positions when the client's ratio of guarantee fell to 136 per cent on the previous day but allowed the client to sell a portion of the shares on 7 July to maintain the ratio of guarantee above 140 per cent; after the ratio of guarantee fell to 136 per cent again on 8 July, it then took measures to close the position on 9 July. As the securities company failed to take measures to close the positions strictly at the prescribed time in accordance with the contract and thus caused the client to suffer additional losses, it should undertake the responsibilities correspondingly. Second, there were some defects when the securities company A notified the client to make up the guarantee and replied to the client's enquiries, and it failed to strictly implement the benchmark for closing positions prescribed in the contract, i.e. it notified the client to make up the guarantee to the benchmark for closing positions of 140 per cent rather than the benchmark of the 160 per cent maintenance margin, thus misleading the client in the judgment of the maintenance margin. Furthermore, when it signed the contract with investor B, its staff failed to have sufficient communication with the client on the business rules and had not delivered the contract to the client; therefore, its client service should be further improved.

Through professional analysis and careful mediation, both parties were able to reconsider their behaviours and responsibilities in the compulsory close. After the securities company A expressed the willingness to compensate investor B properly in line with the principle of resolving the dispute in good faith and improving the client service, the parties finally reached a settlement for a compensation of RMB 50,000 and signed a mediation agreement on 28 September 2015.

3 Innovation of Expedited Dispute Resolution Mechanism of the Free Trade Zone Financial Arbitration Centre

In response to the requirements of 'establishing the international, market-oriented and law-based business environment' and 'developing the international arbitration and commercial mediation mechanism' laid down by the State Council in the 'Overall Plan for China (Guangdong) Free Trade Trial Zone', the SCIA, together with Guangdong Provincial Finance Office and the Authority of Qianhai, established the special financial arbitration centre in the Free Trade Zone, i.e. the Free Trade Zone Financial Arbitration Centre of South China International Economic and Trade Arbitration Commission (hereinafter the 'Free Trade Zone Financial Arbitration Centre'), so as to build the open and law-based financial and business environment of the Free Trade Zone.

The Free Trade Zone Financial Arbitration Centre will take full advantage of the opportunities of enhancing openness in the financial and capital markets in the Free Trade Zone, focus on and strengthen the function of arbitration services in the field of financial and capital markets, and be dedicated to provide high-quality, efficient and professional dispute resolution services (both arbitration and alternative dispute resolution services) in the field of financial and capital markets to domestic and international parties.

The Free Trade Zone Arbitration Centre will further strengthen its characteristics of professionalism and industry-orientation, i.e. it will not only provide the parties with a special panel of financial arbitrators and the professional service of arbitration process administration, but also provide the parties with the corresponding model dispute resolution provisions in line with the features of different financial products and financial disputes. For example, the provision on expedited dispute resolution for typical bank loan disputes is just one of the innovations adopted by the Free Trade Zone Financial Arbitration Centre. In a bank loan dispute, the legal fact is usually clear and the legal relationship is rather simple, while the bank involved in the dispute has a keen demand for the timeliness of the collection of overdue debt. In consideration of these factors, the Free Trade Zone Financial Arbitration Centre puts forward the special model provision on expedited dispute resolution that fully observes the principle of autonomy of the parties. If there is a dispute and the parties agree to submit the dispute to the SCIA to be arbitrated in accordance with the procedure unanimously agreed by the parties, they may agree on the following matters one by one, e.g. the service of documents in the arbitration procedure, composition of arbitration tribunal, hearing of arbitration, cross-examination between the parties as well as reduction of the period of the statement of defence, counterclaims and rendering the arbitral award.

3.1 *Case of Expedited Arbitration*

An applicant, bank A, had signed a comprehensive credit agreement with the first respondent, company B. At the same time, the second respondent, company C, and the third, fourth and fifth respondents, D, E and F, respectively, provided guarantee for all the debts owed under the comprehensive credit agreement if the first respondent failed to repay the debts in full. The applicant released the loan RMB 20 million to the first respondent as agreed; however, the first respondent failed to repay the loan and the other respondents failed to perform the guarantee duty either.

When the dispute arose, to quickly and effectively resolve the dispute, the parties signed the Agreement on Change of the Dispute Resolution Method and adopted the above model provision on expedited dispute resolution by reaching a new agreement on the service of documents in the arbitration procedure, composition of arbitration tribunal, trial of arbitration and reduction of the period of arbitration, etc. Then, the applicant filed the arbitration pursuant to the agreement on dispute resolution, and the SCIA exercised the right to administer the arbitration process as per the specific agreement on arbitration process between the parties. The whole process from the case accepted by the arbitration institution until the issue of arbitration award took only nineteen working days, thus greatly enhanced the efficiency and reduced the cost of dispute resolution for the parties.

In the arbitration award, the arbitration tribunal discussed the validity of the special agreement on arbitration process between the parties: As the applicant and the respondents had signed the Agreement on Change of the Dispute Resolution Method and agreed to submit the dispute under the contract to the SCIA for arbitration, the arbitration shall be conducted in accordance with the special process prescribed in the above agreement, and any matter not provided in the agreement shall be subject to the Arbitration Rules of the SCIA. Article 3(3) of the Arbitration Rules provides that

> where the parties agree to refer their dispute to the SCIA for arbitration but have agreed on the application of other arbitration rules or have agreed on

> a modification of the Rules, the parties' agreement shall prevail unless such agreement cannot be implemented or is in conflict with a mandatory provision of the law as it applies to the arbitration proceedings.

As the above agreement between the applicant and the respondents were consistent with the Arbitration Law of the People's Republic of China and the Arbitration Rules of the SCIA, its validity was recognised by the arbitration tribunal, and the relevant process of this arbitration case was handled in accordance with the special agreement mentioned above and the Arbitration Rules of the SCIA.

The SCIA has always actively explored the diversified dispute resolution mechanism that may satisfy the financial market demand. The Shenzhen Securities and Futures Dispute Resolution Centre, the 'quaternity' dispute resolution mechanism, the Free Trade Zone Financial Arbitration Centre and the model provision on expedited dispute resolution promoted for the banking industry are all valuable explorations and innovations of the SCIA on the basis of the market demand. The SCIA will continue to improve the service quality and provide better services in financial dispute resolution to both the domestic and international parties.

PART III

Common Law Jurisdictions

12

Curbing Managerial Agency Costs

Private Litigation and Its Substitutes in the US

JAMES D. COX AND RANDALL S. THOMAS

1 Introduction

American corporate law is riveted on addressing managerial agency costs. Berle and Means documented the divergence of manager and shareholder interests in their classic dissection of the 1930s American corporation.[1] Subsequently, Jensen and Meckling noted that, within such dispersed ownership systems, shareholders engage in a variety of strategies so as to minimise these divergences.[2] Coining the term 'managerial agency costs', they noted that shareholders may use voting, the threat of a change of control transaction, performance based-compensation and litigation, among other things, to minimise these costs. Over time, the relative value of these different devices for disciplining managers has ebbed and flowed with the changes in patterns of share ownership and constant evolution in corporate law.[3]

Against this paradigm, the debate persists whether private suits, class actions or derivative suits, are useful tools for controlling managerial agency costs.[4] In earlier work, we have argued that shareholder representative litigation has acted as an important policing mechanism of

[1] Adolf Berle and Gardner M. Means, *The Modern Corporation and Private Property* (Transaction Publishers 1932) (typical public corporate owners were dispersed so that equity owners' exercise of oversight was seriously limited by high coordination costs).

[2] Michael Jensen and William Meckling, 'Theory of the Firm: Managerial Behavior, Agency Costs and Ownership Structure', 3 J. FIN. ECON. 305 (1976).

[3] Randall S. Thomas and Robert B. Thompson, 'A Theory of Representative Shareholder Suits and Its Application to Multijurisdictional Litigation', 106 NORTHWESTERN L. REV. 1753 (2012), 1758–1760.

[4] For a positive view of the efficiency of shareholder suits in addressing agency costs, see e.g. James D. Cox, 'Compensation, Deterrence, and the Market as Boundaries for Derivative Suit Procedures', 52 GEO. WASH. L. REV. 745 (1984). But see Daniel R. Fischel and Michael Bradley, 'The Role of Liability Rules and the Derivative Suit in Corporate Law:

managerial abuses at US public companies.[5] Shareholder representative litigation – derivative suits, federal securities class actions and most recently merger litigation – even though it often produces benefits for shareholders, nonetheless raises fears that they are too frequently accompanied by litigation agency costs. This form of agency cost invariably arises with representative suits with no requirement that the named plaintiffs have a substantial ownership interest in the corporation, so that their prosecution are seen as lawyer-driven.[6] And that perception is further underscored in the US where the 'American rule', in contrast to the 'loser pays rule', provides no governor on the suit's initiation and prosecution.

In this chapter, we argue that the recent rise of some important governance developments is a natural consequence of both the ineffectiveness and inefficiency of private suits in addressing certain genres of managerial agency costs. In short, just as one part of a balloon expands when another part contracts, we find that governance responses evolve to fill voids caused by the decompression of shareholder monitoring once supplied by private suits. We claim that as representative shareholder litigation comes under increasing attack, attention has shifted to governance and market mechanisms to address managerial agency costs.

But we also argue that these new governance responses are themselves more efficient due to the rising concentration of share ownership of public companies that attracts and facilitates growing activism among those blockholders.[7] Activist hedge funds are the most obvious manifestation or rising concentration. Hedge fund activism is one of the new policing mechanisms for managerial agency costs in the US,[8] where they function

A Theoretical and Empirical Analysis', 71 Cornell L. Rev. 261(1986); Roberta Romano, 'The Shareholder Suit: Litigation without Foundation?', 7 J. L. Econ. & Org. 55 (1991).

5 Robert B. Thompson and Randall S. Thomas, 'The New Look of Shareholder Litigation: Acquisition-Oriented Class Actions', 57 Vanderbilt L. Rev. 133 (2004); C.N.V. Krishnan et al., 'Shareholder Litigation in Mergers and Acquisitions', 18 *Journal of Corporate Finance* 1248 (2012); James D. Cox and Randall S. Thomas, 'Mapping the American Shareholder Litigation Experience: A Survey of Empirical Studies of the Enforcement of the US Securities Law', 6 *European Company and Financial Law Review* 164 (2009).

6 See e.g. John C. Coffee, Jr., 'Understanding the Plaintiff's Attorney: The Implications of Economic Theory for Private Enforcement of Law Through Class and Derivative Actions', 86 Colum. L. Rev. 669 (1986); Ralph K. Winter, 'Paying Lawyers, Empowering Prosecutors, and Protecting Managers: Raising the Cost of Capital in America', 42 Duke L. J. 945 (1993).

7 Clifford G. Holderness, 'The Myth of Diffuse Ownership in the United States', 22 Rev. of Fin. Studies 1377 (2009).

8 Alon Brav, Wei Jiang, Frank Partnoy and Randall S. Thomas, 'Hedge Fund Activism, Corporate Governance, and Firm Performance', 63 J. Fin. 1729 (2008).

as 'governance intermediaries' by developing and presenting choices for more docile institutional holders who can become supporters but rarely initiators.[9] Institutions are informed by their independent third-party proxy-voting advisors on initiatives teed up by the activist hedge fund. In combination, the hedge funds and institutional investors have driven reluctant managers to take shareholder value-maximising actions.

The passage of the Dodd-Frank Act further armed institutional investors by mandating a non-binding Say-on-Pay vote, thereby filling a corporate governance hole created by the failure of derivative suits to address executive compensation. While its effectiveness as a check on executive pay is still being studied, it has undoubtedly triggered a greater level of engagement between corporate directors and shareholders over compensation issues.

Finally, we consider the rising role of the appraisal remedy within acquisition-oriented shareholder litigation. The appraisal proceeding, an old and historically defunct form of litigation, has been spruced up by a few intrepid investment groups in what some have called 'appraisal arbitrage'. We conclude that each one of these new, or revived, monitoring techniques may be able to stand in for greatly weakened shareholder litigation to curb managerial agency costs.

2 The Shifting Landscape of Private Shareholder Litigation

During the past seventy years, there have been many shifts among the multiple types of shareholder litigation. Close examination reveals both contraction and expansion, with the former involving procedural developments, whereas the latter invariably shows doctrinal innovations. Despite these ebbs and flows, the business community shares the common view that shareholder litigation is vexatious, robust and expanding. As we will see, their concern is partly justified, at least with respect to litigation spawned by acquisitions.

2.1 Shareholder Merger and Acquisition Class Actions

Delaware jurisprudence has for some time placed a bright litigation bull's-eye on acquisition transactions. Initially suits were aimed at cash-

[9] See Ronald J. Gilson and Jeffrey N. Gordon, 'The Agency Costs of Agency Capitalism: Activist Investors and the Revaluation of Governance Rights', 113 COLUM. L. REV. 863 (2013); Paul H. Edelman, Randall S. Thomas and Robert B. Thompson, 'Shareholder Voting in an Age of Intermediary Capitalism', 87 *Southern California Law Review* 1359 (2014).

out mergers with the controlling stockholder[10] but were later extended to multistep transactions with the dominant stockholder[11] for which courts favour the plaintiff by placing the burden of proving entire fairness on the dominant stockholder. Moreover, Delaware law places the burden on management to prove they acted prudently to get the best offer in many sales of control to a third party[12] as well as subjecting defensive actions to heightened scrutiny.[13]

The bull's eye that judicial doctrine places on these transactions has had its effect. In 2012, 111 of the 121 transactions with over $100 million in value experienced deal litigation,[14] with roughly 50 per cent of these deals having litigation filed in more than one jurisdiction.[15] While several commentators have opined on the underlying causes for these developments,[16] we observe that this surge has occurred while the number of securities class actions has declined. While causation is always a difficult challenge, we surmise that the rapid rise in transaction-oriented litigation may, in part, be reflective of otherwise unemployed plaintiff-oriented law firms redirecting their foci.

Just as too much fudge can be a problem, too warm an invitation to challenge transactions creates difficulties. In response to this flood of cases, Delaware has innovated. For example, it removed short-form mergers from close burden-shifted fairness inquiry.[17] More recently, the Delaware Supreme Court held that an acquisition involving the dominant stockholder would be reviewed under the business judgment rule if there is both approval by a majority of the disinterested shareholders of the subsidiary *and* the subsidiary was represented in the negotiations by a truly independent negotiating committee.[18]

10 *Weinberger* v. *UOP, Inc.*, 457 A.2d 701 (1983).

11 In *re Pure Resources, Inc. Shareholder Litigation*, 808 A.2d 421 (Del. Ch. 2002).

12 *Revlon, Inc.* v. *MacAndrews & Forbes Holdings, Inc.*, 506 A. 2d 173 (Del. 1986); *Paramount Comm. Inc.* v. *QVC Network*, 637 A.2d 34 (Del. 1994).

13 *Unitrin, Inc.* v. *American General Corp.*, 651 A.2d 1361 (Del. 1995).

14 Matthew D. Cain and Steven M. Davidoff, 'Takeover Litigation in 2013' (4 January 2014) (unpublished working paper), http://papers.ssrn.com/sol3/papers.cfm?abstract_id=2377001, 1–2.

15 Ibid., at 2.

16 Thomas and Thompson, 'A Theory of Representative Suits', 1758–1760; John Armour, Bernard Black and Brian Cheffins, 'Is Delaware Losing its Cases?', 9 J. Empirical Legal Stud. 605 (2012); Sean J. Griffith and Alexandra D. Lahav, 'The Market for Preclusion in Merger Litigation', 66 Vand. L. Rev. 1053 (2013).

17 *Glassman* v. *Unocal Exploration*, 777 A.2d 242 (2001).

18 *Kahn* v. *M&F Worldwide Corp.*, 88 A.3d 635 (Del. 2014).

Delaware has also innovated procedurally. The most troubling aspect of acquisition litigation captured in the above statistics is that multiple suits are filed in multiple forums. When the same acquisition triggers multiple suits outside of Delaware, the inherent limits on a single court's jurisdiction to resolve disputes in other states makes it problematic.[19]

The antidote appeared, in 2013, when the Delaware Chancery Court upheld a unilaterally director-adopted forum selection bylaw, reasoning that the bylaws, including the board's authority to adopt bylaws, were an extension of the shareholders' contractual rights in the corporation;[20] in 2015, Delaware amended its statute to expressly authorise forum-selection bylaws.

Thus, we see colliding developments in Delaware; the Delaware courts initially developed broad substantive doctrines inviting challenges to acquisitions, followed by approving boards-adopted bylaws that channel those challenges to Delaware.[21] These new bylaws may lead to less accountability on the part of managers and their boards.

2.2 Derivative Suits

Traditional derivative cases raise state law breach of fiduciary duty claims against directors and officers.[22] They were commonly used to attack directors or officers engaging in conflict of interest transactions with the corporation; in earlier years, a good deal of derivative litigation attacked the compensation policies of large public companies.[23] The leading case, *Rogers* v. *Hill*,[24] held that compensation received by the firm's president and directors was excessive, reasoning that stockholder approval of the compensation package 'cannot . . . be used to justify payments of sums as

[19] A further concern that flows from multiforum litigation is a fear that this could feed a reverse auction; this occurs when a cooperative plaintiff collaborates with the defendant corporation to bring all challenges to a swift resolution by a court-approved low-ball settlement that yields a quick return to the lawyers but fails to protect the interest of the shareholders. See *Matsushita Electric Industrial Co.* v. *Epstein*, 515 U.S. 367 (1996).

[20] *Boilermakers Local 154 Retirement Fund* v. *Chevron Corp.*, 73 A.3d 934 (Del. Ch. 2013).

[21] At first it appeared that shareholder representative litigation might be entirely eliminated when the Delaware Supreme Court approved fee shifting bylaws, ATP Tour, Inc. v. Deutscher Tennis Bund, 91 A.3d 554 (Del. 2014), but the Delaware legislature reversed this decision. Del. Gen. Corp. L. § 102(f). This legislation does not preclude other states from adopting fee shifting bylaws though.

[22] Robert B. Thompson and Randall S. Thomas, The Public and Private Faces of Derivative Lawsuits, 57 VAND. L. REV. 1747 (2000).

[23] See Washington, 'A Corporate Executive's Living Wage', 54 HARV. L. REV. 733 (1941).

[24] 289 U.S. 582 (1933).

salaries so large as in substance and effect to amount to spoliation or waste of corporate property . . . If a bonus payment has no relation to the value of the services for which it is given, it is in reality a gift in part, and the majority stockholders have no power to give away corporate property'.[25] *Rogers* undertook an assessment of the overall reasonableness of the compensation package. *Rogers* held promise that the courts could mediate claims of excessive executive compensation.

Rogers' promise has not been fulfiled largely due to the demand requirement: the plaintiff must either make a demand on the board of directors or establish a basis why such a demand would be futile. The ultimate outcome in either case depends on whether the directors are sufficiently independent so that a reviewing court will uphold their decision regarding the fate of the suit. Also, many public companies adopted provisions in the firm's articles of incorporation insulating directors from liability for misconduct that is not a breach of the duty of loyalty, illegal, in bad faith or a knowing violation of the law.[26] These shields limit suits focused on alleged managerial failures to those involving knowing and systematic fiduciary breaches.

A good example of this is *In re Walt Disney Derivative Litigation.*[27] The facts are complicated, but at their core the complaint was that the Disney board hired Michael Ovitz under pressure from Disney CEO Michael Eisner with knowledge that Ovitz had no experience for the position, only to have that confirmed within an admittedly short period of time. The board, without consulting outside experts regarding the corporation's ability to terminate Ovitz without breaching the employment contract, quickly agreed to a $140 million severance package. Even though both the trial and Supreme Court acknowledge grave departures from good corporate practices, each found that the misconduct did not rise to the level of bad faith and, hence, was protected under the firm's immunity shield.[28]

Disinterested director approval of managerial misconduct brings to bear the business judgment rule's strong presumption of propriety. Its impact is illustrated in *Freedman* v. *Adam*,[29] a suit to recover more than $130 million in bonuses approved by the board of XTO Energy. After the plaintiff initiated a derivative suit, complaining that the lack of any performance benchmarks had the consequence under Internal Revenue

[25] Ibid., at 591–592. [26] 8 Del. Code §102 (b) (7).
[27] 907 A.2d 693 (Del. Ch. 2005), aff'd, 906 A.2d 27 (Del. 2006). [28] 906 A.2d at 67.
[29] 58 A.3d 414 (Del. 2013).

Code §162(m) of raising the corporation's taxes, the board prospectively modified the plan. The plaintiff dropped her derivative suit and sought a fee award from the court. XTO Energy's board argued that it was fully aware of section 162(m), but made a conscious decision not to avail itself of it because it believed its approach to compensation decisions should not 'be constrained by such a plan'. The court denied any fee award to the plaintiff because the court reasoned that '[e]ven if the decision were a poor one' as alleged by the plaintiff, 'it was not unconscionable or irrational'.[30]

In addition to its weak substantive standards in the regulation of executive compensation, the derivative suit plaintiff faces typically insurmountable procedural barriers. Derivative suits challenging an executive's compensation are regularly rejected on the ground of failure to make a demand on the board of directors,[31] and even if a demand is excused on a ground of futility, the board can derail the suit through a special independent litigation committee.[32]

Derivative suit litigation has enjoyed modest success with respect to 'failure to oversee' fiduciary duty claims. Chancellor Allen's *Caremark* decision held that the directors' duty of good faith was breached when there is evidence of a 'sustained or systematic failure of a director to exercise reasonable oversight'. A dramatic instance of such a suit is *In re Massey Energy Company Derivative and Class Action Litigation*,[33] where the complaint withstood defendants' motions to dismiss by alleging facts reflecting that the board repeatedly ignored reports and sanctions of mine safety violations in the years preceding the explosion in its Upper Big Branch Mine that killed twenty-nine miners – the deadliest mine accident in forty years. But, there is frequently insufficient evidence that the board has engaged in more than negligent oversight, which is insufficient to overcome the ubiquitous immunity shield discussed above.

Indeed, the Delaware judiciary may even conclude that ignoring red flags is not director negligence. To illustrate, consider *In re Citigroup Inc. Shareholder Derivative Litigation*,[34] holding that the business judgment rule insulated the directors against charges that they failed to take precautions to avoid the ensuing financial losses arising from Citigroup's large exposure to the subprime lending markets. The suit alleged various red flags such as

[30] Ibid., at 418.
[31] See e.g. *Aronson* v. *Lewis*, 473 A.2d 805 (Del. 1984); *Marx* v. *Akers*, 88 N.Y.2d 189, 644 N.Y.S.2d 121, 666 N.E.2d 1034 (N.Y. Ct. App. 1996).
[32] See e.g. *Zapata Corp*. v. *Maldonado*, 430 A.2d 779 (Del. 1981).
[33] 2011 Del. Ch. LEXIS 83. [34] 964 A.2d 106 (Del. Ch. 2009).

an economist's forecast that a speculative bubble was nearing its end, a leading subprime lender closing its 229 offices, another lender filing bankruptcy, analysts downgrading subprime mortgages and a warning of increasing subprime delinquencies by another lender. The court reasoned:

> [The 'red flags'] amount to little more than portions of public documents that reflected the worsening conditions in the subprime mortgage market and in the economy generally . . . Even while admitting that Citigroup had a risk monitoring system in place, plaintiffs seem to conclude that, because the director defendants were charged with monitoring Citigroup's risk, then they must be found liable because Citigroup experienced losses as a result of exposure to the subprime mortgage market. The only factual support plaintiffs provide for this conclusion are 'red flags' that actually amount to nothing more than signs of continuing deterioration in the subprime mortgage market. These types of conclusory allegations are exactly the kinds of allegation that do not state a claim for relief under *Caremark*.[35]

The above reasoning appears consistent with observation made in a widely noted Delaware Supreme Court decision that conduct that offends good corporate governance practices nonetheless is not inherently negligent conduct.[36]

2.3 *Federal Securities Class Actions*

The story of few trials and many tribulations of federal securities class actions is well understood. Cornerstone, the litigation support group, reports that during 2011–2013, companies within the S&P 500 experienced the lowest number of securities class actions. At least since 2005, the trend line in the number of complaints filed has been downward. With the decline in securities fraud class action filings, there has been a concomitant decline in the number of settlements reached each year.

The high risk incident to the filing of a securities class action is embodied in a single data point: the pre-trial dismissal rate of filed suits. In 1996, after the year the PSLRA was enacted, there were forty-two securities class actions dismissed; whereas, in 2013, in an era when many fewer securities class actions were being filed, seventy-nine suits were dismissed. Overall, approximately 42 percent of filed securities class actions are dismissed in response to defendants' motions to dismiss or summary judgment. At the core of these trend lines is the cost curve for

35 Ibid., at 128–130.

36 *In re the Walt Disney Company Derivative Litigation*, 906 A.2d 27, (Del. 2006).

the suits' maintenance, and those costs have, not surprisingly, been impacted by several legal legislative and judicial developments.

The plaintiffs' bar underwent a substantial face-lift with the passage of the Private Securities Litigation Reform Act of 1995. A central provision of the PSLRA was establishing a procedure for the court to select a 'lead plaintiff' that was guided by a rebuttable presumption that the investor with the largest loss is the most adequate plaintiff; as a consequence, the plaintiff in large post-PSLRA securities class actions is often a large financial institution.[37] Because the lead plaintiff selects the suit's counsel, an effect of the lead plaintiff provision has been the concentration of securities class actions among a few plaintiff firms who have the resources to nurture ongoing relationships with many such financial institutions. Nonetheless, the overall objective of the lead plaintiff provision appears to be largely achieved, namely providing the securities class action lawyer with a real client so that there is less evidence of litigation agency costs, for when institutions serve as lead plaintiffs, we have observed that they are associated with larger settlements, larger percentage recovery relative to provable losses, and pre-suit agreements that yield lower relative fees to the suit's counsel.[38]

But the PSLRA did more, much more, than burnish the image of the class action lawyer. The PSLRA added to the Federal Rules of Civil Procedure requirement that a complaint must allege with 'particularity' facts to support an allegation of fraud and that alleged facts must establish more likely than not a 'strong inference' of fraud. Moreover, until all pre-trial motions were resolved, the PSLRA bars any discovery so that the plaintiff no longer can 'fish' through the defendant's records for facts that would support with particularity an allegation of fraud. These developments raise the plaintiff counsel's expenses, and the counsel must be more resourceful prior to filing suit and invest non-trivial sums to investigate possible cases so as to marshal the facts to meet the pleading requirement. The twin effects of heightened pleading and discovery bar drive up the plaintiff's litigation costs with the natural effect of reducing the incidence of securities class action suits and moving some of the litigators into merger litigation.

[37] See generally James D. Cox, Randall S. Thomas and Lynn Bai, 'There Are Plaintiffs and . . . There Are Plaintiffs: An Empirical Analysis of Securities Class Action Settlements', 61 VANDERBILT. L. REV. 355 (2008) 369; James D. Cox and Randall S. Thomas, 'Does the Plaintiff Matter? An Empirical Analysis of Lead Plaintiffs in Securities Class Actions', 106 COLUM. L. REV. 1587 (2006), 1619.

[38] Cox and Thomas, 'Mapping the American Experience'.

The Supreme Court also worked its transformative magic. First, the Supreme Court has dramatically limited who is subject to liability under the antifraud provision. *Central Bank of Denver* v. *First Interstate Bank of Denver*[39] startled the legal community by holding there was no aiding and abetting liability for violations of the antifraud provision of the federal securities laws. More recently, in *Janus Capital Group, Inc.* v. *First Derivative Traders,*[40] the Court further restricted violators in private actions. *Janus Capital Group* held that liability extended only to individuals who had 'ultimate authority over the statement, including its content and whether and how to communicate it'. Thus, the outside lawyer who schemes with managers to fabricate a series of transactions to conceal the firm's financial position would escape liability if the medium for the release of the false information depended on the approval of a board of directors whose members were unaware of the falsity of the information. The judicially narrowed scope of the antifraud provision shields many classic fraudsters (and their employers and their employer's insurance carrier) from private antifraud suits.

The second doctrinal development impacting the plaintiff's costs related to a securities class action flows from Supreme Court decisions addressing the two distinct components of causality in securities litigation. There is a requirement that the misrepresentation induced the plaintiff to purchase or sell the security that is generally referred to as transaction causation and requires the plaintiff to establish reliance on the alleged misrepresentation. Where plaintiff and defendant deal directly with one another, transaction causation is addressed by evidence that the plaintiff *relied* upon the misrepresentation when purchasing or selling the security.[41] However, requiring positive proof of reliance by each member in securities class actions would be inconsistent with the central requirement for class action certification: that common questions of law and fact predominate over issues that are *sui generis* to individual class members.[42] The fraud on the market approach, embraced in the murky reasoning of *Basic Inv.* v. *Levinson,*[43] holds that investor reliance is rebuttably presumed when the security is traded in a well-developed market. In *Erica P. John Fund, Inc.* v. *Halliburton,*[44] a clear majority of the court affirmed the continued use of fraud on the market. *Halliburton,* however, offers something to each litigation camp. The investors' victory

[39] 511 U.S. 164 (1994). [40] 131 S. Ct. 2296 (2011).
[41] See e.g. *Currie* v. *Cayman Resources Corp.*, 835 F.2d 780, 785 (11th Cir. 1988).
[42] FRCP Rule 23 [43] 485 U.S. 224 (1988). [44] 134 S. Ct. 2398 (2014).

lay both in the preservation of fraud on the market as the doctrinal path to satisfying transaction causation and the court's reasoning that fraud on the market does not depend on evidence that the affected security consistently traded in an efficient market but instead that the alleged defendants, obtained a modest victory, as they are able to rebut class certification with evidence, such as costly econometric studies, that the alleged misrepresentation did not affect the security's price. As a consequence, costs to prosecute and defend fraud on the market cases rise as each party necessarily must engage expensive forensic economists to prove or disprove the misrepresentation's effect on the security's price. The Supreme Court has been equally restrictive in the realm of loss causation. *Dura Pharmaceuticals Inc.* v. *Broudo*[45] held that the plaintiff's complaint must set forth facts supporting the claim that the alleged material misrepresentation caused the plaintiff to suffer a material loss. This requirement is typically satisfied by a factually supported allegation that once the truthful information was released, the stock price underwent a noticeable correction. Such proof customarily necessitates that the plaintiff retain a forensic economist to establish such a price change; this task is made more challenging when, as is prevalent, the defendants artfully bundle disclosure of other items with the corrective statement with the goal of making it very difficult for the plaintiff to establish that the alleged misrepresentation caused a net loss.

The result of all the above developments is that much more cherry-picking of suits occurs, with the end result being that the frequency of survival goes down but the outcome for cases that proceed is likely a greater settlement value. The data above supports each of these beliefs.

Despite the significant narrowing of the antifraud provision that has occurred, there is one growing area of antifraud private suits, those whose core complaint is management stewardship. As seen earlier, state fiduciary duty claims that the directors and officers were poor stewards must confront not only the Business Judgment Rule's strong presumption of propriety but more importantly that, at least with respect to directors, the claim is likely insulated by the immunity shield that limits damage actions against directors to breaches of duty of loyalty. The emergence of the antifraud provision in this area illustrates again how a void in one area can be filled. Illustrative of how such oversight suits fall within the antifraud provision is *Omnicare Inc.* v. *Laborers District Council*

[45] 544 U.S. 336 (2005).

Construction Industry Pension Fund.[46] Omnicare stated it 'believed' its various contracts were 'in compliance with applicable federal and state laws' and 'legally and economically valid arrangements'. Subsequent to the public offering, several federal government enforcement suits were initiated against Omnicare, alleging that various aspects of its contractual relationships and arrangements violated multiple provisions of federal health care laws. The plaintiff pension funds that purchased shares in the registered offering sued for securities fraud.

A key analytical step in *Omnicare* is that the securities laws proscribe both what is stated as well as what is omitted. Thus, *Omnicare* observes that 'a reasonable investor may, depending on the circumstances, understand an opinion statement to convey facts about how the speaker has formed the opinion . . . [I]f the real facts are otherwise, but not provided, the opinion statement will mislead its audience'. *Omnicare Inc.* therefore emphasised whether facts related to the opinion needed to be disclosed to prevent the opinion statement from being misleading. Because *Omnicare*'s opinion statements focused on its purported compliance with the law, the opinion applied the above formulation to such statements:

> Consider an unadorned statement of opinion about legal compliance; 'We believe our conduct is lawful'. If the issuer makes that statement without having consulted a lawyer, it could be misleadingly incomplete . . . [A]n investor, although recognising that legal opinions can prove wrong in the end, still likely expects such an assertion to rest on some meaningful legal inquiry . . . Similarly, if the issuer made the statement in the face of its lawyers' contrary advice, or with knowledge that the Federal Government was taking the opposite view, the investor again has cause to complain: He expects not just that the issuer believes the opinion . . . but that it fairly aligns with the information in the issuer's possession at the time.[47]

We therefore find that disclosure-oriented federal securities suits can address errant stewardship, provided that the managers proffer bold claims of their compliance with the law, that their business strategies are yielding great returns or that existing contracts will add immensely to future profits, when behind each assertion is an ongoing violation of

[46] 135 S. Ct. 1318 (2015). See James D. Cox, 'We're Cool' Statements after *Omnicare*: Securities Fraud Suits for Failures to Comply with the Law', 68 S.M.U. L. Rev. 715–726 (2015)(reviewing the implications of *Omnicare* with a focus on puffery and forward looking statements).

[47] 135 S. Ct. at 1328–1329, 1332.

federal or state law that upon detection and compliance will prove immensely unrewarding to the firm. However, outside this realm, the most significant contribution of private and public enforcement of the securities laws is the culture of compliance they compel. Enforcement, public and private, of the securities laws shines a bright light on managers with not only the therapeutic effect of warding some from misbehaviour, but also by alerting investors and regulators of facts warranting inquiry and perhaps enforcement.

3 Evolving Non-Litigation Monitoring Substitutes

The preceding material supports the conclusion that shareholder litigation has a lessening role in addressing certain types of agency cost. Coterminous with the before-described constrictions of shareholder litigation, a number of alternative monitoring techniques have developed that address, to some extent, the voids created by the contraction of shareholder suits. We review below these monitoring developments. Collectively they have brought about significant changes in the relationship between management and shareholders at American public corporations.

3.1 Activist Hedge Funds

In recent years, hedge funds have actively engaged many companies in an effort to boost shareholder value.[48] Empirical studies find that the filing of an activist hedge fund's Schedule 13D filing creates positive average abnormal returns from 7 per cent to 8 per cent.[49] These benefits appear to last: firms targeted by activists see a 1.22 per cent increase in operating efficiency one year after acquisition.[50] Where do these gains come from?

Target firms are generally undervalued by the market, often because of poor management. Hedge funds frequently seek to force companies to pay out dividends or buy back shares as a means of distributing to shareholders 'excess cash'. In other situations, a hedge fund may seek to persuade target firms to spin off less inefficient divisions or assets, or

[48] Brav et al., 'Hedge Fund Activism'.

[49] Ibid., at 1731. But see, Robin Greenwood, and Michael Schor, 'Investor Activism and Takeovers', 92 J. OF FIN. ECON. 362 (2009), 363 (activist targets which do not result in a takeover have abnormal returns statistically indistinguishable from zero).

[50] Christopher Clifford, 'Value Creation or Destruction? Hedge Funds as Shareholder Activists', 14 J. OF CORP. FIN. 323 (2008), 324.

even force the sale of an entire company. The lead hedge fund will often accumulate 6 to 8 per cent of the target company's stock, which by itself is not enough to give them a strong negotiating position if target management resists their efforts. However, other hedge funds and many less-active institutional investors will vote their shares in the target company in support of the lead hedge fund.[51]

Corporate management and their supporters have a less rosy view of hedge fund activism: they argue that hedge funds are pursuing short term profits at the expense of the long term investors in targeted companies.[52] Some advocates of this position have gone so far as to argue that hedge fund shareholders ought to have fiduciary duties to other shareholders as a check on their allegedly opportunistic conduct.[53] Most recent empirical work is inconsistent with the view that hedge fund short-termism is a problem.[54]

Moreover, the argument that hedge funds are systematically ripping off long term investors is hard to reconcile with those investors' actions. Consider that hedge funds seem to have little trouble recruiting institutional investors to support their activist goals;[55] if hedge fund's plans actually only produced a short term gain at the expense of long term profitability, these long term investors would be reluctant to support them.[56] Second, activist hedge fund holding periods average approximately thirty-one months, which is substantially longer than almost all other investors.[57] Finally, one study of hedge fund interventions from 1994 to 2007 found that the initial stock price gains resulting from the initial announcement of a hedge fund's activism were sustained over a five-year period as were improvements in other measures of returns.[58]

51 Gilson and Gordon, 'The Agency Costs of Agency Capitalism'; Edelman, Thomas and Thompson, ' Shareholder Voting'.

52 Martin Lipton, Deconstructing American Business II and Some Thoughts for Boards of Directors in 2007 available at https://ssrn.com.abstract=2017116; Steven M. Davidoff, 'A Standard Criticism of Activist Investors That No Longer Holds Up', *N.Y. Times*, 10 July 2013, B5.

53 Iman Anabtawi and Lynn Stout, 'Fiduciary Duties for Activist Shareholders', 60 *Stanford Law Review* 1255 (2008).

54 Lucian Bebchuk, Alon Brav and Wei Jiang, 'The Long-Term Effects of Hedge Fund Activism' 115 COLUM. L. REV. 1085 (2015).

55 Gilson and Gordon, 'The Agency Costs of Agency Capitalism'.

56 Marcel Kahan and Edward B. Rock, 'Hedge Funds in Corporate Governance and Corporate Control', 155 *University of Pennsylvania Law Review* 1021(2007), 1088.

57 William Bratton, 'Hedge Funds and Governance Targets: Long-Term Results', UNIV. PA. L. SCH. RESEARCH PAPER No. 10–17, 2010, http://ssrn.com/abstract=1677517.

58 Bebchuket al.; see also, Nicole M. Boyson and Robert M. Mooradian, 'Experienced Hedge Fund Activists,' https://ssrn.com/abstract=1787649.

All of this evidence supports the claim that hedge fund activism is not dominated by short term considerations, but rather generates valuable monitoring of corporate management.[59]

Private equity firms interact in important ways with hedge funds and facilitate their activism. One hedge fund strategy that generates substantial shareholder value is persuading targeted firms to put themselves up for sale, often to private equity firms. These sales are generally at a substantial premium over the prior market price and act to discipline management of underperforming companies as well as create ongoing pressure on managers at other firms to aggressively maximise shareholder value.

Private equity firms are also important shareholder monitors in their own right as well.[60] The formation of this control blockholder at newly privatised firms acts to monitor corporate managers and to focus their efforts on increasing stock price. The private equity firm can do this in a variety of ways, including increased levels of pay for performance, smaller and more focused boards and the threat of dismissal for non-performing executives.[61] Simply stated, private equity firms address the separation of ownership from management by becoming *the* blockholder.

3.2 Say on Pay

Excessive compensation payments to top corporate executives is a classic form of managerial agency costs and rising executive compensation has raised concerns whether this form of agency costs is uncontrollable. As discussed earlier, shareholder derivative suits have proven largely impotent to either redress or retard excessive executive compensation. Executive pay challenges are crushed by the deference accorded boards of directors under the derivative suit demand requirement.[62]

The Say on Pay vote by shareholders is a recent regulatory initiative designed to bolster shareholder monitoring of executive compensation

[59] Davidoff, 'A Standard Criticism of Activist Investors', at B5; see also, Dionysia Katelouzou, 'Myths and Realities of Hedge Fund Activism: Some Empirical Evidence', 7 VA. L. & BUS. REV. 459 (2013).

[60] Ronald W. Masulis and Randall S. Thomas, 'Does Private Equity Create Wealth? The Effects of Private Equity and Derivatives on Corporate Governance', 76 U. CHICAGO L. REV. 219 (2009).

[61] Ibid.

[62] See e.g. *Aronson* v. *Lewis*, 473 A.2d 805 (Del. 1984); *Marx* v. *Akers*, 88 N.Y.2d 189, 644 N.Y.S.2d 121, 666 N.E.2d 1034 (1996).

practices.[63] In the US, Say on Pay was adopted when the American Congress passed the Dodd-Frank Act of 2010. Dodd-Frank required, among other things, that US public companies hold an advisory shareholder vote on the compensation of their top executives.[64] In the first set of such votes, held during the 2011 proxy season, shareholders strongly supported existing pay practices at most firms, with Say on Pay votes getting an average of 91.2 per cent support.[65] These average support levels continued to be high in subsequent years with more than three-quarters of companies in the Russell 3000 receiving at least 90 per cent shareholder support in 2012 and 2013.[66] At the other end of the spectrum, only between forty to sixty firms of the Russell 3000 received less than 50 per cent shareholder support during these same years.[67]

Nevertheless, Say on Pay's introduction had a significant effect on American corporate governance.[68] Dodd-Frank's mandated shareholder votes focused directors on shareholders' concerns about executive pay, increased shareholder participation in corporate governance and opened lines of communication between management and shareholders (and proxy advisory firms) regarding executive compensation.[69] Beginning with the US experience, management at many companies made changes to the substance and disclosure of their pay programs in an attempt to more clearly align pay to performance.[70] Many companies revised the content of the CD&A filed with the annual meeting proxy materials.[71] At companies whose pay programs received negative Say on Pay recommendations by proxy advisory firms, management at some firms connected with shareholders following an 'against' recommendation.[72]

[63] Randall S. Thomas and Christoph Van Der Elst, 'Say on Pay Around the World', 92 Wash. U. L. Rev. 653 (2015).

[64] Dodd-Frank Wall Street Reform and Consumer Protection Act, Pub. L. No. 111–203, § 951, 124 Stat. 1375, 1899 (2010).

[65] ISS, *Preliminary 2011 U.S. Postseason Report 2* (updated 8 August 2011). [66] Ibid.

[67] James F. Cotter, Alan R. Palmiter and Randall S. Thomas, 81 George Washington L. Rev. 967 (2013), 979–980.

[68] Randall S. Thomas, Alan R. Palmiter and James F. Cotter, Dodd-Frank's Say on Pay: Will It Lead to a Greater Role for Shareholders in Corporate Governance, 97 Cornell L. Rev. 1213 (2012), 1227.

[69] Luis A. Aguilar, Comm'r, U.S. Sec. & Exch. Comm'n, Speech to Social Investment Forum (10 June 2011).

[70] Michael Littenberg, Farzad Damania and Justin Neidig, 'A Closer Look at Negative Say-on-Pay Votes During the 2011 Proxy Season', *Director Notes (Conference Bd.)* 2 (July 2011), www.srz.com/A-Closer-Look-at-Negative-Say-on-Pay-Votes-During-the-2011-Proxy-Season-07–26-2011/.

[71] Thomas, Palmiter and Cotter, Dodd-Frank's Say on Pay, 1257.

[72] Cotter, Palmiter and Thomas, 995.

Yet, in the United States, Say on Pay has not led to lower executive pay levels or changes in its composition, although internationally its adoption has led to large increases in market value and improvements to long-term profitability.[73] Research on the UK has also found that overall CEO pay levels do not seem to have changed as a result of Say on Pay votes.[74] However, internationally, Correa and Lel find that pay growth rates are lower in their comparative study of twelve countries that have adopted Say on Pay legislation.[75] Their cross-country study of thirty-nine nations – twelve that have adopted Say on Pay and twenty-seven that have not done so – finds that although, 'CEO compensation has increased in several SoP [Say on Pay] countries including the US and UK, the growth in CEO pay is higher for the control group of firms not subject to SoP [Say on Pay] laws, suggesting that SoP laws are associated with lower compensation growth'.[76] Given this split in results, it seems fair to say that the precise effects of Say on Pay on executive compensation levels are still being determined.

3.3 Appraisal Arbitrage

As discussed earlier, merger litigation has played a significant monitoring role in addressing possible agency costs in corporate transactions. There is empirical evidence that class action lawsuits challenging the fairness of merger and acquisition (M&A) transactions had a positive impact on takeover premiums.[77] However, as we discussed above, merger litigation's future has been placed in jeopardy by various judicial and statutory developments.

One investor-oriented development is the modern use of appraisal litigation. In an appraisal proceeding, a shareholder can ask a court to determine the fair market value of their shares. The remedy extends to holders of shares not voted in favour of a pending corporate transaction.

[73] Vicente Cunat, Mireia Gine and Maria Guadalupe, 'Say Pays! Shareholder Voice and Firm Performance', 20 *Review of Finance* (forthcoming 2016), at 5; Peter Iliev and Svetla Vitanova, The Effect of the Say-On-Pay Vote in the U.S., Working Paper (2015), 3.

[74] Martin Conyon and G. Sadler, 'Shareholders Voting and Directors' Remuneration Report Legislation: Say on Pay in the UK', 18 CORP. GOV.: AN INT'L REV. 296 (2010); Fabrizio Ferri and David A. Maber, 'Say on Pay Votes and CEO Compensation: Evidence from the U.K.', 17 REV. OF FINANCE 527 (2013).

[75] Ricardo Correa and Ugur Lel, 'Say on Pay Laws, Executive Compensation, Pay Slice, and Firm Valuations Around the World', 122 J. FIN. ECON. 500 (2016), 501.

[76] Ibid., at 507. Figure 1 illustrates the gap between the two groups of countries. Ibid., 35.

[77] Krishnan et al., 'Shareholder Litigation in Mergers and Acquisitions', 1262.

States vary in how widely appraisal is available. States that are more solicitous of shareholders provide appraisal for amendments to the articles of incorporation that adversely affect the rights of stockholders, the sale of all or substantially all the firm's assets, and mergers and consolidations,[78] whereas Delaware limits its appraisal statute to mergers and consolidations,[79] and the Model Business Corporation Act follows a course between these two positions.[80]

Traditionally, appraisal has been viewed as an ineffective remedy for shareholders that is cumbersome and very limited in its scope. It has three types of disadvantages that commentators have focused on:[81] difficult procedural steps that must be followed in precise order to preserve one's right to the remedy; the lack of a class action procedure that would permit easy joinder of all dissenting shareholders so that the costs of bringing an action could be more widely shared; and the narrow limits of the remedy. As a result, prior research has found that few appraisal actions are filed and even fewer are actively litigated.[82]

Recently, Kahan and Rock have noticed that hedge funds that are dissatisfied with the terms of an acquisition may be adapting appraisal litigation to a new role.[83] Professor Geis[84] and Professors Korsmo and Myers,[85] debate the appropriate role of appraisal litigation as a monitor of M&A deals. Based on some hedge fund litigation over the scope of their appraisal rights, Geis argues that, 'it is certainly possible that a robust after-market for appraisal rights will develop, analogous to the market for corporate control that allegedly disciplines otherwise entrenched managers with the threat of an external takeover'.[86] If so, Geis concludes that 'corporate law might play a meaningful role in enhancing firm value by policing freeze out mergers in a more nuanced and creative manner'.[87] Yet, Geis equivocates about whether it is

78 See e.g. Cal. Corp. Code §§ 181, 1200 et seq., 1300; N.Y. Bus. Corp. L. § 910.

79 See Del. Code Ann., tit. 8 § 262(b).

80 See MBCA § 13.02(a).

81 Charles Korsmo and Minor Myers, 'Appraisal Arbitrage and the Future of Public Company M & A', 92 *Washington University Law Review* 1551 (2015), 1558.

82 Ibid., at 22–23 (finding an average of less than fourteen appraisal actions filed per year from 1977 to 1997).

83 Kahan and Rock, 'Hedge Funds in Corporate Governance', 1038–1039.

84 George Geis, 'An Appraisal Puzzle', 105 *Northwestern Law Review* 1635 (2011).

85 Charles Korsmo and Minor Myers, 'Appraisal Arbitrage and the Future of Public Company M & A', 92 *Washington University Law Review* 1551 (2015). See also, Charles Korsmo and Minor Myers, 'The Structure of Shareholder Litigation: When do the Merits Matter?', 75 *Ohio State Law Journal* 829 (2015).

86 Geis, 'An Appraisal Puzzle', 1638.

87 Ibid., at 1658.

beneficial to target company shareholders because of concerns that opening up the appraisal remedy will lead to more strike suits, and therefore suggests further restrictions on shareholders' (already quite limited) ability to bring these cases.[88]

Professors Korsmo and Myers generate some empirical data on this phenomenon. They find that the dollar value of dissenting shares in appraisal actions spiked sharply in 2013.[89] They document the rise of a small but growing group of investors filing multiple appraisal actions arising out of different transactions.[90] These repeat petitioners 'target deals where the merger premium is low and where controlling shareholders are taking the company private'.[91] Considering these findings, Korsmo and Myers argue that a robust appraisal remedy could be working in a socially responsible way as a 'back-end check on abuses by corporate managers, controlling shareholders or other insiders in merger transactions'.[92]

While this is certainly possible, we are much more cautious about the effects of this potential trend. First, any monitoring effects on M&A activity that will arise out of appraisal litigation will be limited to a small set of deals where appraisal is available. For example, even at the peak of this trend, Korsmo and Myers find that only slightly more than 15 per cent of covered transactions have appraisal actions filed challenging the consideration paid in the deal.[93]

To the extent that appraisal is effective within this narrow class of deals, we expect controlling shareholders and other acquirers to revise existing deal structures to avoid appraisal's reach. This suggests it will be necessary to expand the class of transactions covered by appraisal rights if it is to be truly useful as a monitoring device.

Moreover, appraisal is of value only to large shareholders; small shareholders will not find appraisal to be cost-effective generally. Indeed, small investors will benefit, if at all, from this appraisal litigation only if there is an *ex ante* effect from the potential for appraisal litigation on an acquirers' original pricing of the deal.

Finally, if appraisal litigation is to play a role as a monitor of managerial agency costs in mergers, the market out exception must be eliminated.[94] As numerous critics have pointed out, it makes no sense to say that shareholders who receive marketable securities for their shares

[88] Ibid., at 1676. [89] Korsmo and Myers, 'Appraisal Arbitrage', 17, Figure 3.
[90] Ibid., at 18. [91] Ibid., at 28. [92] Ibid., at 42. [93] Ibid., at 16, Figure 2.
[94] Ibid., at 50.

in a merger do not need appraisal; if they sell those shares in the market after the merger, then they will suffer an uncompensated loss.

4 Conclusions

Litigation's role as an agency cost reducing monitoring device has been controversial over the years. While its fortunes have ebbed and flowed, in recent years shareholder litigation has suffered many setbacks. In its place, a number of new monitoring devices – hedge fund activism, Say on Pay votes and appraisal arbitrage – have arisen and taken center stage. We argue that this is not a coincidence, but that shareholders have found new ways to reduce managerial agency costs to compensate for the loss of old ones.

13

Private Enforcement of Corporate Law

An Empirical Comparison of the UK and US

JOHN ARMOUR, BERNARD S. BLACK, BRIAN R. CHEFFINS AND RICHARD NOLAN*

It is often assumed that strong securities markets require good legal protection of minority shareholders. This implies both 'good' law – principally corporate and securities law – and enforcement, yet there has been little empirical analysis of enforcement. We study private enforcement of corporate law in two common law jurisdictions with highly developed stock markets, the United Kingdom and the United States, examining how often directors of publicly traded companies are sued, and the nature and outcomes of those suits.

We find, based on a comprehensive search for filings over 2004–2006, that lawsuits against directors of public companies alleging breach of duty are nearly non-existent in the UK. The US is more litigious, but we still find, based on a nationwide search of decisions between 2000 and 2007, that only a small percentage of public companies face a lawsuit against directors alleging a breach of duty that is sufficiently contentious to result in a reported judicial opinion, and a substantial fraction of these cases are dismissed.

We examine possible substitutes in the UK for formal private enforcement of corporate law and find some evidence of substitutes, especially for takeover litigation. Nonetheless, our results suggest that formal private enforcement of corporate law is less central to strong securities markets than might be anticipated.

* John Armour, Bernard S. Black, Brian R. Cheffins and Richard Nolan, 'Private Enforcement of Corporate Law: An Empirical Comparison of the United Kingdom and the United States', *Journal of Empirical Legal Studies* Volume 6, Issue 4, December 2009, 687–722. This chapter appears here with permission.

1 Introduction

Nearly a century ago, Roscoe Pound memorably drew attention to the divide between 'law in books' and 'law in action'.[1] The distinction between substantive legal doctrine ('law in books') and enforcement ('law in action') is emerging as an important element in an ongoing debate about the extent to which law explains differences in financial markets around the world. Beginning in the late 1990s, a group of financial economists known collectively as LLSV reported in a series of widely cited studies that corporate and securities laws which protect minority shareholders are associated with deep and liquid securities markets and diffuse share ownership.[2] This research focused almost entirely on 'law in books'. Enforcement – whether by public agencies or private individuals, whether civil or criminal, or whether through formal lawsuits or more informal channels – was left to one side.[3]

The 'law in action' gap is particularly striking because of lively cross-country debate on the value of private lawsuits against company directors. Many in Europe, keen to expand domestic capital markets and improve corporate governance, view stronger private enforcement as desirable and are seeking to change the procedural rules that inhibit private suits.[4] Some in the United States see active enforcement as

[1] Roscoe Pound, 'Law in Books and Law in Action', 44 AMER. L. REV. 12 (1910).

[2] LLSV is shorthand for Rafael La Porta, Florencio López-de-Silanes, Andrei Shleifer and Robert Vishny. See, for example, Rafael La Porta, Florencio López-de-Silanes, Andrei Shleifer and Robert Vishny, 'Corporate Ownership Around the World', 54 J. FIN. 471 (1999); Rafael La Porta, Florencio López-de-Silanes, Andrei Shleifer and Robert Vishny, 'Law and Finance', 106 J. POL. ECON. 1113 (1998); Rafael La Porta, Florencio Lopez-de-Silanes and Andrei Shleifer, 'What Works in Securities Laws?', 61 J. FIN. 1 (2006).

[3] In addition, recoding of corporate laws by lawyers has cast doubt on some of the LLSV results. Holger Spamann, "The 'Antidirector Rights Index' Revisited", 23 REV FIN. STUDIES 467 (2010) (finding only a 0.41 correlation between original LLSV index and his own recoding). This criticism does not extend to their later effort to code securities laws.

[4] See, e.g. Jonathan R. Hay and Andrei Shleifer, 'Private Enforcement of Public Laws: A Theory of Legal Reform', 88 AM. ECON. REV. 398 (1998) (advocating use of private enforcement in transition economies); Guido Ferrarini and Paolo Giudici, 'Financial Scandals and the Role of Private Enforcement: The Parmalat Case', in John Armour and Joseph A. McCahery (eds.), *After Enron: Improving Corporate Law and Modernising Securities Regulation in Europe and the US*, 159, 194–206 (Hart Publishing, 2006) (advocating increased private enforcement in Italy). But cf. Paul Davies, *Davies Review of Issuer Liability: Final Report* (2007), www.hm-treasury.gov.uk/independent_reviews/davies_review/davies_review_index.cfm (opposing significant expansion in private liability of UK issuers for securities misdisclosure).

a core strength of US markets that helps to explain the tendency for firms cross-listed in the US to trade at higher prices than similar non-cross-listed firms.[5] Yet others in the US lament allegedly excessive litigation against companies and directors, or they worry that lawsuit-friendly rules harm the competitiveness of US markets and US firms.[6] In contrast, the United Kingdom is conventionally thought to be less litigious, but not *un*-litigious.[7]

While the need to study private enforcement is obvious, only a handful of previous studies have done so, probably because of the considerable difficulties involved in data collection. This chapter presents new evidence, based on hand-collected datasets from the UK and the US, on the number and outcomes of lawsuits brought against directors of publicly traded companies under corporate law.[8] Our study is, we believe, the first comparative quantitative analysis of the private enforcement of corporate law.

[5] See, for example, John C. Coffee, 'Law and the Market: The Impact of Enforcement', 156 U. Pa. L. Rev. 229–311 (2007); Craig Doidge, G. Andrew Karolyi and Rene M. Stulz, 'Has New York Become Less Competitive in Global Markets? Evaluating Foreign Listing Choices Over Time', 91 J. Fin. Econ. 253 (2009), http://ssrn.com/abstract=982193 (foreign firms which cross-list in the US enjoy a significant cross-listing premium, even after Sarbanes-Oxley Act; London listing provides no premium).

[6] Michael R. Bloomberg and Charles E. Schumer, 'Sustaining New York's and the US' Global Financial Services Leadership', www.senate.gov/~schumer/SchumerWebsite/pressroom/special_reports/2007/NY_REPORT%20_FINAL.pdf (2007); Committee on Capital Markets Regulation, 'Interim Report of the Committee on Capital Markets Regulation', www.capmktsreg.org/research.html (2006); Joseph A. Grundfest, 'The Class-Action Market', Wall St. J., 7 February 2007, A15 (op-ed) (securities fraud class actions are 'an expensive, wasteful and unnecessary sideshow'); Peter J. Wallison, 'Capital Complaints', Wall St. J., 20 March 2007, A19 (op-ed). On the possible effect of the Sarbanes-Oxley Act on corporate risk taking, see Kate Litvak, *Defensive Management: Does the Sarbanes-Oxley Act Discourage Corporate Risk-Taking*, working paper (2009), http://ssrn.com/abstract=994584.

[7] Bloomberg and Schumer, 'Sustaining New York's and the US' Global Leadership', exhibit 20 (63 per cent of respondents to survey on New York's status as a financial center thought the UK was less litigious than the US; 17 per cent thought the US less litigious; 20 per cent thought the two about the same); Coffee 'Law and the Market', 266–268; Peter Montagnon, 'The Cost to Europe of America's Class Action Addiction', Fin. Times, 5 January 2007, 15 ('UK shareholders find themselves less inclined to sue companies').

[8] By 'publicly traded', we mean companies that are listed, and traded, on a stock exchange. Such firms are often simply called 'public' companies in the US; however in the UK, 'public' companies refer to companies formed as PLC's, and thus eligible to become publicly traded – only a small minority of which in fact are. In the UK, publicly traded companies are usually referred to as 'listed' or 'quoted.' The term 'publicly traded' is chosen for its intelligibility to readers from either jurisdiction.

The UK and the US stand out as good choices for such a study. Both are common law jurisdictions with strong judiciaries, low levels of government corruption,[9] and highly developed stock markets.[10] In both, most large business enterprises are publicly traded and many lack a blockholder large enough to exercise continuous, detailed oversight of management.[11] Hence, in the US and the UK the primary corporate governance issue is considered to be ameliorating managerial agency costs rather than limiting self-dealing by major shareholders.[12]

We use our comparative study to test hypotheses about (1) the *role* and (2) the *rate* of private enforcement of corporate law. On the first point, since protection of minority shareholders is thought to be associated with deep and liquid securities markets and dispersed share ownership, one would expect private enforcement of corporate law to be fairly common in both countries. Should this conjecture be incorrect, it follows that robust securities markets can develop without extensive private enforcement of corporate law. Moreover, even if substantive corporate law is converging, as some scholars argue, convergence of the law in action may be far weaker.[13] On the second point, the US is more 'litigation-friendly' than the UK in various respects, so

[9] The US and the UK score well on most measures of legal quality, and also score very similarly, including: efficiency of the judicial system (10 out of 10 for both), rule of law (10 for the US and 8.57 for the UK), corruption (9.10 for the UK and 8.63 for the US), risk of expropriation by the government (9.98 for the US and 9.71 for the UK) and risk of contract repudiation by the government (9.98 for the UK and 9.00 for the US): La Porta et al. 'Law and Finance', 1140–1143.

[10] Over 1998–2007, the US and the UK had mean ratios of stock market capitalisation to GDP of 1.43 and 1.52, respectively, compared with a world mean of 0.99 and an OECD high-income country mean of 1.09. World Bank, *World Development Indicators* (2008), www.worldbank.org.

[11] See La Porta et al., 'Corporate Ownership Around the World', 497 ('in the United States and the UK . . . [even medium-sized] firms remain mostly widely held'). John Armour, Brian Cheffins and David Skeel, 'Corporate Ownership and the Evolution of Bankruptcy Law: Lessons from the United Kingdom', 55 VAND. L. REV. 1699 (2002), 1704, 1715, 1750–1752. Cf. Clifford G. Holderness, 'The Myth of Diffuse Ownership in the United States', 22 REV. FIN. STUD. 1378 (2009) (US public firms are on average no more diffusely held than in many other countries, but ownership of UK firms is the most diffuse in the world).

[12] See, e.g. Reinier Kraakman, John Armour, Paul Davies, Henry Hansmann, Gerard Hertig, Klaus Hopt, Hideki Kanda and Edward Rock, *The Anatomy of Corporate Law,* 2nd ed., (Oxford University Press, 2009), ch. 3.

[13] On convergence of substantive rules, see e.g. Henry Hansmann and Reinier Kraakman, 'The End of History in Corporate Law', 88 GEO. L.J. 439 (2001); Mathias M. Siems, *Convergence in Shareholder Law* (2008*b*).

we anticipate that lawsuits against directors will be more common in the US than the UK.[14]

To test our hypotheses, we examine cases filed in Britain, supplementing existing research on reported cases, and cases that generate reported opinions in the US, supplementing existing research on cases filed. We find that private enforcement of corporate law, through lawsuits against directors of publicly traded companies, is indeed more common in the US than in the UK. However, our results do not support the hypothesis that private enforcement of corporate law is central to strong stock markets and dispersed share ownership.

Most strikingly, our findings indicate that the chances of a director of a publicly traded UK company being sued under corporate law are virtually nil. Indeed, directors of UK public companies which operate in the US may face a greater likelihood of being sued under UK company law in the US than in the UK, though with limited prospects for success. Even in the US, directors face risk from private litigants less than is commonly imagined. There is only a small chance that directors of a publicly traded US company will be sued for damages in a corporate law case serious enough to generate a reported judicial opinion, and many such cases fail to survive a motion to dismiss or for summary judgment.

Our UK findings prompt questions about substitutes. We show that private enforcement of securities and insolvency law do not fill the gap left by corporate law since proceedings are rarely brought against directors of UK public companies under these laws as well. Formal public enforcement against directors, principally under securities law, is also more robust in the US. However, the UK regulatory regime does provide more potent protection than its US counterpart in some important ways, especially for takeovers, with an emphasis on *ex ante* screening as opposed to *ex post* litigation.

The rest of the paper is structured as follows. Section 2 outlines competing theories of the role of private enforcement in corporate law. Sections 3 and 4 then describe prior quantitative studies of private enforcement, our empirical methodology and our results for, respectively, the UK and the US. Section 5 discusses substitutes. Section 6 concludes.

[14] US corporate law is state law; when we consider substantive corporate law doctrine we will assume Delaware law applies because it is standard practice for public companies to incorporate in Delaware. There are not, on the whole, large differences between states in the nature of directors' duties.

2 Theory and Prior Literature

2.1 The Role of Private Enforcement

For publicly traded corporations lacking a dominant shareholder, perhaps the biggest corporate governance challenge is control of managerial misbehaviour, commonly referred to as managerial agency costs. Dispersed shareholders typically lack the incentives and/or the ability to monitor management, so managers have some latitude to manage badly or further their own interests at the expense of other participants in the firm. It is commonly assumed that directors' legal obligations – such as duties of loyalty and good faith, and disclosure requirements – help at least with the problem of self-interested actions. But deterrence presupposes a credible threat that breaches of duty will be sanctioned, which requires enforcement.

Recent literature has debated the relative merits of public and private enforcement of corporate and securities law in serving to promote and sustain stock market development.[15] Proponents of private enforcement argue that private parties have better incentives to bring appropriate actions than public agencies and are thus more effective enforcers.[16] One might call this a 'private enforcement primacy' view.

In contrast, what can be called a 'multiple mechanisms' view treats private enforcement as merely one of a number of mechanisms that can deter manager misconduct and provide the foundation for robust securities markets.[17] On this view, public enforcement by securities regulators, stock exchange rules, shareholder exercise of governance rights, scrutiny of capital-raising transactions by investment intermediaries concerned with reputational capital and the market for corporate control, among others, can all contribute to this outcome. Private enforcement is thus potentially useful,[18] but not essential.

15 See La Porta et al., 'What Works in Securities Laws?'; Howell E. Jackson and Mark J. Roe, *Public and Private Enforcement of Securities Laws: Resource-Based Evidence* (working paper 2008), http://ssrn.com/abstract=1000086.

16 See, e.g. sources cited above in note 2.

17 See Kraakman et al. (2009), *The Anatomy of Corporate Law*, ch.2; Bernard S. Black, 'The Legal and Institutional Preconditions for Strong Securities Markets', 48 UCLA L. Rev. 781 (2001); Brian R. Cheffins, *Corporate Ownership and Control: British Business Transformed* (Oxford University Press, 2008); John Armour, 'Enforcement Strategies in UK Company Law: A Roadmap and Empirical Assessment', in John Armour and Jennifer Payne (eds.), *Rationality in Company Law: Essays in Honour of D.D. Prentice* 71 (Hart Publishing, 2009).

18 Even usefulness is sometimes challenged. See, e.g. Elliott J. Weiss and Lawrence J. White, 'File Early, then Free Ride: How Delaware Law (Mis)shapes Shareholder Class Actions', 57 Vand. L. Rev. 1797 (2004); John C. Coffee, 'Reforming the Securities Class Action: An Essay on Deterrence and its Implementation', 106 Colum. L. Rev. 1534 (2006).

A comparison of the UK and US can shed light on these contrasting theories. Both countries enjoy deep and liquid securities markets and dispersed ownership of many publicly traded corporations. The private enforcement primacy view predicts the following:

> *H1: If private enforcement of corporate law is essential to robust stock markets with dispersed share ownership, there will be vigorous private enforcement of corporate law in both the UK and US.*

A failure to observe vigorous private enforcement in either jurisdiction would contradict the private enforcement primacy view, support the multiple mechanisms view and prompt a search for substitutes.

2.2 *The Rate of Private Enforcement*

The rate of private enforcement of corporate law is likely to be shaped by differences in the legal environment, including the general rules of civil procedure, substantive legal duties imposed on directors and procedural rules specifically governing shareholder litigation. These factors suggest that litigation against directors will be more common in the US than in the UK. For instance, various features of civil procedure, summarised in Table 13.1, are more favorable to plaintiffs in the US. In particular, the facilitation of class actions and the use of contingency fees stimulate entrepreneurial attorneys, whereas the UK's 'loser pays' fees rule will discourage representative litigation.[19]

At the same time, various features of corporate law, summarised in Table 13.2, make it easier for a US shareholder to bring an action against directors than his UK counterpart. In particular, in the US the circumstances under which shareholders can bring a direct action against directors are broader, and the rules governing derivative actions are more lenient. In addition, while much US shareholder litigation involves takeovers,[20] in the UK, takeovers are governed by the Takeover Code, which largely precludes civil litigation concerning takeover bids.[21]

[19] See generally Herbert M. Kritzer, 'Lawyer Fees and Lawyer Behavior in Litigation: What Does the Empirical Literature Really Say?', 80 TEX. L. REV. 1943 (2001).

[20] See Robert B. Thompson and Randall S. Thomas, 'The New Look of Shareholder Litigation: Acquisition-Oriented Class Actions', 57 VAND. L. REV. 133 (2004) [in Table 13.4, Thompson and Thomas, 'Delaware Class Actions' (2004a)].

[21] John Armour and David A. Skeel, Jr., 'Who Writes the Rules for Hostile Takeovers, and Why? The Peculiar Divergence of US and UK Takeover Regulation', 95 GEO L.J. 1727 (2007).

Table 13.1 *Contrasting US and UK civil litigation procedures*

Litigation procedure	US	UK
Class actions	Under Federal Rules of Civil Procedure Rule 23(a), a judge must certify a class action before it can proceed. Relevant criteria include the class being so numerous it is otherwise impractical to join all members, the presence of questions of law or fact common to the class and the risk of varying outcomes that would establish incompatible standards of conduct for those not participating in the litigation. Plaintiffs are routinely granted certifications to bring class actions against directors under corporate and securities law.	No direct equivalent to the US class action. It is possible for litigants to seek a 'group litigation order'. However, while class actions in the US operate on an 'opt out' basis, a group litigation order is an 'opt in' system.
Allocation of legal expenses	Each side pays its own legal expenses, with the exception of successful derivative suits, where the corporation will pay the legal expenses of the shareholder litigant. Directors' legal expenses are commonly both indemnified by the company and covered by D&O insurance.	'Loser pays' fees are typically assessed against the unsuccessful party in legal proceedings on a 'standard basis' that covers litigation expenses 'proportionately and reasonably incurred' and 'proportionate and reasonable in amount.'[22] In the corporate context the 'English rule' will tend to deter (compared to the US rule) litigation in cases where the defendant's legal

[22] Civil Procedure Rules, 1998, S.I. 1998/3132. para. 44.5, ¶ 1; *Lownds* v. *The Home Office*, [2002] 1 W.L.R. 2450, 2453.

Table 13.1 (*cont.*)

Litigation procedure	US	UK
		fees are likely to be large since the plaintiff will realise only a pro rata portion of the recovery if successful, but risks paying all of the defendants' costs in the event of losing, particularly where the defendant can increase his chances of success by outspending the plaintiff and leave it to the plaintiff to pick up the tab.[23]
Contingency fees	Widely used by shareholder plaintiffs, which means that the downside risks associated with litigation are largely shifted to the lawyers.	Prohibited. 'Conditional fee arrangements', which are permitted, are a poor substitute because the maximum 'upside' under such an agreement is a success fee amounting to 100% of hourly fees.

Under US corporate law, directors owe duties of loyalty and care, supplemented by less clearly defined duties of disclosure and of special care when one's company is a takeover target.[24] Cases alleging self-dealing by directors, preferential treatment of 'insiders' (directors, officers and controlling shareholders) and other conflicts of interest are

[23] Edward A. Snyder and James W. Hughes, 'The English Rule for Allocating Legal Costs: Evidence Confronts Theory', 6 J.L. Econ & Org. 345(1990), 349; James W. Hughes and Edward A. Snyder, 'Litigation and Settlement Under the English and American Rules: Theory and Evidence', 38 J. Law & Econ. 225 (1995), 227–228; Michael R. Baye, Dan Kovenock and Casper G. de Vries, 'Comparative Analysis of Litigation Systems: An Auction-Theoretic Approach', 115 Econ. J. 583 (2005), 585, 595–598.

[24] See Bernard Black, 'The Core Fiduciary Duties of Outside Directors', Asia Bus. L. Rev., July 2001, 3, http://ssrn.com/abstract=270749. There is also an even more inchoate duty of 'good faith,' but it is unclear how much this duty adds to the other duties.

Table 13.2 *Aspects of corporate law that are more 'litigation-friendly' in the US*

Subject matter of regulation	US	UK
Standing to bring a derivative action.	Shareholders must seek to be excused from making 'demand' on the board to sue its own present or former members, because the board is unlikely to do so. Demand is generally excused if the plaintiff pleads facts with sufficient specificity showing a likelihood of liability.	Traditionally, standing was very difficult to obtain, particularly in a public traded company. The company had to be under 'wrongdoer control', a requirement that could not be satisfied in many publicly traded companies due to the rarity of blockholders.[25] Also, the misconduct had to constitute 'fraud on the minority', an ill-defined concept involving the wrongdoers benefitting at the company's expense.[26] Under the Companies Act 2006 a court will determine whether to grant leave by applying various statutory criteria, including whether the misconduct has been ratified by the shareholders, whether bringing the suit is likely to promote the

25 *Birch* v. *Sullivan*, [1957] 1 W.L.R. 1247 (Ch.).

26 See Brenda Hannigan, *Company Law* (Oxford University Press, 2003) 458–461; Paul L. Davies, *Gower and Davies' Principles of Modern Company Law*, 377–379, 7th ed. (Sweet & Maxwell, 2003), 458–461 (emphasising, though, the ill-defined nature of the concept).

Table 13.2 (*cont.*)

Subject matter of regulation	US	UK
		company's success and whether the shareholder bringing the suit is acting in good faith.[27]
Shareholders' ability to bring 'direct' suits (with recovery paid directly to shareholders) against directors who breach their duties.	Yes, if there is direct harm to shareholder interests; no, if the harm is to the corporation.	Very difficult. Directors rarely owe duties directly to shareholders and English courts tend to treat losses that shareholders suffer when the company is adversely affected as 'reflective loss' for which the shareholders cannot recover directly.[28]
Disputes concerning takeover bids	Direct lawsuits can proceed over key issues, such as the legality of defensive tactics and the fairness of a freeze out.	The City Code on Takeovers and Mergers ('the City Code') effectively supplants private litigation.

treated as involving the duty of loyalty. In the UK, the Companies Act 2006 codifies directors' duties.[29] Prior to this codification, UK directors owed duties at common law to act in the best interests of the company, to avoid conflicts of interest and to act with care, skill and diligence. Directors of UK companies also face numerous regulatory and

[27] Companies Act 2006, ss. 260–263.

[28] On whom directors owe duties to, see *Peskin* v. *Anderson*, [2000] 2 BCLC 1, 14–15 (Ch.); *Percival* v. *Wright*, [1902] 2 Ch 421, 423–425; Companies Act 2006, § 170(1). On 'reflective loss', see *Johnson* v. *Gore Wood & Co.* [2002] 2 AC 1.

[29] The key duties of directors are to act within their powers, to promote the success of the company, to exercise independent judgment, to exercise reasonable care, skill and diligence, to avoid conflicts of interest, to refrain from accepting benefits from third parties, and to avoid unauthorised self-dealing: Companies Act 2006 (UK), c. 46, §§ 170–177. This statutory statement of duties largely reflects the previous case law: Companies Act 2006, § 170. The statement came into force progressively in 2007 and 2008.

administrative obligations under companies legislation, but these obligations generally do not provide a legal foundation for civil suits.[30]

In many circumstances where directors may have breached their duties, US shareholders are able to commence and sustain litigation. This can be done in the form of a direct suit, if a director's breach of duty has allegedly injured shareholders directly, or a derivative suit, where the harm is principally to the corporation (Table 13.2). In contrast, in the UK, absent exceptional circumstances, direct suits are not available, and derivative suits have also been extremely hard to sustain. Typically, the company is the only 'proper plaintiff' in a suit alleging breach of duty, and the board will control litigation decisions.[31] Directors will rarely sue one of their own, and at common law gaining standing to sue derivatively was very difficult. Statutory reforms introduced in 2006 should make derivative suits moderately easier to sustain,[32] but by how much is not yet known.

When a shareholder in a UK company has had his personal rights infringed, the shareholder can sue in his own name to enforce his own rights.[33] The principal basis for a direct claim is 'unfair prejudice' resulting from the company's conduct.[34] In theory, breaches of duty by the directors of a publicly traded company can amount to unfair prejudice, with a damages award as one potential remedy.[35] However, English courts have generally been unreceptive to unfair prejudice claims involving publicly traded companies.[36]

Since both civil procedure rules and substantive corporate law seem more 'plaintiff friendly' in the US than the UK, we expect that the rate of private enforcement of corporate law, relative to the number of publicly

[30] On the reluctance of English courts to imply civil remedies for the breach of statutory duties, see *Lonrho Ltd.* v. *Shell Petroleum Co. Ltd.*, [1982] AC 173 (HL).

[31] On the difficulty of direct suits, see *Johnson* v. *Gore Wood*, [2002] 2 AC 1. On the 'proper plaintiff' principle, see *Prudential Assurance Co. Ltd.* v. *Newman Indus. Ltd. (No. 2)*, [1982] ch 204. This is an aspect of the board's right to manage the company, typically granted in the company's constitution: see *Breckland Group Holdings Ltd* v. *London and Suffolk Properties Ltd.*, [1989] BCLC 100.

[32] Companies Act 2006, Part 11.

[33] Paul L. Davies, *Gower and Davies' Principles of Modern Company Law*, 8th ed., (Sweet & Maxwell, 2008), 623.

[34] Companies Act 2006, § 994, formerly Companies Act 1985 (UK), c. 6, § 459.

[35] Victor Joffe, David Drake, Giles Richardson and Daniel Lightman, *Minority Shareholders: Law, Practice and Procedure*, 3rd ed., (Oxford University Press, 2008), 235 (breach of duty constituting unfair prejudice); Companies Act, 1985, § 461; Companies Act 2006 § 996. Some commentators argue, however, that the unfair prejudice remedy should normally be confined to relief in respect of harm personal to minority shareholders. See, for example, Davies, *Gower and Davies' Principles*, 689.

[36] See *Re Astec plc*, [1998] 2 BCLC 556; Davies, *Gower and Davies' Principles*, 693–694.

traded firms, will be higher in the US. However, we are unable to say *a priori* by how much.

H2: There should be a greater rate of private enforcement in the US than the UK.

3 The UK

3.1 Prior Literature

Owing in large part to difficulties with data collection, there is little prior empirical research on enforcement in the UK of corporate law or securities law. For public enforcement, one cross-country study examines the budgets and staffing of enforcement agencies in thirty countries, including the UK and the US.[37] Another reports numbers of actions brought and penalties levied in Germany, the UK and the US.[38]

For private enforcement, a few studies have used electronic databases of judgments to determine the incidence of suits against directors that result in a judicial opinion. Cheffins and Black report that the most recent derivative action against directors of a publicly traded company that resulted in a judicial decision was in 1981.[39] Armour finds there were six unfair prejudice petitions involving publicly traded companies that resulted in a judicial decision between 1998 and 2006, three of which involved allegations of misfeasance by the company's directors.[40] In none of these cases did the plaintiff (called a 'claimant' in the UK) seek damages or succeed with their action.

While there are very few cases brought against directors of publicly traded companies under UK company law that have resulted in a judicial opinion, might claims be brought but settle before being adjudicated? Little is known about the incidence of claims filed, as opposed to those resulting in a judicial opinion.[41] Our study addresses this gap.

[37] Jackson and Roe, *Public and Private Enforcement of Securities Laws.*

[38] Coffee *'Law and the Market'*, 261–262.

[39] Brian R. Cheffins and Bernard S. Black, 'Outside Director Liability Across Countries', 84 TEX. L. REV. 1385 (2006), 1407, discussing *Prudential Assurance Co. Ltd.* v. *Newman Industries Ltd. (No. 2)*, [1982] Ch. 204. See also G.P. Stapledon, *Institutional Shareholders and Corporate Governance* (Oxford University Press, 1996), 132 (citing *Prudential Assurance* as the only reported case where a UK institutional investor brought a derivative suit against directors of a portfolio company).

[40] Armour, 'Enforcement Strategies in UK Company Law', 84.

[41] The Law Commission of England and Wales studied the incidence of unfair prejudice claims by hand-collecting data from court records during the period 1994–1995. They reported only six such claims filed against public companies ('plcs'): 'Law Commission of England and Wales, Shareholder Remedies', LCCP 142 235–238 (1996). The Law

3.2 Methodology

Details of claims filed in UK courts – as opposed to judicial opinions to which they may give rise – exist only as confidential paper documents kept by the courts. To study these cases, one must obtain permission from court officials and then review each file manually. On the other hand, unlike the US, there is no need for multi-jurisdictional searching. The UK is comprised of three jurisdictions in which companies can register (England and Wales, Scotland, and Northern Ireland). However, companies registered in England and Wales comprise the vast majority of UK companies traded on the London Stock Exchange. As of October 2008, for those companies traded on the exchange that identified their region, 1,885 (92 per cent) were from England and Wales, 152 from Scotland and 3 from Northern Ireland.[42] Thus, if one can gain access to case files, searching cases filed in English courts will provide a largely complete picture of litigation patterns.

Claims brought under company law against directors of publicly traded companies registered as English or Welsh are almost certain to be brought in the Chancery Division of the High Court, based in London, and most likely in the Companies Court, a specialist list within the Chancery Division. Cases based on statutory remedies, for companies with paid-up capital of more than £120,000 – almost certainly the case for any publicly traded company[43] – must be started in the Companies Court.[44] This includes unfair prejudice claims.[45]

Commission did not report how many, if any, of these claims were against publicly traded companies; nor provide any details about the content of the claims.

42 See www.londonstockexchange.com/statistics/companies-and-issuers/companies-and-issuers.htm (Excel spreadsheet available under List of All Companies, accessed 10 November 2008; archived spread sheets are www.londonstockexchange.com/statistics/historic/company-files/company-files.htm.

43 Companies traded on the main list of the London Stock Exchange will almost surely satisfy this criterion, as a company seeking IPO on the London Stock Exchange main market must have a market capitalisation of at least £700,000. There is no minimum market capitalisation requirement for AIM, a second-tier exchange operated by the London Stock Exchange that allows smaller companies to carry out public offerings under more flexible rules than apply to the Exchange's Main Market: www.londonstockexchange.com/en-gb/products/companyservices/ourmarkets/aim_new/; London Stock Exchange, *AIM Brochure* 3 (2007). However, since only 6 per cent of AIM-listed companies have a market capitalisation of less than £2m, very few, if any, are likely to have a paid-up capital of less than £120,000.

44 See Civil Procedure Rules, 1998, S.I. 1998/3132, Practice Direction 49B (Applications Under the Companies Act 1985 and Other Legislation Relating to Companies), ¶¶ 1(2), 2; *Her Majesty's Court Service, The Chancery Guide 2005* (2005), ch. 20 (The Companies Court).

45 Companies Act 1985, § 459; Companies Act 2006, § 994.

During the period we study, the 2006 codification of directors' duties was not yet operative, so breach of duty claims were equitable in nature. These claims must be brought in the Chancery Division of the High Court,[46] but can be brought in the main Chancery Division as well as in the Companies Court. However, London lawyers advised us that in practice these cases would be filed with high probability in the Companies Court.

We obtained permission from High Court officials to conduct a comprehensive review of all files in the Companies Court list for the years 2004, 2005 and 2006. This encompassed 27,099 claims. Our search strategy was as follows. We looked first for files in which one of the parties was a company legally capable of having publicly traded shares. These companies can be quickly identified because their name must include the suffix 'plc'.[47] For cases involving plcs, we reviewed the file to see whether the suit involved a claim against directors. To find out which plc cases involved a publicly traded company, we cross-checked lists of companies traded on the main market of the London Stock Exchange and on AIM (the Alternative Investment Market).[48]

Searching files in the Chancery Division proved much harder than for the Companies Court. With the Companies Court, all filings are in a single location, so once we gained access to files, we needed no further assistance from court officials. However, mainstream Chancery Division court filings are held in a number of locations. Thus, for us to look at a particular filing involving a plc, court officials had to collect the files manually and bring them to us, which proved highly labour intensive. Chancery Division officials agreed to provide us two months' worth of filings, and we chose October and November 2006,[49] during which time a total of 629 cases were filed.

3.3 *Results*

3.3.1 Companies Court

Table 13.3 summarises the results of our search of files in the Companies Court. Of the 27,090 files surveyed, twenty-four involved claims against

[46] Supreme Court Act (UK) 1981, c. 54, Sch. 1, ¶ 1.

[47] Companies Act 1985, § 25(1), Companies Act 2006, § 58(1).

[48] Companies were classed as 'publicly traded' based on their status when the action was commenced. Their status was determined by consulting the register of public documents kept at Companies House, (www.companieshouse.gov.uk) which indicates whether a prospectus has been filed.

[49] We chose months outside the summer and the holiday season since these are the months when suits are most likely to be filed.

Table 13.3 *Claims filed in UK Companies Court, 2004–2006, in which defendants include directors of public limited companies*
Data on claims against directors of plcs in Companies Court from 2004–2006. The one case involving a claim for damages against directors of a publicly traded company was handwritten and filed without counsel, and was stricken for failure to meet the requirement to provide particulars.

	All plcs				Publicly traded companies			
Year		Public plaintiff	Private plaintiff	Private plaintiff, seeking damages		Public plaintiff	Private plaintiff	Private plaintiff, seeking damages
2004	9	7	2	2	2	1	1	1
2005	11	4	7	0	3	1	2	0
2006	6	4	2	1	1	1	0	0
Total	26	15	11	3	6	3	3	1
Mean	8.67	5	3.67	1	2	1	1	0.33

directors of plcs, of which only six involved companies traded on the London Stock Exchange or AIM. Of these six, three were launched by private plaintiffs. The other three were disqualification actions brought by the government; we discuss these actions later in a section entitled 'Disqualification'. Of the private suits, only one involved a claim for damages.[50] Even this solitary filing did not appear to be a genuine claim, since the plaintiff acted without counsel, and filed only a hand-written statement of claim with no supporting details. The case was struck out by the court when the plaintiff failed to submit full particulars within the stipulated time.

3.3.2 Chancery Division

Our survey of two months' worth of files from the Chancery Division serves as a robustness check on whether our search of the Companies Court missed significant numbers of claims against directors. Of the 629

[50] The other two were: (1) a claim requesting the court to call a shareholders' meeting to pass a resolution to remove and replace the board, which the incumbent board had sought to frustrate, and (2) a petition seeking an injunction regarding how the defendants were managing the company's affairs.

claims filed during this period, only one involved a claim arising under company law in relation to a plc. The company was not publicly traded, and the action arose out of the same facts as one of the claims we found in the Companies Court during the same year. These findings are consistent with plaintiffs not bypassing the Companies Court with any frequency to bring lawsuits against directors of such firms.

To put these findings in context, recall there were as of October 2008 nearly 1,900 UK-incorporated companies based in England and Wales traded on the London Stock Exchange and AIM.[51] If we do not discount the one case brought against directors of publicly traded companies as frivolous, this means the per-year likelihood of directors of a publicly traded firm being sued in English courts for damages under UK companies legislation was 1 out of nearly 6,000, or 0.017 per cent. Hence, the annualised number of lawsuits filed seeking damages against directors of publicly traded companies in the UK is effectively *zero* over our sample period. This suggests that when prior searches of judicial opinions failed to find suits against directors of publicly traded companies, this was not because claims are settled or abandoned before being adjudicated, but rather because such claims are simply not filed.

Suppose we put aside the handwritten case and conclude that there were zero genuine claims against directors over our three-year period in a sample of about 27,000 overall claims. What can we infer from the observed probability of 0/27,090 during this period that a claim, if made, would be against directors of a publicly traded company, about the expected number of such claims in another three-year period? We assume that we can treat corporate suits as existing with probability p in a hypothetical underlying population of suits filed in the Companies Court, with actual suits drawn at random from this population. An Agresti-Coull test for confidence bounds (Stata: cii 27090 0, agresti) provides a 95 per cent confidence upper bound on the true probability that a suit will involve directors of 0.00014, implying a 95 per cent likelihood that there would be four or fewer genuine suits over another three-year period. Thus, we cannot say with confidence that directors of publicly traded UK companies face *no* risk of being named as a defendant in a claim in English courts under UK company law, but can say with reasonable confidence that the risk is very low.

[51] See above note 36 and related discussion.

3.4 *Claims against UK directors filed in US courts*

Many large UK public companies cross-list their shares on a US stock market. Directors of these companies can readily become defendants in securities lawsuits filed in US courts under US securities law.[52] Corporate law, in theory, should be different. US shareholders generally cannot bring an action against directors of UK public companies, even those which are cross-listed, under state corporate law.[53]

US shareholders can potentially sue directors of UK companies for breach of UK corporate law, but must bring the claim in US courts. In the US portion of our research, we found three cases involving a reported decision between 2000 and 2007 where directors of UK public companies were sued in the US for breach of duty. The US courts dismissed two of the three cases on substantive grounds under UK law.[54] However, in *RSL Communications plc* v. *Bildirici*, the defendant directors unaccountably agreed with the plaintiffs that New York law should apply (they sought only to reserve the right to argue later that UK law applied), and the court allowed the claim to proceed.[55] Even though the other two cases were dismissed, it is striking that directors of cross-listed UK public companies could be at a greater risk of being sued under corporate law in the US than in the UK.

4 The US

In the US, a comprehensive search of all filed cases, similar to the one we conducted in the Companies Court of the Chancery Division, is impractical. Finding, let alone examining, every corporate law complaint in all fifty states plus federal courts, would be a daunting task. To make our search manageable, we searched for suits which produced at least one written judicial decision. Our rationale was that directors are likely to contest cases more vigorously where there is a serious prospect they will have to pay out of their own pocket. These contested cases are likely to

52 For background, see Cheffins and Black 'Outside Director Liability Across Countries', at 1413–1414.

53 This is a slight oversimplification. Some states, notably California, apply some provisions of their corporate law to companies principally located in that state, regardless of where in the US they are incorporated. These states might also permit suits against directors of companies incorporated outside the US.

54 *City of Sterling Heights Police and Fire Retirement System* v. *Abbey National plc*, 423 F. Supp. 2d 348 (SDNY, 2006); In *re BP p.l.c. Derivative Litig.*, 507 F. Supp. 2d 302 (2007).

55 *RSL Communications plc* v. *Bildirici*, US Dist LEXIS 67548 (SDNY, 2006), *9–11, 34.

generate a written decision, often on a motion to dismiss or a motion for summary judgment.[56] The principal exception should be for cases where the company is insolvent and cannot pay legal defence expenses, and no D&O insurance is available. The directors might then settle quickly, to avoid incurring defence costs.

A 2006 study by Black, Cheffins and Klausner supports this logic. They searched for cases in which outside directors of publicly traded companies made personal, out-of-pocket payments and found four such cases under corporate law between 1981 and 2005.[57] Of these, three involved a published judicial decision. The fourth seems likely to fit the insolvent company/no insurance exception.[58]

4.1 Prior Literature

Table 13.4 summarises the prior empirical studies of shareholder suits under US corporate law.[59] The studies differ across various dimensions, including the period studied, the state of incorporation considered, and the type of lawsuits considered (derivative suits, class actions or both). Although these differences make comparisons difficult, the studies collectively show that trials are uncommon and plaintiff wins at trial still more so, settlements are reasonably common, the annual odds of a firm being subject to a lawsuit are low, many suits involve takeover bids, and settlements are paid principally by D&O insurance. However, the

[56] An exception, where a director may agree to a personal payment without a written opinion being generated, is where the director is not insured (or insurance coverage is contested) and the company is insolvent, leaving no one to pay legal defence costs. A director might then be willing to settle early and quietly to limit legal expenses.

[57] Bernard Black, Brian Cheffins and Michael Klausner, 'Outside Director Liability', 58 STAN. L. REV. 1055 (2006), 1064–1074.

[58] Black, Cheffins and Klausner (ibid.) found a similar pattern for personal payments by outside directors of public companies under securities law and ERISA law. Of nine such cases, eight had a prior judicial decision; the remainder fit the insolvent company - no insurance exception.

[59] Franklin S. Wood, *Survey and Report Regarding Stockholders' Derivative Suits* (New York: New York Chamber of Commerce, 1944); Thomas J. Jones, 'An Empirical Examination of the Incidence of Shareholder Derivative and Class Action Lawsuits, 1971–1978' 60 B.U. L. REV. 306 (1980), 313–314, 319; Roberta Romano, 'The Shareholder Suit: Litigation Without Foundation?', 7 J.L. ECON. & ORG. 55 (1991), 60–62; Thompson and Thomas, *Delaware Class Actions* (2004a), above note 22; Robert B. Thompson and Randall S. Thomas, 'The Public and Private Faces of Derivative Lawsuits', 57 VAND. L. REV. 1747 (2004), 1772–1777 [in Table 13.4, Thompson and Thomas, 'Delaware Derivative Suits' (2004b)]; Weiss and White (2004), above note 19; Black, Cheffins and Klausner (2006), above note 51, 1090–1091.

Table 13.4 *Prior studies of shareholder suits under corporate law against directors of US publicly traded firms*

Summary of prior empirical studies of shareholder suits under corporate law against directors of US publicly traded companies. Settlement rate and plaintiff court success rate are as % of all filed cases. Settlement rate and plaintiff success rate at trial exclude cases which were still pending at the end of the study period. Plaintiff success rate does not necessarily imply a damages payment. No. of suits is measured after combining multiple complaints involving the same set of facts; these complaints are normally consolidated into a single action in the courts.

			Firms studied		Shareholder suit statistics					
					Suits/year					
Study	Period studied	Courts studied	Type	No.	Total	Per firm	Settlement rate (%)	Plaintiff court success rate (%)	Derivative	Direct/Class action
Wood (1944)	1932–1942	NY	All companies (data summary covers only public companies)		52	–	16.2	2.6	X	
Jones (1980)	1971–1978	All	Sample of Fortune 500 firms	190	29.0	0.15	74.7	–	X	X
Romano (1991)	1966–1987	All	Random sample of 535 public companies traded on NYSE or NASDAQ	535	6.3	0.01	64.8	1.5	X	X

Thompson and Thomas (2004a)	1999–2000	Del. Ch.	All Del. companies (data summary covers only public companies)	–	28.0	–	27.4	0.0	X	
Thompson and Thomas (2004b)	1999–2000	Del. Ch.	All Del. companies (data summary covers only public companies)	–	119.0	–	31.7	0.0		X
Weiss and White (2004)	1999–2001	Del. Ch.	Del. public companies that were merger targets during 1999–2001	564	34.7	0.18	16.0	0.0		X
Black, Cheffins and Klausner (2006)	1981–2005	All	Public companies in which outside directors made personal payments	4	–	–	–	–	X	X

proportion of cases settled (as opposed to being dismissed) appears to be lower today than during the 1970s and 1980s.

Among the more recent studies, we have already discussed the 2006 study by Black, Cheffins and Klausner. A 1991 study by Romano examined shareholder suits against a sample of 535 publicly traded companies between the late 1960s and 1987. She found that most lawsuits settled, with just over half involving monetary recovery and with the vast majority of settlements being paid by D&O insurance. Romano did not examine how often directors were sued or how often they paid damages personally.

Delaware is the state of incorporation for about 60 per cent of US publicly traded companies.[60] In two related 2004 studies, Thompson and Thomas examined all complaints filed in the Delaware Court of Chancery in 1999 and 2000. They found 294 cases involving publicly traded companies where a breach of fiduciary duty was alleged, including 213 class actions (mostly related to takeover bids), fifty-six derivative suits and twenty-five other 'direct' suits. Thompson and Thomas did not offer data on how often the remedy sought was damages as opposed to an injunction – say against a takeover.

A 2004 study by Weiss and White examined takeover-related class actions filed in Delaware courts and found that a majority of complaints are filed very soon after the transaction is announced, and most are dismissed with no recovery. Weiss and White found no trials with plaintiff wins, as well as evidence of attorney reluctance to press claims if substantial time and effort was likely to be required to yield a recovery.

Our study is intended to complement and build upon these prior studies in three key ways: (1) by investigating corporate law litigation nationwide; (2) by examining in greater depth outcomes in cases that met a threshold standard of seriousness; and (3) by focusing specifically on cases where directors were sued. We examine suits against both inside directors (those also serving as company officers) and outside directors.[61]

4.2 Search Methodology

We searched for suits under corporate law that were (1) brought by shareholders, creditors, bankruptcy trustees or the company itself;

[60] Lucian A. Bebchuk and Alma Cohen, 'Firms' Decisions Where to Incorporate', 46 J.L. & Econ. 383, 388 (2003), 391 (data as of 1999).

[61] In theory, a suit could name officers but no directors. In practice, the officers most likely to be sued are typically also directors. Our search found no cases in which only officers were sued.

(2) brought against one or more directors of a publicly traded US company; and (3) produced one or more written decisions between 1 January 2000 and 31 December 2007 but no written decisions before 1 January 2000. We excluded cases which involved investment companies (whether organised as corporations or as business trusts) or publicly traded entities other than corporations (e.g. LLCs, limited partnerships and real estate investment trusts).

We conducted an exhaustive search of Delaware cases. We first accessed all decisions in the Westlaw DEBUS database (Delaware business cases, both state and federal) between 2000 and 2007 which included the term 'director' or 'board'. This generated 368 decisions, which we read, to determine whether the case belonged in our sample.

We discovered that DEBUS is both incomplete (it omits many Delaware corporate law decisions) and unstable (a few cases in our sample that were in DEBUS on one search date were missing at a later date). We therefore also searched all reported decisions on the Delaware Chancery Court website (which contains decisions from 1 July 2000 forward) which involved one of the terms 'director' or 'board' or 'officer' or 'chairman' or 'CEO' or 'CFO'. This produced 637 decisions; we read those which our DEBUS search had not found.

For cases outside Delaware, we first searched the Westlaw MBUS database, the multistate analogue to DEBUS (state only, with no non-Delaware federal cases), excluding Delaware cases. The broad search for 'director' or 'board' which we used for Delaware cases, returned too many cases to read, so we chose narrower search terms that, in test searches, caught a high proportion of the cases found in a broader search that in fact belonged in our sample. We required that a decision include (1) 'director' or 'board'; (2) 'public' or 'stock exchange' or 'NASDAQ'; (3) 'shareholder or stockholder' in the same paragraph as 'derivative' or 'consolidat!' or 'class action'; and (4) 'fiduciary' or 'care' or 'Revlon' or 'fair dealing' or 'buyout'.[62] We carried out a similar search in the LEXIS 'Mega' database, which covers all federal and state cases, and

[62] The broad search for (director or board) (excluding Delaware cases), returned about 10,000 decisions, which was too many to read. In a test read of 250 decisions, only ten (4 per cent) fit the sample criteria. We therefore experimented with more restrictive searches. The search terms we used catch all ten of the 'test read' cases. We used 'Revlon' in our search because duties imposed on directors when a board is on the verge of selling the company are often called 'Revlon duties', after *Revlon Inc.* v. *MacAndrews & Forbes Holdings*, 506 A.2d 173 (Del. 1986).

a supplemental search in this database for cases with 'deriv! litig!' in the title. These searches returned 1,906 cases, which we read.

If an opinion did not state whether the company was publicly traded, we verified its status using the SEC's EDGAR database of filings by publicly traded companies. A single set of facts often prompts multiple lawsuits launched by different law firms, which are often later combined, and sometimes produces multiple judicial decisions. We defined a 'case' as a single set of facts prompting one or more lawsuits and one or more decisions. If the same facts produced both federal and state court decisions, we treated the case as a state case.

Whenever we found a decision, we searched for and read all prior or subsequent decisions in the case through April 2009. If a case produced more than one decision, we assigned the case to a year based on the first decision, and excluded from the dataset cases with initial decisions in 1999 or earlier. When a case referred to another case that seemed as if it might belong in our dataset, we read the other case and added it to the dataset if appropriate. When a case that we read involved a shareholder suing successfully to see corporate books and records, we checked for a later suit against the company's directors or officers, but did not include the books-and-records case in our dataset because these cases do not directly implicate director liability.

4.3 Case Counts

Our searches found 151 Delaware cases, seventy-three non-Delaware state cases and 175 federal-only cases fitting our sample criteria.[63] The total is 399 cases over eight years, or about fifty cases per year, involving 605 discrete decisions. Our Delaware count should be reliable, but we likely failed to find some non-Delaware state cases and some federal cases. Of our 399 cases, 305 (76 per cent) involved Delaware-incorporated companies.

Figure 13.1 shows the annual totals for cases from Delaware, from other states and from federal courts. There is year-to-year variation, but no strong time trend through 2005. There is an apparent increase in decisions 2006–2007, coming almost entirely from a rise in federal cases. There is also a smaller rise in non-Delaware state cases and a decline in Delaware cases. Regression analysis confirms that these trends are

[63] In one instance, the same facts generated reported decisions both in Delaware and elsewhere. We treated the case as a Delaware case.

Corporate Cases, Annual Totals

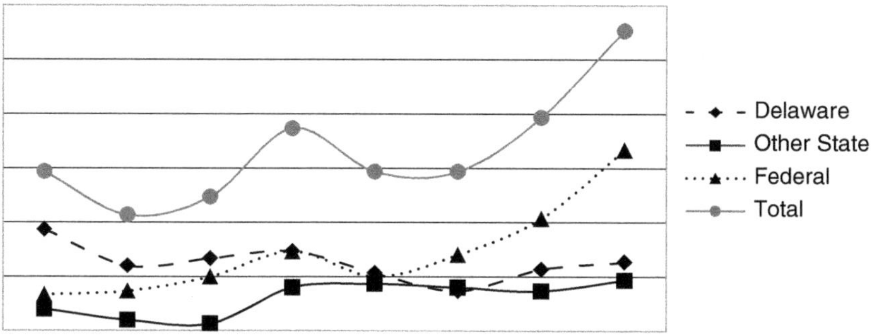

Figure 13.1 US corporate cases: Totals by jurisdiction
Annual number of corporate law cases in database with one or more decisions over 2000–2007, in Delaware state court, other state courts, or federal court. If one case produces several decisions, we use the year of the first decision. Sample = 399 cases. See text for details on search method and sample definition.

statistically significant at the 5 per cent level. The decline in cases in Delaware courts is consistent with a trend just beginning to capture the attention of commentators, in which some plaintiffs bring corporate claims involving Delaware-incorporated companies in other courts.[64]

Of the 399 cases in our dataset, 148 (37 per cent) involved companies listed on the New York Stock Exchange (NYSE); 128 (32 per cent) involved companies listed on the NASDAQ National Market (NASDAQ); 54 (13.5 per cent) involved Pink Sheets-traded companies; 22 (5.5 per cent) were listed on the American Stock Exchange or the NASDAQ bulletin board market. For 47 companies (12 per cent) the decision indicated the firm was publicly traded but we could not locate a trading market.

As of year-end 2007, there were roughly 4,600 US companies listed on the NYSE or NASDAQ.[65] This implies the directors of a company trading on one of these markets faced roughly a 1.1 per cent annual chance of facing a suit under corporate law which generated one or more judicial

[64] See Faith Stevelman, 'Regulatory Competition, Choice of Forum, and Delaware's Stake in Corporate Law', 34 DEL. J. CORP. L. 57 (2009); John L. Latham and Alex Reed, 'Strategies for Mitigating the Hardships of Multi-Jurisdiction Stockholder Litigation', in Practising Law Institute, *Corporate Law and Practice Course Handbook*, 19, 172 (2009).

[65] *World Federation of Exchanges, Focus Report* (January 2008). There were about 2,400 companies listed on the NYSE and another 3,100 on the NASDAQ National Market. Excluding foreign cross-listed companies reduces these amounts to the 4,600 total reported in the text.

decisions. A director's risk of being sued is much lower in a publicly traded firm which is not listed on the NYSE or NASDAQ. While around 9,000 companies have shares traded on the pink sheets, we found only eleven suits per year against directors of these companies, for an annual risk of about 0.12 per cent.

These annual figures overstate to some degree the risk of a director becoming involved in a lawsuit that meets our sample criteria, because often, when a lawsuit is brought against directors of a public company, only some directors will be named as defendants. On the other hand, annual figures do not reflect the 'career risk' that an individual will be named as a defendant in a reported case sometime during his career as a director. There is no data on typical tenure for inside and outside directors, but the median tenure for CEOs in US public companies is seven to nine years.[66] There is also no available data on how many public company boards a typical director serves on, over the course of a career. Given these uncertainties, it seems reasonable to estimate the lifetime risk of a director being named as a defendant in a reported lawsuit at ten times the annual risk, or around 10 per cent.

There is a substantial gap between cases filed and those which yield a judicial decision. Thompson and Thomas report about 150 cases filed per year in Delaware in 1999 and 2000 involving publicly traded companies and claims for breach of fiduciary duty, most of which probably involved claims against directors. In contrast, our dataset includes only about twenty Delaware-decided cases per year. A number of factors likely combine to explain the difference between these figures. First, Thompson and Thomas found that about 40 per cent of their cases were dismissed without prejudice, with no relief.[67] A written opinion in these cases is unlikely, and we found no such opinions in our search. Second, some cases will settle quickly. In the US, unlike the UK, these settlements normally require judicial approval, but approval is often granted without a written opinion. Thompson and Thomas report that 25 per cent of the cases in their sample settled; we do not know how many settled without a written

[66] Eliezer M. Fich and Anil Shivdasani, 'Are Busy Boards Effective Monitors?', 61 J. FIN. 689 (2006), 696 (Table II) (8.68 years); Eliezer M. Fich, 'Are Some Outside Directors Better than Others? Evidence from Director Appointments by Fortune 1000 Firms',78 J. BUS. 1943 (2005), 1951 (9.03 years); James S. Linck, Jeffrey M. Netter and Tina Yang, 'The Determinants of Board Structure', 87 J. FIN. ECON. 308 (2008), 315, (7.1 years) Ivan E. Brick, Oded Palmon and John K. Wald, 'CEO Compensation, Director Compensation and Performance: Evidence of Cronyism?', 12 J. CORP. FIN. 403 (2006), 408–409 (6.9 years).

[67] Thompson and Thomas, 'Delaware Class Actions' (2004a), above note 22, Table 13.4.

Table 13.5 *US corporate cases: Summary data*

Panel A. Nature of claim and status of defendants for 399 corporate law cases resulting in one or more decisions over 2000–2007, in Delaware state court, other state courts or federal court. Cases against directors often name the company as a defendant as well.

Nature of Claim	Insider Only	Outsider Only	Insider & Outsider	Total
Damages only	21	2	258	**281 (70%)**
Damages + another claim	4	0	70	**74 (19%)**
Injunctive + declaratory relief	4	0	37	**41 (10%)**
Other claims only	0	1	2	**3 (1%)**
Total	**29 (7%)**	**3 (1%)**	**367 (92%)**	**399 (100%)**

decision. Third, some cases may sit quietly, with no action. The plaintiffs do not pursue the case, and the defendants either do not seek dismissal or eventually obtain a dismissal order without a written opinion.

4.4 *Who Was Sued and Relief Sought*

Since our primary concern is with director liability, we examined the relief sought. Table 13.5 summarises the breakdown, by type of claim and type of defendant (inside directors, outside directors, or both).[68] In a few cases, the decision refers generically to 'directors', and we could not determine whether outside directors were among the defendants. These 'undetermined' directors probably included outsiders, and we assume this below.

Of the 399 cases in our dataset, 355 (89 per cent) involved claims for damages. Most suits name both inside and outside directors as defendants (367 cases; 92 per cent). All but three of the cases name at least some inside directors.

When a case involved both inside and outside directors, the insiders were usually the primary targets. The plaintiffs' case was often built

68 If the decision named the directors, but did not indicate their status as inside or outside, we verified their status using 10-K filings in the SEC's EDGAR database. We also drew reasonable inferences from the nature of the litigation. For example, in a derivative case in Delaware, the plaintiffs invariably argue that they should be excused from making a demand on the board to sue its own members. To have demand excused, the plaintiffs are effectively forced to sue a majority of the board, which will surely include some outsiders.

around allegations of misdeeds by insiders, described in rich detail, plus approval of the misdeeds by the outside directors, or allegations they failed to notice or respond appropriately to the insiders' actions. One suspects that in many cases, outside directors were named as defendants less because they were likely to be found liable than to put collective pressure on the board to settle, to facilitate the gathering of evidence through discovery or, for a derivative suit, to justify a claim that the plaintiff be excused from the need to demand that the board bring the suit.

4.5 *Outcomes in Damages Cases*

We also assessed case outcomes, focusing on cases which sought damages. Table 13.6 summarises the results of the known outcomes for

Table 13.6 *Outcomes for reported decisions in damages cases*
Principal outcome for 355 corporate law cases with damages claims which result in one or more decisions over 2000–2007, in Delaware state court, other state courts, or federal court. Outcome is based on reported decisions and, where these do not indicate the outcome, a search for settlements (see text for search details).

Case Outcome	Insiders Only	Outsiders Only	Insiders & Outsiders	Total
No relief				
Defendants' motion to dismiss or for summary judgment granted	11	0	173	**184**
Trial verdict for defendants	0	0	5	**5**
Relief				
Trial verdict for plaintiffs	2	0	8	**10**
Settlement	2	1	45	**48**
Outcome unknown. Last known result is:				
Defendants' motion to dismiss or for summary judgment denied or partly denied	8	1	54	**63**
Settlement denied	0	0	6	**6**
Stay granted or denied	0	0	12	**12**
Other	1	0	26	**27**
Total	**24**	**2**	**329**	**355**

the cases in our dataset. The most common outcome was for the defence to succeed on a motion to dismiss or for summary judgment. The defendants succeeded on such a motion in 52 per cent (184/355) of the damages cases in our dataset.[69] We also found fifteen trials, of which plaintiffs won ten against at least one defendant.

In many cases in our sample, the reported decisions did not provide a final outcome. We engaged in an extensive search for outcomes in these cases. We first Sherardized the reported decision(s) in question, to see if any later cases citing them mentioned a settlement. We also examined a company's annual reports on 10-K for mention of a settlement, and conducted a web search for news stories or press releases referring to a settlement or other outcome.[70] We found 48 settlements. Overall, then, plaintiffs obtained some relief in 58 of the 355 damages cases (16 per cent), but there are another 108 cases (31 per cent) for which we could not find the outcome.

The 14 per cent settlement rate implied by our data (48 cases out of 355) is a lower bound on the true settlement rate. If, say, half of the cases with an unknown outcome settle, then plaintiffs would obtain some relief in about 30 per cent of cases that warrant a written judicial decision. This is consistent with other recent studies, but is well below the rates reported in some earlier studies (see Table 13.4).

4.6 Personal Payments

Even when directors are sued for damages, out-of-pocket payments by directors are unlikely due to a series of protective devices that limit both directors' risk of being held liable and their risk of paying personally if they are held liable (as opposed to payment by the company or an insurer). These include the business judgment rule, a 'section 102(b)(7)' provision in the corporate charter which eliminates the personal liability of directors (but not officers) for duty of care violations, company advancement of legal expenses, indemnification by the corporation for

[69] We recorded partial grants of a motion to dismiss or for summary judgment as motion denied. When there was more than one reported decision for a single case, we used the latest result. Some decisions dismiss a complaint, but allow refiling of an amended complaint. We treated cases as dismissed if there was no further opinion arising from the same facts.

[70] Under US securities laws, companies must report annually on their 'material' litigation. Some companies report shareholder lawsuits and the outcomes of these suits, but others treat the suit, the outcome, or both as immaterial and do not report them, either in their 10-K report or in a press release.

damages paid (available for direct but not derivative suits), and D&O insurance.[71] The result is a sharp distinction between 'nominal liability' (the risk of an adverse settlement or court judgment) and the risk of an actual 'out-of-pocket' payment. The 2006 Black, Cheffins and Klausner study found only two instances of out-of-pocket payments by *outside* directors in corporate law cases during the time period of the present study, both of which are outside our sample.[72]

Black, Cheffins, and Klausner argue that the risk of a personal payment by an outside director rises substantially if a company goes bankrupt, because it then may well be unable to indemnify the defendant directors or pay their legal expenses, which takes away one of the shields against personal payment. For the 171 damages cases in our sample which were not resolved on a motion to dismiss or motion for summary judgment, we searched for evidence that the company went bankrupt at a time that could affect its ability to indemnify directors or pay their legal bills.[73] We found twenty-two such cases, or an average of about three per year. However, none of these cases in fact resulted in a personal payment.

Our results confirm Black, Cheffins and Klausner's findings concerning the rarity of outside director personal liability. We found only one case in our sample with personal payments by outside directors, involving ICN Pharmaceuticals. The ICN board approved $50 million in bonuses to both inside and outside directors under circumstances so raw that the award prompted a shareholder revolt. The shareholders installed a new board which sued to recover the bonuses. The former outside directors settled the suit by agreeing to partially repay their bonuses.[74]

We found as well that it is rare for *inside* directors to face out-of-pocket liability in a lawsuit arising under corporate law. In the ICN

[71] For fuller discussion of directors' shields against personal liability, see Black, Cheffins and Klausner, 'Outside Director Liability'.

[72] See ibid., Table 13.2. The first case, Lone Star Steakhouse, is outside our sample because it involves an *ultra vires* repricing of stock options, rather than a breach of fiduciary duty. The second case, reported to Black, Cheffins and Klausner on a confidential case basis, is outside our sample because we are not aware of a reported decision. A third post-2000 personal payment case reported by Black, Cheffins and Klausner, Fuqua Industries, is outside our sample because the first reported decision in this case is before 2000.

[73] The director would be at risk if the firm was bankrupt during the facts relevant to the lawsuit, or went bankrupt after those facts but before the case was resolved. To find relevant bankruptcies, we conducted a web search for the company name and 'bankruptcy' or 'insolven*'; and also searched the company's annual reports on Form 10-K.

[74] See *Valeant Pharmaceuticals International* v. *Jerney*, 921 A.2d 732 (Del. Ch. 2007) (ICN had changed its name to Valeant by the time the case was decided), app. dismissed, 2007 Del. LEXIS 245.

Pharmaceuticals case the corporation secured personal payments from two principal executives in addition to payments by the outside directors. We found two other instances where inside directors made personal payments.[75] One involved HealthSouth. The court awarded summary judgment to the plaintiffs, who sued former CEO Richard Scrushy for restitution of bonuses which were paid based on false financial statements.[76] Scrushy also landed in jail for other misconduct. The second involved Tenet Healthcare, where the CEO paid $1 million personally, and the CFO $500,000, as part of an overall $215 million settlement of a derivative suit and related securities class action suit, with the balance being paid by the company and D&O insurance.[77]

5 Substitutes for Private Enforcement

5.1 *Why Look for Substitutes?*

Our US findings support our second hypothesis that, due to differences in civil procedure and substantive law, there will be more private enforcement in the US than the UK. However, the near-total absence of private litigation in the UK is inconsistent with the first hypothesis that private enforcement of corporate law is critical for the development of strong securities markets or dispersed ownership. It is theoretically possible that the low incidence of private enforcement in the UK shows not that the UK's private enforcement mechanisms do little to deter misconduct, but proves instead that they deter so effectively that no misconduct occurs and hence no enforcement is observed. This implication is at odds, however, with the fact that directors of US public companies conduct themselves in a manner sufficient to generate around fifty cases a year with written decisions involving allegations of breach of duty, despite private enforcement being a *more* credible threat than in the UK due to

[75] We also found one case where a CEO made a personal payment but the source of liability was not corporate law. In *Bansbach* v. *Zinn*, 801 N.E.2d 395 (N.Y. 2003) the company and its founder, majority stockholder and CEO Michael Zinn, were both convicted of violating campaign contribution law, and Zinn served a jail term. The company indemnified Zinn for his legal expenses, but a shareholder sued and the court blocked indemnification, leaving Zinn to pay his own legal expenses.

[76] *Tucker* v. *Scrushy*, 2006 WL 2664197 (Ala. Cir. Ct. 2006), *aff'd*, 2006 WL 932013, (Ala. 2006), see also *Teachers' Retirement System of Louisiana* v. *Scrushy*, 2004 WL 423122 (Del. Ch. 2004).

[77] *Penn* v. *Tenet Healthcare Corp.*, 2007 WL 2729463 (Cal. Sup.); Bloomberg News, 'Tenet Healthcare Agrees to Settle Fraud Lawsuits' (13 January 2008).

the factors identified in Tables 13.1 and 13.2. It is also in tension with our finding that UK company directors are sometimes sued in the US.

Even in the US, private enforcement of corporate law may play a more limited role than is commonly thought in constraining corporate directors. Suits are common enough, as Thompson and Thomas show. However, only a small fraction of the cases filed are sufficiently contentious to yield a single reported judicial opinion. Among those cases filed that generated a written opinion, the judge dismissed the claim in almost half. Trials are rare, averaging only about two per year. While settlements are fairly common, they are almost always paid with other people's money; the risk that directors will make personal payments is small.

Our finding that private enforcement of corporate law is not critical for strong securities markets invites a search for substitutes. Since our most striking empirical finding is the absence of suits against directors of UK publicly traded companies, we focus primarily on what substitutes might exist in Britain. We examine three basic categories: private enforcement of related areas of law (securities and bankruptcy law), public enforcement and shareholder governance rights. Extra-legal substitutes are surely also important, but are beyond the scope of this paper.

5.2 *Private Enforcement of Other Areas of Law*

Our inquiry was limited to lawsuits brought against directors under corporate law. One potential substitute for litigation of this sort is private enforcement of obligations under other bodies of law that also constrain director actions and thus might also address managerial agency costs. Securities law and bankruptcy law are the most likely candidates.

5.2.1 Securities Law

Private lawsuits under securities law can substitute for, or at least supplement, suits under corporate law. Circumstances in the US illustrate this. US securities law is highly protective of investors, both anecdotally and based on the one available quantitative 'law in books' measure (see Table 13.7), while US corporate law is not highly protective by international standards (see Table 13.8). Litigation, moreover, is common, with 150–200 federal securities class actions being brought annually,[78] plus

[78] See, e.g. Cornerstone Research, *Securities Class Action Filings 2008: A Year in Review* (2009), www.cornerstone.com.

Table 13.7 *Quantitative assessment of regulation of securities law*

Aspect of Securities Law	US	UK	Average (49 countries)
Disclosure (based on whether the law requires delivery of a prospectus to potential investors and disclosure, in a public offering of shares, of executive compensation, blockholders, director share ownership, 'large' contracts and contracts with insiders).	1.00	0.83	0.60
Liability standard (based on the burden of proof an investor has to meet to recover damages from a company, its directors, advisers and accountants for misdisclosure in documents supporting a public offering of shares).	1.00	0.66	0.47
Public enforcement (based on the criminal liability for misdisclosure by a company, its advisers, and accountants and on the rule-making powers, independence, investigative powers and enforcement powers of a country's securities regulator).	0.90	0.68	0.52

Source: La Porta, Lopez-de-Silanes and Shleifer (2006), Tables I, II

some number of non-class actions brought in state court. Research in progress by one of us (Black) confirms that almost all name inside directors, and a fair number name outside directors as well.

The situation in the UK is very different. Shareholders in a publicly traded UK company can potentially sue directors under both the Financial Services and Markets Act 2000 and the common law to recover losses caused by false or misleading disclosures in documents supporting a public offering of shares.[79] As a result, UK securities law 'in books' ranks fairly high on investor protection, if one focuses on liability for false

[79] Financial Services and Markets Act, 2000, c. 8, § 90 (creating liability for 'persons responsible' for misleading disclosures; § 79(3); Financial Services and Markets Act 2000 (Official Listing of Securities) Regulations, 2001, S.I. 2001/2956, art. 6, ¶ (1)(b) (naming directors as a 'person responsible'). On common law liability, see *Al-Nakib Investments (Jersey) Ltd.* v. *Longcroft* [1990] 3 All ER 321, and *Possfund Custodian Tr. Ltd.* v. *Diamond*, (1996) 2 All ER 774 (Ch.). Statutory liability is more extensive in a variety of respects: *Encyclopedia of Financial Services Law* ¶ 2A-190 (Eva Z. Lomnicka and John L. Powell eds., 1987–2001).

Table 13.8 *Quantitative studies of shareholder rights*

Study	Variables	Enforcement taken into account?	US score	UK score	Cross-country average
Djankov, La Porta, Lopez-de-Silanes and Shleifer (2008)[80]	Anti-director index (re-coded), based on 1) shareholders voting by mail; 2) absence of a requirement to deposit shares before a vote; 3) cumulative voting for directors; 4) relief to oppressed minority shareholders; 5) pre-emptive rights during share offerings; and 6) shareholder power to call a shareholder meeting.	N/A	3[81]	5	3.29 (72 countries)
Spamann (2010)[82]	LLSV Anti-director index (re-coded).	N/A	2	4	2.80 (46 countries)
Djankov, La Porta, Lopez-de-Silanes and Shleifer (2008)	Anti-self-dealing index, based on regulation *ex ante* (e.g. disclosure, approval by disinterested shareholders) and *ex post* (based on disclosure in periodic filings and ease of proving wrongdoing) of a transaction between a company and a majority shareholder.	'Ease of proving wrongdoing' is one element of *ex post* regulation (based on standing to sue and access to evidence).	0.65	0.93	0.45 (72 countries)

80 Simeon Djankov, Rafael La Porta, Florencio Lopez-de-Silanes and Andrei Shleifer, 'The Law and Economics of Self-Dealing' 88 J. Fin. Econ. 430 (2008).
81 Originally coded as '5' in La Porta et al., 'Law and Finance'.
82 Spamann, 'The 'Antidirector Rights Index' Revisited'.

Lele and Siems (2007)[83]	Shareholder protection index covering 1970–2005, using 60 variables, 42 involving protection of shareholders against boards and 18 involving protection against other shareholders.	Ability to bring derivative litigation is one element of protection against the board.	34 (in 2005)	38 (in 2005)	37.2 (5 countries) (in 2005)
Siems (2008)[84]	Shareholder protection index covering 1995–2005, using 10 variables, six involving protection of shareholders against boards.	Ability to bring derivative litigation is one of the 10 elements.	7.25	7.38	5.3 (20 countries) (in 2005)

83 Priya Lele and Mathias M. Siems, 'Shareholder Protection: A Leximetric Approach', 7 J. Corp. L. Stud. 17 (2007), 31.
84 Mathias M. Siems, 'Shareholder Protection Around the World (Leximetric II)', 33 Del J. Corp. L. 111 (2008).

or misleading disclosure in public offerings (Table 13.7). However, there is no UK equivalent to US Rule 10b-5, the far-reaching provision that creates a private right of action for material misstatements that affect secondary trading of securities. Negligent misstatements in a company's annual accounts and other financial documentation disseminated by directors of a UK publicly traded company can in theory form the basis for a suit by investors against the persons responsible for the disclosure, which can include its directors, but such a suit can only succeed in the rare event that the information was provided to guide a specific purchase or sale of shares.[85] In the US, such reliance is assumed under the 'fraud on the market' doctrine.[86] Finally, several of the UK procedural rules which impede suits under corporate law (Table 13.1) also discourage suits under securities law, including barriers to forming class actions, 'loser pays' fee rules, and lack of a contingent fee system.

The stronger US substantive liability rules and more liberal procedural rules suggest that there should be more securities suits in the US than in the UK, per publicly traded company. This is strongly the case. While around 150 to 200 securities class actions are filed per year in the US, such litigation is rare in Britain. According to searches of electronic databases of judicial opinions, between 1990 and 2006 there was only one reported case involving a claim under statutory rules creating liability for misleading information in public offering documents, and the directors were not named as defendants.[87] Over the same time period, two additional cases, both naming directors as defendants, were brought under common law

[85] See, e.g. *Al-Nakib Investments (Jersey) Ltd.* v. *Longcroft* [1990] 3 All ER 321 and generally *Gore-Browne on Companies* ¶ 43.27 (Alistair Alcock ed., 50th ed. 2004). In 2006, shareholders were given the right to sue the company for compensation for misleading periodic disclosure documentation, but not its directors: Financial Services and Markets Act, 2000, § 90A; for background, see Davies (2007), *Davies Review of Issuer Liability*, at 25.

[86] This difference underscores the hazards in measuring shareholder protection based on 'law in books', as the US 'fraud on the market' rule, which is critical to the viability of securities class actions, is not found in the statute books, but in case law. See *Basic, Inc.* v. *Levinson*, [cite to come].

[87] See Eilís Ferran, 'Cross-border Offers of Securities in the EU: The Standard Life Flotation', 4 Eur. Corp. & Fin. L. Rev 461 (2007), 476–477; Armour, 'Enforcement Strategies in UK Company Law', 85–86. The case was *Axa Equity and Law Life Assurance Society plc* v. *National Westminster Bank* [1998] CLC 1177 (unsuccessful application for discovery of documents in relation to a securities law claim against the company's auditors and directors). Our search also revealed evidence of a second claim, referred to in another decision, which did not itself produce an opinion: see *Re Barings plc (No 6)* [2001] 2 BCLC 159 at [4] (application by creditors of insolvent firm to call a creditors' meeting to replace liquidator; some parties were potentially creditors because they had launched a securities law claim against directors).

principles alleging negligent misstatements in prospectus disclosures.[88] Of these two cases, one was dismissed whilst the other survived a motion to dismiss and likely settled. Thus, while private enforcement of securities law complements private enforcement of corporate law in the US, in the UK, neither body of law receives significant private enforcement.

5.2.2 Bankruptcy and Insolvency Law

Law governing enterprises which cannot pay their debts (principally 'bankruptcy law' in the US and 'insolvency law' in the UK) may create the possibility of claims against the directors of failed enterprises. US bankruptcy law indirectly serves this function. It does not offer important additional substantive rights to shareholders or creditors, beyond those in corporate and securities law, but it does provide a process by which those in charge of a bankrupt firm can pursue those claims. A US bankruptcy trustee will often pursue claims against directors, and these claims are a source of heightened risk for directors of making personal payments.[89]

UK insolvency law could potentially serve this role as well. An insolvent company's liquidator is authorised to bring any action in the name of the company, including a breach of duty claim against directors.[90] UK insolvency law also imposes a duty on directors to refrain from continuing to trade if there is no reasonable prospect of avoiding insolvency.[91] However, in practice, liquidators rarely sue directors of insolvent companies. A study of electronic databases of judicial opinions found only one instance during 1990–2006 where an insolvency practitioner brought a claim against former directors of a publicly traded company, albeit one that resulted in significant personal liability for the defendant directors (all inside directors).[92] The need for the insolvent

[88] The cases were (1) *Al-Nakib Investments (Jersey) Ltd.* v. *Longcroft* [1991] BCLC 7 (claim against company and directors; struck out at preliminary hearing) and (2) *Possfund Custodian Trustee Ltd.* v. *Diamond* [1996] 2 BCLC 665 (claim against company and directors, survived application to strike out, no final judgment so presumably settled). Axa Equity, discussed in the preceding footnote, involved both statutory and common law claims.

[89] See Black, Cheffins and Klausner, 'Outside Director Liability' (most US cases with personal payments by outside directors involve insolvent firms and low, missing, or contested D&O insurance).

[90] Insolvency Act (UK) 1986, c. 45, § 212; Sched. 4, ¶ 4.

[91] This is known as liability for 'wrongful trading': Insolvency Act 1986, § 214.

[92] Armour (2009), 'Enforcement Strategies in UK Company Law', 86. The case was *Bairstow* v. *Queens Moat Houses plc* [2000] 1 BCLC 549, [2001] EWCA Civ 712, [2001] 2 BCLC 531

company to pay the defendants' legal costs ahead of the claims of creditors if the claim fails may be an important reason why liquidators rarely pursue these claims.[93]

In sum, in the US, private enforcement of securities law complements private enforcement of company law, and bankruptcy law contributes to private enforcement of both. In the UK, private enforcement is rare, no matter where one looks. Our initial search for substitutes for private enforcement of corporate law has only deepened the puzzle – what feature of the UK environment might substitute for the near-total lack of civil lawsuits against directors under *any* of the principal bodies of law that might be expected to constrain directors of publicly traded companies?

5.3 *Public Enforcement*

Enforcement by public authorities provides an obvious alternative or supplement to private enforcement. It turns out that in the UK at least one aspect of public enforcement – the UK Takeover Panel – may offer a partial substitute for private enforcement.

5.3.1 Securities Regulators

Jackson and Roe show public enforcement of securities laws, measured via a proxy based on the budget and resources available to regulators, is at least as strongly correlated with stock market development around the world as is private enforcement, measured by reference to an index based on the formal ease of bringing a private lawsuit.[94] These findings imply that even if lawsuits brought by private plaintiffs are uncommon in the UK, enforcement by securities regulators can potentially fill the gap. However, if one looks at measures of regulatory output – the number of public enforcement actions brought and the size of the penalties imposed relative to market size the UK trails the US to a degree comparable to the disparity we report as regards private litigation.[95] Enforcement by securities regulators is thus an unlikely substitute for private enforcement in the UK of corporate or securities law.

(claim against four inside directors for breach of duty in paying dividends out of capital; directors held liable jointly and severally to repay £79m).

93 Insolvency Act 1986, §§ 115, 176ZA; Insolvency Rules (UK) 1986, r. 4.218(1)(a)(i).

94 Jackson and Roe, *Public and Private Enforcement of Securities Laws.*

95 Coffee, 'Law and the Market', 261–263; Armour, 'Enforcement Strategies in UK Company Law', 87–89.

5.3.2 Disqualification

In the UK, the Department for Business, Innovation and Skills has a number of enforcement powers in relation to company directors, notably the ability to seek an order disqualifying individuals from acting as company directors.[96] About 1,500 individuals are disqualified each year from serving as directors, typically on the basis that the manner in which they managed an insolvent company indicates they are 'unfit' to again serve as a director.[97] However, disqualifications of directors of publicly traded companies are rare, in part because it is uncommon for publicly traded companies to enter insolvency proceedings.

Our findings bear this out. If disqualification is by court order, the proceeding must be commenced in the Companies Court.[98] As detailed in Table 13.4 above, over 2004–2006, we found only three cases where disqualification proceedings were commenced against directors of publicly traded companies. A total of six directors were involved, only one of whom was an outside director.[99] Only one of these proceedings resulted in a court order, disqualifying one (inside) director for ten years.[100]

Since 2000, directors have been able to give a 'disqualification undertaking' without a court hearing, a sort of plea-bargain which has the same legal effect as a disqualification order.[101] Over 2001 to 2006, 71 per cent of disqualifications were by means of an undertaking rather than a court order.[102] One would anticipate that a disqualification claim would often be filed before the director gives a disqualification undertaking. If so, our searches should capture these claims. However, some disqualification undertakings appear to be given before a

[96] Company Directors Disqualification Act 1986 (UK), c. 46.

[97] Armour, 'Enforcement Strategies in UK Company Law', at 99; Company Directors Disqualification Act 1986, § 6.

[98] See Company Directors Disqualification Act 1986, § 6(3); Practice Direction: Directors Disqualification Proceedings, ¶ 4.1; Her Majesty's Court Service, *The Chancery Guide 2005* (2005), ¶ 20.1.

[99] Where the claim forms did not indicate whether the defendants were inside or outside directors we determined their status by reference to their Notice of Appointment forms filed at Companies House.

[100] *Secretary of State for Business Enterprise and Regulatory Reform* v *Sullman* [2008] All ER (D.) 238 (Dec).

[101] Company Directors Disqualification Act 1986, §§ 1A, 7(2A), 8(2A).

[102] See Armour, 'Enforcement Strategies in UK Company Law', 99.

claim is filed.[103] Thus, our findings understate the number of disqualifications.[104]

In the US, there is no company law regulator, and hence no public enforcement of corporate law. There is also no general director disqualification regime. However, the SEC has the power to bar individuals from serving as directors of publicly traded companies. A study by Karpoff, Lee and Martin of directors of US public companies who faced public enforcement by the SEC or the Department of Justice for financial misrepresentation over 1978–2006 found proceedings against 2,206 individuals – approximately 76 per year. Of these, 31 per cent (about twenty-five per year) were barred from serving as a director or officer of a publicly traded firm, either permanently or for a period of time. Hence, disqualification trends further deepen rather than resolve the UK director litigation puzzle our findings pose.

5.3.3 The Takeover Panel

While enforcement by securities regulators and director disqualification do not rebalance the private enforcement discrepancy between the UK and US, the manner in which takeovers are regulated does do so to some degree. Takeovers of publicly traded companies are common in both countries and, in the US, lead to a large percentage of the lawsuits under corporate law. In contrast, for UK companies, the actions of all participants in takeover situations relating to UK-registered companies are governed by a comprehensive code of conduct known as the City Code on Takeovers and Mergers ('the City Code'), which is promulgated and administered by the Panel on Takeovers and Mergers ('the Panel').[105] The Panel seeks to enforce the City Code, with a trademark feature being enforcement in real time.[106]

[103] Adrian Walters, 'Bare Undertakings in Directors Disqualification Proceedings: The Insolvency Act 2000, Blackspur, and Beyond', 22 COMP. LAW. 290 (2001), 294–295.

[104] While our searches could not capture claims instances in which all directors gave undertakings before a claim was filed, obviating the need for a filing we checked whether the three reported cases we found provide a full count of the disqualified directors. By searching the Register of Disqualified Directors maintained at Companies House (see www.companieshouse.gov.uk/ddir/) we found three additional inside directors (one named in each of the claims) were disqualified by giving undertakings, one for seven years and two for four years.

[105] Companies Act 2006, §§. 942–59; *City Code On Takeovers And Mergers*, 8th ed., (2006 + updates), www.thetakeoverpanel.org.uk.

[106] Armour and Skeel, 'Who Writes the Rules for Hostile Takeovers', 1729, 1743–1745.

The City Code often imposes tighter constraints on directors than directors' fiduciary duties under corporate law. As a result, compliance with the former will necessarily imply compliance with the latter. Moreover, the Panel normally bars parties from engaging in any litigation (apart from a reference to the antitrust authorities) which might frustrate an actual or potential takeover bid.[107] As a consequence, there is almost no litigation surrounding takeovers in the UK. Enforcement by the Panel is therefore potentially an important UK substitute for private enforcement.

Data on the number of cases in which the Takeover Panel offers guidance confirms that it may offer a substitute for civil enforcement of directors' duties.[108] During the 2004–2006 period covered by our analysis of cases filed, the Panel offered guidance on an average of 287 cases per year,[109] or about 12 per cent of the firms traded on the London Stock Exchange. Moreover, since 1969, the number of Panel engagements since (Figure 13.2, black line) has exceeded the number of actual bids made (Figure 13.2, dashed line) by nearly 50 per cent, meaning the Panel is clearly making rulings both on bids that proceed and often in situations where a bid does not materialise.

5.4 *Shareholder Governance Rights*

Shareholder governance rights – powers enjoyed by shareholders over key decisions in the firm – also likely serve as a substitute for formal civil enforcement in the UK. Governance rights can reduce managerial agency costs by giving shareholders power to remove directors who do not act in shareholder interests as well as *ex ante* decision rights for transactions that could harm shareholders' interests. On both counts, shareholders are better positioned in Britain than in the US.[110]

We have already seen that, in general terms, the UK scores highly on cross-country measures of shareholder rights and outscores the US (Table 13.8). The pattern is the same with respect to key specifics. UK shareholders, in contrast to their US counterparts, generally enjoy pre-

[107] See *City Code On Takeovers* and *Mergers*, Rule 21.1; William Underhill (ed.), *Weinberg and Blank on Take-Overs and Mergers*, 5th ed., (Sweet & Maxwell, 1989, supp. 2006), ¶¶ 4–7114 to 4–7130B.

[108] In the vast majority of cases, the Panel's response to a reference will be given in private. However, in a small minority of cases, the Panel will make a public ruling concerning the conduct of a particular bid situation.

[109] Takeover Panel, *Annual Reports*, 2005–2007, www.thetakeoverpanel.org.uk/statements/reports

[110] Armour, 'Enforcement Strategies in UK Company Law', 104–109.

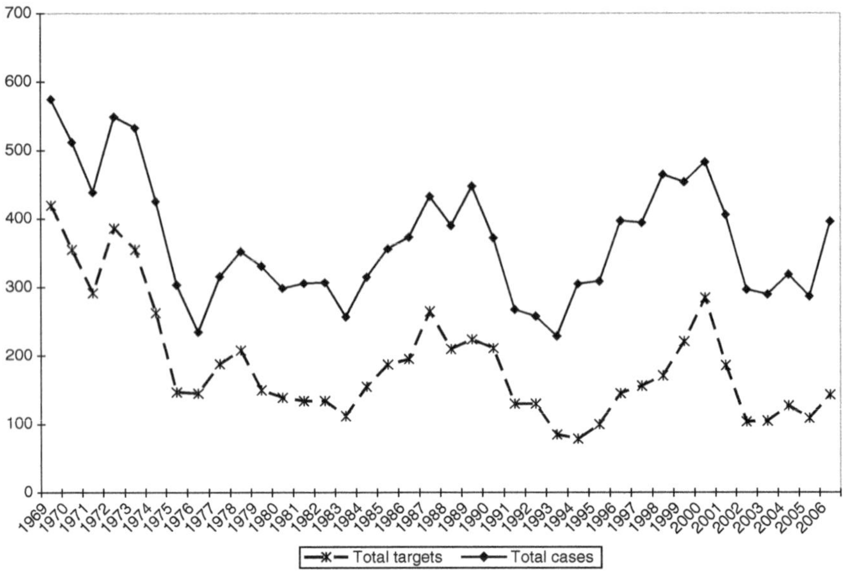

Figure 13.2 Engagements by the Takeover Panel, 1969–2006
Source: Takeover Panel, Annual Reports, 1969–2006[111]

emptive rights when a company issues new shares, and UK institutions see these rights as providing important leverage when a firm needs capital.[112] Moreover, in the UK, shareholders owning 10 per cent or more of the shares can call a shareholder meeting, whereas in the US they generally cannot.[113] In addition, UK directors, again unlike the US, cannot entrench themselves effectively against a resolution for their removal before the end of their term.[114] Moreover, while UK institutional investors can join together informally to change a company's strategy or management with few legal obstacles, similarly minded US institutions face various legal hazards.[115]

[111] Data on total cases for 2005 and 2006 are estimates.

[112] Companies Act 2006, §§ 560–577. See Iain MacNeil, 'Shareholders' Pre-emptive Rights', [2002] J. Bus. L. 78, 78, 84–91, 95–97.

[113] Compare Companies Act 2006, §§303–305 (shareholders owning 10 per cent of the shares collectively can call a shareholder meeting) with Delaware General Corporation Law § 211(d) (board of directors or persons authorised by the articles of incorporation or the by-laws can call a meeting). In most US publicly traded firms, the shareholders have no rights to call a special meeting.

[114] Companies Act 2006, §§168–169; Delaware General Corporation Law § 141(k)(i) (director removal must be for cause when a company has a classified board).

[115] Bernard Black and John Coffee, 'Hail Britannia? Institutional Investor Behavior under Limited Regulation', 92 Mich. L. Rev. 1997–2087 (1994).

Shareholder approval requirements are also more extensive in the UK than the US. In the US, target company shareholders must vote on a merger with another company,[116] but almost all other transactions can be approved by the board alone. In the UK, shareholders have a veto over a range of potentially problematic transactions, such as managerial services contracts of greater than two years in duration, 'substantial property transactions' between a director and his company, loans to directors, and political donations.[117] The London Stock Exchange Listing Rules also require that shareholders must approve transfers of assets to and from a company that exceed designated asset thresholds, or between a company and a related party.[118]

The UK also has a procedure involving a combination of shareholder veto rights and advance judicial clearance for major corporate transactions for which the US has no counterpart. In the UK, a 'scheme of arrangement' can be used to make mergers, share repurchases, debt reorganisations and similar transactions binding on investors.[119] The company must obtain 75 per cent supermajority approval from each class of investors affected by the transaction, and then apply for a court order which makes the arrangement binding on all concerned. The court must satisfy itself of the procedural fairness of the class representation and voting.[120] If it grants an order approving the scheme of arrangement, the ruling effectively bars a later challenge.

To assess how often schemes of arrangement are used in UK public companies, for 2004 to 2007 we searched for court orders for schemes of arrangement (they must be filed with the UK's Registrar of Companies).[121] We matched these records with lists of firms traded on the London Stock Exchange Main List and AIM, then read orders involving these listed firms to determine the nature of the transaction. We found (Table 13.9) that schemes of arrangement are not frequent but are not rare either, with twenty-five such orders being granted over

[116] Delaware General Corporation Law § 251.

[117] Companies Act 2006, §§ 188, 190, 197, 366.

[118] See, e.g. FSA, Listing Rules, LR 10 and 11, particularly LR 11.1.7. Companies listed on AIM, however, do not have to hold shareholder votes in relation to such transactions, and need only disclose their details: see London Stock Exchange, *AIM Rules for Companies*, ¶¶ 12–13 (2007). In the US, under NYSE and NASDAQ listing rules, the issuance of more than 20 per cent of a company's previously outstanding shares requires shareholder approval.

[119] Companies Act 1985, §§ 425–427; Companies Act 2006, §§ 895–900.

[120] See, e.g. *Re Dorman Long & Co* [1934] Ch 635, 655–657.

[121] Companies Act 1985, § 425(3); Companies Act 2006, § 899(4).

Table 13.9 *Schemes of arrangement for UK publicly traded companies, 2004–2007*

Schemes of arrangement entered into by UK companies listed on the UK Official List or AIM, 2004–2007, which receive court approval. 'M&A related' transactions involve either a cash-for-share or share-for-share acquisition, a de-merger or a merger (whether cash-out or otherwise).

Year	No. of schemes	Of which, M&A- related
2004	2	0
2005	4	2
2006	6	4
2007	13	12
Total	**25**	**18**
Mean	6.25	4.5

the four-year period. Most (eighteen) of the twenty-five schemes approved during this period were M&A-related, with ten involving acquisitions of shares, three involving cash-out mergers, three involving share-for-share mergers and two involving de-mergers (corporate 'spin-offs').

5.5 Discussion

Since our results for the UK contradict the private enforcement primacy view, we have investigated potential law-related substitutes for formal private enforcement of corporate law. Across different bodies of law, the private enforcement pattern is similar to that for corporate law – formal private enforcement of securities law is also far more robust in the US than the UK and disqualification is a more potent sanction in the US, at least for publicly traded companies. Public enforcement of securities law offers a similar picture.

However, we did find important areas where the UK regulatory regime provides more potent protection, with the emphasis being on *ex ante* screening as compared with *ex post* sanctions. The Takeover Panel resolves numerous contentious takeover matters by offering 'real time' dispute resolution as takeovers proceed. Shareholders in the UK have greater scope than their US counterparts to dismiss directors not performing up to expected standards and to vote on key transactions.

Finally, schemes of arrangement can be used to obtain advance judicial clearance for fundamental corporate restructuring. The latter two 'shareholder governance' approaches bring us back to 'law in books.' In important ways, the UK has stronger corporate law than the US, in ways that let shareholders protect themselves without the need to file lawsuits.

It is plausible that these substitutes are sufficient so that, in the end, the scope for directors to resist takeover bids, take companies private at below-market prices, self-deal, or otherwise favour themselves are no greater in the UK than in the US. Many American scholars indeed prefer the UK system of takeover regulation.[122] Others have advocated greater reliance on *ex ante* shareholder action and less on *ex post* litigation.[123] It is also possible that directors in both countries are constrained, in significant part, by other factors, not strictly legal. The most we can say is that the mix of constraints in each country is sufficient to support well-developed capital markets and diffuse share ownership, even when, as in the UK, formal private enforcement of corporate law is virtually non-existent.

6 Conclusion

Though this paper has an overall comparative orientation, we have focused more on understanding Britain than the US. The UK has strong substantive corporate law but almost no formal private enforcement of that law against directors of publicly traded companies. The absence of formal private enforcement highlights the importance of procedural rules, often general rules not limited to corporate cases, for the practical operation of substantive rules. Differences in general rules governing class actions, contingency fees and who pays the winner's legal expenses, in tandem with rules specific to corporate law that govern the availability of derivative actions and direct claims by shareholders, may do much to explain the large differences in levels of private enforcement.

The lack of formal enforcement in the UK – and its robustness in the US despite relatively 'weak' corporate law rules – also highlights the

[122] For an early statement of this preference, see Ronald J. Gilson, 'A Structural Approach to Corporations: The Case Against Defensive Tactics in Tender Offers', 33 STAN. L. REV. 819–891 (1981).

[123] For an application of this approach to emerging markets, see Bernard Black and Reinier Kraakman, 'A Self-Enforcing Model of Corporate Law', 109 HARV. L. REV. 1911–1981 (1996).

potential gap between law in books and law in action, which has been understudied in law-and-finance studies of the underpinnings of strong securities markets. US corporate and securities law is often thought of as being highly protective of outside investors.[124] At least for corporate law, this is not because the substantive law is strong – by international standards it is not. The intensity of formal private enforcement may compensate for the modest substantive protections, producing a 'shareholder-friendly' end result.

It is also possible, as some critics charge, that the US suffers from *too much* private enforcement of corporate (and securities) law and might benefit at the margin from fewer – perhaps many fewer – lawsuits and thus lower litigation costs. We are not ready to go this far for two reasons. First, institutional differences between the two countries have to be taken into account. The situation with takeovers, a common source of lawsuits against directors of US public companies, illustrates the point. In the UK, the work done by the Takeover Panel displaces the corrective role that litigation potentially plays in the M&A context. If the US were to limit private lawsuits without introducing a similar regime, sharp practice might become an unwelcome hallmark of the market for corporate control.

Second, our results show that, with respect to corporate law, the risks directors of US public companies face are not as large as is sometimes assumed. The annual odds that a NYSE or NASDAQ national market company would end up in our dataset of suits which generated reported decisions were about 1.1 per cent. The odds were considerably lower for smaller public companies. Also, more than half of the cases we uncovered were dismissed at a preliminary stage of the proceedings. Our findings also suggest that the risk that directors would pay out of pocket is quite small – we uncovered only three instances with this result over an eight-year period. The upshot is that while directors of publicly traded US companies are much more likely to be sued under corporate law than their British counterparts, lawsuits under corporate law are hardly an everyday occurrence and out-of-pocket liability is scarcely to be feared.

Other important points we simply have to leave open. We cannot say on the basis of our results what degree of formal private enforcement is optimal. Nor do we offer a view on how the optimal rate of formal private enforcement might vary depending on levels of public enforcement and

[124] Mark J. Roe, 'Corporate Law's Limits', 31 J. LEG. STUD. 233 (2002), 257.

informal enforcement. On the contrary, we suggest that one likely cannot answer those questions without a great deal of context on a full range of potential substitutes. Nevertheless, we have provided an empirical departure point for debate on these matters by providing empirical evidence showing how markedly rates of private enforcement differ in the US and the UK, and by showing private enforcement of corporate law in the US is not as robust as is often assumed.

14

Securities Law Enforcement and the Rule of Law

JEFFREY G. MACINTOSH

1 Introduction

Most of the dialogue concerning securities regulation deals with the question of efficacy. That is, how can we make securities regulation more effective? In order to answer this question, we have to answer another, higher order question: more effective at what? It has not always been clear that either securities regulators or scholars have been aiming at the right target (or combination of targets).

In Canada, for example, securities regulation has traditionally been defined in terms of 'investor protection'. But investor protection per se cannot be the right target. A simple analogy will illustrate.

Most people would agree that bank robbery is a bad thing. This might lead us into the mistake of therefore believing that the goal of the regulatory apparatus should be to drive bank robbery to zero, or at least vanishingly close to zero. After all, if it is a bad thing, why not seek to entirely eradicate it?

Pursuing this logic, we might adopt rules requiring all banks to be equipped like Fort Knox (the US gold bullion depository), with multiple levels of customer screening, impregnable physical barriers, and armed guards with Doberman pinschers prowling the grounds. We might initially be very happy when we find that the level of bank robbery has indeed been driven to zero. However, we will soon have second thoughts. The capital requirements for building a bank will be so high that the number of banks is likely to be severally reduced, curtailing competition. In addition, because each bank's costs of operation will be very great, the cost of banking services will also be very great. This will make it much more difficult to effect both commercial and personal transactions, with a very significant cost to the economy. The problem is that the regulatory apparatus inhibits not only the kind of activity that we want to discourage, but also a great deal of activity that we want to encourage (or at least, nor discourage).

What we should have been doing is estimating the cost of bank robbery and the cost of various forms of regulatory interventions, and trading off the benefit from each of these forms of intervention (in terms of reduced bank robbery) against the cost of each intervention. Doing so will eventually drive us to an equilibrium where marginal cost and marginal benefit match. While it might sound odd, this, in a sense, gives us an optimal amount of bank robbery.

Regulation of securities markets is not conceptually different. Upon deciding that securities fraud is a bad thing, we might construct our securities regulatory apparatus much as we constructed our banking regulation in the above example; i.e. with the goal of eliminating fraud entirely. But we would run into exactly the same problem; the cost would exceed the benefit. While we would dramatically decrease the incidence of fraud, we would also dramatically decrease the incidence of primary market financings, secondary market trading, corporate reorganisations, etc. The end result would be to increase the corporate cost of capital, making both issuers and investors worse off. Just as there is an optimal amount of bank robbery, there is an optimal amount of securities fraud.

Thus, all regulation must answer to the cost/benefit calculus; that is, does the marginal benefit of a particular regulatory constraint exceed the marginal cost? This constraint is often described in terms of Kaldor-Hicks efficiency and/or allocative efficiency. Kaldor-Hicks efficiency is achieved when a particular regulatory measure generates more wealth than it consumes. Allocative efficiency is achieved when the funds of net savers of capital find their way to those net users of capital that offer the most deserving investment projects, as measured by their net present value (which digests both risk and expected return).

The goal of 'investor protection', *simpliciter*, is thus misconceived. Defining the regulatory objective in terms of Kaldor-Hicks and/or allocative efficiency is a big improvement. However, these definitions still fall short in a critical respect. There are values other than strict wealth maximisation at play in a democratic polity. In particular, I wish to focus on a bedrock principle underlying the legal system in a democratic state – the rule of law (ROL) – and indicate how the conventional economic paradigm may fall short by failing to acknowledge the value of liberty and freedom from arbitrary government action.[1] Indeed, I will

[1] The relationship between securities regulation and the rule of law has provoked relatively little debate in the literature. Notable exceptions include Nicholas C. Howson, 'China's Judicial System and Judicial Reform', LAW QUAD. NOTES 54, no. 1 (2011), 62–64;

also suggest that aside from the independent value of the ROL as a freedom and autonomy-fostering device, it has instrumental value in helping to achieve wealth maximisation.[2] It does so by fostering that high degree of legal certainty that is necessary to facilitate business planning and execution. It also minimises the risk of arbitrary and punitive state action arising out of innovative business undertakings, thus enhancing incentives to innovate and experiment with different business models. It also reduces the likelihood of corruption, which functions as a tax on business.

The ROL cannot be said to be one thing; there are many different views of the content of the rule. Scholars often distinguish between a 'formalist' and a 'substantive' view of the ROL. The formalist view stresses various procedural attributes of the law.[3] It must be publicly declared, prospective in nature, and sufficiently certain to serve as a useful guide for behaviour. It must possess the property of generality (i.e. it must apply equally to everyone). It must be supported by legal institutions that ensure that these attributes are not merely theoretical, but operational. The law must be created by legally authorised persons in a legally authorised manner. Of particular importance to my discussion, the formalist view does not admit a high degree of discretionary authority to be reposed in governmental officials.

The substantive view of the ROL accepts all of the premises of the formalist view, but also insists that the law incorporate individual rights.[4] Dworkin, for example, posits a 'rights' conception of the ROL, which 'insists that . . . moral and political rights be recognised in positive law, so that they may be enforced *upon the demand of individual citizens* through courts or other judicial institutions of the familiar types, so far as this is practicable.'[5] Because of the difficulties of conceptualising and operationalising any substantive view of the ROL in the context of securities regulation, I focus here on the formal view.

Nicholas C. Howson, 'Enforcement Without Foundation? Insider Trading and China's Administrative Law Crisis.' AM. J. COMP. L. 60, no. 4 (2012), 955–1002.

[2] In this respect, the ROL is important not merely in a democratic state, but in any state seeking to have effective financial markets.

[3] See e.g. Joseph Raz, 'The Rule of Law and its Virtue', 93 *Law Quarterly Review* 195 (1977); Joseph Raz, *The Authority of Law: Essays on Law and Morality* (Oxford University Press, 1979).

[4] Brian Z. Tamanaha, *On the Rule of Law: History, Politics, Theory* (Cambridge University Press, 2004).

[5] Ronald Dworkin, 'Political Judges and the Rule of Law', 64 *Proceedings of the British Academy* 259 (1978), 262.

A.V. Dicey's classic formulation of the rule of law is a pithy expression of the formalist view. Dicey states:

> We mean, in the first place, that no man is punishable or can be lawfully made to suffer in body or goods except for a distinct breach of law established in the ordinary legal manner before the ordinary Courts of the land. In this sense the rule of law is contrasted with every system of government based on the exercise by persons in authority of wide, arbitrary, or discretionary powers of constraint.[6]

We may parse the above statement into a number of distinct parts. One is that legal consequences should attach only to 'a distinct breach of law'. This embodies the idea that the law should be both available (i.e. published publicly) and sufficiently clear to offer a reliable guide to citizen behaviour. It should not violate justifiable and reasonable expectations about what is permissible and what is not.

Another element is that the adjudication of whether there has been a breach of law should be 'established in the ordinary legal manner'. Thus, the rules of evidence and procedure should be well known, standardised, and as firmly set in place as the substantive law itself. Substantive law without a reliable mechanism for ensuring its even-handed application is an empty vessel. Substantive law and procedures work hand-in-glove to ensure the impartial, consistent, and equal application of the law to all citizens.

In addition, as expressed in the above quotation, Dicey suggests that the determination that there has been a breach of law must be effected 'before the ordinary Courts of the land'. This adds a lustre to what comes immediately before. We must not have merely a well-known and standardised set of legal procedures, but a set of procedures that look something like that available in a court of law.[7]

Lastly, the second sentence of Dicey's classic formulation stresses the freedom from arbitrary state action. Indeed, he draws a connection

[6] A.V. Dicey, *Lectures Introductory to the Study of the Law of the Constitution*, 'Lecture V: The Rule of Law; Its Nature', from a facsimile of the 1886 Second Edition published by MacMillan & Co., as produced in 1999 by The Legal Classics Library, Division of Gryphon Editions, New York, 174. This is the first of Dicey's three propositions that, together, express his view regarding the rule of law. The second is that 'no man is above the law [and] every man, whatever his rank or condition, is subject to the ordinary law of the realm and amenable to the ordinary jurisdiction of the tribunals'. The third is that the source of personal rights and freedoms is not the constitution, but decisions of the courts. My focus is on Dicey's first proposition.

[7] This construction is not inevitable. Some have interpreted this part of Dicey's edict as merely requiring access to the courts.

between discretion and arbitrariness, stating that 'wherever there is discretion there is room for arbitrariness.'[8]

Other important elements of the formalistic approach, as Raz stresses, are that decisions ought to be 'principled', which means being 'both reasoned and public', and that the legislature, and not the courts, be the primary (although not the exclusive) source of law.[9]

As noted, Dicey's formulation of the ROL embraces the adoption of both substantive and procedural law. In respect of the latter, his view might be interpreted, in modern parlance, as the goal of avoiding type 1 and type 2 errors: that is, 'false positives' and 'false negatives'. This must be done by conditioning the imposition of substantive penalties or liabilities on procedural protections that are themselves well known, prospective, stable, and sufficiently exact to allow the defendant (and plaintiff, in a civil action) an adequate opportunity to advance their view of the law, the facts, and the interaction between the law and the facts in the case at bar.

In this respect, however, as noted in Table 14.1, there are differences between criminal, civil, and administrative actions. Since a primary *desideratum* of criminal law is to avoid convicting the innocent, this places a premium on avoiding type 1 errors (i.e. false positives, or a judgment of guilt where there is none). The desire to avoid type 1 errors is manifest in the high standard of proof required for a conviction – the 'beyond a reasonable doubt' standard. It is also manifest in the exacting rules of procedure and evidence that inhere in a criminal prosecution. While type 2 errors (false negatives, or finding a guilty person innocent) are obviously not unimportant, they nonetheless receive a lower weighting than type 1 errors.

By contrast, in civil litigation we are anxious to preserve a level playing field between plaintiffs and defendants. Hence, neither type 1 nor type 2 errors take precedence; they are equally weighted. This offers perhaps the most compelling explanation for the standard of proof in civil litigation – the 'balance of probabilities' standard – which, in effect, puts equal weighting on type 1 and type 2 errors. In some situations the equal weighting needs to be tweaked to keep the playing field level. We do this by putting the onus of proof on one party or the other. Thus, for example, where much of the relevant evidence is in the hands of one party, we put the onus of proof on that party. If he or she fails to adduce

[8] Dicey, 'Lecture V: The Rule of Law, 175.
[9] Joseph Raz, 'The Politics of the Rule of Law', 3 *Ratio Juris* 331 (1990).

Table 14.1 *Procedural protections*

	Burden of Proof	Onus of Proof	Rules of Evidence	Rules of Procedure	Precedent Binding?	Appeal Rights
Criminal Law	Beyond a reasonable doubt	Prosecutor	Refined	Refined	Yes	Yes: correctness standard
Civil Law	Balance of Probabilities	Plaintiff	Refined	Refined	Yes	Yes: correctness standard
Administrative Law	Balance of Probabilities	Staff	At will	At will	No	Yes: reasonableness standard

any evidence, then even where the other party produces little evidence of its own, that other party wins. The imposition of the onus on the first party thus creates an incentive to adduce relevant evidence.

In the administrative context, the ostensible standard of proof is the same as that in the civil context – a balance of probabilities. However, in this context, the end in view shifts away from punishment or compensation and more toward societal protection. For this reason, the tolerance for type 1 errors is somewhat elevated, while the tolerance for type 2 errors is somewhat suppressed. That is, in allowing regulators to effectively carry out their protective function, we are more tolerant of finding an innocent person guilty than a guilty person innocent. The greater tolerance for type 1 errors is apparent in the relaxed rules of procedure and evidence that predominate in the administrative context.

In Canada, for example, securities regulators decide what evidence they will admit, who has standing to make representations, and (subject to broad 'fairness' constraints) what rules of procedure they will employ. In addition, they are not bound by the doctrine of precedent. Although Canadian securities regulators do, in the main, seek to abide by past decisions (both in relation to substantive and procedural matters), this is not uniformly the case.

The effect of these relaxed rules of procedure and evidence is that those who are accused of regulatory infractions have a greatly truncated set of tools at their disposal to vindicate their conduct, and a correspondingly greater likelihood of being found guilty when innocent.

All of this has important application for the administrative state in general, and securities regulation in particular. The enormous growth in both the range and depth of governmental intrusion in all aspects of life over the past three-quarters of a century necessarily requires a commensurately expanded role for administrative organs and tribunals. Administrative tribunals in the modern state have been given authority by legislatures not only to apply the law as written by the legislature, but to make law of their own via the authority to promulgate rules. They have also been given the authority, via administrative tribunals, to decide when there has been a breach of law and to determine the sanction. It is, indeed, only by vastly expanding the administrative machinery of the state that the manifold and ever-expanding functions of the state can be properly accommodated.

This, however, puts ever-increasing pressure on the ROL. A fundamental aspect of the ROL is ensuring the accountability of those who administer the law. It is more difficult, however, to hold administrative tribunals accountable for their actions than legislators. While legislators may be voted out of office, administrators cannot be. And while senior administrators are typically appointed by their political masters, the performance of any given administrative tribunal under a particular minister's watch is not likely to be a critical election issue. Indeed, many administrative organs, such as Canadian governmental agencies that are set up as Crown corporations, function more or less independently of the Ministries that they are in theory accountable to. Added to this, politicians can disavow responsibility for the actions of administrative agents by taking shelter under the umbrella of the agency's independent operation. They can also deflect public criticism by kow-towing to the specialised expertise of the agency, and proclaiming the impropriety of political interference.

The burden of my argument in the next section is that of all administrative undertakings, securities regulation presents the greatest challenges in fostering and protecting the operation of the ROL.

2 The Securities Regulators' Challenge: Complexity, High-Powered Incentives, and Information Asymmetry

Securities regulatory agencies confront a much more difficult regulatory challenge than virtually any other kind of administrative agency. This is due to a number of factors that distinguish financial markets from other regulated activities. Some of the more important follow.

2.1 The High-Powered Incentives of Private Market Actors to Find Novel Financial Technologies for Generating Profit

In any case in which a great deal of money is at stake, private actors have high-powered incentives to capture a slice of the pie. There is no pie that is quite so large as what might loosely be styled the financial markets, including primary and secondary market trading and mergers and acquisitions.

Table 14.2 indicates that in 2014 alone, US businesses raised $2.2 trillion of debt and equity,[10] although this lagged far behind the banner year, 2006, in which $3.4 trillion was raised.[11]

Also in 2014, $1.5 trillion of mergers and acquisitions were announced, with completed M&A deals totalling $1.2 trillion.[12] The total capitalisation of the NYSE and NASDAQ stock exchanges

[10] SIMFA Fact Book 2015, www.sifma.org/factbook/, 5, 9. [11] Ibid., at 9. [12] Ibid., at 9.

Table 14.2 *Primary market activity in the US in 2014*

TYPE OF SECURITY	$ ISSUED IN 2014
Publicly Issued Equity (Preferred and Common Shares)	$315.4 billion
Publicly Issued Corporate Debt, Asset-Backed Securities (ABS) and Non-Agency Mortgage-Backed Securities (MBS)	$1.8 trillion
Private Placements	$136.6 billion
IPOs	$94.2 billion
Total of All Publicly Issued Debt and Equity	$2.1 trillion
Total of All Issued Debt and Equity (Public and Private)	$2.2 trillion

Source: The Securities Industry and Financial Markets Association (SIFMA), *SIMFA Fact Book 2015*, www.sifma.org/factbook/

was about $28 trillion[13], with secondary market trading at the NYSE and NASDAQ exchanges also running to $28 trillion.[14]

There is no other industry in the United States (or anywhere in the world) that puts as much money in play as the financial markets. It follows that there is no industry that generates such high-powered incentives to find new means of making profits.

2.2 *The High-Powered Incentives of Private Market Actors to Find Ways to Circumvent the Rules (both Licitly and Illicitly)*

Private market actors can profit from financial activity by a wide range of means, some licit and some illicit. In like fashion, attempts to circumvent the rules of the game in order to generate profit carve a wide berth, ranging from out-and-out fraud (such as Bernie Madoff's infamous Ponzi scheme) to activity that is opportunistic and systemically inefficient (such as the expenditure of hundreds of millions of dollars to build private data lines from Chicago to New York in order to communicate stock-price information a few milliseconds faster than the public trunk lines[15]).

[13] Ibid., at 41. [14] Ibid., at 44, 45.

[15] In 2010 Spread Networks spent $300 million to construct a private fibre optic cable running from Chicago to New York in order to shave a mere 2.8 milliseconds off round-trip message latency; Jerry Adler, 'Raging Bulls: How Wall Street Got Addicted to Light-Speed Trading', *Wired*, 3 August 2012, www.wired.com/2012/08/ff_wallstreet_trading/all/. That 2.8 milliseconds was enough to give Spread's high frequency trading customers the ability to outrace other traders' orders to market.

Licit activity that increases overall efficiency, and hence overall wealth, is scarcely a problem. But formally licit activity that seeks to generate private rents that are, in the aggregate, wealth-reducing, is very much a problem. Needless to say, so is illicit activity that seeks to skirt the rules in pursuit of private advantage.

The amount of money at stake creates powerful incentives for an army of Jasons to seek their Golden Fleece by finding creative ways to skirt the rules that govern their behaviour. Moreover, these well-incentivised private actors are well educated, sophisticated in their understanding of the complexities of financial markets, and endlessly resourceful in finding ways to circumnavigate existing rules, both licitly and illicitly.

2.3 *Information Asymmetry*

Information asymmetry is an important determinant of accountability. For politicians, press, and the public to meaningfully evaluate the performance of an administrative agency, there must be some level of understanding of the nature of the activity that is being regulated. Without this, there can be little understanding of whether the agency is regulating in an appropriate manner. Where the subject matter of the agency's concern is both complex and rapidly evolving, information asymmetry rises dramatically. Such is the case with respect to the financial markets.

The complexity of a regulated subject matter can be broken down into static and dynamic complexity. Static complexity refers to the degree of complexity that arises at a particular moment in time, much as a corporate balance sheet is a 'snapshot' of the corporation's financial results on a particular date. Dynamic complexity refers to the manner in which the regulated subject matter evolves and changes over time.

Financial markets are characterised by a high degree of both static and dynamic complexity. Even a relatively straightforward trust indenture, for example, is characterised by a high degree of static complexity. Such documents are often on the order of 100 pages. They are full of arcane language that the average person – and indeed the average lawyer – would find completely mystifying. Untangling the complexities of trust indentures, shareholder agreements, asset securitisations, mortgage backed securities, credit default swaps, merger agreements, prospectus financings, private placements, merger agreements, and so on is a highly specialised job requiring a very high degree of expertise.

This complexity is greatly augmented by dynamic complexity. There is probably no sphere of regulated activity in which the subject matter of the regulation changes with the rapidity of financial markets. New products and new financial engineering techniques appear regularly. The market for asset-backed securities (ABS), for example, did not exist before the 1970s. Between 1996 and 2009, the US ABS market grew from $450 billion to $2.23 trillion.[16] Equally importantly, the techniques for effecting ABS transactions rapidly evolved.[17]

Similarly, the market for credit default swaps (CDS) had its genesis only in the early 1990s. From a $300 billion market in 1998[18], the US market for CDS had grown to a whopping $62 trillion by 2007.[19] As in the case of ABS, financial technologies for effecting CDS also substantially morphed over time.

Globalisation has added to the rapidity with which changes occur. Globalisation substantially broadens the size of the profit pie available to private actors in different national jurisdictions. It also serves as a conduit to disseminate financial innovations with celerity.

2.4 The Complexity of the Regulatory Problem: A Riddle, Wrapped in a Mystery, Inside an Enigma[20]

It is not only securities markets that are highly complex. So is the problem of how to regulate securities markets.

As noted above, there are a variety of adjudicative tools available, including civil, criminal, and administrative law (or some combination of the three). But in addition, regulation of securities markets can serve either (or both) of two goals: compensation for those harmed by improper activity, and the creation of incentives for market actors to act according to some objectively determined standard. The compensation objective is inextricably linked to the incentive objective, insofar as the

16 Sumit Agarwal, Jacqueline Barrett, Crystal Cun, and Mariacristina De Nardi, 'The Asset-Backed Securities Markets, the Crisis, and TALF', *Economic Perspectives*, Vol. 34, No. 4, 101(2010), 106 (Federal Reserve Bank of Chicago).

17 Ibid.

18 Gillian Tett, *Fool's Gold: How Unrestrained Greed Corrupted a Dream, Shattered Global Markets and Unleashed a Catastrophe* (Little Brown, 2009).

19 The market was approximately cut in half, however, as a result of the 2008 credit crisis. See 'Chart; ISDA Market Survey; Notional Amounts Outstanding at Year-End, All Surveyed Contracts, 1987–Present', www.isda.org/statistics/pdf/ISDA-Market-Survey-annual-data.pdf.

20 With apologies to Winston Churchill.

prospect of paying civil damages inevitably impacts on the incentives of market actors. The incentive objective, however, may stand alone. Criminal fines and terms of imprisonment, for example, may create appropriate incentives for market actors to behave themselves, but leave the compensation objective untouched (although this is not inevitable; in Canada, criminal courts are empowered to order that a wrongdoer make restitution to his or her victim). In a similar manner, administrative sanctions may alter incentives while leaving victims uncompensated.

The difference between servicing the compensation objective and the incentive objective is not trivial. Regulation that addresses the incentive objective but which nonetheless leaves victims uncompensated will raise the corporate cost of capital and lower the willingness of people to deal in financial markets.

The regulation problem thus confronts two threshold questions. First, what balance of civil, criminal, and administrative sanctions will be used to achieve the regulatory goal? Second, what relative weight is to be put on the compensation and incentive objectives? The latter problem is made all the more difficult insofar as civil, criminal, and administrative sanctions can function either as complements or substitutes. And, needless to say, particularly as there is a very high number of different types of civil, criminal, and administrative interventions, there is an even higher number of permutations and combinations of civil, criminal, and administrative sanctions that may be employed.

In any legacy legal system (i.e. one that already has some combination of civil, criminal, and administrative sanctions in place), the marginal cost of any given regulatory change will be subject to path dependency. That is, the existing combination of regulatory devices will impact on the marginal cost and benefit of any new intervention (or liberalisation). If, for example, the existing rules impose mandatory capital punishment on one who fraudulently, recklessly, or negligently injures investors, an additional regulatory intervention that imposes mandatory disclosure requirements will probably have relatively little marginal impact on behaviour. On the other hand, if the starting point is no regulation at all, then adding mandatory disclosure rules may result in substantial net benefit.

Securities regulation might be likened to a very complicated analogue computer with a nearly infinite number of mechanical permutations and combinations to achieve its desired output. The addition of a lever here, a larger or smaller set of gears there, will affect how each and every other part of the machine works, and the contribution of each part (and each new part) to the desired result.

Like the analogue computer, securities regulation can work with a variety of different levers and gears. These include civil damages, criminal law fines and/or imprisonment, and administrative sanctions. Each of these in turn has its own internal combination of levers and gears. Civil liability, for example, may be achieved through individual actions, class actions, actions brought by regulators on behalf of investors (whether individually or as a class), or some combination. Each of these forms of action may impose heavy or light procedural and evidentiary barriers. There may or may not be mechanisms for the sharing of costs, indemnification for costs, or for costs to be paid out of a public fund. In respect of each form of action, the mechanism for calculating damages will be critical, and whether there is a possibility of being awarded some multiple of the provable damages (such as triple damages).

Thus, even within the three silos noted above, there are a very high number of permutations and combinations of the various constituent legal elements. Each element will have an impact on the incentive structure of potential plaintiffs to bring an action, and the efficacy of each form of action in addressing the regulatory goals sought to be achieved.

To borrow Winston Churchill's much-quoted statement, what works best 'is a riddle, wrapped in a mystery, inside an enigma'.

2.5 Complexity, Information Asymmetry, and the Role of the Expert Regulator

The complexity and dynamism of financial markets and the high-powered incentives of private actors to circumvent the rules all put a premium on regulatory expertise. If regulation is to be effective, the regulators must possess a high degree of domain-specific human capital. In addition, if markets and financial technologies change quickly, securities regulators must not only be able to learn and to adapt quickly, but they also must be able to change regulatory requirements quickly. Thus, securities market complexity and dynamism put a high degree of stress on the ROL. Efficacious regulation would seem to require that regulators be able to move as nimbly and decisively as financial markets themselves. This in turn suggests not only a broad ability to craft rules without returning to the legislature, but a broad discretionary authority to deal with cases that fall in the interstices of the regulatory edifice.

3 Accountability Barriers

In a system in which we wish the ROL to play a significant role, we must make sure that those people who make and administer securities laws are held accountable for their actions. The very complexity and dynamism of financial markets just explored, however, presents particular challenges in achieving this accountability.

3.1 Politicians

In the normal course of events, politicians take little interest in securities regulation. This is a function of the information asymmetry noted above; few politicians have more than a passing acquaintance with how financial markets work or how they are regulated. Perhaps more importantly, neither do their constituents. Aside from periodic scandals that excite public interest and put the regulation of financial markets in the spotlight, securities regulation is of little interest to the average voter. For this reason, little effective oversight can be expected from politicians.

3.2 Bureaucrats

Government bureaucrats are also stymied by complexity and information asymmetry. In Canada, while securities regulators are nominally accountable to a government Ministry, Ministry bureaucrats typically have little knowledge of securities markets or securities regulation, and supply little useful monitoring or discipline.

3.3 The Courts

Judges are typically no more expert in complex securities regulatory matters than government bureaucrats. While they have training in the law, relatively few have training in business matters, let alone a sophisticated understanding of financial markets.

For this reason, judges are often highly deferential to the decisions of expert regulators, and reluctant to interfere. In Canada, for example, the Supreme Court of Canada has indicated that the courts should accord an administrative tribunal acting within its expertise (such as securities regulators) a high level of deference.[21] Thus, appeals from regulatory decisions are rarely overturned, and little effective oversight occurs.

[21] *Dunsmuir* v. *New Brunswick (Board of Management)*, [2008] 1 S.C.R. 190; *Pezim v British Columbia (Superintendent of Brokers)*, [1994] 2 S.C.R. 557, 114 D.L.R. (4th) 385.

3.4 Private Market Actors and Securities Lawyers

In Canada, private market actors rarely challenge regulatory decisions. Insisting on a hearing before the Commission can be very costly, not merely (or even primarily) because of the direct cost of hiring lawyers, but because of the opportunity cost that an appeal occasions. It can take months for a final decision to be rendered, in which time a market window of opportunity may have closed. If a court appeal from an unfavourable decision is contemplated, the aggregate time to a decision could easily run into a period of years. It is almost always less costly to bend to the regulator's demands even when the regulators overreach their jurisdiction, incorrectly interpret the law, or arbitrarily impose unneeded and costly conditions for proceeding with a transaction. The private market actor's primary concern is to get on with business.[22]

Both private market actors and securities lawyers who engage with regulators on a regular basis also worry that challenging a regulatory edict will jeopardise their reputational capital with the regulators, making it harder to shepherd future deals through the regulatory process.

[22] In Canada, the case of *Re Donnini* (2004), 250 D.L.R. (4th) 195, 76 O.R. (3d) (O.C.A), reversing in part *Donnini, Re* (2003), 37 B.L.R. (3d) 46, (sub nom. *Donnini* v. *Ontario Securities Commission)* 177 O.A.C. 59, 2003 CarswellOnt 3445 (Ont. Div. Ct.); affirming *Donnini, Re* (2002), 2002 CarswellOnt 2314, 25 O.S.C.B. 4697 (Ont. Securities Comm.); additional reasons at *Donnini, Re* (2002), 2002 CarswellOnt 2996, 25 O.S.C.B. 6225 (Ont. Securities Comm.); and varying *Donnini, Re* (2002), 2002 CarswellOnt 2996, 25 O.S.C.B. 6225 (Ont. Securities Comm.) has had a powerful effect on the willingness of market actors and their lawyers to challenge the view taken by Commission staff on a particular issue, or to refuse a staff offer to settle allegations of wrongdoing, even if on unfavourable terms and not supported by pertinent law. Donnini was a trader at an investment banking firm, and Patterson was the president. In connection with the same transaction, both were accused by staff of the Ontario Securities Commission of engaging in insider trading and offered settlements that involved a two-year ban from participating in a professional capacity in securities markets. Patterson elected to accept the settlement, while Donnini elected to go to an administrative hearing to challenge staff's allegations. At the hearing, staff argued for a twenty-five-year ban from securities markets, and the Commission (i.e. the Commissioners acting *qua* administrative tribunal) imposed a fifteen-year ban, which was subsequently upheld by the Ontario Court of Appeal.

Donnini has been interpreted by the financial and legal communities as a statement that failure to accede to a settlement on terms dictated by regulatory staff will result in the aggressive pursuit of a much more severe sanction before the Commission. For this reason, staff settlement terms are almost always accepted regardless of whether the allegations are seen to be justified or not.

3.5 An Unsympathetic Proletariat

In the public eye, well-heeled market actors are an 'unsympathetic proletariat'.[23] In addition to being viewed as 'haves' (as opposed to 'have-nots'), there is in many quarters an abiding suspicion that the mavens of our financial markets are up to no good, that they are parasitical on real economic activity, create no value, and serve mainly to redistribute wealth from honest, hardworking (and much poorer) people to themselves. The vanguard of the financial and corporate worlds are also seen as having privileged access to politicians, and hence an ability to tether the legislative and regulatory processes to their own agendas.

Movies like *Wall Street, Margin Call*, and *The Wolf of Wall Street* do little to dispel these popular perceptions, which have only gotten more acute with the bursting of the dot-com bubble in 2000 and the Global Financial Crisis of 2008. While the popular view is probably wrong more often than it is right, it is not devoid of factual foundation, such as the highly questionable role played by US investment banks in bringing on the Global Financial Crisis of 2008 (by aggressively packaging and distributing to investors mortgage-backed securities and collateralised debt obligations that they knew were of much poorer quality than represented).

That financial market actors are an unsympathetic proletariat is important, for when the government infringes on the liberty of financial and corporate actors, they are not likely to find a sympathetic ear among politicians, the press, or the public at large. This may allow securities regulators greater freedom to engage in practices that violate the rule of law.

In so saying, I do not mean to discount public choice theory. Market actors are well funded, well organised, and have much at stake in regulatory debates. In short, they fit public choice theory's description of a constituency that should be able to get what it wants in legislative and regulatory debates. There is no question that this happens. In Canada, the large investment banks have been able to secure a host of favourable regulatory outcomes over a period of many decades. These include the perpetuation of fixed brokerage commission rates (abolished only in 1983), denial of entry by Instinet to the Canadian market, and most

[23] I borrow the phrase from the American journalist and television commentator George Will, who used the phrase to explain lack of public support for a strike by professional baseball players.

recently, a remarkable decision by the Ontario Securities Commission allowing stock exchanges to treat high frequency traders less favourably than other traders, with a view to regaining lost market share (although of course dressed up as being a measure in the public interest).

The extent to which public choice theory trumps the unsympathetic popular persona of market actors depends, at any given moment, on the array of political forces at work. When major scandals or economic breakdowns occur, such as the bursting of the dot-com bubble, the corporate meltdowns of the early 2000s (such as Enron and WorldCom), and the Global Financial Crisis, populist support for intrusive regulation is likely to trump public choice theory. In other, calmer times, the predictions of public choice theory are more likely to come out on top.

4 Asymmetrical Payoff Distributions

Regulators and politicians have a built-in incentive to overregulate. This is because they face an asymmetrical payoff structure. When scandals occur, both almost inevitably get blamed. However, when things are going well, they receive few plaudits. The source of this asymmetrical payoff distribution is the comparative invisibility of opportunity costs. The direct costs of scandals and other market pathologies are readily observed, but the opportunity cost of overregulation is apparent to few other than those business people directly affected.

Unfortunately, regulation that satisfies the cost/benefit calculus will lead to a higher level of non-compliance and scandals than regulation that over-deters by imposing non-cost-effective regulatory requirements. Thus, the asymmetrical payoff distribution leads regulators (and politicians) to overregulate.

5 The Regulatory Ratchet

Regulatory information asymmetry creates another problem; the ratcheting up of regulatory requirements (often to excessive levels) in response to the random arrival of financial market scandals. I call this the 'ratchet theory' of securities regulation.

Many enhancements of regulatory requirements have been the result of market scandals. Various scandals in the early 1960s, for example, resulted in the Government of Ontario commissioning a major study of securities law that led to major enhancements to the Ontario Securities

Act.[24] More recently, the various corporate scandals of the early 2000s (such as Enron and WorldCom) resulted in the passage of the Sarbanes-Oxley legislation in the United States and a watered-down version of the same in Canada.[25]

In Canada, the 2008 Global Financial Crisis prompted the most radical initiative yet to boost the powers of securities regulators. At present, securities regulation is provincially based.[26] Ostensibly to deal with issues of systemic risk that went unaddressed during the credit crisis, and to simplify the regulatory structure, the federal government began an initiative to create a federal securities regulator.[27] Draft legislation was published in 2010; however, a constitutional challenge by a number of provinces resulted in a decision by the Supreme Court of Canada that the federal government does not have the constitutional power to enact a comprehensive scheme of securities regulation.[28] The Court, however, suggested that the federal government has the power to enact securities laws designed to address nationwide systemic risks, and to collect securities market information on a national basis.

Following this decision, the federal government and Ontario spearheaded an effort to create a cooperative securities regulator jointly run by the provinces and the federal government, called the Cooperative Capital Markets Regulatory System, to which five provinces (out of ten) have signed on.[29] Under the CCMRA, the federal government will adopt legislation known as the 'Capital Markets Stability Act', addressing matters within the federal government's constitutional jurisdiction, and delegate their authority to administer this statute to the Capital Markets Regulatory Authority (CMRA). The participating provincial governments will adopt a uniform statute known as the Capital Markets Act (CMA) that will address matters falling within provincial jurisdiction. Each province will delegate its powers to administer this legislation to the CMRA.

[24] *Report of the Attorney General's Committee on Securities Legislation in Ontario* (Queen's Printer, 1965) (the 'Kimber Report'),

[25] See e.g. Tara Gray, 'Canadian Response To the US Sarbanes-Oxley Act of 2002: New Directions For Corporate Governance', Document PRB 05–37E, Library of Parliament (Canada).

[26] There are ten provincial regulators plus three territorial regulators.

[27] See generally Anita Anand, ed., *What's Next for Canada? Securities Regulation After the Reference* (Irwin Law, 2012).

[28] *Reference re Securities Act*, 2011 SCC 66.

[29] See http://ccmr-ocrmc.ca.

What is striking about the CCMRA proposal is the massive augmentation of regulatory powers that will result.[30] The participating governments have opted for a 'platform' approach to securities legislation. This involves stripping the legislation down to little more than a statutory warrant for the participating governments to manufacture the rules of the game via their administrative rule-making powers. While the current Ontario Securities Act provisions relating to takeover bids, for example, run to 12,000 words, the proposed replacement in the CMA is but 700 words. The continuous disclosure obligations shrink from 3,300 words to a mere 300 words. Virtually everything of substance will be found in the rules.

While various categories of regulated entities are defined in the legislation, the regulators will have discretionary powers to place entire classes of entities, or individual market actors, into one regulatory silo or other – with no power of appeal on the part of those who are affected by these decisions.

Other discretionary powers have been vastly expanded. The federal regulator, for example, will have the power to hand out large fines ($1 million in the case of individual and $15 million in the case of business entities) without holding a hearing or even giving the affected party advance notice. In 'emergency' situations, the regulators will have the power to adopt new rules with no advance notice or opportunity to provide comment. More generally, regulators will have the power, via the decision of an administrative official, to essentially make rules on the fly, with none of the procedural protections that exist when formal rules are adopted.

These and other ambitious changes bear no relation whatever to the ostensible aim of addressing systemic risk by ceding power to a single regulator with a national, rather than merely a provincial perspective on securities markets. They are a remarkable example of the ratchet theory of regulation – and a further remarkable example of how information asymmetry plays a major role in driving the ratchet. Market scandals or meltdowns are not inevitably symptomatic of deficiencies in the regulatory structure; they may simply be examples of determinedly fraudulent behaviour by clever rogues. The public and politicians, however, understanding little about financial markets or how they are regulated, inevitably perceive the problem as indicative of systemic failure, and clamour for reform. In the charged atmosphere that follows, the substantive character of the reform assumes a secondary importance; what matters is that substantial changes appear to have been made.

[30] See generally Jeffrey G. MacIntosh, 'The Grand Market Regulator: Be Afraid, Very Afraid' (2014/15) 11 Exempt Edge 40.

Unfortunately, the ratchet only works in one direction – toward more regulation. Hence, successive scandals and successive turns of the ratchet inevitably breed more intrusive and costly regulation, and regulation that is too frequently untethered to any kind of rational cost/benefit calculus.

6 Accountability, the Rule of Law, and Securities Regulation

As I have noted, securities regulation presents a particularly pressing problem for the ROL. The static and dynamic complexity of financial markets requires a matching degree of complexity at the regulatory level. This complexity manifests itself in a number of different ways. For one thing, the rules of the road will inevitably themselves be complex.[31] Second, those who construct the rules must have a high degree of domain-specific human capital; to regulate financial market complexity requires an understanding of this complexity. Third, regulators must be able to move nimbly in order to respond to fast-paced changes in financial markets.

A number of implications flow from the above. Perhaps the most important is that securities regulation cannot be left in the hands of legislators, who are unqualified to make the rules of the road. In addition, legislative assemblies act far too slowly to deal with lightning-fast changes in financial markets in any meaningful manner. Rather, the bulk of the regulatory edifice must reside in administrative rules promulgated by expert regulators.

This, unfortunately, is bad news for the ROL. In particular, a high level of administrative discretion, particularly if it is unreviewable and relatively unconstrained by procedural protections (such as in the CCMRA proposal):

a) is inconsistent with the requirement that the laws be publicly declared, prospective in nature, and sufficiently certain to serve as a useful guide for behaviour;
b) exposes market actors to the risk of being penalised for something other than 'a distinct breach of law';

[31] There is a lively debate about whether securities regulation should be grounded in 'rules' or 'principles' (i.e. a highly detailed rule structure versus one with few details but broad administrative discretion). Whatever view one takes in this debate, in complex markets, the creation of a modicum of business certainty requires significant complexity in the rules. In my view, the 'rules' versus 'principles' debate is important mostly at the margin, that is, whether complicated rules should stand alone, or be supplemented with broad administrative discretion.

c) violates Dicey's injunction that the 'distinct breach of law' be 'established in the ordinary legal manner' – i.e. pursuant to a comprehensive and well-defined set of procedural protections;
d) poses grave risk to the property of generality; and
e) threatens the foundational principle that the law be created by legally authorised persons in a legally authorised manner, since there is, in effect, no 'legally authorised manner' outside of the bald discretion of administrative officials.

Another casualty is financial market innovation. The value of a business is typically determined by discounting future cash flows using a discount rate reflecting the risk of these cash flows. In exactly the same way, the returns to innovation are dependent on a discount rate that reflects the risk of regulatory rejection (or delay). Uncertainty in regulatory outcome raises the discount rate and lowers the returns to innovation.[32]

The cost of these ROL failures is twofold. As an independent value, the ROL is an important aspect of individual freedom and autonomy in a democratic state. As an instrumental value, it is vital in achieving allocative efficiency since the planning of business endeavours requires certainty, predictability, and freedom from arbitrary state action.

In addition, a high level of administrative discretion inevitably cedes regulators more room to indulge their asymmetrical payoff distributions. This adds to the risk of ratchet regulation, in which the overall regulatory burden increases over time in a manner that is fundamentally detached from any cost/benefit calculus.

7 Is There a Solution?

A solution to the above problems seeks to balance the need for complex and nimble rule-making with the demands of the ROL. This solution is not straightforward. It must necessarily accept the premise that compromise is inevitable; there will be some prejudice to the ROL just as there will be some prejudice to the efficacy of the regulatory apparatus. My preliminary thoughts are as follows:

[32] Just like complexity, certainty has both static and dynamic dimensions. The certainty that is necessary to create a healthy environment for business to operate in pertains not only to what is, but to what might be. By definition, innovation, whether in product or financial markets, pushes past the boundaries of existing technologies. There must be some assurance that novel means of doing things will not be swallowed up in a quagmire of unreviewable administrative discretion, but will be given a fair chance to take root and flourish.

7.1 *Expert Courts*

As noted above, at present, little effective oversight of securities regulators comes from politicians, bureaucrats, private market actors, or the courts. So far as the latter is concerned, the problem is twofold: 1) the lack of expert judges; 2) the high degree of deference shown by judges to the decisions of administrative tribunals. Luckily, however, there is a simple solution to both of these problems – the creation of speciality courts similar in nature to the Delaware Chancery Court. These speciality courts would deal only with securities regulatory matters, and would be staffed by judges with extensive private sector experience. The expertise of the judges would allay the need for a high degree of judicial deference. Rather than a mere 'reasonableness' standard, judges could employ a 'correctness' standard, supplying much more effective judicial oversight.

These same courts should hear civil cases and criminal cases relating to securities regulatory matters.

7.2 *Appeal Rights*

Having expert courts staffed with expert judges will be a Pyrrhic victory unless administrative decisions may uniformly be appealed to the courts – something that is absent, for example, from the CCMRA proposals noted above.

7.3 *Securities Regulators*

A persistent source of poor regulatory decisions is the lack of market experience on the part of regulators. The danger that a lack of market experience poses to securities markets increases as regulatory discretion increases, since a high degree of discretion gives the regulator a wider berth to make mistakes. Asymmetrical payoff distributions exacerbate the problem, as they magnify the natural risk aversion of regulators. An inexpert regulator will be more affected by this risk aversion. Without confidence that he or she is making a decision that will avoid a scandal or some other market pathology, the inexpert regulator will be inclined to err on the side of safety. This is achieved by setting the regulatory bar at an excessively high level.

The securities regulatory authority should have sufficient budget to hire people with a very high level of expertise, with priority given to those who have hands-on market experience. Pay grades should be set at levels similar to those available in the private sector in order to attract talent.

7.4 *Regulatory Procedures*

So far as possible, regulatory discretion must be constrained in scope. It must also be structured, so far as possible, in accord with the dictates of the ROL, allowing affected parties appropriate avenues to make representations and the power to appeal unfavourable decisions in a timely manner to an independent and unbiased tribunal or court.

7.5 *Civil Recoveries*

As noted, civil, administrative, and criminal adjudications are both substitutes and complements. An effective system of civil recovery will incentivise private actors to hold wrongdoers to account, potentially filling lacunae in the public law apparatus.

Certain elements are indispensable to creating an effective civil law system. These include:

a.) an effective class action;
b.) the ability to recover from individuals such as directors, officers, and controlling shareholders who are implicated in the wrongdoing;
c.) an expert judiciary;
d.) costs rules that are capable of surmounting free rider and collective action problems, perhaps including the potential for funding individual or class actions out of the public purse;
e.) timely access to the courts;
f.) timely rendering of decisions;
g.) compulsory non-binding pre-trial mediation; and
h.) the ability of the parties to opt into binding private mediation.

7.6 *The Criminal Law*

Civil litigation is subject to well-known free rider and collective action problems. Thus, a system of securities regulation that relies entirely on the incentive of injured parties to sue is unlikely to result in a sufficient deterrent against wrongdoing. In part, these shortcomings are addressed by administrative oversight of securities markets. Another mechanism for creating appropriate incentives is the criminal law, with the judges who administer the law being the same as those who hear civil and administrative matters involving securities laws.

8 Conclusion

The ROL has both independent and instrumental value. As an independent value, it is part and parcel of the individual liberty and freedom from arbitrary state action that inheres in every democratic polity. As an instrumental value, it facilitates the achievement of allocative efficiency by enhancing certainty about regulatory outcomes, allowing businesspeople to plan and structure their commercial lives with efficacy and predictability.

Securities regulation presents challenges that are probably unique in the world of administrative law. The complexity of financial markets requires matching complexity on the part of the regulatory apparatus, and the ability to react to new developments in a nimble manner. Unfortunately, the means for achieving these goals – wrenching securities regulation away from legislators and giving it to expert regulators, often with a high degree of regulatory discretion – does violence to virtually every aspect of the ROL.

In this chapter, I make a preliminary attempt to identify mechanisms that will best accommodate expert regulation, the rule of law, and administrative accountability. Central to these mechanisms is the creation of an expert court, much like the Delaware Chancery Court, that specialises in securities law and would hear civil, administrative, and criminal matters. With respect to administrative decisions, private market actors must routinely be given rights of appeal from the regulatory body to the court.

Broad, unreviewable discretionary authority is very much at odds with the ROL and quite unacceptable. Regulatory discretion can never be divorced from the chain of accountability and must always be subject to judicial appeal.

Another important aspect of reconciling the ROL and regulatory efficacy is to ensure that regulators possess not merely domain expertise, but pertinent market experience. This will tend to ameliorate regulatory pathologies that result from asymmetrical payoff distributions and regulatory risk aversion. Among these pathologies are excessive and cost-inefficient regulation and the commensurately enhanced burden on individual liberties that results from such regulation.

15

Securities Regulation in Australia

The Role of the Class Action

MICHAEL LEGG*

1 Introduction

Securities regulation, particularly in relation to market integrity and shareholder protection, is an important issue in Australia, with listed Australian corporations being a significant source of Australians' income and retirement investments.

The Australian Securities Exchange (ASX) has a total market capitalisation of around $1.5 trillion. In 1991, only 1.8 million (15 per cent) of Australian adults directly or indirectly held shares. By 2012, 6.7 million (38 per cent) of Australian adults directly or indirectly held shares.[1] Australia also has a superannuation system that mandates contributions from employers to provide for employees' future retirement needs. Superannuation assets totalled $2.0 trillion at the end of the June 2015 quarter. This is the fourth largest pool of superannuation savings in the world. A substantial portion of these funds is invested in Australian equities.[2]

Australia has traditionally relied on a public regulator to enforce its securities laws. However, shareholder class actions have become a growing phenomenon in the Australian legal landscape since around 2003.

* The author would like to thank Nichole Soo, UNSW Law Student for her research assistance.

[1] See Senate Economics Reference Committee, *Performance of the Australian Securities and Investments Commission (June* 2014) 11–12; *ASX, 2012 Australian Share Ownership Study (May* 2013) 4–7.

[2] See Senate Economics Reference Committee, *Performance of the Australian Securities and Investments Commission* (June 2014) 9, 14; Australian Prudential Regulation Authority, *Statistics: Quarterly Superannuation Performance – June 2015* (20 August 2015) 6, 7 (in relation to superannuation entities with more than four members, 24 per cent of $1.3 trillion was invested in Australian listed equities).

Shareholder class actions may be argued to perform two main goals. The first is reactive – compensation for losses suffered by shareholders when there has been a contravention of certain provisions in the Corporations Act 2001 (Cth) (Corporations Act) or the Australian Securities and Investments Commission Act 2001 (Cth) (ASIC Act). The second is proactive – deterrence of future corporate law violations through sanctions for contraventions of the law.[3]

This chapter will explain and critique these rationales in aid of exploring shareholder class actions as a form of securities regulation in Australia.

2 Background

The availability of class actions as a form of shareholder protection is the result of the accretion of three developments in the Australian legal system. First, Parliament's determination to grant standing to private litigants in relation to contraventions of specified provisions in the Corporations Act, and the ASIC Act. Second, is the introduction of a class action regime which provided the procedural framework for the claims of numerous shareholders to be aggregated and pursued by a representative party. Third, a mechanism for financing the class action and bearing the risk of failure so that shareholders would be willing to participate – third party litigation funding.[4]

3 Standing for Shareholders

The Corporations Act, and to a lesser extent the ASIC Act, provide shareholders with standing to seek compensation on their own behalf where there is a contravention of

- a financial services civil penalty provision, which includes continuous disclosure, market manipulation, false trading and market rigging, dissemination of information about illegal transactions and insider trading;[5] or

[3] Second Reading Federal Court of Australia Amendment Bill 1991, Minister for Justice and Consumer Affairs, Australia, *Parliamentary Debates*, Senate, 13 November 1991, 3023; Second Reading Speech Federal Court of Australia Amendment Bill 1991, Attorney-General, Australia, *Parliamentary Debates*, House of Representatives, 14 November 1991, 3176–3177; *Kirby* v. *Centro Properties Limited* [2008] FCA 1505, [8].

[4] Michael Legg, 'Shareholder Class Actions in Australia – The Perfect Storm?', 31(3) *UNSW Law Journal* 669 (2008), 705–707.

[5] Corporations Act ss 674, 675, 1041A-D, 1043A, 1317E.

- misleading or deceptive conduct prohibitions in relation to financial products and services, including securities, takeover documents and fundraising documents;[6] or
- other provisions that may be remedied by an injunction or through 'other orders'.[7]

4 Class Actions

Class actions were introduced into Australia through the enactment of the Federal Court of Australia Amendment Act 1991 (Cth), which provided for 'representative proceedings' through inserting Part IVA into the Federal Court of Australia Act 1976 (Cth) (FCAA).[8] Part IVA commenced on 4 March 1992.

The Australian class action procedures require that a valid class action have seven or more persons with claims against the same person and that those claims are 'in respect of, or arise out of, the same, similar or related circumstances'. The claims must 'give rise to a substantial common issue of law or fact'. The representative party must be a person who has a sufficient interest in the matter to support their own action against the defendant/respondent.[9]

However, even when the requirements for a class action are satisfied, the court has a discretion upon its own motion or on application by the defendant/respondent to terminate the class action where the court is satisfied that it is in the interests of justice to do so because, *inter alia*, the action would be less efficient than separate proceedings or where it is 'otherwise inappropriate that the claims be pursued by means of a representative proceeding'.[10]

The Australian class action procedure also has three distinguishing features that differentiate it from other forms of litigation.

First an 'opt out' or open system where all group members who meet the group definition are automatically part of the class action, but notice is required to be given to group members allowing them an opportunity to

6 Corporations Act ss 670A, 728, 1041H. See also ASIC Act s 12DA.

7 Corporations Act ss 1324, 1325.

8 Class action procedures also exist in the states of Victoria, New South Wales and Queensland. For detailed discussion of the Australian class action regimes, see Damian Grave, Ken Adams and Jason Betts, *Class Actions in Australia*, 2nd ed., (Thomson Reuters, 2012); Michael Legg and Ross McInnes, *Annotated Class Actions Legislation* (LexisNexis, 2014).

9 FCAA ss 33C, 33D.

10 FCAA s 33N(1).

exclude themselves from the action.[11] Group members are not regarded as parties to the litigation, but judgment in the matter will bind all group members except those that chose to opt out.[12] However, the Full Federal Court has held that a closed class action brought on behalf of some, but not all, putative group members is permissible based on its construction of the legislation and because the right to opt out was preserved.[13]

Second is the settlement process. A class action may not be settled or discontinued without the approval of the Court.[14] Further, unless the Court is satisfied that it is just to do so, an application for approval of a settlement must not be determined unless notice has been given to group members.[15]

Third is the alteration to the usual rule on costs. The usual costs rule in Australian litigation is that a losing party is liable for the other side's costs, albeit only a portion of the costs actually incurred.[16] However, in the class action context, the costs rule is limited to the representative party only and does not apply to other group members.[17] This approach to costs has been raised as a disincentive to the commencement of class action litigation, as the representative party remains liable for the cost of legal representation and disbursements (which are arguably incurred for the benefit of the entire group) and, if they are unsuccessful, the costs of their opponent.

5 Litigation Funding

Litigation funding addresses the cost disincentives to the commencement of class action litigation, explained above. Litigation funding is a contractual arrangement between a third party funder (usually a commercial entity) and one or more potential litigants. The funder pays the costs of the litigation (such as the lawyer's fees, disbursements, project management and claim investigation costs) and usually accepts the risk of paying the other party's costs in the event that the claim falls through, providing the plaintiff with an indemnity. In return, if the claim is successful, the funder will receive a certain percentage of any funds recovered by the litigants either by way of settlement or judgment, and the litigants will

[11] FCAA ss 33J, 33X. [12] FCAA s 33ZB.

[13] *Multiplex Funds Management Limited* v. *P Dawson Nominees Pty Ltd* (2007) 164 FCR 275, [44], [194]-[195].

[14] Federal Court of Australia Act s 33V. [15] FCAA s 33X(4).

[16] *Ruddock* v. *Vadarlis* (2001) 115 FCR 229, [11]. [17] FCAA s 43(1A).

assign the funder the benefit of any costs order they receive. The share of the proceeds is agreed with the litigants and is typically between 25–40 per cent of the proceeds (usually after reimbursement of costs).[18]

In *Campbells Cash and Carry Pty Limited* v. *Fostif Pty Ltd* (2006) 229 CLR 386, the High Court of Australia considered the legality of litigation funding for the first time. The High Court majority held that litigation funding was not an abuse of process or contrary to public policy. As a consequence, litigation funding became an accepted part of civil litigation, including class actions.

6 The Goal of Compensation and Class Actions

Class actions in a range of fields have been justified on the basis that they perform the valuable function of compensating large numbers of victims in an efficient manner.[19] The class action facilitates compensation by aggregating claims, levelling the playing field and overcoming the collective action problem. Shareholder class actions change the traditional cost/benefit analysis that applies when an individual shareholder must decide whether to commence legal proceedings. The pooling of claims gives rise to economies of scale and a claim that may be uneconomic to pursue alone can, when combined with other claims, become worth pursuing. In the area of shareholder claims, the class action is an attractive procedural vehicle because many of the claims are small and the class action allows for them to be aggregated to create a single substantial claim. The class action procedure and the substantive causes of action may also be relied upon by large shareholders such as institutional investors, including superannuation funds. An institutional investor's decision whether to commence litigation will depend upon the potential recovery and costs involved. Similar to a retail investor, the costs include direct costs for the fees of legal advisers. However, there are also indirect costs such as management time, complying with discovery (as they have more records) and the

[18] Michael Legg, 'Reconciling Litigation Funding and the Opt Out Group Definition in Federal Court of Australia Class Actions – The Need for a Legislative Common Fund Approach', 30 *Civil Justice Quarterly* 52 (2011), 56.

[19] Martin Redish, 'Class Actions and the Democratic Difficulty: Rethinking the Intersection of Private Litigation and Public Goals', *University of Chicago Legal Forum* 71 [2003], 89; The American Law Institute, *Principles of the Law of Aggregate Litigation* (2010) § 1.04 comment f.

impact on business relationships. With a class action, those costs may be minimised and they can share in any recovery.[20]

7 Compensation Compared to Loss

Australian shareholder class actions have resulted in some large settlement payments. The top five shareholder class action settlements in Australia are listed in Table 15.1, with the $200 million Centro class action settlement being the largest. There have also been small recoveries, as well as a range of settlements in the $30 million to $70 million range (which in aggregate have resulted in settlements of more than $1 billion).[21] However, focussing on the quantum of the settlement misses a more important question: What proportion of shareholders' actual losses is being compensated? This requires a comparison between the settlement amount and the shareholders' losses that are the subject of the claim.

Some judges have included this calculation in the settlement approval judgment. In the GIO settlement approval judgment, Justice Moore observed that the best present estimate of the loss of all group members was approximately $151 million and that $97 million compensation was to be paid so that an individual group member would receive approximately 60 per cent of the loss they suffered.[22] In the Multiplex case Justice Finkelstein observed that the class members would recover in the order of sixty-two cents on the dollar of the reasonable value of their claims.[23] In the Oz Minerals settlement, Justice Emmett stated that the total settlement sum of $60 million equated to about 32 per cent of the value of the claims if they were completely successful.[24] In the White Sands Petroleum class action, Besanko J in approving the settlement calculated that prior to the deduction of lawyer's and funder's fees the shareholders recovered 56 per cent of their claims were they to be completely successful.[25]

[20] Michael Legg, 'Institutional Investors and Shareholder Class Actions: The Law and Economics of Participation', 81 *Australian Law Journal* 478 (2007); Michael Legg, 'Shareholder Class Actions in Australia'.

[21] King & Wood Mallesons, *The Review – Class Actions in Australia 2015/2016* (2016) 8.

[22] *King* v. *AG Australia Holdings Ltd (formerly GIO Australia Holdings Ltd)* [2003] FCA 980, [14].

[23] *P Dawson Nominees Pty Ltd* v. *Brookfield Multiplex Limited (No 4)* [2010] FCA 1029, [22].

[24] *Hobbs Anderson Investments Pty Ltd* v. *Oz Minerals Ltd* [2011] FCA 801, [15].

[25] *Wepar Nominees Pty Ltd* v. *Schofield (No 2)* [2014] FCA 225, [30].

Table 15.1 *Lawyer and litigation funder fees*

Class Action	Settlement Amount*	Lawyer Fees	Lawyer Fees as % of Settlement^	Litigation Funder Fees	Litigation Funder Fees as % of Settlement	Comments
GIO shareholder class action re misleading statements in a takeover	$112 m	$15 m	13.3%	No funder	N/A	Legal fees included a 25% uplift
Harris Scarfe shareholder class action re disclosure to market and in a prospectus	$3 m	$1.55 m	51.6%	No funder	N/A	Respondent's insurance was limited and would be exhausted by defence costs.
Telstra shareholder class action re disclosure to market	$5 m	$1.25 m	25%	No funder	N/A	
Aristocrat Leisure shareholder class action re disclosure to market	$144.5 m	$8.5 m	5.8%	$35 m	24.2%	Settlement occurred after trial.

Multiplex shareholder class action re disclosure to market	$110 m	$11 m	10%	Not disclosed	Est 40%	
Oz Minerals shareholder class actions re disclosure to market	$60 m ($39 m and $21 m)	$3.1 m and $1.8 m	7.9% and 8.5%	$15 m and another amount not disclosed by the funder.	25% (of the total settlement)	Two shareholder class actions
Centro shareholder class action re disclosure to market with additional claims against directors and the auditor	$200 m ($150 m for two class actions and $50 m for the other)	$21.1 m for two class actions and $10.06 m for the other	14% for two class actions and 20.1% for the other.	$60 m for two class actions and another not disclosed by the funder.	40% for two class actions, unknown for the other.	Three shareholder class actions. Largest shareholder class action settlement in Australia.
NAB shareholder class action re disclosure to market	$115 m	$11.8 m	10.2%	Funder paid a percentage of each class member's settlement amount by reference to number of shares held: 40% if less than 1 million shares; 35% if between 1 million shares and 10 million shares; and 30% if more than 10 million shares.		

Table 15.1 (*cont.*)

Class Action	Settlement Amount*	Lawyer Fees	Lawyer Fees as % of Settlement^	Litigation Funder Fees	Litigation Funder Fees as % of Settlement	Comments
GPT shareholder class action re disclosure to market	$75 m	$8.5 m	11.3%	Not disclosed	Est 25–30%	
White Sands Petroleum re disclosure to market and in a prospectus	$3.25 m	$1.04 m	32%	$1.08 m	33%	
Leighton Holdings re disclosure to market	$69.45 m	$3.9 m	5.6%	Not disclosed	N/A	
Billabong International re disclosure to market	$45 m	$5.66 m	12.6%	Not disclosed	N/A	
Newcrest Mining re disclosure to market	$36 m	$10.3 m	$28.6%	$6.78 m	18.8%	

* Includes litigation funder's and lawyer's fees.

^ Percentages calculated to one decimal point.

However, other judgments do not include this important indicia. For example, in the Centro class action, many estimates of the total size of the claim were $1 billion or more.[26] If the $1 billion estimate, or more, is correct, then the $200 million settlement equates to twenty cents on the dollar, or less. Similarly in the NAB class action, the losses were estimated at $450 million by the plaintiffs' lawyers,[27] which would give a recovery of about 26 per cent of losses. No such calculations are included in either judgment approving settlement.

Many factors can impact the size of a settlement relative to actual losses. A significant factor that the parties and the Court are expressly directed to consider by the Federal Court practice note in relation to a settlement is the existence of litigation risk.[28] Litigation risk refers to 'the vagaries of litigation and the risks of failure as well as the expense to be incurred in protracted litigation'.[29] In shareholder class actions that risk is often higher because of the novelty of the law and the need at some point to quantify losses. The law in relation to causation and damages based on a contravention of the continuous disclosure regime or prohibition on misleading or deceptive conduct is unsettled – does there need to be proof of direct reliance, or is indirect or market-based causation sufficient?[30] There is also the prospect of cost and delay because novel points of law are likely to be appealed. Nonetheless the efficacy of shareholder class actions in achieving compensation for shareholders means a comparison between the losses suffered and the settlement or judgment achieved is essential. The aim of compensation is that all of those 'who are entitled to compensation ... actually receive compensation and in the amount to which they are entitled'.[31] Shareholder class actions can

[26] Michael Legg, 'The Price of Settlement? The Centro Class Action and the Divide Between Private and Public Enforcement', Centre for Law Markets and Regulation, University of New South Wales, 9 May 2012.

[27] Maurice Blackburn, *Press Release: NAB in New Class Action Over Toxic Debt Exposure*, 18 November 2010.

[28] Federal Court of Australia, Class Actions *Practice Note (GPN-CA)*, 25 October 2016 [14.4].

[29] *Jarra Creek Central Packing Shed Pty Ltd* v. *Amcor Ltd* [2011] FCA 671, [95]; *Wright Rubber Pty Ltd* v. *Bayer AG (No.3)* [2011] FCA 1172, [12].

[30] See e.g. *P Dawson Nominees Pty Ltd* v. *Brookfield Multiplex Ltd (No 4)* [2010] FCA 1029, [15]-[17]; *Pathway Investments Pty Ltd* v. *National Australia Bank Limited (No. 3)* [2012] VSC 625, [11]-[12]; *Caason Investments Pty Ltd* v. *Cao* [2015] FCAFC 94; Michael Legg and Madeleine Harkin, 'Judicial Recognition of Indirect Causation and Shareholder Class Actions' 44 *Australian Business Law Review* 429 (2016).

[31] Peter Cane, *Atiyah's Accidents, Compensation and the Law*, 8th ed., (Cambridge University Press, 2013), 409.

generate some large headline figures but it is less clear whether those sums truly compensate shareholders.

8 Transaction Costs: Lawyers' and Litigation Funders' Fees

The amount of compensation available for shareholders is much lower that the headline figure discussed above, as any settlement or judgment will be reduced by transaction costs. The two main transaction costs are legal fees and litigation funding fees which are incurred when litigation is employed to seek compensation. Examples of the quantum of lawyer and litigation funder fees are set out in Table 15.1.

Transaction costs are an inevitable aspect of compensation sought through litigation. Shareholder class actions are costly because of the need to address not just the substantive law but the additional complexities created through aggregating claims to be pursued by a representative party. There is also the concern of liability for an adverse costs order that a litigation funder provides protection against. Transaction costs are, from the perspective of lawyer and funder, revenues which provide the incentive for the lawyer to provide their labour and for the funder to undertake the risk of litigation.

While shareholders need to pay to be able to obtain legal and funding services, for the class action to benefit shareholders those costs must be kept to a minimum. In relation to legal fees, Australian courts have power to regulate costs agreements between a solicitor and a client,[32] including in class actions.[33] Legal fees will be subject to approval as part of any class action settlement.[34] In the GPT shareholder class action settlement, Gordon J highlighted the need for the provision of sufficient information to the Court for it to determine if the fees and disbursements charged were reasonable.[35] Further measures may be needed to protect group members from excessive fees, such as replacing the costs expert retained by the lawyers to opine on the reasonableness of their fees[36] with an

[32] *Woolf* v. *Snipe* (1933) 48 CLR 677, 678.

[33] *Johnson Tiles Pty Ltd* v. *Esso Australia Ltd* (1999) 94 FCR 167, [35]–[37]; *Modtech Engineering Pty Ltd* v. *GPT Management Holdings Ltd* [2013] FCA 626, [27].

[34] *Johnson Tiles Pty Ltd* v. *Esso Australia Ltd* (1999) 94 FCR 167, [39]; *Reiffel* v. *ACN 075 839 226 Pty Limited (No 2)* [2004] FCA 1128, [11].

[35] *Modtech Engineering Pty Ltd* v. *GPT Management Holdings Ltd* [2013] FCA 626, [38]–[52].

[36] See *Courtney* v. *Medtel Pty Ltd (No 5)* (2004) 212 ALR 311, [59].

independent, court appointed costs expert.[37] In extreme cases where litigation is commenced to generate legal fees and not vindicate rights, the litigation may be regarded as an abuse of process.[38]

In relation to litigation funding a very different approach has traditionally existed. The quantum paid to the funder was rarely examined. This was the case even when orders were made for the fee charged by a funder to be paid by group members, who although part of an open class action, had not contracted with the funder.[39] However, orders seeking payment from a common fund for a litigation funder were permitted by the Full Federal Court on the condition that the Court would determine the funder's fee at the conclusion of proceedings.[40] However, the funder may choose not to seek an order for payment from a common fund and instead rely on the terms of its funding agreement. A single Federal Court judge has also found that the court had power to directly reduce the funding commission payable as part of the settlement approval process.[41] However, these developments are very recent and untested in relation to whether they reduce transaction costs.

9 The Circularity Problem: Pocket-Shifting?

The circularity problem has been described by one academic in the US as 'the most damaging securities class action criticism'[42] and is a key reason why compensation as a goal of shareholder class actions has been almost abandoned by American academics.[43]

The circularity problem applies to the purchase of shares on-market where an applicant or group member buys from another shareholder. The concern about the utility of compensation in the on-market situation has led to analysis that suggests that when shareholders are diversified the

[37] Michael Legg, 'Class Action Settlements in Australia – The Need for Greater Scrutiny', 38 (2) *Melbourne University Law Review* 590 (2014).

[38] *Treasury Wine Estates Ltd* v. *Melbourne City Investments Pty Ltd* [2014] VSCA 351, [14].

[39] See e.g. *Modtech Engineering Pty Limited* v. *GPT Management Holdings Limited* [2013] FCA 626.

[40] Money Max Int Pty Ltd v QBE Insurance Group Ltd [2016] FCAFC 148.

[41] Earglow Pty Ltd v Newcrest Mining Limited [2016] FCA 1433.

[42] Elizabeth Chamblee Burch, 'Securities Class Actions as Pragmatic Ex Post Regulation', 43 *Georgia Law Review* 63 (2008), 86.

[43] Amanda Rose, 'Reforming Securities Litigation Reform: Restructuring the Relationship Between Public and Private Enforcement of Rule 10B-5', 108 *Columbia Law Review* 1301 (2008), 1312–1314.

payment of compensation is a circular or 'pocket shifting' exercise where the shareholders who traded are paid by the shareholders who did not, but with large transaction costs, being the lawyer's fees and the litigation funder's share of any recovery.[44] The pocket-shifting occurs because most securities class action settle and settlements are funded by the corporate defendant or an insurance policy. Rarely are individual wrongdoers required to contribute financially to a settlement.[45] A diversified shareholder, such as an institutional investor, is equally likely to be the shareholder who traded as the shareholder who did not trade over the long term so that their welfare is not improved.

As the circularity problem poses a grave challenge to a core reason for shareholder class actions, a number of rebuttals or responses have been developed.[46] This chapter will deal with two of those responses.

First the analysis only applies to diversified shareholders and only over the long term. It might therefore be suggested that non-diversified shareholders, usually small retail shareholders, would make a worthwhile recovery through a shareholder class action as they are unlikely to be both within and outside the group definition in any single case nor in a number of cases over time. However, as small investors usually do not trade actively but rather 'buy and hold', they may buy the shares before any contravention (therefore not purchasing as a result of a contravention) and still be holding them once the contravention comes to light. Consequently, the retail shareholder may only fund, but not participate in, a settlement or verdict.[47] The Australian experience is that the majority of participating shareholders in class actions are indeed the diversified institutional investor,[48] but there is also evidence of retail investors participating, albeit in the minority by value.[49]

[44] John Coffee, 'Law and the Market: The Impact of Enforcement', 156 *University of Pennsylvania Law Review* 229 (2007), 304.

[45] Janet Cooper Alexander, 'Rethinking Damages in Securities Class Actions', 48 *Stanford Law Review* 1487 (1996), 1499; Bernard Black, Brian Cheffins and Michael Klausner, 'Outside Director Liability', 58 *Stanford Law Review* 1055 (2006), 1068.

[46] See e.g. Lawrence Mitchell, 'The "Innocent Shareholder": An Essay on Compensation and Deterrence in Securities Class-Action Lawsuits', *Wisconsin Law Review* 243 [2009].

[47] William Bratton and Michael Wachter, 'The Political Economy of Fraud on the Market', 160 *University of Pennsylvania Law Review* 69 (2011), 97.

[48] See *P Dawson Nominees Pty Ltd* v. *Brookfield Multiplex Ltd (No 4)* [2010] FCA 1029, [23].

[49] See *Dorajay Pty Ltd* v. *Aristocrat Leisure Ltd* (2008) 67 ACSR 569, 589–592; Slater & Gordon, 'Thousands of Mum and Dad Investors Poised to Share in Australia's Biggest Shareholder Class Action Settlement' (Media Release, 9 May 2012).

Second it is possible to break the circle by suing directors or advisers.[50] Instead of one group of innocent shareholders paying another group of innocent shareholders, those that are individually culpable are required to compensate the shareholders who suffered loss. This could be by direct or accessorial claims by the shareholder group members, provided they have standing to commence proceedings. Alternatively, the company could cross-claim against directors or advisers, or some of those entities, having been sued, could then cross-claim against the persons they believe are culpable. In Australia most shareholder class actions have been brought against the corporation only. In Table 15.1, this was the case in relation to the proceedings brought against Telstra, Aristocrat Leisure, Multiplex, Oz Minerals, NAB, GPT, Leightons, Billabong and Newcrest. In GIO proceedings were commenced against the company, an adviser and nine directors (one was the CEO and the others were non-executive directors). A similar approach was taken in the White Sands Petroleum class action. This approach may be explained by GIO being a takeover case and White Sands Petroleum being a prospectus case so that both involved regimes where directors and advisers are specifically made liable for particular documents, subject to specified defences.[51] The other cases from Table 15.1 were alleged contraventions of the continuous disclosure regime where liability is placed on the corporation. Persons involved in the contravention may be liable as an accessory only.[52] However, the cases utilising the continuous disclosure regime also included claims involving misleading or deceptive conduct that could be brought directly against a person such as a director or adviser. There are three cases involving alleged continuous disclosure breaches that run counter to the usual approach.

In Centro four corporations were the initial targets, but through a range of cross-claims, other parties were included in the litigation. The corporations cross-claimed against their auditor, PriceWaterhouseCoopers, who in turn cross-claimed against the CEO, CFO and directors.[53] It has been reported that the $200 million settlement was comprised of $95 million from Centro corporate entities, $67 million from the auditor and $38 million from directors' and officers' insurance.[54] The individual directors do not appear to have personally contributed to the settlement.

[50] John Coffee, 'Reforming the Securities Class Action: An Essay on Deterrence and Its Implementation', 106 *Columbia Law Review* 1534 (2006), 1538, 1562.

[51] Corporations Act ss 670A-670D (takeovers), ss 728–733 (fundraising).

[52] Corporations Act ss 674(2A), 675 (2A). [53] Michael Legg, 'The Price of Settlement?'.

[54] Agnes King, 'Red Faces, not Red Ink at PwC Audit', *The Australian Financial Review*, 14 May 2012, 56–57.

The main outliers are the Harris Scarfe and Gunns Limited class actions. In Harris Scarfe proceedings were commenced against six respondents who were all directors.[55] However, this was in the context of the company being insolvent and the proceedings being commenced so as to access the insurance held by the directors. Indeed the settlement was crafted so as to recover up to the amount of the available insurance.[56] Similarly, in the Gunns class action the directors were only sued after the corporation went into liquidation and no recovery from it was possible.[57]

10 The Goal of Deterrence and Class Actions

Deterrence may be defined as the avoidance of a given action through fear of the perceived consequences.[58] Deterrence is usually divided into two categories: specific and general deterrence. Specific deterrence aims to deter 'the particular contravenor who might be tempted to re-offend' while general deterrence is aimed at deterring others 'who might be tempted not to comply with the law'.[59]

General deterrence has particular significance in securities regulation due to the need to protect and maintain market integrity. More generally, investment in public companies depends on the public having confidence in the operation of those companies. Consequently, the significance of the deterrent effect that follows from contraventions of the law being identified and subject to sanction is that other corporations, directors and employees are dissuaded from contravening the law. Indeed, general deterrence may encourage compliance through making the ramifications of a contravention known. However, in the class action context the achievement of general deterrence or compliance is to be achieved through litigation for the payment of damages or compensation. There may also be reputational harm or other indirect costs from litigation.

While deterrence is seen as a goal of class actions and a measure which protects shareholders by hopefully dissuading future contraventions, it is also a goal of the government regulator, ASIC.[60] The interaction of the

55 *Guglielman* v. *Trescowthick* [2004] FCA 326, [13].

56 *Guglielmin* v. *Trescowthick (No 5)* [2006] FCA 1385, [31]; Leonie Wood, 'Class Action Filed against Harris Scarfe Directors', *The Age*, 31 July 2002.

57 *Foley v Gay* [2016] FCA 273, [8]-[12].

58 Arie Freiberg, *The Tools of Regulation* (The Federation Press, 2010) 211.

59 *Australian Securities and Investments Commission* v. *Chemeq* (2006) 234 ALR 511, [90].

60 ASIC has a range of objectives in addition to deterrence, namely, punishment, improving compliance, protecting the public, compensation for investors and deterrence. See ASIC,

class action and the regulator therefore takes on central importance in assessing the role that the class action may play. The optimal deterrence literature provides a schema for examining that interaction.

11 Deterrence and Securities Regulation

The aim of a deterrence-focussed securities regulatory regime according to law and economics scholarship is said to be the achievement of optimal deterrence which means minimising the social costs from breach of the securities regulations as well as the costs of enforcement.[61] The social costs are increases in the cost of capital, reductions in liquidity, inefficient allocation of resources, and additional monitoring costs as confidence in the ability to determine the value of corporate securities is undermined.[62] Enforcement costs may be direct or indirect. Direct costs are the resources consumed in detecting, prosecuting, defending and adjudicating cases. Indirect costs are those associated with over-deterrence. If regulated entities fear an inaccurate determination of liability or an overly broad liability regime, then they may overinvest in precautionary measures or adopt a defensive disclosure policy.[63] In simple terms, under enforcement by a regulator can lead to greater social costs and over enforcement can lead to greater enforcement costs.

The optimal deterrence approach is problematic because of an inability to measure the optimal amount of enforcement.[64] Moreover, both social costs and enforcement costs may be difficult to quantify. Attempts to apply the theory to practice therefore confront grave difficulties. However, the theory does provide a useful analytical tool for examining how public and private enforcement interact and impact upon each other.

12 Class Actions Promote Optimal Deterrence

Class actions impact on the achievement of optimal deterrence because, like a regulator, it can provide an incentive for corporations to comply with the securities laws. It can also impose enforcement costs.

Senate Inquiry into the Performance of the Australian Securities and Investments Commission – Main submission by ASIC (October 2013) [396].

61 Rose, 'Reforming Securities Litigation Reform', 1322.

62 Amanda Rose, 'The Multienforcer Approach to Securities Fraud Deterrence: A Critical Analysis', 158 *University of Pennsylvania Law Review* 2173 (2010), 2179.

63 Ibid., at 2183–2184.

64 James Park, 'Rules, Principles and the Competition to Enforce Securities Laws', 100 *California Law Review* 115 (2012), 128.

In the US, private enforcement through class actions is usually advocated on the basis that it deters misconduct by allowing for the enforcement of statutory requirements for disclosure and prohibitions on misleading conduct as an adjunct to actions by the SEC.[65] The payment of damages in the form of compensation by defendants deters wrongdoing because '[c]orporate decision makers who anticipate bearing the costs of securities fraud, will, ex ante, internalize those costs and engage in efficient levels of care to ensure that their disclosures are accurate'.[66] The class action has the ability to better achieve optimal deterrence by being able to combine all of the claims for compensation (even when losses are small) to ensure that the full social cost is imposed on the defendant, provided group members do not opt out or fail to claim.[67] However, as explained above, the compensation achieved through settlements in Australian class actions has only ever been a portion of the losses alleged.

An evaluation of deterrence cannot be limited to the amount of any settlement or judgment. The size and complexity of class actions means they can be unwieldy and lengthy, giving rise to other substantial costs. Management's time is diverted from the business to defending the litigation. The cost of lawyers and expert witnesses is incurred. The commencement of proceedings, associated press releases by class action promoters and the existence of a contingent liability may dampen corporate performance, including decreasing the share price and attracting media scrutiny with associated effects on reputation. It may also follow that even if corporate management and directors do not make a financial payout, they may still be dismissed from their positions. The class action can significantly add to the costs of misconduct, even if the actual payment of compensation is small. The greater awareness of this amongst Australian corporations and the desire to avoid such costs may evidence the effect of general deterrence.[68]

Another perspective is that private enforcement is a response to the failures of public enforcement. Public enforcement may be sub-optimal,

[65] *J I Case Co* v. *Borack* 377 US 426, 432 (1964), *Bateman Eichler, Hill Richards Inc* v. *Berner* 472 US 299, 310 (1985).

[66] Jill Fisch, 'Confronting the Circularity Problem in Private Securities Litigation', *Wisconsin Law Review* 333 (2009), 336.

[67] David Rosenberg, 'The Regulatory Advantage of Class Action' in W Kip Viscusi (ed.), *Regulation Through Litigation* (AEI-Brookings Joint Center for Regulatory Studies, 2002), 248.

[68] See e.g. Australian Institute of Company Directors, Submission to Productivity Commission on Litigation Funding and Class Actions, 4 November 2013, 1.

not just due to lack of resources, but it may occur due to regulatory capture, complacency or incompetence. These concerns can be overcome by allowing private individuals to sue.[69] The private enforcer can keep the legislature and the regulator honest by showing up these shortcomings. Private enforcement can be a method of accountability for the public regulator.

13 Class Actions Hamper Optimal Deterrence

Class actions seek to maximise the welfare of the private enforcer which may diverge from the social welfare. In particular, litigation will be commenced whenever the private benefit from that litigation exceeds its costs.[70] Moreover, the private enforcer does not bear the costs of over-enforcement. The private enforcer has an economic incentive to act as though all failures to disclose correctly are evidence of the most grievous misconduct.[71] The private enforcer is not concerned with or accountable for the impact of its actions on the social welfare.

The government regulator has a panoply of remedies enabling it to perform its function in a calibrated manner, depending on the facts and circumstances of the particular case before it. If over-deterrence appears to be a problem, the regulator can reduce the level of enforcement; conversely, if under-deterrence appears to be a problem, the regulator can intensify enforcement. Private enforcement, by contrast has no interest in trying to calibrate the level of deterrence.[72] Lawyers and litigation funders only profit when there is litigation to be conducted.

The need for litigation may give rise to what is known in the United States as 'strike suits'.[73] Class actions are settled, even if the case had a low chance of success, because they could impose substantial costs on the corporation that could not be recovered. The 'strike suit' was feasible in the United States because each party bears its own costs.[74] The Australian costs regime where the loser pays is thought to be a deterrent to strike

[69] Steven Ramirez, 'The Virtues of Private Securities Litigation: An Historic and Macroeconomic Perspective', 45 *Loyola University Chicago Law Journal* 669 (2014), 722–723; Burch, 'Securities Class Actions', 99.

[70] Rose, 'The Multienforcer Approach', 2200–2203.

[71] Park, 'Rules, Principles and the Competition', 121–122, 161.

[72] Rose, 'Reforming Securities Litigation Reform', 1329.

[73] The term 'strike suit', coined in the 1930s, refers to litigation whose nuisance value gives it a settlement value independent of its merits. See Note, 'Extortionate Corporate Litigation: The Strike Suit', 34 *Columbia Law Review* 1308 (1934).

[74] See *Alyeska Pipeline Service Co* v. *Wilderness Society* 421 US 240, 247 (1975).

suits. However, a successful company will not recover all of its direct costs let alone any of its indirect costs such as lost management time so that strike suits are possible in Australia.[75] The strike suit may therefore over-deter as corporations adopt an overly defensive approach to compliance.

A government regulator can also adjust the deterrence calculus by adjusting its style of enforcement, taking less of a coercive approach and more of a cooperative approach (or vice versa) if circumstances suggest it would lead to greater compliance. The former approach is primarily concerned with the use of detecting offenses and punishing violators through the courts. In comparison, the latter approach is primarily concerned with preventing violations and remedying underlying problems through encouraging compliance.[76] In the enforcement pyramid these approaches coexist. Private enforcement can undermine the enforcement pyramid by always seeking the greatest amount of damages possible. The shareholder class action is a wedge driven into the side of the enforcement pyramid. Regulated entities may have no incentive to negotiate or cooperate with a regulator as substantial damages claims may still follow. Consequently, the threat of the regulator being able to move 'up' the enforcement pyramid so as to procure cooperation may be lost, or the regulator may need to demonstrate a willingness to use more potent remedies, such as criminal sanctions or increased fines, if they are available. There is then a risk that sanctions are seen as capricious or draconian responses that are not proportionate to the severity of the offence or the harm done.

14 ASIC's View of Class Actions

In 2005, the former Deputy Chairman of ASIC, Jeremy Cooper, told a class actions conference that ASIC cautiously welcomed the emergence of the shareholder class action in Australia as a self-help mechanism.[77] However, after that ASIC appeared to have withdrawn the welcome mat

[75] See Matthew Drummond and Marcus Priest, 'Telstra Settlement Under Court Scrutiny', *The Australian Financial Review*, 16 November 2007, 57 reporting that Telstra Corporation Ltd settled a shareholder class action against it for $5 million because it was cheaper to settle than to defend the proceedings.

[76] Eugene McLaughlin and John Muncie, *The Sage Dictionary of Criminology*, 2nd ed., (Sage, 2006) 346.

[77] Jeremy Cooper, 'Corporate Wrongdoing: ASIC's Enforcement Role', *International Class Actions Conference 2005*, Melbourne. 2 December 2005.

with ASIC commencing its own proceedings for compensation in relation to financial products and advice, most notably in relation to Westpoint and Storm Financial, even though class actions had, or would be commenced.[78] ASIC also vigorously fought requests from class action lawyers for access to information that ASIC had obtained through its investigatory powers. The high-water mark being the Multiplex class action where numerous decisions, including full Federal Court decisions, on public interest immunity were handed down as part of the dispute.[79]

However, in early 2012 ASIC's Chairman, Greg Medcraft endorsed class action litigation as a 'good market-driven solution' that was 'very good at equalling up the tables' and would allow ASIC to 'use [its] resources in other areas'.[80] Further in 2014 when the Federal budget included cuts to ASIC's funding, Greg Medcraft stated that ASIC would 'rely more on individuals, industry and class action litigators to be vigilant and help ASIC do its work'.[81]

The role of class actions as supplementing ASIC has also been recognised by the Federal Attorney-General's Access to Justice Taskforce[82] and the Senate Economics References Committee in its report on the Performance of the Australian Securities and Investments Commission.[83] The deterrence role of class actions is recognised, but the potential to undermine ASIC's role and discretion has not been acknowledged.

15 Conclusion

Class actions have empowered shareholders by allowing for contraventions of the law to be the subject of litigation when previously the cost and

[78] Michael Legg, 'A Comparison of Regulatory Enforcement, Class Actions and Alternative Dispute Resolution in Compensating Financial Consumers' 38(3) *Sydney Law Review* 311 (2016).

[79] Elizabeth Boros, 'Public and Private Enforcement of Disclosure Breaches in Australia', 9 *Journal of Corporate Law Studies* 409 (2009), 434–436; Michelle Welsh and Vince Morabito, 'Public v. Private Enforcement of Securities Laws: An Australian Empirical Study', 14 (1) *Journal of Corporate Law Studies* 39 (2014), 71–77.

[80] Alex Boxsell, 'Regulators Praise Private Court Actions', *The Weekend Australian Financial Review*, 5–9 April 2012, 59.

[81] Shaun Drummond, 'ASIC Chief Sets Sights on Financial Advisers', *The Sydney Morning Herald*, 25 June 2014.

[82] Access to Justice Taskforce, Federal Attorney-General's Department, *A Strategic Framework for Access to Justice in the Federal Civil Justice System* (September 2009) 114.

[83] Senate Economics References Committee, *Performance of the Australian Securities and Investments Commission* (June 2014) 261.

risk of litigation would have dissuaded any action. The need for shareholders to be able to access the remedies in the Corporations Act and the ASIC Act follows from the significance of the listed corporation to the financial well being of Australians. However, there are substantial criticisms of shareholder class actions which undermine both the compensation and deterrence rationales. These criticisms demonstrate the need for greater analysis to identify reforms to ensure that the class action fulfils the goals set for it.

16

Enforcement of Corporate and Securities Laws in India

The Arrival of the Class Action?

VIKRAMADITYA KHANNA

1 Introduction

Corporate governance in Asia has garnered a great deal of recent scholarly attention.[1] One topic that permeates discussions across countries is the enforcement of corporate and securities laws – with some countries

[1] The literature is vast, for a sampling, see e.g. Stijn Claessens and Joseph P.H. Fan, 'Corporate Governance in Asia: A Survey', 3 *International Review of Finance* 71–103 (2002); Donald C. Clarke, 'Corporate Governance in China: An Overview', 14 *China Economic Review* 494–507 (2003); Hideki Kanda, Kon-Sik Kim and Curtis J. Milhaupt, *Transforming Corporate Governance in East Asia*, (Routledge, 2008); Vikramaditya Khanna, 'Corporate Governance Ratings: One Score, Two Scores, or More?', 158 *University of Pennsylvania Law Review* 39–51 (2009); Vikramaditya Khanna, 'Corporate Governance in India: Past, Present & Future?', 1 *Jindal Global Law Review* 171–196 (2009); Vikramaditya Khanna and Umakanth Varottil, 'The Rarity of Derivative Actions in India: Reasons and Consequences' in *Derivative Actions in Major Asian Economies: Legislative Design and Legal Practice*, Harald Baum, Michael Ewing-Chow and Dan W. Puchniak (eds.), (Cambridge University Press, 2012); Vikramaditya Khanna and Umakanth Varottil, 'Board Independence in India: From Form to Function?' forthcoming in *Independent Directors in Asia: A Historical, Contextual and Comparative Approach*, Harald Baum, Souichirou Kozuka, Luke Nottage, and Dan W. Puchniak (eds.) (2016); Curtis J. Milhaupt and Benjamin L. Liebman, *Regulating the Visible Hand? The Institutional Implications of Chinese State Capitalism*, (Oxford University Press, 2015); Curtis J. Milhaupt and Wentong Zheng, 'Beyond Ownership: State Capitalism and the Chinese Firm', 103 *Georgetown Law Journal* 665–722 (2015); Organization for Economic Co-operation and Development (OECD), *White Paper on Corporate Governance in Asia* (2003); OECD, *Corporate Governance in Asia – Progress and Challenges* (2011); OECD, *Public Enforcement and Corporate Governance in Asia – Guidance and Good Practices* (2014); Daniel W. Puckniak, Harald Baum and Michael Ewing-Chow, *The Derivative Action in Asia: A Comparative and Functional Approach*, (Cambridge University Press, 2012). Umakanth Varottil, 'A Cautionary Tale of the Transplant Effect on Indian Corporate Governance', 21 *National Law School of India Review* 1–49 (2009).

relying primarily on public enforcement (i.e. enforcement by government) while others rely on some combination of public and private enforcement (i.e. enforcement by private shareholders). Further, understanding how enforcement is operationalised and its concomitant strengths and weaknesses enables us to better appreciate the actual corporate governance situation in many countries.[2] In light of this, the enforcement of corporate and securities laws in India is examined in this chapter with special attention paid to the recent reforms that allow for class actions, for the first time, under Section 245 of the Companies Act 2013 of India.

To explore this issue in greater depth, this chapter examines the likely value of private enforcement against the background of India's ownership structure and institutional context. This involves laying out what the pre-existing methods of enforcement are and how, if at all, the class action provision builds on their edifice. It also involves a general assessment of how successful this incarnation of the class action is likely to be in the Indian corporate governance space. The overall conclusion is that class actions are likely to be of limited value because of: (1) the glacial speed of the Indian courts, (2) the lack of contingency fees, (3) the limited availability of monetary remedies under the class action provision, and (4) the interaction between ownership structure in India – virtually all

[2] This literature is also voluminous, for a sampling see, e.g. John C. Coffee, Jr., 'Law and the Market: The Impact of Enforcement', 156 *University of Pennsylvania Law Review* 229–311 (2007); Robert Daines and Charles Jones, 'Mandatory Disclosure, Information Asymmetry and Liquidity: The Effect of the 1934 Act', *Draft* (2012); Dhammika Dharmapala and Vikramaditya Khanna, 'Corporate Governance, Enforcement, and Firm Value: Evidence from India', 29 *Journal of Law, Economics, and Organization* 1056–1084 (2013); Howell E. Jackson and Mark J. Roe, 'Public Enforcement of Securities Laws: Preliminary Evidence', 93 *Journal of Financial Economics* 207–238 (2009); Vikramaditya Khanna, 'Law Enforcement & Stock Market Development: Evidence from India', No. 97, Center for Democracy, Development, and the Rule of Law, Freeman Spogli Institute for International Studies, Stanford University (2009). Available at: http://cddrl.fsi.stanford.edu/publications/law_enforcement_and_stock_market_development_evidence_from_india; Vikramaditya Khanna, and Umakanth Varottil, 'The Rarity of Derivative Actions in India: Reasons and Consequences' in *Derivative Actions in Major Asian Economies: Legislative Design and Legal Practice*, Harald Baum, Michael Ewing-Chow and Dan W. Puchniak (eds.), (Cambridge University Press, 2012); Rafael La Porta, Florencio Lopez-de-Silanes and Andrei Shleifer. 'What Works in Securities Laws?', 61 *Journal of Finance* 1–32 (2006); Curtis J. Milhaupt and Katharina Pistor, *Law and Capitalism: What Corporate Crises Reveal About Legal Systems and Economic Development Around the World*, (University of Chicago Press, 2008); Mark J. Roe and Jordan I. Siegel, 'Political Instability: Its Effects on Financial Development, its Roots in the Severity of Economic Inequality', 39 *Journal of Comparative Economics* 279–309 (2011).

firms are controlled – and the absence of fiduciary duties owed by controllers to minority shareholders. The last point suggests that the class action in India is a procedural device that is only weakly tethered to an underlying duty.

This, however, does not mean that significant reform of enforcement should not be pursued in India. Indeed, quite the opposite – this chapter suggests some reforms that are likely to be more useful than the current class action regime in light of the institutional context and ownership structure in India. In particular, reliance on early warning signals provided by regulators and perhaps a version of arbitration that has been tried with measured success in other jurisdictions are worthy of greater consideration.

Section 2 begins by describing the enforcement terrain prior to the enactment of the Companies Act 2013. Public enforcement in India was, until fairly recently, plagued with lengthy delays in obtaining a remedy due to the well-known delays in the Indian judicial system. Indeed, public enforcement only began to move at a *relatively* faster speed in the last few years as the Securities and Exchange Board of India (SEBI) – the securities market regulator – started to take a more active role in examining the governance concerns animating the Indian business context (e.g. controller–minority conflicts). On the private enforcement side, derivative suits were not common (and took a long time to deliver any result), statutory oppression and mismanagement actions were also heavily delayed (perhaps around fifteen years), there was no easy way to aggregate shareholders claims (or to pay attorneys contingency fees)[3] and the remaining causes of action (e.g. contract or tort) had difficult-to-satisfy requirements and lengthy delays as well. Moreover, when SEBI became more active in enforcement, it operated to reduce the scope of private enforcement because of how courts interpreted certain statutory provisions on their jurisdiction once SEBI was involved. Overall, the state of both public and private enforcement in corporate governance in India prior to 2013 was quite ineffectual. This sets the stage for considering whether it might be valuable to enhance private enforcement in the Indian context and what measures might be considered (such as class actions).

[3] There are other ways to potentially aggregate claims (some discussed in this section) that could conceivably be useful in corporate cases. India allows 'public interest litigation' as well, but that is unlikely to be used in the corporate context. On PIL, see generally Surya Deva, 'Public Interest Litigation in India: A Critical Review', 28 *Civil Justice Quarterly* 19–40 (2009); S.P. Sathe, *Judicial Activism in India* (Oxford University Press, 2002).

Section 3 lays out the arguments usually put forward for why private enforcement may add value to a system relying primarily on public enforcement.[4] Two of the key reasons are that private enforcement may incentivise private individuals (i.e. shareholders) to come forward with their corporate governance related information because they stand to gain from it. Moreover, private enforcement – because it holds out the prospect of recovering money for investors – may also aid in deepening liquidity in a market. Both of these features may be particularly important in emerging markets, which frequently suffer from poor public enforcement and thinly traded markets.

Section 4 then examines some of the key features of the Indian context that are relevant for our inquiry. In particular, it discusses the ownership structure in India where virtually all firms are controlled – whether by a family business house, the state, a foreign multinational, or the founders of the firm (who do not belong to the same family or kinship group). This means the key agency problem is not the separation of ownership and control per se, but rather the conflict between the controller and the minority shareholders which should then in turn animate much of the discussion in the Indian context. Second, the other key feature of the Indian landscape relates to the legal system – very long delays in addressing commercial and civil matters and the absence of a contingency fee system (often thought to be valuable in the class action context). This suggests that reliance on timely judicial resolution of corporate governance disputes in India may not be realistic in the current environment.

Section 5 examines reforms that might enhance private enforcement. Section 5.1 starts with the class action provision (Section 245 of the Companies Act 2013) and examines how its structure, the absence of contingency fees, and the absence of fiduciary duties owed by a controller to minorities undermines the value of such an action. Investors may then need to rely on other methods to assuage their governance concerns such as reputation, large holdings, cross holdings, and so forth. Section 5.2 explores some alternatives to class actions that might prove to be useful supplements. Given the institutional conditions and ownership structure

[4] See William Landes and Richard A. Posner, 'The Private Enforcement of Law', 4 *Journal of Legal Studies* 1–46 (1975); Stephen J. Choi and Adam C. Pritchard, *Securities Regulation: Cases and Materials*, 4th ed., (Foundation Press, 2015); Vikramaditya Khanna, 'Law Enforcement & Stock Market Development: Evidence from India'; and George Akerlof, 'The Market for 'Lemons': Quality Uncertainty and the Market Mechanism', 84 *Quarterly Journal of Economics* 488–500 (1970).

in India, it would appear that reliance on non-judicial methods of dispute resolution is going to be important (e.g. arbitration). Moreover, with a respected and more active regulator in the mix (i.e. SEBI) perhaps greater reliance on it as an enforcer or facilitator of enforcement (e.g. through early warning signals) might be very useful.

Section 6 concludes with comments on how even though the changes suggested here may be useful, one should also inquire more deeply into how investors are currently protecting their interests in Indian firms. This is important because when devising enforcement structures and systems, it will be useful to acquaint oneself with the existing structures to examine how they may also prove useful for enhancing investor protection and corporate governance in India.

2 Pre-2013 Enforcement

It is generally well understood that law and enforcement are important for the growth of stock markets. This is because investors are more likely to invest, all else equal, in firms based in jurisdictions that provide investors with some sense of protection so that they are more secure in investing in entities where they have limited control.[5] Investor protection laws (e.g. corporate and securities laws) and their enforcement are ways in which some measure of security may be obtained (as are other sorts of private ordering mechanisms (reputation, reliable intermediaries)).[6]

Prior research has indicated that enforcement of the law is important in a number of spheres ranging from signalling government attitudes to governance issues,[7] providing assurances to investors on the credibility of anti-expropriation measures and firm disclosures,[8] and letting investors know that their concerns can be addressed in some manner.[9]

[5] Daines and Jones, 'Mandatory Disclosure, Information Asymmetry and Liquidity'; Jackson and Roe, 'Public Enforcement of Securities Laws'; Khanna, 'Law Enforcement & Stock Market Development'; La Porta et al., 'What Works in Securities Laws?'.

[6] John C. Coffee, Jr., 'The Rise of Dispersed Ownership: The Roles of Law and the State in the Separation of Ownership and Control', 111 *Yale Law Journal* 1–82 (2001).

[7] Milhaupt and Pistor, *Law and Capitalism*.

[8] La Porta et al., 'What Works in Securities Laws?'; Daines and Jones, 'Mandatory Disclosure, Information Asymmetry and Liquidity'.

[9] Coffee, 'Law and the Market'; Jackson and Roe, 'Public Enforcement of Securities Laws'; Khanna, 'Law Enforcement & Stock Market Development'; Roe and Siegel, 'Political Instability'. For a broader discussion of how these factors interact in the development of active stock markets in India, see Khanna, 'Law Enforcement & Stock Market Development'. For a discussion of important conceptual issues related to corporate law, see Reinier H. Kraakman, Paul Davies, Henry Hansmann, Gerhard Hertig, Klaus Hopt,

In light of this, examining the various kinds of enforcement options available in India becomes critical. This part engages in that inquiry by dividing the discussion into two parts – Section 2.1 addresses public enforcement in India and Section 2.2 discusses private enforcement in India before 2013.

2.1 Public Enforcement of Corporate and Securities Laws in India

Enforcement of corporate and securities laws by the government occurs in multiple ways in India. The two primary methods are enforcement by the securities market regulator – the Securities and Exchange Board of India (SEBI) – and enforcement via the Ministry of Company Affairs and the Registrar of Companies. This is supplemented by occasional reliance on the criminal law.[10]

2.1.1 Securities and Exchange Board of India

SEBI has a broad mandate – to protect 'the interest of investors or orderly development of securities markets'[11] – but for the purposes of this chapter our discussion is limited to its power to impose penalties, grant other remedies (e.g. delisting), and initiate criminal prosecution for violations related to corporate governance requirements under the Securities and Contracts (Regulation) Act 1956 (SCRA), the Securities and Exchange Board of India Act 1992 (SEBI Act), and any rules and regulations promulgated thereunder. SEBI's jurisdiction includes listed firms and their directors, officers, or controlling shareholders, and it has developed a reputation over the years for moving matters rather expeditiously to resolution.[12]

Hideki Kanda, and Edward Rock, *The Anatomy of Corporate Law: A Comparative and Functional Approach*, 2nd ed., (Oxford University Press, 2009).

[10] One might treat stock exchange enforcement as a form of quasi-public or quasi-private enforcement (see Paul G. Mahoney, 'The Exchange as Regulator', 83 *Virginia Law Review* 1453–1500 (1997) and Adam C. Pritchard, 'Self-Regulation and Securities Markets', 26 *Regulation* 32–39 (2003)), but in India stock exchange listing requirements are often enforced by SEBI.

[11] Securities and Exchange Board of India Act 1992, Section 11B.

[12] G. Sabarinathan, 'Securities and Exchange Board of India and the Regulation of Indian Securities Market', Working Paper No 2010-06-309, Unpublished working paper, Indian Institute of Management, Bangalore (2010); Ajit Dayanandan, Sarat Malik and Sneha Nautiyal, 'Effectiveness of SEBI's Complaints Redress Systems (SCORES) in India' (2015), available at: www.sebi.gov.in/cms/sebi_data/DRG_Study/DRG_II_Scores_150920. Praise for SEBI has not been uniform, especially recently – see Dev Chatterjee, 'GIFT to create regulatory crisis for RBI, SEBI: Mistry', *Business Standard*, 23 February

The primary corporate governance provision is Clause 49, promulgated by SEBI in 2000, which bears substantial similarities to the OECD's best practices from around that time.[13] Clause 49 is a mandatory part of the Stock Exchange Listing Agreement, and violations of it can result in SEBI imposing large financial and criminal penalties on firms and directors under Section 23E of the SCRA (1956).[14]

In spite of this, active enforcement in this area has taken some time to get started. Although it was fairly well known that many firms were not in compliance with Clause 49's requirements,[15] SEBI only started investigating violations in September 2007 (SEBI Press Release, 2007) – seven years after Clause 49 came into operation – and to date no sanctions have been imposed.[16]

There are, of course, other regulations that are of import, such as the prohibition of insider trading (and unfair trading), the 'takeover' regulations (relevant in share acquisition cases), and regulation on the failure of firms to address grievances by investors[17] where SEBI enforcement has been more active. However, the issues addressed in these regulations are not at the core of governance concerns in India.[18] Nonetheless, proof that SEBI can be an active enforcer in some areas holds out hope that it could also be an important player in the governance context. Indeed, the increasing breadth of SEBI's powers and its willingness to use certain remedies makes approaching SEBI a popular course of action for investors.[19]

2016, www.business-standard.com/article/economy-policy/gift-to-create-regulatory-crisis-for-rbi-sebi-mistry-116022200637_1.html.

13 Khanna, 'Corporate Governance in India'.

14 SEBI decisions may be appealed through various layers of the Indian administrative and judicial apparatus and all the way to the apex court – the Supreme Court of India.

15 N. Balasubramaniam, Bernard S. Black, and Vikramaditya Khanna, 'The Relation Between Firm-Level Corporate Governance and Market Value: A Study of India', 11 *Emerging Markets Review* 319–340 (2010).

16 A number of these actions were against government owned firms, and to date, only three of these proceedings have been resolved (leading to no sanctions) (SEBI Press Release. 2007. 'SEBI initiates adjudication proceedings against 20 companies for non-compliance of Clause 49 norms'. SEBI PR No.257/2007 (11 September, 2007). Available at: www.sebi.gov.in/Index.jsp?contentDisp=Section&sec_id=1).

17 See Section 23C of the SCRA (1956), Sections 12A, 15C and 15G of the SEBI Act (1992), Sections 3 and 4 of the Securities and Exchange Board of India (Prohibition of Fraudulent and Unfair Trade Practices Relating to Securities Market) Regulations 2003 and Securities and Exchange Board of India (Substantial Acquisition of Shares and Takeovers) Regulations, as amended in 2010 ('Takeover Code') Sections 45(5) and 45(6).

18 SEBI Annual Report. 2008–09, www.sebi.gov.in/annualreport/0809/annualrep08-09.pdf.

19 G. Sabarinathan, 'Securities and Exchange Board of India and the Regulation of Indian Securities Market; Ajit Dayanandan, Sarat Malik, and Sneha Nautiyal,

Having said this, it is noteworthy that private enforcement is usually precluded where SEBI is empowered to act or issue orders because the operation of sections 15Y and 20A of the SEBI Act prohibits civil courts from taking jurisdiction and entertaining a suit in such situations.[20] Thus, the enhancement in public enforcement comes at the cost of limiting private enforcement in this context.

2.1.2 Ministry of Company Affairs

Along with SEBI enforcing India's securities laws, the Ministry of Company Affairs (MCA) administers India's Companies Laws.[21] The MCA primarily investigates matters through its investigations divisions, regional directors, registrars of companies, and more recently the serious fraud office, and promulgates rules under certain statutes (e.g. the corporate social responsibility rules under the new Companies Act 2013). Although the MCA has broad investigatory authority, the cases it could bring are limited to only certain provisions (which are discussed shortly) and have been subject to significant delays leading to MCA's having a substantially weakened ability to play an important and timely enforcement role.

2.1.3 Reserve Bank of India

The Reserve Bank of India (RBI) has the power to regulate a number of things under the Foreign Exchange Management Act 2000 (FEMA 2000) that can have an impact on governance (e.g. acquisitions using foreign currency).[22] Although these might be important in specific cases, they are not generally considered core governance concerns and thus I refrain from discussing the RBI's enforcement role in any greater detail.

'Effectiveness of SEBI's Complaints Redress Systems (SCORES) in India'; Pankaj Vaish, 'Sebi: A Watchful and Efficient Regulator', LiveMint, 22 February 2016. Available at: www.livemint.com/Opinion/isaido0Fv2QYHTBkOCAj3M/Sebi-A-watchful-and-efficient-regulator.html; Anirudh Laskar and Vyas Mohan, 'Sebi's 25-Year Journey', LiveMint, 21 May 2013. Available at: www.livemint.com/Industry/xer1j7wBRbQH1UTOBVrRaL/Sebis-25year-journey.html.

20 Both the courts – in *Kesha Applicances P. Ltd* v. *Royal Holdings Services Ltd* (2006) 130 Comp. Cas. 227 (Bom.), para. 43 – and the Reserve Bank of India (see Report of Committee on Financial Sector (2009) at para. 4.3.4)) – have held that the civil jurisdiction of the courts is excluded in such instances.

21 Ministry of Company Affairs Annual Report (2005), www.mca.gov.in/MinistryWebsite/dca/report/annualreport2005.html.

22 For details, see www.rbi.org.in/scripts/Fema.aspx.

2.1.4 Criminal Liability

Governance concerns can rise to the level of criminal liability in India. In particular, the Indian Penal Code (IPC) makes it a crime to engage in a criminal breach of trust (Section 406) or cheating (Section 420).[23] These provisions have been used at times to police governance issues,[24] but they are generally not used with high frequency. Moreover, conviction rates are fairly low in India,[25] which is likely to weaken the deterrent effect of such laws.[26]

Based on this brief overview, the impression one gets is that, except for SEBI in the last few years, public enforcement in the area of corporate and securities laws in India has been quite lacklustre. That then leads to the discussion on private enforcement.

2.2 Private Enforcement

Although there are multiple bases for private civil enforcement in the corporate governance space in India (e.g. derivative suits, oppression and mismanagement, fraud and so forth) they all largely suffer from lengthy delays in the judicial process and unclear bases for liability. This creates a weak form of private enforcement. This section begins its discussion with derivative suits and then proceeds to examine the other forms of private civil enforcement.

2.2.1 Derivative Suits

Although derivative suits are available in India, they are quite rare for a number of reasons.[27] First and foremost is that India's derivative suit

[23] See *Tristar Consultants* v. *VcustomerServices*, AIR2007 Delhi 157; *Nanalal Zaver* v. *Bombay Life Assurance*, AIR 1950 SC 172.

[24] Vikramaditya Khanna and Shaun J. Mathew, 'The Role of Independent Directors in Controlled Firms in India: Preliminary Interview Evidence', 22 *National Law School of India Review* 35–66 (2010).

[25] Bibek Debroy and Aditya Singh, 'Justice Delivery in India: A Snap Shot of Problems and Reforms', in C. I. Herman (ed.), *Economic Developments in India* (Academic Foundation, 2009); Khanna, 'Judicial Reform in India'.

[26] India's criminal justice system tends to have low conviction rates but fairly relaxed arrest practices (i.e. it is fairly easy to arrest individuals even though convicting them is difficult – see Vikramaditya Khanna and Kartikey Mahajan, 'Anticipatory Bail in India: A Novel Way to Address Misuse of the Criminal Process', in Jacqueline Ross and Steven Thaman (eds.), *Research Handbook on Comparative Criminal Procedure* (Edward Elgar, 2016). This raises concerns for a number of reasons including creating a breeding ground for corruption; Khanna, 'Judicial Reform in India'; Khanna and Mahajan, 'Anticipatory Bail in India'.

[27] Khanna and Varottil, 'The Rarity of Derivative Actions in India'.

system is based on common law, not statute, and is subject to the limitations that come with that.[28] In particular, the rule in *Foss* v. *Harbottle* applies in full force in India.[29] The holding of this case (i.e. that a derivative action belongs to the company) means that if shareholders ratify the complained of activity then the suit becomes infructuous, as the company has effectively said it approves of the underlying activity. This presents an almost insurmountable hurdle for minority shareholders trying to sue controllers, because the controlling shareholder can usually manage to get a majority of the shareholders to ratify the complained about action (e.g. by voting the controller's shares).[30] Although there are exceptions to *Foss*, they are rather limited (e.g. suits based on violations of the charter or underlying legislation, such as *ultra vires* acts, illegal acts, and acts obtained without a required special resolution) or require the minority shareholder to meet difficult burdens (e.g. showing that the controller obtained some benefit at the expense of the *company* (not the minority per se)).[31]

In addition, minority shareholders would face challenges in identifying the underlying fiduciary duties that were violated. Controlling shareholders do not owe fiduciary duties to minorities in India, making a derivative suit on this basis a non-starter.[32] Further, although directors do owe duties to the company in India, these duties are determined by reference to the very thin case law present in India.[33] Moreover, courts can protect directors from liability under Section 633 of the Indian Companies Act 1956 if it is shown that the directors acted honestly and reasonably.[34] This, when combined with the weaker explication of duties and likely controller ratification, leaves the derivative suit mechanism in India with little power.

[28] Ibid. In an earlier study, a co-author and I could only find ten derivative suit cases that reached the High Courts or Supreme Court in India over the last sixty or so years, with only three being permitted to continue.

[29] (1843) 2 Har 461. Indian cases relying on *Foss* include *Nagappa Chettiar* v. *The Madras Race Club* (1949) 1 MLJ 662 (Mad) and *Nirad Amilal Mehta* v. *Genelec* Ltd (2008) 146 Comp. Cas. 481 (Bom).

[30] *See MacDougal* v. *Gardiner* (1875) 1 Ch. D 13.

[31] See *Nagappa*, above note 29; Arad Reisberg, *Derivative Actions and Corporate Governance*, (Oxford University Press. 2007).

[32] See *Rolta India Ltd.* v. *Venire Industries Ltd.* (2000) 100 Comp. Cas. 19 (Bom).

[33] For a more detailed discussion see above note 27.

[34] See above note 27. This is quite frequently used.

2.2.2 Order I, Rule 8, CPC 1908

Another route through which a shareholder may try to initiate private enforcement is through a 'representative' suit under Order I, Rule 8, of the Civil Procedure Code 1908, which states:

> One person may sue or defend on behalf of all in same interest.
> (1) Where there are numerous persons having the same interest in one suit,
> (a) one or more of such persons may, with the permission of the Court, sue or be sued, or may defend such suit, on behalf of, or for the benefit of, all persons so interested.

Generally, a representative suit under this order is thought to be similar to a motion for claim joinder – where similar suits are brought together in one proceeding to avoid duplicative litigation.[35] This is different than the standard background for a derivative suit – where the concern is that most shareholders would not bring a suit unless some form of claim aggregation was permissible. Indeed, the optics are a little stranger still because a derivative suit is permitted when the board is *unwilling* to initiate a suit (perhaps they are conflicted) and thus shareholders are permitted to bring suit, whereas in a representative suit the issue is that all litigants are *keen* to bring suit and for judicial economy these claims will be joined in one proceedings.

In spite of these differences, some courts seem to have allowed what looks like a derivative suit to be conducted as a representative suit with some unusual modifications. Generally, a representative suit requires the permission of the court and notice to be provided to all parties (at plaintiff's expense). The company is included as a defendant (pro forma) and in case the plaintiffs win then the recovery goes to the company (which is again the defendant).[36] Although this results in an awkward fit, it is somewhat understandable given the challenges in bringing a successful derivative suit in the Indian context. Nonetheless, only recently have courts in India begun to discuss the differences between derivative suits and representative actions.[37] In any case, the number of representative suits in the corporate context in India is still vanishingly thin.

2.2.3 Oppression and Mismanagement: Company Law Board

The Company Law Board (and its soon to be successor – the National Company Law Tribunal (NCLT)) is another player in the enforcement

35 Prasad, Mulla, *The Code of Civil Procedure*.

36 See *Jaideep Halwasiya* v. *Rasoi Ltd* (2009) 150 Comp. Cas. 1 (Cal).

37 See *Nagappa Chettiar*, above note 29.

landscape in India. The Company Law Board's (CLB's) governance mandate, for our purposes, is limited to oppression and mismanagement claims under Sections 397 to 399 of the Companies Act 1956 (now replaced by Sections 241 to 244 of the Companies Act 2013).[38] Under the 1956 Act the oppression and mismanagement action was not seen as being too important because the most common remedy available was an injunction and because the CLB, under section 633 of the 1956 Act, could protect directors from liability.[39] Finally, although the CLB may move somewhat faster than the civil courts on commercial matters, it has still been subject to lengthy delays so that any recovery probably has a substantially reduced real value to a litigant.[40]

2.2.4 Contract or Tort?

It is conceivable that a shareholder might initiate a fraud action (under Section 17 of the Indian Contract Act 1872), a misrepresentation claim (under Section 62 of the Companies Act 1956), or a Common Law tort claim for deceit. In all these cases the chances of recovery are slim (because their core elements are difficult to show in modern transactions) and because the endemic delays in litigation would make any judgment worth quite a bit less.

For example, under the tort for deceit the plaintiff must show a fraudulent misrepresentation related to a material fact and that the plaintiff received the shares directly from the company.[41] Thus, secondary market transactions would largely be outside the purview of this tort. Similarly, the cause of action under Section 17 of the Indian Contracts Act 1872 requires that the fraud have been conducted by a party to the transaction thereby exempting most secondary market transactions where the alleged fraud is by the issuing firm.[42]

2.2.5 Impact of Securities Laws on Private Enforcement

India's securities laws might provide for potential causes of action, but as noted earlier, if SEBI is empowered to act on a matter or issue an order

[38] For details, see Companies Amendment Act 2002; *Union of India* v. *R. Gandhi*, in the Supreme Court of India Civil Appeal No. 3067 of 2004 & Civil Appeal No. 3717 of 2005, 11 May 2010.

[39] A. Ramaiya, *Ramaiya's Guide to the Companies Act* (18th edition) (Nagpur: Lexis Nexis Butterworths Wadhwa India, 2014).

[40] Khanna and Varottil, *The Rarity of Derivative Actions in India.*

[41] Avtar Singh, *Company Law* (Eastern Book Company, India 2007).

[42] Avtar Singh, *Company Law.*

then the civil courts are not to entertain jurisdiction for private suits. Thus, as a practical matter these statutory and regulatory provisions do not generate any scope for private enforcement unless SEBI is not empowered to act on a matter – which is fairly rare.

This general overview of public and private enforcement in India leads one to conclude that India has limited public enforcement and almost no effective private enforcement of corporate and securities laws. Indeed, prior surveys of enforcement in India have suggested that it is quite weak.[43] Given these weak protections, one might expect that it would be difficult for dispersedly held firms to develop, and investors might then need to rely on other methods (taking larger stakes, relying on business and social norms) to secure their investment.[44]

This then leads to the key question animating this chapter: What steps can be taken that might enhance enforcement in India? The next two sections begin an inquiry into that question by examining the theoretical case for private enforcement and then examining how it might be operationalised in the Indian business and institutional context. Following that is a discussion of the class action mechanism described in the Companies Act 2013 and other potential enforcement reforms.

3 Potential Value of Private Civil Enforcement

For purposes of obtaining a more thorough understanding of private enforcement in India, this chapter assumes that public enforcement is available and then inquires how might private civil enforcement be a useful supplement.[45] This issue is pursued in two steps – first, examining how private civil enforcement is likely to enhance the availability of information on wrongdoing by incentivising private individuals to come

[43] CII Report (2009), 'Corporate Governance: Recommendations for Voluntary Adoption'. *Report of the CII Task Force on Corporate Governance*, www.mca.gov.in/Ministry/latestnews/Draft_Report_NareshChandra_CII.pdf.; ICSI Report (2009), 'ICSI Recommendations to Strengthen Corporate Governance Framework'. *Institute of Company Secretaries of India*, www.mca.gov.in/Ministry/latestnews/ICSI_Recommendations_Book_8dec2009.pdf); KPMG Report (2008), '*The State of Corporate Governance in India: A Poll*', www.kpmg.com/IN/en/ThoughtLedership/The%20State%20of%20Corporate%20Governance%20in%20India%202008.pdf.

[44] Coffee, 'The Rise of Dispersed Ownership'; Mark J. Roe, *Strong Managers, Weak Owners: The Political Roots of American Corporate Finance* (Princeton University Press, 1996).

[45] For a discussion on public enforcement see A. Mitchell Polinsky and Steven M. Shavell. 'The Economic Theory of Public Enforcement of Law', 38 *Journal of Economic Literature* 45–76 (2000).

forward with their information, and second by examining how the potentiality of recovery for individual investors might aid in deepening the liquidity of stock markets.

3.1 Obtaining Enforcement Relevant Information

Individuals might possess information that is relevant to enforcement efforts (e.g. on wrongdoing) that government agents may not be able to easily access or assess.[46] An example might be when victims of wrongdoing have information about who harmed them and how that government agents would find either difficult or costly to obtain.

By providing these individuals with the prospect of monetary recovery (or the prospect of having the wrongdoer's behaviour adjudged negatively) we provide them with an incentive to bring their information to the attention of authorities thereby increasing the likelihood that the wrongdoer will be punished (and hence deterring her). There are of course other ways in which to incentivise private parties to bring information to light (e.g. bounties, whistleblower duties), but I limit my discussion to private civil enforcement for now.[47]

In the context of corporate governance one can easily see the value of private enforcement. There are likely to be many things related to fiduciary duties about which the putative victim is more likely to have information than the government. Similarly, a shareholder is likely to have a better understanding of the contractual and other relationships between the parties as compared to the government.

3.2 Liquidity Enhancing Features?

Another likely benefit of private enforcement is that by providing an avenue in which investors can obtain monetary remedies for governance wrongdoing, it reduces the downside risk faced by investors when

[46] Landes and Posner, 'The Private Enforcement of Law'.

[47] On bounties and whistleblowing see A. Mitchell Polinsky, 'Private versus Public Enforcement of Fines', 9 *Journal of Legal Studies* 105–127 (1980), Michael Rich, 'Prosecutorial Indiscretion: Encouraging the Department of Justice to Rein in Out of Control Qui Tam Litigation under the Civil False Claims Act', 76 *University of Cincinnati Law Review* 1233 (2008), David F. Engstrom, 'Whither Whistleblowing? Bounty Regimes, Regulatory Context, and the Challenge of Optimal Design', 15 *Theoretical Inquiries in Law* 605–633 (2014). For discussion on the closely associated notion of self-reporting, see Louis Kaplow and Steven Shavell, 'Optimal Law Enforcement with Self-Reporting of Behavior', 102 *Journal of Political Economy* 583–606 (1994).

investing and should attract more investors to the market (compared to if such recovery was unlikely or not timely and no insurance was available), thereby enhancing its liquidity.[48] Of course, the risk of governance wrongdoing or fraud is a risk that investors might also reduce via diversification and thus not require recovery to attract them to the market. Although certainly plausible for some risks, one must keep in mind that systemic risk associated with fraud (that affecting the market) cannot be easily diversified away. If a market is thought to have rampant fraud, then people are likely to simply stay away and that would hurt market development and capital formation.[49] Moreover, if diversification is difficult or costly then that too might hurt market development.[50] This leaves space for private enforcement to play a role in enhancing liquidity by reducing some of the downside risk investors might face.

In the context of India and other emerging markets, if a goal is to encourage the entry of individual investors at the retail level or even to attract them to invest via intermediaries (e.g. mutual funds) then the possibility of recovery for governance wrongdoing might well be an attractive option. India is estimated to have around two million retail investors,[51] but one must keep in mind that the population is over 1.2 billion. Moreover, foreign investors are quite likely to pay close attention to governance issues (as has been observed in the past), and attracting them may involve some measure of private enforcement.[52]

Of course, assessing the value of private enforcement in India will require some understanding of how it might fit within the business and institutional structures in India. It is to those issues that I now turn.

48 Choi and Pritchard, Securities Regulation: Cases and Materials; Khanna, 'Law Enforcement & Stock Market Development'.

49 Akerlof, 'The Market for "Lemons"'; Choi and Pritchard, *Securities Regulation: Cases and Materials.*

50 If there are very few publicly traded firms, then the prospect of diversification is similarly reduced.

51 Rahul Chhabra, Sankar De, Naveen R. Gondhi and Bhimasankaram Pochiraju, 'Is Zero Return a Natural Benchmark for Investors? An Investigation with Individual Trading Records' (20 January 2012). Available at SSRN: https://ssrn.com/abstract=1846474 or http://dx.doi.org/10.2139/ssrn.1846474; For further discussion see 'Indian Retail Investors Tend to Lose in Stock Markets: Study', *Economic Times*, 29 November 2012, available at http://articles.economictimes.indiatimes.com/2012-11-29/news/35433105_1_retail-investors-trade-data-study.

52 Vikramaditya Khanna and Roman Zyla, 'Survey Says. . .Corporate Governance Matters to Investors in Emerging Market Companies', *International Finance Corporation Publication*, World Bank Group 2012. Available at: www1.ifc.org/wps/wcm/connect/dbfd8b004afe7d69bcb6bdb94e6f4d75/IFC_EMI_Survey_web.pdf?MOD=AJPERES.

4 Indian Business and Institutional Context

India's business and institutional structures share some similarities with those in the US and Western Europe, but there are also important differences that will likely influence the desirable structure of enforcement for corporate and securities laws. In this section, I focus on two of the most prominent differences – ownership structure and institutional architecture (i.e. judicial and legal system).

4.1 Ownership Structure: Controlled Firms

India has, depending on how one counts, somewhere around 4,000 publicly traded firms on two major stock exchanges, Bombay Stock Exchange (BSE) and the National Stock Exchange (NSE). However, virtually all these firms are controlled firms. Some are controlled by family business houses (e.g. Birla, Ambani, Adani), some by the State (e.g. Oil and Natural Gas Corporation), some by foreign multinationals (e.g. Nestle India), and others by Indian founders who are neither family nor part of a kinship network (e.g. Infosys). There are few truly dispersedly held firms in India.[53]

This means that the predominant form of governance concerns in India are not the typical concerns between shareholders and management (seen in countries with more dispersedly held firms), but rather the conflict between controlling shareholders and minority shareholders.[54] This conflict raises standard concerns about expropriation of the minority rather than pure executive compensation, about freeze outs rather than hostile takeovers and so forth. In light of this overarching governance concern, what value might private enforcement provide?

First, it seems likely that minority shareholders in a controlled firm (especially larger minority shareholders) are likely to have enforcement relevant information. This is for a number of reasons. First, like shareholders in a dispersedly held firm, minorities are the likely victims of governance wrongdoing and are likely to have useful information about it. Second, some firms may have minority shareholders who are not entirely dispersed – that is, some minorities may have sizeable stakes in

[53] George S. Geis, 'Can Independent Blockholding Really Play Much of a Role in Indian Corporate Governance?' 3 *Corporate Governance Law Review* 283 (2007); Tarun Khanna and Yishay Yafeh, 'Business Groups in Emerging Markets: Paragons or Parasites?', 45 *Journal of Economic Literature* 331–372 (2007).

[54] Lucian A. Bebchuk and Assaf Hamdani, 'The Elusive Quest for Global Governance Standards', 157 *University of Pennsylvania Law Review* 1263–1317 (2009). Khanna, 'Corporate Governance Ratings'; Kraakman et al., *The Anatomy of Corporate Law.*

the firms. These larger positions provide them with the incentive to get informed about the firm – something seen less often in dispersedly held firms – which in turn suggests they should often have enforcement relevant information (because they are monitoring). Moreover, minorities may find it easier to know who to monitor in a controlled firm (i.e. the controller) rather than in a dispersedly held firm (e.g. management, the board, large institutional shareholders, and so forth). This may be even more likely if the minority has other connections with the controller (e.g. belonging to similar business communities (or caste), having intermingled business interests).

Second, even though minority shareholders may have enforcement relevant information, it is likely that their access to and use of it may vary across the different types of controlling structures – whether by controller type (e.g. family business, state-owned) or by how control is maintained (e.g. pyramids, cross-holdings).[55] For reasons of expositional brevity, I do not discuss these variations here, but note it is an interesting area for future research.

Finally, one expects that the potential liquidity enhancing features of private enforcement are likely to be useful in controlled firms in India too. This is especially likely if the government is trying to increase market liquidity (which India's government seems keen to do) by attracting dispersed investors and foreign investors who may not have the other methods of policing governance that larger minorities may possess (e.g. interlinked business, similar business and social networks, and so forth).[56]

In spite of all these benefits of private enforcement, one should be cognizant of the limitations on private enforcement in the Indian business context. The importance of business families, founders, and powerful bureaucrats running most major firms in India may create an atmosphere of reticence in challenging these controllers in open court and may lead to a preference for less visible challenges or for resolutions that keep disputes out of the public view.[57]

4.2 *Institutional Architecture*

Another key issue in assessing the likely value of private enforcement is appreciating the institutional architecture within which it might be

[55] Khanna and Varottil, 'Board Independence in India'.
[56] See Coffee, 'The Rise of Dispersed Ownership'.
[57] Khanna and Varottil, *The Rarity of Derivative Actions in India.*

utilised. This requires us to gain a deeper understanding of the current reality of India's judicial and legal system.

One of the well-known concerns associated with India's legal system is the lengthy delays faced by litigants. Indeed, many judgments occur so long after the alleged wrong that they hardly provide any real recovery.[58] Although there are specialist courts for addressing corporate law matters in India (first the CLB and then the soon to be formed NCLT), they have thus far also suffered from lengthy delays. Moreover, plaintiffs bringing private cases in India must bear court fees (i.e. fees for bringing a civil suit seeking recovery), and these fees can be substantial and may reduce the attractiveness of suit.[59] This makes reliance on private enforcement in the standard court system less attractive as a means to either obtain enforcement relevant information, enhance liquidity, or police governance wrongdoing.

However, even if delays were not endemic, there are other concerns. In particular, it is key to understand who the likely litigants are and what their incentives might be. In the Indian context (as noted earlier), these are primarily minority shareholders in controlled firms. If the minority is composed of shareholders with sizeable stakes in the firm (e.g. 5 per cent), then the minority may consider it worthwhile to bear the costs of bringing suit (including getting informed) and that may make private enforcement more plausible, holding all else equal. However, these larger minorities may also have other extra-legal methods of influencing the controlling shareholder in India making private suits less likely or less likely to lead to a judgment (as opposed to settlement).[60]

On the other hand, if the minority is composed of small dispersed shareholders, then they are unlikely to consider it worthwhile to bear the costs of bringing an individual suit. Simply put, if most minority shareholders own $100 worth of shares, then none of them are likely to hire attorneys (who charge more than $100 for such suits) to initiate litigation. This situation is one in which a typical class action with a

[58] Law Commission of India Report. 2008. *Reforms in the Judiciary: Some Suggestions.* Report No. 230. Law Commission of India; National Mission for Delivery of Justice and Legal Reform. 2009. 'Towards Timely Delivery of Justice to All: A Blueprint for Judicial Reforms'. Available at: http://lawmin.nic.in/doj/justice/National_Legal_Mission-7NOV2009.pdf

[59] Ibid. In addition to the certainty of paying court fees, if the plaintiff loses, he may have to pay some part of the defendant's legal costs (India follows the English rule on legal costs – 'loser pays'), which may be a substantial cost for some retain investors.

[60] See Coffee, 'The Rise of Dispersed Ownership'; and Symposium on Norms and Corporate Law (2001).

contingency fee structure might prove useful. However, in India contingency fees are not permitted.[61]

Finally, even if minority shareholders were willing to sue and the courts provided more timely decisions, private enforcement still faces another hurdle in India – lack of clarity on what the underlying wrong is. Given that most firms in India are controlled, the minority would need some action against the controller (or an action the controller cannot dismiss easily). India does not, at present, provide for fiduciary duties owed by the controller to the minority. Absent the development of such fiduciary duties, any suits against controllers would need to overcome this issue.

In light of the business structures and institutional conditions in India, it seems that private enforcement in the corporate governance space is likely to be quite quixotic. However, that does not mean that reforms might not improve upon the situation.

5 Reform Alternatives?

Many reform efforts have been pursued in India, but with little substantial effect. In this part, I explore the most recent reform effort – promulgating a class action mechanism for corporate law issues – along with other reform efforts that might be pursued. First I explore the attempts to create a class action in India, and then I discuss alternatives to the class action that may generate greater net benefits in India.

5.1 Class Actions Under the Companies Act 2013

Against this background of fairly limited enforcement, the Companies Act 2013 introduced the class action via Section 245, which is reproduced below:

Section 245. Class Action

(1) Such number of member or members, depositor or depositors or any class of them, as the case may be, as are indicated in sub-section (2) may, if they are of the opinion that the management or conduct of the affairs of the company are being conducted in a manner prejudicial to the interests of the company or its members or depositors, file an application before the Tribunal on behalf of the members or depositors for seeking all or any of the following orders, namely: –

[61] See Bar Council of India Rules (Part VI, Chapter II, Section II, Rule 20).

(*a*) to restrain the company from committing an act which is *ultra vires* the articles or memorandum of the company;

(*b*) to restrain the company from committing breach of any provision of the company's memorandum or articles;

(*c*) to declare a resolution altering the memorandum or articles of the company as void if the resolution was passed by suppression of material facts or obtained by mis-statement to the members or depositors;

(*d*) to restrain the company and its directors from acting on such resolution;

(*e*) to restrain the company from doing an act which is contrary to the provisions of this Act or any other law for the time being in force;

(*f*) to restrain the company from taking action contrary to any resolution passed by the members;

(*g*) to claim damages or compensation or demand any other suitable action from or against—

(*i*) the company or its directors for any fraudulent, unlawful or wrongful act or omission or conduct or any likely act or omission or conduct on its or their part;

(*ii*) the auditor including audit firm of the company for any improper or misleading statement of particulars made in his audit report or for any fraudulent, unlawful or wrongful act or conduct; or

(*iii*) any expert or advisor or consultant or any other person for any incorrect or misleading statement made to the company or for any fraudulent, unlawful or wrongful act or conduct or any likely act or conduct on his part;

(*h*) to seek any other remedy as the Tribunal may deem fit.

(2) Where the members or depositors seek any damages or compensation or demand any other suitable action from or against an audit firm, the liability shall be of the firm as well as of each partner who was involved in making any improper or misleading statement of particulars in the audit report or who acted in a fraudulent, unlawful or wrongful manner.

(3) (*i*) The requisite number of members provided in sub-section (1) shall be as under: –

(*a*) in the case of a company having a share capital, not less than one hundred members of the company or not less than such percentage of the total number of its members as may be prescribed, whichever is less, or any member or members holding not less than such percentage of the issued share capital of the company as may be prescribed, subject to the condition that the applicant or applicants has or have paid all calls and other sums due on his or their shares;

(*b*) in the case of a company not having a share capital, not less than one-fifth of the total number of its members.

(*ii*) The requisite number of depositors provided in sub-section (1) shall not be less than one hundred depositors or not less than such percentage of the total number of depositors as may be prescribed, whichever is less, or any depositor or depositors to whom the company owes such percentage of total deposits of the company as may be prescribed.

(4) In considering an application under sub-section (1), the Tribunal shall take into account, in particular—

(*a*) whether the member or depositor is acting in good faith in making the application for seeking an order;

(*b*) any evidence before it as to the involvement of any person other than directors or officers of the company on any of the matters provided in clauses (*a*) to (*f*) of sub-section (1);

(*c*) whether the cause of action is one which the member or depositor could pursue in his own right rather than through an order under this section;

(*d*) any evidence before it as to the views of the members or depositors of the company who have no personal interest, direct or indirect, in the matter being proceeded under this section;

(*e*) where the cause of action is an act or omission that is yet to occur, whether the act or omission could be, and in the circumstances would be likely to be—

(*i*) authorised by the company before it occurs; or

(*ii*) ratified by the company after it occurs;

(*f*) where the cause of action is an act or omission that has already occurred, whether the act or omission could be, and in the circumstances would be likely to be, ratified by the company.

(5) If an application filed under sub-section (1) is admitted, then the Tribunal shall have regard to the following, namely: –

(*a*) public notice shall be served on admission of the application to all the members or depositors of the class in such manner as may be prescribed;

(*b*) all similar applications prevalent in any jurisdiction should be consolidated into a single application and the class members or depositors should be allowed to choose the lead applicant and in the event the members or depositors of the class are unable to come to a consensus, the Tribunal shall have the power to appoint a lead applicant, who shall be in charge of the proceedings from the applicant's side;

(*c*) two class action applications for the same cause of action shall not be allowed;

(*d*) the cost or expenses connected with the application for class action shall be defrayed by the company or any other person responsible for any oppressive act.

(6) Any order passed by the Tribunal shall be binding on the company and all its members, depositors and auditor including audit firm or expert or consultant or advisor or any other person associated with the company.

(7) Any company which fails to comply with an order passed by the Tribunal under this section shall be punishable with fine which shall not be less than five lakh rupees but which may extend to twenty-five lakh rupees and every officer of the company who is in default shall be punishable with imprisonment for a term which may extend to three years and with fine which shall not be less than twenty-five thousand rupees but which may extend to one lakh rupees.

(8) Where any application filed before the Tribunal is found to be frivolous or vexatious, it shall, for reasons to be recorded in writing, reject the application and make an order that the applicant shall pay to the opposite party such cost, not exceeding one lakh rupees, as may be specified in the order.

(9) Nothing contained in this section shall apply to a banking company.

(10) Subject to the compliance of this section, an application may be filed or any other action may be taken under this section by any person, group of persons or any association of persons representing the persons affected by any act or omission, specified in sub-section (1).

Section 245 is largely concerned with restraining the behaviour of the firm and its members rather than compensating shareholders (Sections 245(1)(a) to (f)). The only provisions allowing for monetary remedies are Section 245(1)(g) and (h). However, even here the remedies might be viewed as limited, given that none of the provisions explicitly mention the controller. For example, Section 245(1)(g) allows for monetary remedies primarily against the firm, its directors or advisors for fraudulent, illegal or wrongful behaviour. It is conceivable that controllers might be included in the 'any other person' language in Section 245(1)(g)(iii), but given the general tenor of the Section and the context of this language it does not appear that controllers are the targets. Moreover, because controllers do not owe fiduciary duties to minority shareholders in India, it is not clear whether their behaviour would trigger a class action under Section 245. Indeed, the focus on whether the company has ratified the complained of activity (Sections 245(4)(e) and (f)) and the provision requiring the company to pay for plaintiff's legal expenses (Section 245(5)(d)) appear poorly suited for a typical suit brought by a minority shareholder against a controller and instead seem more suited to a typical derivative action.

However, we are left to speculate on how far Section 245 might go because, as of this writing, no cases have been initiated under Section 245.

This is largely due to the fact that the NCLT has not yet been formally set up. Consequently, it is unclear how the class action mechanism will be operationalised, but given the absence of fiduciary duties owed by the controller and the language in Section 245, it seems unlikely that it would be a very effective tool for generating monetary recoveries to minority shareholders. Indeed, there is no provision permitting contingency fees, which makes Section 245 less appealing for smaller minority shareholders.

Even if the current version of a class action does not provide much solace to shareholders, one could consider alternative reforms. Many might be discussed (e.g. bounties, stock exchange enforcement),[62] but this chapter discusses two reforms that may pay bigger dividends than the current class action regime.

5.2 *Regulatory Early Warning System*

Prior research has suggested that ex ante measures may be particularly valuable in contexts where large harm may be generated from wrongdoing (e.g. the Satyam Fraud).[63] One such measure might be a regulatory early warning system where regulators (such as SEBI) put out information on factors that might be correlated with greater wrongdoing risk so that investors are aware of this and can adjust their behaviour (or initiate litigation and so forth). This may be particularly valuable where wrongdoing is difficult to detect (even with private enforcement) because when regulators provide information on factors correlated with wrongdoing, that may trigger responses by investors and others that might reduce the potential harm or prevent further wrongdoing, if any.

Of course, for such an early warning system to be effective, one must be able to identify some factors correlated with wrongdoing and the current surveillance systems should be able to detect these signs. Although such a list is difficult to provide with finality, below are a list of factors that

62 On bounties, see Polinsky, 'Private versus Public Enforcement of Fines'; Rich, 'Prosecutorial Indiscretion', 1233; and Engstrom, 'Whither Whistleblowing?'; and on stock exchange enforcement, see Pritchard, 'Self-Regulation and Securities Markets'; Mahoney, 'The Exchange as Regulator'; and Stephen Craig Pirrong, 'The Self-Regulation of Commodity Exchanges: The Case of Market Manipulation', 38 *Journal of Law and Economics* 141–206 (1995). Note that bounties have an additional advantage in that even non-shareholders may receive the bounty, providing them with an incentive to bring forth relevant information. This of course comes with costs as noted in the literature on bounties.

63 See Steven Shavell, 'Liability for Harm Versus Regulation of Safety', 13 *Journal of Legal Studies* 357–374 (1984) for more discussion of regulation and liability.

Table 16.1 *Proposed list of possible early warning signals*

Early Warning Signals
If some directors (especially independent directors) resign unexpectedly.
If there are recent off-balance-sheet transactions.
If there was a decision to withdraw an offering of stock or debt.
Any restatement of financial or other important results.
Related-party transactions that exceed some threshold (e.g. 5 per cent of net profit).
If the controller has been selling down her stake in the firm in an unanticipated manner.

would seem useful to someone concerned about potential wrongdoing at a firm (some of these factors arise from studies discussed in previous writings by Khanna).[64]

For an early warning signal system to be effective, we must believe that investors will rely on that system in deciding where to invest or whether to sue. There is little evidence in India about whether either is likely, but in other countries where disclosure based systems have been tried (e.g. 'comply-or-explain' rules in parts of Europe), they have met with some measured success.[65] It is conceivable that if there is sufficient analyst coverage, something similar may occur in India.

5.3 *Arbitration*

Another potential reform is that firms that are publicly traded be allowed (or perhaps required) to have shareholders pursue corporate governance claims in arbitral proceedings rather than in judicial or tribunal proceedings. This has advantages in terms of obtaining expertise in decision making as well as procedural efficiency and speed.[66] Such an approach

[64] Khanna, 'Judicial Reform in India'; Khanna, 'Law Enforcement & Stock Market Development'.

[65] Sridhar Arcot, Valentina Bruno and Antoine Faure-Grimaud, 'Corporate Governance in the UK: Is the Comply or Explain Approach Working?', 30 *International Review of Law and Economics* 193–201 (2010).

[66] Roger S. Haydock, 'Civil Justice and Dispute Resolution in the Twenty-First Century: Mediation and Arbitration Now and for the Future', 27 *William Mitchell Law Review* 745–778 (2000–2001); Keith N. Hylton, 'Agreements to Waive or to Arbitrate Legal Claims: An Economic Analysis', 8 *Supreme Court Economic Review* 209–263 (2000); Steven Shavell, 'Alternative Dispute Resolution: An Economic Analysis', 24 *Journal of Legal Studies* 1–28 (1995).

has been tried in some other jurisdictions. For example, arbitration provisions are available in Brazil for firms listed on the Novo Mercado,[67] and in China for firms domiciled in China issuing stock overseas.[68] Moreover, in India too there are firms that offer arbitration as a method of resolving disputes with shareholders.[69] Under a functioning arbitration system, one expects that the enforcement relevant information and liquidity enhancing effects of private enforcement would both be present because of the prospect of monetary recovery for those providing relevant information (who are most likely to be shareholders). Although conclusive results of these experiments in China and Brazil are not yet available, there is little evidence that arbitration has made the situation any worse than the status quo ante.

6 Conclusion

Enforcement of corporate and securities laws is generally acknowledged to be important to the growth of capital markets, and this may be especially so in emerging markets. In the Indian context, the pre-existing state of both public and private enforcement of corporate and securities laws was fairly weak, and thus attempts to revamp the area via the class action device in Section 245 of the Companies Act 2013 were greeted with some enthusiasm. Indeed, there are good theoretical reasons to think that private enforcement could be beneficial in India, although there may be some limitations in light of India's institutional and business climate.

However, the version of class actions drawn by Section 245 seems constrained in its likely effectiveness. Monetary remedies do not seem to be the primary aim of the provision, and it is not accompanied by other changes that would make it more likely to work in the Indian context. In particular, the prohibition on contingency fees and the absence of

[67] Ira M. Millstein, G. N. Bajpai, Erik Berglöf, and Stijn Claessens, 'Non-Traditional Modes of Enforcement' in *Enforcement and Corporate Governance: Three Views*, 1–17 (2005).

[68] Nicholas Calcina Howson, 'The Doctrine that Dared Not Speak its Name: Anglo-American Fiduciary Duties in China's 2005 Company Law and Case Law Intimations of Prior Convergence', in Hideki Kanda, Kon-Sik Kim, and Curtis Milhaupt, eds., *Transforming Corporate Governance in East Asia* 193–254 (Routledge, 2008).

[69] Balasubramanian, Black, and Khanna, 'The Relation Between Firm-Level Corporate Governance and Market Value'; Francis G.X. Pileggi, 'New Rules Allow for 'Lightning Fast' Adjudication of New Cases Filed in Delaware Court of Chancery'. Litigation Department Alert, Fox Rothschild LLP. (2010). Available at: www.foxrothschild.com/newspubs/newspubsArticle.aspx?id=13596.

fiduciary duties owed by controllers to minorities would appear to hamstring the effectiveness of the class action provision in India. Thus, it appears that the opportunity to enhance investor protection in India is unlikely to be much furthered by Section 245.

Nonetheless, there may be some measures that can be taken that would be beneficial in the Indian context, such as regulatory early warning signals and the increased use of arbitration to resolve shareholder disputes. Early warning signals may help to trigger shareholder monitoring and avert large-scale harms and arbitration helps to address a perennial problem in the Indian legal system – the lengthy delays in the courts and tribunals. Some mix of these measures appear more likely to benefit investors interested in the Indian markets than the current version of class actions exemplified by Section 245.

17

Enforcement of Hong Kong's Securities Law

The Underpinning Philosophy

ALEXA LAM

1 Introduction

Enforcement of the securities law is an important function in serving the communities we live in. Demand for enforcement is not always matched by an increase in resources. In Hong Kong, the securities regulator – the Securities and Futures Commission (SFC), increased its resourcing in terms of headcount by 40 per cent since 2007. But the regulator's workload also increased. Their investigation workload increased by 240 per cent, and litigation work increased by over 500 per cent. And just for the year 2014, their investigation caseload increased by over 50 per cent. This is certainly an exponential increase in demand for enforcement services.

In addition, there are also limitations to what the law by itself can achieve. Existing laws and regulation do not always provide the perfect solutions and tools that policy makers and regulators desire. The regulator simply cannot afford to wait for the perfect powers to be available, if they ever will be, before it does the job it is expected to do. Legal reform and new legislation take time and resources, not to mention the challenges of overcoming the political hurdles and getting the requisite support to pass a bill at the Hong Kong legislative body.

Despite the challenges, this must be right, because there is no guarantee that even an all-powerful regulator with far-reaching powers can achieve its mandate or be able to avoid unintended consequences. In this chapter, I will explore my belief that it is less of a question of how much power you have, and more about how you use what you have to achieve a fair and balanced result of protecting investors and market integrity.

The regulator should have a very clear idea of what exactly it wishes to achieve based on a good understanding of the industry it regulates. The technical challenge for enforcement is how it can continue to be effective without getting bogged down when the workload outstrips its resourcing capacity and how to avoid delays that cause its work to simply be out of time and thus irrelevant. The trite saying that justice delayed is justice denied continues to ring true.

In my view, much can be achieved within the legal confines of the regulatory framework with the judicious use of strategic thinking, creativity and determination. Hong Kong has quite effectively put this into practice. This is my main takeaway.

2 SFC's Enforcement Programme

The first priority of the SFC's enforcement programme is no different from other law enforcement agencies, i.e. the deterrence of crime and misconduct. The SFC does so by bringing criminal prosecution in the Magistrates courts – the junior courts in Hong Kong and proceedings in the Market Misconduct Tribunal against wrongdoers – and taking disciplinary actions against regulated intermediaries. Criminal cases that are required to be brought in the higher courts, i.e. District Courts and the Court of First Instance, are brought by the Department of Justice, to which the SFC refers cases that it has investigated.

While deterrent sanctions are extremely important, they are insufficient by themselves. The SFC firmly believes that the wrongdoer, rather than the victim or the public, ought to pay the costs of the rectification. There is no point in having billion-dollar fines going to the government coffers when the victims themselves are not being remedied. Hence, the SFC has put an equally strong emphasis on dealing with the *consequences* of the misconduct, by this it means providing remedial relief to those hurt by such conduct. The purpose is to help victims and restore investors' confidence in Hong Kong's markets. The SFC's remediation policy holds wrongdoers accountable for their misdeeds and requires them to remediate investors for the loss and damages that they have caused.

Remedial action is a better way to recognise the moral culpability of misconduct.

In the United States, they have class action (and contingency fee is allowed to make such actions feasible). This certainly is an effective tool, as it gives investors a real weapon. However, either the regulator, or the investors, will have to take steps to freeze assets of perpetuators in time, or there may be no money left to compensate investors. Taking swift action to freeze assets is precisely at the core of how Hong Kong's philosophy of remedial protection works. It is also noted that the China Securities Regulatory Commission (CSRC) is very interested in this approach and has sent teams to Hong Kong to learn how it works.

The Securities and Futures Ordinance (SFO) provides tools that SFC uses to pursue remedial action. In particular, I will examine the tools provided under Sections 213 and 201 of the SFO in order for the SFC to provide remedial relief to the victims of market and/or intermediaries misconduct.

3 Section 213 SFO Proceedings

A very effective tool is provided in Section 213 of the SFO. This section is one of the provisions that the SFC has used successfully and with increasing frequency in recent years to obtain remedial relief for the victims of financial fraud and misconduct.

The SFC has been using this section to say that, where a person has contravened the SFO, the court should make an order or take steps to put the parties back where they were before the contravention occurred, i.e. to effectively wind back time as closely as possible, although this cannot be perfect. So on the application of the SFC, the court may make, *inter alia*, the following orders:

(a) a restraining or prohibition order with respect to the wrongdoing or property; or
(b) an order requiring the person to take such steps as the Court may direct, including steps to restore the parties to a transaction to the position in which they were before the transaction was entered into, effectively, rescission under contract law.

Section 213 is a carry-forward from the old law. When we carried out securities law reform in 2000 to 2002 by completely rewriting the law, the relevant provision in the old law was improved and enlarged. We envisaged that the new provision, Section 213, could be used to allow the regulator to ask the courts for a wide range of remedial and protective orders for market and investor protection. When the SFC started to aggressively use Section 213, there were many debates on its application and scope. Essentially, the question was whether relief under Section 213 was entirely free standing and not contingent or conditional on criminal or civil proceedings having first been brought separately to establish that there is a contravention under the SFO. This issue has now been conclusively decided by the Hong Kong Court of

Final Appeal in the case of *SFC* v. *Tiger Asia Management LLC, Sung Kook Hwang Bill & Others.*[1]

In short, the CFA agreed with the SFC's position that Section 213 of the SFO provides for a free-standing remedy and the legislation intended for remedial and preventative orders to be available *separately* from criminal or civil deterrent sanctions. In other words, it is not necessary for the SFC to have first obtained a finding of contravention by another court or tribunal before it could apply to a court for remedial or protective relief separately. This was very significant and, since then, the SFC has successfully obtained remedial orders from the court in a variety of cases. Some recent and notable examples are discussed below.

3.1 Hontex

The case of *SFC* v. *Hontex International Holdings Co Ltd & Ors*[2] is an excellent example of the application of statutory rescission under Section 213. The case concerns the corporate governance of a listed company. Hontex provided false and misleading information in its prospectus that was provided to investors before its initial public offering. The amounts that the company stated in its IPO prospectus in respect of its turnover and profits before tax for several financial years, as well as the total number of its franchise stores stated, were materially false and misleading.

The SFC acted swiftly by first applying to court under Section 213 for an interim injunction *ex parte* freezing the IPO proceeds. Thereafter the SFC engaged in a protracted battle with the company in the Court of First Instance and also on appeal. In the end, the company and its directors entered into a statement of agreed facts with the SFC whereby, without admitting any criminal contravention, they admitted to a contravention of Section 298 of the SFO (a market misconduct provision which prohibits the distribution of false or misleading information that is likely to induce another person to subscribe or buy securities). On the basis of this statement, the court made an order that the company offer to repurchase the shares allotted to or purchased by public shareholders who were then holding the company's shares, i.e. to restore these shareholders to the positions in which they were before their subscriptions and purchases of the company's shares. As a result, a total of HK$1.03 billion (US$132 million) was returned to 7,700

[1] [2013] 3 HKC 600, (2013) 16 HKCFAR 324. [2] [2012] HKCU 1340.

investors. These investors were those who subscribed for Hontex shares in the initial public offering or had subsequently purchased them in the secondary market.

This was the first time that investors in Hong Kong were effectively fully compensated, i.e. made 'whole', by a listed company for false or misleading statements in the company's IPO prospectus.

3.2 *Du Jun*

The second example is the case of *HKSAR v. Du Jun*.[3] Du Jun was a managing director of Morgan Stanley in Hong Kong. Du inside-dealt the shares of CITIC Resources (CRH) while he was part of a team of bankers advising the company on a proposed deal to acquire oil field assets in China. While in possession of inside information, Du bought on separate occasions a total of 26.7 million shares of CRH (for the equivalent of US$11 million), and counselled his wife to buy as well. The SFC used Section 213 to obtain an interim injunction freezing his gains for insider dealing. Du Jun fled Hong Kong to return to Mainland China. He is the son of a Chinese general and lived in a military compound in Beijing with his family. It was difficult to get to him, even for the CSRC. So the SFC went quiet for some time. They went quiet, but they were alert. One day they received notice that Du Jun's wife had returned to Hong Kong and left a couple of days later. The SFC suspected that this might be a dry run for Du Jun to make a visit back to Hong Kong. Sure enough he did.

At the Hong Kong airport, there are automated passport control booths where you put in your Hong Kong identity card, and the gates will open; then you put your fingerprint on the scanner and the gates on the other side of the booth will open to let you through. When Du Jun did this, the gates did not open to let him out. The police arrived with handcuffs. He was then charged with insider dealing.

Du was convicted under a criminal provision of insider dealing under the SFO in the Hong Kong courts and ultimately sentenced to six years of imprisonment. Worthy of note is that on appeal by Du, the court decided that rather than impose a fine calculated on the profits Du made, which would have ended up depriving the counterparties to Du's insider trades of compensation, the appeal court ordered a much smaller fine so that the proceeds seized from Du would be available for compensation under Section 213. Meanwhile, under the Section 213 application separately

[3] [2012] 6 HKC 119.

brought by the SFC, Du was ordered to pay HK$23.9 million (US$3 million) to 297 investors as a result of his insider dealing. The order restored investors who transacted with Du to their pre-transaction positions.

3.3 *Tiger Asia*

The third case is *SFC* v. *Tiger Asia Management LLC & Ors.*[4] This is also an insider dealing case. It is different from other insider dealing cases in that the perpetrators were a New York-based hedge fund and three of its officers. Tiger Asia specialises in equity investments in China, Japan and Korea. All its employees are located in New York. Tiger Asia has no presence in Hong Kong.

Tiger Asia and its senior officers had inside-dealt in the shares of the Bank of China and China Construction Bank (both listed on the Hong Kong Stock Exchange), based on inside information they received from banks and placing agents in Hong Kong and London. The information involved the size and discount range of relevant proposed placements at the time.

The SFC again used Section 213 to seek compensation for investors. The Court of First Instance ruled that it did not have jurisdiction to decide if Tiger Asia and its three officers had contravened insider dealing provisions in the SFO, and without a finding of contravention, the court could not proceed to hear the case and make any order for remedial relief under Section 213 (see *SFC* v. *Tiger Asia Management LLC, & Ors.*)[5]

On a side note, it is worthy to describe Hong Kong's insider dealing regime in this chapter, which will explain why the Court of First Instance believed that it did not have jurisdiction. The SFO provides for two alternative routes for dealing with insider dealing. One is the criminal route, decided in the Hong Kong courts on the criminal burden of proof. If found guilty a defendant could be sentenced to a maximum jail term of seven years. The other alternative is civil proceedings in the Market Misconduct Tribunal (MMT), where the burden of proof is the civil standard of proof. The MMT can make an order for a range of civil penalties including disgorgement of profits and a ban from trading securities in Hong Kong for up to five years. The Court of First Instance in this case took the position that until the market misconduct tribunal or a criminal court had made a finding that insider dealing was

4 [2011] 6 HKC 149. 5 Ibid.

committed, it could not make a decision under Section 213, which is premised upon there having been a contravention under the SFO.

The SFC successfully appealed this decision in the Court of Final Appeal (*Securities and Futures Commission v. Tiger Asia Management LLC & Ors.*)[6] The Court of Final Appeal ruled that Section 213 confers jurisdiction to Hong Kong courts to make a finding of whether there is a contravention (i.e. that market misconduct was committed) and then proceed to make an order for remedial relief. In the meantime, the US SEC also took action against Tiger Asia in the United States.

In 2014, by a statement of agreed and admitted facts, Tiger Asia admitted that they contravened Hong Kong's laws prohibiting insider dealing when they dealt in the shares of Bank of China and China Construction Bank. On the basis of this admission, the SFC succeeded in obtaining a court order under Section 213 that Tiger Asia pay HK$45.26 million (US$5.8 million) to approximately 1,800 investors in Hong Kong and overseas who traded with Tiger Asia in the insider dealing transactions so that they are restored to the positions they were in before the transactions in question took place.

The SFC went on to bring an action against Tiger Asia for insider dealing before the Market Misconduct Tribunal.[7] The tribunal determined that Tiger Asia and its senior officers had engaged in insider dealing and market manipulation in Hong Kong. As the defendants had been made to compensate investors, the SFC did not seek disgorgement of profits (which in any event would have gone to the government coffers rather than the victims). Instead the tribunal ordered that Tiger Asia and two of its officers be banned from trading securities in Hong Kong for four years.

4 Section 201 Resolution

Other than Section 213 of the SFO, the other tool that the SFC uses to pursue remedial action is Section 201 of the SFO. This section allows the SFC to enter into resolution with regulated intermediaries in disciplinary proceedings where the SFC considers it appropriate to do so in the interest of the investing public or in the public interest.

[6] [2013] 3 HKC 600, (2013) 16 HKSFAR 324

[7] See The Report of the Market Misconduct Tribunal into Dealings in the Shares of Bank of China Limited and China Construction Bank Corporation on and between 19 December 2008 to 13 January 2009, dated 7 October 2014 www.mmt.gov.hk/eng/reports/BOC&CCB_Report_e.pdf.

There is considerable room for the SFC and the intermediary to reach agreement, as was demonstrated in the resolutions that the SFC reached with intermediaries with respect to their mis-selling of financial products related to Lehman Brothers. There were over 10 such resolutions. The terms of each of them were different, depending on the facts of the cases.

The other option that the SFC had was to take disciplinary action against these intermediaries, which would have resulted in the imposition of sanctions such as fines, public reprimands or suspension or revocation of their licences or registrations. The maximum level of fine that the SFC can impose is HK$10 million or three times the profit gained or loss avoided by the intermediary. This is for each incident of misconduct.

After considerable deliberation and in view of the large number of retail investors involved and the loss suffered, the SFC considered that reaching a resolution with the banks and brokers for them to repurchase the financial products from the investors was a better option than the imposition of sanctions.

In this case, the SFC felt that focusing too much on the wrongdoer may take away from the consequences of that wrongdoing. The SFC wished to avoid the situation where disciplinary action leaves the wrongdoer unable to remediate the victims. Other factors taken into consideration included the fact that the SFC does not have the power to order compensation from intermediaries to their clients. In addition, there is no class action process in Hong Kong and legal costs are very high and often beyond the means of ordinary investors.

So, the SFC successfully negotiated a significant agreement with 16 banks that sold Lehman Minibonds to the public in Hong Kong in July 2009. The key terms of the agreement were:

- **Repurchase offer** – the banks would make an offer to repurchase from each eligible customer all outstanding Minibonds at a price equal to 60 per cent or 70 per cent of the nominal value of the original investment, depending on the age of the customer.
- **Top up if collateral recovered** – once the underlying collateral was recovered and paid to the Banks, each of them would make a further payment. If recoveries exceeded 70 per cent, the Banks would pay the entire excess amount to eligible customers who had accepted the repurchase offer.

- **Fighting fund** – the Banks' commission income received as a distributor of the outstanding Minibonds was made available to the trustee of the Minibonds to assist in the recovery of the underlying collateral for each outstanding series of Minibonds.
- **Enhanced complaint handling procedure** (ECHP) – the Banks would implement special enhanced complaints handling procedures to resolve, in a fair and reasonable manner, all complaints in relation to the sale and distribution of other structured products.
- **Independent internal control review** of the Banks' systems and processes relating to the sale of structured products.

A total of over HK$10 billion (US$1.28 billion) was returned to investors under the resolution, comprising payments made under the repurchase offers, further payments made after the recovery of the collaterals and payments made under ECHP.

Another example that illustrates the versatile and flexible nature of agreements reached under Section 201 can be seen in the resolutions with Sun Hung Kai Investment Services Ltd[8] and KGI Asia Ltd.[9]

The resolution with brokers in relation to their mis-selling of Minibonds differed from those reached with banks in one significant aspect.

The terms of the resolutions with Sun Hung Kai Investment Services Ltd and KGI Asia Ltd on the repurchase of Minibonds were similar to the one with the banks. However, an additional term was imposed on the brokers, similar to releasing a wrongdoer on parole that states:

> If the SFC finds the same concerns of a materially serious nature, [the broker's] licence will be partially suspended for a period of three years to the extent that [the broker] will not be allowed to sell or distribute unlisted or structured products to clients and provide advice to clients in relation to these products.

Enforcement always follows misconduct, yet the community regards the existence of misconduct as evidence of a failure in enforcement. To help address this misperception, I have shared with you the examples and methods in this article with the hope that they will give the readers some idea of how a regulator has to be innovative in using its

[8] 'Sun Hung Kai Investments Services Ltd Agree to Repurchase Minibonds From Its Clients at Original Value' 22 January 2009, see www.sfc.hk/edistributionWeb/gateway/EN/news-and-announcements/news/doc?refNo=09PR8.

[9] 'KGI Asia Ltd Agrees with SFC to Repurchase Minibonds from Its Clients at Original Value' 5 April 2009, see www.sfc.hk/edistributionWeb/gateway/EN/news-and-announcements/news/doc?refNo=09PR39.

tools to successfully achieve its primary objective to protect investors. To have effective enforcement, the securities regulator needs to take on the challenge of tackling cross-border misconduct and continue to use all the tools available to it in bringing a fair outcome to investors and the market it regulates, as well as to punish wrongdoers.

PART IV

Civil Law Jurisdictions

18

Enforcement of Company and Securities Laws in Germany

An Exercise in Diversity

RAINER KULMS

1 Germany's Corporate Peculiarities

1.1 Diversity of Form and Regulation

Company law enforcement in Germany is an exercise in diversity. Stock corporations figure prominently among the country's enterprises with the highest turnover: Out of the 100 top enterprises, stock corporations take a share of two-thirds.[1] However, when it comes to analysing the GDP, the *Mittelstand* enterprises[2] produce about 53 per cent of the German GDP, employing 78.5 per cent of the workforce.[3] As of 1 January 2014, 16,005 stock corporations (*AGs – Aktiengesellschaften*) and 287 partnerships limited by shares (*KGaA – Kommanditgesellschaften auf Aktien*) did business.[4] But they were by far outnumbered by 1,127,620 limited liability companies (*GmbHs – Gesellschaften mit beschränkter Haftung*).[5]

The German business divide is between public and private business entities. Only some 10 per cent of all German stock corporations are

[1] Deutsches Aktieninstitut, Factbook, Statistiken, Analysen und Graphiken zu Aktionären, Aktiengesellschaften und Börsen (31 March 2012), sub 01–8, www.dai.de/files/dai_user content/dokumente/Statistiken/MAR%202013_Factbook_01_Zahl%20der%20AGs.pdf

[2] I.e. small, mid-size and family-owned businesses: see Carlo Osi, 'Family Business Governance and Independent Directors – The Challenges Facing an Independent Family Business Board', 12 U. PA.J. BUS. L. 181 (2010).

[3] Brian B. Blackstone and Vanessa Fuhrmans, 'The Engines of Growth', *Wall Street Journal*, 27 June 2011, http://online.wsj.com/news/articles/SB10001424052748703509104576329643153915516.

[4] *Udo Kornblum*, Bundesweite Rechtstatsachen zum Unternehmens- und Gesellschaftsrecht (Stand 1.1.2014), GmbH-Rundschau 13/2014, 694 (703).

[5] Ibid.

listed at a stock exchange,[6] whereas the huge majority of German businesses escape direct scrutiny through the capital market. Most of these businesses are owned by families or a limited group of shareholders[7] which combine considerable growth rates with a high degree of profitability.[8] German law does not operate with one single corporate statute or a statutory model for corporate entities. Practising lawyers have to be familiar with the Stock Corporation Act for listed and non-listed corporations (*Aktiengesetz*),[9] the Limited Liability Companies Act (*GmbH-Gesetz*)[10] and the Commercial Code (*Handelsgesetzbuch*).[11]

1.1.1 Listed Corporations and Non-Listed Corporations (*Aktiengesellschaften*)

The current Stock Corporation Act focuses on corporations whose shares are publicly traded at a stock exchange. The traditional listed corporation is two-tier, with the supervisory board holding executive officers liable for breaches of duty.[12] The organisational benefits of a stock corporation with legal personality and limited liability are purchased at the expense of severe restrictions on the freedom of contract.[13] It is virtually impossible to opt out of the mandatory rules for stock corporations. Nonetheless, the

[6] Bundesverband der Deutschen Industrie, Gesellschaftsrecht – Aktienrecht (2014), www.bdi.eu/Aktienrecht9415.htm.

[7] *Wolfgang Köhler*, Lieber nicht an die Börse – Unternehmen wachsen oft schneller, wenn sie keine Aktien streuen, Die Zeit online, 7 April 2007, www.zeit.de/2007/15/G-Familienunternehmen; René Söllner, Die wirtschaftliche Bedeutung kleinerer und mittlerer Unternehmen in Deutschland, Statistisches Bundesamt, Wirtschaft und Statistik, Januar 2014, 40 *et seq.*

[8] Eleven out of twenty-five of Europe's most successful non-listed enterprises are located in Germany: Claudia Tödtmann/Angela Kunze, Europas Top 50: Börsenfern, verschwiegen, erfolgreich, *Handelsblatt* online 25 May 2009, www.handelsblatt.com/unternehmen/mittelstand/ranking-europas-top-50-boersenfern-verschwiegen-erfolgreich-seite-2/3184214–2.html.

[9] For a translation of the *Aktiengesetz*, see Gerhard Wirth, Michael Arnold, Ralf Morshäuser and Mark Greene, *Corporate Law in Germany* (Verlag C.H. Beck München, 2nd ed. 2010), 294 *et seq.*

[10] For a translation of the *GmbH-Gesetz*, see Federal Ministry of Justice, Limited Liability Companies Act, www.gesetze-im-internet.de/englisch_gmbhg/limited_liability_companies_act.pdf.

[11] For a translation of the *Handelsgesetzbuch*, see Thomas Rittler, *Handelsgesetzbuch (HGB) – German Commercial Code* (Verlag Plattform-Compliance Gründau 2014).

[12] See Section 3.1 of this chapter. Limited liability companies (*GmbHs*), which are subject to co-determination law, are also two-tier.

[13] See generally *Karsten Schmidt*, Gesellschaftsrecht, 83 *et seq.; Barbara Grunewald*, Gesellschaftsrecht (Verlag Mohr Siebeck Tübingen, 9th ed. 2014), § 10, 13.

German legislator has attempted to accommodate the specific needs of German family and mid-size businesses.[14] S. 3 (2) of the Stock Corporation Act authorises corporations to opt out of listing rules when the scrutiny imposed by capital market and accounting laws are considered too burdensome.[15] Practitioners have come to devise shareholder agreements as a mechanism to contract around mandatory law.[16]

1.1.2 Limited Liability Companies (*Gesellschaften mit beschränkter Haftung – GmbHs*)

The German limited liability company (*GmbH*) combines limited liability and legal capacity with a greater amount of freedom of contract and exemption from capital market laws.[17] Contrary to listed corporations, the Limited Liability Companies Act authorises stockholders to give binding instructions to the management. Although the German legislator did not intend to restrict transferability of shares in a *GmbH*, limited liability companies are quite remote from traditional capital market influences: Current charters for limited liability companies and supplementary shareholder agreements condition a change of ownership on the consent of remaining shareholders who are regularly entitled to exercise a right of pre-emption.[18]

1.1.3 Limited Partnerships and Hybrids

In exploiting tax benefits for private income, practitioners have added a crossover to company law which combines the freedom of contract under partnership law with the concept of limited liability. The courts have accepted limited partnerships where the general partner is a limited liability company and the limited partners are natural persons (*GmbH & Co. KG's*).[19] Some of these *GmbH & Co. KG's* are

[14] See *Walter Bayer*, Empfehlen sich besondere Regelungen für börsennotierte und für geschlossene Gesellschaften? Gutachten E zum 67. Deutschen Juristentag (Verlag C.H. Beck, München 2008), E 25 *et seq.*

[15] See *Harm Peter Westermann*, in Tobias Bürgers/Torsten Körber (eds.), Heidelberger Kommentar zum Aktiengesetz (C.F. Müller Verlag Heidelberg 2008), § 3 No. 7.

[16] See *Jan Lieder*, in Holger Fleischer/Susanne Kalss/Hans-Ueli Vogt, Aktuelle Entwicklungen im deutschen, österreichischen und schweizerischen Gesellschafts- und Kapitalmarktrecht 2012 (Verlag Mohr Siebeck Tübingen 2012) 232 (244 *et seq.*).

[17] See *Günther H. Roth*, in Günther H. Roth ed., Das System der Kapitalgesellschaften im Umbruch – ein internationaler Vergleich (Rechtsfragen der Handelsgesellschaften 50 (1990) Verlag Dr. Otto Schmidt KG Köln), 2 *et seq.*

[18] *Dirk Eckhardt* in Dirk Eckhardt/Marc Hermanns, Kölner Handbuch Gesellschaftsrecht (Carl Heymanns Verlag Köln 2nd ed. 2014), Chap. 2 No. 286 *et seq.*

[19] See generally *Karsten Schmidt*, Gesellschaftsrecht, 1621 *et seq.*

potent economic players in the country's business scene, assuming *de facto* the role of listed stock corporations where the investors are not shareholders but limited partners. This business model has provoked a debate on how far the law of listed corporations should be applied by analogy to afford a degree of protection to investors comparable to that of (minority) shareholders.[20]

1.2 The Enforcement Scenario

Historically, 'regulation through litigation'[21] and the private attorney-general enforcing statutes are concepts alien to German legal thinking. German corporate legal mainstream theory does not characterise a corporation or any other business organisation as a nexus of contracts.[22] Shareholders are authorised to protect 'corporate legality' by challenging resolutions of the general meeting (including a ratification vote)[23] or by refusing ratification of the boards' activities. Nonetheless, courts and scholars have come to invoke a far-reaching concept of a duty of corporate loyalty owed by members of the board of directors, the corporation and shareholders. This duty of corporate loyalty has been instrumental in expanding shareholders' rights beyond the rigidities of the statutory notion of scrutinising corporate legality.[24] It also operates as a mechanism to block shareholder obstructionism and to accommodate new developments on the market of business ideas and contracting. Moreover, the judge-made duty of corporate loyalty might be seen as

20 *Thomas Liebscher*, in Jochen Reichert/Florian Bortfeldt, GmbH & Co. KG (Verlag C.H. Beck München 7th ed. 2015), § 3 No. 31 *et seq.; Harm Peter Westermann*, Die Verteidigung von Mitgliedschaftsrechten in der Personengesellschaft (einschließlich GmbH & Co. KG), Neue Zeitschrift für Gesellschaftsrecht 2012, 1121 (1122 *et seq.*). See also Federal Supreme Court (Bundesgerichtshof), judgment of 19 October 2009, II ZR 240/08, BGHZ 183,1 *et seq.* ('Sanieren oder Ausscheiden').

21 See the title of the book by *W. Kip Viscusi* ed., Regulation through Litigation (Brookings Institution, Washington, D.C., 2002).

22 Cf. the approach chosen by *Karsten Schmidt*, Gesellschaftsrecht, *Barbara Grunewald*, Gesellschaftsrecht. See, however, Christine *Windbichler*, Gesellschaftsrecht (Verlag C.H. Beck München 22nd ed. 2013), 17 *et seq.*

23 See Section 2.1.1 of this chapter and Federal Supreme Court (Bundesgerichtshof), judgment of 16 February 2009, II ZR 185/07, BGHZ 180, 9 (19 *et seq.*), and decision of 6 November 2012, II ZR 111/12, http://juris.bundesgerichtshof.de/cgi-bin/rechtsprechung/document.py?Gericht=bgh&Art=en&nr=62428&pos=0&anz=1, affirming Court of Appeal (Oberlandesgericht) Stuttgart, judgment of 29 February 2012, 20 U 3/11.

24 This has provoked a call for legislative action to codify the duty of loyalty: *Holger Fleischer*, Reformperspektiven der Organhaftung: Empfiehlt sich eine stärkere Kodifizierung von Richterrecht?, Der Betrieb 2014, 1971 *et seq.*

introducing – albeit cautiously – market-informed thinking into corporate law analysis.[25]

The litigation scenario for listed corporations with dispersed ownership differs from business organisations with a block-holder structure and predominant concerns about minority protection. For a closely-knit group of owners, litigation represents the worst-case scenario because it is likely to precipitate the end of a business which is predicated on cooperative behaviour. In the non-listed context, litigation serves three purposes: Firstly, it operates as an instrument of minority protection.[26] Secondly, it will revolve around the interpretation of a shareholder agreement designed to recalibrate the relationship between various groups of shareholders. Thirdly, litigation scrutinises the economics of the predetermined formula for calculating severance payments (*Abfindung*) to disenchanted shareholders.[27]

German company law theory classifies listed corporations, non-listed corporations and limited liability companies as *Kapitalgesellschaften* ('capital companies') to which common principles are applicable. In the following, the rules on the Stock Corporation Act will be primarily examined, and modifications for limited liability companies will be recognised.

2 Protecting Shareholders' Rights and Beyond

2.1 Legality Control

2.1.1 Suing the Listed Corporation

Under the current statute for stock corporations, a shareholder can apply to the court to have a vote of the general meeting set aside or declared null and void (s. 245 (1) of the Stock Corporation Act).[28] The action for

[25] See Section 2.2.2 of this chapter.

[26] See *Holger Fleischer*, in Gregor Bachmann/Horst Eidenmüller/Andreas Engert/Holger Fleischer/Wolfgang Schön (eds.), Regulating the Close Corporation (Walter de Gruyter GmbH Berlin/Boston 2014), 33 *et seq.*

[27] See *Jens Fleischhauer* in Kölner Handbuch – Gesellschaftsrecht, § 1 No. 645 (*et seq.*) (commercial partnerships) and *Dirk Eckhardt* in Kölner Handbuch – Gesellschaftsrecht § 2 No. 405 *et seq.* (limited liability companies).

[28] On the history of the action to set aside a resolution of the shareholders' meeting: *Markus Emmerich*, Die historische Entwicklung von Beschlussverfahren und Beschlusskontrolle im Aktienrecht im Gesellschaftsrecht der Neuzeit unter besonderer Berücksichtigung des Aktienrechts, Schriften zum Wirtschaftsrecht 130 (Verlag Duncker & Humblot, Berlin (2000)), 131 *et seq.* For a survey of the development of German cases: *Marcus Wandrey*. Materielle Beschlusskontrolle im Aktienrecht – Eine Untersuchung der beweglichen

a declaration of nullity or for setting aside a vote must be directed against the corporation.[29] Nullity may be invoked if substantial procedural requirements have been disregarded, or the vote is in conflict with the essentials of a stock corporation, rules on creditor protection or public policy (s. 241 of the Stock Corporation Act).[30]

Setting aside a resolution of the general meeting for a breach of statutory law (*Gesetz*) or the corporate charter (*Satzung*) is an *ex post* mechanism which can be activated by an individual shareholder.[31] A shareholder who has been unlawfully excluded from the general meeting is entitled to file an action for setting aside a resolution.[32] A resolution to ratify the managerial activities of the board of directors can be attacked if a fundamental breach of statutory law has occurred.[33] Likewise, a shareholder may challenge

Schranken des Aktionärsstimmrechts, Münchener Universitätsschriften (Reihe der Juristischen Fakultät) 238 (Verlag C.H. Beck München (2012)), 54 *et seq.*

29 If shareholders sue, the corporation will be represented by the board of directors and the supervisory board. If the board of directors or an individual director sues, the supervisory board will represent the corporation. The board of the directors will represent if the action has been brought by a member of the supervisory board (s. 246 (2) of the Stock Corporation Act). The right to have a vote of the general meeting of shareholders quashed or declared nil and void extends to resolutions appointing members of the supervisory board (s. 250 (1) of the Stock Corporation Act). A declaration for nullity will be issued where the resolution disregards mandatory provisions of codetermination or stock corporation laws. This includes, *inter alia*, a resolution which appoints a member who already holds a total of ten posts on supervisory boards of corporations under a statutory duty to establish such a board (s. 250 (1) (4) of the Stock Corporation Act). With respect to actions against resolutions appointing members of the supervisory board, shareholders, members of the board of directors and the supervisory board or the boards as an entity, workers' councils or trade unions represented in the corporation or a dependent enterprise have standing (s. 250 (2) of the Stock Corporation Act).

30 Nullity has been found to exist, e.g. if the rules on an increase of the legal capital have been disregarded: Court of Appeal (Oberlandesgericht) München, decision of 14 September 2011, 31 Wx 360/11, Deutsches Steuerrecht 2011, 2308, the corporation practises a sale of its own shares in breach of statutory rules: Court of Appeal (Oberlandesgericht) Oldenburg, 17 March 1994, 1 U 151/93, Neue Juristische Wochenschrift – Rechtsprechungsreport 1995, 1313, or the general meeting passes a resolution for which it has no statutory authority: *Holger Fleischer*, in Holger Fleischer, Handbuch des Vorstandsrechts ed., (Verlag C.H. Beck München, 2006), § 11 No. 88 *et seq.*

31 The right to have a resolution set aside may be exercised by shareholders who were present at the general meeting, shareholders unlawfully excluded from the general meeting or those who have not received an invitation in accordance with statutory provisions (s. 245 (1), (3) of the Stock Corporation Act.

32 Court of Appeal (Oberlandesgericht) Düsseldorf, decision of 11 July 1991, 6 U 59/91, Neue Juristische Wochenschrift-Rechtsprechungsreport 1992, 100.

33 For a survey see *Manuel Lorenz*, Die richterliche Überprüfung unternehmerischer Entscheidungen des Vorstands bei Anfechtungsklagen gegen Entlastungsbeschlüsse, Neue Zeitschrift für Gesellschaftsrecht 2009, 1138 (1139 *et seq.*).

a resolution which is the result of an agreement between the dominant shareholder and the board of directors.[34] A dominant shareholder may not exploit a shareholder resolution for self-dealing.[35] Generally, court action in this context provides the minority with a bargaining chip against a dominant shareholder or a group of powerful shareholders,[36] although courts and the legislator have attempted to limit shareholder obstructionism.[37] Conversely, in staying faithful to the concept of upholding corporate legality, the board of directors or an individual member, may challenge a shareholder resolution if its execution would constitute a felony or a crime (section 245 (4), (5) of the Stock Corporation Act).

Studies have been undertaken to identify plaintiffs and the type of litigation against listed corporations. The litigation industry grew between 2003 and 2011.[38] Between 2005 and 2007 there was an average of six actions per challenged resolution of a general meeting of a listed corporation.[39] A group of ten individuals was found to be most active initiating litigation against various corporations.[40] After the legislator had imposed restrictions on shareholders' rights to sue, individual litigation became increasingly rare. The number of small shareholders jumping on the 'bandwagon' of litigation has decreased.[41] The number of individual plaintiffs is now less than two per litigation.[42] A group of four (plaintiff) companies has acquired notoriety within the litigation industry.[43] Members of the 'professional plaintiffs' have been observed to hold shares in several companies of the litigation industry, thus facilitating a combined effort.[44] The number of individuals behind this corporate litigation machinery amounts to a total of forty-nine, controlling 78 per cent of actions brought[45] and 75 per cent of all interventions in proceedings.[46] It should be noted that these studies do not address litigation

[34] Federal Supreme Court (Bundesgerichtshof), judgment of 1 February 1988, II ZR 75/87, Neue Juristische Wochenschrift 1988, 1579 *et seq.*

[35] Cf. *Pierre-Henri Conac, Luca Enriques, Martin Gelter*, 'Constraining Dominant Shareholders' Self-Dealings, The Legal Framework in France, Germany and Italy', 4 EUR. COMP. & FIN. L. REV. 491 (2007), 514.

[36] Ibid., at 513. [37] See Section 2.2.2 of this chapter.

[38] *Theodor Baums/Astrid Keinath/Daniel Gajek*, Fortschritte bei Klagen gegen Hauptversammlungsbeschlüsse? Eine empirische Studie, Frankfurt, Zeitschrift für Wirtschaftsrecht 2007, 1629 (1639 *et seq.*).

[39] Ibid., at 1634. [40] Ibid., at 1634.

[41] *Theodor Baums/Florian Drinhausen/Astrid Keinath*, Anfechtungsklagen und Freigabeverfahren, Eine empirische Studie, Zeitschrift für Wirtschaftsrecht 2011, 2329 (2332 *et seq.*).

[42] Ibid., at 2233. [43] Ibid., at 2334. [44] Ibid., at 2335.

[45] The total of proceedings which were analysed was 584: Ibid., at 2352.

[46] Ibid., at 2336.

strategies for a declaratory judgment censuring the corporation and its board(s) for a breach of the duty of corporate loyalty or for outsourcing schemes without shareholder approval.[47]

2.1.2 Limited Liability Companies

The courts are charged with fleshing out rules for scrutinising the legality of resolutions of the meeting of shareholders of a limited liability company.[48] Judges rely on an analogy with the provisions of the Stock Corporation Act. Although the shareholders enjoy considerable freedom of contract under the Limited Liabilities Act, they may not redesign the statutory toolkit for actions for nullity or setting aside a shareholder resolution.[49] On the other hand, a shareholder agreement signed by all shareholders may be used to directly attack a resolution of the general meeting.[50] As a corollary, an interim injunction may be issued against a shareholder who intends to deviate from his duties under a voting[51] or pooling agreement.[52]

2.2 Transcending the Limitations of Legality Control

2.2.1 Outsourcing

Shareholder litigation is conditioned on the statutory requirement that the board of directors has to seek a shareholder vote (and should not fail

[47] See Section 2.2.1 of this chapter. For a comprehensive analysis of the procedural possibilities at the disposal of shareholders: Federal Supreme Court (Bundesgerichtshof), judgment of 10 October 2005, II ZR 90/03, Neue Juristische Wochenschrift 2006, 374 (375 *et seq.*) („Mangusta/Commerzbank II').

[48] *Christoph Teichmann* in Markus Gehrlein/Jens Ekkenga/Stefan Simon, GmbHG-Kommentar, Anh. Zu § 47 GmbHG, No. 1 *et seq.; Karsten Schmidt* in Scholz, GmbHG, II §§ 35–52 (Verlag Dr. Otto Schmidt Köln 10th ed. 2007), § 45 No, 35 *et seq.; Hartmut Rensen*, Beschlussmängelstreitigkeiten in der GmbH (Nomos Verlagsgesellschaft Baden-Baden 2014), 25 *et seq.* See generally on legal remedies for minority shareholders: Holger Fleischer, in *Regulating the Close Corporation*, 28 (63 *et seq.*).

[49] The corporate charter of the limited liability may, however, extend the statutory deadlines for filing an action: Federal Supreme Court (Bundesgerichtshof), decision of 13 July 2009, II ZR 272/08, Neue Zeitschrift für Gesellschaftsrecht 2009, 1110; *Hartmut Rensen*, 212 *et seq.*

[50] Federal Supreme Court (Bundesgerichtshof), judgment of 20 January 1983, II ZR 243/81, Neue Juristische Wochenschrift 1983, 1910 *et seq.*

[51] *Hartmut Rensen*, 252 *et seq.*

[52] See Federal Supreme Court (Bundesgerichtshof), judgment of 22 January 2013, II ZR 80/10, Mitteilungen der Bayerischen Notarkammer 2013, 254 (255) and decision of 15 March 2010 II ZR 4/09, Neue Juristische Wochenschrift 2012, 3718 (3719 *et seq.*); Court of Appeal (Oberlandesgericht) Hamm, judgment of 12 April 2000,8 U 165/99, Neue Zeitschrift für Gesellschaftsrecht 2000, 1036 *et seq.*; and *Hartmut Rensen*, 264 *et seq.*

to do so).[53] Judges are reluctant to interfere with managerial prerogatives as long as there was a proper exercise of business judgment.[54] But in the interest of minority protection and a proper discharge of directors' duties the courts may (on a case-by-case analysis) impose a duty to call for a vote even though the statute is silent.[55] In a case decided by the Federal Supreme (*Bundesgerichtshof*) Court in 1982, the management had outsourced most of the profitable business of a corporation to a newly established, wholly owned subsidiary, thereby watering down claims for dividends flowing from activities of the (original) corporation. The Court classified this strategic outsourcing as a *de facto* change of the corporate charter since it redefined shareholders' rights to a dividend. The plaintiff shareholder was granted a declaratory judgment against the parent corporation which stated that the latter was under a duty to seek the consent of the general meeting of shareholders.[56] The Court was criticised for encroaching on managerial prerogatives.[57] In 2004, the Federal Supreme Court explained its 1982 holding. An unwritten duty to seek a vote of the shareholders' meeting should be read into the statute whenever a restructuring scheme recalibrates the division of powers and rights between the board and the shareholders, thereby fundamentally interfering with the membership status of a shareholder.[58] If so, a quorum of three-quarters for an approving vote of the general meeting is required. Strategic measures of lesser importance will remain within the province of exclusive management powers.[59]

[53] See Pierre-Henri Conac, Luca Enriques and Martin Gelter, 4 EUR. COM. & FIN. L. REV. 491(2007), 514.

[54] Federal Supreme Court (Bundesgerichtshof), decision of 8 October 2013, III ZB 26/12, Neue Zeitschrift für Gesellschaftsrecht 2013 1342 (1343 *-*et seq.*) ('Frosta'), see *Michael Brellochs*, Der Rückzug von der Börse nach „Frosta' – Rechtsdogmatische Einordnung, Durchführung und Rechtsschutz in zukünftigen Fällen, Die Aktiengesellschaft 2014, 633 (638 *et seq.*).

[55] See Pierre-Henri Conac, Luca Enriques, and Martin Gelter, 4 EUR. COM. & FIN. L. REV. 491 (2007), 515; *Holger Fleischer* in Fleischer (ed.), Handbuch des Vorstandsrechts (Verlag C.H. Beck München 2006), § 21 No. 70 *et seq.*

[56] Federal Supreme Court (Bundesgerichtshof), judgment of 25 February 1982, II ZR 174/80, BGHZ 83, 122, (130 *et seq.*) („Holzmüller').

[57] See discussion of critique in Federal Supreme Court (Bundesgerichtshof), judgment of 26 April 2004, II ZR 155/02, BGHZ 159, 30 (37 *et seq.*) („Gelatine').

[58] Ibid.

[59] There is no duty to seek the approval of the general meeting of shareholders if just the participation in another company shall be sold: Federal Supreme Court (Bundesgerichtshof), decision of 20 November 2006, II ZR 226/05, Deutsches Steuerrecht 2007, 586. Under the influence of the Federal Constitutional Court (Bundesverfassungsgericht, judgment of

2.2.2 Abuse of Rights and Corporate Loyalty

In applying the Stock Corporation Act the courts attempt to strike a balance between shareholder protection and a ban on delaying tactics which obstruct corporate decision-making processes. In 1989, the Federal Supreme Court reiterated that shareholders were entitled to police corporate legality.[60] Nonetheless, they have to refrain from blackmailing the corporation into making payments without a corresponding legal right to demand consideration for withdrawing their brief. In handling shareholder obstruction, the Court did not invoke the duty of corporate loyalty. Instead, it relied on a general duty to abstain from an abuse of rights (*Rechtsmissbrauch*).[61] The courts have made it clear that this duty is owed on a basis of reciprocity. A minority shareholder is under a duty of loyalty to exercise his membership rights in accordance with the corporation-related interests of his fellow shareholders.[62] Usually, a shareholder's willingness to evidence loyalty will be tested when the corporation has to master a critical financial situation.[63]

Under the Stock Corporation Act, a shareholder is entitled to attacking a resolution of the general meeting to increase or decrease the legal capital or to enter into an enterprise agreement with another corporation. However, the corporation may ask the court to unblock the delaying effects of an action to have the resolution set aside if the action is evidently unfounded, the plaintiff holds shares of nominal value of not less than 1,000 € or the corporation has an interest in averting considerable harm (*Freigabeverfahren*).[64] Considerable harm has been found to

11 July 2012, 1 BvR 3142/07, 1 BvR 1569/09, BVerfGE 132, 99 (119 *et seq.*)) the Federal Supreme Court (Bundesgerichtshof) applies a comparable logic to delistings: A shareholder vote is not required for a delisting since neither membership rights nor the balance of power between the board of directors and shareholders is affected: judgment of 8 October 2013, III ZB 26/12, Neue Zeitschrift für Gesellschaftsrecht 2013, 1342 (1343 *et seq.*) ('Frosta'). See comment by *Stephen Lambert/Mario Weichel*, Wegfall der 'Macrotron-Trias' – Folgen für Umstrukturierungskonstellationen in Konfliktlagen des Aktien- und Kapitalmarktrechts, Wertpapiermitteilungen 2014, 1024 (1025 *et seq.*).

60 Federal Supreme Court (Bundesgerichtshof), judgment of 22 May 1989, II ZR 206/88, BGHZ 107, 296 (308 *et seq.*) („Kochs Adler').

61 Ibid. See also the analysis by *Johannes Georg Jacobs*, Der Missbrauch der aktienrechtlichen Anfechtungsklage im Lichte des ARUG (Verlag Dr Kovač, Hamburg (2012)), 87 *et seq.*

62 Federal Supreme Court (Bundesgerichtshof), judgment of 13 March 1978, II ZR 142/76, BGHZ 71, 40 (48 *et seq.*) („Kali & Salz).

63 Ibid.

64 S. 246a of the Stock Corporation Act. For an economic analysis of the unblocking procedure: *Florens Sauerbruch*, Das Freigabeverfahren gemäß § 246a Aktiengesetz – Eine rechtsökonomische Untersuchung (Gabler GWV Fachverlage Wiesbaden 2008), 163 3t *seq.*

exist if the corporation would otherwise be faced with continued debt or illiquidity.[65]

Under partnership law, the Federal Supreme Court has reinterpreted the duty of loyalty, requiring a partner to accept a pre-insolvency reorganisation plan in the interest of fellow shareholders: In a 2009 case on a commercial partnership, an illiquid property fund organised as a *de facto* publicly held company, the reorganisation plan provided for a substantial decrease of capital and a subsequent injection of fresh capital from consenting partners.[66] The partners faced a clear choice: accept the decrease and leave, or accept the decrease, inject new cash and stay.[67] The Court reiterates that no partner can be forced to inject fresh money. But on the other hand, the duty of loyalty owed to the other partners tilted the scales in favour of acceptance of the reorganisation plan.[68] The Court weighs the interest of the partners who want to continue with new contributions against those who reject the envisaged increase of capital. The alternative is to reorganise or leave.[69] Nonetheless, a partner may legitimately withhold acceptance when a previous plan, adopted three years earlier, had not produced any substantial reorganisation benefits.[70] There is little doubt that this holding would also apply to limited liability companies.[71]

2.2.3 Injunctive Relief

In the daily business of a stock corporation a shareholder action asking the court to set aside a resolution of the general meeting may not attain the desired objective within the necessary timeframe. Courts have granted interim injunctive relief (*Einstweilige Verfügung*)[72] unless the special

[65] See discussion by the Court of Appeal (Oberlandesgericht) Jena, decision of 12 October 2006, 6 W 453/06, Neue Zeitschrift für Gesellschaftsrecht 2007, 147 (151 *et seq.*).

[66] Federal Supreme Court (Bundesgerichtshof), judgment of 19 October 2009, II ZR 240/08 („Sanieren oder Ausscheiden'), BGHZ 183, 1 (3 et seq.)

[67] Ibid., at 3 et seq. [68] Ibid., at 14 et seq.

[69] Ibid.; See comment by *Wulf Goette*, 'Sanieren oder Ausscheiden' – Zur Treuepflicht des Gesellschafters in der Sanierungssituation, Gesellschafts- und Wirtschaftsrecht 2010, 1 (2 *et seq.*). This jurisprudence has been extended to partnerships established under the Civil Code ('*BGB-Gesellschaften*'): Court of Appeal (Oberlandesgericht) Stuttgart, judgment of 11 July 2013, 19 U 11/13, Zeitschrift für Wirtschaftsrecht 2013, 1661.

[70] Court of Appeal (Oberlandesgericht) München, decision of 16 January 2014, 23 AktG 3/13, Der Betrieb 2014, 943 *et seq.*

[71] *Benedikt* v. *Schorlemer/Matthias Stupp*, Kapitalerhöhung zu Sanierungszwecken – zur Reichweite der Zustimmungspflicht der Minderheitsgesellschafters mit Sperrminorität, Neue Zeitschrift für Insolvenzrecht 2003, 345 (348 *et seq.*, 354).

[72] See the facts in the case decided by the Court of Appeal (Oberlandesgericht) München, decision of 28 July 2010, 7 AktG 2/10, Wertpapiermitteilungen 2010, 1859. For

unblocking rules of the Stock Corporation Act apply. An order for interim relief will be issued after a summary assessment of the merits, but applicants face considerable financial risk. If subsequently, the interim relief is recognised as unjustified and the court order is lifted, s. 945 of the Code of Civil Procedure imposes a statutory duty of compensation. While courts will grant interim relief against the deficient implementation of resolutions of the general meeting,[73] they are much more reluctant to issue a temporary injunction restraining shareholders from exercising their vote in a specific manner during the general meeting of a listed corporation.[74] A less restrictive approach is applied in the context of shareholder agreements signed by all shareholders (i.e. a voting or pooling agreement).[75]

2.2.4 An *Actio pro socio* or Derivative Action?

The supervisory board plays a pivotal role in policing deviant managerial behaviour. A shareholder can only directly sue a director if there is evidence that a shareholder has suffered damages through individual action by the director in addition to losses sustained by the corporation.[76] If, however,

a comprehensive survey see *Ingo Drescher*, in Martin Henssler/Lutz Strohn et al. (eds.), Gesellschaftsrecht (Verlag C.H. Beck München 2nd ed. 2014), § 246 AktG No. 52 *et seq.*

[73] *Wolfgang Zöllner* in Baumbach/Hueck, GmbH-Gesetz – Kommentar (Verlag C.H. Beck München 20th ed. 2013), Anhang nach § 47 No. 195.

[74] Court of Appeal (Oberlandesgericht) München, judgment of 13 September 2006, 7 U 2912/06, Neue Zeitschrift für Gesellschaftsrecht 2007, 152 (153 *et seq.*), see also for a takeover context Court of Appeal (Oberlandesgericht) Frankfurt am Main, decision of 27 May 2003, WpÜG 2/03, Neue Juristische Wochenschrift 2003, 2180 (2181 *et seq.*) (capital market law). See also for limited liability companies *Christoph Teichmann* in Markus Gehrlein/Jens Ekkenga/Stefan Simon, GmbHG – Gesetz betreffend die Gesellschaften mit beschränkter Haftung – Kommentar (Carl Heymanns Verlag Köln 2012), Anhang zu § 47 GmbHG No. 85 *et seq.* The decision of the District Court (Landgericht) Duisburg, judgment of 27 June 2001, 21 O 106/02, Der Betrieb 2003, 441 ('Babcock/HDW'), blocks the sale of a substantial participation without a vote of general meeting of shareholders, but does not appear to be in line with subsequent cases decided by the Federal Supreme Court (Bundesgerichtshof), For a comprehensive analysis see: *Thomas Liebscher/Matthias Aller*, Einstweiliger Rechtsschutz im GmbH-Recht, 36 Zeitschrift für Insolvenzrecht 1 (3 *et seq.*) (2015) and *Michael Kort*, Einstweiliger Rechtsschutz bei eintragungspflichtigen Hauptversammlungsbeschlüssen, Neue Zeitschrift für Gesellschaftsrecht 2007, 169 (170 *et seq.*).

[75] Federal Supreme Court (Bundesgerichtshof), judgment of 27 October 1986, Zeitschrift für Wirtschaftsrecht 1987, 293 (295); Court of Appeal (Oberlandesgericht) Köln, judgment of 16 March 1988, 6 U 38/87, NJW-RR 1989, 352 *et seq.* (limited liability company). Cf. passim *Thomas Liebscher/Matthias Aller*, 36 Zeitschrift für Insolvenzrecht 1 (3) (2015).

[76] This is the case when a member of the board of directors has been found guilty of embezzlement (see Section 3.2 of this chapter) which causes losses to a shareholder: cf. *Uwe Hüffer*, Aktiengesetz – Kommentar, § 93 No. 19 *et seq.*

a majority of shareholders refrains from instructing the supervisory board to initiate court proceedings against a deviant director, individual shareholder action (on behalf of the corporation) may be envisaged. Under s. 148 of the Stock Corporation Act, shareholders, who own one per cent of the legal capital of a corporation or a total of shares of € 100,000 or more, may apply to the court for permission to file a claim for damages against a member of the board of directors or the supervisory board on behalf of the corporation irrespective of whether the general meeting of shareholders has passed a resolution in favour of litigation.[77] If the court grants permission, the applicant shareholders have to invite the corporation to take action. If the corporation declines, the applicant shareholders may sue on behalf of the corporation. This procedure is overly burdensome,[78] but proposals to develop a more expansive derivative suit or an *action pro socio* for stock corporations have been greeted with little enthusiasm.[79]

Under the statutory provisions for limited liability companies, shareholders and partners are expected to protect themselves *ex ante* by negotiating solutions which protect the minority against shareholder oppression. The *actio pro socio* for shareholders of a limited liability company has had to overcome considerable difficulties. Initially, it was thought that charters of limited liability companies might be so construed as to accommodate a right to bring a derivative suit.[80] Currently, an *actio pro socio* is recognised as a type of litigation where a shareholder sues on behalf of the limited liability company if internal mechanisms for redress fail.[81]

Cost rules for a derivative suit or an *actio pro socio* operate as an incentive to bring only those suits which are likely to succeed.[82] Both, the rules on derivative suits under s. 148 of the Stock Corporation Act

[77] On this *Klagezulassungsverfahren* ('lawsuit admission procedure'): *Pierre-Henri Conac/ Luca Enriques/Martin Gelter*, 4 Eur. Com. & Fin. L. Rev. 491(2007), 507.

[78] *Barbara Grunewald*, Gesellschaftsrecht, 266.

[79] See the criticism by *Christine Windbichler*, 315.

[80] For a detailed analysis, see *Matthias Habersack*, Die Aktionärsklage – Grundlagen; Grenzen und Anwendungsfälle, Deutsches Steuerrecht 1998, 533 (535 *et seq.*).

[81] Under the specificities of German law on limited liability companies where the managing director is under a statutory duty to take instructions from a majority of shareholders, legal theory requires the shareholder envisaging a derivative action to invite the managing shareholder to take action before filing a brief for litigation (*Barbara Grunewald*, Gesellschafterklage, at 70). See generally on the action pro socio with respect to limited liability companies: *Frank Ebbing*, in Lutz Michalski/Henning Blaufuß (eds.), GmbH-Gesetz (Verlag C.H. Beck München 2nd ed. 2010) § 14 No. 99 *et seq.*, *Holger Fleischer*, in *Regulating the Closed Corporation*, 28 (65 *et seq.*).

[82] See generally on cost rules Section 4.2 of this chapter.

and on unblocking procedures provide for exceptions from the general rule, but do not achieve full internalisation of costs.[83]

3 Company Law Enforcement by Deterrence

3.1 *Management Liability*

The legislator has entrusted the supervisory board with assessing and litigating management liability whereas shareholders face factual and legal obstacles to directly challenge the board of directors. The statutory toolkit suggests that company law enforcement by the supervisory board operates by deterrence. The supervisory board may either terminate the contract with a disloyal director or file an action for damages. Supervisory boards subject to codetermination laws have brought forth multiplayer games with coalition-building between the management and shareholders' representatives or labour respectively.[84] Communications between the board of directors and the chairman of the supervisory board are often informal.[85] To switch from a cooperative game to a strategy of confrontation requires a certain momentum on the supervisory board. Members of supervisory boards may lack the necessary qualifications for exercising any meaningful control of managerial activities.[86] In the face of such inhibitions, the Federal Supreme Court has made it clear that the supervisory board is under a duty to commence litigation against directors whose business decisions have caused huge losses to the corporation: In a 1997 case, the supervisory board had declined to sue the members of the board of directors for damages although they had operated a Ponzi scheme to the detriment of the corporation. The Court insisted on a liability assessment by the supervisory board irrespective of a future vote of the general meeting of shareholders.[87] If managerial risk-taking behaviour demonstrates a considerable degree of irresponsibility the supervisory board must sue, unless substantial business interests would be jeopardised by court

[83] Cf. *Florens Sauerbruch*, 201 *et seq.*

[84] Katharina Pistor, in Margaret M. Blair and Mark J. Roe eds., *Employees and Corporate Governance* (Brookings Institution Press Washington, DC, 1999), 163, 179 *et seq.*

[85] For a detailed analysis see *Johannes Semler*, Der Aufsichtsrat – Die Karriere einer Einrichtung, Neue Zeitschrift für Gesellschaftsrecht 2013, 771 (776 *et seq.*).

[86] The Federal Supreme Court (Bundesgerichtshof), judgment of 15 November 1982, II ZR 27/82, BGHZ 85, 293 (295 *et seq.*), imposes a duty on the Supervisory Board to seek expert advice if special knowledge is required to judge a business decision of the board of directors.

[87] Ibid.

action.[88] Settlement agreements with deviant members of the board of directors take effect upon the approval of the general meeting.[89]

S. 93 (2) of the Stock Corporation Act imposes liability on members of the board of directors who breach their duties. S. 93 defines the duty of care owed by each member of the board of directors in the light of the business judgment rule. In corporate practice, managerial duties have been further fleshed out by corporate governance codes and specific compliance schemes.[90] More recently, the duty to establish a compliance management system has been characterised as a duty sanctioned by the liability regime under s. 93 (2).[91] There is an ongoing debate on how to reconcile a strict rule of policing negligent managerial misbehaviour with the business judgment rule.[92] It is suggested that the Stock Corporation Act should allow for more freedom of contract in the corporate charter. Corporations should be free to lay down their own liability rules for its directors, excluding liability for simple negligence (*einfache Fahrlässigkeit*).[93]

[88] Ibid. See also case analysis by *Jens Koch*, Die schleichende Erosion der Verfolgungspflicht nach ARAG/Garmenbeck, Neue Zeitschrift für Gesellschaftsrecht 2014, 934 (935 *et seq.*).

[89] See s. 93 (4) (1) of the Stock Corporation Act and MAN SE, Bekanntmachung der Einberufung zur Hauptversammlung am 15.5.2014 mit dem Ziel der europaweiten Verbreitung gemäß § 121 AktG and Annexes (17 March 2014, available at http://www.dgap.de/dgap/News/hauptversammlung/man-bekanntmachung-der-einberufung-zur-hauptversammlung-hannover-mit-dem-ziel-der-europaweiten-verbreitung-gemaess-aktg/?companyID=136&newsID=792537) and D&O ISAR Vergleich zwischen Allianz Global Corporate & Specialty AG, AIG Europe Ltd., HDI Gerling Industrie Versicherung AG, CNA Insurance Company Ltd., Chubb Insurance Company of Europe S.E. und MAN SE (2014), available at www.renk.de/cms_media/module_ob/1/554_1_RENK_HV_2014_TOP_5_D_O_Vergleich_ISAR_d.pdf.

[90] See *Christoph E. Hauschka* (ed.), Handbuch der Haftungsvermeidung im Unternehmen (Verlag C.H. Beck München 2010); *Sharon Oded*, Corporate Compliance – New Approaches to Regulatory Enforcement (Edward Elgar Cheltenham 2013), 105 *et seq.*

[91] District Court (Landgericht) München I, judgment of 10 December 2013, 5 HKO 1387/10, Der Betrieb 2014, 766 (769) and case note by *Robert Oppenheim*, Die Pflicht des Vorstands zur Einrichtung einer auf Dauer angelegten Compliance-Organisation – Zugleich eine Besprechung von LG München I; Urteil vom 10.12.2013, 5 HK 1387/10 (n.kr.), Deutsches Steuerrecht 2014, 1063 (1065 *et seq.*). See also *Holger Fleischer*, Aktienrechtliche Compliance-Pflichten im Praxistest: Das Siemens/Neubürger-Urteil des LG München I, 2014 Neue Zeitschrift für Gesellschaftsrecht 321 (322).

[92] See debate during the 2014 reunion of the German Confederation of Lawyers: 70. Deutscher Juristentag Hannover 2014, Beschlüsse [Resolutions], www.djt.de/fileadmin/downloads/70/140919_djt_70_beschluesse_web_rz.pdf, and the comments by *Bernd R. Meyer*, Die aktienrechtliche Organhaftung – Reform durch juristische Methodik oder gesetzgeberisches Handeln?, 2014 Neue Zeitschrift für Gesellschaftsrecht 1208 *et seq.*, and by *Kai Hasselbach/Felix Ebbinghaus*, Anwendung der Business Judgment Rule bei unklarer Rechtslage, 59 Die Aktiengesellschaft 873 *et seq.* (2014).

[93] 70. Deutscher Juristentag Hannover 2014 Beschlüsse [Resolutions].

The statutory recognition of the business judgment rule was first thought to counterbalance litigious shareholders and judicial activism.[94] Under German law, however, the business judgment rule does not qualify as a safe harbour provision. Where the statute has codified express behavioural duties these will prevail over the business judgment rule. There have been a number of *causes célèbres* where 'delinquent' directors had to pay substantial amounts of damages.[95] A study commissioned for the 2014 meeting of the German Confederation of Lawyers has suggested that the statute should address decision-making scenarios where the law is unclear and the board of directors has sought expert advice although a court subsequently disapproves of the legal analysis.[96] Directors should then escape personal liability for damages once they have sought proper advice.[97] In fairness to current case law, it appears that director will *de facto* only be liable for gross negligence whereas light cases of negligence in the discharge of the duties of the board of directors will go unpoliced.[98] The principles of management liability under Stock Corporation Law have been extended to limited liability companies.[99]

[94] See *Holger Fleischer*, Ruinöse Managerhaftung: Reaktionsmöglichkeiten de lege lata und de lege ferenda, Zeitschrift für Wirtschaftsrecht 2014, 1305 *et seq.; Klaus J. Hopt*, Die Verantwortlichkeit von Vorstand und Aufsichtsrat: Grundsatz und Praxisprobleme – unter besonderer Berücksichtigung der Banken, Zeitschrift für Wirtschaftsrecht 2014, 1793 *et seq.*

[95] See Wirtschaftswoche 9 May 2008, Siemens wird ehemalige Vorstände auf Schadensersatz verklagen, www.wiwo.de/unternehmen/korruptionsskandal-siemens-wird-ehemalige-vorstaende-auf-schadensersatz-verklagen/5424490.html, District Court (Landgericht) München I, judgment of 10 December 2013, 5 HKO 1387/10, Der Betrieb 2014, 766 (769), settlement agreements in the MAN SE case MAN SE, Bekanntmachung der Einberufung zur Hauptversammlung am 15.5.2014 mit dem Ziel der europaweiten Verbreitung gemäß § 121 AktG and Annexes (17 March 2014, www.dgap.de/dgap/News/hauptversammlung/man-bekanntmachung-der-einberufung-zur-hauptversammlung-hannover-mit-dem-ziel-der-europaweiten-verbreitung-gemaess-aktg/?companyID=136&newsID=792537; D&O ISAR Vergleich zwischen Allianz Global Corporate & Specialty AG, AIG Europe Ltd., HDI Gerling Industrie Versicherung AG, CNA Insurance Company Ltd., Chubb Insurance Company of Europe S.E. und MAN SE (2014), available at www.renk.de/cms_media/module_ob/1/554_1_RENK_HV_2014_TOP_5_D_O_Vergleich_ISAR_d.pdf.

[96] *Gregor Bachmann*, Reform der Organhaftung? – Materielles Haftungsrecht und seine Durchsetzung in privaten und öffentlichen Unternehmen – Gutachten E zum Juristentag 2014 (Verlag C.H, Beck München 2014), E 47 *et seq*. See also *Kai Hasselbach/Felix Ebbinghaus*, 59 Die Aktiengesellschaft 873 (878 *et seq.*) (2014).

[97] See Federal Supreme Court (Bundesgerichtshof), judgment of 20 September 2011, II ZR 234/09, NJW-Rechtsprechungs-Report Zivilrecht 2011, 1670.

[98] *Gregor Bachmann*, Gutachten zum Juristentag 2014, E 4.

[99] *Holger Fleischer* in Münchener Kommentar zum GmbH-Gesetz (Verlag C.H. Beck München 2012), § 43 No. 71.

3.2 *Criminal Liability for Embezzlement*

Risky business strategies and the loss of corporate funds have come to arouse the interest of shareholders claiming compensation, public prosecutors and the general public. Under section 266 of the German Criminal Code (*Strafgesetzbuch*),

> whosoever abuses the power accorded him by statute, by commission of a public authority or legal transaction to dispose of assets of another or to make binding agreements for another, or violates his duty to safeguard the property interests of another incumbent upon him by reason of statute, commission of a public authority, legal transaction or fiduciary relationship, and thereby causes damage to the person, whose property interests he was responsible for, shall be liable to imprisonment not exceeding five years or a fine.[100]

Embezzlement cases are based on the belief that corporate law sanctions against management failure and waste are not exhaustive. This is not an issue of efficiency.[101] Instead, there is a school of thought insisting that corporate liability for damages should be supplemented by penal deterrence.[102] Recent statistics suggest that the total amount of fraud and embezzlement cases is declining in spite of increasing damages per case.[103] Crime prevention authorities do not have data on risky business strategies or bribery schemes leading to a conviction.[104]

When it came to light that managers of the German electronics conglomerate Siemens had maintained unofficial, hidden cash chests for financing bribes to foreign officials, they were accused of having disregarded the property interest of shareholders:[105] The Federal Supreme Court explained that the system of hidden cash accounts had gone beyond a mere exercise in risk-taking. Money had been withheld from shareholders which should

[100] S. 266 (1) (Embezzlement and abuse of trust) of the Criminal Code, English translation available on the homepage of the Federal Ministry of Justice at www.gesetze-im-internet.de/englisch_stgb/englisch_stgb.html#p2195.

[101] Cf. *Ralf Peter Anders*, Untreue zum Nachteil der GmbH (2012 Springer-Verlag Berlin, Heidelberg), 171.

[102] See *Ralf Peter Anders*, 122 *et seq*., 171 *et seq*.

[103] Bundeskriminalamt, Wirtschaftskriminalität – Bundeslagebild 2013, p. 5 et seq. (available at www.bka.de/nn_193360/DE/Publikationen/JahresberichteUndLagebilder/Wirtschaftskriminalitaet/wirtschaftskriminalitaet__node.html?__nnn=true).

[104] Ibid.

[105] For the international dimension of the Siemens case US Federal Department of Justice, Transcript of Press Conference Announcing Siemens AG and Three Subsidiaries Plead Guilty to Foreign Corrupt Practices Act Violations, Washington, D.C., 15 December 2008, www.justice.gov/archive/opa/pr/2008/December/08-opa-1112.html.

have accrued to them or the corporation.[106] In the Mannesmann-Vodafone takeover case,[107] managers of the target corporation had succeeded in staving off a hostile takeover by negotiating a friendly takeover. Afterwards, the supervisory board of the target company awarded additional cash premiums to corporate executives for the successful conclusion of the deal. The Federal Supreme Court opined that there was sufficient evidence for a breach of s. 266 (1) of the Criminal Code.[108] Under their employment contracts, the Court explained, the managers had not been entitled to additional payments. Thus the extra-contractual payments were deprived of any incentive function and just reduced the funds of their companies. On remand, the case was settled,[109] but the risks for managerial criminal liability remain. Embezzlement may also be found in conglomerates where the dominant parent company siphons off funds from the subsidiary thereby causing damage to creditors of the subsidiary.[110] When the members of the supervisory board of a Berlin bank had approved risky, loss-incurring real estate transactions, they were indicted under s. 266 (1) of the Criminal Code because the public prosecutors disapproved of bank guarantees which had caused substantial damages to the bank.[111] The courts rejected this logic because appropriate risk control mechanisms had been operative and the damages sustained had not jeopardised vital funds of the bank.[112]

The Federal Constitutional Court (*Bundesverfassungsgericht*) has noted that embezzlement and the notion of breaching a fiduciary relationship build on extra-penal norms, potentially liable to abuse.[113] The Court requires clear evidence on a breach of duty, demonstrated

[106] Federal Supreme Court (Bundesgerichtshof), judgment of 29 August 2008, 2 StR 587/07, Neue Juristische Wochenschrift 2009, 89 *et seq.*

[107] For a detailed account see Michael Hoffmann-Becking, Vorstandsvergütung nach Mannesmann, Neue Zeitschrift für Gesellschaftsrecht 2006, 127 et seq.

[108] Federal Supreme Court (Bundesgerichtshof), judgment of 21 December 2005, 3 StR 470/04, Deutsches Steuerrecht 2004, 284 et seq.

[109] Zeit on-line 29 November 2006, Mannesmann – Prozess eingestellt, available at www.zeit.de/online/2006/48/Mannesmann-eil.

[110] See *Markus Roth*, in Reinhard Bork/Carsten Schäfer (eds.), GmbHG – Kommentar zum GmbH-Gesetz (2nd ed. 2012, RWS Verlag Kommunikationsforum GmbH Köln), § 82 No. 21 *et seq.*, Federal Supreme Court (Bundesgerichtshof), decision of 31 July 2009, 2 StR 95/09, NJW 2009, 3666 *et seq.*

[111] See Federal Supreme Court (Bundesgerichtshof), judgment of 13 May 2013, 5 StR 551/11, NStZ 2013, 715 *et seq.*

[112] Ibid.

[113] Federal Constitutional Court (Bundesverfassungsgericht), decision of 23 June 2010, 2 BvR 2559/08, 2 BvR 105/09, 2 BvR 491/09, BVerfGE 126, 170 (200 *et seq.*).

by an insufficient risk assessment. Moreover, the detriment must have materialised. It appears from the reasoning of the Court that proper expert advice might substantially reduce the risk of a criminal law indictment.[114] As a corollary, the absence of a compliance management system or the disregard for internal compliance procedure does not automatically trigger an indictment for embezzlement.[115]

Civil litigation courts are aware of the interface between company and criminal laws. Nonetheless, they will not automatically stay proceedings for damages until criminal law convictions for embezzlement have become unappealable: Despite the evidentiary problems in a legal system without pre-trial discovery, a demand for a stay will be rejected if the criminal proceedings are unlikely to produce new information.[116]

4 Procedure

4.1 Burden of Proof Rules

The efficiency of private enforcement of corporate law is predicated on the information available once a suit has been filed.[117] Under regime of pre-trial discovery fact-finding is delegated to private parties.[118] Thus discovery invites early negotiations between the parties if a request for discovery is challenged.[119] This is not to deny that the 'discovery game' might easily turn into 'a circle of blame' with high cost.[120] But under the

[114] Ibid.

[115] Federal Supreme Court (Bundesgerichtshof), judgment of 29 August 2008, 2 StR 587/07, Neue Juristische Wochenschrift 2009, 89 *et seq.*, cf. *Ute Bottmann*, in Tido Park/Ute Bottmann (eds.), Kapitalmarktstrafrecht (Nomos Verlag Baden-Baden 3rd ed. 2013), Kapitel Compliance, no. 64 *et seq.*

[116] See Court of Appeal (Oberlandesgericht) Braunschweig, decisions of 20 January 2014 (Oberlandesgericht Braunschweig, Press Release, Schadensersatz gegen Porsche Automobil Holding SE wegen vermeintlich unrichtiger Ad-hoc-Mitteilungen: Oberlandesgericht Braunschweig weist Beschwerden von drei Klägern zurück, available at www.oberlandesgericht-braunschweig.niedersachsen.de/aktuelles/pressemitteilungen/schadensersatz-gegen-porsche-automobil-holding-se-wegen-vermeintlich-unrichtiger-Ad-hoc-Mitteilungen-OLG-Braunschweig-weist-Beschwerden-zurueck-121259.html.

[117] For a twenty-first century perspective, see Richard Marcus, 'Looking Backward to 1938', 162 U. Pa. L. Rev. 1691 (2014), 1695 *et seq.*, 1721 *et seq.*

[118] See Erica Gorga and Michael Halberstam, 'Litigation Discovery and Corporate Governance: The Missing Story about the 'Genius of American Corporate Law', 63 Emory L. J. 1383 (2014), 1415 *et seq.*

[119] Ibid., at 1416.

[120] Robert L. Nelson, 'The Discovery Process as a Circle of Blame: Institutional, Professional, and Socio-Economic Factors That Contribute to Unreasonable, Inefficient, and Amoral Behavior in Corporate Litigation', 67 Fordham L. Rev. 773 (1998), 795 *et seq.*, see also:

German rules of civil procedure, choices for corporate litigation are radically different from their US counterparts since discovery does not exist.[121] Parties with severe problems of evidence might either take a free ride on criminal proceedings against a corporate official where the facts will be investigated *ex officio*. Alternatively, parties may leak what little information they have to the press, hoping that reputational concerns will induce the corporation to negotiate an out-of-court settlement. If none of this produces the desired outcome, the plaintiff will have to rely on specific burden-of-proof rules designed to address informational imbalances to some degree. These rules attempt to accommodate the implications of the business judgment rule and alleviate the difficulties of plaintiffs who are naturally unaware of what has been discussed on the board of directors or the supervisory board.[122]

Although s. 93 of the Stock Corporation codifies the business judgment rule, it does not create a rebuttable presumption that a member of the board of directors or the supervisory board has exercised his business judgment properly and is therefore exempt from liability. Rather, burden of evidence rules under s. 93 of the Stock Corporation Act introduce a shifting mechanism in order to protect managing executives from unduly burdensome pleading requirements. The corporation suing an executive has to state its case and offer evidence that damage has been incurred due to a breach of duties by the member of the board of directors.[123] Once these requirements have been met, the defendant manager will have to establish that in implementing the – now incriminated – business decision, he did not breach his duties[124] since he could

Timothy Wilson, 'Comment – A Mandate for Failure: The Sedona Cooperation Proclamation and Modern Discovery Under the Federal Rules of Procedure', 35 U. La Verne L. Rev. 165 (2013), 172 *et seq.*

[121] For a public law perspective see: *Rüdiger Breier* in Heinz-Peter Mansel/Barbara Dauner-Lieb/Martin Henssler (eds.), Zugang zum Recht: Europäische und US-amerikanische Wege der privaten Rechtsdurchsetzung (Nomos Verlagsgesellschaft Baden-Baden 2008), 29 *et seq.*

[122] See generally *Walter G. Paefgen*, Die Darlegungs- und Beweislast bei der Business Judgment Rule, Neue Zeitschrift für Gesellschaftsrecht 2009, 891 *et seq.*

[123] See Federal German Supreme Court (Bundesgerichtshof), judgments of 22 February 2011, II ZR 146/09, Neue Zeitschrift für Gesellschaftsrecht 2011, 549 (550 *et seq.*), and of 22 June 2009, II ZR 143/08, Neue Juristische Wochenschrift 2598 (on liability rules for limited liability companies) and decision of 18 February 2008, II ZR 62/07, Neue Zeitschrift für Gesellschaftsrecht 2008, 314 (on liability under the statute for limited liability companies).

[124] The section on director liability of the 2014 meeting of the German confederation has proposed to eliminate this burden of proof rule from the statute book.

reasonably believe to have acquired the relevant information before taking his decision. Under the burden of proof rule the defendant manager does not have to rebut the presumption that he committed an error or a breach of duty unless he can establish that he applied the reasonable care and skills of an average businessman in a comparable decision-making situation.[125] Courts have sought to protect business people from overstretched burden of proof rules.[126]

4.2 Cost Rules

Under the German law of civil procedure a successful plaintiff is entitled to a full recovery of costs, including court fees and those for his attorney.[127] Due to the cost/risk associated with an action for setting aside a resolution of the general meeting of shareholders or having it annulled, individual shareholders rarely commence proceedings.[128] Today's proceedings are brought by financially potent groups of shareholders or hedge funds protecting the interests of their investors.[129] The current Stock Corporation Act attempts to introduce a cap on the cost of litigation. Under s. 247 (1) the courts have discretion to fix the amount in controversy. According to s. 247 (1) (2) the amount in controversy is normally assumed not to exceed one-tenth of the legal capital. Although the statute envisages a cap of 500,000 € on the

125 The section on director liability of the 2014 meeting of the German confederation of lawyers would add a rule whereby a member of the board of directors may rely on the business decisions taken by a fellow member as long as there is no indication to the contrary.

126 See analysis by *Gregor Bachmann*, Gutachten zum Juristentag 2014, E 36 *et seq.*

127 This does also apply to an *actio pro socio* where the shareholder sues on behalf of the limited liability or a commercial partnership: *Dirk Verse* in Martin Henssler/Lutz Strohn, Gesellschaftsrecht (2nd ed. 2014), GmbHG § 14 no. 127.

128 See the economic analysis by *Michael Adams*, Reform des Kostenersatzrechts bei Aktionärsklagen mit Drittwirkung, Die Aktiengesellschaft 2000, 396 (397 *et seq.*, 409 *et seq.*).

129 See *Financial Times*, 2 February 2014, 'Hedge Funds File € 1.8 bn Lawsuit against Porsche Board Members', www.ft.com/cms/s/0/7d0af122-8bfd-11e3-bcf2-00144feab7de.html #axzz3QKExkLxa; *Handelsblatt*, 2/3 February 2014, Hedgefonds attackieren Piëch und Porsche, www.sbr-online.de/pdfarchive/einzelne_pdf/sbr_2011_apr_151–185.pdf). On shareholder activism in Germany, see Mark Mietzner, Denis Schweizer and Marcel Tyrell, 'Intra-Industry Effects of Shareholder Activism in Germany – Is There a Difference between Hedge Fund and Private Equity Investments?', 63 SCHMALENBACH BUS. REV. 151 *et seq.* (2011), www.sbr-online.de/pdfarchive/einzelne_pdf/sbr_2011_apr_151–185.pdf and *Thomas Bunz*, Vorbereitungs- und Reaktionsmöglichkeiten auf Shareholder Activism, Neue Zeitschrift für Gesellschaftsrecht 2014, 1049 (1050 *et seq.*).

amount in controversy, this limit may be disregarded if the importance of the matter for the plaintiff requires a higher valuation. Courts have shown little inhibition in setting the amount in controversy well beyond this threshold if a major shareholder sues.[130]

5 Company Law Enforcement and Capital Market Laws

In spite of globalisation, traditional regulatory philosophies continue to hold their grip on company law enforcement. The advent of institutional investors, (foreign) private equity and hedge funds has shaken up the litigation scene, but it has not ushered in major changes in legal theory on private law enforcement. The focus is on corporate legality issues, mitigated by judicial creativity on the duty of corporate loyalty. More than once, corporate legality has been protected indirectly by criminal law, capital maintenance rules and their sanctions, and insolvency law. Capital market legislation does not compensate private investors for what might be bemoaned as a surprising lack of exclusive focus on shareholder wealth-maximisation under company law statutes. Instead, German capital market law has opted for a government-led enforcement system which is in stark contrast to the US combination of privately brought lawsuits, SEC-led litigation and criminal law proceedings.[131]

5.1 Basics

Current capital market law has been shaped by the EU's rules on primary and secondary trading. The regulatory scenario for listed stock corporations has changed considerably with the EU's rules on primary and secondary trading[132] and their transposition into Members State law.

[130] For a survey over the case law, see *Uwe Hüffer*, Aktiengesetz, § 247 No. 8.

[131] Stavros Gadinis andHowell E. Jackson, 'Markets as Regulators', 80 So. Cal. L. Rev. 1239 (2007), 1271 *et seq.*, 1312 *et seq.*

[132] See Directive 2003/71/EC of the European Parliament and of the Council of 4 November 2003 on the prospectus to be published when securities are offered to the public or admitted to trading and amending Directive 2001/34/EC, O.J. L 345/64 of 31 December 2003, and Directive 2004/109/EC of the European Parliament and of the Council of 15 December 2004 on the harmonisation of transparency requirements in relation to information about issuers whose securities are admitted to trading on a regulated market and amending Directive 2001/34/EC, O.J. L 390/38 of 31 December 2004. For a comprehensive analysis see Niamh Moloney, *EU Securities and Financial Markets Regulation*, 3rd ed., Oxford University Press, 2014), 71 *et seq.*, 425 *et seq.*

Under the Securities Trading Act (*Wertpapierhandelsgesetz*)[133] a domestic issuer of securities has to disclose insider information as soon as he becomes aware thereof and cannot claim a privileged interest to withhold them.[134] A prohibition on market manipulations is to ensure that the board of directors of a listed corporation will refrain from making false and misleading statements which bear on the rating of a security.[135] The law imposes (additional) disclosure and notification duties if the acquisition of shares of a listed corporation reaches certain thresholds. Moreover, s. 25a of the Securities Trading Act mandates a disclosure by a listed corporation whenever it obtains an option right under a financial instrument to purchase shares, thus crossing statutory notification thresholds.[136] The notification duty extends to shareholder agreements which provide for coordination mechanism within voting pools enabling a party or several parties to control the decision-making process of the general meeting.[137] The notification has to be lodged with the German Federal Financial Supervisory Authority (*BaFin/Bundesanstalt für Finanzdienstleistungsaufsicht*).[138]

Under ss. 37b, 37c of the Securities Trading Act, the issuer has to pay damages sustained due to omission of disclosing or disclosure of untrue ad-hoc information. However, ss. 37b, 37c do not confer a direct claim for damages against the board of directors or an individual member of the board.[139] If a corporation is held liable under the Securities Trading Act, it may in turn sue its directors under the established liability

133 For an English translation of the Act see Federal Financial Supervisory Authority: www.bafin.de/SharedDocs/Aufsichtsrecht/EN/Gesetz/wphg_101119_en.html;jsessionid=385162988155BB9E51E4F4BBE5A9095E.1_cid363?nn=2821360#doc2684270bodyText1

134 S. 15 (1) of the Securities Trading Act (*Wertpapierhandelsgesetz*).

135 S. 20a Securities Trading Act (*Wertpapierhandelsgesetz*).

136 For a combination of an option and a pre-emption right see the shareholder agreement of a listed corporation: Turbon AG Veröffentlichung gemäß § 26 Abs. 1 WpHG mit dem Ziel der europaweiten Verbreitung of 26 June 2013, available at www.presseportal.de/pm/9052/2501462/dgap-pvr-turbon-ag-veroeffentlichung-gemaess-26-abs-1-wphg-mit-dem-ziel-der-europaweiten-verbreitung, see also for a call-option in a shareholder agreement: MPC Münchmeyer Petersen Capital AG, Veröffentlichung gemäß § 26 Abs. 1 WpHG/ of voting rights pursuant § 41 para. 4d WpHG), available at www.mpc-capital.de/contell/cms/server/mpc-capital_de/MPC_Capital/Investor_Relations/Jaehrliches_Dokument/?&format=print.

137 *Uwe H. Schneider* in Heinz-Dieter Assmann/Uwe H. Schneider (eds.), Wertpapierhandelsgesetz (6th ed. 2012 Verlag Dr. O. Schmidt), § 22 No. 178.

138 S. 21 of the Securities Trading Act (*Wertpapierhandelsgesetz*)

139 *Rolf Sethe* in Heinz-Dieter Assmann/Uwe H. Schneider, Wertpapierhandelsgesetz, §§ 37b, 37c, No. 160 *et seq.*

rules of stock corporation law to recover the damage sustained.[140] Apart from ss. 37b, 37c, civil law theory has taken a complicated approach towards private enforcement under the Securities Trading Act. Although many provisions of the statute impose duties on the issuer, courts are reluctant to confer individual claims on a shareholder or a potential investor on the capital market.[141] Ultimately, a case-by-case approach applies.[142] Public enforcement will be undertaken by *BaFin*, whose regulatory toolkit stretches from moral suasion to findings that an offence or a crime has been committed.[143] In calculating administrative fines for offences under the Securities Trading Act, *BaFin* applies a catalogue which builds on the size of the issuer, the severity of the offence, the need for a special deterrence factor and the financial capacity of the infringer.[144]

In transposing the European Takeover Directive,[145] Germany has enacted the Securities Acquisition and Takeover Act (*Wertpapiererwerbs- und Übernahmegesetz*),[146] which imposes disclosure and corporate governance duties on the board of management of bidder and the target corporations. From a comparative law perspective, s. 33 of the Act on defensive action taken by the board of the target company needs to be

[140] *Rolf Sethe*, in Heinz-Dieter Assmann/Uwe Schneider, Wertpapierhandelsgesetz, §§ 37b, 37c No. 163; *Matthias Haas*, Die persönliche Haftung von Vorstandsmitgliedern für falsche ad-hoc Mitteilungen, LMK 2004, 181 *et seq.*

[141] Federal German Supreme Court (Bundesgerichtshof), judgments of 19 February 2008, XI ZR 170/07, BGHZ 175, 276 (279 seq.), of 22 June 2010, VI ZR 212/09, BGHZ 186, 58Neue Zeitschrift für Gesellschaftsrecht 2010, 1071 (1072 *et seq.*), and of 13 December 2011, XI ZR 51/10, BGHZ 192, 90 (96 *et seq.*).

[142] See ibid. and *Holger Fleischer*, Das Vierte Finanzmarktförderungsgesetz, Neue Juristische Wochenschrift 2002, 2977 *et seq.*

[143] See ss. 4, 38 *et seq.* of the Act and e.g. Schreiben der Bundesanstalt für Finanzdienstleistungsaufsicht zur Auslegung einzelner Begriffe der §§ 31 Abs. 2 S. 4, 34b Wertpapierhandelsgesetz (WpHG) in Verbindung mit der Verordnung über die Analyse von Finanzinstrumenten (Finanzanalyseverordnung – FinAnV), WA 36 – Wp-2002–2007/0006, 21 December 2007 (available at www.bafin.de/SharedDocs/Veroeffentlichungen/DE/Auslegungsentscheidung/WA/ae_071221_34bwphg.html).

[144] BaFin (Federal Financial Supervisory Authority, Section for Administrative Offence Procedures, WpHG Guidelines – Guidelines on the Imposition of Fines in Administrative Offence Proceedings for Breaches of the Provisions of the Securities Trading Act, Berlin November 2013, available at www.bafin.de/SharedDocs/Downloads/EN/Leitfaden/dl_lf_bussgeldleitlinien_2013_en.pdf?__blob=publicationFile.

[145] Directive 2004/25/EC of the European Parliament and of the Council of 21 April 2004 on Takeover Bids, O.J. L 142/12 of 30 April 2004.

[146] For an English translation of the Act see Federal Financial Supervisory Authority: www.bafin.de/SharedDocs/Aufsichtsrecht/EN/Gesetz/wpueg_en.html;jsessionid=46EA0FD5ADC7A88DE426FFB88FFDC55B.1_cid381?nn=2821360#doc2684280bodyText1.

mentioned. Although the board of directors of the target company may not take defensive action, it is authorised to solicit a competing offer, provided that the board observes the duties normally arising from the business judgment rule. S. 33 (2) of the Act authorises the general meeting to exempt the board of directors from the prohibition against defensive measures for a maximum period of 18 months. A minimum quorum of 75 per cent of a general meeting, at which at least 75 per cent of the subscribed capital are present, is required.[147]

S. 35 (2) of the Securities Acquisition and Takeover Act introduces the mandatory offer after the bidder has acquired the control of the target company. Legal theory does not qualify this duty as an obligation which arises under the law of corporation. Rather, capital market law imposes this duty in the interest of the capital market and investors.[148] Once the bidder has obtained shares which constitute more than 95 per cent of the legal capital of a corporation, he can apply to the court to have the remaining shares transferred to him and pay an adequate compensation.[149]

According to s. 4 (1) of the Securities Acquisition and Takeover Act, *BaFin* is charged with controlling whether bids (including mandatory bids) have been made in accordance with the law. But *BaFin* will only use its powers if the public interest so dictates.[150] Law enforcement under the Act takes the form of an administrative order (*Verwaltungsakt*)[151] which can be attacked in court. However, minority shareholders of the target company do not have a right to be heard if the bidder asks *BaFin* to dispense with the statutory requirement of a mandatory bid.[152]

147 S. 33 (2) of the Securities Acquisition and Takeover Act.

148 *Roland Steinmeyer* in Roland/Steinmeyer/Michael Häger (eds.); WpÜG – Wertpapiererwerbs- und Übernahmegesetz – Kommentar (Erich Schmidt Verlag Berlin 2nd ed. 2007), § 35 No. 8.

149 S. 39a (1) of the Securities Acquisition and Takeover Act.

150 See s. 4(2) of the Securities Acquisition and Takeover Act.

151 See the facts of the case decided by the Court of Appeal (Oberlandesgericht) Frankfurt, decision of 24 November 2009, WpÜG 11, 12/09, Neue Zeitschrift für Gesellschaftsrecht 2010, 63. In a worst case scenario this may include a prohibition of proceeding with the takeover bid if there is an evident breach of the law (see *BaFin* Homepage on Supervision under the Securities Acquisition and Takeover Act – 'Aufsicht über Wertpapiererwerbs-, Übernahme- und Pflichtangebote nach dem WpÜG', available at www.bafin.de/SharedDocs/Standardartikel/DE/bieterpflichten_wpueg.html?nn=2798666#doc2677528bodyText4.

152 Court of Appeal (Oberlandesgericht) Frankfurt, decision of 27 May 2003, WpÜG 1/03, Neue Zeitschrift für Gesellschaftsrecht 2003, 729 *et seq*.

5.2 *Collective Redress Mechanisms*

With respect to collective redress mechanism in corporate settings, current German legislation falls behind the EU's non-binding recommendation on 'common principles for injunctive and compensatory collective redress mechanisms'.[153] When German Telekom was partially privatised, thousands of retail investors bought shares under the influence of alleged misrepresentations in the prospectus. More than 17,000 individual actions for damages were filed, paralysing a local district court.[154] A Capital Markets Model Case Act was passed, applicable to claims for damages for inaccurate, misleading or omitted public capital information.[155] After an amendment in 2012, the Act also covers claims for damages flowing from the *use* of inaccurate or misleading information and from the failure to inform the public about a deficiency of the information.[156] In its current form, the statute is a bundling device whereby parallel proceedings on a similar *factual* setting will be stayed until a test case has been decided.[157] Investors who have a similar claim, but have not commenced litigation yet, may join the test case proceedings and the statute of limitations will be tolled.[158] A local court of appeal (*Oberlandesgericht*) will then decide on the issues of the model case. The decision of the court will be binding on those claimants who joined

[153] See Commission Recommendation of 11 June 2013 on common principles for injunctive and compensatory collective redress mechanisms in the Member States concerning violations of rights granted under Union Law (2013/396/EU), O.J. L 201/60 of 26 July 2013.

[154] *Thomas Möllers/Bernhard Pregler*, Zivilrechtliche Rechtsdurchsetzung und kollektiver Rechtsschutz im Wirtschaftsrecht, 176 Zeitschrift für das gesamte Handels- und Wirtschaftsrecht 144 (148) (2012); Brigitte Haar, 'Investor Protection Through Model Case Procedures – Implementing Collective Goals and Individual Rights Under the 2012 Amendment to the German Capital Markets Model Case Act (KapMuG)', 15 Eur. Bus. Org. L. Rev. 83 (2014), 84.

[155] Kapitalanleger-Musterverfahrensgesetz KapMuG, current version of 19 October 2012, BGBl. I 2182. For a critical assessment of the 2005 version of the law: *Axel Halfmeier/Peter R'ott/Eberhard Feess*, Kollektiver Rechtsschutz im Kapitalmarktrecht (Frankfurt School Verlag, 2010), 80 *et seq.*; and *Thomas Möllers/Sabine Seidenschwann*, Der erweiterte Anwendungsbereich des KapMuG, NZG 2012, 1401 *et seq.*

[156] *Brigitte Haar*, 15 Eur. Bus. Org. L. Rev. 83 (98 *et seq.*) (2014); *Matthias Söhner*, Das neue Kapitalanleger-Musterverfahrensgesetz, Zeitschrift für Wirtschaftsrecht 2013,7 *et seq.*

[157] ss. 5,8 of the Act. See: *Gregor Vollkommer* in Burkhard Hess/Fabian Reuschle/Bruno Rimmelspacher, Kölner Kommentar zum KapMuG (Carl Heymanns Verlag Köln 2008), § 4 No. 9.

[158] ss. 10 (2), 11 (1) of the Act, see: *Johannes Wigand*, Zur Reform des Kapitalanleger-Musterverfahrensgesetzes (KapMuG), AG 2012, 845 (846).

the test case. Once the model case ruling has become unappealable, the stay on the individual (parallel) proceedings will be lifted and the respective courts will have to decide the individual cases on the basis of the test ruling.[159]

Test case proceedings are initiated by an application for a model case ruling. The local court of appeal has discretion to choose the lead plaintiff of the test case.[160] Seemingly, test cases proceed on an opt-in basis. Those who opt in will be registered and the local court of appeal publishes a notice to alert other potential participants. However, even those who decline to join the case may be affected by the case. In an individual litigation, the court has power to stay proceedings *sua sponte* if it feels that the test has some bearing on its decision, even if the individual claimant disagrees because of the potential delay in getting a judgment in his own case.[161] Participants who are not recognised as lead plaintiffs are entitled to make submissions, but only to the extent they do not conflict with declarations of the lead plaintiffs.[162] *Res judicata* applies and the model case ruling may only be disregarded under very limited circumstances.[163] The statute expressly authorises parties to settle their dispute by a court-approved settlement which will take effect if less than 30 per cent of the non-lead party participants opt out of the settlement.[164] After a very slow beginning, model case proceedings seem to have picked up. But very often, they do not get beyond the stage of admissibility. One of the major drawbacks of this collective procedure is its lack of speed.[165]

5.3 *Conclusion*

In enforcing company law and securities regulation, the German legislator has opted for a bifurcated approach, relying both on private and public enforcement. Private litigation prevails in company law, although managers should not underestimate the risks of an indictment for embezzlement under criminal law. Securities law enforcement is largely assured by public authorities, although activist shareholders and investors are attempting to lower the threshold for private damage claims under the capital market statutes. But courts remain reluctant to expand the concept of private securities litigation. In 2014, the annual meeting of the

[159] S. 22 (4) of the Act. [160] S. 9 (2) of the Act.
[161] Brigitte Haar, 15 Eur. Bus. Org. L. Rev. 83, (2014), 98 *et seq.*, *Axel Halfmeier/Peter Rott/Eberhard Feess*, 80 *et seq.*
[162] s. 14 of the Act. [163] s. 22 (2), (3) of the Act. [164] See s. 17 (2) of the Act.
[165] Cf. Brigitte Haar, 15 Eur. Bus. Org. L. Rev. 83, (2014), 97 *et seq.*

German Confederation of Lawyers debated whether judicial activism should be counterbalanced by relaxed statutory liability rules for members of the board of directors and the supervisory board. In spite of globalisation and the current debate on statutory shortcomings, the fundamental concepts of company law enforcement for public and private companies have not seen much change. Moreover, the German corporate governance is informed by a stakeholder approach which goes beyond the statutory concept of codetermination.[166]

The focus of German company law is on legality. Legality from a shareholder perspective is to maintain the distribution of powers between the board of directors and the general meeting.[167] This includes protection of minorities against a board of directors who are seen as advancing the interest of a dominant shareholder or a group of shareholders.[168] The courts have transcended the limits of the legality concept by recognising a duty of corporate loyalty,[169] which could also be instrumental in introducing market-oriented principles into what is essentially a principal-agent relationship. More than once, courts have pointed out to the constitutional underpinnings of shareholders rights in order to cure rigidities of the statute.[170] Nonetheless, the constitutional reference does not exclusively serve to buttress shareholder wealth maximisation, but to accommodate evolutionary developments within the legislative concept of legality, including codetermination.[171] However, 'legality' within non-listed corporations and limited liability companies

[166] Klaus J. Hopt, 'Comparative Corporate Governance: The State of the Art and International Regulation', 50 AM. J. COMP. L. 1 (2011), 7 *et seq.*, 20 *et seq.*

[167] See Section 2.2.1 of this chapter. [168] See Section 2.1 of this chapter.

[169] See Section 2.2.2 of this chapter.

[170] See Federal Constitutional Court (Bundesverfassungsgericht), judgments of 7 August 1962, 1 BvL 16/60, BVerfGE 14, 263 (277 *et seq*), and of 27 April 1999, 1 BvR 1613/94, BVerfGE 100, 289 (301 *et seq.*); Federal Supreme Court (Bundesgerichtshof), decision of 20 May 1997, II ZB 9/96, Neue Juristische Wochenschrift 1997, 2242 (2243 *et seq.*), noting the constitutional underpinnings of the statutory duty to compensate outstanding shareholders for their loss of dividends after the corporation has entered into a profit transfer agreement with another, and judgment of 25 November 2002, II ZR 133/01, BGHZ 153, 47 (54 *et seq.*) ('Macroton'). For an analysis of the jurisprudence of the Federal Constitutional Court: *Alexander Schiel*, Aktionärsschutz zwischen Aktienrecht und Kapitalmarkt (Duncker & Humblot, Berlin (2009)); 85 *et seq.; Michael Becker*, Verwaltungskontrolle durch Gesellschaftsrecht – Eine vergleichende Studie nach dem deutschen Verbandsrecht und dem amerikanischen Recht der corporation, Beiträge zum ausländischen und internationalen Privatrecht 62 (Verlag Mohr Siebeck Tübingen (1997)), 406 *et seq.*

[171] Cf. Lucian A. Bebchuk and Mark J. Roe, 'A Theory of Path Dependence in Corporate Ownership and Governance', 52 STANF. L. REV. 127 (1999), 150 *et seq.*, 168 *et seq.*, Janis

has a different connotation once litigation is not a viable option. Negotiated, cooperative strategies are likely to prevail as long as there are regrets that a business might exit from the market.

The board of directors is responsible for assuring corporate legality. S. 4.1.3 of the German Corporate Governance Code expects the board of directors, *inter alia*, to assure that law and internal policies will be complied with within the company and, if applicable, within the conglomerate group.[172] S. 4.1.4 provides for appropriate risk management.[173] Although the code operates on a comply-or-explain basis for listed corporations,[174] its recommendations are likely to be regarded as stating an important aspect of corporate legality.[175] The pronouncements of the Corporate Governance Code will also make their way into the law on non-listed stock corporations and limited liability companies.[176] The directors' duty to observe corporate legality is flexible enough to adapt managerial duties to changing economic circumstances. Conversely, too much judicial flexibility provokes calls for limiting liability within the corporate charter *ex ante*, lest boards of directors become risk-averse.[177]

Sarra, 'Corporate Governance in Global Capital Markets, Canadian and International Developments', 76 TUL. L. REV. 1691 (2002), 1716 *et seq.*

172 Regierungskommission Deutscher Corporate Governance Kodex, German Corporate Governance Code (as amended, 24 June 2014), available at www.dcgk.de//files/dcgk/usercontent/en/download/code/E-CorpGov_2014.pdf.

173 Ibid. 174 See s. 161 of the Stock Corporation Act.

175 Cf. *Holger Fleischer*, Neue Zeitschrift für Gesellschaftsrecht 2014, 321 (322 *et seq.*); *Klaus J. Hopt*, 59 AM. J. COMP. L. 1 (2011), 37.

176 Cf. *Ingo Theusinger/Oliver Jung* in Volker Römermann/Heino Büsching (eds.), Münchener Anwaltsbuch GmbH-Recht (Verlag C.H. Beck München (3rd ed. 2014)), § 24 No. 8 *et seq.* (on limited liability companies).

177 See debates and resolutions during the 2014 meeting of the German Confederation of Lawyers: 70. Deutscher Juristentag Hannover 2014, Beschlüsse, available at www.djt.de/fileadmin/downloads/70/140919_djt_70_beschluesse_web_rz.pdf.

19

Liability for Misstatements to the Market

The Post-Parmalat Years

GUIDO FERRARINI AND PAOLO GIUDICI

1 Introduction

On 27 December 2003 Parmalat was declared insolvent. The case shocked Italy and Europe because it was immediately apparent that this was one of the biggest accounting scandals in recent history and the first big one in Europe after the American frauds that were discovered in 2001 with respect to Enron, WorldCom, etc. In a previous article written immediately after the scandal,[1] we argued that the deficiencies of private enforcement in Italy had a role in the Parmalat scam, because at the time in the Italian financial market, deterrence was entirely focused on public enforcement, meaning the Securities Commission's administrative actions and criminal actions. Public enforcement, however, is far from being perfectly efficient. Since issuers were not sufficiently deterred by investors' civil actions, deterrence was not working on a day-by-day basis.

The fact that Parmalat's Extraordinary Commissioner and investors brought civil actions in the US rather than in Italy led the Italian public to believe that this was a form of modern forum shopping which was based on the search for the more convenient substantive rules and ignited, as far as investors suits were concerned, by the class-action mechanism, which at the time was missing in Italy. The political discussion then focused on the introduction of class actions in Italian civil procedure law and on amending existing substantive rules in order to make them even stricter.

We argued, however, that the poor state of Italian private enforcement did not depend on substantive rules or the simple absence of class

[1] Guido Ferrarini and Paolo Giudici, 'Financial Scandals and the Role of Private Enforcement: The Parmalat Case' in *After Enron* (John Armour and Joseph A. McCahery eds., Hart Publishing, 2006), 159.

actions. We made two main points. First, and contrary to what many observers thought at the time, Italian substantive rules are, somewhat surprisingly to those accustomed to the law and finance concepts of strong and weak law, even stricter than their US equivalents. Second, we pointed out that the introduction of mechanisms similar to class action would not have been enough to change the poor record of private enforcement. Attorney fees rules had to be altered. Even more importantly, discovery rules had to be introduced and pleading rules amended, while civil litigants should have been given easier access to supervisory agencies' factual findings in administrative proceedings against regulated entities and issuers.

After more than ten years, things have changed to some extent, and private enforcement is today more important, but it is still not working properly as a deterrence mechanism, mainly for the reasons we have just mentioned. Courts respond to investors' problems concerning the launch and sustainability of long-term civil actions in Italy by offering an interpretation of substantive rules that is generally favourable to plaintiffs. We explain this approach as a way to rebalance the inherent disadvantage that investors face in the Italian civil procedure system, even though we argue that in a recent decision concerning insider trading liability, the Cassation Court maybe went too far in stretching the boundaries of damage actions.

In this chapter, we analyse the most significant cases on liability for market misstatements that were decided by Italian courts in the last twelve years, and we show how Italian courts cope with problems that are typical of this kind of liability around the world. In Section 2 we describe Italian Law on issuers' and gatekeepers' liability. In Section 3 we analyse the most significant cases and compare their approach with that followed by US Courts.

2 Italian Law

2.1 *General Liability Regime for Omissions and Misstatements*

Many of the current disclosure obligations that are found in Italian law were implemented from European law, even though many others had pre-existed.[2] Accordingly, we are not presenting here Italian rules on

[2] At least four European Directives cover issuers' disclosure duties: the Prospectus Directive (Directive 2003/71/EC as amended by Directive 2010/73/EU, with all the delegated regulation); the Listing Particulars Directive (Directive 2001/34/CE); the Transparency

disclosure obligations. Instead, we are concerned with the Italian rules under which civil liability attaches to the breach of disclosure obligations or to misstatements to the market, because those rules are left to EU member states.

Traditionally, the liability rules concerning issuers' misstatements and omissions have been governed by tort law,[3] by general standards concerning pre-contractual liability,[4] and by a specific rule of the Civil Code regarding promoters' misrepresentations.[5] All the statutory rules that were subsequently enacted with explicit reference to liability for inaccurate disclosures are therefore considered as specifications of these two main rules.

Liability in tort covers any deliberate or negligent act that causes unfair damage. The undisputed interpretation is that tort liability covers inaccurate information and omissions of mandatory disclosure obligations, at least by issuers to creditors and investors.[6] Inaccurate information contained in financial reports, that companies are obliged to make public through deposits with the public company register, is covered as well.

The Anglo-American debate over pure economic loss is far away from the Italian tradition, because at least one rule of the Civil Code that lies in the area of tort law makes implicit but clear reference to liability for misstatements to creditors and market investors. The provision[7] states that the director liability regime (directors' liability to the company and to its creditors as a class) does not prejudice the right to damages of individual shareholders and third parties that have been directly damaged by negligent or deliberate acts of the directors. The history of this provision shows that it mainly refers to culpable or intentional misstatements and omissions by the directors.[8] Those misstatements and omissions are therefore considered a case of tort.[9]

Such provision is a key rule in this area of law because it touches upon another very important matter which is constantly discussed in the

Directive (Directive 2004/109/EC); the MAD directive (Directive 2003/6/EC, now repealed by Directive 2014/57/EU).

[3] Article 2043 Civil Code. [4] Article 1337 Civil Code.

[5] Article 2339 Civil Code. See Guido Ferrarini, *La responsabilità da prospetto. Informazione societaria e tutela degli investitori* (Giuffrè, 1986).

[6] Ibid., at 141 ff. [7] Article 2395 Civil Code.

[8] But also statutory auditors are considered liable (Article 2407, last paragraph, Civil Code).

[9] Gustavo Minervini, *Gli amministratori di società per azioni*, 363 (Giuffrè, 1956). Cassation Court, 28 February 1998, n. 2251, Foro it., 1998, I, 3246; Guido Ferrarini, *La responsabilità da prospetto*, 150 ff.; Ugo Carnevali, 'La responsabilità civile degli amministratori per danno ai risparmiatori', *Contr. impr.* 83 (1988).

international literature. It implicitly states that directors are personally liable for misstatements. Thus, the directors are liable even though they disclosed inaccurate or false information on behalf of the company and irrespective of whether the inaccurate or false disclosure was to the benefit of the company. Under Italian law, accordingly, directors are not shielded by the corporate entity. The purpose of this departure from general principles of corporate law is deterrence. The undisputed interpretation is that the company remains liable as well, as the directors were acting as a body or as representatives of the legal entity;[10] and since the provision's *raison d'être* is deterrence, the company cannot waive liability in the corporate charter.[11]

At least two other statutory provisions concerning company information confirm that inaccurate information is a civil wrong, at least in a financial market environment. Since 1975 a provision attaches liability of auditors to third parties for non-compliance with auditor duties.[12] Article 154-*bis* CSFA attaches the directors' liability regime to managers charged with preparing companies' financial reports. These rules are considered specifications of the general liability rule grounded in Articles 2043 and 2395 of the Civil Code on the question of directors' liability for financial information, either episodic or periodic.

All these rules, which make no distinction between primary markets and secondary markets, are governed by the joint and several liability principle where liability is also extended to aiders and abettors. Some authors have argued that at least some of these rules can be construed as a contractual liability regime for misrepresentation.[13] Indeed, in the SCI case, the Cassation Court assumed that the disclosure duties might be constructed as contractual in nature.[14] However, the difference between tort law and contract law in this area of law should not be overemphasised, as we will

[10] Ferrarini, *La responsabilità da prospetto* (1986), 68 ff. e 142 ff.

[11] Andrea Tina, *L'esonero da responsabilità degli amministratori di s.p.a.* (Giuffrè, 2008), 160 ff.

[12] Currently the provision is Article 15 of the Legislative Decree no. 39/2010, which implements a provision of the Italian law that implements the Auditor Directive, i.e. Directive 2006/43/CE. See Paolo Giudici, 'Auditors' Multi-Layered Liability Regime', 13 *EBOR* 501 (2012), comparing the Italian liability regimes concerning auditors with the US and UK.)

[13] Eugenio Barcellona, *Responsabilità da informazione al mercato: il caso dei revisori legali dei conti* (Giappichelli. 2003); Paolo Giudici, *Regolazione finanziaria ed esternalità del contratto: i contratti rivolti ai terzi*, Riv. reg 2014, 46.

[14] Cassation Court, 3 July 2014, no. 15224, *Soc.*, 2014, 1378.

discuss with regards to the main difference between the two regimes, namely the burden of proof.

2.2 Prospectus Liability

Prospectus liability, today, is governed by specific rules. Previously, the general rules on pre-contractual liability and company promoters' liability were invoked with regards to misstatements in the placing of securities accompanied by a prospectus prepared by the issuer and the underwriters. The argument was that the relationship between each investor and whoever had prepared the prospectus and was soliciting investment was pre-contractual in nature.[15] An important extension of this argument was that pre-contractual liability has a contractual nature that entails the need to call for the application of contractual principles concerning evidence and statutes of limitations, which are more favourable to investors.[16] Initially court cases followed this reasoning.[17] However, the Cassation court held that prospectus liability, and more in general pre-contractual liability, is a case of tort.[18] In the meantime, however, prospectus liability has been specifically targeted by securities regulation, which now explicitly considers the prospectus (and the KIID) as a pre-contractual document (Article 98-*ter*, para. 3). In fact, a prospectus liability regime has been inserted in the Legislative Decree no. 58/1998 (Consolidated Services and Financial Act – CSFA), largely to implement Article 6 of the Prospectus Directive (Directive 2003/71/EC). The relevant provision states that the issuer, the offeror, the guarantor and any person that contributes to the information contained in the prospectus is liable for the information provided towards any reasonable investor who relied on this information, unless it can be proved that

[15] At the time, the mainstream view was that pre-contractual liability was applicable only to cases where a party abandons the negotiations after having induced the other party to rely on the signature of the contract. Some scholars argued that pre-contractual liability was applicable also to situations where an investor had been induced to rely on untrue information concerning the issuer and had thereafter entered into an investment contract: see Ferrarini, *La responsabilità da prospetto* (1986).

[16] More specifically, under contractual liability the plaintiff can claim that the defendant has failed to perform; it is on the defendant to prove that the opposite is true. In tort actions, instead, the burden of proof is entirely on the plaintiff's shoulders. The statute of limitation is ten years in contractual liability, five years in tort.

[17] See Milan Tribunal, 11 January 1988, in *Giur. comm.*, 1988, II, 585; Milan Court of Appeal, 2 February 1990, in *Giur. comm.*, 1990, II, 755

[18] Cassation Court, 11 June 2010, no. 14056.

sufficient due diligence was performed in order to ascertain that the information was true and there were no significant omissions. The lead manager is also liable unless due diligence can be demonstrated.[19] Underwriters are not liable for prospectus liability instead. The liability is on who participated in the prospectus drafting, not on distributors – who can be held liable under MiFID rules concerning the sale of financial instruments, in a completely different liability scenario.

The prospectus liability regime is similar, in structure, to a contractual liability regime, because it is on the defendant to prove that due diligence was duly performed. In other words, the plaintiff should show that he or she relied on wrong information or that there was a material omission, and then it is on the defendant to show that he or she acted with due diligence.[20] The prospectus liability regime is mainly addressed to primary markets, but it is also applicable to misrepresentation contained in the listing particulars.[21]

In sum, and with reference to investors' claims, liability stems from a set of different rules that have a common ground. When there are prospectuses or listing particulars, the prospectus liability regime is applicable to issuers, offerors, auditors and whoever provided information contained in the prospectus. Liability attaches to the lead manager as well. With reference to directors (and the company itself), statutory auditors ('collegio sindacale'), auditors, and the manager charged with preparing the company's financial reports, liability stems from the different tort provisions that we have already mentioned. Accordingly, there is no distinction between primary and secondary market claims under Italian law. Thus, there is no distinction between information contained in selling documents and information contained in financial reports or press releases. From this perspective, the Italian law took a path very different from the UK one, where a distinction was traditionally drawn between information contained in prospectuses and in other documents.[22]

2.3 *Burden of Proof concerning Negligence*

On paper a distinction should be drawn between the prospectus liability regime and the episodic or periodic information liability regime

19 Article 94 CSFA.

20 The statute of limitation is five years, like in tort, but also like in all company law matters.

21 Article 113 CFSA.

22 Paul Davies, 'Davies Review of Issuer Liability – Liability for misstatements to the market: A discussion paper by Professor Paul Davies QC' (2007). 16ff, hm-treasury.gov.uk/davies.

governed by tort. As mentioned, under prospectus liability the plaintiff can claim damages caused by misstatements in the prospectus, and the defendants have a due diligence defence. Accordingly, the standard is negligence, with a shifting of the burden of proof to the defendant that is more typical of liability arising from contract obligations. It is on the defendant to prove that his actions or words were not negligent. Under tort principles, the standard is negligence as well – but the burden of proof is on the plaintiff. In practice, however, this difference should not be overstated. Courts are never very formalistic on this point, and are prepared to use various doctrines, amongst which the 'vicinity to evidence' doctrine is the most egregious, to shift the burden of proof required in tort.[23]

The 'vicinity to evidence' doctrine must be acknowledged, taking into consideration the fact that Italian civil procedure does not offer instruments that can be compared to US discovery or UK disclosure (except in a limited number of cases, which are not relevant in misrepresentation cases). Thus, the court can recognise that it is excessively difficult for the plaintiff to offer evidence of facts that occurred in the defendant's sphere of action, such as facts in the sphere of action of management and auditors. For this reason, Italian courts are allowed more freedom in allocating the burden of persuasion and the burden of proof through rebuttable presumptions than common law courts. Accordingly, an Italian court can consider the facts mentioned by the defendant as sufficient circumstantial evidence to assert that '*res ipsa loquitur*', and shift on the defendants the burden of proving that there was no negligence. The result is that the two regimes are not so different in terms of burden of proof.[24]

Accordingly, Italian liability rules may appear more complicated than they really are. We have a general rule concerning misstatements and omissions in capital markets, which finds some apparent specifications that actually do not say anything special, except that they clarify, basically following international standards, who can be held liable: directors, lead managers, statutory auditors, auditors, and any expert or party who took responsibility for a part of the prospectus.

[23] See below, Section 3.

[24] Some scholars have asserted that since Article 113 CSFA, which refers to liability for information contained in the listing particulars, mentions Article 94 CSFA liability regime, the reversal in the burden of proof should be applied by analogy to any market information.

2.4 Consumer Class Actions

Italy has adopted a class action instrument with regard to consumers' rights.[25] The rule, however, does not refer to actions in tort or to pre-contractual liability, and therefore it is very doubtful whether retail investors can bring a securities class action in cases concerning misstatements to the market. In a decision concerning the issuance of new equity by Monte dei Paschi di Siena, a very old Italian bank and one of the biggest Italian banking groups, a consumer association brought a claim on behalf of retail investors. Those investors had exercised their option rights and had purchased new shares of the bank, relying on the information contained in the prospectus, which was allegedly false. The Florence Tribunal decided in favour of the bank, dismissing the class action on the ground that the shareholders are not consumers and that the action was in tort, thereby falling outside the boundaries of the class action instrument.[26]

3 Post-Parmalat Cases and Issues

3.1 The Major Cases

After Parmalat, many significant cases were decided. The majority of them started after Parmalat's collapse, even though at least one very important case that was recently decided by the Cassation Court had started well before Parmalat.

The first Italian case ever concerning a false prospectus in an IPO setting was *Freedomland*, decided by the Tribunal of Milan in 2008.[27] There were previous court decisions concerning prospectus liability,[28] but never in an IPO setting. Freedomland was an internet-television company that went bankrupt. A large number of investors (the final number was 1,165) who had purchased its shares in the course of the IPO and in the secondary market sued the lead manager and sponsor, the auditor and the securities watchdog (Consob). The Milan Tribunal held everybody liable toward investors. After a few months the Milan Tribunal

[25] Article 140-*bis* Legislative Decree 6 September 2005, no. 206 ('Consumer Code').

[26] Firenze Court of Appeal, 15 July 2014, *Foro it.*, 2015, I, 2782.

[27] Milan Tribunal, 25 July 2008, *Freedomland.*

[28] See Milan Trib., 11 January 1988, II *Giur. Comm.* 585 (1988); Milan Court of Appeal, 2 February 1990, II *Banca borsa* 734 (1990); Guido Ferrarini, *Sollecitazione del risparmio e quotazione in borsa*, G.E. Colombo – G.B. Portale (eds.), Trattato delle società per azioni, 10**, Utet: Torino, 1993, 289.

decided *Italaudit*, one of the many cases arising from the Parmalat scandal.[29] The case concerned the auditor of some of Parmalat's subsidiaries which were used to hide the negative results of the dairy group. The court accorded damages to the investors who had bought Parmalat shares and bonds on the market in the period interested by the inaccurate audit.

The two most interesting cases of the post-Parmalat era so far are *Italease* and *SCI*. The first case concerned a bank that had concealed its trade in derivatives, which had generated huge losses.[30] A professional investor brought a claim, arguing that the purchase price it had paid was highly inflated. The defendant argued that there was lack of standing, since the investor was seeking redress for losses to the company that had an indirect impact on its investment. The court rejected this defence, holding that the investor was claiming damages for information that, if known, would have changed its investment approach, and therefore direct damages under Article 2395 were recognised. The defendant then argued that the directors were liable under Article 2395 of the Civil Code, not the bank, which had suffered because of their decisions. The court rejected this defence, following the well-established view that the company is liable for its own directors' inaccurate information released to the market, independently of the reasons that led the directors to provide the market with inaccurate or false information. Thus the defendant argued that the plaintiff had to prove reliance; but the plaintiff provided evidence of the manner in which the information had been collected, elaborated, and the investment decision had been taken. The damages were measured on the basis of the difference between the purchase price and the sale price after the disclosure of the truth about the company. Thus, in the *Italease* opinion we find all the plethora of issues commonly discussed in this kind of action around the world.

The *SCI* case is even more interesting, because it is an insider trading case and because it was decided on the grounds of arguments that (we submit) were unconvincing. It concerned the insolvency of a listed building company and the insider trading transactions that ensued.[31] *SCI* was a small-cap that negotiated a debt restructuring plan with banks, which were also shareholders of the company following a previous conversion of debt into equity aimed at saving the firm from insolvency. At a certain

[29] Milan Tribunal, 4 November 2008, *Italaudit.*

[30] Milan Tribunal, 22 luglio 2010, *Italease, Soc.*, 2015, 862.

[31] Milan Tribunal, 14 February 2004, *SCI, Foro it., 2004, I, 1581.*

point in time, however, it appeared clear that there was no way to save the company. The information was kept confidential both by the company and the creditor banks, but the latter gradually sold their shares in the company on the market. At the time, there were also rumours that the company was a potential takeover target (the court decisions do not discuss if this was a 'pump and dump' scheme organised by the banks). Investors who purchased the shares, unaware of the truth and in the hope of a takeover bid, brought claims against the banks, alleging that increased market activity had induced them to buy SCI's shares and that the banks, as controlling shareholders, should have informed the market about their decision to sell the shares.

Both the Milan Tribunal and the Milan Court of Appeal held the banks liable for damages suffered by investors, but the banks brought an appeal against these judgments to the Cassation Court. Somehow surprisingly, the Italian supreme civil judicature held that insiders have a general 'disclose or abstain' duty, based on general principles of civil law and European capital markets law about transparency, and on the investors' right to operate in a fair and transparent marketplace. We will return on this decision in a subsequent paragraph, when discussing causation issues.

What is still missing in the now rather developed Italian jurisprudence in capital markets law is a case of corrective disclosure of a solvent company, followed by a sharp price drop and by investors' suits. *Italease* was close to this situation, but in reality the company was already on the edge of insolvency.

3.2 *Italian Courts and Transaction Causation*

It is now interesting to analyse how Italian courts have dealt with causation problems and damages. Causation is highly debated in US academia and case law, and it may be instructive to compare the US approach with that followed in a traditional civil law jurisdiction such as Italy.

Under Italian law and on paper, it is for the claimant to prove that, in acquiring or disposing of securities, it acted in reliance on the published information, and that this reliance was reasonable. The reliance element attaches both to prospectus liability regime and to the traditional tort regime. However, courts are induced to establish an inference of reliance from the facts. In all the main Italian cases concerning investors' claims for inaccurate or false disclosure, proving reliance was not an obstacle indeed. Basically, the courts ascertained that there was a misstatement or an omission in a situation where the issuer had a duty to disclose. Then the courts observed that without the misstatement or the omission, the plaintiff would have purchased or sold at a different value because the true information would have had an impact on prices. Evidence that the investor had actually acquired and elaborated the wrong information has not been considered an issue, since courts constantly presume that the wrong information reached the investor through financial advisors or other financial intermediaries, or that the market price reflected the lack of right information.[32] Italian courts have been wary not to conceptualise this point too much, and they avoid any reference to the fraud-on-the-market theory. When non-institutional investors are concerned, there is probably more influence by the old German doctrine of 'investment atmosphere', which asserts that misstatements can generate a sort of investment euphoria that is independent from specific reliance on the misrepresented facts.

This approach to causation issues is particularly clear in two recently published decisions concerning the *Italease* case, where the Tribunal of Milan and the Court of Appeal of Milan applied to secondary market transactions the principles of law stated by the Cassation Court in a 2010 decision concerning prospectus liability.[33] In that decision the Cassation Court held that the 'untruthfulness of the prospectus gives rise to a presumption of relevance concerning the impact of the information distortion over the investor's choices. The investor cannot face the burden of a negative proof concerning other potential factors that might have influenced his investment choices.'[34] Accordingly, the burden of proof is reverted. It is on the issuer to provide evidence that the plaintiff did not rely on the misstatement (or would have not relied on the complete and true information). The Court of Appeal of Milan and the Tribunal openly took the presumption approach with regard to secondary market transactions as well, adopting what is, in fact, a US-style rebuttable presumption.

This approach to transaction causation issues has greatly facilitated the permissive joinder of claims, both in prospectus liability cases (see *Freedomland*) and in other cases (see *Italaudit* and *SCI*). For instance, in *Italaudit* investors' reliance on Parmalat group consolidated accounts

32 Only in one case, *Italease*, the investor was asked to provide evidence of transaction causation.

33 Trib. Milano, 17 January 2014, in *Soc.*, 2015, 855; Milan Court of Appeal, 15 January 2014, n. 118, in *Soc.*, 2015, 7, 849.

34 Cass., 11 June 2010, no. 14056, in *Soc.*, 2011, 411.

was not even discussed in the court's opinion. Reliance was taken for granted because the court reasoned that the inaccurate accounts provided the whole market with inaccurate information regarding the group situation, and the investors had, therefore, purchased financial instruments unaware of the truth. Investors were not required to prove that they had read and relied on the group financial statements.

Thus, the scenario is very similar to the US one, and US dissatisfaction with the FOTM theory, considered as the result of a peculiar trajectory taken by US law somewhere in history, might sound strange from an Italian perspective. Of course, Italian courts do not deal with large class actions. Accordingly, claims concerning mainly a group of investors and courts and academics might be unable to foresee the sheer dimension of a securities class action and the problems that it raises. But this point should not be overemphasised. As already mentioned, in at least one post-Parmalat decision, *Freedomland*, more than a thousand claimants joined their actions and won the case.

3.3 *Insider Trading and Causation: SCI*

With regards to causation, however, *SCI* is a special case, for the Supreme Court held that an insider has a 'disclose or abstain' duty. In particular, the Court held that banks selling their shares in a company on the brink of insolvency, while in possession of inside information concerning the same, were obliged to disclose this information to investors before transacting with them. The Court, in a sense, set aside all transaction and loss causation issues that are typical of insider trading liability cases, without considering that under Italian and European law, insiders do not have a disclosure duty, which is rather on the issuer and its controlling shareholder. Therefore, the Supreme Court made improper recourse to the US 'disclose or abstain' maxim, no doubt in an effort to enhance private enforcement, but eluding causation issues, such as those regarding the link between insider negotiations on the market and investors' reliance and losses.

3.4 *Italian Perspectives on the US Critical Analysis of Securities Class Actions*

US commentators' critique concerning securities class actions looks, from an Italian perspective, far less convincing than it appears to be in American academia. Arguments about the inability of securities class actions to result in compensation are focussed on data that do not match with the Italian, and more generally European, experience. Italian cases settle much less frequently than US ones. The pressure to settle is basically inexistent in the Italian environment; from an Italian perspective one might even wonder why so many cases are settled in the US and if this excessive settlement propensity is not the real problem instead. In Italian cases which reached a final judgment, investors were awarded damages by the court, but it is difficult to assess whether they were really able to recover the money due from the defendants (see below: insolvent issuer scenario).

The pocket-shifting scenario is less convincing as well. Some cases (such as *Italease* and, before Parmalat, *Fingem*) were brought by big investors, who were significant shareholders in the company. Other cases concerned small investors acting against insolvent issuers, their directors and gatekeepers. The policy implications of large class actions where – absent liable gatekeepers – a class of shareholders gets compensation from the company, and therefore from another class of shareholders, is lost in an environment where there are no large class actions and often there is no solvent company to pay the damaged party.

As to the deterrent value of securities actions, Italian courts emphasise it more and more, and in a recent Cassation Court decision, the court explicitly referred to it before awarding damages to investors who had suffered losses because of a massive elusion of mandatory takeover rules.[35] In this area of law, moreover, there can be the growing impact of the European action in favour of private enforcement of antitrust law. In a recent decision, the Cassation court explicitly argued in favour of the interpretation of civil procedure rules concerning evidence in a matter that would make private enforcement in antitrust cases effective.[36] We believe that this approach will influence securities litigation, where the arguments in favour of private enforcement are very similar and equally strong.

3.5 Damages

In the US, as two scholars recently pointed out, 'one of the most striking features of FOTM jurisprudence is the absence of case law on damage

[35] Cassation Court, 10 August 2012, no. 14392, 14399 and 14400. See also Cassation Court, 13 October 2015, no. 20560.

[36] Cassation Court, 4 June 2015, no. 11564.

calculations.'[37] In Italy, court cases have dealt with this issue, even though not within a clear theoretical framework. Under Italian law, it is for the claimant to prove a loss in respect of securities purchased or sold, caused by the inaccurate disclosure, its delay or omission. This is the loss causation requirement. As to quantification of damages, the loss is the difference in value between the inflated price and the value of the securities at the moment the truth made its way into the marketplace. Since it can be difficult to understand what part of the depreciated value is attributable to the emergence of the truth rather than to market conditions, Italian courts are usually prepared to adopt quantifications in equity and to accord some interest on the amount of the recognised loss.

Accordingly, the plaintiff must prove the purchase at inflated price and, if there was a sale after the truth emerged, the sale, through any available documentary evidence. If there was a sale before the truth emerged, theoretically the investor cannot claim damages, because she sold at inflated prices as well. In-and-out traders should have no right to claim damages. However at least in one case, *Freedomland*, the court apparently accorded damages to in-and-out traders as well.[38] More specifically, the court considered the investors' position in classes and calculated the damage in equity, generally as the difference between the purchase price and the average price of the shares in the ninety days following the discovery of the truth. However, the court accorded damages for the difference in value also to investors who had resold the shares before the moment where the truth started to make its way into the market place. The mere fact of having purchased shares under the influence of incorrect information was considered to be enough to redress the investor of any negative consequence deriving from the investment.

In *SCI* the court accorded damages, but not proportionate to the whole loss suffered by investors. The court reasoned that investors had taken a lot of risk because the company perspectives appeared already uncertain, and there were conjectures about a possible takeover bid. Hence, the judges argued that the investors were risk-takers and would have bought the shares nevertheless, even though at a different price. Accordingly, the court calculated damages in equity.

There are no direct cases on whether the plaintiff can claim damages for losses attributable to the decision not to sell the shares at a certain

[37] William W. Bratton and Michael L. Wachter, 'The Political Economy of Fraud on the Market', 160 U. Pa. L. Rev. 69 (2011), 84–85.

[38] *Freedomland.*

point in time on the grounds of the positive, misleading information provided for by the issuer at that moment in time. However, if the plaintiff can show that there was a decision-making process to keep the shares, and this process was causally influenced by the information setting, loss causation can be proven and damages can be awarded. The Tribunal of Milan in the 1999 *Fin.Ge.M.* case[39] briefly touched on this point. Indeed, the court held that the right to damages is also connected to the decision to keep the shares, where this decision had been induced by inaccurate or false information.

4 Conclusions

After Parmalat, Italian courts have decided some very significant cases concerning liability for misstatements to the market; therefore there is now a wide corpus of decisions in this area of law. The Italian Cassation Court recently decided also an insider trading civil liability case.

The lack of effective class actions mechanisms is not an insuperable problem, but it is obvious that many potential cases were not launched because it is doubtful whether the class action mechanism can go to the benefit of retail investors in securities cases. The organisation of a large group of plaintiffs as a permissive joinder is obviously a big task, with huge transaction costs in terms of collecting the powers of attorney, the money to finance the action, the documents concerning each single plaintiff.

Access to information is a problem and that might explain why Italy has, up to now, a significant court decision on all issues except a case of corrective disclosure of a solvent company followed by a sharp price drop. Indeed, if the company is solvent and there is no public investigation or intense press coverage, obtaining information is very difficult in the absence of discovery rules.

Issues concerning transaction causation are mostly resolved through the rebuttable presumption that the misstatements created a market environment that induced the investor to enter the market. As to lack of disclosure, transaction causation is never an issue. Courts never refer, however, to FOTM or any other economic model, and this lack of an expressed rationale with regard to transaction causation creates uncertainty. With regard to damages, in many significant cases they have been accorded on equity grounds.

[39] Milan Tribunal, 21 October 1999, *Fin.Ge.M.* v. *Price Waterhouse and other defendants*, *Giur.it.*, 2000, 554.

In a very recent case concerning the sale of shares on the market by insiders, the Italian Cassation Court has boldly transplanted the American 'disclose or abstain' rule into the Italian environment in order to overcome reliance and loss causation issues. The case, in our opinion, went a bit too far in asserting that anyone who trades while possessing inside information is liable to anonymous counterparts on the other side of the trade. However, it clearly shows that the Italian Supreme Court wants to stress that private enforcement of securities regulation is a value.

20

Growing Securities Litigation against Issuers in Japan

Its Background and Reality

GEN GOTO*

1 Introduction

Securities litigation against issuers is growing in Japan. In the latter half of the 2000s, many suits by investors in the secondary market were filed against issuers that made material misrepresentations, and in many of them, plaintiffs were granted judgments in their favour.[1] Before then, such litigation was very rare, and no published court decision had imposed liability on defendant issuers.[2] Some might claim that Japan has now started to follow the litigious United States in this area of the law – in a similar manner to Japan's rise in shareholder derivative suits.[3]

* The author would like to thank Dan Puchniak, Masakazu Shirai, and the participants of the Conference on Public and Private Enforcement of Company Law and Securities Regulation – China and the World, held at the Chinese University of Hong Kong on 13–14 December 2014 for their valuable comments and advice. Also, the author would like to thank the Japan Society for the Promotion of Science for financial supports to this research through the JSPS Postdoctoral Fellowship for Research Abroad and Grants-in-Aid for Scientific Research (A) No.24243001. The research for this article was conducted while the author was a visiting scholar at East Asian Legal Studies of Harvard Law School. Unless noted otherwise, the websites cited in this article were last visited on 7/1/2016.

1 See Section 3.1.1 and Section 3.2.1 of this chapter.

2 Takahito Kato, 'Ryutsu Shijyo ni okeru Fujitsu Kaiji to Toshika no Songai' [Misrepresentations in the Secondary Market and Investors' Damage], 11 *Shin-sedai Ho-seisaku-gaku Kenkyu* 303 (2011), 304. The absence of securities litigation does not mean that there were no window-dressings before 2005. To name a few examples, there are cases of *Sanyo Special Steel Co.* (1965), *Fuji Sash Co.* (1978), *Yamaichi Securities Co.* (1997) and *Kanebo* (2005) (years in parentheses are those in which window-dressings became public).

3 Japan is known as a country where shareholder derivative suits are actively used, only next to the United States. For derivative suits in Japan, see, Dan W. Puchniak and Masafumi Nakahigashi, 'Japan's Love for Derivative Actions: Irrational Behavior and

This article analyses this phenomenon from three perspectives. First, it looks into the legal background that caused this sudden increase of securities litigation. The largest factor is the 2004 reform of Securities and Exchange Act (now named Financial Instruments and Exchange Act, hereinafter, FIEA), which introduced Article 21–2 – a special provision for the statutory liability of the issuer to investors in the secondary market. Based on the experience in the United States, however, we know that the driving forces behind securities litigation are often plaintiffs' lawyers, and that civil procedural rules are as important as substantive rules on liability in shaping the incentives of lawyers. In this regard, more analysis is necessary to explain the increase in securities litigation, as Japanese rules on civil procedure differ from those of the US in that there are neither class actions nor discovery.

Second, although many commentators in Japan state that securities litigation against issuers is increasing,[4] these observations are largely based on the accumulation of decisions regarding three large misrepresentation cases, namely, Seibu Railway, Livedoor and Urban Corporation.[5] Before any evaluation, it would be worthwhile to take a look at the actual degree of the increase and its driving force.

Third, keeping the second point above in mind, this article reviews recent critiques of Article 21–2 that arose in response to the increase, and the following reform of FIEA in 2014 that slightly weakened Article 21–2.

The above three problems will be addressed in Sections 2, 3 and 4, respectively, followed by a short conclusion in Section 5.

2 The Backgrounds of the Increase

2.1 FIEA, Article 21–2: Japanese Fraud-on-the-Market

Before the 2004 reform of the Securities and Exchange Act, investors in the secondary market were only able to sue issuers based on Article 709 of the Civil Code, which is the general provision for tort liability. Under this

Non-Economic Motives as Rational Explanations for Shareholder Litigation', 45 VAND. J. TRANSNATIONAL L. 1 (2012).

4 See for example, Hideki Kanda, 'Fujitsu Kaiji to Toshisha no Songai' [Misrepresentation and Damage of Investors], in *Kigyoho Kinyuho no Shinchoryu – Maeda Shigeyuki Sensei Koki Kinen* [New Trends in Enterprise Law and Finance Law – Festschrift for Professor Shigeyuki Maeda's 70th Birthday] (ed. Atsushi Koide, Souichirou Kozuka, Gen Goto and Aken Ban, Shojihomu, 2013) 313, 315.

5 In each of these three cases, more than one suit had been filed by different plaintiffs, and the Supreme Court decided on at least one of them.

regime, plaintiffs are required to establish intention or negligence of the wrongdoer (i.e. the issuer) regarding the wrongdoing (i.e. the misrepresentation) and the causation between such intention or negligence and the plaintiffs' damage. These burdens of proof, especially the one for causation, were difficult to fulfil.[6]

The Financial Services Agency (hereinafter, 'FSA') viewed this situation as an under-enforcement of securities regulations, and introduced Article 21–2 to strengthen the right of investors in order to promote public trust in the fairness of the capital market and to foster investment by the public.[7] This article is applicable to misrepresentation made in disclosure documents that were submitted after 1 December 2004.[8]

The liability of issuers under Article 21–2 of FIEA differs from the tort liability above in several aspects. First, the only things that a plaintiff needs to prove to succeed in a claim for compensation of damages under Article 21–2 are that there was a material misrepresentation[9] in documents disclosed to public under Article 25, paragraph 1 of FIEA,[10] and that she acquired[11] securities issued by the person who submitted the document, not through a public offering, after that document was disclosed to public.[12] Although the provision does not state it explicitly, the plaintiff does not need to prove that she relied upon the document in making her investment decision.[13] In other words, the liability under Article 21–2 is based generally on the fraud-on-the-market theory in the US.

6 For example, see Tokyo District Court, 20 December 2001, 1133 Hanrei Taimuzu 161.

7 Hidenori Mitsui ed., *Kachokin Seido to Minji Baisho Sekinin– Jyokai Syoken Torihiki-ho* [Administrative Fines and Civil Liability: Securities and Exchange Act Annotated] (2005) 2–11, 31. Note that the report of the Financial Systems Council proposing such reform (see ibid., at 9–11) was published on 24 December 2003, before misrepresentations of Seibu Railway, Kanebo and Livedoor, the major scandals of the mid-2000s, came to light in 2004, 2005 and 2006, respectively.

8 Art.5, Supplementary Provisions to the Reform Act of the Securities and Exchange Act. www.fsa.go.jp/houan/159/hou159.html.

9 Material misrepresentation includes both fake statements on important matters and a lack of a statement on important matters that should be stated or on a material fact that is necessary to avoid misunderstanding.

10 The list of documents of Article 25, paragraph 1, FIEA, includes, but is not limited to, the annual report, semi-annual report, quarterly report, extraordinary report and internal control report. Importantly, Article 21–2 is not applicable to misrepresentations made in disclosures required by stock exchanges or in voluntary disclosures.

11 See note 79 below for the amendment on this point by the 2014 reform.

12 Art.21–2, para.1, FIEA.

13 Tomonobu Yamashita and Hideki Kanda (ed.), *Kinyu-shohin Torihikiho Gaisetsu* [Financial Instruments and Exchange Act] (Yuhikaku, 2010), 209.

Second, this Japanese version of the fraud-on-the-market theory is more powerful than its original US version under Rule 10b-5 in that liability under Article 21–2 is a strict liability, and plaintiffs do not have to establish the intention or negligence of the defendant issuer regarding misrepresentations.[14] As discussed in Section 4.2, however, this point was amended in 2014 and the standard of liability became negligence liability with burden of proof for non-negligence on defendants.[15]

Third, the plaintiff's burden of proof is also eased substantially by a statutory presumption of the amount of damages caused by the material representation, which also has the effect of a presumption of causation. When there is a public announcement that there was a misrepresentation,[16] the amount of damage caused by the material misrepresentation is presumed to be the difference between the average market price of the one-month period before such an announcement and the average market price of the one-month period after such an announcement.[17] Eligibility for this presumption is limited to investors who have acquired the shares of the issuer within one year prior to the day of the public announcement and continue to hold the shares at the day of such announcement.[18] This presumption of damage is rebuttable, and the defendant issuer is not liable for all or part of the damage suffered by the plaintiff if the loss in share value was caused by reasons other than the decline of value of shares that should arise from the material misrepresentation.[19]

Of course, there are some limits. The amount of damage recoverable under Article 21–2 is limited to the difference between the amount paid by the plaintiff to acquire the security and the market value of that security at the time when the plaintiff claimed damages under Article 21–2.[20] Such an upper limit does not apply for claims under Article 709 of the Civil Code.

[14] Compare Art.21–2, para.1, FIEA with Art.21, para.2 and Art.22, para.2, FIEA.

[15] See notes 79–80 below and accompanying texts.

[16] The definition of 'a public announcement of the fact of misrepresentation' is given in Art. 21–2, para.4, FIEA (paragraph 3 before the 2014 reform). See also Supreme Court, 13 March 2012, 66 Saiko Saibansho Minji Hanreishu 1957.

[17] Art.21–2, para.3, FIEA (paragraph 2 before the 2014 reform). This presumption is based on the idea of out-of-pocket damages. Plaintiff is free to claim recessionary damage by proving that she would not have purchased shares of the issuer but for the misrepresentation in question.

[18] Art.21–2, para.3, FIEA (paragraph 2 before the 2014 reform).

[19] Art.21–2, para.5 and 6 (paragraphs 4 and 5 before the 2014 reform), FIEA. See also Section 4.1 of this chapter.

[20] Art.21–2, para.1 and Art.19, para.1, FIEA.

Also, there is a shorter prescription period than that for claims based on general tort law.[21] The right to claim damages under Article 21–2 is extinguished by prescription when the right is not exercised within two years from the time when the person who is entitled to claim the damages comes to know, or is able to know by exercising reasonable care, about the material misrepresentation, or when the right is not exercised within five years from the time when the document is submitted.[22]

Overall, Article 21–2 has substantially eased the burden of proof for plaintiffs to sue the issuer in comparison to suits based on general tort law. One point that claims based on Article 21–2 share with claims based on general tort law is that, unlike in the US, both claims are not subordinated to other debts of the issuer corporation even in bankruptcy.[23] This reinforces the point that based on the substantive law, Japanese investors are in stronger position than those in the US.

The liability of issuers under Article 21–2 also stands out in comparison to that of directors and outside auditors. Although FIEA has special provisions for the liability of directors, statutory auditors, executive officers and outside auditors against investors in the secondary market,[24] they do not include a presumption of damage.[25] Thus, plaintiffs suing directors, statutory auditors, executive officers and outside auditors must establish the amount of damage and the causation between the damage and the material misrepresentation, which is not an easy task.[26] Also, the standard of liability is not strict liability, and directors, statutory auditors, executive officers and outside auditors can escape from liability by proving that they were unable to discover the misrepresentation even though they had exercised due care.[27]

21 Claims based on general tort law are extinguished by prescription when the right is not exercised within three years from the time when the person who is entitled to claim the damages comes to know the damage and the tortfeasor, or when the right is not exercised within twenty years from the time of the tort. Art.724, Civil Code.

22 Art.21–3 and Art.20, FIEA.

23 In the US, claims against the issuer corporation for misrepresentation are subordinated in the bankruptcy procedure of the issuer. See, 11 U.S.C. 510(b).

24 Art.24–4 and Art.22, FIEA.

25 On the other hand, there is neither an upper limit of the amount of damage nor a short prescription period.

26 This difficulty may be eased if the plaintiff sued directors and outside auditors together with the issuer. Also, courts may consider the idea behind Article 21–2, paragraph 3 when dealing with the liability of directors, statutory auditors, executive officers and outside auditors. See for example, Tokyo District Court, 22 June 2014, 1397 Kinyu Shoji Hanrei 30.

27 Art.24–4, Art.22, and Art.21, para.2, no.1 and 3, FIEA.

2.2 *Procedural Limits under Japanese Law*

The experience in the United States shows that the driving forces behind securities litigation are often, if not always, plaintiffs' lawyers and that civil procedural rules are as important as substantive rules on liability in shaping the incentives of lawyers. In this regard, Japanese rules on civil procedure differ from that of the US in two important respects.

2.2.1 Lack of Discovery

First, as Japanese civil procedure does not have a system for comprehensive compulsory disclosure of evidence like discovery in the US, the ability of plaintiffs in Japan to collect evidence in the hands of defendants is very limited. The lack of US-style discovery, however, would not be crucial for claims based on Article 21–2 since plaintiffs do not need to establish the intention or negligence of the defendant issuer.[28]

2.2.2 Lack of US-Style Class Actions

Second, and more importantly, US-style class actions, which are the major form of securities litigation in the US, are not permitted in Japan. Japan did introduce its first collective redress procedure in 2013,[29] but the scope of this new procedure is limited to claims for compensation of damages suffered by consumers and related to consumer contracts. Thus, it is generally unavailable for investors in the secondary market who suffered damages through misrepresentations.

Therefore, a Japanese lawyer motivated to replicate a US-style securities class action must persuade a large number of investors to become a plaintiff at the outset. Somewhat surprisingly, such attempts are not uncommon, which demonstrate that US-style class action is not a prerequisite for securities litigation. As we will see in Section 3.2 below, several law firms are trying to build a large group of plaintiffs by setting up websites to invite 'victim-shareholders', who have been harmed by misrepresentations, to join lawsuits. These lawsuits could be called 'quasi-class actions'. The implicit adoption of the fraud-on-the-market theory by Article 21–2 and its presumption of the amount of damage and causation must have contributed to the practicability of such

[28] This point would apply equally to suits against directors, statutory auditors, executive officers or outside auditors as these defendants bear the burden of proof for non-negligence.

[29] Act on Special Provisions Regarding Civil Procedure for Collective Redress of Property Damages to Consumers, Law No.96 of 2013.

attempts by eliminating the necessity of establishing causation for individual investors, just as the fraud-on-the-market theory eased class certification in the US. Still, the scale of such litigation is likely to be smaller than class actions in the US.[30]

2.2.3 Rules on Lawyer's Fees

Two aspects regarding lawyer's fees under Japanese law, which are similar to US law, are also worth noting. First, contingency fees are not prohibited, and there is no limit on the quantum of contingency fees.[31] Second, Japan basically adopts the so-called American rule regarding lawyer's fees. That is, each party of a lawsuit is responsible for its own lawyer's fee and does not have to pay the other party's lawyer's fee even if it loses.[32] While there is a chance that plaintiff investors are awarded all or a part of their lawyers' fee as their damages caused by the issuer's tortious act (i.e. misrepresentation),[33] such opportunity for the defendant issuer is limited to cases in which it succeeds to prove that the plaintiffs were intentional or reckless in filing a lawsuit without merit.[34]

3 Actual State of Securities Litigation against Issuers

To summarise the previous part, Japanese investors suing issuers face less of a burden of proof than their counterparts in the US, and a weaker form of class action is theoretically possible. Thus, the question that arises is: in

[30] See Section 3.2.1 of this chapter.

[31] Until 31 March 2004, Japan Federation of Bar Associations had set the standard tariff of lawyer's fee, which comprised of sliding scales for retainer and contingency fee. For contingency fee, the table was 16 per cent for amount of up to 3 million JPY, 10 per cent for amount over 3 million to 30 million JPY, 6 per cent for amount over 30 million to 300 million JPY, and 4 per cent for amount over 300 million JPY. See (Kyu) Nihon Bengoshi Rengokai Hosyu-to Kijyun [Former Standard Tariff of Japan Federation of Bar Associations on Lawyers' Fee], www.miyaben.jp/consultation/pdf/expenses_kijun.pdf. This standard tariff was abolished, as Japanese Fair Trade Commission viewed it as potentially in violation of anti-trust law.

[32] While the costs and fees payable to the court are placed on the losing party unless the court determines otherwise (Art.61 and Art.67, Civil Procedure Code), compensation to lawyers is not included in such costs and fees. See, Act on Costs of Civil Procedure, Art.2, no.10 (including compensation for lawyers appointed by the court only).

[33] See for example, Tokyo High Court, 28 August 2014, 367 Shiryoban Shoji Homu 20; Osaka District Court, 21 July 2015, 1476 Kinyu Shoji Hanrei 16. However, some courts deny awarding lawyers' fee in addition to the amount of damage calculated by presumption under Article 21–2, paragraph 3, FIEA. Tokyo District Court, 27 November 2014, LEX/DB25505951.

[34] Supreme Court, 26 January 1988, 42 Saiko Saibansho Minji Hanreishu 1.

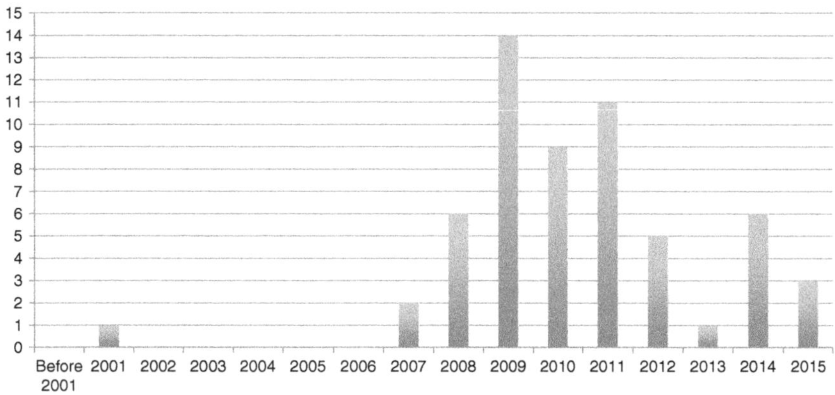

Figure 20.1 Number of published court decisions per year
*Made by the author from LEX/DB Internet and Westlaw Japan

reality, has Japan developed a US-style securities litigation system or do substantial differences still remain? This part provides a preliminary overview on the actual state of securities litigation against issuers in Japan.

3.1 How Big Is the Increase?

The first question is, how big is the increase in securities litigation against issuers in Japan? As information regarding the number of suits filed is not publicly available in Japan,[35] this chapter tries to approach this question from two directions: the number of published court decisions and records of public enforcement.

3.1.1 Number of Published Court Decisions

As of 15 August 2016, a search on LEX/DB Internet and Westlaw Japan, two of the most commonly used databases for case law in Japan, generates fifty-eight decisions regarding liability of issuers against investors in the secondary market.

Figure 20.1 shows the number of court decisions issued in each year. With the exception of the oldest decision on Yamaichi Securities case

[35] Japan does not have a system like the Public Access to Court Electronic Records (PACER) in the US (www.pacer.gov), let alone a specialised database like the Securities Class Action Clearinghouse of Stanford Law School (http://securities.stanford.edu/index.html).

Table 20.1 *Number of court decisions and of suits on the liability of issuers*

Name of the issuer	Number of decisions	Number of suits	Art. 21–2 FIEA
Yamaichi Securities	1	1	Before 2004 reform
Japan System Technology	3	1	Not entered into force
Associent Technology	1	1	Not entered into force
Seibu Railway	23	7	Not entered into force
Livedoor	8	5	Applicable
NIWS Co.	4	3	Applicable
Urban Corporation	14	9	Applicable
Senior Communication	1	1	Applicable
IHI	1	1	Applicable
Olympus	2	2	Applicable
Total	58	31	

* The name of the issuer is in the chronological order of the date of the first issued decision regarding that issuer.

** Made by the author from LEX/DB Internet and Westlaw Japan.

issued in 2001, all other fifty-seven decisions were issued on or after 2007. Out of these fifty-seven decisions, twenty-seven decisions dealt with cases filed after the 2004 reform but before it entered into force,[36] and thirty decisions dealt with cases filed after Article 21–2 entered into force. Apparently, the introduction of Article 21–2 in the 2004 reform affected investors' decisions to sue the issuer, even for cases in which Article 21–2 was not applicable.[37] It is no wonder that there is a public perception that securities litigation is on the rise.

When decisions by the upper courts for the same suit are consolidated, however, the total number of the cases decreases to thirty-one. Also, some of these cases dealt with suits filed by different plaintiffs against the same issuer for the same misrepresentation.[38] Table 20.1 shows that even

[36] Although the exact date of filing is not noted in court decisions, their docket numbers indicate the year of filing.

[37] The announcement of the policy that an issuer corporation should be liable for its misrepresentation in the secondary market and adoption of the presumption of damage by Article 21–2 might have urged investors to file suits.

[38] As Japan does not have the US-style class action, different suits filed by different plaintiffs against the same issuer for the same misrepresentation can proceed independently and are not bound by each other.

after the 2004 reform, securities litigation has been filed against only nine issuers, and that three major misrepresentations (Seibu Railway, Livedoor, and Urban Corporation) account for twenty-one out of thirty cases (70.0 per cent) and forty-five out of fifty-seven decisions (78.9 per cent). After Article 21–2 entered into force, securities litigation has been filed against only six issuers, and two major misrepresentations (Livedoor and Urban Corporation) account for fourteen out of twenty-one cases (66.7 per cent) and twenty-two out of thirty decisions (73.3 per cent).

Of course, this is still a large change from the prior situation where almost no decision regarding liability of issuer corporations was published. It would be fair, however, to say that securities litigation against issuers is not as widespread a phenomenon as it appears to be at the first blush.

3.1.2 Public Enforcement against Misrepresentations

As there might be securities litigation that ended in a settlement, and there might be unreported decisions or cases that are currently ongoing, looking at published court decisions may not provide the entire picture. Also, it is necessary to see how many cases of misrepresentations there are in order to judge whether securities litigation is raised in only a small proportion of cases. For this purpose, this chapter turns to records of cases of public enforcement against material misrepresentations by FSA and the Securities and Exchange Surveillance Commission (hereinafter, SESC),[39] and conducts an Internet-based search for information of securities litigation for those cases.[40]

Public enforcement in this context takes two forms in Japan. First, issuers who have made material misrepresentations are subject to administrative fines, which were introduced by reforms in 2004 and 2005.[41] Orders to pay these fines are issued by the Commissioner of FSA,[42] and SESC makes recommendation to the Commissioner to

[39] SESC is an independent committee set up under FSA as an independent enforcer of securities regulation modelled after the Securities and Exchange Commission in the US.

[40] This was done by searching for news on each issuer on NIKKEI Telecom 21, a database covering newspaper articles published on Nihon Keizai Shinbun, the most-read business newspaper in Japan. In addition, the author checked each issuer's website for press release as supplement.

[41] Art.172–2 and Art.172–4, FIEA. Administrative fines were first introduced by the 2004 reform for misrepresentation in disclosure documents upon issuance of securities, and were expanded to periodic disclosure documents in 2005.

[42] Art.185–7, FIEA.

do so.[43] Second, material misrepresentations are subject to criminal sanctions,[44] and SESC makes requests for criminal prosecution to the prosecutors' office when it is convinced that a crime has been committed.[45] As the standard for order of payment of administrative fines or criminal sanctions are the existence of material misrepresentation,[46] which is also the standard for the liability of the issuer under Article 21–2, the burden of proof of plaintiff investors suing issuers will be further reduced when they can rely upon SESC's recommendation for order of payment of administrative fine or request for criminal prosecution. In other words, plaintiffs should be able to 'piggyback' on SESC.

As of 15 August 2016, SESC has made recommendations for orders of payment of administrative fines or requests for criminal sanctions against 109 issuers for material misrepresentation.[47] Article 21–2 was applicable in ninety-nine of these cases. In addition, FSA has individually started trial proceedings for administrative fines against one issuer,[48] to which Article 21–2 was applicable. As we have seen in the previous section, published court decisions can be found for six out of these one-hundred cases.[49] This is clearly not a high ratio.[50]

To conduct an Internet-based search, the author took a sub-sample of twenty-three cases regarding issuers that are listed in the First Section of Tokyo Stock Exchange, which is the top-tier market in Japan.[51] This is

[43] Art.20, para.1, the Act for Establishment of the Financial Services Agency. Although trial procedures usually begin from recommendations from SESC, FSA can start them by its own decision. Art.178, FIEA.

[44] Art.197, para.1, no.1 and Art.197–2, no.6, FIEA. [45] Art.226, para.1, FIEA.

[46] To be precise, administrative fines are not applicable to misleading statements, and criminal sanctions are not applicable to omissions and misleading statements. However, this does not affect the point in the text, as the civil liability under Article 21–2 has a wider scope than those of administrative fines or criminal sanctions.

[47] Information regarding enforcement actions by SESC can be found in Annual Reports of SESC, www.fsa.go.jp/sesc/english/reports/reports.htm.

[48] Information regarding orders for payment of administrative fines by FSA can be found at FSA, Kachokin Nofu Meirei Ichiran [List of Orders for Payment of Administrative Fine], www.fsa.go.jp/policy/kachoukin/05.html.

[49] In other words, public enforcement was present in all of the cases with published court decisions to which Article 21–2 is applicable.

[50] The reason why 'piggybacking' on SESC seems to be not prevalent remains for future research.

[51] These corporations are, in chronological order of enforcement by SESC and FSA, Nikko Cordial Group, Tonichi Carlife Group, Nittoc Construction Co., Sanyo Electronics, Maruzen Co., IHI Corporation, Magara Construction Co., Urban Corporation, Futaba Industrial Co., Bic Camera, Japan Victor, JVC Kenwood Holdings, M3, Mercian Corporation, Olympus Corporation, Oki Electric Industry Co., OBIC Co., Riso Kyoiku

because these corporations are more likely to be sued by quasi-class actions, as they have larger assets and thus are less likely to become insolvent (i.e. they have deep pockets) and as they have a larger number of shareholders, which makes it easier for lawyers to gather plaintiffs. Also, these corporations are more likely to be in the media spotlight.

Out of twenty-three issuers, however, the author was only able to confirm filings of securities litigation for only five issuers, namely, IHI Corporation, Urban Corporation, Olympus Corporation, Riso Kyoiku Co.[52] and Toshiba Corporation.[53] Although the non-exhaustive nature of this research leaves the possibility that securities litigation has been filed against the other eighteen issuers but not reported,[54] this finding coincides with the result from the previous section that securities litigation is now beginning to be filed in Japan, but at a rate that is not so high. This current situation of Japan seems to differ from that of the US, especially before the enactment of Private Securities Litigation Reform Act of 1995, where class actions led by plaintiffs' lawyers became the dominant form and strike suits without merits were allegedly prevalent.

3.2 *Who Is Suing?*

Next, the question becomes: who is filing securities litigation in Japan? This section analyses characteristics of plaintiffs and their lawyers in recent securities litigation filed after the enactment of the 2004 reform and how these lawyers are being paid.

Co., Sanei Architecture Planning Co., AGORA Hospitalities Group, Japan Best Rescue System, Toshiba Corporation, and Shinnihon Corporation.

52 'Riso Kyoiku wo Moto-Kabunushi ga Baisho Teiso, Funsyoku de Kabuka Geraku', [Former Shareholders of Riso Kyoiku Filed Suit against the Company for Compensation of Loss as Stock Price Declined for Window Dressing], Nihon Keizai Shinbun (16 June 2014, 13:31 JST), www.nikkei.com/article/DGXNASDG1601R_W4A610C1CR0000/.

53 Makiko Yamazaki, 'Toshiba Shareholders Sue in Tokyo for $2.45 Million after Stock Plunge', *Reuters* (Sun 6 Dec 2015 11:52pm EST), www.reuters.com/article/us-toshiba-accounting-idUSKBN0TQ0D020151207.

54 Interestingly, in two cases, namely, Sanyo Electronics and Bic Camera, shareholders have filed derivative suits against directors and statutory auditors for damages suffered by the corporation in relation to misrepresentation, such as illegal payment of dividends, excessive payment of corporate tax or administrative fines, instead of securities litigation against issuer corporations. See, Osaka District Court, 28 September 2012, 2169 Hanrei Jiho 104 (denied liability of directors and statutory auditors of Sanyo Electronics for illegal payment of dividends, holding that accounting in question was not illegal); Tokyo District Court, 26 December 2013, 1451 Kinyu Shoji Hanrei 17 and Tokyo High Court, 24 April 2014, 1451 Kinyu Shoji Hanrei 8 (both denied liability of directors and statutory auditors of Bic Camera, holding that accounting in question was not illegal).

3.2.1 Types of Plaintiffs and Their Lawyers

As summarised in Table 20.2 below, lawsuits against issuers filed after the 2004 reform can be classified into three categories. First, there are suits filed by institutional investors. Second, there are quasi-class actions, in which lawyers gathered a group of investors as plaintiffs. And third, there are suits filed by individual investors.

3.2.1.1 Lawsuits by institutional investors Lawsuits filed by institutional investors can be found in the cases of Seibu Railway, Livedoor, Olympus and Riso Kyoiku. The first three cases were major corporate scandals in Japan, while the last case received relatively less coverage in the media.

The amount claimed in these lawsuits are large, often in the order of tens of billions JPY (which is hundreds of millions USD).

In three out of four lawsuits against Seibu Railway and the lawsuit against Livedoor, lawyers of Mori, Hamada & Matsumoto, which is one of the four largest law firms in Japan, represented the plaintiff institutional investors. The lawyers in lawsuits against Olympus and Riso Kyoiku are undisclosed.

3.2.1.2 Quasi-class actions Quasi-class actions can be found in the cases of Seibu Railway, Livedoor,[55] Olympus,[56] Riso Kyoku,[57] IHI,[58] Eneres[59] and Toshiba.[60] Sometimes, there are two or more groups of

[55] See, Livedoor Kabunushi Higai Bengodan [Attorneys for Victim-Shareholders of Livedoor](www.livedoor-higaibengodan.jp/index.htm, already closed); ITJ Law Office (http://blog.livedoor.jp/itjlawoffice/)

[56] See, Olympus Kabunushi Higai Bengodan [Attorneys for Victim-Shareholders of Olympus] (www.olympus-higaibengodan-tokyo.jp/index.html); Olympus Kabunushi Bengodan [Attorneys for Shareholders of Olympus] (www.olymben.jp/), Kabunushi Songai Baisho Seikyu Sosho Sodan Saito [The Website for Consultation on Lawsuits for Compensation of Damages by Shareholders], The Olympus Case (www.kabunushi-sosyo.com/olympus).

[57] Riso Kyoiku Kabunushi Higai Bengodan [Attorneys for Victim-Shareholders of Riso Kyoiku] (http://aoi-law.com/article/risou/); Kabunushi Songai Baisho Seikyu Sosho Sodan Saito [The Website for Consultation on Lawsuits for Compensation of Damages by Shareholders], The Riso Kyoiku Case (www.kabunushi-sosyo.com/riso/).

[58] IHI Funsyoku Kessan Higai Kabunushi Bengodan [Attorneys for Victim-Shareholders of IHI's Window Dressing] (www.ihi-higaibengodan.jp).

[59] Kabunushi Songai Baisho Seikyu Sosho Sodan Saito [The Website for Consultation on Lawsuits for Compensation of Damages by Shareholders], The Eneres Case (www.kabunushi-sosyo.com/eneres/).

[60] Toshiba Jiken Kabunusi Bengodan [Attorneys for Shareholders of Toshiba's Case] (http://東芝粉飾.com).

Table 20.2 *Lawsuits against issuers by different types of investors*

	Name of issuer	Type of the plaintiffs	No. of plaintiffs	Plaintiffs' lawyers	Amount claimed (JPY)	Amount awarded or settled (JPY)	Source
1	Seibu Railway	institutional	4	Mori, Hamada & Matsumoto	12,097,884,247	1,921,261,231	Tokyo High, 2014/3/27
2	Seibu Railway	institutional	6	Mori, Hamada & Matsumoto	3,887,413,112	825,421,657	Tokyo High, 2014/6/25
3	Seibu Railway	institutional	16	Mori, Hamada & Matsumoto	24,874,221,973	2,918,495,280	Tokyo High, 2014/8/28
4	Seibu Railway	institutional	1	Shinozuka & Noda	136,552,126	86,689,028	Tokyo High, 2014/7/16
5	Seibu Railway	quasi-class action	290	Masaaki Takehashi et al.	1,322,699,965	* (judgment partially in favour of plaintiffs)	Tokyo High, 2014/1/30
6	Seibu Railway	individual	1	Yoshiaki Kawai et al.	17,179,000	0	Tokyo Dist., 2007/8/28
7	Seibu Railway	individual	1	none	56,492,000	0	Tokyo Dist., 2008/2/21
8	Livedoor	institutional	6	Mori, Hamada & Matsumoto	10,903,817,119	9,905,230,416	Supreme, 2012/3/13

Table 20.2 (*cont.*)

	Name of issuer	Type of the plaintiffs	No. of plaintiffs	Plaintiffs' lawyers	Amount claimed (JPY)	Amount awarded or settled (JPY)	Source
9	Livedoor	quasi-class action	3345	Attorneys for Victim-Shareholders of Livedoor	23,072,237,007	* (judgment partially in favour of plaintiffs)	Tokyo High, 2011/11/30
10	Livedoor	quasi-class action	409	ITJ Law Office	4,435,392,397	** (judgment partially in favour of plaintiffs)	Tokyo Dist., 2009/7/9
11	Livedoor	quasi-class action	20	ITJ Law Office	84,577,140	** (judgment partially in favour of plaintiffs)	Tokyo Dist., 2009/7/23
12	Livedoor	individual	2	Kinki Chuou Law Office	151,056,802	58,778,682	Tokyo Dist., 2009/6/18
13	Olympus	institutional	1	unknown	undisclosed	4,360,000,000	issuer's press release
14	Olympus	institutional	86	unknown	37,674,068,436	11,000,000,000	issuer's press release
15	Olympus	institutional	68	unknown	5,892,443,184	lawsuit in progress	issuer's press release

Table 20.2 (*cont.*)

	Name of issuer	Type of the plaintiffs	No. of plaintiffs	Plaintiffs' lawyers	Amount claimed (JPY)	Amount awarded or settled (JPY)	Source
16	Olympus	institutional	6	unknown	27,914,567,399	lawsuit in progress	issuer's press release
17	Olympus	quasi-class action	11	Attorneys for Shareholders of Olympus	33,774,940	20,850,568	Osaka Dist., 2015/7/21
18	Olympus	quasi-class action	146	Attorneys for Shareholders of Olympus	approx. 580,000,000	lawsuit in progress	lawyers' website
19	Olympus	quasi-class action	4	Attorneys for Shareholders of Olympus	45,065,240	lawsuit in progress	lawyers' website
20	Olympus	quasi-class action	100	Attorneys for Victim-Shareholders of Olympus	911,240,790	lawsuit in progress	lawyers' website
21	Olympus	quasi-class action	undisclosed	Hibiya Station Law Office	unknown	lawsuit in progress	lawyers' website
22	Olympus	individual	1	Mitsutoshi Hoshide	111,772,009	48,180,000	Tokyo Dist., 2015/3/19
23	Riso Kyoiku	institutional	2	undisclosed	367,434,930	lawsuit in progress	issuer's press release
24	Riso Kyoiku	quasi-class action	undisclosed	Hibiya Station Law Office	undisclosed	lawsuit in progress	lawyers' website

Table 20.2 (*cont.*)

	Name of issuer	Type of the plaintiffs	No. of plaintiffs	Plaintiffs' lawyers	Amount claimed (JPY)	Amount awarded or settled (JPY)	Source
25	Riso Kyoiku	quasi-class action	7	Aoi Law Office	approx. 18,000,000	lawsuit in progress	lawyers' website
26	IHI	quasi-class action	192	Attorneys for Victim-Shareholders of IHI's Window Dressing	418,546,253	48,176,110	Tokyo Dist., 2014/11/27
27	Eneres	quasi-class action	undisclosed	Hibiya Station Law Office	undisclosed	lawsuit in progress	lawyers' website
28	Toshiba	quasi-class action	454	Attorneys for Shareholders of Toshiba's Case	approx.		
				1,900,000,000	lawsuit in progress	lawyers' website	
29	Urban Corporation	quasi-class action?	1	Aoi Law Office	410,850	197,900 or less (case remanded)	Supreme, 2012/12/21
30	Urban Corporation	quasi-class action?	1	Aoi Law Office	132,500	77,592	Tokyo High, 2012/3/29
31	Urban Corporation	quasi-class action?	1	Aoi Law Office	56,170,000	22,299,200	Tokyo Dist., 2011/2/7

Table 20.2 (*cont.*)

	Name of issuer	Type of the plaintiffs	No. of plaintiffs	Plaintiffs' lawyers	Amount claimed (JPY)	Amount awarded or settled (JPY)	Source
32	Urban Corporation	quasi-class action?	288	Aoi Law Office	undisclosed	** (judgment partially in favour of plaintiffs)	Tokyo Dist., 2011/4/11
33	Urban Corporation	individual	1	none	45,500,000	2,615,000 or less (case remanded)	Supreme, 2012/12/21
34	Urban Corporation	individual	1	Toyohisa Muramatsu	2,915,000	481,368	Tokyo Dist., 2010/1/12
35	Urban Corporation	individual	1	none	762,400	216,000	Tokyo Dist., 2010/1/13
36	Urban Corporation	individual	1	none	250,000	40,000	Tokyo Dist., 2010/3/26
37	Urban Corporation	individual	1	Akira Suzuki et al.	2,332,000	1,200,000	Tokyo Dist., 2011/8/29
38	Japan System Technology	individual	1	none	860,000	0	Supreme, 2009/7/9
39	Associent Technology	individual	2	Eiichi Yokokawa et al.	15,873,700	15,873,700	Oita Dist., 2008/3/3
40	NIWS Co.	individual	1	Tomoyuki Matsuba et al.	156,398,000	5,866,020	Tokyo Dist., 2009/2/9
41	NIWS Co.	individual	1	Tomoyuki Matsuba et al.	155,198,921	153,788,127	Tokyo High, 2011/4/13

Table 20.2 (*cont.*)

	Name of issuer	Type of the plaintiffs	No. of plaintiffs	Plaintiffs' lawyers	Amount claimed (JPY)	Amount awarded or settled (JPY)	Source
42	NIWS Co.	individual	1	Akira Suzuki	24,090,985	7,788,355	Tokyo Dist., 2009/12/3
43	Senior Communication	individual	1	Credo Law Office	18,765,413	2,596,239	Tokyo Dist., 2013/2/22

* Total amount awarded is unavailable as some of the plaintiffs decided to settle after the decision of the lower instance courts, while the others went on appealing.

** The exact amount awarded is unavailable, as the annex to the judgment is not included in the database.

*** Two other suits against Olympus filed by two corporate shareholders (Terumo Corporation and Funai Electric Co.), both settled already, are not included in the table above as they seem to claim compensation for damages as investors of the primary market.

**** Made by the author from the sources noted in the table.

lawyers filing quasi-class actions separately against one issuer. It would be fair to say that quasi-class actions are gradually spreading.

Still, their size is small in comparison to class actions in the US.[61] The largest of Japanese quasi-class actions to date is the one filed against Livedoor, representing more than 3,000 investors and claiming approximately 23 billion JPY (approximately 200 million USD).[62] In other quasi-class actions, the number of the plaintiffs is mostly in the order of hundreds, and the amount of their claim is correspondingly smaller.

When one takes a look at composition of plaintiffs' lawyers filing these quasi-class actions, there are some overlaps. This suggests that a couple of groups of lawyers have formed the beginning of an entrepreneurial plaintiffs'-bar in Japan.

For example, the Attorneys for Victim-Shareholders of Livedoor, which comprises forty-two lawyers, and the Attorneys for Victim-Shareholders of Olympus, which comprises thirty-six lawyers, are led by the same lawyer, Mr. Chouhei Yonekawa, and their members largely overlap although not exactly the same.[63] Also, the Attorneys for Victim-Shareholders of IHI's Window Dressing are led by those who participated in the above two quasi-class actions against Livedoor and Olympus.[64] This loose group of lawyers is a mixture of those from many small and medium-sized law firms.[65]

On the other hand, some law firms are filing quasi-class actions on their own. Aoi Law Office, which employs eight lawyers and the lead partner of which had participated in the Attorneys for Victim-Shareholders of

61 In the US securities litigation, the median of the settlement value for 1996–2013 was 8.3 million USD, and the largest settlement value in 2014 was 265 million USD. See Cornerstone Research, 'Securities Class Action Settlements: 2014 Review and Analysis' (2015), www.cornerstone.com, 1.

62 *Kyu Raibudoa Shudan Sosyo Shuketsu* [Class Action against Former Livedoor Ends], Nihon Keizai Shinbun, 19 July 2012, p. 34. It has been reported that more than 90 per cent of the plaintiffs decided to settle after Tokyo District Court's decision holding the amount of damage as 200 JPY per share, which is about one third of the initial claim. The appellate court increased the amount to 550 JPY per share. Ibid.

63 See, the list of lawyers in Tokyo District Court, 21 May 2009, 2047 Hanrei Jiho 36 and www.olympus-higaibengodan-tokyo.jp/group.html.

64 See www.ihi-higaibengodan.jp.

65 This group has also filed quasi-class action in relation to the misrepresentation by FOI upon its listing to Tokyo Stock Exchange, not against the issuer corporation but against its directors, statutory auditors, outside auditors, underwriters, and Tokyo Stock Exchange. The reason for omitting the issuer corporation from defendants was its bankruptcy. See Efu-O-Ai Higai Kabunushi Bengodan [Attorneys for Victim-Shareholders of FOI], www.foi-higaibengodan.jp/index.html and www.foi-higaibengodan.jp/pdf/101203.pdf.

Livedoor, had filed quasi-class actions against Riso Kyoiku,[66] and also against the directors of Urban Corporation.[67] Also, Hibiya Station Law Office, which comprises seven lawyers, has also filed quasi-class actions against Olympus, Riso Kyoiku and Eneres, and suggests the possibility of doing so against Toshiba.[68] This could be the beginning of the emergence of law firms that specialise in quasi-class actions.

Another point worth mentioning is the fact that securities litigation by institutional investors is clearly different and filed separately from quasi-class actions. While the lawyers of the latter lawsuits belong to small and medium-sized law firms, institutional investors tend to be represented by those from leading established corporate law firms. With the exception of one lawsuit against Riso Kyoiku, which was filed by two trust banks claiming 367 million JPY, institutional investors have filed lawsuits only in Seibu Railway, Livedoor and Olympus cases, which all had a large impact on Japanese society compared to other cases,[69] while quasi-class actions also target smaller cases. In addition, even when institutional investors had not filed suits by themselves, as in the case of IHI, it seems that they did not join quasi-class actions, as the total amount of claims of quasi-class actions in those cases are relatively small.

3.2.1.3 Lawsuits by individual investors Interestingly, a significant number of lawsuits have been filed by one or a few individual investors, sometimes even without being represented by a lawyer. Indeed, this type of lawsuit accounts for at least fifteen out of thirty lawsuits filed after the

[66] Riso Kyoiku Kabunushi Higai Bengodan [Attorneys for Victimised Shareholders of Olympus], http://aoi-law.com/article/risou/, 'Riso Kyoiku wo Moto-kabunushi ga Baisyo Teiso, Funsyoku de Kabuka Geraku' [Former Shareholders of Riso Kyoiku Filed a Suit against the Company for Compensation of Drop of Share Price Caused by Window Dressings], Nihon Keizai Shinbun, www.nikkei.com/article/DGXNASDG1601R_W4A610C1CR0000/.

[67] Tokyo District Court, 22 June 2014, 1397 Kinyu Shoji Hanrei 30.

[68] Kabunushi Songai Baisho Seikyu Sosho Sodan Saito [The Website for Consultation on Lawsuits for Compensation of Damages by Shareholders], The Toshiba Case (www.kabunushi-sosyo.com/toshiba/). This law firm also filed lawsuits based on Article 21–2 against Celartem Technology (www.kabunushi-sosyo.com/celartem/). This case is not counted in the previous section, as the SESC's request for criminal prosecution on Celartem was based on a different kind of charge (use of fraudulent measures regarding private placement of shares).

[69] This attitude may resemble that of institutional investors in the US described in James D. Cox and Randall S. Thomas, *Letting Billions Slip through Your Fingers: Empirical Evidence and Legal Implications of the Failure of Financial Institutions to Participate in Securities Class Action Settlements*, 58 Stan. L. Rev. 411 (2005).

2004 reform with published court decisions.[70] In the cases of Japan System Technology, Associent Technology, NIWS Co. and Senior Communications, this type of lawsuit is the only one that can be found.

As the amount of claims in this type of lawsuit tends to be small, often less than 100 million JPY (approximately 1 million USD), in comparison to that of lawsuits by institutional investors or of quasi-class actions,[71] the impact of such suits should not be overestimated.

3.2.2 *Compensation of Lawyers*

The experience in the US tells us that compensation of plaintiffs' lawyers is a very important factor that shapes the landscape of securities litigation. Unfortunately, information on how lawyers are actually paid is generally not publicly available. In some quasi-class actions, however, lawyers have disclosed their tariffs on websites that they set up to invite investors to join as plaintiffs. These are summarised in Table 20.3.

The largest difference between Japanese quasi-class actions and typical US class actions ascertainable from Table 20.3 is that while plaintiffs' lawyers in the US incur all the expenses without taking retainers in expectation of being reimbursed *ex post* by substantial contingency fees, all groups of lawyers in Japan require payment of a retainer at the outset. In the Olympus case, Hibiya Station Law Office did offer an alternative tariff with no retainer by doubling the rate for contingency fee, they still require plaintiffs to make a deposit of 2 per cent of amount of their claims, which will be used for actual expenses and adjusted when the case ends. The reason behind this Japanese practice may be the lack of financial resources of plaintiffs' lawyers as they mostly belong to small to medium-sized law firms, and the difficulty of setting higher rate for the contingency fee as explained in the next paragraph. Also, it is practically possible to require the payment of retainer in an opt-in system, as plaintiffs must individually contract with lawyers to be represented by them. As the amount of retainer (or deposit) is calculated in relation to

70 While all nine lawsuits filed against Urban Corporation are those by individual investors, four of them are represented by Aoi Law Office, which had filed a quasi-class action against directors and statutory auditors, and presumably are a part of such attempt. The reason for not filing a quasi-class action against Urban Corporation itself would be the fact that it was undergoing insolvency proceedings at that time. Individual lawsuits took the form of claim assessment in the insolvency procedure.

71 This is not to deny that the amount of claim is often, but not always, quite large for an individual to make it worthwhile to file a lawsuit.

Table 20.3 *Compensation for plaintiffs' lawyers in quasi-class actions*

Issuer	Plaintiffs' Lawyer	Retainer	Contingency Fee	Other Fees
Olympus	Attorneys for Victim-Shareholders of Olympus	10,000JPY +1% of the difference between the purchase price and the selling price (when the shares are sold) or 1% of 1/2 of the purchase price (when the shares are still held) +VAT	10% of the amount recovered +VAT	None
	Attorneys for Shareholders of Olympus	10,000JPY (for 100 shares or less) + 2,000JPY per 100 shares (up to 10,000 shares) +1,000JPY (per 100 shares over 10,000 shares) +VAT	10% of the amount recovered +VAT	None
	Hibiya Station Law Office	Following percentage of the amount of claim + VAT 6% (0–3million JPY), 4% (3–30million JPY), 2% (30–300million JPY) 1% (over 300 million JPY)	Following percentage of the amount awarded (not the amount recovered) +VAT 10% (0–3million JPY) 8% (3–30 million JPY) 4% (30–300 million JPY) and 3% (over 300million JPY)	2% of amount of claims (1% for the amount exceeding 30 million JPY), as initial deposit for expenses (remainder reimbursed when the case ends)

Table 20.3 (*cont.*)

Issuer	Plaintiffs' Lawyer	Retainer	Contingency Fee	Other Fees
		None	Following percentage of the amount awarded (not the amount recovered) +VAT 20% (0–3 million JPY) 15% (3–30 million JPY) 9% (30–300 million JPY) 6% (over 300 million JPY)	2% of amount of claims (1% for the amount exceeding 30 million JPY), as initial deposit for expenses (remainder reimbursed when the case ends)
Riso Kyoiku	Hibiya Station Law Office	Following percentage of the amount of claim +VAT 8% (0–3million JPY) 5% (3–30million JPY) 3% (30–300million JPY) 2% (over 300 million JPY)	Following percentage of the amount awarded (not the amount recovered) +VAT 16% (0–3 million JPY) 10% (3–30 million JPY) 6% (30–300 million JPY) 4% (over 300 million JPY)	5% of amount of claims as initial deposit for expenses (remainder reimbursed when the case ends)
	Aoi Law Office	30,000JPY + 2% of the purchase price (- the selling price) +VAT	10% of the amount recovered +VAT	None
Toshiba	Attorneys for Shareholders of Toshiba	40,000JPY + 5JPY per share + VAT	10% of the amount recovered +VAT	None

* Made by the author from the websites of the plaintiffs' lawyers.

the amount of claim of each plaintiff, this also may be one of the causes of the reluctance of institutional investors to join quasi-class actions.

Second, the percentage used for calculating the contingency fee is quite modest.[72] It is either a fixed rate of 10 per cent (plus value-added tax), or a regressive rate starting from 10 per cent, 16 per cent or 20 per cent, with the highest rate applicable only to amount below 3 million JPY (approximately 25,000 USD).[73] These rates are seemingly affected by the former standard tariff of the Japan Federation of Bar Associations,[74] which was the same with the tariff of Hibiya Station Law Office in the Riso Kyoiku case. One of the reasons for not setting a higher rate is presumably to avoid an impression among prospective plaintiffs that lawyers are pursuing their own fortune rather than rescuing victims of financial fraud. Such an impression would adversely affect the size of the group of plaintiffs in Japan, as lawyers need to be appointed by individual plaintiffs in order to represent them.

4 Recent Critiques of Article 21-2 and the 2014 Reform of FIEA

4.1 *Recent Critiques of Article 21-2*

Although securities litigation against issuers is still not a widespread phenomenon in Japan, as we have seen in Section 3.1, the increase of published decisions was enough to induce academic discussion, which centered on how to determine the amount of compensation.[75]

Considering the classic case where the stock price has been inflated by misrepresentation and later falls when the misrepresentation is revealed, one of the main problems is whether investors should be compensated only for the damages caused by the inflated stock price, or also for the damage that accompanies the misrepresentation being made public (e.g. loss of reputation). Although several commentators have strongly

[72] According to Theodore Eisenberg and Geoffrey P. Miller, 'Attorney Fees and Expenses in Class Action Settlements: 1993–2008', 7 *Journal of Empirical Legal Studies* 248 (2010), 262, the median ratio of the attorney's fee in securities class actions is 25 per cent of the class recovery in the settlement.

[73] Note that the contingency fee will be calculated in relation to the recovery for each plaintiff as each plaintiff contracts individually with the lawyers. Thus, the highest rate would be often applicable to small investors.

[74] See note 31 above.

[75] This discussion was inspired by adoption of different calculation methods for the same case (Seibu Railway and Livedoor) by lower courts.

supported the former view,[76] the Supreme Court in the Livedoor case adopted the latter view.[77]

The rationale relied on by the supporters of the former view is a critique that imposition of liability on issuer by Article 21–2 is tantamount to transfer of assets from one group of investors who had held shares of the issuer before the misrepresentation and thus were not eligible to sue the corporation, to another group of investors who acquired shares after the misrepresentation and thus were eligible to sue. From this standpoint, it would not be fair to permit the latter group to recover incidental damages such as the loss of reputation from the former group as such damages are born by both groups. The strict-liability standard of Article 21–2 was also criticised for exacerbating this problem.

These commentators have also asserted that the appropriateness of issuer's liability should be judged from the viewpoint of optimising the deterrence of misrepresentations, by taking other measures such as the liability of directors into consideration.[78]

4.2 Reform of 2014

Article 21–2 was amended in the 2014 reform of FIEA.[79] This was an indirect response to the above discussions in that it did not amend the method of calculating the amount of damages, abolish issuer's liability under Article 21–2 nor strengthen director's liability under Article 22 and Article 24–4 by introducing a presumption of damage. Instead, it changed the standard of liability from strict liability to negligence liability with the burden of proof for non-negligence on defendant issuer.[80]

[76] See for example, Kato, 'Ryutsu Shijyo ni okeru Fujitsu Kaiji to Toshika no Songai', 335–337.

[77] Supreme Court, 13 March 2012, 66 Saiko Saibansho Minji Hanreishu 1957.

[78] Kato, 'Ryutsu Shijyo ni okeru Fujitsu Kaiji to Toshika no Songai', 332–335.

[79] See generally, Jun Otani et al., *Heisei Nijyu-roku Nen Kaisei Kinsyoho-to no Kaisetsu (3) – Shinki Jyojyo Kigyo no Futan Keigen oyobi Jyojyo Kigyo no Shikin Chotatsu no Enkatsuka ni Muketa Sesaku [Commentaries on the 2014 Reform of FIEA (3) – Measures for Reducing the Burdens of Newly Listed Corporations and Smoothing Finance of Listed Corporations]*, 2040 *Shoji Homu* 67 (2014), 71–74. This reform also expanded the eligibility of Article 21–2 to investors who disposed of the issuer's securities during misrepresentation. The availability of the presumption of damage, however, is still limited to those who acquired the issuer's securities during misrepresentation. Compare, Article 21–2, para.1 and para.3 (both as amended).

[80] Art.21–2, para.2, FIEA (as amended). Former paragraphs 2 to 5 of Article 21–2 are now paragraphs 3 to 6 accordingly.

In comparison to the claims under Rule 10b-5, this new standard is still more favourable to plaintiff investors in that simple negligence suffices and that the burden of proof for non-negligence is placed on the defendant. The difference from the former regime, however, is that defendant corporations now have a chance to rebut this point, which will prolong suits.

This change may affect the current practice of securities litigation in Japan, especially that of quasi-class actions, as some groups of lawyers try to achieve speedy relief by filing against issuers only and leaving their directors aside.[81] The value of such tactics will be diminished by the 2014 reform, but not eliminated, as negligence of a representative director or a director responsible for financial reporting would be sufficient for the liability of issuers, while the negligence of each director will be examined in suits against directors. Also, directors have been named as defendants in some quasi-class actions.[82]

5 Conclusion

This article is an initial attempt to grasp the reality of securities litigation in Japan. Securities litigation against issuers clearly increased in Japan after the introduction of Article 21–2 of FIEA, but such lawsuit is not yet commonplace or abundant. On the other hand, in a limited number of highly publicised cases, multiple suits by different plaintiffs have been filed concurrently against the same issuer for the same misrepresentation by different plaintiffs. Also, there are three different types of plaintiffs, namely, institutional investors, a group of other investors (i.e. other than institutional investors) gathered by lawyers via the Internet, and individual investors. Although the second type, to a certain extent, resembles class action in the US, their lawyers' compensation differs as they take retainers and set modest contingency fees. Also, the focus of discussions that followed the increase of securities litigation was not on an increase of strike suits without merits, but rather on the theoretical rationale of issuer's liability.

These findings show that securities litigation is possible even without US-style class actions if there is a strong substantive law, but ultimately it may develop differently than in the US. Of course, securities litigation in

[81] See for example, www.olymben.jp/olymben_activity/?p=32 (Attorneys for Shareholders of Olympus) and www.kabunushi-sosyo.com/riso/index.html (Hibiya Station Law Office on the Riso Kyoiku case).

[82] See for example, Tokyo District Court, 21 May 2009, 2047 Hanrei Jiho 36.

Japan is still in its embryonic development, and might resemble the US more closely in the future. It is too early to judge what securities litigation in Japan will become.

An important question, which this article could not discuss, is: how large is the deterrence effect of securities litigation in Japan? Answering this question will require taking the above characteristics into consideration.

21

Private Enforcement of Company Law and Securities Regulation in Korea

HWA-JIN KIM

1 Introduction

This chapter offers a brief overview of the private enforcement of corporate law and securities regulation in Korea, with particular reference to the current legislative efforts in the Korean National Assembly and recent court cases. This chapter also talks about Korea's ill-fated and misguided adoption of the fraud-on-the-market theory in securities fraud litigation.

2 Private Enforcement of Corporate Law

2.1 Shareholder Derivative Suit

The Korean Commercial Code (KCC) provides that where a director (1) has acted in violation of any laws and regulations or in violation of the company's articles of incorporation or (2) has neglected to perform his or her duties, such director shall be jointly and severally liable for damages to the company resulting from such acts or omissions.[1] This rule is privately enforced through the shareholders derivative litigation under Articles 403, 404, 405 and 406 of the KCC.

The shareholders derivative suit mechanism has been in place since the enactment of the KCC in 1960. However, up until 1997, for the thirty-five years since the enactment, not a single lawsuit was filed. After the Asian

[1] Art. 399 Para. 1 KCC. The director's basic duty of care is provided in Art. 382 Para. 2 KCC that refers to Art. 681 (fiduciary duty in the agency relationship) Korean Civil Code. In practice, the duty of care shall require the directors of the following actions: duty of attention on the activities of the company; duty to attend meetings; duty to review corporate information and documents; duty to thoroughly discuss major policies and business issues; and duty to review all major filings with the regulatory agencies. See generally Hwa-Jin Kim and Sung-Joon Park, 'Directors' Duties and Liabilities in Korean Companies', in *Korean Business Law*, Hwa-Jin Kim ed., (Edward Elgar, 2012), 1.

economic crisis in 1997, some shareholder activist groups started to use the derivative litigation to improve corporate governance of large Korean companies.[2] Still, the genuine derivative suits are rare. Ordinary shareholders hardly have incentives to file the suit. Private enforcement of corporate law in Korea is more to improve corporate governance of Korean firms than for legal remedy. For that reason, current policy discussion focuses rather on the introduction of double derivative lawsuit.

2.2 Double Derivative Suit

The discrepancy between cash-flow right and control right in big Korean conglomerates (*Chaebols*) is quite substantial. For instance, the average ownership of the controlling shareholders of non-public member firms of Samsung Group was 78.43 per cent, whereas their cash-flow rights were as low as 19.43 per cent.[3] For public member firms the number was 13.52 per cent and 1.14 per cent, respectively.[4] Since Korea does not allow dual-class commons, the discrepancy comes from control over affiliated firms, including financial firms, and circular shareholdings. Those affiliated firms are quite often non-listed private firms that are not subject to the disclosure obligations of the Korean Capital Markets Act (KCMA). In such a complicated ownership structure with a lack of transparency, there is a risk that non-listed subsidiaries may be used for tunneling and other questionable rent-seeking acts. Even if something were to happen at the subsidiary level, the only shareholder is the parent controlled by the controlling minority shareholder. He or she won't cause the firm to sue managers of subsidiaries. Reformist groups are trying to rectify the situation through introducing the double derivative lawsuit into the KCC.

Surprisingly, in 2003, the Seoul High Court ruled that shareholders of a listed company can sue the directors of non-listed subsidiaries.[5] The case involved a manager of an 80 per cent subsidiary who committed embezzlement. The court pointed out the possibility and risk of

2 See Bernard Black, Brian Cheffins and Michael Klausner, 'Shareholder Suits Against Korean Directors', in *Korean Business Law*, Hwa-Jin Kim ed. (Edward Elgar, 2012), 27, 35–40.

3 For the corporate governance issues of Samsung Group, see Hwa-Jin Kim, 'Concentrated Ownership and Corporate Control: Wallenberg Sphere and Samsung Group', 14 *Journal of Korean Law* 39 (2014).

4 See James Jinho Chang and Hyun-Han Shin, 'Family Ownership and Performance in Korean Conglomerates', 15 *Pacific-Basin Finance Journal* 329 (2007).

5 Judgment of 22 August 2003, 2002-Na-13746.

wrongdoings through subsidiaries under common control of the managers of the listed parent. The court also opined that the definition of the shareholder under Article 403 of the KCC shall include the shareholder of the parent company.[6] However, the Korean Supreme Court quickly reversed the decision of the Seoul High Court in 2004 by ruling that the shareholder of the listed parent company does not qualify as the shareholder of its subsidiaries.[7]

The case reignited the policy discussion, and a revision of the KCC has been the subject of a lively debate since then. Finally in 2013, the Korean Ministry of Justice submitted a bill to the Korean National Assembly which included, among others, the double derivative lawsuit. However, the controversial bill did not go through the final stage of the legislative procedure and is still pending. The Korean National Assembly is currently discussing ways to reform the corporate governance of large conglomerates. The double derivative lawsuit is very much on the agenda of the relevant committees of the legislative body.

The concern is that private companies may more or less become public companies through strike lawsuits, thus losing the privilege and benefit of being private.[8] When introduced, if at all, the court shall take a conservative approach to the double derivative suit. The judgment of the Seoul High Court was based on the compensation and deterrence theory.[9] In this particular case, veil piercing was not available because there existed no 100 per cent relationship between the parent and the subsidiary. It should be noted, however, that in the United States most court cases adopt the veil piercing theory in allowing a double derivative suit.[10] As Korean case law is already familiar with veil piercing,[11] the double derivative suit may not be that necessary after all.

[6] See Ok-Rial Song, 'The Double Derivative Suits under the Commercial Code', 28 *Korean Civil Law Case Studies* 528 (2006) (Kor.) (supporting the judgment).

[7] Judgment of 23 September 2004, 2003-Da-49221.

[8] There is a report that from 2000 to 2004, 81 per cent of the lawsuits filed against business corporations were dismissed or withdrawn. See Hwa-Jin Kim, *Corporate Finance and Governance*, 2nd ed., (Pakyoungsa, 2012) (Kor.), 304.

[9] There are scholarly opinions that the shareholder derivative lawsuit does not deter wrongdoings of corporate managers, see, e.g. Roberta Romano, 'The Shareholder Suit: Litigation without Foundation?', 7 *Journal of Law, Economics, and Organization* 55 (1991).

[10] See David W. Locascio, 'The Dilemma of Double Derivative Suits', 83 *Northwestern University Law Review* 729 (1989), 743–746.

[11] See, e.g. the Korean Supreme Court Judgment of 19 January 2001, 97-Da-21604. See generally Joseph Cho and Eun Young Shin, 'Piercing of the Corporate Veil in Korea: Case Commentary', *Korean Business Law*, Hwa-Jin Kim ed. (Edward Elgar, 2012), 101.

3 Private Enforcement of Securities Regulation

3.1 Securities Fraud Litigation

With respect to public companies in Korea, any director who provides false or misleading statements or fails to indicate material concerns shall be liable to the party for any damages incurred as a result of such false statements or material omissions. They have a due diligence defence.[12] This rule applies to frauds in the primary as well as secondary markets, and has been well enforced privately, creating sizable case law and professional literature.[13] Therefore, in terms of the private enforcement of securities regulation in Korea, the 'new' securities class action has received more attention.

3.2 Securities Class Action

The controversial Securities Class Action Act (SCAA) was passed by the Korean National Assembly in December of 2003 with the aim of providing a more effective means of relief for small investors in the capital markets while at the same time enhancing the transparency of corporate governance. The SCAA came into full effect on 1 January 2007. The cause of action is narrower than which is available in the United States. Claims for damages under the SCAA are limited to the recovery of loss arising from false statements in the registration statements, business prospectuses, annual, semi-annual and quarterly reports, insider trading, stock price manipulation, and faulty auditing.

The first class action lawsuit was filed in April of 2009. The second and third lawsuits were filed in December of 2011 and in June of 2014, respectively. Only nine lawsuits have been filed in the past ten years. In other words, it looks like the law has become almost ineffectual. It should be noted though that the law went into effect in 2007, i.e. after a three-year waiting period. When the law was enacted, Korean firms were understandably horrified and substantially improved accounting practices during those three years. The law stipulated that if firms confess past sins, it won't be applied retroactively.[14] In that sense, the law contributed to the improvement of corporate governance of large Korean firms.

[12] Art. 125 and Art. 162 of the KCMA. These provisions will be discussed below.

[13] See Hwa-Jin Kim, *Theoretical Foundations of Securities Regulation*, (Pakyoungsa, 2004), Ch. 3.(Kor.).

[14] See Kim, *Corporate Finance and Governance*, 349.

Unfortunately, the future of the SCAA does not look bright. There is no Milberg (Weiss) in Korea. Furthermore, no contingency fee arrangement is allowed.[15] Since no discovery is available in civil procedure, plaintiffs regularly have a hard time proving the claim despite the fact that Korean law is quite accommodating, as discussed below. In addition, no institutional investor may want to play the lead plaintiff due to their relationships with potential fee-paying corporate clients.[16] Perhaps the introduction of the securities class action in Korea will remain and be recorded as too hasty and ambitious a reform effort.

4 *Halliburton* in Korea?

4.1 *Importing the Fraud-on-the-Market*

As far as the securities fraud action is concerned, Korea imported all the elements of the cause of action from the United States except scienter: Materiality, misrepresentation or omission, reliance, causation and damages.[17] Korean law does not know the concept of scienter. The focus here is on reliance, which is the single most controversial requirement in securities fraud litigation in Korea, and any jurisdiction for that matter.

Basic Inc. v. *Levinson*[18] introduced the rebuttable presumption of reliance in securities fraud litigation (transaction causation requirement) based on the fraud-on-the-market theory.[19] However, the US Federal

[15] See Black, Cheffins and Klausner, 'Shareholder Suits Against Korean Directors', at 42. The SCAA provides for attorney's fees to be paid out of the recovery to the plaintiff class. Art. 44 of the SCAA.

[16] *Cf.* Ronald J. Gilson and Jeffrey N. Gordon, 'The Agency Costs of Agency Capitalism: Activist Investors and the Reevaluation of Governance Rights', 113 *Columbia Law Review* 863 (2013).

[17] For cause of action, see generally James D. Cox, Robert W. Hillman and Donald C. Langevoort, *Securities Regulation: Cases and Materials*, 7th ed., (Wolters Kluwer, 2013) Chs.9 and 13.

[18] 485 U.S. 224 (1988). See Donald Langevoort, 'Basic at Twenty: Rethinking Fraud on the Market', *Wisconsin Law Review* 157 (2009); Jonathan R. Macey et al., 'Lessons from Financial Economics: Materiality, Reliance, and Extending the Reach of Basic v. Levinson', 77 *Virginia Law Review* 1017 (1991).

[19] *Cf.* Note, 'The Fraud-on-the-Market Theory', 95 *Harvard Law Review* 1143 (1982); Brad M. Barber et al., 'The Fraud-on-the-Market Theory and the Indicators of Common Stocks' Efficiency', 19 *Journal of Corporation Law* 285 (1994); Daniel R. Fischel, 'Use of Modern Finance Theory in Securities Fraud Cases Involving Actively Traded Securities', 38 *Business Lawyer* 1 (1982); Jonathan R. Macey and Geoffrey P. Miller, 'Good Finance, Bad Economics: An Analysis of the Fraud-on-the-Market Theory', 42 *Stanford Law Review* 1059 (1990); Jonathan R. Macey, 'The Fraud-on-the-Market Theory: Some Preliminary Issues', 74 *Cornell Law Review* 923 (1989). For the

Supreme Court decision has been very controversial. For example, some voices were raised to reconsider the case in *Amgen Inc. et al. v. Connecticut Retirement Plans and Trust Funds.*[20] And, in 2014, it once again became the hot issue in *Halliburton Co. et al.* v. *Erica P. John Fund, Inc.* (23 June 2014).[21] Although *Halliburton* did not change precedent, it seemed evident that the fraud-on-the-market theory was still facing tough challenges from new perspectives in contemporary economics.[22]

Halliburton was a wake-up call whereas *Basic* was an inspiration for the Korean legislature and judiciary. The Korean Supreme Court adopted the fraud-on-the-market theory not only in the securities fraud litigation, but also in litigations in tort law claims. It is interesting to note that under the KCMA there is no transaction causation requirement at all.

> **Article 125 (Liabilities for Damages Caused by False Statements, etc.)**
> (1) The following persons shall be liable for damages inflicted upon any person as a result of acquiring securities by including a false description or representation of any material fact in a registration statement (including a corrective registration statement and supplements thereto; hereafter the same shall apply in this Article) and an investment prospectus (including a preliminary investment prospectus and a short-form investment prospectus; hereafter the same shall apply in this Article) or omitting a material fact therefrom: Provided, that such person shall not be liable if he/she proves that he/she was unable to discover such inclusion or omission even if he/she exercised reasonable care or that the person who acquired the securities knew the fact at the time when he/she made an offer to acquire them: . . .
>
> **Article 162 (Liability for Damages Caused by False Description, etc.)**
> (1) The following persons shall be liable for damages sustained by a person who acquired or disposed of securities (including securities depositary

Efficient Capital Market Hypothesis, see Ronald Gilson and Reinier Kraakman, 'The Mechanisms of Market Efficiency', 70 *Virginia Law Review* 549 (1984); Donald Langevoort, 'Theories, Assumptions, and Securities Regulation: Market Efficiency Revisited', 140 *University of Pennsylvania Law Review* 851 (1992); Reinier Kraakman, 'Taking Discounts Seriously: The Implications of 'Discounted' Share Prices as an Acquisition Motive', 88 *Columbia Law Review* 891 (1988).

20 133 S. Ct. 1184 (2013). See Donald C. Langevoort, 'Judgment Day for Fraud-on-the-Market?: Reflections on Amgen and the Second Coming of Halliburton', *Georgetown Public Law and Legal Theory Research Paper* No. 13–058 (2013).

21 See Lucian A. Bebchuk and Allen Ferrell, 'Rethinking Basic', 69 *Business Lawyer* 671 (2014); Merritt B. Fox, 'Halliburton II: What It's All About', 1 *Journal of Financial Regulation* 135 (2015).

22 *Cf.* Cass R. Sunstein et al., 'A Behavioral Approach to Law and Economics', 50 *Stanford Law Review* 1471 (1998); Ryan Bubb and Richard H. Pildes, 'How Behavioral Economics Trims Its Sails and Why', 127 *Harvard Law Review* 1593 (2014).

> receipts related to such securities and other securities specified by Presidential Decree; hereafter the same shall apply in this Article) issued by a corporation obligated to submit a business report due to a false description or representation of a material fact in such business report, half-yearly report, quarterly report, or material fact report under Article 159 (1) (hereinafter referred to as 'business report, etc.') or a document attached thereto (excluding audit reports prepared by an accounting auditor), or due to an omission of a description or representation of a material fact therein: Provided, That a person held liable for such damages shall not be liable if he/she proves that he/she was unable to know such fact although he/she exercised reasonable care, or that the person who acquired or disposed of such securities knew the fact at the time he/she acquired or disposed of the securities . . .

The Korean Supreme Court adopted the fraud-on-the-market theory in a more plaintiffs-friendly way because of the statutes' wording. Reliance is not even presumed; it is given. As a result, it cannot be rebutted.[23] The provisions in the KCMA were not a drafting error of some sort. It was the 1997 financial crisis, which created a scenario last observed in the 1930s in the United States. Plaintiffs had to be strongly protected at that time. As there was no discovery available in Korea, this was how the country decided to respond. The Korean Supreme Court went one step further in that it adopted the fraud-on-the-market theory even in tort law cases,[24] whereas the US state courts never adopted the fraud-on-the-market theory in such cases.[25]

4.2 *Comparison: German Law*

In Germany, only *ad hoc* disclosures are regulated by the German Securities Exchange Act (Gesetz über den Wertpapierhandel – WpHG) whereas fraud through periodic disclosures is regulated by tort law, i.e. the German Civil Code (Bürgerliches Gesetzbuch: BGB). Registration statements are regulated by other statutes.[26] To be sure, fraud in the

[23] Judgment of 25 October 2007, 2006-Da-16758, 16765; Judgment of 11 October 2002, 2002-Da-38521.

[24] Judgment of 12 September 1997, 96-Da-41991; Judgment of 28 January 2010, 2007-Da-16007.

[25] *Cf. Mirkin* v. *Wasserman*, 23 Cal. Rptr. 2d 101, 858 P.2d 568 (Cal. 1993). See Christopher Boffey, 'Mirkin v. Wasserman: The Supreme Court of California Rejects the Fraud-on-the-Market Theory in State Law Deceit Actions', 49 *Business Lawyer* 715 (1994).

[26] Registration statements are regulated by Verkaufsprospektgesetz and Börsengesetz. See Barbara Grunewald and Michael Schlitt, *Einführung in das Kapitalmarktrecht* 235–261 (3.Aufl., C.H.Beck, 2014).

primary market and fraud by ad hoc disclosure can also be actionable by tort law and a sizable body of case law has been developed.[27]

Even though Germany has actively imported many principles and case law in corporate law and securities regulation,[28] the German law and Federal Supreme Court (Bundesgerichtshof: BGH) explicitly reject the fraud-on-the-market theory.[29] Fraudulent *ad hoc* disclosure is regulated by Articles 37b (material omission) and 37c (misrepresentation) of the WpHG. Article 37c requires the reliance element by stipulating that the plaintiff shall have trusted the misrepresentation. In terms of Article 37b, the transaction causation exists through the proposition that without the material omission, the plaintiff would not have purchased the securities.[30] These Articles also require loss causation as an element of the cause of action.[31] The burden of proof on causation lies on the plaintiff.[32]

German courts treat securities fraud litigations almost like general tort law litigations.[33] This is partly because frauds in the primary markets are regulated only by the BGB. The German Federal Court once directly referred to the 'fraud-on-the-market theory in the US securities regulation' and rejected an adoption of the theory in fraudulent ad hoc disclosure cases in that such an adoption would expand the scope of liabilities under Article 826 of the BGB too far.[34]

[27] For the German law of securities fraud, see generally, Alexander Hellgardt, *Kapitalmarktdeliktsrecht* (Mohr Siebeck, 2008); Stefan Richter, *Schadenszurechnung bei deliktischer Haftung für fehlerhafte Sekundärmarktinformation* (Mohr Siebeck, 2012). For other European jurisdictions, see Klaus J Hopt and Hans Ch. Voigt (Hrsg.), *Prospekt- und Kapitalmarktinformationshaftung: Recht und Reform in der Europäischen Union, der Schweiz und den USA* (C.H.Beck, 2004).

[28] See Jan von Hein, *Die Rezeption US-amerikanischen Gesellschaftsrechts in Deutschland* (Mohr Siebeck, 2008).

[29] See Kim, *Theoretical Foundations of Securities Regulation*, 88–92.

[30] Peter O. Mülbert and Steffen Steup, 'Haftung für fehlerhafte Kapitalmarktinformation', in Mathias Habersack et al. (Hrsg.), *Unternehmensfinanzierung am Kapitalmarkt* 915, 985 (2. Aufl., DrOttoSchmidt, 2008).

[31] Mülbert and Steup, 'Haftung für fehlerhafte Kapitalmarktinformation', 986; Grunewald and Schlitt, *Einführung in das Kapitalmarktrecht*, 288.

[32] Mülbert and Steup, 'Haftung für fehlerhafte Kapitalmarktinformation', 987; Grunewald and Schlitt, *Einführung in das Kapitalmarktrecht*, 288.

[33] See BGH 28.11.2005 – II ZR 80/04, NZG 2007, 345, 346: BGH 4.6.2007, ZIP 2007, 1560, 1562.

[34] BGH, Beschluss vom 26. Juni 2006 – II ZR 153/05; BGH, WM 2007, 1557, 1559 (ComROAD Case). Art. 826 of BGB applies to frauds in the secondary markets. Richter, *supra* note 27, 82–83. To be actionable under Art. 826 of BGB, the transaction causation between defendant's misrepresentation and plaintiff's investment decision. Mülbert and Steup, 'Haftung für fehlerhafte Kapitalmarktinformation', 992.

In addition to the conventional developments in tort law, German academia and some court decisions have been referring to the concept of 'Investment Atmosphere' (Anlagestimmung). According to this line of scholarly opinion and cases, the investors are presumed to have relied on misrepresentation when the investor made an investment decision based on an inflated investment atmosphere created by an investment prospectus or memorandum.[35] This is reminiscent of *Basic*. There have been discussions in Germany on a possible expansion of the concept to strengthen the liabilities out of misrepresentation in the capital markets. The discussion was obviously influenced by the Efficient Capital Market Hypothesis.[36] However, the German Federal Supreme Court rejected the concept. According to the Court, an investment decision depends upon building of intent on an individual level to which many reasonable and unreasonable factors contribute. Those factors cannot be easily generalised.[37] Many commentators support the Federal Supreme Court's rejection of the Anlagestimmung.[38]

4.3 A New Perspective

Now is the time to reconsider the whole thing. Circumstances have significantly changed since 1997. Investor protection mechanisms are relatively well in place in the Korean capital markets. Financial regulation and supervision work reasonably well.[39] Korea also needs a strong and sound securities industry. The ultimate purpose of the KCMA has not received the attention it needs. The primary purpose of the securities regulation is the protection of investors. There is no debate about that. But, the scope of the KCMA is much broader as its Article 1 stipulates.

The burden of proof is on the plaintiff. *Ibid.*, at 993. Plaintiff must prove that the particular misrepresentation did constitute the core element of plaintiff's investment decision. Richter, *Schadenszurechnung*, at 88.

35 OLG Frankfurt a.M., WM 1994, 291, 198; OLG Frankfurt a.M., WM 1996, 1216, 1219.

36 See, e.g. Theodor Baums, 'Haftung wegen Falschinformation des Sekundärmarkts', 167 *Zeitschrift für das gesamte Handelsrecht und Wirtschaftsrecht* 139 (2003); Knut Sauer, 'Kausalität und Schaden bei der Haftung für falsche Kapitalmarktinformationen', *Zeitschrift für Bankrecht und Bankwirtschaft* 24 (2005).

37 Richter, *Schadenszurechnung*, 89–92.

38 Matthias Casper, 'The Significance of the Law of Tort with the Example of the Civil Liability for Erroneous ad hoc Disclosure', in Reiner Schulze ed., *Compensation of Private Losses*, (De Gruyter, 2011) 91, 98; Richter, *Schadenszurechnung*, 91.

39 *Cf.* Hwa-Jin Kim, 'Financial Regulation and Supervision in Corporate Governance of Banks', 41 *Journal of Corporation Law* 707 (2016).

Article 1 (Purposes)

The purpose of this Act is to contribute to the development of the national economy by facilitating financial innovation and fair competition in the capital market, protecting investors, fostering the development of the financial investment business, and heightening the fairness, reliability, and efficiency of the capital market.

The Korean Supreme Court's adoption of the fraud-on-the-market theory in its current fashion must be changed. The KCMA should also, at the very least, adopt *Basic*, i.e. the reliance requirement of the cause of action must be added as German statute has already done. On a separate note, there have been academic voices that express concern over the trend that securities law is becoming a little too much like consumer protection law.[40] Balance is needed.

Korea has adopted many things from the United States law, including the squeeze-out merger,[41] the corporate opportunity doctrine[42] and securities class action. Others are waiting in line, such as the poison pill and the dual-class commons. Unfortunately, some are misguided and ill fated. The fraud-on-the-market theory in the KCMA in its current form and tort law cases is the most conspicuous example.

[40] *Cf.* Zohar Goshen and Gideon Parchomovsky, 'The Essential Role of Securities Regulation', 55 *Duke Law Journal* 711 (2006), 713; Jeffrey N. Gordon and Lewis A. Kornhauser, 'Efficient Markets, Costly Information, and Securities Research', 60 *New York University Law Review* 761(1985), 802. See also the German literature Grunewald and Schlitt, *Einführung in das Kapitalmarktrecht*, at 3; Petra Buck-Heeb, *Kapitalmarktrecht* 3–7 (6.Aufl., C.F.Müller, 2013).

[41] See Hyeok-Joon Rho, 'New Squeeze-Out Devices as a Part of Corporate Law Reform in Korea', in *Korean Business Law*, Hwa-Jin Kim ed., (Edward Elgar, 2012), 52.

[42] See Hwa Jin Kim, Seung Hwan Lee and Stephen Woodcock, 'Favoritism and Corporate Law: The Confused Corporate Opportunity Doctrine in the Hyundai Motor Case', 3 *Michigan Journal of Private Equity and Venture Capital Law* 41 (2013).

22

The IPC Model for Securities Law Enforcement in Taiwan

WEN-YEU WANG

1 Introduction

The individual investor's private right of action against securities fraud has long been statutorily recognised in Taiwan. Since its enactment in 1968, the Securities and Exchange Act (SEA) has provided actionable rights for fraud in connection with the public offering, issuing, private placement, or trading of securities – and for fraud arising from misleading prospectus, as well.[1] Arguably, for as long as the securities market has been statutorily regulated, an investor's right to sue has been part of the regulation scheme. The enforcement of these laws, besides finding compensation for the plaintiffs, can be viewed as producing an external benefit of general deterrence, which in turn brings about 'a more efficient environment for economic activity',[2] because the potential wrongdoers may be kept at bay when they realise that the illicit transaction they had in mind might not be worth their gamble. In other words, a 'public good' is provided by such enforcement: the benefits of the enforcement effort accrue to persons who are not required to bear their share of the enforcement costs.[3] While different jurisdictions may apply a varying concoction of different proportions of public enforcement to private enforcement to deliver this good, Taiwan's enforcement, while clearly providing private right of action for private actors in the SEA, has come to rely exclusively on the government-sanctioned Securities and Futures Investors Protection Center (IPC).[4] That is, despite expressly

[1] Zhengquan Jiaoyi Fa [Securities and Exchange Act] 1968 art. 20 § 2, art. 31 § 2 (Taiwan).

[2] Curtis J. Milhaupt, 'Nonprofit Organizations as Investors Protection: Economic Theory and Evidence from East Asia', 29 YALE J. INT'L L. 169 (2004), 184; Wen-Yeu Wang and Jhe-Yu Su, 'The Best of Both Worlds? On Taiwan's Quasi-Public Enforcer of Corporate and Securities Law', 3 *The Chinese Journal of Comparative Law* 1 (2015), 1.

[3] Milhaupt, 'Nonprofit Organizations as Investors Protection', 172.

[4] Wang and Su, 'The Best of Both Worlds?', 15.

recognising private investors' right to sue substantively, the actual suits are brought not by these investors themselves, but by the IPC.

Since the author's 2008 analysis, in which transparency and independence were identified as key areas for improvement via a public choice analysis,[5] other scholars have similarly voiced their concern over IPC's reform,[6] and the author has since made a more in-depth analysis in the agency cost context,[7] as well. While these works targeted the IPC's function as a whole, including derivative actions stemming from corporate law, this chapter strives to narrow the discussion to put the spotlight on the IPC's role in securities class action litigation in order to present a clearer picture. The result is that, the author has come to identify two areas warranting a revisit after a survey of recent works. By building on the author's prior works and expanding the depth of the analysis, this chapter will explore the following notions: one, the IPC's derivation of compensation to the investors plaintiffs via settlement as opposed to judgment award as detrimental factor in the provision of

[5] Wen-Yeu Wang and Jian-Lin Chen, ' Reforming China's Securities Civil Actions: Lessons from PSLRA Reform in the US and Government-Sanctioned Non-Profit Enforcement in Taiwan', 21 Colum. J Asian L. 115 (2008), 143–151 (recognizing the IPC as an appropriate improvement in an enforcement environment where privately litigated civil suits are traditionally not emphasised, but ultimately expressing concern due to the IPC's close ties to the government, thereby rendering it dangerously akin to a typical government administrative branch).

[6] See, e.g. Ching-Ping Shao, 'Representative Litigations in Corporate and Securities Laws by Government-Sanctioned Nonprofit Organizations: Lessons from Taiwan', 15 *Asian-Pacific Law and Policy Journal* 58 (2014) (explaining the creation of the IPC via public choice theory, while refuting traditional theories on the creation of NPOs. Shao thereby applies by extension that same public choice context to the analysis of the IPC's operation, ultimately arriving at a suggested reform of separating the IPC's status as lead plaintiff from its function as class counsel); Jen-Guang Lin, 'The Challenges and Contemporary Issues of Taiwan's Investor Protection System – A Model to Learn or to Avoid', 11 *National Taiwan University Law Review* 129 (2016), (offering a more affirmative view on the IPC's value in investor protection through a pragmatic lens, while still noting several areas for improvement, such as calling for the involvement of non-executive directors and for the requirement for judicial approval in the securities fraud class action settlement process as one way to ease the concern of undue influence from the government. However, Lin holds that such concern may be too speculative; and supports the IPC's litigation practice of settling the disputes to 'increase the possibility of recovering compensations from the defendants').

[7] Wang and Su, 'The Best of Both Worlds?', at 5.(demonstrating that the existing regulatory scheme 'does not recognise the inherent agency problems' with the FSC running freely unchecked and able to affect 'its own political agenda beyond simply protecting investors', and ultimately reiterating the 2008 suggestions with added suggestion of lifting restrictions on attorney contingency fees as way to 'create meaningful competition in the presentation of corporate shareholders and thereby check and balance the IPC's power').

public good;[8] and two, agency problems stemming from inherent misalignment of interests between the government and investors under public choice analysis.[9] We begin by providing an overview of the IPC.

2 Overview of the IPC

In an effort to strengthen the securities market by way of investor protection improvement, the Taiwanese government enacted the Securities Investor and Futures Trader Protection Act (the Act) on 17 July 2002,[10] which went into effect on 1 January 2003. Not long thereafter, on 22 January of the same year, the IPC was formally formed pursuant to Article 7 of the Act, with funding contributed by the prescribed market participants pursuant to the Act.[11] However, it is worth noting that the IPC is not an entirely new invention for Taiwan. The IPC's predecessor, the Investor Service and Protection Center (ISPC) was formed in 1998, which served to assist investors in their filing of class actions against securities market misconduct, albeit under a drastically different class action scheme than the present-day IPC.[12] By the time the IPC came about in 2003, most of the ISPC simply rolled over to the IPC.[13] The following overview focuses on three fronts: the IPC as a government-sanctioned entity, the IPC as an alternative to the US class action scheme, and the IPC as a fee-shifting mechanism – each identified as a characteristic atypical to either a pure public or private enforcer of securities law. Together, they will tell the tale of a public-good provision scheme falling between the public and private dichotomy.

[8] See Wang and Su, 'The Best of Both Worlds?', 19. [9] See Ibid., at 25.

[10] See Lin, 'Challenges and Contemporary Issues', 7–8 ('. . . [creating] a viable system to help investors redress their losses owing to market misconducts has become an important task for the government.').

[11] Funding contributions, in terms of both dollar amount and contributing sources, varied between the initial round for the formation of the foundation and the subsequent continuing contribution. The extent of contributions varied for the different contributors, as well. For more discussion on this, see Lin, 'Challenges and Contemporary Issues', 12–13.

[12] In the ISPC-era, the individual plaintiff remains as the named plaintiff, with the ISPC's lawyer appointed as the agent to carry out the litigation; In the IPC-era, the individual plaintiff empowers the IPC to bring the suit in its own name as the only named plaintiff. See Lin, 'Challenges and Contemporary Issues', 8–10, n.54.

[13] See Lin, 'Challenges and Contemporary Issues', 12 n.48 ('[a]ll businesses, including the office desks and chairs, or ISPC were transferred to the [IPC]').

2.1 As a Government-Sanctioned Entity

The IPC took on the form of a foundation since its inception, as opposed to an extension of the administrative or executive branch of government. Its legal status as a foundation does not mean, however, that the regulatory body takes on a distant role. On the contrary, although the IPC is a distinct legal entity and enjoys autonomy to a certain extent, the IPC's internal affairs are significantly externally regulated by the Financial Supervisory Commission (the Commission) under the Act. This level of external regulatory intervention is much greater than typical foundations formed under Taiwan's Civil Code.

In terms of its organisation, the board of directors and the board of supervisors are not selected by the contributors. Articles 11 and 15 of the Act dictate that both the board of directors and the board of supervisors are to be selected by the Commission (with a term of three years and successive terms permitted)[14] amongst candidates put forth by the financial contributors and independent candidates not representing the contributors, but either from academia, experts in the field, or impartial members of the public, with the independent group making up at least two-thirds of the respective board. The election of the chairperson by the board is also subject to the Commission's approval under Article 12's stipulation. In practice, for the year 2014, there were eleven directors and three supervisors.[15] Following the two-thirds criteria, besides the chairperson and general manager, who also holds the position as a director, the remaining nine directors were selected from the latter group.[16]

Another way the Commission becomes involved is via the promulgation of governance rules under the power granted by Article 8 of the Act, especially under the catch-all clause permitting the Commission to effect all necessary management or operational rules pursuant to the Act. In practice, this means that the IPC is mandated to initiate or promulgate self-regulatory bylaws for approval or recordation, respectively, with the Commission.[17] To date, the board has approved and adopted self-regulatory bylaws in several key areas of the IPC's operation: class action, settlement, arbitration, mediation, compensation fund, management regulation, and services regulation.[18]

[14] Zhengquan Touziren Ji Qihuo Jiaoyiren Baohu Fa [Investor Protection Act] art. 11 § 2 (Taiwan).

[15] Securities and Futures Investors Protection Center, 2014 Annual Report, 12–13 (2014).

[16] Ibid. [17] *See* Lin, 'Challenges and Contemporary Issues', 22. [18] Ibid., at 22, 55.

In terms of more detailed operation, the IPC is again unable to free itself completely from the Commission's intervention. Procedurally, the IPC must undergo internal review before a class action suit or derivative suit is filed.[19] The general manager and the chairperson, excluding the nine 'outside' directors, must approve the decision to sue based on studies conducted by the internal Legal Service Division[20] before seeking final approval from the board. Upon the board's final approval, the IPC must next file the decision with the Commission within five days.[21] So, it is under such heavy regulatory influence that the author has come to label the IPC as a government-sanctioned non-profit organisation.[22]

With the task of investor protection, the Act provided the IPC with a formidable arsenal: consultation regarding relevant regulations or civil disputes,[23] mediation service,[24] and class action litigation.[25] In 2009, the Act was revised to further expand the IPC's role, effectively making mediation before IPC Mediation Committee compulsory for small claims[26] and adding on the power to initiate derivative suits against or for the removal of the issuer's director or supervisor.[27] Visiting briefly the

19 See Lin, 'Challenges and Contemporary Issues', 33–34, 62. 20 Ibid., at 34.

21 Ibid., at 62 n.254.

22 See Wang and Chen, 'Reforming China's Securities Civil Actions'; Wang and Su, 'The Best of Both Worlds?', 2.

23 See Wang and Chen, 'Reforming China's Securities Civil Actions', 144; Lin, 'Challenges and Contemporary Issues', 25–26.

24 Zhengquan Touziren Ji Qihuo Jiaoyiren Baohu Fa [Investor Protection Act] art. 22 (Taiwan).

25 Zhengquan Touziren Ji Qihuo Jiaoyiren Baohu Fa [Investor Protection Act] art. 28 (Taiwan).

26 Zhengquan Touziren Ji Qihuo Jiaoyiren Baohu Fa [Investor Protection Act] art. 25–1, art. 25–2 (Taiwan). These two articles were added in the 2009 revision to the Act, making mediation effectively compulsory. For small claims cases (disputed claim amounting to NT$1 million or less), in the case that one party to the dispute fails to appear before the Mediation Committee without due cause, the Mediation Committee, considering the relevant circumstances, may put forth a mediation proposal, binding to the parties of the dispute, if the parties to the dispute fail to express explicit dissent from the proposal within ten days, or if the dissenting party fails to appear before the Mediation Committee for mediation after expressing dissent.

27 Zhengquan Touziren Ji Qihuo Jiaoyiren Baohu Fa [Investor Protection Act] art. 10–1 (Taiwan). Typical shareholder derivative suits come in three forms under the Company Law: one, against the directors or supervisors for violation of fiduciary duties to the corporation; two, for the removal of directors or supervisors in the case of their substantial violation of the law or the corporate charter; and lastly, for the nullification of shareholder meeting resolution when such resolution was reached in violation of procedural requirements set forth by the law or the corporate charter. Gongsi Fa [Company Law] art. 214, art. 200, art. 189 (Taiwan). Whereas the Act focused on enforcement of regulations pertaining to securities market prior to this revision, the IPC now also takes on an expanded role in corporate governance, as well.

notion of public choice theory[28] as a government-sanctioned entity, the expansion of the IPC's role would suggest that, not only has the legislature found the IPC at least non-detrimental to its political agenda, the legislature may potentially find the IPC as an attractive venue to affect its political agenda. Because, as personal utility maximisers, the government is sure to abstain from getting in its own way by expansion of the IPC, if the IPC ran counter to its utility maximisation calculus.

So, in addition to the IPC's characteristic as a government-sanctioned entity, its relationship with the government may potentially extend beyond simple external regulatory intervention. Though the IPC as a non-profit may be sufficiently guarded from abuse of power due to the board members' self-interest in preservation of personal reputation, thereby preventing their alignment with the government's political interest; the government is always unchecked from exerting its political preference in this other direction. In other words, while the IPC is not motivated to align with the government, the government remains free to attempt to align the IPC with its own interest.

2.2 *As an Alternative to US Class Action*

Under the Act, the IPC may initiate a representative class action in its own name with respect to a securities or futures matter arising from a single cause that is injurious to multiple securities investors or futures traders, so long as the IPC is empowered by no less than twenty such investors or traders who can retract their respective empowerment any time prior to the end of oral arguments in the first instance of trial.[29] Even after the conclusion of the first instance of trial, the investors or traders can still withdraw their respective empowerment and file for an appeal independent of the IPC's case.[30] The extent of empowerment includes the power for compulsory execution, provisional attachment, provisional injunctions, and for participation in reorganisation or bankruptcy proceedings, so long as they are performed for the realisation of the right of action[31] and

[28] See Dennis C. Mueller, *Public Choice III* (1st ed. 2003), 473. Political actors are viewed as utility maximisers, whose determination of a particular policy is the product of utility calculation, influenced by interest groups' exertion of their agenda or preference.

[29] Zhengquan Touziren Ji Qihuo Jiaoyiren Baohu Fa [Investor Protection Act] art. 28 § 1 (Taiwan).

[30] Zhengquan Touziren Ji Qihuo Jiaoyiren Baohu Fa [Investor Protection Act] art. 32 § 1 (Taiwan).

[31] Zhengquan Touziren Ji Qihuo Jiaoyiren Baohu Fa [Investor Protection Act] art. 28 § 3 (Taiwan).

include the power to perform all procedural acts to make waivers, accept liability, withdraw the case, or to enter into settlement, unless restricted by the investors or traders.[32]

As a corollary to the empowerment scheme, plaintiffs are required to opt into the class before IPC can initiate the litigation, but once they do, all the legal legworks are done by the IPC.[33] In sharp contrast to this opt-in scheme is the US securities class action's opt-out scheme, under which the judgment or settlement of the class is directly and automatically binding on any persons who did not opt out of the class within a certain period of time.[34]

Another area of difference is in terms of attorney fee arrangement: the Act prohibits the IPC from making any such arrangement with the plaintiffs. The IPC, as bearer of the litigation costs, can only deduct from the trial proceeds any legitimate expenses, excluding attorney fees.[35] Whether as a contingency or flat fee, the IPC is barred from soliciting remuneration or fee award from the plaintiffs.[36] In contrast, contingent attorney fee is very much a critical part to the US securities class action scheme. The US model confers extraordinary leverage and power on the plaintiff attorneys, who, in exchange for a significant portion of the potential proceeds, bear a substantial portion of the litigation risk in the initiating and organising of the suits.[37] This arrangement relieves the plaintiffs from having to pay attorney fees up front and 'enables a plaintiff's attorney to undertake litigation as a joint venture with the client'.[38]

In terms of the IPC's litigation practice, by November 2015, for the seventy-eight ongoing cases pertaining to securities law, forty-eight civil suits were filed as supplementary suit to the criminal case after indictment, and twenty-eight civil suits were filed parallel to the criminal case but initiated after indictment. That is, an overwhelming number of cases

32 Zhengquan Touziren Ji Qihuo Jiaoyiren Baohu Fa [Investor Protection Act] art. 31 § 1 (Taiwan).

33 Wang and Su, 'The Best of Both Worlds?', at 14–15.

34 Wang and Chen, 'Reforming China's Securities Civil Actions', at 133.

35 Zhengquan Touziren Ji Qihuo Jiaoyiren Baohu Fa [Investor Protection Act] art. 33 (Taiwan).

36 Ibid.

37 See John C. Coffee, Jr., 'Litigation Governance: Taking Accountability Seriously', 110 Colum. L. Rev. 288 (2010), 293.

38 See John C. Coffee, Jr., 'Understanding the Plaintiff's Attorney: The Implications of Economic Theory for Private Enforcement of Law through Class and Derivative Actions', 86 Colum. L. Rev. 669 (1986), 670.

were filed following criminal indictment. Only one civil suit was filed before criminal indictment, and the remaining one case is absent a criminal indictment.[39] Ease of access to evidence has been cited as reason for following on the prosecutor's heels.[40] Due to the lack of an evidentiary discovery process in civil trials, plaintiffs in general may find it difficult to gather evidences.[41] However, it is uncertain whether this reasoning applies in the IPC's scenario. Under the Act, the IPC may request relevant information for the purpose of initiating a securities class action suit from issuers, securities firms, securities service industries, and futures- or securities-related entities.[42] Understandably, the market participants may be hesitant, to say the least, to offer any aid in the filing of suits against themselves. To combat this, the Act provides that in the case that the IPC's information request was not fulfiled, the IPC must report to the Commission for further action,[43] thereby granting the IPC quasi-investigative power.[44] The IPC's preference over utilisation of criminal findings may therefore be indicative of either: lack of intent for full enforcement,[45] or undersized staff for its *de facto* status as the 'monopoly enforcer'.[46] The latter may be the more likely explanation.

39 Securities and Futures Investors Protection Center, 團體訴訟案件進行中案件彙總表, www.sfipc.org.tw/main, last visited 10 December 2015. Ongoing cases not related to securities law violation are excluded by the author. For a complete picture, concluded cases should also be incorporated into this statistical analysis. But due to difficulty in data collection, this chapter regrettably makes do with the readily available information.

Besides the procedural differences between supplementary and parallel civil actions, the major difference lies in the rule on court fees: supplementary civil actions are exempted completely from having to pay court fees. This may partially explain its significant utilisation. But, as later discussion will show, this is not without its corresponding drawbacks.

40 Lin, 'Challenges and Contemporary Issues', 49; Wang and Su, 'The Best of Both Worlds?', 21.

41 Lin, 'Challenges and Contemporary Issues', 50–51.

42 Zhengquan Touziren Ji Qihuo Jiaoyiren Baohu Fa [Investor Protection Act] art. 17 § 1 (Taiwan)

43 Zhengquan Touziren Ji Qihuo Jiaoyiren Baohu Fa [Investor Protection Act] art. 17 § 2 (Taiwan)

44 Shao, 'Representative Litigations', 83. But see Yu-Hsin Lin, 'Modeling Securities Class Actions Outside the United States: The Role of Nonprofits in the Case of Taiwan' 4 NYU J. L. AND BUS. 143 (2007), 183 (pointing out that 'because there is virtually no penalty for violating this clause, the quasi-investigation power of the IPC is relatively weak').

45 Shao, 'Representative Litigations', 83.

46 Wang and Su, 'The Best of Both Worlds?', 15. By the end of July 2015, the IPC employed nine lawyers, with an average of four years of experience in the IPC, and fourteen paralegals. Lin, 'Challenges and Contemporary Issues', 31. With the number of ongoing cases at eighty, this translates to roughly nine cases per lawyer simultaneously.

Despite the IPC's being funded in no small part by these market participants, the IPC's attorneys are not financially tied to these funds in their receiving of a fixed remuneration. Complemented by their tendencies for preservation of personal reputation in the industry, the notion that the IPC staff would purposefully refrain from deploying an available investigative tool becomes weak.

In terms of the IPC's result from litigation, by the end of 2014, the IPC had brought 187 securities class action claims (inclusive of those rolled over from the ISPC), seeking an aggregate claim of approximately NT$43.9 billion on behalf of approximately 112,000 investors,[47] of which eighty-four class action claims were ongoing in the courts.[48] The other 103 were either settled or awarded final and binding judgments on behalf of more than 18,000 investors, with compensation (via both settlement and judgment award) reaching approximately NT$6.6 billion.[49] Of this NT$6.6 billion amount, approximately NT$2.93 billion came from settlement.[50] This means that approximately NT$3.67 billion have been awarded in favour of the IPC, though of this amount, only NT$0.31 billion have been actually recovered,[51] amounting to a recovery rate of approximately 8 per cent.[52] For the year 2014 alone, the recovery rate was approximately 7 per cent.[53]

2.3 *As a Fee-Shifting Mechanism*

In the Pre-IPC era, the enforcement was wholly dependent upon private actors.[54] The most promising mechanism to achieve efficient enforcement

47 Securities and Futures Investors Protection Center, 4. 48 Ibid., at 20. 49 Ibid.

50 Ibid. 51 Ibid., at 5.

52 For the accumulated figure by the end of 2013, the recovery rate was also approximately 8 per cent. Wang and Su, 'The Best of Both Worlds?', 19.

53 Accumulated by end of 2013, NT$2.84 billion was awarded, of which NT$0.25 billion was recovered. See Wang and Su, 'The Best of Both Worlds?', 19. For the year 2014, the rate is determined as: (0.31–0.25) / (3.67–2.84) x 100% = 7%.

54 In the same year that the Act was imposed, the Civil Procedure Code also saw revision, in part by adding Article 44–2, facilitating a civil class action suit for a single cause injurious to multiple plaintiffs by way of public notice by the court for other investors who suffer from the same injury to opt into the class. Prior to this addition, aggregated suit can only be achieved via the 'vanilla' Article 41, making the plaintiffs, or the plaintiffs' lawyers, responsible for finding other injured investors. The Code is constructed to make class action suits possible to the extent by allowing for delegating of the litigation to one or more persons to represent the plaintiffs.

However, for the ISPC-era (i.e. since its inception in October 1998 until the IPC's takeover in 2003), class-action styled suits were initiated, with the ISPC bearing the attorney fee and court fees. There were a total of twenty-four such suits brought by the

was a contingency fee arrangement permissible under the Attorney's Code of Ethics[55] by way of attorney-organised class action similar to the US model. Yet in practice, such an arrangement was far too restrictive to achieve meaningful entrepreneurialism by attorneys to take on litigation costs and risks.[56] A low ceiling in the amount of remuneration the attorney could seek in relation to the claim amount meant that the potential return for the attorney is not significantly more, if not less, than the litigation costs and risks.[57] While the award for attorneys in US securities class actions are generally 20 per cent to 30 per cent of the trial proceeds,[58] the Taipei Bar Association provides a suggested cap at NT$0.5 million for claims less than NT$5 million, and only increasing this by 3 per cent of the claim for claims greater than or equal to NT$5 million.[59] With substantially limited upside, a capital-intensive upfront investment to organise the litigation is out of the question. In the IPC-era, costs and risks shifting became available by its financing of the entire litigation upfront.[60]

For ease of effecting legal action, the Act further provides the IPC with several economic advantages in its trial procedures: exemption from court fees for the portion of the claim in excess of NT $30 million;[61] exemption from security deposit for provisional attachment or provisional injunction;[62] and similarly exemption from

ISPC, typically initiated by the ISPC as a plaintiff (ISPC holds shares to all listed corporations on the exchange), then joined by other investors, appointing the ISPC's attorney as their attorney, for a joinder action under Article 53 of the Civil Procedure Code. See 游志煌, 論投資人保護法與證券詐欺訴訟之發展, 499 證文資料 2, 5 (2003); Lin, 'Challenges and Contemporary Issues', at 9–10; Lawrence Liu, 'Simulating Securities Class Actions: The Case in Taiwan', Vol. 3 No. 4 *Corporate Governance* 4 (2000), 8.

55 Lushi Lunli Guifan [Attorney's Code of Ethics] 1983 art. 35 § 2 (Taiwan).

56 See Wang and Su, 'The Best of Both Worlds?', 9. 57 Ibid.

58 See, e.g. Janet C. Alexander, 'Do the Merits Matter? A Study of Settlements in Securities Class Actions', 43 STAN. L. REV. 497 (1991), 536; John C. Coffee, Jr., 'Rescuing the Private Attorney General: Why the Model of the Lawyer as Bounty Hunter Is Not Working', 42 MARYLAND L. REV. 215 (1983), 239; Coffee, 'Understanding the Plaintiff's Attorney', 685; Elliott J. Weiss and John S. Beckerman, 'Let the Money Do the Monitoring: How Institutional Investors Can Reduce Agency Costs in Securities Class Actions', 104 YALE L. J. 2053 (1995), 2080.

59 Taipei Lushi Gonghui Zhangcheng [Taipei Bar Association Charter] art. 29 (Taiwan). The same contingency arrangement limitation remains in effect to date.

60 Investor Protection Act.

61 Zhengquan Touziren Ji Qihuo Jiaoyiren Baohu Fa [Investor Protection Act] art. 35 §1, §2 (Taiwan). This has been changed in the 2009 revision of the Act, as well. The superseded article allowed for exemption from court fees for portion of the claim in excess of NT$100 million.

62 Zhengquan Touziren Ji Qihuo Jiaoyiren Baohu Fa [Investor Protection Act] art. 34 (Taiwan).

provisional execution.[63] Court fees are typically calculated based on a graduated percentage of the claim with a fixed lower end,[64] and the security deposits are typically one-third of the claim.[65] For securities fraud, the relevant costs could be significant due to the large number of defrauded investors typically. In comparison to the typical class action suits under the Article 44–2 of the Civil Procedure Code, the typical civil action sees only temporary exemption from court fees in excess of NT$0.6 million, with no additional provision for relaxation in security deposit requirement. From an economics standpoint, it is apparent that investors or traders find no incentive to initiate the action in any way other than through the IPC. As a result, the IPC has grown to gain a *de facto* monopoly over serving as the lead plaintiff and lead counsel in the securities class action suits.[66]

3 The Benefits in Enforcement via the IPC

3.1 Mitigating Agency Cost

While the US scheme may stress access to judicial relief for all and the maintaining of a more efficient judiciary process for implementing an opt-out scheme, it leaves room to be desired by opening a door for potential abuse by the entrepreneurial lawyers,[67] potentially allowing for the entrepreneurial lawyers to run unchecked because, one, the access to judicial relief justification's premise on the plaintiffs' inability to seek judicial relief due to lack of resources also necessarily prevents them from exerting any meaningful monitoring on the entrepreneurial lawyers; and, two, though PSLRA incorporated a lead plaintiff provision in search of meaningful supervision on the lawyer's self-interest,[68] the results have been mixed.[69] Though studies have shown that cases with institutional investors as lead plaintiffs resulted in higher settlement amounts than cases without, it may be the result of institutional investors 'cherry picking their cases'.[70] By

[63] Zhengquan Touziren Ji Qihuo Jiaoyiren Baohu Fa [Investor Protection Act] art. 36 (Taiwan).

[64] Minshi Susong Fa [Civil Procedure Code] art. 77–13 (Taiwan). For a claim of NT$30 million, the court fees range between NT$276,000 to NT$414,000 depending on the instance of the trial. Shao, 'Representative Litigations', at 71 n.86.

[65] Ibid., at 71. [66] Wang and Su, 'The Best of Both Worlds?', 15.

[67] Wang and Chen, 'Reforming China's Securities Civil Actions', 133.

[68] Securities Act of 1933 § 27(a)(3)(B); Securities Exchange Act of 1934 § 21D(a)(3).

[69] Wang and Chen, 'Reforming China's Securities Civil Actions', 139–140.

[70] Stephen J. Choi and Robert B. Thompson, 'Securities Litigation and Its Lawyers: Changes During the First Decade after the PSLRA', 106 Colum. L. Rev. 1489 (2006), 1505–1506.

adopting an opt-in mechanism, it at least forces the disclosure of relevant information to a certain extent, in that the default on the side of independent litigation forces the attorney side to disclose information in order to motivate the conversion by the potential clients. This reduces initial assessment costs on the client side.

Furthermore, the contingency fee arrangement adopted by the US widens the misalignment of interest between the entrepreneurial attorney and the clients. Though the US model sees benefit in enabling the plaintiffs, who otherwise would be unable to sue, to initiate action,[71] which is arguably similarly accomplished via the IPC's bearing of all litigation costs up front, the US model suffers from heightening agency cost as the result of the misalignment of interests between the attorney and plaintiffs in what each party is ultimately after. While the plaintiffs are interested in the size of the proceeds, the attorney is motivated by the legal fees he or she is able to collect.[72] This apparent misalignment of interest between the attorney and plaintiffs is arguably absent under the IPC scheme, in which the IPC attorney finds no financial stake in the venture due to his or her inability to collect remuneration from the plaintiffs.

With the goal of creating 'a viable system to help investors redress their losses owing to market misconducts',[73] it is unsurprising that such a contingency scheme was not adopted in lieu of the IPC model. However, it is worth mentioning that from the viewpoint of provisioning a public good in deterrence, whether the plaintiffs find meaningful recovery becomes perhaps secondary to the overall deterrence effect. In other words, as long as deterrence can be achieved, contingency arrangement or not, the policy can sway in either direction. But, whether deterrence is, in fact, achieved is uncertain at best.[74]

3.2 *Providing a Fee-Shifting Mechanism*

In the Pre-IPC era, despite the law making it a clear substantively private right of action against securities fraud in various settings,[75] there was

[71] Ibid. [72] Wang and Su, 'The Best of Both Worlds?', 4.

[73] See note 10 and accompanying text.

[74] For discussion on US securities class action's failure to deter, see John C. Coffee, Jr., 'Reforming the Securities Class Action: An Essay on Deterrence and its Implementation', 106 COLUM. L. REV. 1534 (2006), 1547–1556; Eric Helland, 'Reputational Penalties and the Merits of Class-Action Securities Litigation', 49 J. L. AND ECON. 365 (2006), 367. For Taiwan, see Section 4.

[75] See note 1 and accompanying text.

a gap between substantive rights and enforcement of those rights.[76] Those claims, when viewed from an individual's perspective, present as a negative enforcement value, in that even when they may very well be meritorious, the cost of enforcement exceeds the potential reward.[77] It has been said that these claims are economically feasible only in the aggregate.[78] But, as seen in the previous part of this chapter, limitations on the contingency fee arrangement prevent this organisation in the securities fraud setting for Taiwan.[79] Leaving it to the individual investor to bring the lawsuit, the aggregated setting exacerbates the negative enforcement value in that the class device increases the cost for the plaintiff.[80] To compound this, a free-riding problem prevents any rational individual from volunteering to be the lead plaintiff.[81] The US adopts this entrepreneurial fee system that incentivises plaintiff attorneys to remedy this collective action problem.[82] The IPC, then, can be viewed as an alternative to address this collective action problem.

The IPC finances the entire litigation, only to extract from the trial proceeds the relevant expenses in the end.[83] Once the investors empower the IPC to bring the suit, they take a backseat in the litigation, and all costs and risks are transferred to the IPC.[84] Similar to the contingency fee arrangement model adopted by the US, but with essentially no downside from agency problems,[85] investors are greatly motivated to join the class by empowering the IPC, regardless of how remote they may be from compensation,[86] because the worst outcome is that they wasted a few minutes of their time in filing with the IPC.

4 Dilution of Deterrence due to Reliance on Criminal Investigation

In Section 2.2, we saw the IPC's overwhelming tendencies to bring suits following criminal indictment.[87] Simply put, given the way IPC operates under its current scheme, both pursuant to the Act and in accordance to its internal guidelines, leaving evidentiary investigation to the prosecutor

[76] Wang and Su, 'The Best of Both Worlds?', 6. [77] Ibid.
[78] See Coffee, 'Litigation Governance', 292. [79] See Section 2.3.
[80] Wang and Su, 'The Best of Both Worlds?', 7. [81] Ibid. [82] Ibid., at 8.
[83] Investor Protection Act. [84] Wang and Su, 'The Best of Both Worlds?', 15.
[85] See Section 3.1.
[86] See Dan W. Puchniak et al. eds., *The Derivative Action in Asia: A Comparative and Functional Approach* (1st ed. 2012), 33, n. 99 and accompanying text.
[87] See note 39 and accompanying text.

results in great dilution to the general effect of deterrence, thereby greatly discounting the provision of public good. Under a public choice analysis, it is perhaps even plausible to say that such a reliance on criminal investigation may be part of the design if the cost of evidentiary investigation is indeed too great for the IPC to handle in its current state.[88] This highlights the potential misalignment of interest between the government's political aspiration and the investors' protection or achieving deterrence.

4.1 *Giving the Primary Actors a Head Start to Hide*

From the previous part of this chapter, it is shown that the IPC requires opting in from at least twenty investors before it can initiate a securities class action in its own name. Viewed optimistically, safeguarding fair treatment can be offered as an explanation. Pessimistically, it becomes a way for the Commission to keep the IPC on a tight leash. But, regardless of the justification, the end result is the same in that the opt-in scheme, and the associated internal procedural steps to complete before a class action suit can be filed, in combination of its reliance on criminal investigation for evidences result in the perfect storm: allowing the would-be civil suit defendants a great head start in making themselves judgment proof.[89] Potential defendants may dispose of their assets during the period of time between criminal indictment and the filing of civil suit.[90] The low recovery rate for judgment awards in the single digits, percentage wise, suggests this occurrence.[91]

Viewed from an economic standpoint, deterrence works when the costs of a violation are raised.[92] For the violators, compensation awarded to the plaintiff but not collected precludes the raising of the cost of violation,[93] thereby greatly depreciating the deterrence effect.[94] Previously, by the author's own review, it was observed that the solicitation process for the

[88] Though in Section 2.2, this article has made the point that the IPC's disregard for its quasi-investigative power may be explained by its intention against full enforcement or understaffing, and that no clear justification can be offered to sway the conclusion one way or the other, for the sake of this discussion, it is assumed that the IPC intends full enforcement of law, at least to the extent it's capable. Because if it were otherwise, then the associated 'harm' by letting the criminal investigation do the work would be just what the doctor ordered, therefore making the point moot.

[89] See Wang and Su, 'The Best of Both Worlds?', 20. [90] Ibid. [91] Ibid.

[92] Ibid., at 19. [93] Ibid.

[94] See Margaret H. Lemos and Max Minzner, 'For-Profit Public Enforcement', 127 HARV. L. REV. 853 (2013), 885 (pointing out that failure to collect is 'hard to square with a pure

requisite number of defrauded investors typically lasts one month.[95] While it was hoped that this one-month period may serve as a glimpse into just how long it takes to file a civil suit after criminal indictment, current review shows that the one-month period is far short of the average time frame. By way of analysis of the ongoing securities class action cases published on the IPC's website,[96] accounting for all such cases with clear criminal indictment date and civil suit filing date, the author has found that on average, it takes the IPC 300.7 days to file its civil suit after criminal indictment, with the fastest at twenty-two days, and slowest at 691 days. This is to say, between board approval and solicitation for empowerment, the IPC on average spends 300.7 days on its internal processes. If tempering asset relocation seemed plausible under the one-month period, it now seems more probable than ever.

To ameliorate this problem, the article turns to the opt-in scheme as a start. While the opt-out scheme under the US securities class action model suffers criticism from the potential for entrepreneurial attorney's abuse,[97] there is significant reduction in agency problem potential in the IPC model, because the IPC attorney does not hold a financial stake in the venture.[98] As such, conversion to an opt-out scheme would be a great first step toward cutting down the transitioning period in order to revive the deterrence effect. But, ultimately, performing its own investigation alongside criminal investigation, for example, remains the Holy Grail.

4.2 *The Confusion in Burden of Proof*

Under SEA, a violation of the securities law may give rise to civil liability, administrative penalty, and/or criminal liability.[99] Due to inherent differences in the standard of proof required to establish liability, a defendant not criminally liable may still theoretically be held civilly liable.[100] By relying on the criminal investigation, there may be two problems: one, in overlooking cases that may satisfy the burden of proof under civil trial, but are not indicted due to prosecution's concern for failing to meet the burden of proof in criminal proceeding;[101] and two, in exposure to heightened risk of unfavourable judgment decisions

deterrence theory of enforcement, [in that] [e]conomic theories of deterrence assume that punishment is imposed, not just announced').

95 Wang and Su, 'The Best of Both Worlds?', 20.

96 Securities and Futures Investors Protection Center.

97 See Section 3.1, 16–17.

98 Ibid.

99 Wang and Su, 'The Best of Both Worlds?', 21.

100 Ibid.

101 Ibid.

due to the court's affinity to decide affirmatively to criminal trial results for a particular subset of civil trial type.[102]

Under the Criminal Procedure Code, the prosecution bears the burden of proof.[103] Criminal indictment, however, is not explicitly stipulated as requiring the accused's conviction. But, with the prosecution taking on an objective duty to be mindful of both incriminating and exonerating circumstances surrounding the accused,[104] the prosecution is barred from filing an indictment if under its own review, the available evidence prevents a conviction. Additionally, the court has power to make a ruling to dismiss the indictment prior to the examination of evidence if it determines *prima facie* that the evidence put forth by the prosecution is obviously insufficient to establish guilt, and if the prosecution fails to deliver additional evidence establishing guilt.[105] Once the ruling becomes final and binding, the prosecution cannot initiate prosecution for the same case, except for limited circumstances.[106] So, it is not difficult to see the prosecution as motivated to only present cases that have at least a shot at criminal conviction. This is to say, for cases not charged by the prosecution due to their not meeting the criminal evidentiary threshold, the IPC under the current operation scheme has no way to review whether civil liability may arise therefrom. Because, the evidence has not been made known to the IPC via indictment. Viewed thusly, there is a systemic risk of under-deterrence, in that the IPC's securities class action suits bring little to the overall detection of illicit behaviour by following criminal trials. They only intensify the penalty that the accused may already be facing.[107] This is the first problem.

Next, for suits brought by the IPC as supplementary to (or 'piggybacking' on) the criminal action,[108] the risk of under-deterrence is exacerbated. Besides the aforementioned problem in only intensifying penalty already facing the criminally accused, such intensifying of the penalty may be absent altogether in supplementary suits. In a recent survey of forty-three concluded supplementary class actions, it was shown that if the criminal defendants were found not guilty, 100 per cent of the supplementary

102 Yu-Hsin Lin, 'The Noah's Ark for Investors: An Empirical Study of Investor Protection Center and Securities Class Actions', 229 Taiwan L. Rev. 75 (2014), 82.

103 Shingshi Susong Fa [Criminal Procedure Code] art. 161 § 1 (Taiwan).

104 Shingshi Susong Fa [Criminal Procedure Code] art. 2 § 1 (Taiwan).

105 Shingshi Susong Fa [Criminal Procedure Code] art. 161 § 2 (Taiwan).

106 Shingshi Susong Fa FA [Criminal Procedure Code] art. 161 § 3 (Taiwan).

107 Wang and Su, 'The Best of Both Worlds?', 21.

108 See note 39 and accompanying text.

civil cases rendered judgment in favour for the defendants.[109] Unless the prosecution has consistently, while preventing outright dismissal by court ruling, initiated criminal action with a level of evidentiary support not quite sufficient to establish criminal liability nor civil liability, the result would suggest external factors at play to compel the civil trial results to align with the criminal's. And, as long as the IPC continues to rely on supplementary civil actions, its securities class actions suits remain exposed to such factors.

4.3 Public Choice Analysis

As shown, there are quite a few problems associated with the IPC's current reliance on criminal investigation. In the case that it is the IPC's lack of resources that has led to such reliance,[110] the lack of resources viewed through the lens of public choice theory could mean that the government is motivated by considerations other than investor protection and provision of deterrence as a public good, thereby giving rise to a IPC with inadequate resources for full enforcement.

The public choice theory holds that political actors are viewed as utility maximisers, whose determination of a particular policy is the product of utility calculation, influenced by interest groups' exertion of their agenda or preference.[111] Here, interest groups are individuals with common interest, with policy preferences and bargaining powers to exert an influence on government policy-making.[112] In the case of securities law enforcement, instead of incentivising private parties to sue, the government has created an enforcer to represent the private parties.[113] Via public choice theory, this is viewed as the end result of the government's utility calculation in consideration of the relevant interest groups' attempt to sway the policy its way. So, if the hypothesised lacking in resources is indeed responsible for the IPC's reliance on criminal investigation, and that funding of the IPC is stipulated by the Act, and that the IPC created in accordance to the Act is the product of the government's utility calculation, then it is logical to say that in the government's utility calculation, other factors, besides investor protection and provision of deterrence as a public good was at play. Because had those been the only factors affecting the government's

[109] See Lin, 'The Noah's Ark for Investors'. [110] See note 88 and accompanying text.
[111] See Mueller, *Public Choice III*. [112] Ibid.
[113] Wang and Su, 'The Best of Both Worlds?', 24.

utility calculation, it would not be the case that accumulated recovery rate is a lowly 8 per cent.

Thus, when viewed in the public choice theorem light, there is a real concern for inherent misalignment of interest between the government's aspiration and the goal of investor protection and deterrence. Returning to this chapter's previous review of the tie between the government and the IPC,[114] which characterised the government as free to attempt to align the IPC with its own interest, this becomes worrisome, given the above potential for misalignment of interest.

5 Dilution in Deterrence due to Compensation via Settlement as Opposed to via Judgment Award

By the end of 2014, of the NT$6.6 billion compensation obtained by the IPC via settlement and final judgment award, NT$2.93 billion came from settlement,[115] or approximately 44 per cent. In relation to the actual recovered amount, this figure jumps to approximately 90 per cent.[116] It is clear that whatever deterrence effect there might be, it is largely derived from settlement, as it is overwhelmingly accountable for the real increase in the perpetrators' cost of violation. Given the lack of resources hypothesis,[117] coupled with the unfavourable judiciary environment for its supplementary civil actions,[118] it may be understandable why the IPC has taken on settling instead of going all the way through trial. Had the IPC gone the latter route, the actually recovered amount might have been less. In terms of getting money for the injured investors, settling is okay. In terms of achieving deterrence, however, there are some concerns for reliance on settlement to do so.

5.1 Deep-Pocket Strategy

While settlement as a way to achieve deterrence is not inherently problematic, it becomes so under the IPC's practice, in which secondary actors are the targets in a 'deep-pocket' strategy.[119] One justification for this

[114] See Section 2.1, 5–8. [115] See Section 2.2, 8–13.

[116] Ibid. With a 100 per cent recovery rate for the settlement at an amount of NT$2.93 billion, the recovered amount from judgment award was calculated to be NT$0.31 billion. The percentage calculation is as follows: (2.93) / (2.93+0.31) x 100% = 90%.

[117] See note 88 and accompanying text. [118] See Section 4.2.

[119] See Wang and Su, 'The Best of Both Worlds?', 22.

strategy is that due to the timing for the initiation of civil suits following the criminal indictment, which for the ongoing securities class action cases took an averaged 300.7 days after criminal indictment,[120] potential civil class action defendants may attempt to relocate their assets to prevent payout to the investors.[121] But, for the targeted secondary actors, such as underwriters and CPAs, due to their stake in the continuation of their respective business, asset relocation is difficult. So settlement becomes a viable option for them, but lacking completely in incentive for the primary actors, e.g. the directors. Because, the directors, although they may be similarly interested in continued employment in the business, find no problem in partitioning their assets elsewhere and find no reason not to do so. For the former, there is no capital requirement for being a director, meaning that there are no external forces to compel the primary actors to leave his or her assets as is in order to finance future business. In the latter notion, US experience shows that even when a board is accused of fraud in shareholder class actions, the director's personal reputational capital remains unscathed in most cases.[122] In the face of certain losses by settling with the IPC vis-à-vis a worst-case scenario of personal reputational harm at a low probability, potentially a positive net present value transaction, it is no surprise that settling poses no attraction to the directors.

With punishment directed only at secondary actors, the deterrence effects are not felt by the primary actors. And arguably, it is the primary actors who possess the scienter to defraud investors.[123] The secondary actors are parties colluding to the illicit enterprise, no less. But, increasing the penalty on the latter (i.e. civil settlement on top of potential criminal liability) while not addressing the former, such a formula does not lend itself to deterrence. As long as the primary actors can be economically persuasive, there will be secondary actors willing to join in the fraudulent behaviour, so long as the payout to the secondary actors vis-à-vis potential gain through fraud remains a positive net present value transaction (at least in the potential wrongdoer's own estimation). Thus, the provision of public good is greatly discounted by settling with an emphasis on secondary actors, as opposed to obtaining judgment awards.

[120] See note 96 and accompanying text.

[121] See Lin, 'Challenges and Contemporary Issues', at 38; note 89 and accompanying text.

[122] See Helland, 'Reputational Penalties', 74.

[123] See Wang and Su, 'The Best of Both Worlds?', 25 (expressing sentiment that the underwriters who settle are not the real wrongdoers).

To force settlement upon the primary actors, the issue is tied to the supposedly general lack of resources hypothesis that has resulted in the 300.7-day 'waiting period' before civil suits were filed. If this time can be significantly reduced, or an alternative internal procedure established for timely provisional attachment to allow for meaningful early intervention by the IPC, asset relocation for the primary actors may become improbable altogether. Thusly, they can be either forced to settle just the same as secondary actors or await judgment and take their chances.

5.2 *Public Choice Analysis*

From Section 4.3 (at 24–25), it was shown that there exists a potential misalignment of interests between the government's political aspiration and the goal of investor protection or provision of deterrence. This political aspiration, to reiterate, is the product of interest group forces at play. The author has previously expressed concern for political intervention in the settlement process,[124] and the public choice analysis conducted thus far has not ameliorated this concern. As discussed in Section 2.1 (at 5–8), while the IPC is not motivated to align with the government, the government remains free to attempt to align the IPC with its own interest. And, stemming from its own political interest, be it to showcase the IPC as a champion in the protection of investors' rights while underhandedly conforming to the interest groups' demands or other motivations, it was shown that there is at least a departure from the supposed investor protection or provision of public good.

This potential misalignment of interest may bring additional concerns of abuse in a litigation scheme with significant emphasis on finding compensation or deterrence through settlement. While some have pointed to the IPC's internal settlement guideline promulgated by the board as a way to ensure fair settlement results,[125] an internal guideline alone does not sufficiently curb the author's concern. First, this guideline remains mysterious and accessible by the IPC only,

[124] Wang and Su, 'The Best of Both Worlds?', 23 (citing the high profile case of Procomp Informatics as an example, in which it was revealed that the Commission, as the regulatory body over the audit firms who settled, had intervened in the settlement process). See Lin, 'Modeling Securities Class Actions', 190.

[125] See Lin, 'Challenges and Contemporary Issues', 57–58.

without even a hint of what types of factors are at play.[126] There is no way to tell just what type of potential abuse the guideline may prevent. Secondly, even assuming the guideline as able to establish a fair settlement amount *arguendo*, it fails to address the concern on whether the defendant should settle in the first place. Based on a formula for the determination of settlement figure alone, a truth-finding objective is absent as a basis for the guarantee of entirely fair results. Inherently, settlement makes do with the asymmetry of information and even makes use of this disparity to compel the parties to reach mutually agreeable terms. As such, it logically cannot function as the saviour of all potential for abuse because it thrives on a disparity of information. At best, this guideline prevents the IPC from throwing away cases by settling too leniently, or it prevents the regulatory body by forcing the defendant to settle at exorbitant terms. While this concern for potential abuse remains one regarding a systemic risk, there is a real concern in leaving the abuse safe-guards to personal ethics in that there is no systemic solution in place to address this issue.

To combat this, transparency and independence have been suggested.[127] Interestingly, suggestions of outsourcing the legal counsel function via a bidding process, though intended as a way to increase market participation to realise the IPC's full potential, may also fit the general idea for the prevention of undue political intervention[128] because the legal actions are now done by outsiders. The government is subsequently less incentivised to force a settlement if it cannot claim the settlement as its own contribution via association with the IPC due to its quasi-public nature. That is, it no longer promotes personal utility for the government. Another suggestion has been to remove the restrictions on contingency fee arrangements.[129] Similarly, this was done to create additional market-oriented mechanisms to check and balance the IPC's litigation as a way to ensure the quality of the IPC's performance.[130] Such competition for representation in class action may also translate to the disincentivisation for the government to force a settlement, because it similarly cannot claim those settlements with non-IPC suits as its contribution.

[126] Ibid., at 55 (stating vaguely that the guide 'include[s] a list of factors and establish[es] a formula allowing the SFIPC staff to settle case[s] with certain degree of flexibility and certainty').

[127] Wang and Chen, 'Reforming China's Securities Civil Actions', 150–151; Wang and Su, 'The Best of Both Worlds?', 25–26. See Lin, 'Challenges and Contemporary Issues', at 62–63 (calling for more board involvement).

[128] See Shao, 'Representative Litigations', 89–93.

[129] Wang and Su, 'The Best of Both Worlds?', 26.

[130] Ibid.

6 Conclusion

In creating a quasi-public enforcer of securities law in the provision of a public good, Taiwan has addressed concerns about the high transaction costs for individual action and collective action problems for the enforcement of securities law via private right of action. Viewed thusly, the IPC greatly enhanced the provision of public good; without it, there might be none altogether for Taiwan. But, this NPO model contains inherent and systemic flaws that require systemic solutions. While available facts do not strongly suggest abuse or intentional under-deterrence by the IPC, this review has shown that there is danger for the former, and there is strong evidence indicating greatly discounted deterrence provision. While there are many things the IPC brings to the table in the investor protection arena, it suffers from many ailments as well.

This review has suggested potential solutions against each identified problem. Returning to the public choice context, it is hoped that this review will help invigorate an interest group to influence the political actors' decision-making process in order to usher the IPC into a more intricate organisation that addresses not only the 'what-has-happened', but also the 'what-could-happen'.

23

Building Enforcement Capacity for Brazilian Corporate and Securities Law*

JOHN ARMOUR AND CAROLINE SCHMIDT

1 Introduction

In this chapter, we study the development of enforcement institutions for Brazilian corporate and securities law. In common with many other emerging markets, Brazilian equity markets channel only a relatively modest proportion of funding into public firms. Persuading financiers to commit funds on an arm's-length basis to public companies requires effective corporate and securities laws and associated institutions. This implies both appropriate rules and effective enforcement institutions. Brazilian policymakers and regulators have sought, over the past fifteen years, to improve the quality of the corporate governance and securities rules protecting outside investors in such companies. However, it is well established in the literature that the quality of enforcement institutions are at least as important as the substantive law in facilitating investment.

A central challenge for Brazil, however, concerns the limitations of the regular courts as forums for adjudicating complex business law disputes. They are slow to decide cases, and the judges lack relevant business expertise. Moreover, they are uncertain as regards outcomes, and do not produce clear guidance for parties to plan their affairs without recourse to litigation. These limitations create two linked problems for corporate law: a lack of certainty *ex ante*, because of the discretionary nature of much decision making and the lack of expertise of judges, and a delay in getting a decision *ex post*.

In this chapter we document four strategies employed by Brazilian actors to improve adjudication institutions for corporate law. These can

* This research was funded by an ESRC Grant under the *Rising Powers and Interdependent Futures* initiative. We are grateful to those we interviewed in the course of conducting this research.

be pursued independently, but in a way that overlaps, such that they mutually reinforce each other's efficacy. Our research draws on data collected through interviews with Brazilian lawyers and market participants.[1]

First, there has been a vast growth in the use of arbitration to resolve commercial disputes generally in Brazil. This bypasses the ordinary court system to some degree, giving parties access to expert dispute resolution rapidly. Second, the São Paulo Court of Appeal (*Tribunal de Justiça de São Paulo*) was restructured in 2010 to create a specialist panel of expert business law judges. Third, the Brazilian Securities and Exchanges Commission (*Comissão de Valores Mobiliários* or CVM), operates a dedicated 'administrative' court, with power to enforce CVM regulations and public company law. Fourth, a recent initiative seeks to create a new player: the Mergers and Acquisitions Committee (*Comitê de Aquisições e Fusões* or CAF), intended to provide a decision-making body for M&A transactions.

The weakness of legal institutions in supporting finance is a problem shared by most emerging markets and indeed many developed markets. An appreciation of the Brazilian experience in overcoming these problems may therefore yield insights to policy makers elsewhere.

The remainder of this paper is structured as follows. Section 2 reviews the literature on law and finance highlighting the importance of effective institutions, especially as regards enforcement, for the growth and development of arm's-length finance. Section 3 presents background on the Brazilian context: the economy and capital markets, and the challenges faced by judicial infrastructure. Section 4 describes the four mechanisms used to build enforcement capacity, in Brazilian corporate and securities laws, and Section 5 discusses the extent to which the findings are capable of generalisation to other countries.

[1] We conducted thirty-eight semi-structured and open-ended interviews with professional subjects connected to law and finance in Brazil, including legal practitioners, judges, arbitrators, investment bankers, in-house lawyers, regulators, and officials at the Brazilian development bank (BNDES). Interviews were conducted in London, Brasilia, Rio de Janeiro and São Paulo. Interviews were held in English and Brazilian Portuguese, in person and without liaison. They were typically around 1.5 hours in length and recorded upon request, followed by note-taking. Interviews were held with Brazilian nationals, selected through purposeful snowball sampling, where interviewees recommended their peers based on their judgments about levels of expertise and reputation – leading to a sample that includes many of the key actors. Subjects were sent an *aide memoire* containing a series of questions in advance, and the interviews began with this agenda but were allowed to develop in line with the interests of the subjects. Confidentiality was secured as requested.

2 Law and Finance: The Importance of Institutions

A large body of literature has explored the links between legal institutions and the raising of finance. As a matter of theory, legal institutions matter because they facilitate arm's-length contracting. Suppliers of capital fear opportunistic behaviour by those controlling the firm. Once finance has been raised, controllers may divert resources to themselves at the expense of the investors, a practice sometimes referred to as 'tunnelling'.[2] In theory, legal protection for minority shareholders can reduce the extent to which such expropriation takes place. Of course, expropriation might be constrained even in the absence of credible legal enforcement, because of a controller's concern about their reputation. However, establishing a reputation takes time, creating a barrier to entry. Effective legal institutions, by enabling financiers to enforce arm's length contracts – that is, not relying on reputation or prior dealings – can help firms to raise finance more easily.

An influential body of empirical literature has explored links between legal protection offered to investors and the raising of finance. Seminal contributions from La Porta, Lopes-de-Silanes, Shleifer and Vishny reported a correlation between legal protection of outside investors, as measured by an index of 'quality of law', and the depth and liquidity of stock markets.[3] While the particular construction of the initial index has been subject to criticism,[4] the methodological innovation has spawned a new literature. A subsequent refinement focuses on situations of self-dealing, precisely the type of issue that will occur between controlling shareholders and a minority.[5]

Of course, not all transactions between controlling shareholders and their firms are harmful for minority shareholders. Consequently, many

[2] See e.g. S. Johnson, R. La Porta, F. Lopez-de-Silanes and A. Shleifer, 'Tunneling', 90 *American Economic Review* 22 (2000); V. Atanasov, B. Black and C.S. Ciccotello, 'Law and Tunneling', 37 *Journal of Corporation Law* 1 (2011).

[3] R. La Porta, F. Lopez-de-Silanes, A. Sheifer and R.W. Vishny, 'Legal Determinants of External Finance', 52 *Journal of Finance* 1131(1997). See also, for a more recent survey, R. La Porta, F. Lopez-de-Silanes and A. Shleifer, 'The Economic Consequences of Legal Origins', 46 *Journal of Economic Perspectives* 285 (2008).

[4] See e.g. J. Armour, S. Deakin, P. Sarkar, M. Siems and A. Singh, 'Shareholder Protection and Stock Market Development: An Empirical Test of the Legal Origins Hypothesis', 6 *Journal of Empirical Legal Studies* 343 (2009); H. Spamann, 'The "Antidirector Rights" Index Revisited', 23 *Review of Financial Studies* 467 (2010).

[5] S. Djankov, R. La Porta, F. Lopez-de-Silanes and A. Shleifer, 'The Law and Economics of Self-Dealing', 88 *Journal of Financial Economics* 430 (2008). However, c.f. D.M. Klerman, P.G. Mahoney, H. Spamann and M.I. Weinstein, 'Legal Origin or Colonial History?', 3 *Journal of Legal Analysis* 379 (2011).

jurisdictions regulate self-dealing by specifying a procedure through which approval may be granted: whether by minority shareholders, independent directors, or even a court. Direct court decision making makes heavy demands on the judiciary. Minority shareholders must be able to launch a petition for judicial scrutiny cheaply, and courts must be able to review the transaction quickly. The court must be free from actual or apparent bias, and the judge must have sufficient business knowledge to be able to make sense of relevant expert evidence.

In the presence of limitations on courts' ability to meet these challenges, delegation of review of self-dealing transactions to independent directors and/or shareholders may seem attractive. However, this creates additional pressures. Independent directors must in fact *be* independent. And for shareholder voting to work, the vote must be free from coercion, and shareholders secure in the belief that a vote against the controller will not result in some form of retaliation. Each of these mechanisms consequently requires some second-order judicial support – reviewing the appointment of supposedly independent directors, and/or the conduct of shareholder votes. If courts cannot supply such support, then these mechanisms will not function effectively.

3 The Brazilian Context

3.1 Economy and Finance

Brazil is the world's seventh largest economy by GDP. It experienced rapid growth in the early twenty-first century, peaking at 7.5 per cent in 2010.[6] In common with many emerging markets, Brazil's capital markets represent only a modest portion of GDP, with finance for industry being sourced largely from retained earnings or from the state in the form of loans from the Brazilian Development Bank (BNDES).[7]

From the mid-1960s until 1985, Brazil was ruled by a military regime. Hyperinflation was endemic from the early 1970s, with annualised rates peaking at over 2,000 per cent in the early 1990s. During this time, capital markets languished. A key component of successive authoritarian governments' strategy for maintaining public order was to guarantee that

[6] Source: Instituto Brasileiro de Pesquisa Econômica Aplicada (data available at www.ipeadata.gov.br).

[7] M.H. Santana, M. Ararat, P. Alexandru, B. Yurtoglu and M. Rodrigues da Cunha, 'Novo Mercado and Its Followers: Case Studies in Corporate Governance Reform', *IFC/Global Corporate Governance Forum Focus* 5 (2008), 2.

household savings would not be dissipated by inflation, achieved through indexation of savings accounts. A byproduct, however, was to crowd out investment in industry: given an attractive risk-free real rate of interest on savings accounts, domestic investors were not interested in equities, still less corporate bonds. At the same time, capital controls choked off foreign investment. The combined result was that Brazilian businesses had little access to private capital. Consistently with this picture, most significant businesses were state-owned and much of the debt finance was channelled through BNDES.

Following Brazil's return to democracy in 1985, successive governments tried a variety of measures to bring inflation under control, which succeeded in gaining traction only by the mid-1990s. At around this time, Brazil embarked on a massive privatisation programme.[8] This coincided with the opening of the economy internationally, triggering an influx of foreign portfolio investment.

The next decade saw substantial progress in the development of Brazilian capital markets. This has been associated with the introduction by the Brazilian Stock Exchange (Bovespa) in 2000 of the *Novo Mercado* ('New Market') listing segment, with higher associated corporate governance standards.[9] From 2004 to 2008, the Brazilian Stock Market experienced unprecedented growth. During this period, 113 companies filled IPOs with the Brazilian Securities and Exchange Commission (that is, the CVM).[10] The average daily trading volume on Bovespa increased from BR$1.2 billion in 2004 to BR$5.5 billion in 2008. Stock market capitalisation deepened enormously, growing from 35 per cent of GDP in 2000 to 100 per cent by 2007. There are currently 525 public companies listed on Bovespa, but the ratio of their market capitalisation to GDP trailed off somewhat from the high point of 2007, falling to 55 per cent in 2012.[11]

8 F. Anuatti-Neto, M. Barossi-Filho, A.G. de Carvalho and R. Macedo, 'Costs and Benefits of Privatization: Evidence from Brazil', *Inter-American Development Bank Research Network Working Paper No. R-455* (2003).

9 See e.g. E. Gorga, 'Changing the Paradigm of Stock Ownership from Concentrated towards Dispersed Ownership: Evidence from Brazil and Consequences for Emerging Countries', 29 *Northwestern Journal of International Law & Business* 439 (2009); B.S. Black, A.G. de Carvalho and E. Gorga, 'Corporate Governance in Brazil', 11 *Emerging Markets Review* 21 (2010); B.S. Black, A.G. de Carvalho and E. Gorga, 'What Matters and for Which Firms for Corporate Governance in Emerging Markets? Evidence from Brazil (and Other BRIK Countries)', 18 *Journal of Corporate Finance* 934 (2012).

10 BM&FBovespa, *Public Offerings and IPOs* (www.bmfbovespa.com.br/pt-br/mercados/acoes/ofertas-publicas/ofertas-publicas.aspx?idioma=pt-br).

11 World Bank, *World Development Indicators 2013*, Table 5.4 (wdi.worldbank.org/table/5.4).

3.2 *Law Enforcement: The Problem of Judicial Backlogs*

Brazilian courts present a bottleneck to litigants. There is a huge backlog in judicial caseloads. Our interviewees recounted that lawsuits could take ten or more years until a final trial.[12] They viewed the large backlog of cases as in part a function of the litigation rate, and in part a function of courts' difficulties in closing cases. Others spoke of the use of litigation, at least after the return to democracy, as a means of challenging executive overreaching in fields such as taxation. Consideration of litigation statistics allows us to distinguish between these accounts.

In 2012, Brazil's annual litigation rate was 12.8 new suits filed per 100 citizens.[13] This is high, but not exceptionally large by international comparison: the average across the EU in 2010 was 11.3,[14] and for the US the equivalent number was 5.8.[15] Much of the litigation in Brazil is between the business sector and the state, with tax foreclosure proceedings accounting for 32 per cent of all cases.[16] Data from 2011 disclose that federal public bodies were the most frequent litigants, plaintiffs in 12 per cent of new cases filed that year, followed by the financial sector (11 per cent), municipal authorities (7 per cent) and other state public bodies (4 per cent).[17] When tax and employment cases are removed from the picture, the total level of litigation appears much more modest. Together, this suggests that the high backlog is not primarily a function of 'litigiousness' of Brazilians. The high numbers of tax and employment cases, on the other hand, seem consistent with the use of litigation in these sectors as a means of challenging executive overreaching.

[12] One spoke vividly of a matter in which his law firm was acting between corporate parties, in relation to which none of the natural persons originally involved was still alive, making it very hard to determine what had happened.

[13] See Conselho Nacional de Justiça ('CNJ'), *Executive Summary: Courts in Figures 2013 – The Base Year 2012* (Brasilia: CNJ, 2013), 9 (filing data); World Bank, *World Development Indicators 2013*, Table 2.1 (wdi.worldbank.org/table/2.1).

[14] CEPEJ (European Commission for the Efficiency of Justice), The Functioning of Judicial Systems and the Situation of the Economy in the European Union Member States, Report prepared for the European Commission (DG Justice), January 2013, 629 (Table 5). A number of EU countries have significantly higher rates of case filing than Brazil, including Austria, Denmark, Germany, Poland and Slovenia.

[15] J.M. Ramseyer and E.B. Rasmusen, 'Comparative Litigation Rates', Harvard John M. Olin Center for Law, *Economics & Business Discussion Paper No 681* (2010), 5 (Table 1).

[16] CNJ, *Executive Summary: Courts in Figures 2013*, 13. These have a particularly high non-completion rate, with only eleven tax foreclosure cases out of 100 annually remanded or dismissed: ibid., 9.

[17] CNJ, *100 Maiores Litigantes* (Brasília: CNJ, 2012), 8.

Where Brazil stands out internationally is in its *backlog* of pending cases. Countries with high litigation rates generally have court systems that are able to manage the caseload, resulting in only modest backlogs carried across from year to year. That is not the case in Brazil, which in 2012 had an astonishing 29.3 lawsuits pending per 100 citizens,[18] nearly seven times higher than the EU-wide average of 4.4.[19] The high backlog relative to the litigation rate suggests that courts have difficulties in completing cases.[20]

The source of this difficulty does not seem to be lack of judicial resources. Brazilian judges are well paid, with typical salaries similar in absolute terms to judicial pay in Germany, and equivalent to thirty-two times average annual salaries in Brazil.[21] Moreover, Brazil has 8.8 judges per 100,000 citizens,[22] significantly more than the UK (3.6) and nearly as many as the US (10.8).[23] Although it is less than half the average in the EU (18.9),[24] the difference is nowhere near as large as the sevenfold difference in pendency. The large number of well-paid judges means that Brazil's expenditure on the judicial branch accounts for 3.2 per cent of total public expenditure,[25] far more, for example, than the average of 0.44 per cent across the EU.[26] Both quantity and – by inference from salary – quality of the Brazilian judiciary are comparatively high.

Another possible cause could be corruption. If Brazilian judges were not performing their function effectively because of bribery or political influence, this would greatly undermine the efficacy of the legal system. Yet we consider it unlikely that this is a complete explanation for the observed pattern of backlog, for two reasons. First, as we have seen, Brazilian judges are well paid, whether by relative or even absolute standards. If officials' pay exceeds what they might earn from bribes,

18 CNJ, *Executive Summary: Courts in Figures 2013*.

19 CEPEJ, The Functioning of Judicial Systems.

20 To be sure, the litigation rate likely under-represents demand for litigation, or 'litigiousness', because the long backlog will reduce parties' expectations as to outcomes. Nevertheless, the causal mechanism would still be the difficulties faced by courts in completing cases.

21 M. Dakolias, 'Court Performance around the World: A Comparative Perspective', *World Bank Technical Paper No 430* (1999), 21.

22 CNJ, *Executive Summary: Courts in Figures 2013*, 7.

23 See CEPEJ, The Functioning of Judicial Systems, at 631 (UK data: Table 6); Ramseyer and Rasmusen, 'Comparative Litigation Rates', 5 (US data: Table 1).

24 CEPEJ, The Functioning of Judicial Systems.

25 CNJ, *Executive Summary: Courts in Figures 2013*, 5.

26 CEPEJ, The Functioning of Judicial Systems, 631 (Table 6).

then corruption is likely to be reduced.[27] Second, and consistently with this, Brazil does not fare particularly poorly on cross-national indicators of corruption, in comparison to other emerging economies. For example, the World Bank's indicators suggest that corruption in Brazil is only half that in Russia, less than a quarter of that in India and approximately a seventh of that in China.[28]

Why then do Brazilian courts struggle to close cases? Our interviewees spoke of a procedural law that was considered highly 'ritualistic', so as to permit too many rights of appeal. Plaintiffs were said to pursue all their rights to appeal, facilitated in this regard by low court filing fees.[29] However, this does not explain *why* parties pursue these options. In most cases it would be cheaper for parties jointly to settle, so there would be a good reason for doing so.

Another problem frequently mentioned by interviewees, namely uncertainty, could provide the explanation. As a matter of theory, uncertainty over the outcome of a judicial decision makes settlement less likely, as parties are less able to estimate how much they give up – in expected value terms – by not electing to pursue their suit to trial.[30] There are several potentially relevant sources of uncertainty. One is that judicial decisions do not have the force of binding precedents, at least in the common law sense, in Brazil.[31] The absence of precedents means that prior decisions are not 'coded' so as to enable subsequent parties to arrange their affairs. This in turn makes it harder for parties to anticipate outcomes to litigation.

However, the absence of precedents cannot be the whole story. Brazil's legal system shares this feature with most civil law systems around the world. Moreover, certainty in Brazilian jurisprudence is to some degree enhanced by a form of judicial pronouncement known as a *súmula*. *Súmulas* have the function of harmonising court jurisprudence, and can be described as a series of concise legal pronouncements made by

[27] See eg J. Svensson, 'Eight Questions about Corruption' 19 *Journal of Economic Perspectives* 19 (2005), 32–33.

[28] World Bank, *World Development Indicators 2013*, Table 5.2 (wdi.worldbank.org/table/5.2) (percentage of firms reporting making informal payments to public officials: Brazil 11 per cent, China 72 per cent, India 48 per cent, Russia 20 per cent).

[29] This seems similar to observations made in the context of India: see J. Armour and P. Lele, 'Law, Finance and Politics: The Case of India', 43 *Law & Society Review* 491 (2009), 509–511.

[30] The theoretical literature is surveyed in Ramseyer and Rasmusen, 'Comparative Litigation Rates'.

[31] See ibid.

the court, normally one or two lines in length, about the holding of the court on a particular matter. These are defined once the court has judged similar case laws and has confirmed a position. The Supreme Court has been publishing *súmulas* since 1964,[32] and most Appellate Courts now do so also. Traditionally their status was simply to summarise rather than oblige subsequent courts to follow them. However, since 2004, the Supreme Court has published what are known as *súmulas vinculantes*, which are treated as binding on subsequent courts.[33]

A second source of uncertainty, as regards business decisions, comes from the fact that Brazilian judges typically lack expertise in business matters. Brazilian judges are recruited by public exams soon after they graduate from law school, with purely legal qualifications. The professional experience they develop is solely that gained from adjudicating cases. Brazilian courts traditionally have generalist jurisdiction in relation to a particular geographic region, meaning that the judges do not usually have the opportunity to develop a specialism in business law over the course of their careers. This makes them poorly situated to pass judgment on complex commercial matters. The majority of our interviewees were in agreement that courts in Brazil lack expertise to appreciate cases involving matters related to business laws or complex business transactions, with leading lawyers and legal professionals speaking more strongly about the judiciary institutional failure to properly address highly complex commercial cases and, therefore, their preference for arbitration.[34] However, whilst this is a plausible source of uncertainty as regards litigation outcomes, it too is similar to the position in many civil law countries, where generalist judges recruited directly from law school are the norm.[35]

A third source of uncertainty, which is specific to Brazil, has to do with the way in which courts approach their interpretative functions. In contractual interpretation, judges may take into account the 'social and economic consequences' of their decisions. The Brazilian Civil Code of 2002 unified the Civil Code of 1916,[36] and the Commercial Code of

[32] *Emenda Regimental*, de 28 de Agosto de 1963, published by the Supreme Federal Court.
[33] Constitutional Amendment No 45/2004, Art 103-A.
[34] See also B.M. Salama and V.M. Prado, 'Legal Protection of Minority Shareholders of Listed Corporations in Brazil: Brief History, Legal Structure and Empirical Evidence', 4 *Journal of Civil Law Studies* 147 (2011).
[35] G.K. Hadfield, 'The Levers of Legal Design: Institutional Determinants of the Quality of Law', 36 *Journal of Comparative Economics* 43 (2008).
[36] Código Civil, *Lei 3017, de 1 de Janeiro de 1916.*

1850,[37] incorporating rules on business activity. Among other changes, the 2002 Civil Code provided, in the section on general provisions applicable to contracts, that, 'the freedom to contract should be exercised by reason and within the limits of the social function of the contract.'[38] This resonates with Article 5(XXIII) of the Brazilian Constitution of 1988, which provides that 'property shall observe its social function'.[39] The 'social function' of property and contracts so defined brings public law considerations into the adjudication of private contracts and property. It follows that consequences to third parties may be taken into consideration during legal disputes. Brazilian law does not clearly define the limitations of this concept and legal scholars and courts have been developing its interpretation. The broad application to contracts means that decisions are subject to wide-ranging judicial discretion. Our interviewees reported that court decisions based on the notion of the 'social function of contract' tended to interfere with contractual relations in favour of the party who appeared to the court to be the weaker. Consistently with this, a study of the consequences of litigating breaches of contract reported that affected traders and industries subsequently increased the number of explicit warranties in their contracts, presumably seeking to restrict judicial discretion.[40] Such interference is also reported to be prevalent prevailing in attempts to enforce debts by creditors, in which courts act as champions of borrowers against financial institutions.

4 Building Capacity in the Enforcement of Brazilian Securities and Corporate Law

We turn now to consider a series of institutional developments which are deployed in Brazil to seek to overcome the limitations of the courts. We apply a simple analytical framework to understand the ways in which institutional arrangements relevant to securities and corporate law are developing in Brazil, and how key actors perceive they operate. This draws from political science the idea of *institutional layering*, that is, the incorporation of solutions that overcome institutional limitations

[37] Código Comercial, *Lei 556, de 25 de Junho de 1850.*

[38] Código Civil, *Lei 10.406, de 10 de Janeiro de 2002*, Art 421.

[39] Constitution of the Federative Republic of Brazil (1988); See also A. de Santos Cunha, 'The Social Function of Property In Brazilian Law', 80 *Fordham Law Review* 1171 (2011).

[40] C.L. Rezende and D. Zylbersztajn, 'Quebras Contratuais e Dispersão de Sentença', *Revista Direito GV* 7 (2011).

without eliminating old institutional structures.[41] Often institutional change can be described in terms of 'breakdown and replacement':[42] historical events lead to critical juncture moments where institutional change or reproduction takes place. 'Layering', however, favours a more nuanced analysis to institutional transformation. In such cases, new arrangements induce incremental changes in the old institutional structures leading to institutional advancements or complementarities. This approach traditionally looks at social processes as they unfold over time and in relation to other processes, specially looking to the ways in which adaptation contributes to institutional continuity.[43] In our study, we look at legal processes and each of the institutional developments in Brazil can be seen as a 'layer' in which new arrangements are created, based on the foundation of the basic system of corporate law enforced through state courts. Each derives its legality to some extent from the underlying foundations. Yet each offers a way of overcoming some of the limitations of the underlying system. None is able completely to transcend these limitations, and so each is, by itself, an incomplete solution. However, the fact that all four approaches can be pursued simultaneously means that they overlap to a significant degree, especially in relation to areas crucial for facilitating outside investment such as the control of tunnelling by majority shareholders.

4.1 *Arbitration: The* Novo Mercado *Arbitration Chamber*

Arbitration is widely used by commercial parties in emerging markets as a way of sidestepping long delays in the regular courts. Moreover, it permits the selection of decision makers with expertise in the field, thereby allowing for decisions of better quality than those offered by generalist judges who may have little knowledge of business practice. However, Brazil had no tradition of arbitration until the passage of the Arbitration Law of 1996.[44] Before then, arbitration was viewed as an improper delegation of the decision-making authority entrusted to the courts.

Arbitrators have no coercive powers of their own, instead relying on the ordinary court system for enforcement. Nevertheless, the workload

[41] See e.g. K. Thelen, *How Institutions Evolve: The Political Economy of Skills in Germany, Britain, the United States, and Japan* (Cambridge: Cambridge University Press, 2004); J. van der Heijden, 'Institutional Layering: A Review of the Use of the Concept', 31 *Politics* 9 (2011).

[42] Thelen, *How Institutions Evolve*, 52. [43] Ibid.

[44] Lei de Arbitragem (Arbitration Act). *Lei 9.307, de 23 de Setembro de 1996.*

for the courts is greatly reduced, as all the judges need do is enforce the arbitral award. The benefits of arbitration could easily be undermined if courts retained power to review the validity of arbitration clauses, or of decision making by arbitrators in accordance with them. To minimise the potential for such challenges, the Brazilian Arbitration Act recognises the principle of 'competence-competence': that is, that arbitration chambers are *themselves* competent to confirm the extent and scope of their own competence – namely, the validity and interpretation of arbitration clauses.[45] Moreover, the Act makes clear that, as regards domestic awards, the arbitrator 'is the judge in fact and in right, and his/her award is not subject to appeal or homologation by State Courts'.[46] Nevertheless, parties to arbitration can still seek precautionary injunctions in state courts, which can be appealed, therefore, holding up the proceedings until a final decision by the court. Our professional interviewees however felt that even in such cases arbitration was preferable to ordinary litigation, because of the arbitrators' superior business expertise.

Arbitration has a particular manifestation in relation to Brazilian securities law. In December 2000, Bovespa (the São Paulo Stock Exchange) launched the *Novo Mercado*, special listing segment open to publicly traded companies willing to commit to additional standards of corporate governance. For a company to list on the *Novo Mercado*, it had to adopt governance practices significantly beyond those required by Brazilian corporate law, including rules expanding shareholder rights and enhancing the scope of issuer disclosure. Adherence to the *Novo Mercado* is achieved through a private agreement between Bovespa, senior managers, controlling shareholders, and the company itself.[47] The agreement includes a statement of consent and acceptance of personal liability for non-compliance with the relevant rules.[48]

The story of the *Novo Mercado* is well known in the corporate law literature.[49] Here, we focus on a feature that has not received much attention: that companies listing on the *Novo Mercado* must include an arbitration clause in their articles subjecting intra-corporate disputes to the jurisdiction of the *Novo Mercado* Chamber of Arbitration (*Câmara de Arbitratgem do Mercado* or CAM).[50] The CAM was instituted in 2001 as a complementary arrangement for listed companies to settle disputes in

[45] Ibid., Art 8. [46] Ibid., Art 18.

[47] BM&FBovespa, *Regulamento de Listagem do Novo Mercado: Atualizado em Fevereiro de 2008*, Item 2.1.

[48] Ibid. [49] Gorga, 'Changing the Paradigm of Stock Ownership'.

[50] Regulamento de Listagem do Novo Mercado, Item 3.1, IV.

the markets managed by Bovespa. The Brazilian Arbitration Act permits parties, if they elect to do so, to adopt rules from a specialised arbitral body.[51] In addition, a 2001 reform to the Corporations Act made clear that companies were authorised to choose arbitration as a means to solve disputes between shareholders and the corporation, or between majority and minority shareholders.[52] The *Novo Mercado* listing agreement requires the submission of all disputes between the company, shareholders, senior managers, fiscal council members and Bovespa to CAM arbitration.[53]

Bovespa's expressed goal in mandating arbitration clauses for *Novo Mercado* firms was to sidestep the limitations of the general courts.[54] The CAM is composed of a minimum of thirty arbitrators,[55] who are appointed by Bovespa's Board of Directors.[56] Bovespa undertakes only to select persons with unblemished reputations and well-established knowledge of the capital markets, business law, and relevant technical areas necessary for the resolution of the disputes.[57] By increasing expertise, and reducing the delay associated with dispute resolution, the CAM was intended to reduce investors' perceptions about the risks associated with weaknesses of enforcement in the regular courts. Our interviewees suggested that Bovespa played an important role in ensuring that listed companies understood the advantages of these arbitration clauses.

Arbitration in general – and the CAM in particular – represents the first example of the 'institutional layering' we describe in this paper. The arbitrator has no inherent legal power, save that which is derived from the courts' recognition of his authority. Yet the introduction of the Arbitration Act of 1996 permitted parties largely to opt out of dispute resolution in the ordinary courts, in favour of privately selected experts. The arbitrator – whose expertise permits a more predictable and better-

[51] Lei de Arbitragem, Art 13 § 3. [52] *Lei 10.303, de 31 de Outubro de 2001.*

[53] Regulamento de Listagem do Novo Mercado, Item 2.1 (disputes submitted to arbitration proceedings include matters related to 'enforcement, validity, efficacy, violation and related effects of: a) the provisions in the Corporation Law, Company's articles, b) rules issued by the National Monetary Council, Central Bank of Brazil and the Securities and Exchange Commission of Brazil, c) all other rules governing capital markets in general, and d) the directives in the listings rules, arbitration rules and the Novo Mercado agreement.')

[54] Santana et al., 'Novo Mercado and Its Followers', 16.

[55] Regulamento de Listagem do Novo Mercado, Item 2.2.

[56] Ibid., Item 4.3. Appointment is for a term of 5 years, with the possibility of reappointment. The members of the Body of Arbitrators then appoint, for a term of two years, a president and two vice presidents for the Arbitration Chamber: Item 2.2.1.

[57] Ibid., Item 4.1.

informed decision – provides the substantive direction, which is then fitted into an enforcement framework that relies upon the domestic courts. As such, it lowers the demands on the judiciary and consequently increases the prospect of effective decisions. Because the arbitrator's authority is derived from that of the court, we can view it as 'layered' on top of the court's underlying jurisdiction.

Arbitration is far from a complete solution, however. First, for arbitration to be invoked, there must be an underlying action launched in the ordinary courts. Consequently, CAM can only improve outcomes conditional on litigation being launched. In order to be capable of protecting minority shareholders against self-dealing and other ways of extracting private benefits, it must be straightforward for shareholders to launch suits alleging a breach of duty by controllers. Yet this does not appear to be the case in Brazil. Many of our interviewees emphasised that shareholder litigation was actually a rarity. Correspondingly, CAM has had an average of only 8.5 new cases per year from 2010 to 2013.[58] Although the number of cases is small, their average value is very high, reaching R$57 million per case over this period.

Second, arbitration proceedings are generally confidential. Whilst the Brazilian Arbitration Act does not mandate confidentiality,[59] it is common for commercial parties to seek it. Parties generally prefer confidentiality so that sensitive details about the claim and/or its resolution are not released to the public. CAM follows this preference, with its internal rules expressly granting confidentiality to parties.[60] However, an important drawback to confidential decisions is that they do not permit arbitrators' reasoning to be available to guide future parties as to the likely outcome of disputes. Consequently, while confidential arbitration can make proceedings cheaper *ex post*, and likely improve the quality of decision making, it does little to assist parties in planning their affairs *ex ante*. There is a concern among legal professionals – echoed by some of our interviewees – that overreliance on confidential arbitration might in the long run make matters even worse, because not only does arbitration not produce precedents, but it may reduce courts' ability to produce new precedents as well, by diverting disputes that might otherwise generate them. In a bid to provide more guidance for future parties regarding decision outcomes, CAM has modified its rules to provide that the

58 Data provided to the authors by the CAM, for the purposes of this research, in June 2014.

59 Lei de Arbitragem, Art 13, §6 (arbitration should be exercised with impartiality, independence, competence, diligence and *discretion*: emphasis added).

60 BM&FBovespa, Internal Rules of the Market Arbitration Chamber, Item 6.1.

arbitration award, the thesis and legal grounds established in the award may be disclosed, regardless of parties' consent, provided that their identities are not disclosed.[61] However, this provision has not yet been implemented.

4.2 Specialised Business Chambers in the São Paulo Court of Justice

The second change we consider is not so much the introduction of an additional institutional layer as a re-ordering within the existing institution of state courts. It consists of the establishment of a specialist business chamber within the regular courts sitting in São Paulo.

In 2005, following the enactment of the new Brazilian Bankruptcy law, the São Paulo Court of Justice approved the creation of a specialised bankruptcy chamber (*Câmara Especial de Falências e Recuperações*) and two specialised trial courts in bankruptcy law (*Varas Especializadas de Falência e Recuperação*). The improvement in the institutional arrangement had various rationales. The most obvious, confirmed by our interviewees, was to provide faster and more expert decisions in commercial (insolvency) cases. There was also an institutional objective of influencing the formation of jurisprudence in higher courts in Brazil. At the time, the backlog of cases in the São Paulo Court of Appeal was not allowing faster decisions and important commercial cases in São Paulo were slower to reach higher courts in comparison to other State Courts, thus failing to influence national precedents. São Paulo is the wealthiest state in Brazil, contributing almost 40 per cent of the national GDP. So the institutional understanding was that the significance of the state in the national economic market, associated with its industry and extensive business transactions, required not only a faster response from the state courts, but also a stronger contribution to national precedents based on specialised decisions in commercial cases.

The Bankruptcy Chamber has established a high reputation among legal professionals, and in 2010 the São Paulo Court of Justice extended the initiative to create a general Business Law Chamber (*Câmara Reservada de Direito Empresarial*). The new general chamber was responsible for deciding cases involving corporate law, matters related to business transactions,[62] and industrial property. Later the chambers dealing with bankruptcy and business law were unified into the current

[61] Ibid., Item 6.3. [62] Specifically those regulated in the Civil Code, Arts 966 to 1195.

arrangement, consisting of two Business Law Chambers (*1a e 2a Câmara de Direito Empresarial*). Judges are selected for these Chambers based on their expertise in business law. Our legal professional interviewees were of the opinion that these Chambers have contributed to an increase in legal certainty in the State of São Paulo. The Business Law Chambers have now also produced a body of *sumulas* (summary precedents) that provides a clearer direction to future parties about the position of the Court.

The establishment of specialist business law chambers seems an obviously desirable innovation, given the institutional context of judicial enforcement in Brazil. To the extent that it serves its function of providing quicker and more certain decisions, it may also be expected to reduce the demand for arbitration. One might ask whether, therefore, there would be any need for further institutional innovations. A partial answer lies in the still-significant limitations of even a specialist business chamber. Such chambers must still apply the constitutional canons of interpretation; they simply do so with a greater background of business expertise. Thus, while they will tend to increase certainty, at least relative to non-specialist state courts, it is less clear whether they do so by more than could be achieved through other institutional innovations. In the next two subsections, we will consider two further 'institutional layers' governing related party transactions, in parallel with state courts. The agencies concerned each supply – in whole or in part – additional rules, and initiate their own enforcement actions. These are two further dimensions not offered by specialist chambers: specialist rule production *ex ante*, and subsidisation for enforcement activity.

4.3 Processo Administrativo *in the CVM Court*

Brazil's financial system is regulated and supervised by the National Monetary Council (*Conselho Monetário Nacional* or CMN), the Brazilian Central Bank (*Banco Central do Brasil* – Bacen) and the Brazilian Securities and Exchanges Commission (*Comissão de Valores Mobiliários* or CVM).[63] The CVM is an independent government agency, linked to the Ministry of Finance but not subordinate to it, and enjoys financial and budgetary autonomy.[64] The CVM has a general mandate for promoting the development of Brazil's securities market, encompassing securing its efficient

[63] Capital Markets Law, *Lei 6.385, de 7 de Dezembro de 1976.*

[64] Ibid., Art 5. This enhances its credibility as a neutral decision maker in cases involving state-owned firms.

operation, protecting market participants against irregular and illegal activities, reducing information asymmetry, and promoting legal enforcement,[65] by controlling and inspecting publicly-traded corporations.[66]

Importantly for our purposes, the CVM has enforcement powers encompassing the whole of securities and corporate law, as well as its own resolutions and any other law under which it is granted supervisory jurisdiction.[67] It can consequently address self-dealing transactions constituting breaches of corporate law. In addition, the CVM has supervisory responsibilities in relation to fundamental transactions involving significant risks for minority shareholders – in particular, corporate restructurings. In 1999, the CVM regulated disclosure procedures on the selling of control, or consolidation of existing control, of a company.[68] A new regulation in 2000 introduced special procedures, such as disclosure of information, economic use and the accounting treatment of premium and discount, to govern the legal relationship for share substitution for non-controlling shareholders.[69] Later regulations characterised any restructuring that only benefitted the controlling shareholder as an abuse of power;[70] also addressing tender offers,[71] and more recently, takeover bids.[72]

CVM enforcement powers – whether in relation to the CVM's own regulations or the general corporate law – are not exercised in the ordinary courts, but through a specialist tribunal, the CVM Administrative Court. Thus there are two parallel enforcement mechanisms for breaches of corporate law: shareholder class actions, launched in the ordinary courts, which would in an appropriate case result in arbitration proceedings; and CVM proceedings. This two-track process is legally possible because the CVM's jurisdiction is classified as being 'administrative'.

It is worth expanding a little on the notion of administrative proceedings (*processo administrativo*). In Brazil, institutions under federal

[65] Ibid., Arts 4 and 8. [66] Ibid., Art 8, incise V. [67] Ibid., Art 11.

[68] *CVM Instrução Normativa 299, de 09 de Fevereiro de 1999.* Before 1997, Brazilian corporate law required the acquirer of a controlling stake in a public company to make a (mandatory) tender offer for the shares held by minority shareholders, at the same price as that offered to the controlling shareholder. This requirement was removed in a 1997 reform intended to facilitate the privatisation process. In a series of subsequent regulations, however, CVM sought to restore the protection of minority shareholders in corporate restructurings.

[69] *CVM Instrução Normativa 319, de 03 de Dezembro de 1999.*

[70] *CVM Instrução Normativa 323, de 19 de Janeiro de 2000*, Art 1, incise II.

[71] *CVM Instrução Normativa 361, de 05 de Março de 2002.*

[72] *CVM Instrução Normativa 487, de 25 de Novembro de 2010.*

administration[73] have jurisdiction to initiate *processo administrativo* with a view to controlling their own activities, the protection of the rights of individuals and the performance of the Federal Public Administration.[74] Institutional activities are embedded in the notion of internal control of the state and public management supervision.[75] In general terms it also implies that institutions should, in the performance of their duties, follow the principles of legality and efficiency, aiming to promote the public good and respect for individuals' rights.

The CVM has power to investigate, through *processo administrativo*, illegal acts and inequitable practices of members of publicly traded companies and other market participants.[76] *Processo administrativo* can be initiated by the various supervision departments at the CVM.[77] The CVM promotes external routine inspections through its Compliance Inspection and Examination Office (*Superitendência de Fiscalização Externa* or SFI). The CVM describes its enforcement strategy as following a risk-based supervisory approach (*Supervisão Baseada em Riscos* or SBR), identifying risks as the product of the expected probability of a participant committing an illegal act and the severity of the act's impact on the market.[78] A general feature of *processo administrativo* is that interested parties can submit petitions, within the relevant institutional jurisdiction, for the opening of proceedings or the clarification of their own legal obligations. Consequently the CVM is willing to launch an administrative inspection following a request by a private party, if there is evidence of irregularity. This permits administrative enforcement by the CVM to function as a (partial) substitute for private enforcement through the ordinary courts.

73 Institutions directly linked to the central federal, state or municipal governments are said to be under the direct administration of the state. Entities with their own legal personalities but performing state activities, such as state-owned or state-controlled companies, are said to be under the indirect administration of the state.

74 Processo Admnistrativo no Âmbito da Administração Pública Federal, *Lei 9.784, de 29 de Janeiro de 1999*, Art 1.

75 H.L. Meirelles, D.B. Aleixo D.B. and J.E. Burle Filho, *Direito Administrativo Brasileiro* (São Paulo: Malheiros Editores, 2014), 759.

76 Capital Markets Law 1976, Art 9, incise V.

77 These include the Corporate Relations Office (*Superintendência de Relações com Empresas* or 'SEP'), the Institutional Investors Supervision Office (*Superintendência de Relações com Investidores Institucionais* or 'SIN'), the Trading and Markets Supervision Office (*Superintendência de Relações de Mercado e Intermediários* or 'SMI') and the Accounting and Auditing Ruling Office (*Superintêndencia de Normas Contábeis e de Auditoria* or 'SNC').

78 Comissão de Valores Mobiliários, *Relatório Anual 2012* (São Paulo: Comissão de Valores Mobiliários, 2012), 54.

Administrative proceedings must follow federal rules, principles of law – including due process – and the relevant institution's internal procedural rules.[79] Following a *processo administrativo*, the CVM has power to seek the imposition of penalties including warnings, fines and suspensions,[80] which are payable independently of civil or criminal liability.[81] The initial decision regarding imposition of a penalty is made by the relevant part of the CVM with oversight of the party under investigation. That party can then appeal to the full Board of Commissioners,[82] and from their decision to the Council of Appeals of the National Financial System (*Conselho de Recursos do Sistema Financeiro Nacional* or CRSFN),[83] or the Ministry of Finance, depending on the subject matter. If a CVM investigation concludes that a crime occurred, the Public Attorney Prosecutor's Office is notified, to permit it to file a criminal suit,[84] which will be heard in the regular courts.

The CVM's Annual Report gives a snapshot of its annual enforcement activity. In 2012, the CVM received more than 35,000 requests for investigations from investors and members of the general public. Detailed analyses were carried out in 900 cases and the department responsible for publicly-traded companies investigated 350 complaints.[85] From these, SFI launched 238 external inspections, of which just over half (54 per cent) related to investment funds. These in turn led to eighty-four administrative proceedings being initiated, most of which related to market manipulation and insider trading. Of the cases initiated, twenty-one were resolved through administrative agreements (*Termo de Ajustamento de Conduta*), twenty-five were heard by the Board, and ten were resolved at the Supervisory Level.[86]

The CVM Board are both expert in the relevant subject-matter and – by the standards of Brazilian public agencies – independent of government.[87]

[79] Processo Admnistrativo no Âmbito da Administração Pública Federal, Lei 9.784, de 29 de Janeiro de 1999. See also Meirelles et al., Direito Administrativo Brasileiro.

[80] The CVM's enforcement competence is defined in the Capital Markets Law 1976 (as amended by Law 9.457 of 5 May 1997, Decree-Law 3.995 of 31 October 2001 and Law 10.303 of 31 October 2001), Art 10 §10 and Art 9, incise V, § 5.

[81] Capital Markets Law 1976, Art 9, incise V. [82] Ibid., Art 11, § 12.

[83] Ibid., Art 11, incise III, § 4. The CRSFN was created in 1985 under *Decreto 91.152, de 15 de Março de 1985.* On rights of appeal, see also 'Processos Adminsitrativos Sancionadores', in Mobiliários CdV (ed) *Deliberação CVM 538, de 05 de Março de 2008* (Brasília Diário Oficial da União, 2008), art 37.

[84] Capital Markets Law 1976, Art 12.

[85] Comissão de Valores Mobiliários, Relatório Anual 2012, at 55. [86] Ibid., at 64.

[87] See *supra* note 61 and text therein.

By law, CVM Board members should be experts in the capital markets and have a good reputation.[88] Board members are appointed by the president of Brazil following their approval by the Federal Senate. The term is for five years, with no reappointment, and appointments are staggered such that a single member is appointed each year.[89] An important guarantee of independence is that Board members cannot be removed mid-term other than for criminal or administrative misconduct.[90]

Not only do CVM officials possess more specialist expertise than the regular judiciary, but – according to our interviewees – *processo administrativo* is likely to produce a result far more quickly. As a result, while the overlapping jurisdictions mean parties may have a choice of enforcement channel, our interviewees thought that petitioning for *processo administrativo* was generally preferred to launching a suit in the state courts. In their view, it would be quicker and more expert than the state courts, and consequently a better route to a decision.

CVM enforcement thus provides a third 'institutional layer' in relation to the enforcement of minority protection. In principle, *processo administrativo* runs in parallel with the enforcement of private rights of action in the state courts. It does not rely on them for enforcement, but in contrast is an alternative route to enforce the same underlying rights, at least as respects aspects of corporate and securities laws giving rise to private rights of action. Administrative proceedings do not result in compensation of investors, but do serve an important deterrent function for controllers. Consequently they can be used to protect outside investors from harmful related party transactions. The public funding of CVM, and its control of proceedings, assists private investors by overcoming the costs of launching litigation.

CVM decisions and the state courts do not so much function as substitutes (as with courts and arbitration) but rather as complements. This is because the CVM's administrative jurisdiction and state court civil (or criminal) jurisdiction are not mutually exclusive. After an administrative decision by the CVM, the parties may still bring the case to the regular state courts. Although the CVM Board publish written decisions, technically speaking, their legal consequences are limited to administrative proceedings and only a court decision renders a matter *res judicata* for civil proceedings.[91] Yet because *processo administrativo*

[88] Capital Markets Law 1976, Art 6. [89] Ibid., Art 6, § 1.

[90] Ibid., Art 6, § 2. Such misconduct could comprise administrative improbity or non-observance of their duties or other prohibitions associated with their positions: Art 6, § 3.

[91] See Meirelles et al., *Direito Administrativo Brasileiro*, 772.

moves more quickly than civil litigation, and the CVM Board have specialist expertise, state courts treat CVM decisions as highly influential.[92] This means that parties generally can look for guidance on corporate and securities law to the growing stock of CVM written precedents. Moreover, the expertise of the personnel involved means that the precedents thereby produced – and the guidance to parties they convey – are likely to be of higher average quality than state court decisions.

4.4 CAF: The Brazilian Takeover Panel

A fourth 'institutional layer' in enforcement may come to be constituted by Brazil's newly established Mergers and Acquisitions Committee (*Comitê de Aquisições e Fusões* or CAF). The CAF, which formally began operations in January 2014, is a self-regulatory initiative aimed at securing equitable treatment for shareholders of publicly traded companies during tender offers (*ofertas públicas de aquisição de ações* or 'OPAs') and corporate restructuring transactions (*operações de reorganização societária*).[93] Although the CAF does not have any statutory basis, its founders – which include the CVM, Bovespa, the Brazilian Financial Market Association (*Associação Brasileira de Entidades dos Mercados Financeiro e de Capital* or ANBIMA), the Brazilian Institute of Corporate Governance (*Instituto Brasileiro de Governança Corporativa* or IBGC) and the Association of Capital Markets Investors (*Associação de Investidores no Mercado de Capitais* or AMEC) – hope that it will come to be highly influential in relation to CVM and state court decision making.[94]

The CAF's regulatory and institutional function is intended to complement those of the CVM. The CAF's *Self-Regulatory Code on Mergers and Acquisitions* (the CAF Code) sets out a series of rules and principles for mergers and acquisitions, which are expressly described as cumulative with, rather than substituting for, applicable legal provisions,

92 Moreover, the CVM often plays a role of *amicus curiae* in securities cases in state courts: see Capital Markets Law 1976, Art 31.

93 Comitê de Aquisições e Fusões, *The Self-Regulatory Code on Mergers and Acquisitions* (2014) (the 'CAF Code'), Preamble 1, I.

94 Discussions leading to the establishment of the CAF were first initiated by the CVM, and later continued by the São Paulo Stock Exchange (BM&Bovespa). The Brazilian Association of Publicly Held Corporations (*Associção Brasileira das Companhias Abertas* or 'ABRASCA') was also initially involved but subsequently withdrew participation.

including Brazilian corporate and securities law. Similarly, the CAF's activities are expressed not to substitute for the role of CVM administrative oversight in these transactions.[95] The CAF and its Code, respectively, bring procedural and substantive *additions* to the pre-existing protections for shareholders.

As far as substance is concerned, the CAF Code applies a 'principles-based' approach in relation to takeovers and corporate restructurings. Key principles include the equal treatment of shareholders,[96] and the provision of sufficient information for shareholders to make decisions.[97] There are two main innovations in the CAF Code that go beyond the underlying legal requirements, as regards the protection of minority shareholders. First, it introduces a requirement for a mandatory tender offer whenever an acquiror makes a purchase taking their stake above a threshold of the voting stock of the target company.[98] This is understood as a way of protecting minority shareholders against tunnelling by controllers, because the controller must offer the same price in the mandatory bid to minority shareholders as they have paid to acquire their controlling stake. This gives minority shareholders an option to exit following a change in control, if they are concerned that the acquirer is going to engage in tunnelling.[99]

The second innovation is to give minority shareholders the opportunity to demand a second valuation opinion on restructuring transactions involving related parties, most notably 'freezeout' transactions by a controlling shareholder.[100] Once the first valuation is released, the companies involved should convene special meetings of the non-controlling ('outstanding') shareholders at which the non-controlling shareholders decide whether they would like to call for a second valuation.[101]

[95] CAF Code, Preamble 1, II. [96] Ibid. Art 29, incise I.

[97] Ibid., Art 29, incise III (provision of information); incise VIII and IX (consistent and conflict-free provision of information in valuation reports). Another stated principle is that shareholders should make decisions about takeovers or restructurings (incise II). However, this does little to protect minority shareholders as it is satisfied by majority decision making.

[98] Ibid., Arts 65–70. The threshold level, in the range of 20–30 per cent, is set in the articles of a company adhering to the CAF Code. On the history of mandatory tender offers in Brazil, see note 65.

[99] However, there is an exemption for cases where control is already in the hands of a person holding more than 50 per cent of the voting rights: ibid, Art 65, para 5.

[100] Ibid., Sections II to V.

[101] Ibid. Art 84. A special procedure should follow if the special meeting decides to require a second valuation report (Art 85). If the second valuation is more favourable to holders of outstanding shares of the adherent companies or the other way around, but as long the

The regular shareholder meetings that would decide on the corporate restructuring itself are not to be called until procedures regarding the valuation have been completed.[102]

Turning to process, the CAF introduces a new decision-making and enforcement agency, the CAF Takeover Panel. The Panel's operation is to some degree modelled on the UK's Takeover Panel.[103] Thus it operates in 'real time' during a restructuring or takeover to provide the parties with guidance as to appropriate actions. The Panel also offers prior consultations to parties contemplating relevant transactions.[104] The CAF's Chief Executive is a well-known M&A practitioner from an investment bank, with many years of experience, and members of the Panel, which will adjudicate disputes, consist of expert arbitrators. Thus what is envisaged is a decision that will be produced *ex ante*, involving as much input as possible from minority shareholders through the voting rules, and moderated by experts with credibility in the market.

As the CAF has no statutory basis, its decisions cannot be directly enforced other than through reputational sanctions, such as public censure,[105] or in more extreme cases, withdrawal of the CAF's oversight. However, the CVM offers an important indirect channel of enforcement. The CVM has entered into Cooperation Agreement with the CAF whereby it provides that related party corporate reorganisations undertaken in accordance with the CAF Code will attract a presumption of regularity in administrative proceedings.[106] Moreover, for companies that opt into the CAF Code by changing their articles, breach of the Code would be a breach of their articles, which could be enforced by the CAF.[107]

The CAF's innovations are only applicable to companies that have elected to submit to its jurisdiction. Such election may take one of two

exchange ratios do not differ more than 10 per cent, parties can proceed to revise the share exchange ratio, provided that the no share exchange implemented is not lower than the average between the two valuations.

102 Ibid., Art 84, §2. At that meeting, shareholders can approve the transaction or request a third valuation of the companies involved (Art 85, §5) and a final decision should consider the average among the three valuations (Art 88, § IX).

103 See The Takeover Panel, 'About the Panel' (www.thetakeoverpanel.org.uk/structure). On the history of the UK Takeover Panel, see J. Armour and D.A. Skeel, Jr, 'Who Write the Rules for Hostile Takeovers, and Why? – The Peculiar Divergence of U.S. and U.K. Takeover Regulation', 95 *Georgetown Law Journal* 1727 (2007), 1756–1764.

104 Comite de Aquisições e Fusões, *Directive Release 2014/001* (2014), Item 24.

105 CAF Code, Art 136, incise II.

106 CVM/CAF Cooperation Agreement of 27 August 2013 (cafbrasil.org.br/site/en/normative-ruling/cooperation-agreement/).

107 CAF Code, Art 136, § 2.

forms. The first is *corporate* election, where the company through its articles commits to abide by the CAF Code, and the second is a *transactional* election, whereby the parties to a particular transaction agree to submit the process to the CAF's jurisdiction. Our interviewees were positive about the CAF initiative but explained that companies are resistant to include provisions on their articles. Amending a company's articles to incorporate the Code would benefit the company's minority shareholders were it to be a target but might cost them more were it to be an acquirer. Moreover, it likely would not benefit the controlling shareholder if the company were a target, as they would need to share any control premium with minority shareholders. Consequently most Brazilian companies might be expected to eschew such amendments of their articles: indeed so far, only one company has done so. In the case of a transactional agreement, submitting to the CAF's jurisdiction may be in the interests of both sides in an arm's-length transaction, as it will bring greater expertise and speed to the resolution of disputes. For related party transactions, the primary incentive would seem to be to benefit from the CVM's presumption of regularity.

The CAF is an ambitious attempt to create a new institutional layer for control transactions, which has significant implications for minority investors. Staffed by experts, and making public its decisions, the CAF has the potential to become a source of information for parties wishing to order their affairs in relation to control transactions and restructurings. At least at this early stage of its inception, it is clearly layered on top of the legal authority of the CVM. If it comes to function as conceived, it will represent a sort of outsourcing of decision-making and rule-writing authority by the CVM that bears some resemblance to the way in which arbitration functions in relation to state courts, save that the CAF will produce written decisions, which will be made public. However, at the time of writing it is not entirely clear how the overlapping performance of the CAF and the CVM will work in practice.

5 Conclusion

We have seen that four distinct strategies for institutional development are being employed in Brazilian corporate and securities law to overcome the problem of the inefficacy of state courts in resolving business disputes: arbitration, specialist judicial chambers within the regular state courts, administrative enforcement by the CVM and, most recently, the establishment of the self-regulatory CAF. Each of these developments can be seen as a 'layer' based on the foundation of the basic system of corporate law enforced through state courts. Each derives its 'legality' to some extent from the underlying foundations. Yet each offers a way of overcoming some of the limitations of the underlying system. None is able completely to transcend these limitations, and so each is, by itself, an incomplete solution. However, the fact that all four approaches can be pursued simultaneously means that they overlap to a significant degree, especially in relation to areas crucial for facilitating outside investment such as the control of tunnelling by majority shareholders. None, individually, could be described as an ideal or fully functional enforcement mechanism. Yet collectively, they are mutually reinforcing, and their operation together is greater than the sum of their parts.

We consider that the account of institutional layering in Brazil offers insights that may usefully generalise to other emerging markets. Weak enforcement is an endemic problem for building legal institutions in emerging markets. The Brazilian approach suggests a focus on the art of the possible. Simultaneously pursuing whatever solutions which can be implemented, despite manifest limitations, may be more effective in aggregate than trying to pursue a single optimal solution which fails to get executed.

Conclusion

ROBIN HUI HUANG AND NICHOLAS CALCINA HOWSON

1 A Big Gap between 'law in books' and 'law in action'

Any attempt to comprehensively analyse the enforcement of corporate law and securities regulation is difficult, not only because there are so many distinct national systems in play, but also because, we need to examine both formal enforcement mechanisms and the way in which such mechanisms are applied in practice. If nothing else, the expert analyses presented in the foregoing chapters of this book confirm that with respect to enforcement issues a rather large gap does exist between what Roscoe Pound memorably called 'law in books' and 'law in action'.[1]

Across the globe, there certainly appears to be a discernible trend toward encouraging private enforcement in recent years. As this collection demonstrates: the PRC formally allowed private claims against securities misrepresentation in 2002;[2] after the Parmalat case of 2003, Italian courts have adjudicated several very significant civil cases concerning securities misrepresentation;[3] Germany introduced a model case mechanism to provide collective redress for securities investors in 2005;[4] in 2004 Japan introduced a special provision enabling investors to pursue liability of securities issuers for misrepresentation in disclosure documents;[5] Korea passed a law in 2003 (effective from 2007) to introduce a class action mechanism designed to enhance protection for small investors in the Korean securities markets;[6] in 2003, Taiwan established a non-profit organisation successor to a similar body created in the late 1990s, the Securities and Futures Investors Protection Center, which can by itself bring a representative action with respect to an alleged securities

[1] Roscoe Pound, *Law in Books and Law in Action*, 44 AMER. L. REV. 12 (1910). See John Armour, Bernard S. Black, Brian R. Cheffins and Richard Nolan, Chapter 13.

[2] See Liming Wang, Chapter 6. [3] See Guido Ferrarini and Paolo Giudici, Chapter 19.

[4] See Rainer Kulms, Chapter 18. [5] See Gen Goto, Chapter 20.

[6] See Hwa-Jin Kim, Chapter 21.

or futures-related breach which has harmed multiple securities investors or futures traders;[7] and India reformed its company law statute to allow for class action in 2013.[8] Of course, the trajectory in the US, the motherland of private enforcement of corporate and securities law in a decidedly common law context, has been in the opposite direction as a result of both statutory amendment and jurisprudential developments, and notwithstanding the scandals that gave rise to Sarbanes-Oxley and then the Global Financial Crisis.[9]

However, it is one thing to stipulate a private right of action in statute or regulation, and it is quite another to see it implemented or pursued in practice. In all countries and legal systems, the successful implementation of a private enforcement scheme depends on various procedural, institutional, political and cultural factors.[10] In some jurisdictions that have actually gone as far as introducing a class action mechanism, such as Korea and India, its effectiveness has been severely curtailed by the lack of rules allowing or governing contingency fee arrangements. In emerging economies such as the PRC, India and Brazil, private enforcement has in many ways been frustrated by the judiciary. For instance, the PRC had long provided a regulatory-statutory 'legal basis' for civil liability for false and misleading disclosure in its securities markets, but this could not even begin to be implemented until 2002–2003 when the PRC Supreme People's Court (SPC) reversed its initial ban on acceptance of such cases and started to allow Chinese courts to take such cases under intense public pressure. And even after the SPC's switch in 2002–2003, the Chinese judicial bureaucracy has continued to use all manner of tricks to stymie the handling of civil compensation claims for misrepresentation in the securities markets, which at least one of the authors in this collection sees as the reason for the lower-than-expected number of securities civil claims to date.[11] Similarly, in India and Brazil, limitations

[7] See Wen-Yeu Wang, Chapter 22. [8] See Vikramaditya Khanna, Chapter 16.

[9] See Judge Jed Rakoff, Chapter 1; James D. Cox and Randall S. Thomas, Chapter 12; and John Armour, Bernard S. Black, Brian R. Cheffins and Richard Nolan, Chapter 13.

[10] See Judge Jed Rakoff, Chapter 1; Mathias Reimann, Chapter 2; and Xianchu Zhang, Chapter 7.

[11] Robin Hui Huang, Chapter 8. We should note that in some cases the PRC judiciary acts creatively when faced with doctrinal and institutional constraints. For instance, in the distinct area of private enforcement of corporate law fiduciary duties, one of our authors theorises that PRC judges have enforced basically common law transplanted fiduciary duty doctrines using the traditional civil law analytical framework for tort liability. See Jiangyu Wang, Chapter 10. Similarly, the spirit of judicial innovation has been demonstrated in the enforcement of China's statutory corporate veil piercing regime. See

associated with the functioning of the courts are identified as one of the central challenges facing private enforcement.[12]

However, if something is not 'in the books' or is subject to some level of regulatory or institutional constraints, one need not jump to the conclusion that there results a complete vacuum, as there may be in operation effective functional substitutes for what appears to be missing. This volume reveals that phenomenon in spades. For instance, China does not have class action and severely restricts both 'group' actions and contingency fee arrangements,[13] but the Chinese People's Courts have come up with a procedural innovation – something with a function similar to the German model case regime – which allows the PRC People's Courts to efficiently hear multiple cases arising from the same securities misrepresentation.[14] In Japan and Italy, the lack of a class action has not proven a fatal problem either.[15] Likewise, while Australia does not formally allow the kind of contingency fee arrangements which are considered crucial for private enforcement, in practice a third party litigation funding mechanism has served as a functional substitute for contingency fee arrangements.[16]

While it is hard to determine the relative significance of public and private enforcement in quantitative terms, from the chapters in this book it would seem that across the globe – with the notable exception of the US[17] – private enforcement is far less important than public enforcement. In Hong Kong, for example, while a private right of action is available, it has not really been used to date, partly due to the lack of class action, partly because of the effectiveness of public enforcement in protecting investors. The Hong Kong securities regulator, for example, has instead ordered issuers to repurchase from aggrieved investors the

Robin Hui Huang, 'Piercing the Corporate Veil in China: Where Is It Now and Where Is It Heading?', 60 *American Journal of Comparative Law* 743 (2012).

12 John Armour and Caroline Schmidt, Chapter 23 (stating that 'Brazilian judges are overworked, with a long case backlog. They are also under-trained in business matters . . . '); Vikramaditya Khanna, Chapter 16 (noting 'the glacial speed of the Indian courts').

13 See Liming Wang, Chapter 6. 14 See Robin Hui Huang, Chapter 8.

15 Guido Ferrarini and Paolo Giudici, Chapter 19 (contending that 'the poor state of Italian private enforcement did not depend on substantive rules or the simple absence of class actions'); Gen Goto, Chapter 20 (opining that 'US-style class action is not a prerequisite for securities litigation').

16 Michael Legg, Chapter 15 (stating 'litigation funding addresses the cost disincentives to the commencement of class action litigation . . . ').

17 Even in the US, it is claimed that ' . . . [as] representative shareholder litigation comes under increasing attack . . . attention has shifted to governance and market mechanisms to address managerial agency costs'. James D. Cox and Randall S. Thomas, Chapter 12.

shares sold to them at inflated prices caused by misrepresentation in public issuance documents, and ordered insiders to pay money to their trading counterparties to restore such counterparties to the same position, in financial terms, they were in before the insider trading prohibition-breaching trades.[18] We may conclude therefore that public enforcement in Hong Kong – rapidly becoming one of the world's most important securities markets – has been very effective in protecting investors, largely obviating the need for private enforcement. Further, in many jurisdictions where there is some allowance for private enforcement in varying degrees, such as the PRC, Taiwan, Japan and Korea, a 'piggyback' can be employed, whereby private enforcement always follows after or operates in parallel with public enforcement. As many of the authors in this collection note, this kind of piggybacking helps private claimants overcome the evidentiary difficulties caused by the lack of discovery rules in those jurisdictions and allows private enforcement to benignly free ride on public enforcement.

Hence, although private enforcement seems to have become increasingly important and popular amongst the national jurisdictions examined in this book, it has not yet played a very significant role in enforcing corporate and securities laws, at least judging from the number of cases observed to date. Of course, we recognise that it may not be appropriate to measure the significance of private enforcement simply by reference to the private cases which are actually brought. In Korea, for instance, the introduction of class action is said to have generated strong deterrence so that many Korean listed companies rushed to improve their disclosure practices before the law took effect three years after its enactment.[19]

The above observations divined from the chapters presented in this book have important implications for a more critical understanding of the widely-accepted 'law and finance' literature.[20] On the one hand, methodologically, it is simply not adequate to solely identify formal rules for investor protection on the books, both substantive and procedural, and

[18] See Alexa Lam, Chapter 17. [19] See Hwa-Jin Kim, Chapter 21.

[20] Rafael La Porta, Florencio Lopez-de-Silanes, Andrei Shleifer and Robert Vishny, 'Law and Finance', 106 *Journal of Financial Economics* 1113 (1998) (reporting that the common law outperforms the civil law in encouraging financial development); Rafael La Porta, Florencio Lopez-de-Silanes, Andrei Shleifer, 'What Works in Securities Laws?', 61 *Journal of Finance* 20 (2006) (arguing that compared with private enforcement, the importance of public enforcement is at best modest); Simeon Djankov, Rafael La Porta, Florencio Lopez-de-Silanes, Andrei Shleifer, 'The Law and Economics of Self-dealing', 88 *Journal of Financial Economics* 430 (2008) (conducting a cross-country empirical study of law and finance).

then assign value to them as independent variables in cross-country and allegedly empirical studies of 'law and finance'. This book reveals that although many jurisdictions have had the same or similar formal rules on the books, the enforcement of such norms and implementation of such procedures in practice vary greatly, always depending on the respective institutional, political, cultural and economic environments in which they operate. Moreover, the simple valuing of such norms or formal practices as independent variables so characteristic of this literature completely ignores the possibility that a given jurisdiction might use equally or more effective substitute mechanisms, the implementation of which is invisible in these tabulations.

On the other hand, the robust 'legal origins' conclusions drawn by the 'law and finance' studies, seem rather weak in the face of the material presented in this book. Under the 'legal origins' argument, common law jurisdictions make more use of private enforcement which correlates to deep and more liquid securities markets. However, this book suggests that the initial premise upon which the 'legal origins' edifice is built is overly simplistic: indeed, apart from the US, all other common law jurisdictions discussed in this book, including the UK, Australia, Canada, India and Hong Kong, clearly put more reliance on public enforcement than private enforcement.[21] At present, these non-US common law jurisdictions seem to rely on private enforcement at a level comparable to that in civil law jurisdictions, both in terms of the availability of the class action regime and the actual cases produced to date. In fact, one of the chapters in this book demonstrates that historically the level of investor protection in the UK and Germany was actually similar over the nineteenth century.[22]

In short, what seems apparent from the discussion in this book and the conference in which it is rooted is the divergence in the approaches to enforcement of corporate and securities laws – certainly across national jurisdictions, but more importantly even among jurisdictions sharing the same 'legal origins', within the same geographical locations, or tagged into the same developmental categories. Accordingly, rather than celebrating the perhaps false dream of convergence in what all admit are increasingly globalised capital markets, this book hopes to contribute to

21 See John Armour, Bernard S. Black, Brian R. Cheffins, and Richard Nolan, Chapter 13 (empirically examining the role of private enforcement in the two leading common law jurisdictions, namely the US and the UK, and finding there is divergence).

22 See Carsten Gerner-Beuerle, Chapter 3.

a deeper and less synthesising understanding of persistent divergence, and the reasons for it.[23]

2 A New Taxonomy of Enforcement Strategies

Enforcement strategies of corporate and securities law have traditionally been divided into two broad categories, namely public enforcement and private enforcement. In general, public enforcement is initiated by a state official such as a regulator or a prosecutor, while private enforcement is by a private party in the form of civil actions for compensation or rescission. The public vs. private enforcement divide is based on two general criteria: first, public and private enforcers may have differing incentives: the former is usually paid a public servant's salary regardless of case outcomes, whereas the latter is primarily motivated by the prospect of financial gain contingent upon success in litigation; second, public enforcers are relatively centralised and subject to explicit political control, whereas private claimants are not.[24] Both enforcement strategies, however, take the form of court proceedings.

As this book makes clear, the simplistic dichotomy between public and private enforcement may not fully capture the complexity and diversity of how corporate and securities laws are enforced in practice. For instance, how do we understand efforts made to enforce the law but without recourse to court proceedings? Professor John Armour of Oxford University, one of the contributors to this book, has come up with a new taxonomy of enforcement strategies, introducing a formal vs. informal divide according to whether the law is enforced through state judicial institutions. Under this two-dimensional taxonomy, there are four types of enforcement strategies, including: formal public enforcement, informal public enforcement, formal private enforcement and informal private enforcement.[25]

[23] See Donald Clarke, Chapter 5 (arguing that the purported 'bonding' effects of cross-listings by PRC issuers might be illusory).

[24] The Securities and Futures Investors Protection Center in Taiwan shows the blurring of boundaries between public and private enforcement mechanisms: The Center can bring private litigation for compensation on behalf of aggrieved investors but has close ties to the government which render it 'dangerously akin to a typical governmental administrative branch'. Wen-Yeu Wang, Chapter 22.

[25] John Amour, 'Enforcement Strategies in UK Corporate Governance: A Roadmap and Empirical Assessment', (April 2008) *ECGI Working Paper Series in Law* (No 106/2008). And see Nicholas Calcina Howson, 'Enforcement Without Foundation? – Insider Trading and China's Administrative Law Crisis', 60 AM. J. COMP. L. 955 (2012)

This categorisation of enforcement strategies represents a significant improvement over the simple public-private dichotomy, but still has inadequacies. To start with, the criterion used for the formal vs. informal divide may need refinement. As noted above, the formal vs. informal dimension is introduced to take account of those enforcement activities which are not affected through state judicial institutions. This informal type of enforcement activity has the advantage of economising on the considerable costs of judicial or quasi-judicial proceedings. These advantages, however, cannot be taken as absolute, because enforcement by regulators may be subject to judicial review, and thus state judicial institutions may ultimately be involved.

Importantly, the scope of enforcement activities a public regulator is able to carry out without seeking judicial orders is a 'rule of law' issue.[26] For instance, in the PRC the securities regulator has a wide range of powers to freeze or seal up assets, restrict securities transactions, and impose administrative penalties such as warnings, fines and revocation of licences, as well as orders prohibiting the subjects of enforcement from certain activities.[27] It would be inappropriate to refer to those enforcement activities as 'informal'. The reputational sanction imposed by stock exchanges in the form of public censure is commonly understood as a mode of informal enforcement, but in fact, when stock exchanges impose public censure, they need to go through the same procedure as other disciplinary measures such as fine, suspension or delisting of securities. Again, it would be remarkable to understand delisting decisions as 'informal enforcement' as well. The same could be said of the enforcement activities carried out by public regulators or stock exchanges in many other jurisdictions such as Hong Kong, where the regulator has power to impose public censure, fine licensed persons, and suspend or revoke business licenses.

Under the new taxonomy, another example of informal enforcement by regulators is a private conversation between the regulator and the firm or securities trading party in question. This can occur in the context of either an investigation after an alleged violation, or during an application

(demonstrating how China Securities Regulatory Commission civil enforcement of the PRC's insider trading prohibition is *ultra vires* and a breach of 'administration according to law' [*yifa xingzheng*]).

26 See Jeffrey G. MacIntosh, Chapter 14 (discussing enforcement modalities from a rule of law perspective).

27 Robin Hui Huang, *Securities and Capital Markets Law in China* (Oxford University Press, 2014), Chapter 2.

for enforcement action in the future. In the former case, private conversations can be seen as 'informal' to the extent that they are not done through any formal proceedings. It seems doubtful, however, that private conversations regulator to regulate should be treated as a form of enforcement in some cases. Private conversation is something like the threat of sanctions, rather than actual sanctions, and in such cases sanctions are not imposed presumably because the alleged violation is deemed too minor to warrant enforcement. Under these circumstances, private conversation is more like education than enforcement in the strict sense. In the latter case, the regulator provides guidance or even approval to market participants in relation to matters which have captured regulatory attention. This might be more properly labelled a kind of '*ex ante* enforcement', a regulatory technique which has been used extensively in the PRC of course where the government had maintained a tight grip on the securities market via a host of approval requirements. For instance, up until now, China has used a merit review regime for public markets' fundraising transactions, notably initial public offerings. The non-action letter mechanism used in many jurisdictions such as the US might be another example.

Informal private enforcement refers mainly to the exercise of corporate law-based or securities law-mandated voting rights by shareholders, which for this context we include the 'Wall Street Walk' (voting with their feet by unloading). For many, this so-called informal private action might be more appropriately associated with 'governance' rather than 'enforcement' per se.[28] Even if this can be seen as enforcement in its broad sense, it might be better addressed as 'self-enforcement', which usefully emphasises that corporate and securities law is rather uniquely enforceable by shareholders themselves without recourse to any public institutions such as the judiciary.[29]

There is, however, an urgent need to pay very close attention to private enforcement activity which is not carried out in the courtroom. For

[28] Oliver E William, *The Mechanisms of Governance* (Oxford University Press, 1996), 145–170; see also James D. Cox and Randall S. Thomas, Chapter 12 (referring to institutional shareholder activism and the Say-on-Pay voting mechanism as 'governance developments').

[29] Bernard Black and Reinier Kraakman, 'A Self-Enforcing Model of Corporate Law', 109(8) *Harvard Law Review* 1911 (1996). For the PRC case, see Nicholas Calcina Howson, '"Quack Corporate Governance" as Traditional Chinese Medicine – The Securities Regulation Cannibalization of China's Corporate Law and a State Regulator's Battle Against Party State Political Economic Power', 37(2) SEATTLE U. L. REV. 667 (2014).

instance, securities arbitration has long been an important way to settle securities disputes.[30] Indeed, that mechanism is discussed in several chapters in this book as an alternative to court-based private enforcement.[31] Further, many jurisdictions have special mechanisms for settling securities markets disputes, such as the Financial Services Ombudsman in the UK and Australia, the Financial Dispute Resolution Centre recently established in Hong Kong,[32] and the Shenzhen Securities and Futures Dispute Resolution Centre in the PRC. Although arbitration, mediation, and such special mechanisms can play a role similar to that of court-based private enforcement, they are not currently covered in the taxonomy of enforcement strategies/mechanisms. We submit here that they might be included in the discussion under 'alternative private enforcement'.

In sum, this book and global practice alike teach us that the traditional dichotomy between public and private enforcement is far too crude, and does not adequately reflect how corporate and securities laws are enforced in practice. In the multiplicity of global norms, procedures and practices discussed herein, this book supports the idea that a new, four-way taxonomy of enforcement strategies is a better starting point for understanding – either in isolation or comparatively – the enforcement of corporate law and securities regulation across the globe.

[30] Shahla Ali and Robin Hui Huang, 'Financial Dispute Resolution in China: Arbitration or Court Litigation?', 28(1) *Arbitration International* 77 (2012). Further, China has recently tried to resolve securities disputes through mediation. Robin Hui Huang, 'Securities Dispute Mediation in China', 10(2) *Journal of Comparative Law* 177 (2016).

[31] See Michael Barr, Chapter 4 (stating that 'mandatory pre-dispute arbitration clauses are pervasive in consumer financial and investor contracts'); Xiaochun Liu, Chapter 11 (discussing the newly established Financial Arbitration Centre under China's Free Trade Zone policy); Junhai Liu, Chapter 9 (stating that 'arbitration is faster, cheaper, more confidential, more professional'); Vikramaditya Khanna, Chapter 16 (contending that one potential reform is to 'have shareholders pursue corporate governance claims in arbitral proceedings rather than in judicial or tribunal proceedings'); John Armour and Caroline Schmidt, Chapter 23 (noting the growing role of arbitration in Brazil which is part of 'a mutually reinforcing system of enforcement').

[32] Robin Hui Huang, 'In the Aftermath of the Global Financial Crisis: The Proposed Establishment of a Financial Dispute Resolution Centre in Hong Kong', 85 *Australian Law Journal* 726 (2011).

INDEX

Lightning Source UK Ltd.
Milton Keynes UK
UKHW05n0250290518
323278UK00020B/137/P

9 781107 164994